WAKEFIELD PRESS

Roma the First

Kerrie Round and Susan Magarey, photograph by Mick Bradley

Susan Magarey AM, FASSA, PhD, has degrees in English Literature and History from Adelaide University and the Australian National University. She was Director of the Research Centre for Women's Studies at Adelaide University where she is now Adjunct Professor in History. She is the author of two monographs – the prize-winning biography of Catherine Helen Spence, *Unbridling the Tongues of Women* (1986) and *Passions of the First-Wave Feminists* (2001) – and more than sixty articles and book chapters. She has edited eight collections of articles – including *Women in a Restructuring Australia: Work and Welfare* (1995) with Anne Edwards, and *Debutante Nation: Feminism Contests the 1890s* (1993) with Sue Rowley and Susan Sheridan, and was the Founding Editor of the tri-annual journal, *Australian Feminist Studies*.

She is currently President of the Friends of the Library at the University of Adelaide, a member of the Board of the History Trust of South Australia, and founder of the Magarey Medal for Biography. She is writing a history of the Women's Liberation Movement in Australia. For fun, she swims, gardens, cooks and listens to music. She describes her life in the words of Australian poet Jennifer Maiden: 'Ambivalent, ambidextrous, ambiguous, androgynous, amorous, ironic'. In her next life she will be a trapeze artist.

Kerrie Round received a BA (Hons) and PhD in history from the University of Adelaide. She has lectured in Australian history and heritage at the University of Adelaide and Vanderbilt University, USA and taught in the graduate diploma and masters program in applied historical studies in the Department of History, University of Adelaide. She has written and edited books and articles on the history of South Australia and was managing editor of *The Wakefield Companion to South Australian History*. She now works as an editor and consultant historian and spends her spare time reading, walking and killing pot plants.

A biography of Dame Roma Mitchell

Susan Magarey
& Kerrie Round

Wakefield Press
1 The Parade West
Kent Town
South Australia 5067
www.wakefieldpress.com.au

First published 2007
Reprinted in this revised edition with revised index 2009

Photograph facing title page: Roma Mitchell in court, photograph by Stewart Cockburn, published with kind permission of the *Advertiser*.
Designed by Liz Nicholson, designBITE
Printed and bound by Hyde Park Press

National Library of Australia
Cataloguing-in-publication entry

Author:	Magarey, Susan.
Title:	Roma the first: a biography of Dame Roma Mitchell/ authors, Susan Magarey; Kerrie Round.
Publisher:	Kent Town, S. Aust.: Wakefield Press, 2007.
ISBN:	978 1 86254 780 3 (pbk.)
Notes:	Includes index. Bibliography.
Subjects:	Mitchell, Roma, Dame, 1913–2000. Women lawyers – South Australia – Biography. Women judges – South Australia – Biography. Governors – South Australia – Biography. Women in public life – Australia.
Other Authors:	Round, Kerrie.
Dewey Number:	340.092

Contents

Acknowledgements

We have many people to thank for their help in learning to know Dame Roma Mitchell. We must thank everyone who was involved in producing the book, *Dame Roma: Glimpses of a Glorious Life* (Axiom Press), Adelaide, 2002, for it was this that in the beginning persuaded us of the need for a biography. Among them, we are particularly grateful to the Honourable Justice Tom Gray, Master Peter Norman and Helena Jasinski. We must thank Cyril Brown and Linda Knobben of the Research Branch of the University of Adelaide; the arithmetic required in preparing an application for funding to support our project depended entirely on them. Professor Margaret Davies of the Faculty of Law at Flinders University gave us good advice about the assessment of our grant application for which we are most grateful. And we must thank the Australian Research Council for the grant that enabled us to afford three of the six years of research and writing that have gone into this book.

In the course of that research, we incurred many debts. First, we are especially obliged to the staff of the Law Library, the Special Collections in the Barr Smith Library (particularly Cheryl Hoskin), the Barr Smith Library generally (and especially Margaret Hosking) and the Archives – all of the University of Adelaide.

We are grateful to the Special Collections Librarian at Flinders University, Gillian Dooley, and to Joan Stephenson of the Faculty of Social Sciences Office at Flinders University for translating into English a notebook of shorthand from among the Don Dunstan papers. We want to thank everyone who helped us at the State Library of South Australia, at State Records of South Australia, at Catholic Archives and Mercy Archives in Adelaide, at the Supreme Court Library and at the Library of the Law Society of South Australia. In particular, we are indebted to Jenny Scott of the State Library of South Australia, and, again, to the Honourable Justice Tom Gray for help in gaining us access to the Law Society. We thank Patricia Summerling, the Adelaide City Council, Sharon Polkinghorne and Ron Courtvriend of the *Advertiser*, and the Law Society for many of the pictures which appear in this book. Thanks, too, to the South Australian Parole Board, and the South Australian members of the Ryder-Cheshire Foundation, and to the Canberra staff of the Winston Churchill Memorial Trust. The National Library of Australia was always hospitable. We are especially grateful to Margie Burn, now of the National Library, who drew upon her experience of being the Special Collections Librarian at the University of Adelaide in the past to advise us to read the papers of Sir Walter Crocker, and to Jill Stevens who gained Sir Walter Crocker's permission for us to read his diary, held in Adelaide University's Special Collections.

Many people kindly gave us their time in interviews, telephone conversations and email exchanges. Thank you. You are listed in the Bibliography at the end of the book. Dr. Kylie O'Connell gave us advice about reading on the South Australian Police Force, and former Police Educator Daryl Anderson read a draft of Chapter Six and offered encouragement: thank you, too. Our gratitude to Dr Barbara Wall who rescued us from a dead-end over translations from Latin into English; to Dr Roma Varoneckas who gave us advice about Ruth Mitchell's health; to Tim Reeves who made copies for us of his articles concerning the tragic death of George Duncan; to Nick Jose who told us gossip about Don Dunstan's origins; to Anna Ragosa of the History Trust of South Australia who found and copied for us an article about Patricia Hackett; to Greg McCarthy who lent us a copy of his invaluable book about the South Australian Bank crisis; and to Mary Lyons who transcribed the recorded interviews, scanned a host of photographs, and lent us her mother's missal. Other friends talked with us about Dame Roma's life, about biography generally, and about the history of the twentieth century: Margaret Allen, Margaret Anderson, Desley Deacon, John Emerson, Fay Gale, Jill Roe, Ashley Marshall, Anne Levy, Linda Matthews, Carolyn Pickles, Judith Roberts, Tim Rowse and Kensington Gallery's Susan Sideris: thank you very much, all of you.

Once we had composed our story of Dame Roma's life, we wanted someone to read it. We are grateful to the Honourable Justice Catherine Branson for the time that she spent on it. To Laureate Professor Stuart Macintyre, the Honourable Justice David Bright, Professor Susan Sheridan, Associate-Professor David Hilliard and our publisher Michael Bollen, we owe a great debt and offer our heart-felt thanks. We are also profoundly grateful to our partners, David Round and Susan Sheridan, for incorporating our involvement with this work into the occasional dinner over the years.

‘I suppose generosity of spirit is more important really than anything else’

Roma Mitchell

Australian Biography II, p. 93

‘I certainly call myself a feminist, yes’

Roma Mitchell

Australian Biography II, p. 60

Timeline
Life of Roma Flinders Mitchell

1913	Born
1920	Starts school
1931	Starts university
1934	Admitted to the Bar
1935	Begins work as a barrister and solicitor
1938	Mother dies
1952	Elected to the Council of the Law Society of South Australia (FW)
1957	Appointed Convenor, Laws and Suffrage Committee, National Council of Women
1962	Appointed Queen's Counsel (FW)
	Elected to the Standing Committee of the Senate, University of Adelaide
1963	Elected Vice-President, Law Society of South Australia (FW)
1964	Appointed to the Executive, Law Council of Australia
1965	Appointed to the Winston Churchill Memorial Trust
	Appointed a Justice of the Supreme Court of South Australia (FW)
	Elected to Council, University of Adelaide
1968	Appointed to the Committee of Enquiry into Education in South Australia (the Karmel Committee)
	Appointed to the Board of Directors, Winston Churchill Memorial Trust (FW)
1969	Appointed Vice-President, (new) Friends of the Art Gallery
1971	Appointed Chairman, Criminal Law and Penal Methods Reform Committee (the Mitchell Committee)
	Awarded CBE
1972	Appointed Deputy Chancellor, University of Adelaide (FW)
1973	First of the five reports of the Mitchell Committee published
1975	Appointed Chairman, Parole Board of South Australia
	Presented the Boyer Lectures on the ABC (FW)
	Appointed one of the Deputy National Chairmen, Winston Churchill Memorial Trust
1977	The final Mitchell Committee Report published
	Awarded Queen's Silver Jubilee Medal

1978 Appointed a Royal Commission into the 'Salisbury Affair'
Appointed Chairman, State Heritage Committee
1980 Joined the Board of Governors, Adelaide Festival of Arts
1981 Appointed Chairman, Human Rights Commission (F)
Appointed to the Council of the Order of Australia
Appointed National President, Ryder-Cheshire Foundation
1982 Hugh and Ruth Gooch die
Created DBE
Built holiday house at Carrickalinga
1983 Appointed Chancellor, University of Adelaide (FW)
1984 Appointed to head the Social Security Royal Commission (Federal)
Appointed Chairman, Review of Services for Behaviourally Disordered Persons
Appointed National Chairman, Winston Churchill Memorial Trust
1985 Awarded Doctor of the University of Adelaide
1987 Delivered Meals on Wheels
1988 Appointed National President, Winston Churchill Memorial Trust
Appointed Chairperson, Aboriginal Legal Rights Movement Review Committee
Appointed Chairperson, South Australian Child Protection Council
Recorded a Bicentennial Boyer Lecture
Appointed to the Court of Appeal, Kiribati
1991 Appointed Governor (FW)
Made Companion of the Order of Australia
1993 Awarded Doctor of Laws honoris causa, Flinders University
1994 Awarded Doctor of the University of South Australia
Awarded Institution of Engineers Medal
1996 Appointed Chair, Ministerial Board of the Ageing
1997 Appointed Commandeur dans l'Ordre de la Légion d'Honneur
Invested with the Distinguished Cross of Merit with Crown of the Sovereign Military Order of St John (FAW)
1998 Appointed a Founding Trustee, Don Dunstan Foundation, University of Adelaide
2000 Presented with the Commander of the Royal Victorian Order (CVO) award
Dies

F: First
FW: First Woman
FAW: First Australian Woman

Chapter One

Growing Up Caring, Competitive and Catholic

In the Beginning

The dreaded telegram arrived. 'Missing, believed killed in action.' Roma, only just over four, would not believe it. She adored her tall handsome father. As the youngest of three, the first of whom had died as an infant, she competed for the affection he lavished on the precious next child, Ruth. She would rush to the front door to greet him, clamouring to be picked up – 'a younger member of a family is always fighting for recognition in some way', she said years later.[1] She still had the letter that he had sent her from England for her fourth birthday, asking after her teddies and if they were ever naughty. Daddy would bring her a little dog when he returned.[2] But then came the confirmation: Harold Flinders Mitchell had been killed in action, during the Battle of Dernancourt in France, on 5 April 1918.[3] Amid her own anguish, Roma's mother Maude determined to try to lessen the shock for seven-year-old Ruth, at school at St Dominic's Priory down the road: she would wait and tell her after tea. But she had not reckoned on little Roma.

Had Daddy told her to look after her mother while he was away? Maude suffered from headaches. Roma had taken to waiting at the door to meet Ruth when she came home from school, to warn her not to make any noise when their mother's head was hurting. This time, though, she pattered along the street to meet her – to tell her that their father was dead. After they had eaten that evening, Maude began to tell Ruth that there was, now, no hope of her father returning. Ruth burst into tears. There was no need to go on, she sobbed, Roma had already told her. Later, when Maude asked Roma why, the child replied, 'I wanted to save you having to do so': 'I had a very strange protective feeling', she was to recall. 'My mother and I were very close.'[4]

It was as though a great gong had sounded, a note that would reverberate throughout her life. Her mother would now be the single most important adult in her world until she was herself grown up, and she would protect her mother, take care of her with all her heart and mind and soul, because her father was no longer there to do so.

This was Roma Flinders Mitchell, born on 2 October 1913, under the sign of Libra. Her story takes place in Australia – 'the last of lands, the emptiest', wrote poet A.D. Hope – spanning a period that historian Michael Ignatieff has deemed '"the worst century there has ever been" in wanton destruction of human life and in murderous unreason masking itself as reason'.[5] A highly local story, it is, yet also and simultaneously a global story resonating with the great issues, the shifts and changes, across the world throughout that century. It begins in the city of Adelaide, core of a British colony founded less than a century earlier, on the plain that – by no means empty – had been home to the Kaurna people before the arrival of the ships from Britain, roughly in the middle of the southern curve defining the Australian continent. The forms that appear in her story derive from those origins: the British law that the colonists practised, with all its theatrical paraphernalia and terminology; a gradually developing copy of Westminster Parliament and Whitehall Government, but with deference to British rule and allegiance always observed; education adopted from schools and universities in England and Scotland, mostly. Only in its churches was it distinct, for, among all of Britain's colonies in Australia, South Australia was the 'paradise of dissent', with all the echoes such a phrase brought, of the Roundheads in

England, the Pilgrim Fathers – and Mothers – in New England in north America.

Roma Mitchell was baptised with three Christian names, the second – Alma – the name of Maude's younger sister. She would drop the Alma later, but during her early years she carried middle names that declared her allegiance to the families of both of her parents, neither of whom was a dissenter.

Theirs was an unlikely union. Maude Imelda Victoria Wickham was the oldest living child of William Wickham and Susanna Turley. Susanna died of tuberculosis in 1886, when Maude was only eight years old, and William – a groom – moved to the state of Victoria and re-married. Maude, her sister Alma, and possibly their baby brother, ten-month-old Harry, went to live with their maternal grandmother in Mount Gambier, a town of about 2,000 people, the culturally vibrant, social, commercial and administrative centre of a prosperous agricultural and pastoral district in the south-east of South Australia. There, Maude and Alma attended the Convent of Mercy. Their older sister, May, was brought up by her paternal aunts in Parkside, an inner suburb of Adelaide. Twenty years later, May Wickham – who might have been working as a barmaid, a frequent means of upward social mobility for women – married the witty, exuberant and glamorous young law student, Francis Villeneuve Smith, whose repartee at the expense of some of his lecturers almost, but not quite, resulted in his being forbidden to sit his final-year exams. He would go on to become the doyen of the South Australian legal profession.[6]

Harold Flinders Mitchell was a law student one year behind Frank Villeneuve Smith. But Harold was a reluctant lawyer, in spite of his heritage. His father, Samuel, had tossed in a successful commercial career – during which he served a term as mayor of the northern South Australian town of Port Augusta – to study law at the University of Adelaide, beginning in 1885 when he was thirty-three, the year in which Harold was born. He went on first to a distinguished practice in the law, then to election to the House of

Harold Flinders Mitchell, copied from Dame Roma Mitchell's Scrapbooks at Master Peter Norman's chambers, 2001.

Assembly, the lower house of the South Australian legislature. He was the member for the Northern Territory, a vast terrain – the largest electorate in the world – at that time governed from Adelaide, as one of the parliamentary group of progressive liberal wheat farmers, no doubt with connections from his days in Port Augusta. This group would, in 1906, become the Liberal Democratic Union [LDU] which achieved government that year, in alliance with the Labor Party. The alliance collapsed, leaving the LDU heading a government in which Samuel Mitchell served briefly as Attorney-General. Subsequently, he was made Government Resident of the Northern Territory, a position equivalent to the Lieutenant-Governor of South Australia. It also made him a judge in a court 'clothed with all the powers of a Supreme Court'. Not for long, though: the territory was handed over to the government of the Commonwealth of Australia in 1911, with Samuel Mitchell officiating over the occasion. Back in Adelaide, he was appointed first a police magistrate, then Commissioner – later Judge – of Insolvency.[7] It was a stellar career. Harold, his third child and second son, a prize-winning student at the exclusive St Peter's College, followed in his footsteps, but without great enthusiasm. Harold's interests were in milch cows and bee-keeping. He wanted to live in the countryside.[8] And, it soon became clear, he wanted to live in the countryside with Frank Villeneuve Smith's striking, dark-eyed sister-in-law, Maude Wickham.

Maude Imelda Victoria Mitchell, c. 1935, published with permission of the State Library of South Australia, PRG778/23/8, p. 40.

Harold had been articled to his father in 1903. Four years later, he moved to the town of Kingscote on Kangaroo Island off the south coast of South Australia to set up a practice for his father among a population of fewer than 1,300, a practice that his father transferred to him in 1908, the same year in which he graduated, a week after his marriage to Maude. Harold was a stalwart of local community life: secretary of the tennis club, a member of the Kingscote Literary Society, secretary of the local Agricultural, Horticultural and Pastoral Society, treasurer of the Kingscote Trades and

Progress Association. He was also a warden of St Alban's Church of England in Kingscote, and at times acted as a lay preacher.[9] This was the principal reason for his union with Maude Wickham being so unlikely, for she was a Catholic.

Did it matter? Yes, it did, even in South Australia where the proportion of Catholics in the population was considerably smaller than in other Australian states: 14% of the population in 1901, for instance, compared with 25% in New South Wales and 22% in Victoria.[10] Did this lessen the likelihood of tension between Catholics and Protestants in South Australia? The short answer to that question is yes. South Australia's Catholics were not all working class. They accounted for a large proportion of the state's publicans, and had a small but respected presence in the elite professions of law and medicine, as well as in political life. One of the early governors of South Australia – the local representative of the British monarch in the colony – had been Catholic, Sir Dominick Daly, from 1862 until 1868. The editor of the Catholic weekly, the *Southern Cross*, W.J. Denny, held the seats of West Adelaide and Adelaide in the lower house of the South Australian Parliament for the first thirty-three years of the twentieth century; he was also a minister in several governments. It would seem that there was no absolute barrier fashioned by religious prejudice to social or political advancement.

Yet Catholic clergy developed the cohesiveness of their community by emphasising its distinctiveness. They built up a network of Catholic schools, founded exclusive Catholic organisations, promoted their Irish heritage – with large and exuberant celebrations of St Patrick's Day on 17 March – and encouraged Catholics to keep their distance from other forms of Christianity. In South Australia only Catholics and Methodists formed communities that were sufficiently large and unified to sustain a weekly paper. The masthead of the *Southern Cross* announced it to be 'A Weekly Record of Catholic, Irish and General News'. During the twentieth century there may have been little overt or public antagonism between members of different Christian denominations. But there was, as historian David Hilliard has observed, a good deal of hostility among evangelical Protestants to the doctrines and rituals of the Catholic religion ('Romanism'), and a good deal of quiet discrimination against Catholics in some businesses and government departments. Roma Mitchell, herself, recalled that when she was a child there was, 'to a substantial extent, distrust on the part of adherents to one Christian religion of the religious practices of other Christian religions'. Her paternal grandparents would not associate with her mother and her children, because they were Catholics.[11]

At almost exactly the time when Maude Wickham and Harold Mitchell met, probably at May's aunt's house in company with Frank Villeneuve Smith, fresh regulations could have heightened tensions over religious difference. In 1908 the papal decree *Ne Temere* came into effect. This stipulated that no marriage involving a Catholic was valid unless it was celebrated before a Catholic priest or a bishop. Mixed marriages were to be strongly discouraged; Australian Catholic bishops determined that such marriages should not be solemnised before the main altar of a church but in a side chapel or sacristy. The service uniting Maude and Harold on 8 August 1908 was conducted in Archbishop's Court, behind the Catholic St Francis Xavier's Cathedral at the centre of the City of Adelaide, rather than before its altar or that of an Anglican church.[12]

This young couple was not alone. Maude Wickham may have been raised in the Catholic faith, but her older sister, May, had been brought up as an Anglican. And May had married Frank Villeneuve Smith, who was a Catholic, in St Oswald's Church of England in Parkside, an inner suburb of Adelaide. Alma, too, brought up as a Catholic with Maude, married an Anglican, successful salesman, Cecil Jenkins. The sisters were, and remained, good friends. Besides, Maude and Harold were in love. Their firstborn, Mignon, was born just seven and a half months after their wedding – a promise, perhaps? May and Frank Villeneuve Smith came to Kingscote and stayed at the Ozone Hotel just a month later – a celebration, perhaps, of two mixed marriages.[13]

But baby Mignon contracted meningitis. There was no doctor on Kangaroo Island. She died on the *Karatta* as Maude and Harold tried to get her to Adelaide for treatment, in March 1910.[14] They did not return to the island.

Instead they quartered, briefly, in Alberton, a working-class suburb with a high proportion of Catholics north-west of the city, near to Port Adelaide. Harold would have caught the train into the City of Adelaide to work with his father's firm in Queen's Chambers, in Currie Street. Maude was already pregnant. Ruth Flinders Mitchell was born on 20 July 1910 at Mrs Bartlett's Maternity Home, Buller Terrace, Alberton. They moved soon afterwards to Knightsbridge, east of the city, at the foot of the Mount Lofty Ranges, but in March 1911 were off to the country again. This time they stayed on the mainland, in Cowell, a wheat-shipping centre midway between Port Augusta and Port Lincoln on the dry stretches of Eyre Peninsula. Samuel Mitchell's connections, with the Masons from his time at Port Augusta and with the progressive wheat growers from his time in Parliament, would have furnished introductions. Harold launched himself into work, and a similar round of civic activities as on Kangaroo Island, with one, very modern, difference: he was treasurer and secretary of the new Jervois Automobile Club; he probably drove a car when he went to work in Cleve on Saturdays and Arno Bay on Wednesdays. Cowell also offered another modern moment: moving pictures were shown at the skating rink every Thursday night, followed by dancing until midnight.[15] Did they get out at night, Harold and Maude? Difficult with Ruth still so small.

At Cowell, Harold made a stab at a different life. Not cows and bees, this time. Instead, following one of his father's occupations in Port Augusta, he made a tentative beginning at supplementing his legal practice by buying and selling real estate. It went nowhere. They moved again, several times, Harold hanging up his shingle in Mannum then Renmark, offering consultations to the fruit growers in the towns along the River Murray.[16]

In 1913 Maude was pregnant again and determined that her third confinement, like her second, would take place in the city. She came to Adelaide to stay with sister Alma, and Cecil, in the exclusive suburb of Medindie. Roma Alma Flinders Mitchell was born at Quambi Nursing Home, Pennington Terrace, North Adelaide.[17] Then Maude took the new baby back to the Riverland.

Roma Mitchell would recall a moment of their time there. 'I must have been two', she said,

> and we lived in Renmark on the River Murray and I remember ... that it [the house] had a fairly large entrance hall and it was either my

> birthday or Christmas time and somebody had given me a mechanical toy. And I remember my father and another man whom I can't identify down on their hands and knees playing with the toy ... Somebody had given me the toy and they, in learning how to work it, were enjoying it themselves.[18]

Hardly the first or last child to be irritated by adults taking over her playthings.

Harold was restless, and not surprisingly. All of Anglo-Australia was in a ferment of jingoistic loyalty to the King of England and the British Empire. Australians had begun joining the Australian Imperial Forces within a week of Britain's declaration of war against Germany on 4 August 1914, and in less than two weeks 10,000 men had enlisted in Sydney alone. Even Irish-Australian supporters of Home Rule were caught up in the frenzy; the *Southern Cross* publicised accounts of Irish regiments and their heroism. But the initial rush of volunteers gradually dried up so the Federal Government organised recruitment drives. Then these, too, began to fail. In January 1916 recruits numbered 22,101, but by August of that year – with Catholic Irish reaction to the Easter Rising in Dublin in 1916 slowly lessening enthusiasm for all things English – there were only 6,170.[19] Conscription was on the horizon. Harold resolved to go to war.

On 17 July 1916 he was found medically fit to join the permanent military forces, and on 9 August he enlisted for service in the Great War. By the beginning of 1918 he was a second lieutenant with the 45th Battalion of the Australian Imperial Forces, engaged in some of the fiercest fighting of the war. He died in a counter-attack against German soldiers, 'one of the finest ever carried out by the Australian troops'. A gift that he had sent to Maude, the Anzac Book written and illustrated in Gallipoli by the Australian soldiers, reached her five weeks after his death.[20]

After the War

Maude and Ruth and Roma were living in Hill Street, North Adelaide, across the parklands from the Jenkinses in Medindie, on the brow of a gentle hill in a city known for its flatness. Ruth's school, St Dominic's Priory, was nearby, and on one side of the road was the splendid great pile of sandstone that was St Laurence's

Church. It was a pleasant house, newly painted with dainty wallpaper, and the usual outside bathroom. The Mitchells did not have it to themselves. Harold had allocated two-thirds of his allowance, the maximum amount allowed, to his family. As a private he received five shillings a day plus a tiny separation allowance; once he was an officer he earned fifteen shillings a day, but this amount was still small.[21] Maude Mitchell needed help with the rent, so they shared the house with two sisters, Katherine and Honoré Lenihan, who were studying for their Arts degrees at the University of Adelaide. The Lenihans looked after the children when Maude was ill; her headaches were a serious affliction that Ruth would inherit. They read to them, too, and played with them and took them on outings. Katherine Lenihan kept notes about precocious, round-cheeked, bright-eyed young Roma.

The house had no garden at the back, only about a metre of asphalt:

> Mother and Roma are going to town. 'What would you like me to bring you Miss K?' the little one runs into my room to ask me, and then, without waiting for an answer – 'Oh! I know – I'll bring you a yard!' 'A yard of what, Roma?' 'A yard of nuffin – just a nice back yard!'
>
> ... Mother is clearing away the high tufts of grass growing in the cracks of asphalt, and stands beside the last one by the bathroom door. 'Mother' pleads an earnest little voice – 'Please don't cut that one down!' 'But it's so untidy, Roma,' objects Mother. 'But the fairies won't come here to play at all if you do!' Tuft left standing.[22]

The girls had plenty of toys. Harold's younger sister, Jean, passed on to them a Noah's Ark that she had been given when she was a child and travelled with her parents to Germany, and perhaps, too, a jacket and trousers that the Chinese community in Darwin had given her in 1911, when she was about thirteen.[23] And there were dolls.

> A colony of dolls lives behind Mother's dining room door. Every now and then when the family gets too numerous, Mother makes a swoop, and the dolls retire to the big trunk in the bathroom where the other toys live.

> Then, one might observe the small mother retrieving them one by one, by slow degrees and very unobtrusively.
>
> Many journeys to the bathroom have resulted in a well-populated colony this morning. 'What a lot of children you have, today, Roma!' I remarked looking at the tribe. 'Yes!' responded the small parent bitterly 'and every one of 'em's playing up!'
>
> ... Later that afternoon Roma began journeys to the trunk in the bathroom of her own accord, and many favourite toys disappeared from public gaze.
>
> This, I knew, forecasted a visit from Baby Beryl – a twelve month old cousin. Roma loved her – but the colony did suffer.

Little Beryl Jenkins bit a piece out of one of the dolls that afternoon. Another day, when Roma was dealing none too gently with the dolls herself, Katherine Lenihan protested.

> 'Roma' said I, 'don't spoil those toys. Keep them for when you have little Romas of your own.' The child gave a roguish laugh: 'Oh, but' she said 'I'm not going to have any little Romas of my own!' Knowing how fond she was of younger children I was surprised. 'But you are fond of babies – how is this?' 'Well' she answered, with her adorable lisp. 'I've been finking things over. I'd love them so much, I couldn't help spoiling them and I hate spoilt children, so I've made up my mind not to have any at all!'

One morning, Honoré noticed her standing at the door as she and Katherine recited Wordsworth's 'Ode on the Intimations of Immortality' to each other, committing it to memory. Roma 'clasped her hands together and stood as if she had seen a vision: "Oh, please say that again!" she implored.'

> Our birth is but a sleep and a forgetting:
> The Soul that rises with us, our life's Star,
> Hath had elsewhere its setting,
> And cometh from afar:
> Not in entire forgetfulness
> And not in utter nakedness,
> But trailing clouds of glory do we come
> From God, who is our home:
> Heaven lies about us in our infancy!

One night, she persuaded Katherine into 'an entirely new and unorthodox Highland fling' with her. This was fun. But then it turned sour. Roma wouldn't let Ruth join in, and when Katherine scolded her for this, refused to say she was sorry. Even the next morning, she still wouldn't apologise, and when Katherine told her she thought her behaviour selfish, Roma replied, 'in a perfectly judicial tone': 'I'm not sorry, and if I said I was it would be telling a lie. And surely you don't want me to tell a lie!' Impossible little prig! She did give in, later, whispering in Katherine's ear, 'I've been sorry all the time, but I just couldn't say it.'

A relief for grief-stricken Maude, these two adult women must have been. She never recovered from Harold's death, and never contemplated remarrying. The subject did come up, but as a joke. 'My sister and I, as we got older, were little horrors', Roma Mitchell recalled. 'We'd say, "oh, we'd leave home"' – threatening to abandon their mother to the delights of some fancied new nuptial bliss.[24] But now, Maude was going to have to make some decisions and arrangements. Not for her a return to the country; that had been Harold's dream. She would stay in the city, and she would stay in one place. She had slightly more money: widows of lieutenants received £91 a year, the equivalent of a private's pay, plus £12 annually for each child under sixteen. No doubt her brothers-in-law helped, too. For Maude had not been educated to earn a living, herself, despite her schooling by the Mercy nuns in Mount Gambier. 'She had to struggle along, keeping up appearances', her youngest daughter reflected later. Women of her generation 'tolerated things modern women would not put up with'.[25] What she could do, though, was to make sure Ruth and Roma would learn how to win their livelihoods.

First, Ruth must stop attending St Dominic's Priory. This was 'where Catholics sent their daughters to be educated as ladies'; there was 'a large concentration on fancy work', rather than anything useful. Maude enrolled both Ruth and Roma in a school run by the Mercy nuns, St Aloysius College, in Angas Street in the centre of the City of Adelaide, next to St Francis Xavier's Cathedral. Second, she moved them to 48 Kyre Avenue, Kingswood, a villa with an extensive rambling garden close to the foothills of the Mount Lofty ranges to the south of the city. From here, on Sunday afternoons, they could walk past the Mitcham Reserve and up, up the hill to Brownhill Creek.[26] Here at Kyre Avenue, they were only a few streets away from 'Halsbury', the house that May and Frank Villeneuve Smith built at 13 High Street, Unley Park, named after the foundational legal text, Halsbury's *Laws of England*.

The Villeneuve Smiths were themselves having children: their daughter, Lindley, born in 1910, their first son, Inglis, in 1913, and a second son, Cairns, in 1923 – all of them named after English and Scottish Law Lords. Frank's spectacular practice meant that they were doing very well. He worked extremely hard; he once protested that he knew 'what it is not to be with my family on Sunday for a whole year', and to work 'five nights a week after midnight'. He coupled such labours with his forceful personality, his good looks, his extraordinary command of the English language, his ready wit, and the large pince-nez that he kept attached to a long black silk ribbon around his neck, and used to impress members of a jury. It is often said that there is a narrow border between the practice of the law and a career on the stage; Frank Villeneuve Smith showed just how narrow it could be. His partner, Harry Alderman, once asked a member of a jury 'what he had thought of Mr Villeneuve Smith's address. "Truly, Mr Alderman", the juror replied, "I didn't understand what all those words meant, but I only had to look at Mr Smith to know what he was driving at."' His most legendary exploit dated from his student days.

Francis Villeneuve Smith copied from Dame Roma Mitchell's Scrapbooks in Master Peter Norman's chambers, 2001

After a late night, the youthful Villeneuve Smith was on his way home from a student gathering. He stopped and thumped on the street door of a two storey building at the corner of Grote and Brown Street calling out repeatedly for 'Paul, Paul'. Villeneuve Smith knew only that someone named Paul lived at this address. In time, a drowsy Paul appeared at the upstairs window. Villeneuve Smith called up, 'Have I the honour of addressing Paul?' 'Yes', replied Paul, testy over this early morning disturbance. 'I've often wondered, old man', said Villeneuve

> Smith, 'whether you ever got an answer to that long letter you wrote to the Ephesians.'

He was also known for his inability to manage a tap, 'turning them into fountains by his touch', and for drinking binges after bouts of intense pressure in the courtroom – not uncommon in the profession – leaving Harry Alderman to maintain order in the practice. Francis Villeneuve Smith was made King's Counsel in 1919 at the age of thirty-six, one of the youngest silks then practising in Australia, and only the second Catholic appointed to silk in South Australia.[27] May maintained order at home when he was working – or drinking.

Domestic life at the Villeneuve Smiths was not exclusively about the law. Maude would go to the races with Frank and May on Saturdays, and – since Frank did not drive – Ruth and Roma could ride about in their chauffeur-driven car, Roma getting irritated with Lindley when she was familiar with the chauffeur, and bored when the children were left in the car while the adults ran errands, grouchy at not being the centre of attention. Ruth and Roma stayed with the Villeneuve Smiths often; a safety-net, perhaps, for times when Maude had a headache. They spent time with their Jenkins cousins, too – Cecil born in 1907, Merle in 1908, Rex in 1910, and Beryl, the only one of this family younger than

Roma Mitchell, Merle Jenkins, Beryl Jenkins, Ruth Mitchell at Brighton, c. 1923, published with permission of the State Library of South Australia, PRG778/23/9, p. 10

Roma Mitchell, young enough to be a threat to Roma's dolls, born in 1917. They stayed with them in the summer when Alma and Cecil would rent a house at Seacliff and take the little Mitchells with them to spend two weeks or so in the sun and the sand and the sea.[28]

From Kyre Avenue, the Mitchells could walk to Mass at Our Lady of Dolours in Cambridge Terrace, scarcely two blocks away. Mass was celebrated in the parish school room until 1928 when the present church, a Spanish mission-style building, was opened. From 1923, their parish priest was Father Cornelius Crowley, a 'legendary friend of battlers', known for having arrived for Mass barefooted because he had given his shoes to a swagman on the road. 'What's happened to your coat, Father?' enquired Maude one mid-winter day, when he arrived to visit the Mitchells. It was the same story: someone had come to the presbytery who needed it more than he did. He was a great reader, Roma Mitchell remembered, and 'very interesting intellectually'. Maude was a keen reader too; just as well, with long lonely evenings once the children had gone to bed.[29]

Young Roma had a number of *Play Box Annuals*, collections of British story books published each year, including one her father had sent her from Cambridge in 1917. Better food for the imagination in her copy of *Alice in Wonderland*.

> 'There is no use trying,' said Alice; 'one can't believe impossible things.' 'I dare say you haven't had much practice,' said the Queen. 'When I was your age, I always did it for half an hour a day. Why, sometimes I've believed as many as six impossible things before breakfast.'

She kept her devotional books: *The First Christmas. The Infant Jesus* by F.W. Faber, D.D., and *The Child's First Prayer Book*, which Maude gave her for her tenth birthday. In it Roma kept the death notice that Maude had inserted in the daily paper for Harold. She read the weekly *Southern Cross*, too, and regularly won its children's competitions. One was for a book review published under the heading 'My Favourite Book'. The book, *Nellie Doran. A Story of Australian Home and School Life* by one Miriam Agatha, depicts characters who, fourteen-year-old Roma Mitchell decided, 'are fitting models for school girls to follow'. The central character, Nellie, finally overcomes her parents' poverty to go to school, where Sister Mary Cecilia recognises her innate talent as a violinist. She shows her 'sweetness of disposition' at one point, and at another reveals her talent with the violin when playing 'Ave Maria' at a concert in honour of the Reverend Mother's feast day. Then she is summoned to play for a visiting musician, who offers to send her to Germany where she would become a famous musician. But that would mean leaving her beloved parents. 'It was a great opportunity, but Nellie declined, for she knew that it would be a great grief to her parents to have to part with her, and so she sacrificed all for love of them.'[30] It is saccharin moralising, no doubt, but also an affirmation that must have gladdened Maude Mitchell's heart.

The youngest in a household of women, Roma Mitchell was the centre of attention throughout the years of her formation, growing into a capacity and power to protect. She drank in her faith with her mother's milk. The Catholic faith – beliefs, rituals and sacraments rich with antiquity – formed a bedrock for her being, imparting a certainty in the fundamental ordering of the world, a sureness of belonging in it, as secure as her mother's love. Learning, amid the cultured, musical and educationally distinguished Mercy nuns – another environment almost exclusively of women – she would find the elements that made up that capacity to take care, to protect. She would, too, develop a fierce ambition; success inspires competitiveness and the desire for greater success, and Roma Mitchell would succeed, from the word go. She would also – for was she not born under the star most often represented by the scales of justice – hone a fine sense of right and wrong, a spin-off from a competitiveness that extended even to her teachers.

Saint Aloysius

From Kingswood, Ruth and Roma could catch the tram to school. The school, officially renamed St Aloysius High and Boarding School in 1904, but usually referred to as Angas Street, was the work of a community of Sisters of Mercy who had migrated from Dublin to Buenos Aires in the 1850s, then at the beginning of the 1880s to both Adelaide and Mount Gambier in South Australia. In

St Francis Xavier's Cathedral, before spire added, published with permission of the Adelaide City Council.

Adelaide, they bought a two-storey house in Angas Street next to St Francis Xavier's Cathedral, established a fee-paying school upstairs, and downstairs, St Cecilia's, a school for the poor. It is possible that the nuns helped the Mitchells by foregoing fees for them even though Ruth and Roma attended the fee-paying school; they did so for a few other families. Ruth Mitchell began attending the upstairs school on 2 February 1919. Roma was still too young, so Maude taught her to read at home. Roma Mitchell started school on 3 February 1920, a few months after her sixth birthday. The school was small: thirty-two nuns, forty-six boarders and 183 day pupils. Even after its new buildings opened in 1922, including the magnificent Italianate Memorial Chapel, it had only 221 day pupils and fifty-two boarders. The girls knew each other, and their teachers, as individuals. The nuns, too, for all their remoteness – they lived in the Sisters' House, always wore their habits, refrained from eating in front of their pupils – knew each of their students. Sister Teresa (Dunlevie) awarded Roma Mitchell an Honour Badge in grade two or three, saying quietly to an older student, 'That little girl will go a long way.'[31] A star in a small firmament shines especially brightly.

School days were saturated with religion. Each day began with morning prayer, everyone kneeling on the floor beside her desk. Each lesson began with a prayer. They all recited a Hail Mary each time the clock struck:

> Ave Maria, gratia plena, Dominus tecum; benedicta tu in mulieribus, et benedictus fructus ventris tui, Jesus. Sancta Maria, Mater Dei, ora pro nobis peccatoribus, nunc et in hora mortis nostrae. Amen

Everyone joined in reciting the Angelus at noon:

> . . . Ora pro nobis, sancta Dei Genitrix.
> Ut digni efficiamur promissionibus Christi . . .

Everyone joined in singing a hymn at the end of the day.[32] The church's liturgical calendar governed their year: the Annunciation of Our Lady in March, and prayers for Saint Joseph, Spouse of Our Lady; All Saints in November; the Immaculate Conception of the Blessed Virgin Mary in December. The younger girls learned the catechism by heart. All students heard stories from the Bible, prayed, sang hymns, often and every day. They attended lessons on Christian doctrine. They competed with each other for prizes for attendance, for good conduct, for amiability, awarded at the monthly assemblies before the whole school. They visited the new chapel for Mass and Benediction. Mass was celebrated in Latin by a priest, standing alone and remote at the high altar – a challenging mystery. They undertook a retreat each year: one or two days of silence, prayer and reflection under the watchful eye of a priest. Roma liked the peace and quiet; she also liked being allowed into the chapel, usually off-limits for the schoolgirls. They made their first Confession and their first Communion in the Cathedral next door. They learned their parts for the performance of a play at lunch time to mark a nun's patronal feast day. Only boarders could be prefects. Day girls established their capacity to be leaders by belonging to the sodality of the Children of Mary. Roma joined, wearing the blue cloak, ribbon, badge and veil for the first time at her consecration ceremony. She was expected to emulate the Virgin and pray to her for the virtues of purity and modesty. And each year – marking the school's specifically Irish heritage and allegiances – the girls took part in the city-wide celebration of St

Patrick's Day, helping to decorate the floats drawn by draught horses and later motorised lorries, joining in the sports that were held on the Adelaide Oval, singing at the evening concert.[33]

After ten years or so, it would feel as though the ritual was hard-wired into your heart and your brain, as essential to your being as breathing. So it was for Roma Mitchell. She attended Mass every week of her life, no matter where she was, and, in her later years, every day.

In 1920 Mother Mary Cecilia Cunningham inherited a fortune from her mother in Argentina. She gave it to the Sisters of Mercy and they used some of it to have the Angas Street school and convent expanded. It was a large fortune – £120,000. They used it, as well, to have their agent outbid the Catholic archbishop at the auction of a palatial house that had belonged to Robert and Joanna Barr Smith, also in Angas Street, so that the palace became part of a convent instead of the episcopal residence of his desires.[34]

Nuns are bound by a vow of obedience, the Sisters of Mercy no less so than any others. But these were also independent-minded women, accustomed to a leadership that made 'judicious use of subversion' in the service of their ministry, and that was 'passionately committed to the dignity and worth of women'. The younger sisters who had joined the order in Argentina brought into the school curriculum a cultured, elegant and musical emphasis, derived from wealthy upper-class South American families, with a focus on languages and painting. Roma Mitchell was to recall her childhood favourite pictures being Bouguereau's *Virgin and Child*, Waterhouse's *Circe Invidiosa*, Tom Roberts' *The Breakaway* and E. Philips Fox's *Alfresco*. Her recollection, made in a gubernatorial speech some seventy years later, offered a judicious mix of sacred and profane, European and Australian, appropriate to her occasion no doubt. But it did nevertheless include in its list a representation of Circe, the woman who turned men into beasts, and this could have been an allusion to the Mercy nuns' willingness to encompass the profane as well as the sacred in their education.[35] Newer recruits from the Australian state of Victoria included well-educated sisters, some of whom had university degrees. They designed the curriculum to encourage academic excellence and achievement, as well as the Christian virtues of devotion and selflessness. 'The Sisters were ambitious for those of their students who could do well.'[36]

As little girls, Ruth and Roma went to school with white pinafores over their everyday clothes, graduating by the mid-1920s to the standard uniform – a navy blue pleated tunic over a white long-sleeved blouse with a navy tie. In summer they wore white panama hats, and in winter navy felt ones; there were blazers for the winter, too, with the school motto on the pocket: 'Loyal en tout'. Hats and gloves were compulsory in the street. They were to speak properly: the nuns tried to teach Roma to overcome the lisp Katherine Lenihan had found so enchanting; it remained, though, as a slight curl of the tongue, forward in her mouth. They were to be well-behaved: their schooling included manners, behaviour and obedience, with respect for the sisters to be evident at all times; the girls carried their books for them, opened doors for them, stood up when they arrived for class. They learned deportment with a book balanced on the head to make them stand up straight. St Aloysius did teach needlework, but – to Maude's relief – for only an hour a week in junior secondary school. Roma was to confess:

Roma Mitchell in her new school uniform, St Aloysius College, published with permission of the State Library of South Australia, PRG778/23/1, p. 1.

> I didn't shine at sewing. We had to make a pillowcase to teach us all the different stitches. My pillowcase got dirtier and dirtier and it never was finished. So I wasn't a star at that at all. I must say, digressing, that you do imbibe things from your parents a bit. When my sister went to St Dominic's Priory ... my mother was slightly put off by the fact that they had a very large concentration on fancy work and I suppose I heard that and it must have impressed me as I was never very enthusiastic about fancy work ... I never, never completed my pillowcase.

She was hopeless at sport, too: 'I was skinny and small until I was 13 or 14 when I sprang up.' She grew tall, but was never especially physically adept. Someone took a photograph of her in school uniform with a golf club – once, but never again, and she 'gave up tennis after deciding it did more to amuse her friends than help her'. But she did learn to ride a horse. During her first years at school, she made friends with another Angas Street pupil, Lorna Lumbers, and would visit her at home. The Lumbers family lived in the countryside at Salisbury where they owned orange orchards and grape vines. Young Lorna and Roma used to spend their time careering about on horseback.[37]

Lorna Lumbers and Roma Mitchell at Paradise, c. 1922, published with permission of the State Library of South Australia, PRG778/23/9, p. 4.

Roma learned to swim, as well, but not at school. During the long hot Adelaide summers, she and Ruth spent time at the beach with other friends as well as their Jenkins cousins. Roma would stay with the Lumbers family, if they took a house at Seacliff or Glenelg. And both Mitchell girls spent a number of holidays with younger friends who had a large house on a hillock at Brighton: the Whytes, who escaped from life on a station beyond Port Augusta to spend the summer at the seaside. These were Jean and Phyllis, 'Phyllis' translated into 'Billie'. Their mother, born Kitty Macully, must have relished these holidays. She was a powerful swimmer who had been awarded the Grand Diploma of the Royal Life Saving Association, and was famous for having saved the life of a drowning woman in 1919. She spent the summer giving swimming lessons from the Brighton Jetty, and doubtless taught Ruth and Roma to swim. But then tragedy struck. On 18 March 1926, Kitty Whyte dived off the jetty into the jaws of a four-metre white pointer shark, and died minutes later. When someone asked young Roma Mitchell how the shark had taken Mrs Whyte – surely a strange question to address to a twelve year old – she thought for a moment, then gave a wonderfully literal and unemotional reply: 'By the femur bone', she said. The Whyte girls were younger than Roma and Lorna Lumbers; Lorna recalled Roma being teacherly with them, insisting that Billie rehearse her lessons, even on the beach.[38]

Jean and Billie Whyte with their dog, published with permission of the National Library of Australia

Lessons at Angas Street were in English literature; ancient history, which meant the empires of the Greeks and Romans two thousand and more years ago; modern history, which meant a history of England, though Catholic histories presented Henry VIII, his wives and the 'Reformation' in a very different light than did histories written by Protestants; Latin; French; geography; geology; physiology; and arithmetic – where the enlightened nuns set the tables to music 'in triple or duple time'. It was not a curriculum especially shaped to the interests that girls were supposed to cultivate. In English, as well as learning grammar and how to parse and analyse a sentence, they read such boys' adventure stories as Robert Louis Stevenson's *Treasure Island* and *Kidnapped* and Shakespeare's *As You Like It* in which the heroines run away to live, cross-dressed, in the Forest of Arden. Does such reading encourage girls to be tomboys? To develop a robust sense of adventure themselves? They went to performances of Shakespeare by local actors Allan Wilkie and his wife – called Miss Hunter-Watts for the stage – performances 'given in difficult circumstances', Roma tactfully decided later. They were also subjected to Oliver Goldsmith's two best-known poems, 'The Traveller' and 'The Deserted Village', rhyming couplets of mind-numbingly arcane reflection. But there was, as well, Dickens and *A Christmas Carol*. Roma won prizes: *Round the Fire Stories* at the end of Grade IV, and *Golden Annual for Girls* at the end of her time in primary school, and in the senior school, histories of the Athenian, Macedonian and Roman empires, Sydney Herbert's *Modern Europe 1789–1914*, and – a progressive innovation – Ernest Scott's *Short History of Australia*. In the senior school she escaped the classes that involved 'getting hearts and eyes to cut up from the abattoirs', though Ruth took Physiology and won a prize for it. Roma's forte was Latin, a field depending primarily, at least in the early stages, on diligence and a good memory – rehearsing her lessons, just as she made Billie Whyte do. She won the school's prize for Latin in 1929; the mysteries of the Latin Mass would no longer be so unknowable. She was also dux of the school, not merely once but twice: in 1928, when she took her Leaving Certificate and gained three credits, and then again in 1929, when she did Leaving Honours, gained two credits and won the Annie Montgomerie Martin Medal for topping the state in French. Maude decided that, as an October child, Roma was too young to go on to the university, and would benefit from an extra year at school. So Roma repeated Leaving Honours and topped the state in Latin in 1930, a source of special satisfaction for this competitive young woman because it was usually a boy from St Peter's College, Harold's *alma mater*, who took that honour.[39]

From the beginning, she shone brightly. She would shoot questions at her teachers, and sometimes they were difficult to answer. She could be distinctly sharp. When Mother Magdalene criticised her for whistling, Roma snapped back that Queen Mary was a great whistler. Reverend Mother was reduced to 'Well, I suppose people have their faults.' She would argue with Sister Camillus, her music teacher, too. She told Lorna Lumbers that, as the youngest of thirteen children, Sister Camillus had probably joined the convent because she couldn't get any personal attention any other way. She developed respect and affection for some of the other nuns: Sister Margaret Mary, who supervised her first three years in the primary school, Sister Angela, Mother Cecilia, and Sister Ignatius who taught French. But respect or not, 'if there was ever any question of having to speak up for somebody, I always found myself doing it. I was the one saying "That wasn't fair".' She competed fiercely, especially with Molly Brazel, Lorna Lumbers was to recall. 'I was competitive at school', Dame Roma remembered; she remained friends with Molly Brazel long afterwards, nevertheless. She joined the St Aloysius Girl Guide troop. The Girl Guide movement aimed to create a sense of belonging to the British Empire for each individual, regardless of class or politics or religion. Roma went further: setting out to care for the young, she initiated a Brownie pack and was its first Brown Owl. She also had a brief spell as a member of a branch of the Junior Catholic Women's League, established at St Aloysius late in 1929, where she may have developed further her taste for debating.[40]

Mercifully, she had a sense of humour, as well, or she would have been altogether too like Mary Bennett, the priggish sister in *Pride and Prejudice*. She delighted in the informality of an encounter with Archbishop Spence, when he was walking through the school grounds one day, and said, 'Well, I hope you kids have a good holiday'. She was generous; she did Beryl Pickhaver's Latin homework for her. She could be fun; she and Lorna Lumbers sang a duet at a school concert, 'Old Friends are the Fairest, Old Friends are the Rarest'. She developed a remarkable gift for friendship; she and Lorna remained friends all her life. And she had fun. At the elaborate operetta and concert produced to celebrate the opening of St Cecilia's Hall on 20 September 1925,

Ruth was Tamborina, one of two Spanish dancers, and Roma and Lorna were dancing fairies.[41]

School took up most of her time. But not all of it. She learned eurhythmics at school, but went to dancing classes run independently. She learned to Charleston. She danced with her cousin, Cecil Jenkins. She waltzed with another friend, Kay Brownbill; they trod on each other's toes, watched by their proud mothers. The girls danced with each other at school socials; they were not allowed to invite boys to join them. She learned to play the piano at school, principally to please Maude who longed for a daughter to graduate from Adelaide University's Elder Conservatorium of Music. She gave up those lessons when she was fifteen or sixteen, telling Maude that she would never make a musician. But she loved music, all the same. She remembered listening, when she was still at school, to a St Aloysius old scholar, Hilda Gill, singing at a children's party, marvelling at how lovely she and her voice were. She and Ruth went to hear the Czech violinist, Jan Kubelik, when he visited Adelaide in about 1925. She and Ruth went with the Villeneuve Smiths to watch the superlative Russian ballerina, Anna Pavlova, when she danced – floating through the air like thistledown – at the Theatre Royal in Hindley Street in 1926. The school organised excursions: train rides to Belair National Park for picnics, for instance. The family organised others: a visit to Wirths Circus to see lions and flying trapeze artists, and in 1927, Maude took the girls to watch George and Elizabeth, Duke and Duchess of York – future British monarchs – drive through the streets of Adelaide in an open carriage.[42]

A Legal Ambition

'Always', she said. 'Always I intended to be a barrister.'[43] She said so, remarkably, when she was only twelve and being interviewed for her suitability for financial assistance from the McCaughey Bequest for the education of children of servicemen killed in the Great War.[44] There were obvious examples before her in her family: her father, however reluctant a lawyer he had been, and her scintillating Uncle Frank. But they were men. School offered other, female, examples: Mary Tenison Woods (née Kitson), a St Aloysius old scholar, graduated in law from the University of Adelaide in

1916, the first woman in the state to achieve a law degree, and another Angas Street old scholar, Clare Sparkes Harris, also graduated in law, in 1923. The Mercy nuns were proud of them, and of other pupils who gained academic distinction, and held them up as salutary examples. When the wonderfully combative and victorious Mother Mary Cecilia Cunningham asked Roma, then aged about fifteen, what she intended to do when she left school, Roma replied, 'Go to the varsity to study law.' Mother Cecilia corrected her, but not to discourage her ambition, merely to require her to say the full word, 'university'. Moreover, she had Maude with her, like wind in her sails. Quite a number of well-meaning people, Roma Mitchell would recall, 'had the temerity to tell me and my mother that the law was not a career for a young girl to aspire to. Fortunately, she and I ignored their advice.'[45]

Roma had even more reason, now, to take care of Maude. Did she know it? She had been only twelve when Maude found she had breast cancer. Did Maude try to protect both daughters, this time, from information that would render them apprehensive, fearful for her? What she certainly did protect them from was the knowledge that the doctor had said he could operate on her, and that might deal with the disease for some time, but the operation was risky. And risk leaving Ruth and Roma as orphans? Oh no! Maude refused the operation. The doctor said she would be able to manage for some time, even without an operation. But she would die before her allotted span. All the more reason, then, for young Roma to go to the university and study law and make a good living.

It was as though Roma's sails caught a great gust of wind: a great surge bore her forward. For Maude was wholly and whole-heartedly with her tall, angular, clever daughter. Decades later, Kay Brownbill, of the dancing classes, wrote to Roma of the look on her mother's face: 'I saw when she looked at you that she had no fear, because she TRUSTED you.'[46]

Intelligent, ambitious, competitive and hard working, Roma Mitchell would have had the world at her feet – if she had been a man. Being a woman, the best thing to do, it seemed, was to ignore the difference as much as possible, at least so far as learning and work were concerned. Her abilities gave her a measure of distance on some of the teaching instilled by the nuns. She had thought Sister Camillus, who taught her Latin, was 'a pretty broad-minded nun for those times'. But Sister Camillus told her to translate 'nymphae nudae' as 'the nymphs in light attire'. When it came to the exams, Roma Mitchell didn't do anything of the sort. 'I wouldn't have got first place if I had.'[47] And getting first place was immensely important, for this showed her – to herself, and to the world – to be a star, shining brightly in a larger firmament.

A good girl, but capable of ignoring her teachers; an intensely devoted daughter, drawing strength from her mother's love just as she gave her mother her protectiveness and her caring. A complex person, with several selves already: Roma Mitchell was ready to move out of the sheltered enclave of her schooling and into the world.

Chapter Two
Courses in Law, and Life

A British Society in the Great Depression

It was a larger world than Roma Mitchell had known, to be sure, beyond St Aloysius College. But it was not so very large. In the early 1930s, Adelaide had a population of roughly 312,000 almost entirely Anglo-Saxon people, and that represented more than half of the population of the whole of South Australia. Adelaide was a

King William Street, 1930s, published with permission of the Adelaide City Council

city-state.[1] A 'German *Residenzstadt*' decided Sidney and Beatrice Webb, visiting Fabian socialists from England in 1898:

> the capital of a little principality, with its parks and gardens, its little court society, its absence of conspicuous industrialism, and its general air of laying itself out to enjoy quietly a comfortable life.[2]

But, despite the German settlers in the Barossa Valley to the north of the Adelaide plain – grotesquely reviled during the Great War – most people thought the culture of this city the most Anglophile of all in Australia. Middle-class accents were Australian versions of the English southern counties: in Adelaide people said 'chance' and 'dance' with long 'a's, to rhyme with 'darn' or 'farm'. 'Apart from its sunnier climate', recalled former country lad, Walter Crocker, in town to finish his education in the 1920s, 'the Adelaide of those days belonged in all things to the English world – in its temperament no less than in most of its practices'.[3] Others pointed to the excellence of the Scots as colonists, personified by pioneering nineteenth-century journalist, feminist and electoral reformer, Catherine Helen Spence.[4] The first statue carved in Adelaide was of Robbie Burns, unveiled on the corner of Kintore Avenue and North Terrace in 1894.[5] Whichever – it was British.

It was also small, and divided into a hierarchy that accorded social primacy to wealth derived from ownership of land – large acreage, up country – on which people pastured sheep and cattle, conducted agriculture and viticulture, or mined for copper; that workforce had initially been imported from Cornwall. Social cachet attached to early arrival in a colony whose British population – unlike that of the eastern colonies, or the west – was free of convicts: these people belonged to Old Adelaide Families. It took the irreverently democratic late twentieth century to point out that such a soubriquet yielded the acronym 'OAFs'. But it was not a rigid or closed hierarchy. Historian Hugh Stretton has pointed out that the Adelaide Establishment was

> an open oligarchy, willing to recruit talent; and they seem to have conserved, in at least a few of themselves, some of the radical propensities that had founded the colony in the first place.

Another historian, Dirk Van Dissel, agreed. The 'gentry group did not have rigidly defined boundaries' he noted, 'its edges were blurred and there were groupings of various kinds within it': dissenters, especially Methodists (a quarter of South Australia's population by 1901), as well as Anglicans; doctors and lawyers as well as graziers, for instance. For men, attendance at the Arnoldian Anglican St Peter's College, founded in 1847, contributed social eminence as well. St Peter's College – 'Saints' – educated a majority of the Adelaide Establishment; 36 per cent of South Australian men born before 1918 who appeared in *Who's Who in Australia* in 1988 had been taught there, a higher proportion than from all of the other South Australian Protestant schools combined. Such concentration was exceptional: private Anglican schools dominated the upper ranks of the social hierarchy of all the capital cities in Australia, but only in Adelaide was that domination achieved by a single school.

Walter Crocker grew up in South Australia, schooled in Adelaide, and then went on to become an eminent diplomat on an international stage. But when he retired, he returned to Adelaide, considering its smallness an advantage.

> The size of Adelaide was manageable socially as well as administratively. This meant an inter-penetrating knowledge of groups and persons of a kind which kept the charlatan, the crook, and the climber, in his place . . . The cost was snobbery . . .

Snobbery, indeed. 'Briefly summed up', wrote 'Thistle Anderson', *nom-de-plume* of satirist Mrs Herbert Fisher,

> the creed of Adelaide so-called Society runs:–
>
> 'I believe in Lewis Cohen, Mayor of Adelaide, and in Sir George LeHunte (or any other man), Governor of South Australia, from whom much hospitality may be expected. He was appointed in England, and ascended into Government House. From thence he shall issue many invitations. I believe in the social laws, in much going to Church, in doing unto others as they would do unto you if they could, in the charity that will be beneficial to our social position, and in the Life of the Everlasting, Amen.'

Certainly, Government House, with all its connections with Britain, was an important centre of social life for the gentry: they were invited there for luncheons, dinners, garden parties and children's parties; many of their daughters made their debuts there. But Mrs Fisher could also, evidently, ignore what her own pen told all who read her: Anglo-Saxon snobs, the Adelaide Establishment might well have been, but that did not prevent the citizens of the city electing a Jew as their mayor. And Cohen was not the only one; Judah Moss Solomon, first president of the Adelaide Hebrew Congregation, had been Adelaide's mayor from 1869 to 1871. Further, political scientist Dean Jaensch has noted, an 'ethos of Burkean independence' remained strong among those elected to the South Australian Parliament, and its lower house has a history boasting 'the presence of strong and committed progressives'. Bookish mild-mannered jurist John Bray might have hated being at Saints, but he achieved outstanding results there and went on to success both in the law and in literature. That same education produced the most radically democratic of South Australia's premiers, arguably of all Australian premiers in the twentieth century.[6]

Temperance advocates had brought early closing to all public hostelries providing alcoholic drinks following the Great War: pubs closed at six o'clock in the evening; glasses of wine were swept off the tables of hotel dining rooms at eight. 'I went to South Australia', ran a popular saying, 'and it was closed'. Slightly unfair: early closing applied across the country in the 1930s. But in Adelaide, isolated from the other cities of Australia by the vast Nullarbor Plain to the west, miles and miles of mallee scrub to the east, desert to the north, and ocean to the south, early closing seemed an integral part of a slow, conformist and regimented everyday life. Artist Stella Bowen remembered the city as a

> queer little backwater of intellectual timidity – a kind of hangover of Victorian provincialism ... It lies shimmering on a plain encircled by soft blue hills, prettyish, banal, and filled to the brim with an anguish of boredom.

Sundays were confined to going to church and devotional reading. During the week, the butcher, the baker and the milkman arrived in suburban streets with their horses and vans to make deliveries.

The bottle-oh came, too, to remove a household's empties. Food was good, but ruined by its cooking, and meals followed a uniform regimen: roast beef or roast mutton, hot on Sundays, cold on Mondays, hash on Tuesdays, rissoles on Wednesdays, and occasional deviations into meals of pork, or chicken – a luxury – followed by a stodgy pudding of sago or tapioca. Not too difficult for Maude Mitchell to teach her two daughters to make, then. You couldn't eat out: there were very few genteel cafés and grill restaurants. There were two night clubs, John Bray remembered,

> where you could eat and drink and dance. Theoretically they were private clubs and so outside the law but police winked at them. Cheaper than going out to dinner was to meet at one of these clubs at about 10 pm, pay the admission fee, buy a couple of bottles of beer and a plate of bacon and eggs.

Men 'tended to congregate by themselves', he noted, and 'all males drank heavily', beer usually. Prices remained stable throughout the decade: a penny for an ice cream, threepence for a meat pie, six pence for a schooner of beer, six pence on the tram from the city to Glenelg on the shore of Gulf St Vincent, where stretched those endless and entrancing beaches of Roma Mitchell's childhood summers. She went to the seaside further afield, too; sprawling on the sand at Chiton Rocks, the fashionable surfing beach at Victor Harbor on the Fleurieu Peninsula, about a hundred kilometres south of Adelaide, with lively, theatrical, fellow student Roxy Simms, probably two in a group who, as Dame Roma was to recall, would pile into 'a car that the family had been able to give him or her' and go off for a drive.[7]

There were diversions from the regimentation, of course. Sport, above all. Cricket bats had arrived on the boats that brought the first British settlers, and even economic hardship could not keep everyone away from the Adelaide Cricket Ground when the English Test team toured in 1932–1933, following their attempt to defeat Don Bradman with bodyline bowling. Racing, too, still drew crowds; Roma Mitchell's mother went to regular race meetings with the Villeneuve Smiths. There was also a non-British local phenomenon: Australian Rules football; it gained its earliest individual award in Adelaide in 1930, when arrangements for the annual presentation of the Magarey Medal for the best and fairest player were formalised. People went dancing – at the Palais Royal on North Terrace, the Palais at Glenelg or the Palais at Semaphore. People went to the moving pictures. As early as 1911 a little theatre in Rundle Street had begun running newsreels on a continuous loop. Rundle Street also boasted the Grand Picture Theatre, Hoyts Regent Theatre (deemed to be 'Australia's most luxurious' when it opened in 1928 with Greta Garbo and John Gilbert in the silent *Flesh and the Devil*), the York Picture Hall and the Pavilion (the Pav). The Wondergraph in Hindley Street became the Civic in 1932. And there was the tribute to the 'imperishable memory' of Australia's first *prima donna*, Dame Nellie Melba, for which no fewer than 50,000 people squeezed onto the Adelaide Oval in 1931. But economic depression had thinned the crowds at the cricket, the football and the races, and almost halved the numbers at the movies where patrons sat in the cheaper seats.[8]

Even such diversions could confirm the sense of unchangeable stability, despite current financial stresses and strains. Yet there were also hints of a shift in pace, an expansion of perspective, signs of a gathering modernity. There were more cars on the roads, more households had telephones, and the movies were talkies these days. Hoyts Regent showed its first in 1930: *The Jazz Singer*, starring Al Jolson. A few people bought wireless sets, and gathered around them to hear commentaries on the cricket or 'Bringing Up Sally' or a church service or a concert. Or news from overseas: in 1932 George V initiated the Christmas Day broadcasts designed to link the countries of the British Commonwealth of Nations in a common bond with England. Gramophones made an appearance, a new status symbol. American music – the Big Bands, Swing and Jazz – dominated. And there were songs, one – 'Brother, Can You Spare a Dime' – giving melody to the anguish of the times. Norman Lindsay's scandalous paintings of naked nymphs and satyrs were hung at the Argonaut Galleries in 1930, and in 1934 a local, the wonderful and exotic Patricia Hackett, daringly played the title role of Oscar Wilde's *Salome* – banned in England in the previous year – in the Torch Theatre that she had established in the basement of Claridge's Arcade.[9]

In her first year at university, Roma Mitchell could travel there by tram, just as she had to school, staying aboard for another stop or two then catching another, or walking along North Terrace. On the way, she crossed Kintore Avenue where a long line of unemployed men queued to collect ration tickets so that they could get

North Terrace, published with permission of the Adelaide City Council

food: six and a quarter pounds of meat, ten loaves of bread, four tins of jam, and a little oatmeal and rice for two people for a fortnight, those ration tickets bought them. They often had to travel several miles to buy their rations from specified tradesmen. Further along North Terrace, past Adelaide University's Mitchell Building and Elder Hall, was the city's Exhibition Building, built for the Jubilee International Exhibition in 1887, but more recently used to house parts of the annual Agricultural Show. Now four to five hundred men were camping there, for want of rent or a roof; expelled during the day, with nothing to do but roam the city. Destitution and despair, exacerbated by drought, made rank the very air they breathed. Camps of makeshift huts and humpies of newspapers, hessian bags and bits of board crowded the bank of the River Torrens, stretching from the Adelaide Zoo to the City Weir. Roma Mitchell saw them. 'Men used to come around to the ... back door of the houses', she remembered, 'asking if they could chop wood or do anything for food. You'd give them a meal.'

Cardboard humpies along the Torrens during the Great Depression, published with permission of the *Advertiser*

Everywhere you saw toeless boots and patched clothes, patched again, and again. Some people actually starved. For this was the depth of the Great Depression, worse in South Australia than anywhere else in the nation, with 70,000 in a population of 575,000 dependent on welfare. Young Roma had learned about it at school: the day girls at the fee-paying school used to leave any sandwiches they did not eat at lunch to be taken downstairs to the poor children, and those day girls turned up their noses at the smell of the poor children as they passed them to go up the stairs. Roma remembered the Kintore Avenue queues: 'it was pretty ghastly'. The University of Adelaide was not quarantined from the desperation: staff took a major cut in salary, and day-to-day maintenance of the buildings was curtailed.[10]

Law and Life in a Patriarchal Institution

This one, perhaps even more than other universities around Australia, prided itself on its Britishness. Such institutions were trans-national manifestations across the red map of empire of traditional British Culture that invoked 'Britain as the cradle of freedom and order and as the repository of maturity and wisdom'. Staff and students alike took great pride in the University's standing and heritage. They glowed when the *Manchester Guardian* claimed that Adelaide University's Rhodes Scholars 'had attained a uniformly higher standard of scholarship at Oxford than those from any other part of the world'. When Roma had said at school that she wanted to go to the varsity, she was merely echoing general usage around that institution that implied that it was

> a very superior and exclusive facsimile of the very grandest institution on this planet, 'The Varsity' – of Oxford or Cambridge . . . nowhere, we passionately believed, not even in New Zealand, could there be a better, because more loyally British, varsity than ours.

Copying the verbal usage, and sentiment, of her cousin, Lindley Villeneuve Smith, most likely. Lindley was taking Law, probably to please her illustrious father. Or Ruth, who, a prize-winner in Physiology at school, had wanted to do medicine. This had proved impossible. Ruth suffered an illness that – inadequately understood and inadequately treated, probably endometriosis – left her suffering irregular and debilitating menstrual periods. She joined the Education Department instead, took three subjects towards an Arts degree between 1928 and 1930, then went off to be a kindergarten teacher.[11]

Roma Mitchell arrived at the University of Adelaide trailing clouds of glory from her French and Latin results. They won her a government bursary that exempted her from university fees, and that was a great help to the family finances: an Arts subject cost £5.5.0; Law subjects £7.7.0 each; and there would be a further £7.7.0 to pay when she completed her degree. The bursary brought her an annual maintenance allowance of £20, too, and she still had support from the McCaughey Bequest. Life at the Mitchells', paradoxically, was financially easier during the worst of the Depression, with Roma's bursary and Ruth's earnings added to Maude's war widow's pension. The University granted Miss Mitchell status in Latin and part of first-year French, so – already off to a flying start – she would take the remainder of first-year French and also second-year French, as well as Elements of Law I and Contracts I. The French classes taught her to translate between French and English, to compose essays and understand lectures in French, and something of the history of French literature. They taught her to converse in French, too, a facility that won her a place on the stage in French plays. Contracts was about agreements giving rise to legal obligations and the nature and extent of those obligations. Elements of Law introduced her to the general principles of legal interpretation, and to the history of English Law, written and unwritten – the English Common Law that enmeshed so many countries around the globe in the cultural and political web of that red map of the British Empire.[12]

She began the year, though, in a quite different environment. On 16 February 1931, she attended a dance at Halsbury, the Villeneuve Smith's beautiful, spacious house, for Lindley and pretty, slender Ruth, and another friend, Marjorie Clayton, to make their debut. The *Penny Post* waxed lyrical about the 'brilliant cushions' studding the steps of 'the exquisite staircase that rose out of the great hall with beamed ceilings', the dance room, also 'brilliant' with 'gold and yellow balloons, lines of small gold baskets filled with orange poppies strung across the room' and the Collegians' Orchestra strumming rhythmically.

> Miss Ruth Mitchell looked very attractive in a white crepe satin, long and flared, and with a cape effect at the back. Her posy was pink, and she wore a pink necklace, the gift of her aunt.

Roma Mitchell in her ball dress, copied from photograph in Dame Roma Mitchell's Scrapbooks in Master Peter Norman's chambers, 2001

Roma had already cut off the plaits that she had worn at school; now she had her hair shaped into a fashionable bob, with a curl in onto each cheek, and wore a floor-length, straight-up-and-down dress with vertical pleats. But what she remembered best about this occasion was that she danced with a Saints boy only a year older than she was, John Jefferson Bray, like her already a committed devotee of the Law.[13]

In this, Roma Mitchell's first year at university, she kept her head down. She knew how to work hard and efficiently and that is what she did in what was for her a newly secular environment. From the beginning she was an outstanding student. A bright star, and now shining in a wider firmament. She finished 1931 with a credit in second-year French and the Intermediate Certificate in Law. This would allow her to begin articles – the lawyer's apprenticeship – in her second year, whereas most students had to wait another year, until they had satisfied the requirement of two Arts subjects and first-year Latin. It put her a year ahead of most of the other students who had begun at the same time as she had.

Time for a change, decided Maude Mitchell. In spite of the impression of peace and plenty at the coming-out dance in February, by the end of that year the Villeneuve Smith household was suffering major disruption. May was dying of cancer, and Inglis was, unfeelingly, carrying on with a housemaid. Better for Maude's girls to be out of easy reach. Ruth stopped teaching infants and began working on the social pages of Adelaide's daily newspaper, the *Advertiser*, with a friend from St Aloysius, one of Roma's classroom competitors, Molly Brazel. The harshness of the times meant that Ruth did more than write about the Adelaide Establishment at play, the usual fare in the social pages: once she wrote an article about how to dye wheat bags to make children's clothes. Maude moved them to the other side of town, 36 LeFevre Terrace in North Adelaide, a house with a telephone, looking across the road to the parklands with the Jenkinses on the other side. Maude had another change in view as well for her academically stellar daughter, another course to tackle. Now it was time for tall, skinny Roma Mitchell to be launched upon the world as a young woman.[14]

She had already had to begin negotiating the gender politics of an institution – so unlike the Mercy Sisters' school – filled with and dominated by men. It was not that being a woman at the University of Adelaide was unprecedented. Women had been admitted to classes (even in Anatomy, a major sticking point at universities in Britain) since 1874, and to degrees since 1881. The new Cloisters, Refectory and Lady Symon Building facing Victoria Drive along the River Torrens included pleasant facilities exclusively for women. The Women's Union welcomed women freshers with a tea, followed by singing and jokes. It was not even that being a woman in the Law School was unprecedented. By the time Roma Mitchell enrolled, the Adelaide University Law School could boast twenty women graduates, and nine of them had been admitted to the Bar. Moreover, five other women enrolled in Law at the same time as she did; that *was* unprecedented – six women in a class of thirty taking first-year Law. But the gender politics of the University at large, and of the Law School in particular, were not only a matter of numbers.[15]

The culture of the whole institution was patriarchal, even masculinist. This was not the sharp polarisation of the sexes that characterised gender relations during the campaigns for votes for women during the late nineteenth and early twentieth centuries. Those campaigns combined a demand for equality between women and men with a plea for recognition of women's distinctively female special needs, particularly concerning marriage, reproductive control and maternity. South Australia had passed legislation enfranchising women as early as 1894, well before anywhere else in Australia, and had introduced a number of the changes that feminists had sought: married women were allowed to retain ownership of their own property; the age of consent was raised; divorce law reform enabled some women to sue for divorce. South Australian mothers had also benefited from the Commonwealth Government's provision of a maternity allowance. Even so, equality was (as it still is) a long way off. But ways of thinking about it had changed. By the 1930s, historian Marilyn Lake relates, 'it came to be understood that women must win equality through disavowing sexual difference and by emulating men'.[16]

It was not quite like that in South Australia. The three young women who founded the Tatler's Club in Adelaide in 1932 could not disavow sexual difference; they wanted to belong to a literary club, and there was no question of the men of the Pickwick Club admitting them as members. So, instead, they founded their own club, an intellectual endeavour that Roma Mitchell's friend and colleague, Beryl Linn, joined in 1933. This was emulating the men, no doubt, but such emulation also acknowledged and, perforce, mimicked the separatism and homosociality of the men's club. Similarly, Roma Mitchell wanted to join the Aquinas Society, a body for Catholic students formed at the University of Adelaide in 1929 to contest the dominant Protestant influence on campus and the spread of 'atheistic communism'. But that society, too, was open only to men. What she did eventually join was the Aquinas Society (Women's Branch) established in 1933, again perforce a separate, and separatist, body. Conversely, the culture of the University at that time was based on the unspoken assumption that, while it was no longer an exclusive masculine stronghold, those women who might attend classes there had a real task in life and that was not to emulate men but, rather, to become the wives of the present students, and mothers of the next generation.[17]

Women could not attend tutorials because tutorials were provided only for students in residence, and the only residences were St Mark's College in North Adelaide and St Andrew's College at Mitcham, residences exclusively for men. (Men who were not in residence were also disadvantaged.) Even with the advantage of such extra teaching, a man could complain.

> The women are fitting objects for a rather dubious congratulation, for they have achieved the seemingly impossible task of eating their cake and having it. They are the recipients, and they insist on being the recipients, of many favours the acceptance of which precludes any application of their much vaunted doctrine of the equality of the sexes.

The source of his unhappiness was a lower subscription charge for women to join the University Union. Well, the women could have replied, when we have wages or salaries equal with those of men, then we will happily pay the same membership fees. Another grumbler mocked:

> I had never seen a Yo-Yo until I met one in the Barr-Smith library. One of the girls was playing with it. She said she liked doing it, since it appealed to the old feminine passion for having something on a string. She explained to me the symbolism of the game. The idea is, you get the Yo-Yo thoroughly wound up, and then drop him with a jerk. By all natural law he should stay dropped – but no! The player jerks her finger again, and he climbs meekly up the string. This can be repeated to taste.

Or, and more seriously, he pontificated on the phenomenon known as 'butterflies': 'one-subject co-eds'. These may well have included Lindley Villeneuve Smith in their number: she did not pass one subject in all of her four years at university. She was probably one of the young women who enrolled for the social life and the possibility of finding a mate, which was, when all's said and done, still the principal means to a livelihood for women. No-one reminded the grumbler of the young men at university primarily for the sport, or those sent by parents who could afford the fees but could not find work for their sons during the Depression and did not want them idle. Students could attempt a subject as many times as they wanted, so pressure to study could be avoided altogether, if there were not also financial imperatives.

Mitchell Building, University of Adelaide, published with permission of the State Library of South Australia, B4189.

In the Law School, the separation of the sexes was literal and physical: the men sat at the back and sides of the lecture room, and the women grouped together at the front. Men complained that since the passage of the *Female Practitioners (Legal) Act* in 1911, allowing women to practise Law, they found their lecturers overcome by shyness.

> The first year I attended lectures on the laws of contracts the professor gave us several pages of notes on the question of 'unmoral considerations'. The following year, when a woman was in the class, the subject was avoided, and I understand the question was similarly avoided this year ... Judging from my notes large portions of the criminal law and

> the law of evidence will have to be deleted if women are admitted to the classes; and I think it will be unfair to make students pay heavy fees for lectures and then have important questions missed because females invade the classroom.

The men admitted to the Supreme Court in April 1934 went to the Supreme Court Hotel to drink lots of beer and sing 'doubtful songs'. Those men knew that the number admitted that day included three women: Beryl Linn, Vivienne Judell and Shirley Morris. They did not merely forget them; they were excluding them: they had already refused to have their photographs taken with them.[18]

The point at which such separatism mattered most was the point of admission to the Law Students' Society. It was open only to men. And such exclusion mattered for any woman wishing to become a barrister – an advocate – for the training in legal argumentation necessary to become a barrister took place in moots, and the moots were organised by the Law Students' Society. In the past, the women had dealt with such disadvantage by getting hold of the book of moots produced by the Law Students' Society and tackling some of the problems themselves. But this did not give them the experience, credit or recognition that the men gained through mooting in the society. On 13 May 1932, the student newspaper, *On Dit*, reported that the women in the Law School had founded the Women's L.S.S.

> A constitution was adopted. Professor Campbell was asked to be President. The first committee was Helen Solomon, Secretary; Shirley Morris, Treasurer; Vivienne Judell, Jean Gilmore and Gladys Matthews.

The problems to be debated were set by someone already in practice. The consequence for him – and it was him – was, Roma Mitchell remembered, that 'We used to get the unfortunate practitioner who had set the problem to come over twice – once to adjudicate for the men, once for us.' These women were going to the Bar, despite the men in the Law Students' Society.[19]

The gender politics of the times at the University of Adelaide were not always or uniformly antagonistic, though. It was a small university, with about 2200 students on the books (many of whom were evening students and not around during the day) and 320 members of staff, on the smallest campus in Australia. It felt intimate – something like family: 'we really did know everybody', Roma Mitchell was to recall, 'and not only did we know everybody in our own faculty, but we knew a lot of people in the rest of the university'. The refectory was its hearth. At one end there was a long 'high' table with a white cloth, and the rest of the space was filled with bare tables for four. The professors and the few full-time lecturers lined up with the rest at the counter for their pies with sauce and sometimes chips, took their plates and sat wherever there was a space. A student might find herself sitting next to the tall, dignified Antarctic explorer, Douglas Mawson, or his fellow geologist, Cecil Madigan, or to Kerr Grant, the Professor of Physics who rejoiced in 'an unruly mop of hair, a flowing walrus moustache, and twinkling deep-set eyes under bushy eye-brows'. A student might find herself sitting next to witty musician, John Horner, or to J.I.M. Stewart, Professor of English who also wrote detective novels under the pen-name 'Michael Innes' and whose rakish dress and ever-present pipe drew many imitators.

Talk had the fizz of students encountering modernity: Frazer's *Golden Bough*, Freud's *Interpretation of Dreams*, Einstein's *General Principles of Relativity*, the Nobel Prize-winning research of the Curies, T.S. Eliot's *The Waste Land*, Ezra Pound's *Cantos*, Virginia Woolf's *Jacob's Room*, Gertrude Stein's 'a rose is a rose is a rose', F. Scott Fitzgerald and 'a lost, drunk, jazz generation', wrote John Miles the poet.

> Throughout the 1920s the outpouring progressed. By halfway through the next decade, Modernism, omnibus brew of artistic tendencies alternately simmering then boiling over in the northern hemisphere on both sides of the Atlantic since the last decade of the 19th century, finally spilled to Australia.
>
> And the literary, particularly poetic, upsurge that it brought began in Adelaide in 1935, centred around that city's university.

Artistic modernism had touched down in Adelaide as early as 1907, when 'a red-headed little firebrand of a woman', Rose MacPherson, just back from Paris, laid the foundations for what would later be her career as leading Australian modernist painter,

Margaret Preston. But she left again in 1912 taking it with her, at least for then. It was during the 1930s that Australian literary and artistic modernism burst into bloom among the middle-class bohemians around the *Phoenix*, a journal produced in the Adelaide University Students' Union, 'pilot ship', wrote Miles, for the *Angry Penguins* of the early 1940s and the counter-modernist Ern Malley hoax, brain-child of scholarship boys in the east.[20]

The refectory was also where the Dance Club held its fortnightly gatherings during the winter. During the summer, it organised cabarets and dances on the lawns outside. A band played romantic melodies.

> You're the cream in my coffee,
> You're the salt in my stew,
> You will always be my necessity –
> I'd be lost without you.

Men wore dinner jackets, women wore long dresses and carried tiny dance cards with little pencils attached to enter the names of the men asking them for dances. The highlight of each year was the University Ball. The University Wives' Club decorated the refectory with wattle, geranium, marigolds and poinsettia, and set out a sumptuous supper. There was punch to drink, 'laced once with several bottles of Chartreuse or Benedictine', remembered one Law student. The Chancellor of the University of Adelaide, the Registrar and all the professors unbent from their classroom formality and joined in. Host was the president of the Sports Association, Professor of Law, Arthur Campbell. At eight o'clock, he and his partner for the night welcomed the young women dressed in white and carrying bouquets of flowers – white mixed with the University colours – who were making their debut, attended by young undergraduate men togged up in academic gowns. They formed themselves into a guard of honour for the Governor of South Australia, and after that steered through the debutante's waltz. Then everyone took to the floor. They danced the Lambeth Walk. They played the Monte Carlo: a pointer spun in the middle of the dance floor eliminating dancers until only one couple – the prize winners – remained. ('I danced with your mother, at one of those gatherings', eminent historian, John La

Nauze, told Susan Magarey.) Supper lasted from half past ten until midnight, time enough for couples to sneak away for a kiss in the cloisters, and dancing continued until two in the morning.[21]

Barr Smith Library, published with permission of the Adelaide City Council

The second course that Maude wanted Roma embarked upon, now that her trajectory as an exceptional student was securely set, was about being a young woman, perhaps finding a suitor, a future husband. So Roma would go to the dances. She tried to put on more weight, because she was so skinny. 'I don't think I ever had any illusions that I was any great beauty', she said. Yet she had no problem securing partners. She loved dancing. This was the girl who had learned to Charleston while she was still at school. She would have been a regular at the Aquinas Society's annual ball in the Refectory, too, once it had become a highlight of the Catholic calendar. And dancing could often be, as English novelist Mary Wesley put it so delicately, 'hugging upright'. At the end of one of these evenings, Roma stayed so late that she found that the University's gates had been closed, locking her in.

How did this happen? Had she and her partner been kissing each other in the shadows of the newly built Barr Smith Library? Who could such a partner have been? One good friend of her student days was Ken

Litchfield, another Law student and one of the founding editors of On Dit; *later he would marry Ruby Skinner, a champion tennis player. But Beryl Linn said that the men and women taking Law did not associate with each other outside the classroom. Perhaps Roma Mitchell was kissing someone who was nothing to do with the Law.*

How was she to get home? She had to climb the gates in her ball dress.

Surely she must have thought of sex, and marriage, and children at some time, around now? Regimentation and conformity did not prevent sexual experimentation. At about this time, John Bray (who usually preferred the exclusive company of men) managed to father a son while engaging in a sexual romp after a wedding with a married couple. Her

John Bray and friends, taken from the back cover of *A Portrait of John Bray: Law, Letters, Life* (Wakefield Press) Adelaide, 1997.

good friend, Lorna Lumbers, thought that if Roma had married it would have been Jim Brazel, brother of Roma's classroom competitor and Ruth's friend and colleague at the Advertiser. *Jim Brazel would have been eminently suitable. He was also a Catholic, an old scholar of the Christian Brothers' College, where he is still regarded as one of their best students; he had to take his Leaving exams twice, not because he had failed to achieve outstanding results the first time, but because he was too young to enter university. He was only twenty when he graduated in 1926, reputed to be one of the two youngest graduates in Law in Australia. By the time that Roma Mitchell was embarking upon her life as well as her Law subjects, Jim Brazel was established in a new legal partnership in the chambers previously occupied by Roma's uncle Frank Villeneuve Smith. He maintained strong ties with the Law School. He was the practitioner who came to the University more than once to adjudicate the women's moots, and subsequently in 1933 and 1934 to referee debates between the Men's and the Women's unions – debates in which Miss Mitchell performed with wit and distinction. He would have been a spectacular dancing partner: he was known in the legal profession as 'Gentleman Jim' for his striking good looks, piercing blue eyes and immaculate dress. He was fun, too, with a dry and often cynical wit.*

Photograph of Jim Brazel at a tennis party, published in J.A. Cassidy & J.F. Corkery, *Alderman's, Barristers & Solicitors: History of the Firm 1928–1988* (The Firm) Adelaide, 1988

But it would have been surprising if it had been Jim Brazel helping Roma Mitchell over the locked University gates. For he married Kathleen Jones at St Ignatius' Church in Norwood on 2 September 1932.

Besides, Roma Mitchell was very occupied with her Law courses, and her new work as an articled clerk, even if she did also enjoy dancing – fulfilling her mother's desire to launch her on the world as a young woman. If she was to practise the Law as she desired, then the kind of marriage she would need to make was extremely modern, more modern than the pilot ship Modernists could imagine, perhaps too modern for even Roma Mitchell herself to envisage. 'I think in those days it would have been difficult indeed to have achieved what I achieved with a family', she reflected later. She was very young. Such questions could wait. Besides, there was Maude to care for; that great gong still sounded; Maude and Roma were, said Roma, very close.[22]

There were distractions from both of the courses she was set upon. For three days each year the University Exhibition and Students' Carnival took over the campus with sports, displays and exhibitions of the work of the various academic departments, and, finally, 'the night of Carnival' when – as in all carnivals – the traditional order of authority could be overturned. Law students arrested various prominent citizens, found them guilty and fined them. Dental students put on a display in which forceps, drills, masks, probes and toothpaste figured prominently. The Footlights Club presented three performances of their Carnival Revue in which 'the girls are girlish, the songs are snappy, and the patter pure – or thereabouts'. The Dance Club ran a Palais de Dance in the Refectory; students came wearing fancy dress, and Commerce and Economics students took the money at the gate.[23]

Roma Mitchell's second year, 1932, brought three courses, all in Law: Wrongs (which included Torts – civil, as distinct from criminal, injuries – and Criminal Law), Property I and Constitutional Law, which included the constitutions of both Australia and South Australia as well as English Constitutional Law. Arthur Campbell taught two of them; he was the Bonython Professor of Law and the one full-time member of staff in the Law School. 'I think he was a very good professor for his time,' Roma Mitchell reflected, 'when you think that he coped with five or six subjects'. He was a polymath. He had gained university medals in no fewer than three subjects at Sydney University: Mathematics, French and German. He had also gained a first-class degree in Mechanical and Electrical Engineering as well as his Arts degree. Sydney University wouldn't allow him to enrol in Law while he was also taking Engineering, so he took the exams of the Barristers Admission Board in New South Wales instead. At Adelaide University he enjoyed high regard among his students. ' "We're going to learn this together," he told his first class in Constitutional Law – not a bad way of learning it and teaching it for a well educated and very able man.' Many praised the grounding that he gave them in Elements of Law, the first-year subject. All rejoiced in his extra-curricular life.

> He was a portly man, a bachelor, a *bon vivant*, a character. He kept a Chinese cook and drove a baby Austin. His cellar was excellent, an uncommon thing in those days. He liked social gatherings, mixing easily without losing authority. He regularly attended student functions, was president of the Union, president of the Sports Association, played hockey for years, was closely interested in both Men's and Women's Law Students' Societies, and in general presided with benevolence over the life of the law school.

His shape caused anguish when he played in goal on the hockey field, and delight at other times:

> Prof. Campbell has a new Austin,
> He finds it very exhaustin',
> For his elbows and knees
> Go in with a breeze
> [But] his abdomen has to be forced in.

Roma Mitchell remembered his friends calling him 'old bull-frog'. He was, she recalled, interested in 'different foods', 'things like capsicum and eggplant – most unusual'. Some years later, she remembered, her brother-in-law, who was twenty years older than her sister, and a friend of Campbell's, wanted to invite him to dinner. Ruth was nervous. Whatever was she going to talk with him about? 'Oh, just talk to him about food', advised her younger sister. 'He'll be fine'. And so was she, because, as Dame Roma recalled, 'he was otherwise rather a shy bachelor'.

Roma Mitchell believed that he had contracted a marriage at some time when he had been in the South Sea Islands. Years later, she said, he had a German housekeeper who gave birth to a son: 'and he went over to Melbourne with her and they registered the child, but he didn't marry her'. He would have, she was sure, if he had been free to do so. Campbell was also generous and hospitable. He regularly attended the meetings of their new Women's Law Students' Society and often, when business was done, would 'entertain the entire company for supper at an exclusive restaurant conveniently situated on North Terrace'.[24]

Third year meant classes with other teachers as well, part-time lecturers who were also practitioners. Students had met E.W. 'Teddy' Benham in second year; he taught Property – Real and Personal Property, and in third year Equity and Conveyancing, and Company Law. 'Grave' was the word most often associated with Benham and his teaching, and his standards were so high it was difficult to gain even a low pass. He switched off his hearing aid and gave his lectures at dictation pace, insisting that students write down everything that he said, even if they were taking the subject for the second time.

> Probably there is not a student who sat under him who does not still have that mental picture of Teddy Benham at the lecturer's desk, his hair sparse and grey, head up, eyes shut with spectacles pushed up on his forehead, that eternal pencil being rolled up and down, up and down, between the palms of his upright hands which faced each other like two confronting gothic windows – while behind those closed eyes that learned and acute mind ran on with its penetrating speculations ...

In third year they met Charles Brebner, a man of a sharp, dry sense of humour, who taught them Roman Law, and Herbert Mayo, who taught them Jurisprudence, the philosophy of law: 'he had the problem of not being able to read his own hand-writing' noted Roma Mitchell, so 'he used to spend a little of his lecture time in trying to probe that'. In their fourth and final year, Law students learned about Evidence & Procedure, and Private International Law from the popular Geoffrey Reed. The Law itself, like the Law School, was smaller then than it would become. As Dame Roma Mitchell was to point out, 'there were no trades practices and intellectual property was really much less important without the electronic media'. The external affairs power in Constitutional Law, at a time when Australia was still a part of the British Commonwealth and therefore could not make treaties on its own behalf, was negligible. She echoed one of the grumblers, too, though not in tones of complaint: 'My recollection is that the sexual crimes were really treated more in the breach than the observance. The lecturers were much too polite to go into details on that at all. They were very much glossed over.'

Despite the fizz heralding the arrival of Modernism in the refectory, Law students gained a strong sense of tradition and certainty. One of them, Malcolm Playford, was to recall these years as

> life in an atmosphere of permanency and security. One walked through the city surrounded by buildings which had been there since the beginning of time and would undoubtedly remain there until the end of time. Social conventions were equally immutable and were accepted without question. And so with the law ... my overwhelming recollection is the sense of permanency which had particular application to the law and its administration and practice. The law, once revealed, was as sure and certain as the Ten Commandments engraved on stone.

Future judge Charles Bright made a similar observation: 'It was the last period when judges were certain'.[25]

The gathering forces of modernity would take some time to sweep up the generation of lawyers among whom Roma Mitchell learned the Law. Yet, as a woman, and a woman studying the Law, she herself was both symptom and symbol of those very forces.

She made good friends during her time as a student. With the number of women in the Law School so small, they formed a tight-knit group; the other women found her good company. They would go to the theatre as a group, taking seats in the gods at the Theatre Royal in Hindley Street to watch Dame Sybil Thorndike and her husband and son, Lewis and Christopher Casson, performing in *Macbeth* and in a new play, Bernard Shaw's *Saint Joan*. She invited her friends home, too; her friends liked her mother, 'she entered into the fun of things'. Walking between the University, the courts and the chambers of their principals, once they were in articles, they stopped and watched the excitement of the auctions in the Brookman Building Wool Exchange. And she went with both the Rangers and her Brownie pack on camps, sleeping in tents and making a great hash of trying to cook in a camp oven.[26]

Roma Mitchell was, of course, a member of the Women's Law Students' Society; she held office as its secretary during 1934. She brought to it all her talents as a debater, shaped during her years in the Junior Catholic Women's League. The Women's Law Students' Society organised their first debate almost as soon as they had managed to form their organisation. On 20 June 1932 Roma Mitchell and Jean Gilmore debated against Pat Frick and Jean Wilson, *On Dit* reporting mockingly that the warmer the debate waxed, the colder became the audience in the unheated building, so that at the conclusion, victory for Frick and Wilson – announced by adjudicator Jim Brazel – the entire audience was shivering. Two years later they initiated a debate against the men's Law Students' Society, an event that was to become an annual occasion. This time Roma Mitchell and Gladys Matthews argued against Charles Bright and Eric McLaughlin, Miss Mitchell's team losing again, but gaining praise from adjudicator Brazel. Already they had moved into a wider competition. In July 1933, in the first debate ever to take place between the Men's and the Women's Student Unions, Roma Mitchell, Joan Hawker and Nancy Newland argued against Otto Nichterlein, Eric Janzow and Bill Irwin. The proposition for debate was 'That men would be more incompetent at housework than women are at business', and the women had to argue the negative case, against their own sex. This time Mitchell's team triumphed, amid general hilarity. Her team won again 'by an innings' the next year, when she and Gladys Matthews, joined this time by Hope Crampton from the French Department, defeated Max Serjeant, Frew Bonnin and George Amos, with Jim Brazel once again in the adjudicator's chair. The Women's Law Students' Society prized Roma Mitchell's debating skills, literally: they gave her their prize for debating in both 1933 and 1934. In 1934 when the Australian High Court was sitting in Adelaide, the Law School invited Justice Owen Dixon to present a lecture on Advocacy. The two Law Students' Societies presented separate votes of thanks, Miss Mitchell remarking that it was 'a unique occasion in that she was able to agree with any remarks made by Mr [Colin] Moodie in his capacity as Secretary of the L.S.S.' [27]

Law and Life in a Protestant World

For a budding barrister, she was not only well away, but moving swiftly, the wind full in her sails. Maude was proud, and as protective as her shining bright daughter was of her: she went with Roma to see the principal of a law firm to which Roma sought to be articled. He asked if she was Catholic. Maude replied for her. That is not a proper question to ask, she observed, an answer that told her interlocutor what he wanted to know and ensured that Roma was not taken on in that firm.[28]

However bright she was, and however many prizes she might win for debating, she could not experience the same certainties as Malcolm Playford and Charles Bright. For she was a woman making her way in a patriarchal world, and she was a Catholic in a world dominated and run by Protestant gentry and OAFs – Insiders – who, however committed to religious toleration, nevertheless held an array of assumptions about Catholicism meaning working-class Outsiders. The very Britishness of the culture of the city of Adelaide, and of its University, did not so much discriminate against a member of the Catholic faith as dismiss them. Walter Crocker's family 'thought of Catholic *as being synonymous with* Irish. *They saw a single entity, Irishromancatholic, and it was anti-British and therefore disloyal.' Maude, Ruth and Roma Mitchell knew this with some intimacy: Harold's distinguished, Anglican father and mother seldom associated with their son's Catholic widow; 'my grandparents were bigoted as far as my mother was concerned' Dame Roma was to remark caustically. Yet, even though Maude's war widow's pension was meagre, the Mitchell women's kin, the Jenkinses and the Villeneuve Smiths, were firmly established in the middle class. Moreover, Maude, Ruth and Roma were not Irish, not anti-British, and far from disloyal. The social space that they occupied in the muscular, masculine paradise of dissent, then, was liminal – spiking its uncertainties with possibilities of self-definition and political self-determination.*

From the end of 1931 when, ahead of others in her year, Roma Mitchell went off to seek entrance to a firm as an articled clerk, the centre of gravity in her working world shifted back to the part of town near her old school, to the streets near the courts where law firms had their offices, Grenfell, Currie, Waymouth and Pirie streets, just to the north of Victoria Square, and in Victoria Square itself, centre of the city. She did not 'invade' the Law School's library any longer; all the books that she needed were in her principal's offices. Her Catholic uncle Frank Villeneuve Smith helped her find a firm that would take her on. On 10 December 1931 she began work with W.A. (Bill) Rollison of Rollison & Rollison in Scottish House on the corner of King William and Waymouth streets, opposite the offices of the *Advertiser* where Ruth worked, and where up to thirty of the Depression's jobless men at any one time lingered in the hope of a hand-out from the paper's proprietor, Langdon Bonython. Now, lunch times meant the Quality Inn, not the Students' Union.[29]

Bill Rollison was, like Jim Brazel, an old scholar of Christian Brothers' College, and had been Villeneuve Smith's articled clerk.

Articled clerks usually paid a lump sum to their principals when they were taken on, but Roma and Maude were spared this expense because Roma was the child of a lawyer. This did mean, though, that she could not earn the small weekly stipend articled clerks usually received in return. She did not earn the pocket money articled clerks usually picked up, either. They did this by serving summonses or appearing on unsatisfied judgment summonses against debtors, tracking down debtors who had not presented at court and cross-examining them. When serving a summons, they had a list of questions they had to ask, in a prescribed order. Those boys thought it side-splittingly funny that a young woman among the clerks asked a debtor, first, if he was married, and second, and even though he had replied 'no' to the first question, if he had any children. Miss Mitchell was not subjected to such mockery because, she said, 'I never got a summons to serve. The men used to serve the lot.' That made her all the more eager to finish her degree in the four years, rather than the usual five. Then she could be admitted to the Bar almost immediately after she had turned twenty-one, the minimum age for admission.

Rollison & Rollison was a small firm, so Roma Mitchell learned little about general law during her time with them. 'I have never been able to find my way about the Lands Titles Office', she commented, later. But about three-quarters of the firm's work was in the courts, and Bill Rollison tossed her in the deep end. He would, she remembered, 'throw me the documents and say "Get a Brief up in that"', and then take her with him to the Police Court, presided over by a magistrate, the kindly Bonnie Muirhead. There he performed impressively, examining and cross-examining witnesses in a stentorian voice, and from time to time making disparaging remarks about the opposing barrister, booming to Miss Mitchell, 'Good lesson to you on how not to cross-examine.' Embarrassing! Nevertheless, 'I still think that you learn more about advocacy from watching and listening than any other way', she noted. One time, when she was back at the University attending a lecture, but still thinking about the brief she was preparing for Rollison, she bailed up Professor Campbell and asked his advice. Days later, Bill Rollison ran into Arthur Campbell and said, 'Thanks for that opinion you gave, I'm not sure whether I agree with it or not.'[30]

Learning from Rollison lasted only a year, however; he was, said Roma Mitchell, a 'libertyman' – not 'libertarian' but rather one who took liberties: 'you know, drinking too much and women around the place' – and had to cease practice, temporarily. Roma Mitchell's articles were transferred to his nephew G.D. (Gerry) Rollison from 24 December 1932.[31]

'We did have a pleasant life in articles', she later reflected. There were some memorable moments. Another student, younger than Roma Mitchell, recalled her own 'life in articles' for which life in a girls' school had failed to prepare her, the first moment concerning the aroma of yeast – ingredient of beer as well as bread.

> Going … to file a document in court and remarking 'What a lovely smell of fresh bread' and Miss Chapple dissolving almost into giggles and a tipstaff, just back from a little session at the pub, leaning over the counter. Walking to the court with G- who said, 'I don't care for cross-examining a girl who's in the family way' – wondering how on earth G- could be related to such awful people, thinking he should probably not have anything to do with a case involving relations, still admiring his courage in admitting to the connection – and getting it straightened out with Roma Mitchell. Checking my first transcript, a divorce case, with a fellow clerk and saying, 'I wouldn't have thought that people like that would even know French'; the other clerk leaving the room abruptly and Roma coming in to explain about French letters.[32]

And how did Roma Mitchell know about French letters, then? She, too, had been to an all-girls' school. But that was no guarantee of such ignorance. If she had not picked it up at school, then Maude would have told her; Maude Mitchell was too sensible to have accepted the view that ignorance ensured innocence, and too concerned to protect young Roma from anything that could hinder or halt her outstanding progress. There was, moreover, the protection of her faith.

It was a source of certainty, different from Malcolm Playford's and Charles Bright's, grounded in a history far older than that of Protestant Adelaide. Yet even this tradition was showing signs of change. She and Ruth – and probably Maude as well – became involved with the Catholic Guild for Social Studies. Father James O'Doherty, a Dominican priest, established this body in 1933 in the

Mitchells' local parish in North Adelaide, in company with Paul McGuire and his wife, Margaret, a recent and enthusiastic convert to Catholicism. The McGuires had been in England and Europe and had been inspired there by the Catholic Evidence Guild in London, and movements of Young Christian Workers and Young Christian Students in Belgium, all efforts to combat Communism. Back in Adelaide in 1932, they became exponents of a new expression of the Catholic faith: lay people participating in public life in the name of the church, redeeming the world. They encouraged women and men together to study social fact and theory, promote their faith in the community and work together in study groups. Like its European sources of inspiration, the Guild was formed to fight what its members saw as the menace of Communism.

This was not complete fantasy; there was a clear Communist presence in Adelaide. Two members of the Communist Party of Australia contested the state elections in 1930, and at one point during the Depression a crowd of no fewer than 5,000 gathered outside the Communist Party headquarters in Franklin Street to hear speeches delivered from second-floor windows. Members of the Communist Party of Australia were busy with direct action, too; they organised three demonstrations during 1930, and the Beef Riot of 1931, protesting the withdrawal of beef from the meat rations, leaving only sausages and bony mutton. The press claimed that 2000 Communists organised this action.

But the Guild combined its abhorrence of Communism's atheism with a condemnation of industrialism's exploitation of workers. It drew its membership principally from the unemployed and believed that Catholic teachings about society were the only solution to the economic and social hardship of the time. It organised study circles, set up a book club, and mounted lectures that attracted large audiences. Father O'Doherty also wrote plays dealing with the problem of being Christian and formed the Calaroga Players to perform them in the Calaroga Hall in Jeffcott Street, North Adelaide. In one of these, Ruth Mitchell played the lead in *Mary, Queen of Scots*, never failing to be 'charmingly natural, a fact that made her work doubly convincing'. There was a murmur of admiration as she made her entrance dressed in 'black velvet, long and beautifully cut'. She and Roma designed the period dance to be performed, in this and in a later production, *King Hal's Divorce*, and taught the dancers how to do it.[33] English history as parable, this was, paradoxically pressing the narrative of England's kings and queens into the service of what had become a most un-English faith.

In the early 1930s, the Catholic Guild for Social Studies offered Roma Mitchell a community to which to belong, separate from the University. It must have been a relief. For the ascendancy of men from the Anglican St Peter's College, in residence at the Anglican St Mark's for their undergraduate years, was marked – and powerful – at this time. In 1931, the year in which she enrolled at university, Archie Grenfell Price, famous geographer and foundation Master of St Marks, swept all the anti-Labor forces together with a fiery speech protesting against the strategies adopted by the state and federal governments to combat the Depression. He and his allies formed an Emergency Committee to hold the various conservative groups together and focus them on contesting elections to the Federal Parliament later that year. They succeeded, too, Price directing the campaign from his rooms at St Marks.[34]

Roma Flinders Mitchell graduated in what was then a cavernous Elder Hall on 12 December 1934. Her superlative memory had served her well: she finished with top place in Evidence and second place, with a distinction, in Private International Law. The

Roma Mitchell and fellow law graduates, published with permission of the State Library of South Australia, PRG778/23/7.

University awarded her the David Murray Scholarship of £25 for the student who had consistently maintained the highest level of results throughout the degree. She was the first woman to win this scholarship. She was admitted to the Bar, with nine others, on 15 December 1934, six weeks or so after her twenty-first birthday, the only woman among them. These boys did not refuse to be photographed with her; they might even have been quite pleased to have her with them.[35]

Roma Mitchell was an outstanding individual, they believed, and not a symptom of incipient social change. She was the exception. Indeed, she was exceptional, though not as unique as they might have liked to think. There were other women practising as solicitors or barristers in other parts of Australia: Joan Rosanove and Grata Flos Grieg in Victoria, Agnes McWhinney and Katherine McGregor in Queensland, Alice Cummins in Western Australia, and of course Mary Kitson and Dorothy Somerville in South Australia. But the very fact that we can name them, individuals, shows how their achievement stands out. Like these women, Roma Mitchell did not represent the women those men would seek to marry.

And what did Roma Mitchell think about this? Bright-eyed with conscious achievement, brimful with knowledge, and confident in the recognition of her talents, she was single-mindedly on the brink of the career she had wanted ever since she knew what a career was, the career that would win her a livelihood, and a livelihood for her beloved mother as well. Now, perhaps, Maude could relax. Now perhaps her headaches would ease. Perhaps. How much longer did Maude have?

Triumphant Maude Mitchell gave a luncheon party – a very different kind of debut for her clever daughter – at the Arcadia Café in the basement of Bowman's Buildings, King William Street. This was a grand place, with 100 tables seating 400 people, and a string orchestra in the afternoon. There were eighteen guests, all women – cousins, aunts, friends and fellow students. Beryl Jenkins, the doll-biter, was there, and Lindley Villeneuve Smith, too. They sat at a long table set with primrose covers and decorated with tall vases of deep pink gladioli. The Arcadia's menu offered a choice between consommé a la royale, crème of asparagus soup or crème of barley soup, followed by hors d'oeuvres, again a choice, ritz toast, canapé fifi, canapé blanc, or canapé Anglais, and for the main course they chose between iced lobster salad in lettuce shell, jellied salmon or veal and ham pie, finishing with a dessert of waffles or trifle, jelly or apple pie. Maude wore an ensemble of marine blue crepe with a white blouse and hat to tone. Ruth wore a frock of flowery printed crepe in vivid colours. Roma was in a suit of white crepe de chine printed with a georgette design in china blue and a wide-brimmed white hat. It was an occasion that brought together in one quite wonderfully all-female moment, like an epiphany, the two courses that she had just completed – in the Law, and in growing into her life as a woman. Presiding over it all was her proud mother. My bluebird of happiness, Maude called her.[36]

Chapter Three

World War Two

Becoming a Lady Lawyer

Now came a time of great changes – in the world at large, and in Roma Mitchell's life. Former colonies of the British Empire became self-determining Dominions of the British Commonwealth of Nations. Air travel and wireless communications brought these Dominions closer to each other, and closer to events in Europe and in what members of the British Commonwealth still called 'the Far East', to the north of Australia. Those events were spiralling into a maelstrom of bellicose atrocities, unthinkable even for those who had suffered the nightmare of the trenches in Europe during the Great War of 1914–1918. Fascism surged into power in Italy, Spain and Germany, and then roared into north and east Africa, into the demilitarised zone of the Rhineland, into Austria, the Sudetenland, Czechoslovakia, Poland, with divisions of *panzers*, fleets of bombers and fighter planes. Across the northern hemisphere, an imperialist Japan stormed into Manchuria, also with bombers and fighter planes. Pacts between Germany, Italy and Japan guaranteed that when the democracies took up arms against these imperialist totalitarian regimes, the ensuing conflicts would engage the whole world, including – extensively and horrifically – its civilians.

Britain and her Dominions were distracted during 1936 and 1937 by ructions in the sex lives of their royal family. After a crescendo of speculation, the as-yet uncrowned Edward VIII abdicated so that he could marry American divorcée, Wallis Simpson, broadcasting his decision personally, by wireless, to the world. In May 1937 his younger brother was crowned George VI. But even the most ardent and unpolitical royal watcher could not have failed to notice the British Prime Minister, Neville Chamberlain, busy in his attempts at 'appeasement' in Europe, efforts Australia supported. Chamberlain was more afraid of the Soviet Union than of the growing power of Hitler, and his peace-making efforts were less and less successful as the Nazis conquered ever more territories and cultures, and instituted increasingly destructive measures against Jewish people. Even far-off Australia sent government representatives to a meeting in France in July 1938 to discuss ways of helping Jews to flee Hitler, though that meeting did nothing of any practical use. But in March 1939 Britain and France promised to support Poland against any threat to its independence. Accordingly, when Hitler invaded Poland, Britain had no choice but to declare war on Germany.

On 3 September 1939, Miss Mitchell recalled, 'I and others ... went to the House [of Parliament] to hear that fateful pronouncement'.[1] 'It is my melancholy duty' declared Prime Minister Menzies, broadcasting from Melbourne, 'to inform you officially that in consequence of a persistence by Germany in her invasion of Poland, Great Britain has declared war upon her and that as a result, Australia is also at war.' By this time, Miss Mitchell had managed not only to find herself a job, and not only to fashion for herself a practice as a lawyer – solicitor and barrister, both – but also to win herself a partnership in a firm of lawyers.

None of these achievements was easy, even for someone with her outstanding academic results, her drive and her self-confidence. For she was a woman, she was a Catholic, and the Great Depression made the end of 1934 a bad time for anyone to look for work.

The world beyond the University and articles was incontrovertibly a man's world. She ran smack into prejudice against employing women while she was still an undergraduate. During her final year a circular arrived from the Australian Department of External Affairs inviting new graduates in law with good results to apply for training for the diplomatic corps. Miss Mitchell applied. In response she received a letter telling her that the Federal Government would employ only men in this capacity.[2] Even the legal profession, for which she had made herself so eminently qualified, could accept her only as an exception. It was a 'brotherhood', a fraternity; how was such bonding to function if one of the brothers was a sister? Other women lawyers knew it was a strenuous calling. Dorothy Somerville declared:

> Very few girls are fitted, either physically or temperamentally, to be lawyers. She who intends taking it up seriously should, above all things, have an exceptionally strong constitution, especially if she wishes to do Court work. She must be capable of taking a wide survey of the case under discussion, have a logical mind, and plenty of assurance, and must be able to inspire her clients with confidence – not the easiest thing in the world.[3]

By these criteria, young Roma Mitchell was perfectly fitted to be a lawyer. She did not suffer from the headaches that plagued her mother, and now her sister, Ruth. Nor did she suffer from irregular or excessive menstrual periods, as Ruth did. Her undergraduate coursework and her time in articles with Rollison & Rollison showed that she had a ready grasp of the complexities of a case and was perfectly and quickly logical. She had, as well, considerable charm and an engaging sense of humour.

She could not remain with Rollison & Rollison, though; they were too small to afford a paid solicitor. She cast about, 'eager to get going and to make some money. Not that we made much in those days.' Then she learned, 'more by good luck than anything', that the firm of Nelligan & Angas Parsons was looking for a managing clerk, that is, a solicitor who would be employed by the firm, but not a partner in it. She applied. J.W. Nelligan, known as Joe, was another graduate of Christian Brothers' College, like Bill Rollison, and moots adjudicator Jim Brazel, and Harry Alderman, who was for a time in partnership with Roma Mitchell's uncle, Frank Villeneuve Smith. Joe Nelligan was also married to Nora, formerly Nora Maguire, an old scholar of St Aloysius College. So

Roma Mitchell was applying for a job in the heartland of the distinctively Catholic branch of the Adelaide legal profession of which her uncle Frank was so eminent a member. But even then, Joe Nelligan delayed and delayed making a decision. Eventually Roma Mitchell's patience snapped: she telephoned Mr Nelligan and told him that she had been thinking of joining another firm, but would prefer joining his. 'What about it?' she asked. 'So', she reported, 'he decided that he would take me.' She began work on 19 February 1935.

On every anniversary of that day for the next twenty-seven years, she would prance into Joe Nelligan's office saying, 'Isn't this a lucky day for you?' and he would reply, 'I'm not too sure that it is such a lucky day.' 'It was, it was a lucky day for both of us', she declared, 'because he was a very good barrister'. And she was an exceptional junior, clearly exceptional: in June 1935, only four months after beginning work with that practice, she was made a partner, the firm becoming Nelligan, Angas Parsons & Mitchell.[4]

This was an extraordinarily rapid rise – for a woman, even for a man during the later years of the Great Depression. Most of the women who had taken law at the University of Adelaide abandoned it when they married, leaving only those rudely described by the brotherhood as a 'few oddities': Dorothy Somerville, Sheila Maddeford, Thelma Bleby, Beryl Linn, Jean Gilmore and Pepita Saunders.[5] Yet the Depression meant that the nine men admitted to the Bar on the same date as Roma Mitchell encountered even greater difficulty: only two remained in the law. Charles Bright went on to become a judge of the Supreme Court, and Colin Rowe moved on from a country legal practice to a seat in the South Australian Parliament, including a period as Attorney-General in one of the Playford governments of the 1950s. For the others, making a living in the law was always going to be difficult, and in the end proved impossible.[6]

With Joe Nelligan, Roma Mitchell was in practice with a well-known friend of the underdog. He was the barrister retained by the unemployed arrested during the Beef Riot of 1931. He was a member of the United Labor Party (Lang Movement), a breakaway group from the Australian Labor Party named after Jack Lang, Premier of New South Wales 1925–1927 and 1930–1932, most famous for his efforts to counter the Depression by suspending interest payments to British bond holders. In March 1931 he had refused to pay the bond-holders' interest, announcing that it was more important to pay the dole. In March 1932, he forestalled the conservative Australian Government's efforts to enforce such payments by, literally, emptying the state's coffers. In Adelaide, the United Labor Party (Lang Movement) grew rapidly as people reacted against the Federal Labor Government's Financial Emergency Bill, which would mean reductions in wages, pensions and social services. The United Labor Party (Lang Movement) was still a labour party, nationalist and populist, but, in the opinion of Communist historian, Jim Moss, it was not only pro-Catholic but also conservative, and its antagonism to the banks had a distinctly anti-Semitic edge.[7]

Nelligan was an outstanding barrister and skilful cross-examiner, second only to Roma Mitchell's uncle Frank in courtroom bombast and drama. Len King, later himself an eminent QC, described Nelligan's 'persuasive style' as being 'in the great tradition of Irish advocacy, eloquent and persuasive with a distinctive thespian quality'. His cross-examination had 'dramatic effect' and – remembered King – his influence on juries 'bordered on the mesmeric'. Jack Elliott, a barrister younger than Roma Mitchell by three years, described him as

> a short man, nearly as broad as he was tall with the barrel chest of an opera singer. Atop his square body was a big head with a ruddy face, black hair and big black eyes. But most peculiar to him was the great volume of his voice. He did not speak. He bellowed. It was said that when Nelligan was on his feet in the Criminal Court you could hear him outside in King William Street. I do not know whether judges or magistrates had ever tried to induce him to moderate his delivery, but after hearing him during an entire case I was convinced that it was natural and habitual.

Perhaps he was slightly deaf. Elliott also described Nelligan's appearance in a case in which an elderly greengrocer was charged with indecent assault. The quietly spoken Roderic Chamberlain was the prosecuting counsel and Nelligan appeared for the defence. The principal witness was a little girl. Chamberlain elicited her story in gentle and encouraging tones: 'she had gone into the accused's van with her mother and stayed there when her mother had left to answer the telephone. In the mother's absence the accused had felt her "wee wee".' Joe Nelligan stood up to cross-examine.

> His appearance alone was enough to frighten a child. It was rendered even more disconcerting by streams of perspiration coursing down his cheeks from under his wig, for it was a hot day and warm even in court.
>
> The child peered over the top of the witness box into the great black eyes of what must have looked to her like a giant troll in a wig. And when it spoke to her in an enormous voice she was plainly startled.

It was enough, it turned out. The poor child was terrified into contradicting her earlier story. Whatever did Miss Mitchell think of that result? Such bombast was a style on its way out, though, in Roderic Chamberlain's view. He thought that as juries became better educated, they were less impressed by courtroom theatricalism, an esoteric vocabulary such as Villeneuve Smith deployed – 'bamboozling the jury with big words' in niece Roma's view – and a domineering manner. Chamberlain held that juries were now finding his own quiet, restrained, though deadly, manner more convincing. Roma Mitchell thought that Nelligan would have adapted to the changing manner, 'because he wasn't florid in style', as her uncle Frank was.[8]

Their theatre had once been quite literally a theatre. In 1843, all jurisdictions were combined under the same roof, that of the former Queen's Theatre in Gilles Arcade. The stage housed the Supreme Court, one of the green rooms provided a robing room for counsel and the other made 'a very decent cell in which to lock up a refractory jury', while 'a lower dungeon which formerly served for ghosts and wizards to rise from or sink into in the melodrama or pantomime' became a 'temporary prison for the rough and rugged old convicts from Sydney or Van Diemen's Land' who, it was perhaps erroneously claimed, formed the majority of the prisoners. The pit was the Police Court. After several moves, the Police Court – the Court of Summary Jurisdiction, also known as the Magistrates' Court, which dealt with traffic and minor offences – moved into what was commonly called the Greek structure in Angas Street. By the mid-1930s the Police Magistrate was so busy that two Special Magistrates were appointed to assist him, and sometimes additional justices, too. Another magistrate handled traffic and Children's Court matters in the old Glenelg railway station on the west side of King William Street, and there was an 'overflow' Police Court room in the National Bank building opposite. The Local Court – in which Local Court judges and special magistrates presided over cases involving workers' compensation, landlords' and tenants' disputes and the like – had settled into 288–299 King William Street.[9]

The Supreme Court, eventually in Victoria Square, dealt with serious crime. Here was where judges and barristers wore wigs and gowns. This court was divided into civil and criminal jurisdictions. The civil jurisdiction heard a range of non-criminal cases including those involving probate, divorce and defamation. Since 1927, when the South Australian Parliament abolished the use of juries in civil cases, including divorce and defamation proceedings, one judge presided over this court, usually without a jury. The criminal jurisdiction dealt with major criminal cases. A judge presided, with a jury of twelve men – literally; women were not allowed to sit on juries until 1965.

Dissatisfied litigants could appeal: from the Magistrate's Court to be heard by a single judge in the Supreme Court; from the Supreme Court to three judges sitting together, called the Full Court in civil appeals, and the Court of Criminal Appeal for criminal cases. From there, any further appeal had to gain leave to proceed. If it succeeded, it went to the High Court, Australia's highest court. Any appeal from the High Court also had to obtain leave to proceed higher – to the Privy Council in England, the ultimate authority, sign of the continuing precedence of Britain, and the imperial reach of the English Common Law.

Miss Mitchell was not her uncle's niece, perhaps even her grandfather's granddaughter, for nothing. Even though she found her first court appearances 'quite terrifying', it being 'a fearsome thing at first to fight for people in front of a judge and jury', she learned to enjoy appearing in court:

> there's a certain amount of excitement in court work ... It, the bar and the acting profession are to some extent allied it seems to me. There's a lot of preparation for a case. And although some people appear flamboyant they're not going to be successful unless they've done that preparation. So there's a lot of getting ready for a case which is a big case. Then there's the court atmosphere which is an atmosphere of its own. And then there is either the high of success or the low of non-success.[10]

And she appeared in court often. The legal profession was fused in South Australia, as it was in Western Australia and Tasmania, though not in the other Australian states. That meant that Roma Mitchell appeared in court as a barrister as well as working as a solicitor. As a junior, she had to do most of the preparation for each case, criminal and civil, interviewing clients and witnesses, as well as attending in court. She had to 'manage' Joe Nelligan, too. He tended to be obsessive about his cases. He would advise his juniors what to do, but would then badger them to see if they had completed their tasks before they had had time to begin. And then she had to stand up and perform in court. 'It was right for me', she said; 'there's a lot of excitement attached to it'.[11]

She presented her first case about a month after she had started working. A client came into the office, limping. He had severe leg injuries that he said he had suffered at work. He also had no money, so he had been referred to Nelligan & Angas Parsons under the Poor Person's Legal Assistance Scheme.[12] The case would be heard in the Local Court, and as there would be no fee, Miss Mitchell could not afford to pay for medical reports. Instead, she subpoenaed the relevant doctors and sent them into the witness box cold – without having interviewed them first – a cheeky procedure, and risky as well, as she had no idea what those witnesses would say under cross-examination. She was lucky. Those doctors gave the evidence that she needed to win her case. So she chalked up her first victory. It was also a win against the experienced Arthur Blackburn VC, a war hero, father of Richard Blackburn who was still in Law School. Roma Mitchell would recall this case as 'a rather traumatic experience for a counsel newly admitted to the Bar'.[13]

She worked in the Police Court. She worked in the civil jurisdiction of the Supreme Court, appearing alone in undefended divorce cases, on insurance matters, workers' compensation cases, union work – 'Joe had several unions we used to act for', she noted; 'I did quite a bit of union work' – and in appeal cases, on such matters as contempt of court, patents, motor vehicle accidents and fraud. In the latter cases, and in an increasing number of divorce and custody disputes, she acted as junior for both P.B. (Phil) Angas Parsons and Joe Nelligan. John Bray later remarked: 'When I was young at the bar it almost seemed as if a trial lawyer did nothing but endeavour to salvage the wrecks of motor cars and the wrecks of marriages.'

The wrecks of marriages presented Roma Mitchell with profound injustice in the lives of women. She found herself acting for 'a lot of women who were … subjected to domestic violence who had literally nowhere to go because nobody had the power to put the husband out of the house if the house [was] either his or was rented in his name'. She acted for women who were 'deserted wives', women whose limited education left them either with no way of earning a living or with access only to work earning minimal pay, at a time when there were no pensions and no women's shelters. Following the passage of the new *Matrimonial Causes Act* of 1929, people could sue for divorce on the grounds of cruelty, desertion, insanity and habitual drunkenness. But in all cases of divorce, one party had to be found to be at fault, and that fault was often proved with evidence procured by private investigators, some of whom got themselves into trouble by being sleazily over-zealous. If the fault was the woman's adultery, especially if she remained with the co-respondent, then she usually lost custody of her children; indeed all custody of children disputes were manifestly unjust for women, until legislation in 1940 gave women equal right with their husbands to the guardianship of their infant children.[14]

Was there not a direct conflict between acting in such cases, and Roma Mitchell's commitment to the Catholic religion? There was no falling off in her faith. On the contrary. In November 1936 she spoke at the first Australian Catholic Education Congress, held in Adelaide, indicating her continuing involvement with the Catholic Guild for Social Studies, declaring the promulgation of Church doctrine to be the most sublime social service, recommending the Catholic philosophers and Papal encyclicals as inspiring reading and Catholic newspapers as sources of important information on international affairs.[15]

Only four months later, in March 1937, the Papal encyclical *Divini Redemptoris* – which was to sell 87,000 copies in Australia – called for international support for General Franco and the bishops in Catholic Spain in their battle against what the encyclical called 'the fury of Communism'. In Australia 'the complexities of the conflict were often overlooked in the polemical battle between militant Catholics and sections of the Left', noted historian Bruce Duncan: 'many Australian Catholic commentators depicted the conflict in Spain as a "crusade" against the forces of evil, as a conflict between God and Satan'. Catholic supporters of Franco, notably members of the Catholic Young Men's Society, took to breaking up meetings of the Spanish Relief Committee, including one in the Adelaide Town Hall being addressed by Congregational Minister, Aubrey Stevens.[16]

At such moments the gulf between Roma Mitchell's belief and the views of her non-Catholic contemporaries could yawn widely. For non-Catholics usually focused on atrocities committed by Franco and his Catholic allies, and wrote about them. Two South Australians, H.M. Seppelt and B.R. Gee, in Europe to study the wine industry, inadvertently witnessed the Badajoz massacre – three hundred bodies piled up to make a bonfire over which a priest presided – and wrote an appalled account for the Australian press. Another South Australian, Paul Pfeiffer, one of the firebrand students fomenting modernist art in company with left-wing Jewish wordsmith Max Harris, was struck with horror at Franco's German allies bombing a Basque town out of existence – subject of Pablo Picasso's representation in *Guernica*. He wrote a long poem about it, titled simply 'Spain'. It won him Adelaide University's Bundey Prize for English Verse.[17]

That gulf gaped over matters of far more immediate concern to a practising lawyer, as well. One encyclical issued in 1930 was *Casti Connubii* in which Pius XI reiterated the Catholic Church's abhorrence of divorce, associating it with 'perverted morals', 'vicious habits' and 'contagious disease'. And in *Divini Redemptoris* he declared the emancipation of women and the education of children by the state to be among the great evils leading to a 'humanity without God'. However could Miss Roma Mitchell adhere to such teachings, and at the same time, endeavour to lead an emancipated life herself, working for her *living, and spending so much of her working life involved in cases of divorce and custody?*

The best answer comes from Len King, fellow Catholic, articled to Miss Mitchell in 1948 and 1949, who would go on to become Attorney-General in the governments of Don Dunstan in the 1970s and subsequently Chief Justice. 'She was a person of independent mind', he affirmed,

> *and at times out of sympathy with ecclesiastical moral rulings, particularly intrusive rulings affecting the practice of her profession in the family law area, which seemed to her, and to others, to show scant understanding of the ethical framework of the Australian legal profession and the way in which it operated in Australian society.*[18]

Did this mean that it was the Law that was supreme for Roma Flinders Mitchell? Or is this a moment when we are in company with not merely one self, but two, or even three, a moment when she is not going to choose priorities between her faith, her vocation and her quietly developing commitment to justice for women?

Proceedings in family law cases were sometimes extremely coarsely expressed. Miss Mitchell was known for remaining cool and collected. Edward Morgan was to recall an occasion when he was sitting as a magistrate and she appeared before him in No. 2 Police Court. The witness she was cross-examining, he reminded her, 'gave you an answer which was as indelicate as it was unexpected. And you didn't bat an eye-lid.'[19]

Miss Mitchell did little work in the criminal jurisdiction when she first went into practice. She regretted this: 'I think that is a very good court in which to start to get experience.' But the criminal court was manned – manned – by men; 'you have to remember', she said,

> that women did not serve on juries ... So it was an all male jury, a male judge, the only female person in court would be some unfortunate witness who would be accompanied by a member of the women police force, because the women police in South Australia were a sort of separate body of the police. They did only what would now be regarded as welfare work, virtually. And it was not thought appropriate for a

> woman to hear and still less to use some of the language that might be used in the court.[20]

She thought that, as a woman, she would herself be regarded as 'an object of curiosity' in a court so exclusively masculine. That would distract everyone from the proper object of attention, she considered, so 'I would be doing a disservice to the client'. No doubt she was right. Sexual segregation, and thence sexual polarisation, was so extreme, even as late as the mid-1960s, that when union official, Clyde Cameron, sent one of his fellow unionists to talk with Miss Mitchell about a case in which she was to represent them, all his distracted mate could report afterwards was that he had been too busy 'looking at her three-pennies'.[21] 'Threepenny bits': rhyming slang for 'tits', however well-covered; a distraction better avoided.

Such a rarity, she was. One day when she was crossing from one court to another, a man stopped Miss Mitchell and asked, 'Are you a lady barrister?' Maybe he wanted to offer her a brief, she thought. But no. It was what he encountered as a contradiction in terms that interested him. 'Yes', she told him. To which he replied, simply, 'I've never seen one', and walked away. Crushing? Perhaps. But, then, she had not offered any feminine attempt to make him feel more important than she was. Perhaps it was the man who felt crushed? Roma Mitchell insisted that – unlike, for instance, barrister Joan Rosanove in Victoria – it was fatal for women 'to play on their sex by asking for concessions': 'You neither ask nor give quarter. You don't play that sex game as far as your work is concerned. That can be left for other times.'[22] No quarter, then; she might have been prepared to 'pander ... to the men a fair bit' when she was a student, but not any longer. Her height added authority to her self-possession. Tall, 169 centimetres even without her high heels. Nevertheless, she engaged in what she called 'managing' Joe Nelligan, a very feminine procedure, and she looked entirely feminine and very elegant. You look 'as though you'd stepped out of a Vogue Magazine with your umbrella swinging along', an old client told her. Clyde Cameron admired her 'walk and elegance' on her way between Waymouth Street and the Supreme Court. It was an elegance that the rules of court attire put to the test: when it became very hot 'the judge would suggest we might like to remove our wigs', recalled Roma Mitchell: 'I was always hoping he might say "Let's remove our stiff collars" but he never did.'[23]

She did do some criminal work. One case concerned a young man charged with a criminal offence by the Taxation Department. Nelligan defended him with Miss Mitchell acting as his junior, and, against all expectations, they won. Another case concerned Arthur Durrant, charged with murdering his employer in the rural hamlet of Bugle Ranges. This was a hanging offence. The defence was carried by Phil Angas Parsons with Miss Mitchell as his instructing solicitor. She had to interview the defendant at Adelaide Gaol. Arthur Durrant was considered dangerous. Maude Mitchell worried about her daughter's safety. No need for concern, Roma assured her mother, there are warders everywhere. What she didn't mention was that those warders were outside a closed door; she always had to ask Arthur Durrant to open the door for her to leave. Angas Parsons and Mitchell got their client off; Durrant was acquitted on the grounds of insanity. But then, Dr H.M. Birch – who was both the expert psychiatrist called by the prosecution and the Director of Parkside Hospital, South Australia's principal hospital for the mentally ill – insisted that this young man was sane and refused to accept him as an inmate. The prosecuting barrister, the quiet but deadly Roderic Chamberlain, was so furious at the verdict that he brought Durrant to trial for a second time, this time for the murders of two other victims, his employer's wife and daughter. This time Miss Mitchell appeared in court, acting as Angas Parsons' junior counsel. But this time the defence arranged a deal: Durrant pleaded guilty to manslaughter. He was sentenced to life imprisonment, which in the 1930s meant he would spend the remainder of his days in prison.[24]

Such a story raises questions about telling the truth: a client telling a lawyer the truth, or not, and the lawyer then representing that client in court, truthfully, or not. At the beginning of the twenty-first century, popular conceptions of the practice of the English and North American law often depict it as gladiatorial, the skill being in winning the battle, questions about who might or might not be telling the truth being largely irrelevant. Roma Mitchell saw this interaction rather differently. It was her job to defend her client, and that did not mean believing or not believing that person, but simply representing that person's case. Her account may also help explain the separation that she achieved between her religion and her work. An interviewer asked her: 'Have you ever been in a situation where you in your heart didn't believe your client and really felt that they were guilty when … they were pleading that they were not?' 'No', she replied:

> I wouldn't have ever let myself feel that. I think that is one of the elements that you have to train yourself in. That you do not, you are not the judge. There have been odd occasions when I've said to a client, well, I believe you because I'm bound to believe you, but it may be very hard to convince a court that way. So I suppose you expect, you're expressing some disbelief in that respect but then you do know that it's not for you to decide whether you believe or don't believe because if that were not the situation some people would never get a defence. They'd never get a Counsel to defend them if Counsel allowed himself or herself to be the judge also.

But that system depends, the interviewer continued, 'on your speaking for somebody who may in fact be lying'. 'Quite', replied Dame Roma, tersely. 'And you have to act as if you don't think that he or she is lying', the interviewer pressed on. 'Does that bother someone who's so concerned with fairness?' Dame Roma explained:

> I don't think you act as though you don't think he's lying. I think you act as though your opinions are not what is at issue. It's his, it's what he says, what his instructions, that's what's at issue. You see, otherwise you confuse the task of the judge and the task of the defending counsel … Of course, on the other hand, I think the public sometimes thinks that a barrister puts forward a defence knowing that it's not true. Well, of course, that … is completely unethical, and nobody with any ethics would do that. If the client says, well I'm going to say this, but it's not really the fact, well, then … you say well I'm sorry I can't appear for you.

'Have you ever been in a situation where you've declined a case?' the interviewer asked. 'No', replied Dame Roma, 'I don't think I have, no'. 'But you would have been perfectly prepared to do that?' 'Oh you'd have to', she answered, 'you'd have no alternative. No alternative at all.'[25]

It was not until 1943 that Miss Mitchell acted in an appeal case by herself, a probate matter, a case that she won. Before that, though, in 1938, when she was still only twenty-five years old, she appeared before the High Court – the first woman to do so. She acted as Nelligan's junior in *Maeder v Busch*, a patent case that the judges dismissed unanimously, with costs. The case is a landmark, legal historian Margaret Thornton has pointed out, because it marks the first time in thirty-five years, and fifty-nine volumes of the *Commonwealth Law Reports*, that a woman became visible, even if she did not speak. At least, not yet.[26]

Starting in an established firm saved Roma Mitchell the expense of finding and furnishing premises and buying equipment – 'a typewriter or two, a telephone', no dictaphones. All correspondence was taken in shorthand and from that the stenographers typed the documents, using carbon paper to make copies; if more originals were necessary, they had to type the document again. A new lawyer might have the expense of setting up accounting systems that met with the approval of the Law Society, as well. Only after that, could he or she set about finding fee-paying clients to pay the bills. Saved from all this, Roma Mitchell worked in an established office in Scottish House, a small two-storey building on the corner of King William and Waymouth streets, a short walk from the court buildings. It was just as well it was not further; there was no lavatory for women in the Supreme Court building. There was a public lavatory in Victoria Square, but the typists in the Supreme Court would avoid having to visit it, so Miss Mitchell avoided it too, since five more minutes would have her back in Scottish House.

When she began she was on a salary. Beryl Linn's salary as a Managing Clerk in 1936 was £2 a week, less than that of the typists. Roma Mitchell thought that she 'started off on much the same sort of terms as the men who went into other firms, which was very minimal in those days'. So she probably did not suffer any financial discrimination, though such 'minimal' payment would have been all the more reason for her to be glad of being made partner and able to take briefs. The fused profession meant that she gained briefs more readily than in those states where the Bar was separate. The 'brotherhood' within the profession made male solicitors reluctant to brief any barrister who was not a brother lawyer; Roma Mitchell herself observed that there was 'a certain barrier to getting work as a barrister as a woman – I think a lot of solicitors were very prejudiced'. By contrast, she noted, 'the lay client has never worried about the sex of the barrister'; they wanted someone who would work hard and succeed.[27]

And she did work extremely hard. At this time, those most exploited of middle-class women workers, nurses, worked between forty-four and fifty-two hours a week, over six days (at most, averaging just under a nine-hour day). Miss Mitchell worked twelve to thirteen hours a day on at least three days a week, having a quick evening meal at the Quality Inn in Grenfell Street before going back to the office for a few more hours. She worked at the weekends, too.[28]

She also went on country circuit. Following in the footsteps of the law in Britain in the eighteenth and nineteenth centuries, circuit brought from the city to the provinces all the theatre and majesty of the law. The Judge, his Associate and the Crown Prosecutor travelled in a special train with their own food. The Police Inspector greeted them when they arrived. They went to the local hotel where they dined together, upstairs, separately from the general dining room. They wore tails and silk top hats to walk in procession to the court, accompanied by the Sheriff in a frock coat, and preceded by two unmounted Troopers with drawn swords. Once in the court house they donned their courtroom regalia. Such pageantry was designed to inspire awe and terror. In Mount Gambier it never recovered after a street urchin referred to the circuit party, audibly, as a 'group of undertakers who had been arrested by the troopers'.[29]

Life and Loss

Roma Mitchell's life was not all consultations and court appearances. Joe Nelligan's example showed how important it was to look further afield: his health suffered, she decided, from his failure to take holidays, and the narrowness of his interests aged him prematurely. By the time they worked together, he had lost interest in anything but the law, his family and football, so he seemed to her to be like someone of a previous generation. He and Roma were fond of each other, but, as she recalled, 'he used to say to me that ... I had too many interests in too many other things, and I'd say, I'd never know what was going on if I didn't have them.'[30]

Every week, Roma and her female law colleagues – Viv Judell, Jean Gilmore, Beryl Linn – would lunch in Dorothy Somerville's office in the Epworth Building in Pirie Street, a solidarity in reaction against the separatism of the brotherhood, and its habit of lunching in pubs where women were not admitted. They called themselves the Thursday Girls. In 1937 Sesca Anderson joined them, when she was articled to her aunt, Dorothy Somerville – called 'Dumps' because the doctor attending her birth said that she looked like a dumpling; the Thursday Girls called Sesca their Girl Friday. These lunches were a good way of staying in touch with the gossip. Later they were good ways of staying in touch with other serious matters, too. At the University an ardent pacifism was surfacing in debates in the Students' Union, against which other students argued the dangers of not being ready for war. In 1940, a rush of conservative blood to the collective student head led to three people, one of them modernist poet Max Harris – who would later and temporarily join the Communist Party of Australia that, by then, numbered all of twenty – being tossed into the River Torrens for arguing that the University should form a core of strike-breakers to help the war effort.[31]

Of course long hours of work were not always possible. In summer the extreme heat, and lack of air conditioning, would drive Roma Mitchell out of the office.[32] She might telephone Jean Gilmore to join her in catching a tram to the seaside at Glenelg where they could change into their bathers in a bathing box and go for a swim. Or she could catch a different tram immediately in front of her office, north along King William Street just past North Terrace to the City Baths for a swim – or stay on the tram and swoop down the hill across the River Torrens and up again to O'Connell Street in North Adelaide. From there, it was only a short walk to LeFevre Terrace, along the parklands, where she lived with Ruth and Maude in their 'cocoon'.[33]

Did Maude usually cook her two daughters a meal? Or did they take it in turns? Maude might have needed to rest; she was suffering from arthritis. Did they discuss their visits to the dressmaker? Both Ruth and Roma went to one they referred to as 'F.B.' or 'Mr B'. He made Roma a dinner dress that drew admiring comment: 'Marie Brown told me I had a good dress sense so I forbore to say that it was going to London next year.' Mr B. was making another dress for her when she 'ran into him and "his friend" in town', she wrote to Ruth. Even though Roma had disliked sewing at school, they took up their own needles and thread on occasion: Roma told Ruth that she 'came home and made a white frill for my Lucas frock (which now looks quite wearable)'. Did they wash and set each other's hair, these women? When Ruth was away, Roma told her about going to have her hair washed at the hairdressers and running into a friend who was waiting for attention, her head tied up in a scarf because she had already washed it herself. She must have looked like a pudding; catty Roma remarked: 'I refrained from enquiring whether she had boiled it'. 'Roma is ironing', Maude wrote to Ruth one day in the heat-wave stricken January of 1935, 'isn't she a good girl.'[34] Ruth was away, no doubt at the seaside. She still worked on and off at the *Advertiser*.

They went to the movies: Hollywood's *Mutiny on the Bounty*, and a local product, as well, Charles Chauvel's *Heritage*. There were evenings at the Palais de Danse on North Terrace where no drinking was allowed: Old Style dancing on Monday nights, when they danced to the music of Clarrie Young's band; Modern Dancing on other nights, with Harry Boake Smith and his Orchestra. An all-female band of sixteen, all with red hair, played at the '"swank"' John Martin's Department Store during afternoons of shopping. There were concerts of classical music; E. Harold Davies, Professor of Music at the Elder Conservatorium, organised a South Australian Orchestra and its performances. There were the little theatres and their daring experiments. During 1935 at her Torch Theatre, Patricia Hackett produced and played in *The Song of Songs*, an arrangement of the Biblical text in conjunction with other poetic pieces and music; her production, wrote one reviewer, could be 'criticised for eroticism'.[35] Somewhere amongst all this, Ruth Mitchell met a dashing Englishman called Hugh Gooch, and fell in love.

Tall, he was, and handsome, and, twenty years older than she was, almost old enough to have been her father. He was an 'Old Contemptible', that is a member of the first British forces sent into France at the beginning of the Great War. He was admitted to the Honourable Artillery Company in London on 6 August 1914, two days after the declaration of war. He went to France as a private in the 1st Battalion (Infantry) on 18 September 1914 and came home a captain in 1917. After the war, when he was about thirty, he, his father and his younger brother, Gerald, who was still an adolescent, migrated from London to Adelaide. For they had kin in South Australia. Their father was a cousin of Sir Sidney Kidman, the famous cattle king whose pastoral holdings added up to an area larger than all of England. Kidman had a policy of employing members of his family, so he engaged Hugh Gooch as an accountant in the family firm that ran their vast commercial enterprise from Adelaide. He employed Gerald Gooch, too, as a bookkeeper on Thargomindah, a cattle property 193 kilometres east of Cunnumulla, on the banks of the Bulloo River in south-west Queensland, a station that Gerald Gooch would, in time, purchase for himself. From this beginning, Hugh Gooch established himself among the Adelaide Establishment, the OAFs. Some years later he set up independently as the first chartered accountant in South Australia, and did the books for some of Adelaide's top businesses, among them G & R Wills, a multinational company with subsidiaries in Perth and Broken Hill, Britain and the United States.[36]

Besides his love, he offered Ruth the kind of care that young Roma – being like her father, Maude Mitchell thought[37] – had endeavoured to provide for her widowed mother, and her sister. It was even more secure, Hugh Gooch being a man, and an Anglican. He offered her, as well, financial comfort, an extended family in England, and a place among the always permeable ranks of Adelaide's Establishment, the kind of place that her paternal grandparents could have provided for them all, had they been less rigidly opposed to Maude Mitchell's Catholicism.

Back in the 1920s, those grandparents, Samuel and Eliza Mitchell, and their daughter Jean, had decided to live in the newly opened Grosvenor Hotel. Very New York! Very Paris! Except that this was a temperance hotel. It was on North Terrace, opposite the Adelaide Railway Station, only a quick walk from their

Anglican parish church, Holy Trinity, the oldest church in Adelaide. The Mitchells joined others taking permanent rooms, with shared bathrooms on each floor. Another resident, Mrs Simon Harvey, kept her suburban mansion even while she lived in the Grosvenor, and had her uniformed chauffeur bring her fruit and flowers from its garden each day, and take her on outings. Roma Mitchell had met her grandfather. She thought him 'a nice little man actually' – a view that abruptly, and with all the unconscious arrogance of the tall, shrank to a midget the patriarch who had scorned her beloved mother. 'I should suspect he would have been horrified if he'd known what I was going to do', she thought. But he died in 1926, while she was still at school. Eliza Mitchell lived long enough to see her granddaughter practising the law, but never expressed any view about it. She 'was a pretty unbending sort of a person', noted Roma: 'her father was British Army in India, and she was typical'. Against all expectations, when she died on 9 July 1938, Eliza Mitchell bequeathed £150 each to Ruth and Roma, and a memento to the approximate value of £10.[38] The Mitchell girls would have been hypocritical to have expressed grief, though they seem to have drawn closer to their aunt, Jean Mitchell, who was now alone. Besides, they had concerns of their own.

Their mother's arthritis seemed to have got worse, or perhaps something else was the matter. So she went to see a doctor, and since he couldn't tell what it might be, he referred her to a surgeon. The surgeon decided to open her up and see what he could find. Maude Mitchell went into hospital, and into the operating theatre, and there the surgeon found that she had cancer of the liver. Secondaries, presumably, from the cancer diagnosed when Roma was only twelve. And fatal. Even worse for Roma and Ruth – Maude never recovered consciousness. She lapsed into a coma, and died on 2 September 1938. 'Really', Roma was to say, 'it was the better thing to happen, but you don't think it at the time.'

You don't think it at the time. No. Everything goes grey and small and distant – except for the one enormous aching absence. The reverberations of that great gong echoed hollowly in a void.

They hadn't even had a chance to say goodbye.

'Comforter, where, where is your comforting?'

Roma inherited a lot from Maude, she believed: 'her will to survive and to maintain standards' for a start, and 'I think courage and strict honesty', and 'the desire to learn'. We had, she said:

> a great affinity. I don't think it always happens with mother and daughter, but we did. And – oh, she had wonderful qualities! She had staying power. She had courage. She was always encouraging. She entered into the fun of things. She was ... just a great person, I thought. And other people thought so too. My friends thought so. I wasn't the only one. A lot of people, a lot of my friends were very fond of her.

And now she was gone. Yes, said eighty-year-old Dame Roma, remembering her twenty-five-year-old self – a boat on a suddenly windless sea with its sails gone limp – 'it was a great grief to me. It's still, even at this stage, I have to remind myself that it was many years ago. It's, I still feel on the anniversary of her death, I still feel a grief.'[39] No-one would ever fill that place in Roma Mitchell's life.

For Ruth Mitchell, though, there was Hugh Gooch. There was a wedding to be arranged. Another mixed marriage for the Mitchells: Father James O'Doherty, friend in the Catholic Guild for Social Studies, would marry Ruth and Hugh at St Laurence's Church in North Adelaide. Then Roma and her aunt, Jean Mitchell – the two spinster relations, without other financial commitments – would host a reception at the South Australian Hotel – 'the South' – Adelaide's top place for fine dining and Establishment entertaining. Friends who helped were connections from Roma Mitchell's work, for Roma had already begun to blur the boundary between the domestic and the professional. Nora Nelligan helped arrange the flowers in the church: camellias, antirrhinums, roses and blossoms filled the altar with white. But this was the side altar, because it was a mixed marriage; Father O'Doherty declined to bless the ring, to Hugh Gooch's chagrin. Joe Nelligan escorted Ruth up the aisle to give to Hugh; she was 'charming in wide-skirted white American marquisette over taffeta, trimmed on the skirt with rouleaux of Valenciennes lace'. Roma and Joan Gooch – Gerald's daughter, with whom Ruth and Roma had become friends while she was boarding at the small, private, non-denominational Wilderness School – were the 'attendant maids', wearing wide-skirted white tricotine with finely tucked marquisette bodices and Peter Pan collars. Kenneth Wills, a hero from the Great War, and John Ayers, a Kidman, both OAFs, were Hugh's groomsmen. Bill Gunson and David Hogarth, both lawyers and devout Catholics – friends of Roma's – were ushers. After the party, some of the guests, including Nora Nelligan, and Roma Mitchell still in her bridesmaid's dress – and presumably well lit up – scampered east along North Terrace to dance at the Palais Royal where Laurie Grealy crooned into the microphone.

Now Roma was alone. From being the heart of a doting domestic cocoon, she had become an independent career woman, working and playing hard, but without the ease and familiarity of any intimate relationship. For most of the rest of her life she would come home to an empty dwelling. During the first couple of weeks she moved into a guesthouse called Alanda in Brougham Place, just round the corner from the family household on LeFevre Terrace. Immediately after the wedding she spent an afternoon cutting up the remains of the wedding cake, packing the pieces into tins to be posted to the two dozen or so people who had not been able to be there, then sharing the leftovers with Hugh's father in his nursing home, and the other guests and staff at the guesthouse. 'You know how good I am at cutting cake', she wrote to Ruth, 'and the icing would fall off'.[40] Then she moved again, into 'Greenways', a red brick block of flats – apartments – with rounded corners and a slight air of Art Deco, at 45 King William Road, North Adelaide, just down the hill from Brougham Place and opposite the Children's Hospital. The tram from her office stopped almost directly outside, making it easier to get home now there were no street lights.

World War

For the war had begun, a month before Ruth Mitchell's wedding. Menzies' announcement had followed Chamberlain's within an hour. 'The Second World War', writes historian Joan Beaumont,

> stands astride the twentieth century like a Colossus. It was a truly global war, with a toll of human life of at least 60 million. It devastated Europe, triggered massive movements of populations, unleashed irresistible forces of nationalism in Asia, and left the international order irrevocably changed.[41]

Men began enlisting in the Second Australian Imperial Force, which sent soldiers off to the Mediterranean as early as February 1940. One in six men of military age in Australia had volunteered by the end of March 1940, and between June and August that year, following Germany's defeat of France and the threat of invasion of Britain, a further 102,000 men volunteered. As its members enlisted as soldiers or nurses, the Catholic Guild for Social Studies dwindled into an off-shoot of the Catholic United Services Association. Most Australian armed forces initially went to support the British campaigns in the Mediterranean, in north Africa, and in Syria, among them Roma Mitchell's good friend and fellow lawyer, David Hogarth. At home, people gathered outside wireless shops listening anxiously for news, or sat beside wireless sets listening for news bulletins and knitting socks, scarves and pullovers to be sent to the troops – 'over there'. But on 7 December 1941 the Japanese attacked the United States Fleet in Pearl Harbor in Hawaii. On 11 December 1941 Japanese planes sank two British warships in Malaya, and the Australian Government called up single men aged between eighteen and forty-five and married men between eighteen and thirty-five for military service. Then on 15 February 1942, Singapore – the centrepiece of imperial defence strategy that proved almost indefensible – fell to the Japanese, who also moved swiftly and with deadly effect through the Netherlands East Indies, Dutch Borneo and Sulawesi, Rabaul, Ambon, Dutch Timor, Sumatra and Java. They appeared poised to invade Australia. Indeed, they bombed Darwin only four days after they took Singapore. Labor Prime Minister John Curtin ordered the Australian forces back to engage in the war in the Pacific and the defence of their homeland, and mobilised the entire civilian population.

The Government introduced rationing of meat, sugar, butter, clothing and petrol. The streets began to fill with men in khaki. In Adelaide, trams stopped running at midnight; lights on the foreshore – along the city beaches – were banned; people dug air-raid trenches; the Volunteer Defence Corps marched in the parklands surrounding the city, preparing to defend it against Japanese attack. The Country Women's Association led the drive to establish the Women's Land Army, which then organised hundreds of women as grape pickers, fruit pickers, graders and packers, as harvesters of vegetables to be canned or dehydrated. They milked cows. They made packing cases. At Port Noarlunga, Morphett Vale and Laura they harvested flax that was then made into webbing for parachute harnesses. To the north of the city, around the village of Penfield in the district of Salisbury, the Federal Government compulsorily acquired the farms subsequently covered by No. 2 Explosives and Filling Factory, a giant complex of 1405 buildings covering 1486 hectares, eventually, as historian Carol Fort relates, 'employing 6400 people' roughly a third of whom were women, including married women with children. Other munitions works in Adelaide included the Small Arms Factory at Hendon, the Fuse and Cartridge Case Factory at Finsbury, and the Stores and Transport Section at Finsbury North, for during these years South Australia became the chief Australian producer of explosives and small arms ammunition. It was dangerous work. A transport clerk at Salisbury, described one of the damage limitation measures:

> They used to have the horse trolley and it would have another one, like a trailer on behind ... sitting in that would be a little box of explosive so that if it did go off, it would be far enough away. All that would get hurt might be a couple of horses and the horse driver.

And the women who did it worked for no more than sixty per cent of the wage that men earned for the same job.[42]

Phil Angas Parsons had signed up, and a year or so later, so did the partners' managing clerk, George Walters. That meant there were only Miss Mitchell and Mr Nelligan to hold their firm together. It was the same for other firms. So many of Roma's contemporaries donned uniforms and vanished from Adelaide – some of them forever. Lawyers at home picked up the briefs left by lawyers who had enlisted. Resolved to give financial support to the members of their profession who had gone to war, they returned part of their fees to the firms where the briefs originated. It meant those still at home worked harder and for less, even while they were, as Roma Mitchell pointed out, 'preserving the practices of those who were away on service'.[43] It could be strenuous. Howard Zelling remembered that there were, as well as the run-of-the-mill problems, American ships – Liberty Ships and others. The sailors arrived,

> and they had a bit too much to drink and broke windows and assaulted people. Things of that sort. And it was nothing to be called up at, say, two o'clock in the morning, to get yourself to Port Adelaide the best way you could, deal with them, and the boat had to go. The convoy was ready and you had to help it.[44]

He had not passed the medical – problems with his eyes – so he could not enlist. Instead he was 'kept scrambling' to get the work done when there were too few lawyers to do it.

Roma Mitchell worked harder than ever. So did others. Beryl Linn took over Bill McCann's practice when he became Prices Commissioner, and then when his partner went off in the Air Force, Beryl Linn had to carry on alone.[45] The Poor Person's Legal Assistance Scheme was extended to members of the armed forces. Solicitors were rostered to attend military training camps in the suburbs and the Adelaide Hills to prepare wills and give advice. At least ninety per cent of the lawyers who remained in South Australia took part in this scheme.[46] Roma wrote regularly to her friend, the clever lawyer and fellow Catholic, David Hogarth, who had been an usher at Ruth Mitchell's wedding. He was captured by the Germans on the shores of the Peloponnese in April 1940 and sent to a succession of prisoner-of-war camps in Germany where he remained for the ensuing four years. Conditions for prisoners of war were governed by the Geneva Convention, and were therefore not as diabolically terrible as those in the concentration camps; the Red Cross in Switzerland made it possible for David Hogarth to enrol in courses towards a Bachelor of Arts degree by correspondence through London University. He completed all but one subject by the end of the war. But such conditions were, nevertheless, a nightmare: on two occasions Hogarth could not take his examinations because he was too weak from lack of proper food; he weighed just on fifty kilograms by the time he was released. Letters from home were an important way of keeping his spirits up, and letters from Roma added legal news to the family bulletins from his wife, Toby.[47]

Roma Mitchell also embarked on voluntary war service as an

air raid warden. Thought to be urgent, this was positively ludicrous. Her beat was on the western side of King William Street; she had to patrol it to make sure that the black-out restrictions had been followed and no lights were visible. One night she returned home from doing this to find a light blazing from the window of her flat at Greenways; she had left home in the daylight without drawing her blackout curtain. There were no wardens about to reprimand her, she noted. Another time, there was a 'giant exercise', she related, 'to test the efficacy of the emergency services in Adelaide'. This became a farce.

> When the alarm was sounded we proceeded to our posts. Mine was the General Post Office, only a block away from my legal office. When we arrived ... we received notification that the Post Office had been struck by a bomb, and the air raid wardens had to take all appropriate actions, among them to exclude the public and the employees from the building, and report. Something had gone amiss with the emergency fire fighters who, although summoned by my group, failed to arrive in time to save the Post Office. I had just completed a report to this effect and stated in it that the Post Office was totally destroyed when the fire fighters arrived and, notwithstanding my protest that it was too late to do any fire fighting, proceeded to lay out their hoses and 'save' the building.

Even at the time, she noted, they thought it all 'comical'.[48]

Other young women helped the war effort by going to the dances at the Palais Royal where, one recalled, 'we danced cheek to cheek with men in khaki, and many a glowing face was kissed under those lights, turned obligingly low for just that purpose'. She was not the only young woman to have danced at the Red Cross fund-raisers at the Burnside Town Hall, clasped in the arms of a boyfriend before he went off to the war. 'Night and Day', they hummed, 'Begin the Beguine' and 'Deep Purple', she might sing, with a catch in her throat, 'Wish Me Luck as You Wave Me Goodbye', and 'There'll be Bluebirds over the White Cliffs of Dover'. Rosemary Blackburn was probably a student of English at the University of Adelaide during these years; she did not marry Dugald Wighton until three years later. During the war, she remembered making cakes for the Red Cross, sewing up food parcels in unbleached calico, listening to serials on the wireless like *Dad and Dave*, or the comedies *Fruity Melodrama* and *Mal and Ginger*, or quiz shows like *Information Please*, starring John Bray.[49]

At last it was over. 8 May 1945, VE Day, signalled the end of the war in Europe. On 6 August 1945 a United States plane dropped an atomic bomb on the Japanese city of Hiroshima; on 9 August another dropped a second atomic bomb on another city, Nagasaki. Japan surrendered. VJ Day, 15 August 1945, signalled the end of the war in the Pacific. 'Those of us who can recall that moment', Dame Roma was to say,

> will never forget the sense of jubilation and relief, even in the face of so much personal loss, which overwhelmed the entire population. Recently, our television screens have been showing newsreel film of those momentous times. We have been able to watch anew the crowds surging onto the streets, laughing, singing and dancing. I was one of the diners at the South Australian Hotel who joined the crowds dancing in North Terrace ... it was a spontaneous social eruption the like of which we may never see again.[50]

Jubilation, no doubt. It would take time for people to begin to question some of the means by which those victories had been achieved, specifically the civilian deaths following the Allied attack on the Ruhr dams (of 'Dam Busters' fame), the annihilation of Hamburg and Dresden by Allied bombing,[51] and the atomic

Crowd rejoicing at the end of World War II, published with permission of the *Advertiser*

bombs dropped on Hiroshima and Nagasaki. Roma Mitchell would encounter just such questions very directly when she met Leonard Cheshire and Sue Ryder and became involved in their international philanthropic work. But that was not until a quarter of a century later. In August 1945 there was also immense relief, for the end of the war meant that the soldiers could come home. Australia lost a total of almost 40,000 during World War II. It lost, too, much of its confidence in the capacity of the British Commonwealth of Nations to come to its defence. What it gained was a new independence in foreign policy and a new, if interruptive, alignment with the United States of America, and a fresh momentum for social reform.[52]

Here women were in the forefront. There was the continuing matter of unequal pay, now more than ever a subject of objection, given the work that women had done, and in men's jobs too, during the war. There were all the issues raised at the National Women's Conference for Victory in War and Peace in 1943, revised and extended at a second conference, the Australian Women's Charter Conference, a major international event held in Sydney in 1946. Historian Marilyn Lake lists the charter's recommendations, beginning with its reaffirmation of 'the need for the immediate application of the principle of equality as between men and women in all laws, regulations and usage'.[53]

There were also other, more subtle but no less humiliating discriminations to be overcome. One that had served to keep the young Roma Mitchell firmly in her place was the exclusion of women from the dinner of the Australian Legal Convention, an assembly at which all the senior members of the profession in the country gathered, sometimes with luminaries from Britain as well. The second Australian Legal Convention was held in Adelaide – where there were celebrations for the centenary of the foundation of white South Australia – in 1936. She was but 'a fledgling member of the profession', she recalled, and could remember only one business meeting and a cocktail party at Mount Osmond. 'I did not attend the Dinner', she observed: 'Young female practitioners did not then have the temerity to attend formal dinners of the profession.'[54] Nor did she attend a dinner held at the South Australian Hotel on 29 April 1938, organised by the Council of the Law

Society of South Australia, at which there was to be a toast to Sir George Murray, by that time Lieutenant Governor and Chief Justice of South Australia, and Chancellor of the University of Adelaide. The toast was to commemorate the fiftieth anniversary of Murray's call to the Bar by the Inner Temple of the Inns of Court in London in 1888. Murray would respond. Roma Mitchell was eager to hear Murray's speech in reply, but unwilling to make a fuss about being excluded. So she went to the hotel and stood in a doorway where she was shielded from the assembly by a curtain, able to hear, but not to be seen.[55]

Undignified! Degrading even? Yes, indeed! Roma Mitchell's chosen profession was patriarchal, masculinist, at times profoundly misogynist. It still denied her a place among the brotherhood at their rituals of celebration and solidarity. But that was not going to prevent her learning what she wanted to hear from Murray's address, young Roma Mitchell told herself. And she was not going to draw attention to her difference from them, appearing in a dress among all those smoky and inebriated white ties and tails. 'I think my main reason for not wanting to draw too much attention to myself was in case they put other obstacles in my way', she noted. But having to resort to such a measure, this time, ignited a long fuse that finally exploded, uncomfortably, thirteen years later. At a legal convention in Sydney, Roma Mitchell and Sesca Zelling, youngest of the Thursday Girls before she had married Howard, bought tickets for the dinner. When they arrived at the door, they were told that they could not enter: it was a function for men only. 'Nonsense', said Miss Mitchell. 'We've paid to go in to this event, so we are entitled to attend it.' They swept in and found the seats that had, indeed, been allocated to them. And they stayed for the whole evening, too, though it cannot have been especially pleasant. The brotherhood was not about to abandon its exclusivity and separatism easily; one of the men told Sesca Zelling that she looked as though she was in a men's bathing house.

Chapter Four
Out of the Frozen Fifties

A Modern Woman

Roma Mitchell was gregarious. She said so herself.[1] Now that she was living alone she would look beyond her own household for company. Of course she and Ruth remained very close. Her cousins, too, were in touch, sometimes more than she liked. And she had always had friends beyond the household: some from her schooldays and her time as a student were still in frequent and fond contact, even though many were also by this time absorbed in their own households, with husbands and children. Now, though, there was an added intensity to all of these connections. It was up to her to maintain them; she couldn't simply rest in a social ambience that she and her mother and sister generated together. There were newer friends from among her colleagues as well, forming a new kind of extended family.[2]

One friend was especially precious: Lorna Lumbers, the little girl who had sung 'Old Friends are the Fairest' with her at school. She and her husband, Harold Williams who was with General Motors-Holdens, had spent time in New Zealand but then settled in Melbourne. They stayed in close contact; Lorna had known Roma's mother – 'a wonderful person', she said. So when Lorna Williams had her first child, Adrienne, within days of Maude

Mitchell's death, Lorna and Harold Williams reached out to comfort with a gesture of great affection and understanding. Perhaps, thought Lorna, 'perhaps Roma would like – she had nobody then you see, although Ruth was alive. But she had nobody then and I thought perhaps she might like to be Adrienne's godmother. And my husband, of course, urged me on. "Oh, yes" he said, "That would be wonderful".'[3] It was a life-long bond, an important one. Roma would visit the Williamses in Melbourne, and go riding with Lorna. Her mount was called Rex; beside the photograph of herself and Rex in her album, Roma Mitchell wrote a self-mocking acclamation: 'Quelle derrière'.[4]

At the end of 1948 Ruth and Hugh Gooch set off for England, first-class passengers on the Orient Line's R.M.S. *Orion*, a journey of a little less than a month. They were to be away, meeting Hugh's family and exploring in England and Europe, until August 1949. The web of connection binding the elements of the former British Empire and the world of the Common Law across the globe was now, for Roma Mitchell, rendered denser by emotional links. 'Ruth darling', she wrote: 'Having been obliged to post the letter to you at Fremantle by 11.30 am this morning, I am now obliged to post this one and also the one to Aden by 4.30 am tomorrow'. Every four or five days or so she wrote, sometimes to both of them together, sometimes to each separately. She missed them, though she did also let them know that she had no time to be lonely. Nevertheless, for two nights in a row, she dreamed that they had come home early, in the second dream because Ruth was ill. She worried about Ruth's headaches, asking about her eyes and sending her packages of Vincents APC powders (a lethal combination of aspirin and caffeine), a dozen at a time, parcelled up with the orders that she asked Ditters, Adelaide's specialist glacé fruit and nut store, to send them. When they had been gone for but two of the eight months, she wrote to say, 'I know it seems silly to mention it yet, but when you know your return ship and the date of your sailing don't forget to mention it, will you.' A date to look forward to.

She 'wondered about Church' and how it was managed, on board ship; perhaps she and Ruth Gooch had continued going to Mass together, even after Ruth was married. Roma reported to Ruth that this year, 1949, the Law Year's beginning was for the first time to be marked by two religious ceremonies: 'We are to have the Red Mass in St Francis Xavier's Cathedral, and the rest of the profession are to attend a service at St Peter's Cathedral. Afterwards', she added, 'the Chief Justice and Judges are to receive the profession in the Lady Mayoress' parlour (odd place).' Ruth sent Roma clippings from English newspapers: one an article by Bishop Bell of Chichester on Communism and the Churches, others giving accounts of the Hungarian Communist Party's persecution of Cardinal Joseph Mindszenty – 'truly horrifying are they not?' commented Roma. The Cold War was already well under way, and her perspective on Communism had taken shape during her time in the Catholic Guild for Social Studies.

She took care of her sister and brother-in-law, even from such a distance. She extended the insurance policy on Ruth's jewellery for being overseas.[5] She reported to Hugh on his investments, and a change that required her to exercise a power of attorney for him. She paid his accounts, too. Him she teased: 'Dearest Hugo', she wrote, 'Am pleased to hear that you are in the exalted company which you mention.' Hugh Gooch was a terrible snob; was she mocking him for name-dropping? Or did 'exalted company' carry a different meaning? 'Trust it is not too much of a strain upon your and Ruth's language', she continued, 'or does the navy expect to hear a little strong language now and then'. They were, it seems, travelling with one very conservative Captain Buchanan. There was an almost brotherly – not sisterly, brotherly – note in her letters to Hugh: 'Have you adopted any seagulls or other feathered birds yet? I take it that Ruth will not permit you to adopt any other sort.'[6]

She told Ruth about her visits to the hairdresser, writing with her new Biro minor while she was under the dryer, and complaining about having to have her hair permed.[7] She often had difficulty making her hair presentable.[8] She told Ruth about her visits to the dressmaker: Mr B. made her a 'mustard frock' which she wore on Christmas Day, and later a dress of raspberry-coloured wool, 'very plain for subsequent office wear' but with 'an additional full back which buttons on to the skirt' to give it some 'back action'. Mr B. wanted to know if the Gooches had any news of 'the Court' in England. She told both Ruth and Hugh about visiting Mr Mansell to buy a new hat. 'It is an enormous one in a natural straw with flat crown and straight brim and black satin ribbon trimming. I liked it', she remarked, 'but thought it was too enormous so he took an inch off all round. It is still enormous but quite nice, I think.'

Her cousins rallied to make sure she did not feel lonely. Merle Jenkins, a social work student, was concerned at her cousin's long hours at work.

> Merle rang at the office when I was working – said I really shouldn't, she must talk to me about it – got very short shrift – was told I had always done it and had no intention of stopping now – so she rang off after about 2 instead of 30 mins. Will wait a week or so to ring her.

Even so, she spent Boxing Day with Merle, and Beryl who was working as a nurse – 'enduring' – at the Royal Adelaide Hospital, and the Paternosters – Noel and Cecil, formerly Jenkins, and their children. Another time, she had 'the Jenkins girls' to dinner and took them to *The Big Clock*, an American thriller starring Charles Laughton, Ray Milland and Maureen O'Sullivan; 'I was quite home-sick for you to dig your fingers into my arm', she told Ruth. But she also had to turn down several of the cousins' invitations. 'Am afraid', she wrote to Ruth, 'the Jenkins girls will be writing again to tell you of my engagements'.[9]

Other cousins did not try to look after her; rather, the reverse – which she preferred. She invited Lindley Villeneuve Smith, now married to Tommy Garnett, for drinks. It was quite a party. She listed the guests: some North Adelaide neighbours, Geoffrey and Anne Kenihan, who seem to have been friends of the Garnetts. The Mainwarings – 'not because they will want to say goodbye to the Garnets [sic], but because I have them on my list of people who should be entertained'; he may have been the Geoffrey Mainwaring who painted 'a bewitching portrait of her'. Molly Trait, editor of the 'Marian March' section, later the Women's Pages, of the *Advertiser*, was a friend from the Guild for Social Studies. Roma saw her almost weekly together with Molly's sister, usually for a midday meal on Sundays. Ray Want, probably a neighbour at Greenways, was there, but without his wife, Stella, because she was too tired. Lindley's younger brother Cairns came along, too. Eleven people in all, 'and they did not depart until about 10 pm'.[10]

She was surrounded by friends, including some from Ruth's days with the *Advertiser*, just across Waymouth Street from her own office. From work, she walked home, north along King William Street, past the disabled old soldier sitting on the pavement playing his accordion and the newsboys shouting 'Pa-a-a-p-er',[11] and then down the hill and across the river, past the Adelaide Oval and St Peter's Cathedral to Greenways, sharing the journey with Noel Adams (from the *Advertiser*) who then strode on to Prospect. She made the most of her holidays. One day she swam at the City Baths, went to the races, and then to the Kenihans for a chop picnic – predecessor of the barbecue – in the garden. On another, she had midday dinner with the Trait sisters, spent the afternoon wrapping Christmas presents, sallied forth in the evening, calling on Kenneth and Vic Wills with a book that Hugh Gooch had left with her to return to his groomsman, finally arriving at Joan and Noel Adams's for drinks at half past nine. She travelled by public transport, so getting from one party to the next took time. Nor was such a social whirl exclusive to Christmas. On another evening, this time in January, she went to a party at the Willses – 'I regret to say that Vic (who was in very good form) was wearing the old white lace', she reported – and then on to dinner with Maj Frick, a contemporary from the Law School, and her husband Ted Povey; they had said 'they did not mind waiting for me until late'. Roma was 'a great fun lover', said her younger colleague, Pam Cleland: 'We often congregated at her flat in Greenways at North Adelaide after legal dinners and functions – male and female practitioners alike.' Other friends from university days, now also married – Roxy Simms had become Roxy Byrne – threw parties. Law School friend Joan Atkins, now married to Phil Garrood, had a party in the house that they had borrowed while their own was being built in Medindie that – stated hard-working Miss Mitchell – 'did not break up until the ungodly hour of 1.30 a.m.'[12] The street lights would have been turned off by then! But she was not complaining. Boasting, rather.

For this was a new, racy and extremely modern life that she was leading: a professional woman in her mid-thirties, earning enough – herself – to employ someone to clean her flat; to have her clothes made; her hair washed and set, even permanently waved; to meet her friends for lunch at the South; to take her cousins off to the movies. Independent, she was; untrammelled; self-determining. Free of domestic obligations, she could organise her time to allow herself a swim at the City Baths on her way into work, or spontaneously to skip out of the office to buy a pair of shoes; she was waylaid on that expedition, distracted into having afternoon tea with a friend at a club.

She embraced such modernity, identifying with it; it offered a context for her modern exceptionalism – as an unmarried professional woman. She explicitly chose to go to a new, modern and 'challenging' Musica Viva concert instead of the concert and speech day at her old school. She looked forward to the arrival of an exhibition of modern art being brought to Australia by the British Council, went to listen to one of Adelaide's own pioneering modernist painters, Ivor Francis, talking about it at the Art Gallery, and decided it would shock traditionalists; perhaps she had in mind the 1939 Herald *Exhibition of French and British Contemporary Art, well-received in Adelaide, but occasion for a public row about its 'indecency' in Sydney. She quizzed Ruth about sculptures by Jacob Epstein in London. She had a friend undergoing the very new and modern shock treatment. She went to a new, experimental Italian film, and was impressed. She was to move, in 1962, into another block of flats, designed by early Modernist architect Jack McConnell, a new, clean-lined, fresh-smelling white building in Melbourne Street, North Adelaide – across the parklands from Greenways, past the Koala Farm, another five minutes' walk from her office. She was a modern, independent woman – with the world opening out before her.*

Among all these friends were two she had known since they were babies. On Christmas afternoon she went on to have tea with the Whytes, father Prim and step-mother Eileen, and the two girls she and Ruth and Lorna Lumbers had played with on the beach at Brighton, under the shadow of their mother's tragic death. Jean and Billie had gone on to school, boarding at the Anglican St Peter's Girls' School. When she left school, Jean found that she was supposed to go back to Yadlamalka, the station that Prim managed, and work there; tall and rangy, she was deemed to be 'a useful stockman'. But this was not life as Jean Whyte envisaged it.

By the end of the 1940s she was back in Adelaide, a librarian, one of the first Australians to achieve such a qualification, embarked on a career as a teacher of librarians, and working part-time towards a degree in Arts. Billie went directly to university, where she was also to earn academic honours. 'Arts results out this evening', Roma Mitchell wrote to her sister: 'Phyllis Whyte – 1st place (credit) English and Tormore essay prize, 2nd place (credit) psychology, and pass history. Good wasn't it?' Unfortunately Jean 'missed on her Latin' for this year. She would make up for it later. Meantime, Roma took her young friend to the races, to the polo, and off for a swim when the weather was warm enough. Billie, gifted with a wicked sense of humour as well as her academic talent, related a story that depended for its punch on everyone knowing that the current vice-regal incumbents of Government House were Sir Willoughby and Lady Norrie. 'Talking of Govt House', wrote Roma Mitchell to Ruth and Hugo Gooch, 'reminds me of a good story I heard from Billy Whyte'. She was doing a vacation job in John Martin's department store.

Jean Whyte graduating, published with permission of the National Library of Australia

> There was some doubt as to whether a certain comb was selling for 9d or 1/-, so Billy was exercising her discretion according to the apparent affluence or otherwise of the customer. The other day one of the assistants called to her, 'What's the price of this comb?' Billie glanced at the prospective customer and said '9d.' Later the girl came up to Billie and said, 'Do you know whom I was serving just now'. Billy, 'No.' Girl, 'Lady Norrie.' (!!)[13]

There were, too, the Thursday Girls and her Law School friends. She went to the last night of a production of Noel Coward's semi-autobiographical *Present Laughter* with Jean Gilmore. She went to the Musica Viva concert with Beryl Linn.

Musica Viva were new and experimental: founded by immigrant Austrian Jew, Richard Goldner, on the model of an ensemble in Vienna, they first performed in Sydney in December 1945. Their repertoire included works by composers considered contemporary and difficult – Schoenberg and Korngold. Even Elgar. She went to see *The Secret Life of Walter Mitty*, starring Danny Kaye, with Jean Gilmore. She went to see *Open City*, a film co-written by Federico Fellini, directed by Roberto Rossellini and starring the incomparable Anna Magnani, about Italian underground workers defying the Nazis towards the end of the Second World War. Its vivid newsreel quality convinced her of 'its obvious truth and sincerity': 'It was a film which left me dry-eyed but feeling the shock of having been present at the horrors portrayed – an amazing film.'

She had watched it with two Law School friends, Chris Walker, and Jessie Badger who was now Jessie Jansen and had two small children. With Chris Walker, Roma performed in a sketch for the Lyceum Club called 'The Case of the Cow'; she had picked the cow up one morning ready for a rehearsal at lunchtime. Then came the performance.

> We all put in bits that were not in the script. At one stage when the front and the back of the cow did not seem to be co-relating I asked Chris if the animal was a cow or a dromedary. The audience, however, seemed to enjoy it all and particularly the cow whose antics were very funny.

After Christmas, though, Chris Walker had to go into hospital to have some fibroids removed, an event prompting fears of malignancy – and for Roma, no doubt, memories of her mother's last days. On the day Chris Walker was to be admitted, she spent the afternoon and evening with her, and went with her into Calvary, the Catholic hospital on the crest of a hill in North Adelaide. Chris Walker recovered. But Jessie Jansen, who had not seemed anything but healthy, shocked everyone:

> her husband came home to lunch and when he left Jessie was on the floor playing with their two children (boy aged four and girl ten months). When he came home in the afternoon Jessie was still where he had left her, but dead, and the children had cried themselves to sleep.[14]

A heart attack, they surmised, appalled at the tragedy.

And there were the colleagues who became friends. She had a strong sense of indebtedness to the men who had gone off to fight in the war against fascism. She was good friends with her articled clerk, Tom McGovern – an airman who had been shot down over Europe and spent the last few months of the war in prisoner-of-war camp – and his wife, and with the handsome George Walters who had come back from the war to join the firm where he had served his articles. Walters invited Miss Mitchell to join him and his fiancée for dinner at the South. He invited her to his wedding. Charles Bright, with whom she had graduated, and his wife Betty – a medical doctor – invited her to a New Year's Eve party. An 'erstwhile confrere', John McFarlane, who had been to a party and was, presumably, especially cheerful, rang to invite her to a show – at a quarter to nine on an evening when she had decided to have an early night.[15]

She formed a strong bond with her young cousin, Cairns Villeneuve Smith. When his mother died, Cairns had been sent to board at St Peter's College. There he lapsed into apparent apathy. 'He is', his housemaster reported, when he was fifteen, 'a well of idleness in which his personality is drowning. It is a wonder to me that his complete inactivity, mental, physical and spiritual, has not bored him to death long ago.' This was a pedagogical regime not capable of recognising a boy's grief and misery, it seems. His headmaster washed his hands of him, predicting that he would never matriculate: 'if he is to be a lawyer I recommend that he leaves and be privately tutored'. Perhaps the threat was enough. Or perhaps the war had begun, giving Cairns a quite different impetus to achieve. He had his revenge on both schoolmasters by matriculating with high honours, then going directly off to war, enlisting in the most glamorous arm of the Australian military, the air force, in 1942. But he did want to be a lawyer, and he did not have the pass in Latin he still needed to be admitted to Adelaide University's Law School. So when he returned in 1945, Roma Mitchell took him on. She and Tom McGovern tutored him in Latin. He went on to join the other ex-servicemen in the Law School where he completed his Law degree with top honours in Constitutional Law in 1948. He remained such good friends with his cousin Roma that his widow would later describe their relationship as more like that between a brother and sister.[16]

Other ex-servicemen in the Law School immediately after the war included Len King, who had studied and passed English I while serving in the air force in New Guinea, 'his only guide and mentor being the complete works of Shakespeare'. Back in Adelaide, he enrolled in the Law School under the Commonwealth Reconstruction Training Scheme, won the Andrew Scott Prize for first-year Latin and completed his Law degree with one top place and five seconds, going on to serve his articles first with George Walters and then with Roma Mitchell.[17]

Roma was to continue taking care of David Hogarth, too. He was haunted by his four years as a prisoner of war in Germany. 'They were starving', he told barrister Jack Elliott, about the Soviet prisoners crowded into the enclosure next to their camp. 'It was horrible to see them trying to survive by eating grass. When we received our Red Cross parcels most of us took the food out of them and threw it over the wire to the poor devils. It was the least we could do for them.'[18] He was suffering badly from depression when he came back to his wife Toby and to Adelaide. So Roma would visit them and sit with David and talk with him – or, perhaps, listen to him; David, it seems, was a talker[19] – for hours at a time until his mood lightened. Toby believed that this help was pivotal to David's recovery and return to his legal practice, which was to prove generally most successful.[20]

The Lady Lawyer at Work

As was Miss Mitchell's. For, as her Jenkins cousins complained, Roma Mitchell was working harder than ever, her clientele growing as she fulfilled that early imperative to take care of people; the great gong still echoed, however faintly. Her office, like others, was open five and a half days a week; they saw clients on Saturday mornings. And that was only the office hours. Ted Mullighan remembered that

> she usually worked seven days and four nights a week. She stopped work at about 6.45 pm and had a brief meal with one of her colleagues … and resumed work about an hour later … At about 10.00 pm she would go home and prepare for the next day in court. When not in

> court she had a heavy workload of seeing clients. She had appointments for them each 15 minutes. She was able to get to the nub of matters quickly. Her secretary, always a competent shorthand writer, sat with her so that work generated by the consultation could be done the same day.

Technological innovations helped, like her post-war plastic biro – a Christmas present from Chris Walker. They improved conditions in the office: 'when I got air conditioning if I wanted to stay on working, I stayed on working', she noted. They began using dictating machines: her first was 'a great ugly affair', and she got 'awfully muddled' the first time she used it, but after that it made a marvellous difference to the work of the typists.[21]

Her work included insurance and personal injury cases, family estates and some work for industrial unions. One case involved kleptomania. The client later wrote to her:

> It is not the huge and very obvious things you have done but all the 'tiny' kindnesses that will go unsung, because you will never mention them and those who received them pay you the honour of silence. I remember when you helped me with a friend whose elderly mother was in strife through absent-minded shop-lifting. You saved a fine family from undue distress with a skill and graciousness that I shall not forget. Deeds like that must run into the hundreds during the many years you have used your various skills on behalf of others.[22]

She also appeared in court as Joe Nelligan's junior, taking on some of the cross-examination of witnesses. But it was her reputation as a specialist in matrimonial law that was growing most, in a field of the law that was itself growing. 'Yes, I always found it very interesting', she allowed. She had a capacity for empathy with her clients, an imaginative sitting alongside them, as she did when she sounded brotherly in her letters to Hugh Gooch. It enabled her to help – to take care of – a great many people; they wrote later to tell her how much they owed her. You 'acted for me when I was in the process of divorcing my husband', wrote one former client. 'I was very confused and unhappy at the time and you were a great help to me'. Another client changed her own and her children's last name to Mitchell, because she regarded Miss Mitchell 'as the only person who had ever been kind to her'. Still another told her,

> you gave me back my life ... and I have never forgotten it ... You represented me in 1950 in a divorce action ... (it was habitual cruelty and drunkenness). I was a mess physically and mentally and it was only through your little pep talks I regained self confidence and the ability to go on.

Most of these clients were women, but there was occasionally a man: 'I will always remember your great kindness to me in the very unhappy war years when my first venture into matrimony almost ran into alimony'.[23]

'Matrimonial litigants have to have some way of casting fault', she observed. But it was far from easy to assign moral blame unquestionably to only one party in such cases, open-minded, perceptive Miss Mitchell pointed out.

> Certainly the establishment of a ground for divorce does not in itself prove that the other party is blameless. Adultery, for example ... is frequently capable of clear proof, but how can one be satisfied that the adulterous party is the more blameworthy? Coldness, meanness of spirit, acerbity, a relentless lack of charity or forgiveness on the part of the other spouse, may be morally at least as blameworthy as the adultery. Yet the stigma (if stigma it be) of being the 'guilty' party in the suit, falls on only the one party.[24]

In matrimonial practice she could encounter serious personal menace. 'Because she had this large female matrimonial clientele', her colleague Len King was to recall, 'of course she had a few recalcitrant husbands who appeared on her doorstep'. This provoked a steely command.

> I always remember one particular fellow obviously had ... belted his wife around and he was there to belt her solicitor around, too, if he could – verbally at any rate. And he was absolutely objectionable and shouting and carrying on and brow-beating and swearing at her. And it was really an education to watch how she handled him. She just bounced him out of that office with an absolute assurance.

Later, Ted Mullighan, a junior partner, recalled that when she was appearing as leading counsel for a woman suing for divorce on the grounds of habitual cruelty, a man began ringing her up in the early hours of the morning, day after day, abusing her and 'speaking indecently'. Mullighan suggested that she raise the matter with opposing counsel and the judge; she did not have to put up with such behaviour. But she decided not to: she didn't want them thinking that 'she was "being a woman"'.[25]

Indeed, she was not 'being a woman'. She was being an extremely effective lawyer: a hard-working solicitor, and a talented barrister as well. Her ambition required a cool and entirely professional performance. She endeavoured to eliminate any thought of sexual difference in her interaction with her colleagues. She was opposed to separate robing rooms for men and women at the Supreme Court. 'She ensured that the nature of her barrister's jackets and paraphernalia were such that men would not be embarrassed when she changed', noted Ted Mullighan. 'She regarded the occasions in the robing room as an excellent opportunity to discuss the case with her opponent with a view to settlement or, at least, an agreement which would save time and expense at trial.'[26] *It was the case, the client and the law that mattered, not her sex.*

But culture and tradition are not so easily set aside. By specialising in family law, Roma Mitchell was focusing on a broad terrain – human relationships – traditionally considered to be the domain of women, and establishing her reputation in a field of legal practice that was held to present few technical or intellectual challenges. Contradictorily, then, she was *allowing her sex to inhibit her ambition, whether she recognised this or not.*

'Incisive is probably the word that springs to mind', said Len King, thinking of her style in cross-examination. 'She was a very efficient person and she expressed herself very lucidly and with an economy of expression and she was very direct in her questioning style.' It was effective, he noted: 'she framed her questions succinctly and directly'. None of the verbal showing-off that her uncle Frank engaged in, then, nor – however much she owed to his inspiration – any

Len King

of the Irish eloquence of Joe Nelligan. But her style was not without artifice. In a lecture on cross-examination she told the students:

> Don't just remind your witness, if you think he's not telling the truth, that you are going to bring him to this point or the other, move around a bit in cross-examination and come back and forth, that is the best way to catch out anybody who is not truthful or who is forgetful.[27]

The organisation of their firm had been changing. In 1947 Joe Nelligan took silk – he became a King's Counsel – an honour bestowed by the government on the recommendation of the Chief Justice, in this case Sir Mellis Napier. It was awarded to only a few, considered intellectually exceptional, with a record of hard work and varied experience. A KC or a QC, depending on the sex of the monarch on the throne of England, worked exclusively as a barrister. They enjoyed higher incomes and status than other barristers, and undertook the most difficult litigation and the more responsible advisory work. They were governed by strict rules that, as barrister Jack Elliott explained, kept them apart from the people who were the clients of a law firm.

> They had no clients, held no trust funds, and appeared in court [only] on the instruction of other lawyers ... They could not interview parties or witnesses except in the presence of the solicitors who were instructing them. This was to protect the barrister from any suggestion of 'addressing' – that is telling people what to say in court – and to preserve the distance between the barrister and those he represented.

Because South Australia had a fused profession, Elliott pointed out, the only people who practised like this were KCs or QCs – until the 1960s, when an Independent Bar was established. Silks were a select company, which would be studded with knighthoods: since 1930 the largest number created silk in any one year had been the four in that year; then there were no more until her former Law lecturer Sir Geoffrey Reed took silk in 1937; two more who would become knights in 1943; and another two who would also be knighted in 1945; and then there was Nelligan's year, 1947, when another four were made silk, including Roderic Chamberlain, whom many expected to go on to become the Chief Justice.[28] Joe Nelligan must have been proud. But, then, in 1952 he suffered a minor stroke. He continued working, but couldn't do as much as he had. Miss Mitchell had to work harder than ever to make up the difference in the firm's income.

Phil Angas Parsons had not returned to the law after the war. George Walters was a partner by 1946, but moved on, away from the over-powering Nelligan, in 1950, beginning his rapid rise in the profession to Master of the Supreme Court in 1965 and Judge in 1966. During the succeeding decade, Nelligan and Mitchell had a number of other partners, mostly solicitors practising in country towns and briefing Nelligan. The post-war generation of Law graduates – McGovern and King – were succeeded by yet another generation: Pam Cleland, Ted Mullighan, David Haese and Doreen Curnow. McGovern and King thought Miss Mitchell 'excellent' on a personal level. She 'took you under her wing', explained Len King.

> She was a sort of mother figure, I suppose, and very kind and considerate and very anxious to help you on your way and take an interest, take an interest in you personally. She was a good teacher, and very lucid in her explanations of why she was doing things, what she was doing ... And she gave me, anyway, and I suppose Tom McGovern, too ... a good deal of responsibility, jobs to do, that we were left to do on our own initiative and of course we had to report back, but she wasn't looking over your shoulder all the time for fear you'd made a mistake.[29]

It was much the way Bill Rollison had taught her.

She could be fierce, Pam Cleland found. Miss Cleland was a beautiful exotic in a legal office. Before taking to the law, she had studied with water colourist Gwen Barringer and oil painters Jeffrey Smart, Dorrit Black, Jacqueline Hick and Ludwig Dutkiewicz, and she had exhibited not only in Adelaide but also in London. Dame Roma was to recall, long afterwards, 'She was artistic in her approach to the law, sometimes reducing me almost to despair, because the law does not encourage the originality in pleadings which Pam was inclined to exhibit.' Pam Cleland went home one day very cast down by Miss Mitchell's criticism of her work. But that night, quite late, Miss Mitchell rang her to say, 'Look, I was all wrong. I read through those notes. They are all right.' Forthright, Len King said, with 'the happy knack of being

Pam Cleland

able to call a spade a spade without offending anyone'. But sharp, too: 'she had a quick temper' said Pam Cleland, she 'wouldn't suffer fools gladly'.[30]

Miss Mitchell had, of course, joined the Law Society of South Australia when she first began to practise. This was the legal profession's equivalent of a trade union: a body that cared for the profession and its members, and regulated their behaviour. In 1952 she was persuaded to stand for election to its Council. She mentioned this to Crown Solicitor Tacky Hannan when she ran into him. He had been christened Albert James, but he was a chatterer; his Classics professor, Darnley Naylor, used to admonish him in Latin, 'Tace, Hannan', and the nickname had stuck. Hannan had not succeeded in his first attempt at membership of the Council, and he told Miss Mitchell that she should not expect to do so, either. She was not intimidated: 'Well, I'm only doing it the first time'; she would not bother to pursue it if she failed. But she did succeed, elected by ballot on 29 September 1952, taking her place with the six men also elected at the same meeting, the first woman in the Law Society Council's seventy-five year history. Within two months she was president of its Etiquette Committee, a body that met only about twice a year, to determine questions of proper procedure. These could be quite delicate.

> A Solicitor having been instructed by a Client to take proceedings for divorce learns from the Client of the Client's own adultery and seeks instructions to disclose it to the Court. The Client thereupon terminates his retainer and instructs another Solicitor to take or continue the proceedings. Is the first Solicitor then under a duty to disclose the facts either to the Court or to the second Solicitor. <u>Answer</u>: The duty of disclosure ceases on the termination of the retainer whether or not the writ has been issued. Furthermore, the disclosure whether to the Court or to the second Solicitor or to anyone else would be a breach of the Client's privilege.[31]

A world of secrets and confidences.

She was also a member of the Legal Assistance Committee. This committee was hard work, for it administered the Poor Person's Legal Assistance Scheme. Jack Elliott believed this scheme had been inspired by 'the health system operating in the public hospitals, where specialists and surgeons were available on certain days or in emergencies to the poor free of charge'. Perhaps there were some who wanted to emulate the doctors. But the Law Society's own account is of an effort in 1933 to overcome what had become the impossible workload of the Public Solicitor's Office, created under legislation in 1925, to render legal assistance to the poor. After discussion, negotiation, and some strident expressions of opinion in the press, the legislation was amended. The government agreed to make a small payment to the Law Society to administer the scheme, and provide it with offices; in return, the Law Society undertook that

> the Society, its Council and its members [would carry out the work] as a voluntary charitable effort [which would] see that no person [would] be left without proper legal assistance, if he [was] deserving of such assistance, and would be unable to obtain it without the help of the Society's members.

The scheme saved the government the costs of the Public Solicitor's Office. It enabled new lawyers to gain some experience, even if it earned them almost nothing. It ensured a voluntary provision of legal aid to all who needed it. Most importantly for the profession, it ensured such assistance was organised by lawyers themselves, rather than by the state, something conservatives rejected as 'socialistic', maintaining the profession's autonomy, independence of government, and 'gentlemanly' distance from any association with a salary – an issue that was to become a source of great strife between the medical profession and the Federal Government in the 1970s. Howard Zelling put it succinctly: 'we ran it ourselves and we were never going to be kicked around by politicians'.[32]

Roma Mitchell would write a paper about the Legal Assistance Scheme. People would come to the Law Society's office to explain their difficulty. Or, if they were in gaol, then Alphonse Barbier, the Keeper, would take their application and ring the office. In that case the Secretary might have to go to the Adelaide Gaol to interview the prisoner. The Secretary would assess their case. They could give advice on a simple matter themselves. If it needed more consideration, 'we would assign them off to a younger member of the profession'. If it was seriously complicated, 'we'd appoint a Senior Counsel who'd then do it again for very little, or almost nothing, and he'd do what was necessary'. If it was difficult for the Secretary to decide what to do, then the location of the Law Society's offices helped, as Sesca Anderson explained. She became the Secretary after the Australian Government ordered that women in its employ were to be replaced by the men returning from the war; she had been working in the Commonwealth Deputy Crown Solicitor's Office. The Law Society 'had a very convenient stairway at the back, behind the Secretary's room', she pointed out,

> down into the office of Browne, Rymill & Stevens, and Mr Edgar Stevens, who was the Vice President of the Law Society, was the lifesaver of every Secretary. Because if you didn't know what to do, and it was urgent, you nipped down the back stairs into Mr Stevens' office and asked him.[33]

From each initial interview, the Secretary made a file, and at the end of the week distributed them to the three members of the Legal Assistance Committee. There would 'usually be 8 or 10 files over the weekend for each person', recalled Brian Magarey, Councillor of the Law Society from 1949, President in 1970–1971, and such homework was constant throughout the year. First thing on Monday morning, the three would meet and make decisions about accepting or refusing the assignment – 'the latter was very rare', Magarey observed.[34] Miss Mitchell's paper about the system explained it to a conference to be held on the other side of the world in the mid-1950s.

Out, Out into a Modernising World

The 1950s are – retrospectively – depicted as a period of rampant repression. The conservative Menzies Government was endeavouring to silence political dissent, trying – unsuccessfully – to outlaw the Communist Party. The Labor Party was riven by anti-

Communist factionalism. Men's identities focused increasingly and exclusively on their work; women's on their contribution to the baby boom, and their capacity as consumers, not only of the makings of the family meals but also of a growing array of consumer durables. Creative talent fled: 'Peter Finch, Leo McKern, Keith Michell, Joan Sutherland, Marie Collier', wrote George Farwell, were to find in British theatre an acknowledgement and appreciation that did not exist in Australia at this time. Artists Sidney Nolan and the Boyds, too, departed for Europe. 'British cynics said you had to sing Italian with an Australian accent now to make good at Covent Garden or Sadler's Wells', Farwell reported.[35] In Australia, this decade has been held to have been a period of crushing conformity and suburban littleness, satirised subsequently by Barry Humphries in the immortal Edna Everidge of Moonee Ponds and Sandy Stone of Gallipoli Crescent, Glen Iris. Books banned for 'indecency' included *Moll Flanders*, Huxley's *Brave New World* and the *Kama Sutra*.

In Adelaide the fifties stretched from the early forties well into the sixties. In 1944, leftist modernist Max Harris was prosecuted for publishing 'indecent advertisements' in the Ern Malley issue of *Angry Penguins*. The trial – which Harris thought to have been initiated by anti-Communist Catholic Crown Prosecutor Tacky Hannan in league with Catholic Action – resulted in his conviction, despite the support of such an eminence as Professor Charles Jury, prepared to argue for the literary merit of Malley's, and Harris's, work. The proceedings included a quite wonderful exchange between Harris and Detective 'Dutchie' Vogelesang. The detective read out some lines of verse:

Max Harris, published with permission of the Barr Smith Library

> New Year brought its concertinas in,
> The redundant festivities of piano and song
> For the flatchested women of the camp,
> Whose genitals ached like very hell

For the passionate copulation in satin
And passivity by the low-tuned radio,
Waking to the morning aubade of trams.

'Does it mean that the woman's sexual parts are aching for an evening dress?' he asked.

> Harris, perhaps in amazement, agreed.
> 'Don't you think that is immoral?' asked Detective Vogelesang.[36]

Even two decades later, such stultification prevailed that Daniil Granin, a writer visiting from the Union of Soviet Socialist Republics in 1967, found Adelaide entirely empty.

> Suddenly John Brey [sic] popped up. He was carefully hugging several cans of beer. We had liked John Brey from the first moment we met him, but now he was the finest person in all Adelaide.
>
> 'What's happened?' I asked.
>
> 'Where's everybody? Where are the workers, where are the capitalists?'
>
> 'Sunday,' said John Brey.

He – John Bray – elaborated on what Sunday meant in Adelaide.

> 'The triumph of loneliness and abandonment. You can die of hunger in the middle of a town. Or of thirst. Nobody ventures to disturb anyone. Most suicides occur on Sundays.'
>
> 'But where are all the people?'
>
> 'Those who don't commit suicide go to the beach, or watch TV, or potter about in their gardens.
>
> 'Once a week a person has to get away from the crowd and be alone,' said John. 'It's good for you. Get ready, we're going on a picnic.'[37]

But there were also, concurrently, distinct stirrings of something very different. The impetus to industrialisation embraced in South Australia in response to the need for munitions works during the Second World War found continuing support under the Liberal-Country League Government of orchardist, Thomas Playford, in the following years. That impetus expanded into production of automobiles and white goods. Playford's regime was assisted by an electoral arrangement that gave a weighting of at least 2:1 in favour of the rural areas (some have called it a gerrymander; some, a 'playmander'), which kept him in power for a record-breaking twenty-eight years. Playford's governments gave important state support to industrial development. They established a program of accelerated immigration to help supply the basic labour requirements of the new industries, and among those migrants were some from Europe – the 'New Australians' blamed for any suburban disruption from upset rubbish bins to a Peeping Tom, in writer Barbara Hanrahan's memories – who gradually brought about a transformation of the monochrome Britishness of Adelaide society and culture, including its eating and drinking habits.[38]

Premier Tom Playford leading the Anzac Day march down King William Street, published with permission of the *Advertiser*

The products of some of the industries that required the new immigrants' labour needed markets that were local as well as interstate, even – in time – international: now was the moment when every household had to have its own Holden motorcar, Hills Hoist rotating clothesline and Simpson Pope washing machine, in Adelaide as well as in Melbourne and Sydney. And if each household was to afford such items, then the mothers of the baby boom would have to find jobs that brought in earnings, as well as being at home to contribute to that population explosion. This was an economic imperative that counteracted government regulation and cultural prescription confining women to their hearths and households. Hugh Gooch would not allow Ruth to return to paid employment with the *Advertiser* after they were married, even when it became clear that she was not going to bear the children they both had hoped for – but he was both rich and old fashioned.[39] The need for women, including wives and mothers, in the labour market, and concomitantly, those women's need for an income, was a yeast beginning to work in the social and cultural dough.

In the meantime, people set out to explore the world. 'I don't ever remember such an exodus of Adelaide people', wrote Roma Mitchell in 1949. Merle Jenkins, armed with a double degree, won a grant to spend two years doing research at the University of Manchester in England. Jean Whyte, who had finished her Arts degree with the John Howard Clark Prize for first place in English, gained – with supporting references from Roma Mitchell – two awards: one a Fulbright Travel Grant to take her to the United States, the other a fellowship awarded by the American Association of University Women to enable her to study at the University of Chicago where she also spent 1954–1955 as a Fellow of the Graduate Library School.[40]

To Jean Whyte, travel brought another kind of new experience as well. It was in Chicago, a few years later, that she also found, at least for a moment – if her poem can be read as autobiographical – sexual passion.

> You come to tea. Your fingers turn the key,
> Your lips on mine, your arms encircling me.
> Scones, cups and teapot at the bedside stand
> A little space my female bed is manned.
>
> Your clothes are off, and with joy ever-new
> My eager thighs rise to be joined to you.
> Your lips are at my nipple, and on fire
> From breast to cunt I burn with deep desire,
> And in the summer-naked curtained room
> Your pulsing penis burst into my womb.
> . . .
> Then with my whole being throbbing at my need
> One quick deep spurt – my earth receives your seed.[41]

She continued to rhyme to the end of her days. She was not to marry, though late in her life she set up house with the philosopher Hector Monro.[42] Did she ever show this poem to her dear and supportive friend, Roma Mitchell? Why would she not? They were like sisters.

By that time, Jean's younger sister, Billie, had also had an early brush with desire, though without leaving Adelaide. In the mid-1950s, Phyllis Whyte was working at the Wilderness School – where Joan Gooch had earlier been a boarder – a popular and prized teacher of English Literature. Susan Magarey recalls that

> she used to write hilarious skits on Shakespeare's plays for the senior girls to perform at the end-of-term concert. She would adjudicate debates, too. She adjudicated one in which I was a speaker, in my first year in the senior school, aged thirteen. Afterwards, I longed for the time when I would be old enough for her to teach me as well. But it was not to be. During a school expedition to the pictures, Billie Whyte made the mistake of holding hands with a student, curly-headed Jill Holden. Jill Holden would later marry Tony Gibbs who was to become professor of English at the University of New England. Sadly, we did not see Miss Whyte at Wilderness after that.

From 1961 to 1985, Miss Whyte taught at Adelaide Girls' High School, an establishment that became co-educational in the late 1970s. Deborah McCulloch taught there too and told us that Billie Whyte had relationships with at least two of the other women on the staff, both at the same time.[43]

Would Roma Mitchell have told either Jean or Billie Whyte if she had had a similar experience of her own? Her younger friend and colleague, Pam Cleland, had famously raunchy parties at which the guests would drink a lot, fling off their clothes, plunge into her hot pool and disappear in various combinations among the rhododendrons. At one such gathering, visiting gay ballet supremo Rudolph Nureyev looked at 'all those women in that pool' and announced that he'd 'like to whip them'. At another, Pam Cleland presided over the dinner table – stunningly – stark naked; a reaction against her Methodist mother who had made her undress under her school uniform, she explained. Roma Mitchell 'was very good at a party' another friend, Mary Bleechmore, was to remember. 'And she'd let her hair down quite enough, you know. She'd be very informal.' But she was always entirely discreet, said Pam Cleland. Being discreet doesn't mean that she did not frolic in the shrubbery. But Miss Cleland's remark is a tease: it does not mean that she did, either. Is it, perhaps, a double tease? Did Pam Cleland have a fling with Roma Mitchell, herself? After all, Pam Cleland considered Roma Mitchell 'a sort of a "renaissance woman"'. What did that mean? 'Well', she continued,

> if people are fairly developed human beings I don't see why they shouldn't be on the borderline of bi-sexuality, quite frankly. I mean, really what you really like are people, not anatomy, don't you?

Yet sexual relationships between women were considered immoral, even if they were not illegal, and Mary Bleechmore said that Roma Mitchell 'never put a wrong foot forward', not once in her whole life. Pam Cleland, herself, said of Roma Mitchell that 'she was quite prepared to drink to excess but she knew when to stop'; compared with 'the rest of us', she declared, Roma Mitchell was 'on the verge' of being a prude.

And then, there was still the handsome, blazing blue-eyed and immensely intelligent Jim Brazel, a widower since 1951. 'I always thought that Jim Brazel was a bit keen on her actually', said Pam Cleland. Many of their colleagues, too, thought there was definitely a tendresse between them; Alec Genders, at one time junior to John Bray, declared unequivocally of Jim Brazel, 'Now, for your information, he was on with Roma.' Did she harbour a secret longing for the entirely traditional, even as she was so thoroughly modern? If she did, then that combination was not to work. Brazel married his second wife, Lynette O'Brien, in January 1959, shortly before he was elevated to the Bench of the Supreme Court, the first Catholic to achieve such an eminence.

But by this time, Roma Mitchell was in her mid-forties. She clearly considered questions of marriage to have belonged well in the past: 'You must remember that I'm a war-generation person'. 'Circumstances', she told interviewer Susan Mitchell, 'dictated the fact that I never married. It wasn't a matter of a definite decision. Gradually one path closes and another one opens.'[44] Even so, did she long for emotional intimacy, so missing from her modern, professional life, however crowded it was with friends and work? It is always possible to love, *without love necessarily leading to marriage. That would have been an extraordinarily modern relationship. Did she and Jim Brazel have an extremely modern fling?*

Is it only the un-married who prompt such intrusive speculation about their sex lives?

In the early 1950s, Roma Mitchell was exploring the world. Her first adventure was to Western Australia, to visit her paternal cousin, Bill MacDonald, three years older and son of her father's older sister, Maud. He lived at Fossil Downs, an enormous – 600,000 hectare – property in the Kimberley region, 3200 kilometres north of Perth. It was the last of the hundred or so cattle stations in the north-west still to be privately owned, and it was 'the showplace of them all'. Being a modern woman, Miss Mitchell set out by aeroplane, a DC-3, from Parafield Airport, just to the north of Adelaide, only three years after the air service began. This was an adventure in itself.

The journey to Perth took eleven hours, and the plane landed three times, at Ceduna, Forrest and Kalgoorlie, before it reached Guildford Airport. 'Don't listen to anyone who tells you the air trip to Perth is boring', she told Ruth. For part of the journey they flew into the sunset, 'and you can imagine how lovely it was with the red brown of the Nullarbor Plain beneath'. From Perth, she flew north to Derby, on the coast, thence to Fossil Downs. It was a once-a-week trip, the plane journey to the Kimberley stations, bringing mail, newspapers, fresh food, mail-order goods and the occasional visitor, for this was a vast territory, covering about a sixth of the total area of Western Australia, with about 100 Aboriginal communities and 100 pastoral properties, but no bitumen roads. The only regular communication came from Radio Australia, which crackled and spat. The DC-3 left Derby at six in the morning and stopped at Mount House, Glenroy and Halls Creek, before it reached Fossil Downs. At each stop there was a magnificent morning tea with little pies and pasties, scones and iced cakes, and pots of boiling tea, laid out on spotless white cloths under a bough to protect them from the sun. When cousin Roma reached Fossil Downs, she faced her fourth morning tea.

The station complex was huge.

> There is no place like it anywhere in the North. Bill and Maxine MacDonald puddled all the concrete blocks themselves in the river bed, built a large two-storey home, furnished it with elegance and fashioned about it an independent settlement that has almost a Mediterranean character; stockman's quarters, storerooms, saddler's shop and harness[,] station offices pleasantly set about a pink-washed courtyard and enlivened by tropical shrubs and trees. Embedded in the flagstones of the homestead verandah are fossils dating back 250,000 years.

The author of this account was another friend that Roma Mitchell made on her journey, the English travel writer George Farwell, there on assignment from the Commonwealth Information Bureau in Sydney.[45]

Three years later, Roma Mitchell was on a plane again; not for her the gradual and heart-wrenchingly slow departure of the passenger ship from Adelaide's Outer Harbour, with passengers holding streamers by one end and their friends and relations on shore the other end, until the streamers broke. This time she was heading off to London. She was not going to visit the queen, although there was, now, a new monarch on the British throne, a young Queen who had visited Australia in 1954. Rather, she went as an official Australian delegate to attend the first Commonwealth and Empire Law Conference, a new source of international bonding among members of what had been Britain's Empire, based, as Miss Mitchell reported later, on 'the one thing [that] the British Commonwealth has retained intact ... the common tradition in law'. This was the conference to which she took her paper on the Poor Person's Legal Assistance Scheme, and another on an earlier distinctively South Australian legal innovation, the Torrens Land Title System. She would not be away for as long as Beryl Linn, who arranged for someone to take over her practice for seven months and travelled by sea. But Miss Mitchell would be away for all of three months, doing a good deal of exploring, meeting Hugh Gooch's relations, and making friends and winning admirers among other legal colleagues. She took a prodigious quantity of luggage, something to wear on every kind of occasion:

red & blue denim
blue & white sleeveless
Cream & brown frock & jacket
Garden frock
Orange Italian – to wear
Navy blue & white
Italian 3 piece
? 2 piece blue
cream shirt & jacket
3 piece navy
white cotton cardigan
blue late afternoon
black late afternoon & black jacket
blue & pink long
long green & navy
red batile green
long black [crossed out]
beige slacks – 2 tops
long towelling gown [crossed out]
cream shoes
navy (ditto)
gold (ditto)
beige walking (ditto)
blue coat
? Burbury
stoles – 2
turban[46]

She paused in Europe on her way, and spent a few days in Scotland, too, concluding with the Scottish Bar's reception for her in Edinburgh. Then the conference opened with great pomp and circumstance at a ceremony in the Great Hall in Westminster with the British legal establishment resplendent in 'their black robes encrusted with silver', their full-bottomed wigs and their black silk stockings and silver-buckled shoes. People liked Miss Mitchell's two papers, especially her account of the Poor Person's Legal Assistance Scheme, which would in time influence the legal aid system introduced in Britain. There were receptions in the Gallery of the House of Lords, the London County Council's chambers on the banks of the Thames, and at the Fishmongers' Guild. The conference concluded with a banquet in the Guildhall, where they listened to Sir Anthony Eden, the British Prime Minister; the Archbishop of York, Cyril Forster Garbett; the Master of the Rolls, Sir Raymond Evershed; and the Lord Mayor of London, Cuthbert L. Ackroyd, all presided over by Sir Hartley Shawcross, President of the Bar Council and of the conference. It was a dazzling display of theatrical majesty for which the British seem to have a special talent, of particular appeal to members of so theatrical a profession. Roma Mitchell was impressed and delighted: 'unforgettable', she told a newspaper reporter on her return to Adelaide.[47]

She stayed at the Sesame Ladies' Foreign and Imperial Club in Grosvenor Street in Belgravia. There she might have encountered an ageing T.S. Eliot or a younger Osbert Sitwell, both of whom favoured the dining room. She visited all of the most famous imperial landmarks: the Tower of London, Madame Tussaud's, Westminster Abbey, Windsor Castle, the British Museum and the National Gallery. Denise Brazel, Jim Brazel's daughter, was also in London, visiting her great-aunt Eileen and great-uncle Sir Charles McCann, South Australia's Agent-General. The Brazel connection was warm: Roma Mitchell took them to the theatre to see Michael Redgrave and the Australian Diane Cilento performing in *The Tiger at the Gate*, a new adaptation by Christopher Fry of Jean Giraudoux's *La Guerre de Troie n'aura pas Lieu*. She would overcome cultural parsimony at home: she took herself to Covent Garden to see two new ballets choreographed by Frederick Ashton, *The Lady and the Fool* and *Madame Chrysantheme*, which she loved. She visited Hugh Gooch's relations. And she spent a morning at the Bow Street Magistrate's Court, watching how the business was despatched, impressed with the way they made use of a probation officer, but 'quite shocked' at how they dealt with the prostitutes.

> [A]ll that happens is that each is fined 30/- or 40/-. It seemed to be 40/- where they had had a previous conviction within the past 2 weeks, 30/- if longer. I am told that many of them have had more than 200 convictions. It seems to me that either they should not be prosecuted at all if they are not causing a disturbance, or more appropriate penalties (such as imprisonment) should be imposed after frequent convictions.

> There is much discussion here (and I agree with it) that the present system of fines week after week savours too much of a licence fee.[48]

It also made a travesty of the law prohibiting working women from plying their trade, something any but the most cynical lawyer would find objectionable.

Then she flew to the United States of America. This flight proved dangerous and frightening; it ran into the tail end of a hurricane that had been inflicting extensive damage in the US.

> We were five hours late arriving in America. We could not land at Boston and went on to New York. For two and a half hours we had no contact from the front of the plane. Even the air hostess – one of whom was completely incapacitated – had none. You get an impression of moving at terrific speed and bounce all over the place. Everyone except myself was violently ill. And I was scared to the extent that I thought we would not get out of it. But once it was over it was over, as far as I was concerned.

So curtly does she dismiss hours of believing that she was facing death! A testament to the power of prayer? After that she could cope with being stuck in a lift halfway up the Empire State Building without turning a hair. She climbed back into other planes, too, including a four-passenger sea plane over the Great Lakes in Canada, before chugging off by train for the Rockies and then Vancouver. From there she flew again, to San Francisco, Honolulu and then home.[49]

These two expeditions generated an appetite that was never sated. There was another Australian expedition, then in 1960 she went to the second Commonwealth and Empire Law Conference, in Ottawa, Canada, again as an official Australian delegate. On her way, she attended a conference of the International Federation of Women Lawyers in Manila, flying out of Sydney at midnight, arriving just in time to attend a luncheon given by Manila's Chief Justice, then chairing a panel discussion on family relations among hundreds of international lawyers, lasting several hours. Some of the South East Asian delegates thought she was Queen Elizabeth.

She paused on the way to Canada for a holiday in London, staying at the Forum Club in Belgrave Square, where she met other Australians: Winnie and René Levy, parents of Anne, at that time a tutor in Genetics at Adelaide University; Zeta Walsh, a member of the National Council of Women as was Roma Mitchell, all from Adelaide; and Pat Kennedy, a solicitor from Melbourne. Except for one morning when she stayed talking with the Levys and saw the horse guards pass by, she was out and about by 10.30 am, having already telephoned an array of people to arrange to meet them. She had only twelve days, so she set a cracking pace: lunch with Zeta Walsh at the Vendome in Albemarle Street; with the Clover family, relations of Hugh Gooch, at an Italian restaurant; with Theo Ruoff, Senior Registrar at the Land Registry, Lincoln's Inn, and also a legal author who wrote witty commentaries on the British legal scene for the *Australian Law Journal*, at the Angel, 'a nice pub on the river bank' at Bermondsey where they watched Tower Bridge and the shipping; and various others. She spent a day on someone's farm, and a weekend visiting Hugh's relations at Torquay. She went to the hairdresser twice. And she must have been out almost every night, taking on board the current theatrical mixture of the newly classical (Chekhov) with the new and jazzed-up from the United States. She saw Stephen Sondheim's *West Side Story*, the Romeo and Juliet story set in a New York dockland to Leonard Bernstein's music ('very good'); Brecht's *Galileo* at the Mermaid ('very sardonic, but has a lot of wit and is beautifully acted'); *Oliver*, the musical that Lionel Bart made from Dickens' heart-rending novel ('excellent with many catchy tunes'); the wonderful husky Judith Anderson, originally a South Australian, in Chekhov's *The Seagull* at the Old Vic ('I think the play is boring, but it is beautifully acted. The young girl ... was excellent and received an ovation'); a dramatised version of E.M. Forster's *A Passage to India* ('I remember finding the book difficult to read because it was so diffuse. But the play was excellent'); *Follow that Girl* ('a musical by Julian Slade who did *Salad Days*. It was similar in style and we thoroughly enjoyed it'); Alec Guinness as *Lawrence of Arabia* ('truly magnificent. But I don't know how it would be if the lead were changed'); and the Festival Ballet ('some gay new ballets'). As always, she looked for the new and modern. She went to the Picasso Exhibition at the Tate Gallery. She went to *Pieces of Eight* ('a gay witty revue with eight players which would probably not pass the censor at home. It seems to me that our people will let in any vulgarity but not sophisticated wit if it is near the bone and this is certainly near the bone').[50]

It all sounds very brisk and determined: the habit of efficiency trespassing from her work into her pleasures. 'As you can see I am not sitting at home and pining', she told Ruth. But she was missing her all the same. Roma had not been well: in hospital the year before, suffering from ulcers, and then a chest cold before she arrived in London. And she was missing her mother, too. 'Remembering that it is the anniversary of Mother's death', she wrote to Ruth,

> *I felt that I should like particularly to write today. I have been wishing that the three of us could have been in London to-gether. Not that I have had a spare minute, but other people could have jumped in the lake.*

Later, she thanked Ruth for telling her about 'the Mass for Mother': 'I was thinking about her and you so much'.

Perhaps it is not surprising, then, that she did not enjoy the Canadian conference, finding it 'heavy going' and 'not comparable with the English one': 'The papers and discussions are the usual mixture of interesting and dull', and people tended to mix only with others from their own countries. There was a dinner dance, though, which kept her up and out until two in the morning, and on another evening, following a reception given by the Australian High Commissioner, she joined a party of eight determined to defeat Ontario's draconian liquor licensing by dining across the river in Quebec. After that they went to a nightclub to hear Della Reese, an 'American negress pop singer', wrote Roma to Ruth. They liked Della Reece so much they stayed for the second show, arriving back at their hotel at 1.40 am, with a wake-up call booked for 6.15 am. Miss Mitchell catnapped between sessions.

This visit to north America enabled her at least to see Margaret Hyndman of Toronto, a pioneer, for she had taken silk in 1932, a mere six years after she had been called to the Ontario Bar, the first woman QC in the British Empire: now *there* was an ambition to match, you could expect an intrinsically competitive observer to note. And on their way home, she and Pat Kennedy and another Melbourne solicitor, Mary Cameron, visited San Francisco Municipal Judge Lenore D. Underwood at her court in the Hall of Justice, ostensibly to learn something of the United States' justice system; no doubt, also, to see a judge who was also a woman.[51] Being a woman was about to assume a far larger place in Roma Mitchell's life. The 1950s in Adelaide had been fermenting to considerable purpose, changing her world professionally, artistically, and personally.

The World Arrives in Adelaide

The legal profession had been embroiled in a case beginning in 1958 that called into question an array of assumptions held by some of its most senior members – about its entitlement to protect itself; to do as it saw fit, however irregularly; and to maintain its independence of the state. The profession had encountered, too, a new force in the disposition of the affairs it had previously considered its own exclusive domain – the press. Indeed, hindsight would date from this case the rise of the most important and powerful media baron in the world – Rupert Murdoch. This was the case of Rupert Max Stuart, an Aboriginal man of the Aranda people, charged with murdering nine-year-old Mary Hattam, a Caucasian girl, near Thevanard, a small town on the west coast of South Australia, on 21 December 1958. The ensuing succession of trials, appeals and inquiries exposed to public critique and outrage everything initially taken for granted about Stuart's ability to understand questions put to him in English, and Chief Justice Napier's right to determine judgment on an appeal against his own sentence. Appallingly, Stuart was first sentenced to hang, then that sentence was postponed no fewer than six times before Premier Playford was finally persuaded by public outcry to commute it.

Roma Mitchell took no part in this case, but her cousin Cairns Villeneuve Smith did. Afterwards, he and his wife Pamela moved to Melbourne, not, as was rumoured, because the case had compromised his career, but rather because he wanted to practise solely as a barrister, and the only way he could do that in the fused profession in Adelaide was by becoming a QC. He was still too young to have acquired the distinguished experience necessary for that. Pamela had vetoed going to Sydney because she did not like the weather there, and thought the property prices too high, but she was quite happy to go to Melbourne. Roma missed them, but telephoned weekly and visited them often, as they did her.[52]

The Stuart case speeded up the changes under way in the Law School at the University of Adelaide. The newly appointed Professor of Law, Norval Morris, and Alex Castles, another fresh face around the Law School, set about changes to the curriculum and the introduction of new people to lecture to their students. They separated Family Law from its previous inclusion with Partnership, Companies, Bankruptcy and Divorce, and appointed Miss Roma Mitchell the first part-time lecturer in the new subject. She enjoyed this, walking up to town with students after classes, sharing gossip about the profession and talking with them about their careers.[53]

Cartoon of Cairns Villeneuve Smith copied from the Order of Service for his funeral

Her cultural environment was becoming richer, too. For George Farwell, the writer she had met at Fossil Downs, and his wife Noni, moved to Adelaide in 1958, Noni to work for the *Women's Weekly* and George to promote the first Adelaide Festival of Arts. This was the consummation of a desire long nourished by John Bishop, Professor of Music and Director of Adelaide University's Elder Conservatorium of Music. Sir Lloyd Dumas, Managing Director of the *Advertiser*, took the idea to the Adelaide Club–heartland of the OAFs–and there won support from, as George Farwell described them,

> Sir William Hayward, modern art collector and head of John Martin's department store; Sir Ewen Waterman, grazier and company director; Sir Arthur Rymill, the Bank of Adelaide's musically-inclined chairman;

> Brigadier Sir Kenneth Wills … and Sir Roland Jacobs, of the S.A. Brewing Company.

The Gooch-Wills connection ensured that Miss Mitchell was apprised of these developments from the beginning, including, no doubt, the row that developed over the proposal that the principal drama to be performed would be Alan Seymour's *One Day of the Year*, a 'broadside against Anzac Day sentimentalities'. In the end, that play was rejected, winning the Festival Board a reputation for philistine stuffiness. But the Festival was an immense success.

Bishop persuaded the Australian Broadcasting Commission to send orchestras from both Sydney and Melbourne to join the Adelaide Symphony Orchestra; a combination, conducted by Nicolai Malko, opened the Festival in Elder Park on the banks of the River Torrens, 'frightening the black swans with *Ride of the Valkyries* and Handel's *Fireworks Music*, suitably followed by rockets and falling stars'. Farwell listed a dazzling array of international artists appearing in Adelaide: the pianist Philippe Entremont from Paris; the Janaçek String Quartet from Prague; Joan Hammond in Strauss's *Salome*; the great Shakespearean Sir Donald Wolfit; Robert Speaight in Eliot's *Murder in the Cathedral*; and Dave Brubeck, 'whom students persuaded me to take to the university to debate his philosophy of cool jazz', said Farwell. Roma Mitchell's good friend John Bray, poet and by then a QC, helped organise the Festival's Writers' Week; his first published collection of poems would be launched at the second Writers' Week in 1962. 'Sober Adelaide was transformed', wrote Farwell:

> Queues formed at the box office weeks before opening day. Newspapers put the arts on their front page. Bright banners enlivened its thoroughfares, and coloured lights were strung along North Terrace. Gaily-dressed girls boarded interstate and country trains, handing out flowers. Others were at the airport, where every plane brought in musicians, painters, writers, singers, actors, critics. Not a day went by without its art opening, first night, folk display, wine tasting, reception or cocktail party.[54]

Never again would Roma Mitchell have to wait for a trip to London for an artistic feast. The Adelaide Festival of Arts has taken place every two years ever since. And George and Noni

Farwell – clever, highly literate, witty, cultured and informed – were to become close and life-long friends with Roma, both of them also born under the sign of Libra, the scales of justice, an extra bond.

Then, two years later, on 20 September 1962, Miss Mitchell was made a Queen's Counsel, a silk. This was a rank of attainment depending on professional pre-eminence. Ironically – since such an achievement could be thought to have affirmed her practice of making as little as possible of sexual difference in her career – that meant, too, that now she was going to have to pay more attention to being a woman.

Chapter Five
Roma the First

Becoming a Silk

A Queen's Counsel. This was 'a mark of recognition by the Sovereign of the professional eminence of the Counsel upon whom it is conferred'.[1] For Roma Mitchell it was the pinnacle of her career: 'The only thing that I really felt was an achievement on my own' she said, 'was when I became a silk, a Queen's Counsel ... That was an achievement in work.'[2] In this, she took immense pride.

There could never have been any doubt that she deserved such recognition. She had an extensive practice that had won her widespread and warm approval. The *Advertiser* commented,

> She is a gifted woman and greatly respected and admired in the solemnity of the courts and the law generally for her outstanding ability. With it she combines a generous understanding that has made her an authority on the letter and the spirit of family law in Australia.[3]

She was lecturing on Family Law at the University of Adelaide. She was contributing long hours of voluntary labour to the Council of the Law Society of South Australia. She had represented Australia at two British Commonwealth and Empire gatherings, in London and Ottawa, and had won plaudits for her paper at the first.

She was acquiring an international reputation for her work in family law. There had been the FIDA conference in Manila in 1960.[4] Then in May 1962, as senior Australian delegate, she presented a paper to a major seminar on the Status of Women in Family Law in Tokyo, jointly hosted by the United Nations and the government of Japan. By the time the third Commonwealth and Empire Law Conference took place in Sydney in 1965 Roma Mitchell had a vocal international following. Jamaican barrister K.C. Burke declared 'I came here this afternoon to hear Miss Mitchell, and I have not been disappointed' – she had presented a paper on uniformity of law within the Commonwealth. English QC, Tom Kellock, prefaced his reply on behalf of the paper givers with the salutation, 'Mr Chairman, gentlemen and members of the Roma Mitchell fan club'.[5]

She would not miss her attendance at Mass when she was travelling, no matter how difficult it might be to get there. It was Sunday while she was in Tokyo. Fellow Australian, Aline Fenwick, noted that they had not seen a church. 'Look', she said to Roma, 'while we're travelling I don't think we're supposed to go.' But Roma was determined. 'Oh, we must never miss', she replied. 'So we got a taxi', related Miss Fenwick,

> and in some extraordinary way she conveyed what we were after and we finished up on the outskirts of Tokyo about an hour later at the back of someone's house where there was a shed, and in the shed Mass was being celebrated. There are very few Catholics in Japan, and in we went, these two tall, fair people. They just froze, these little women at the back, and it was almost over. A couple of times en route I'd said to Roma, 'Look, I'm sure –'. 'No, we must try.' ... I wouldn't have gone on with it. There's a moment when you just don't have to. But no, she ... was meticulous.[6]

Even when it was insupportably uncomfortable. In Greece in 1963, Roma reported that 'The Cathedral is ... as airless as the Church Ruth and I walked into in Melbourne and promptly left. Fortunately Mass is being said at one of the altars all the time. So it is only about 30 minutes endurance.' By the time she left, she was so hot and wet that she had mopped off all her make-up.[7]

Her church was changing, though. The Second Vatican

Council of 1962–1965 approved a number of decrees that reshaped Catholic theology, opening its windows 'to an ecumenical, theologically plural, even secular world', wrote historian Katharine Massam. Liturgical change brought the vernacular into church services, and rearranged the furniture, bringing the altar forward so that Mass could be celebrated facing the congregation.[8] Roma Mitchell would now learn to worship in English.

Her achievements and the recognition they brought set her firmly – securely – beside the men who were her closest peers. John Bray had taken silk three years earlier than she did. This erudite, mild-mannered lawyer, a poet 'with slightly larrikin recreational tastes', was gaining a reputation as a champion of the underprivileged – as long as that underprivileged was male – 'a fearless and most learned fighter ... The acknowledged leader of the Bar, appearing in almost every jurisdiction.'[9] The others made QC at the same time as Roma Mitchell were Keith Sangster, Howard Zelling and Andrew Wells. Sangster, the same age as Roma, was, like Bray, committed to justice for the oppressed and disadvantaged. He was a pacifist, his reputation building from his war service and subsequent investigations of war crimes in the Pacific in the 1940s through to his expertise in tax law and pioneering work on the responsibilities of company directors in the 1950s, to revisions of liquor licensing and innovative analysis of white-collar crime in the 1960s. Howard Zelling was three years younger than Roma Mitchell. He was the lawyer with the photographic memory whose eyesight kept him out of the forces so he spent the war years picking up cases for his friends and colleagues. He had married the youngest of the original Thursday Girls, Girl Friday Sesca Anderson, Secretary of the Law Society, immediately after the war. His reputation was to prompt his appointment as Chairman of the Law Reform Committee of South Australia in 1963. The reputation that Andrew Wells built was, primarily, for his outstanding scholarship: awarded a Rhodes Scholarship in 1940–1941, he took it up when he left the Australian Imperial Forces after the war and gained first class honours in both a Bachelor of Arts (Jurisprudence) and Bachelor of Civil Law at Magdalen College, Oxford. Back in Adelaide he was snapped up by the Crown Law Office. He was six years younger than Miss

Mitchell.[10] They were all much of a generation, then; it could not be said that her elevation had been delayed.

But that made it all the more surprising, for a woman had never been made silk in Australia before, no matter how deserving she might have been. So how did it come about?

Let us tell you two stories.

The first begins with Sir Mellis Napier. In Britain, and in New South Wales and Queensland in Australia, someone wishing to take silk had to petition the government. In the other Australian states, such appointments were made on the recommendation of the Chief Justice to the Governor in Council. The government was expected simply to endorse that recommendation, reinforcing the independence of the law from the state, and ensuring that such appointments were free of political interference. In South Australia in 1962 the Chief Justice was the eighty-year-old Sir Mellis Napier.

He had been born in Scotland, educated in London, and had come to Adelaide with the rest of his family, following his father who had accepted a post as senior resident physician at the Royal Adelaide Hospital in 1896. This was not a happy start. The hospital needed Dr Napier because its entire honorary medical staff had resigned in protest against the radical-liberal government of C.C. Kingston in a protracted row over appointment of nurses. The Adelaide doctors had been supported by the British Medical Association placing a world-wide ban on their own members working at the hospital, a ban that Dr Napier ignored. The Adelaide doctors were also supported by the OAFs – indeed, some were OAFs themselves – opposed to Kingston's government. The OAFs never forgave Dr Napier for his part in enabling the government to keep the hospital open, some resorting to an ugly smear campaign. There were, Dame Roma recalled, 'the most scurrilous articles ... published about Napier, who they said was an abortionist'; then, decades later, medicos in the Adelaide Club with long memories objected to Chief Justice Napier being elected their president because they weren't going to have the son of 'that doctor' presiding over them.

Nevertheless, Mellis Napier (his first name was his mother's family name), the doctor's third son, enrolled in Law at Adelaide University, gained his degree in 1902, when he was only twenty and articled to Kingston, and was admitted to the Bar in October 1903. He rose rapidly. He took silk in 1921 and was appointed to the Bench of the Supreme Court in 1924. Moreover, he was elected to the Adelaide Club, and elected its president in 1928. In 1935 the United Australia Government of former Labor politician, Prime Minister J.A. Lyons, appointed him chairman of a royal commission into the nation's banking systems; it reported in 1937, presenting a set of recommendations that fellow commissioner, future Labor Prime Minister J.B. Chifley, endorsed, and – on the other side of politics – Robert Menzies approved. Napier succeeded Sir George Murray as Chief Justice of South Australia in 1942, a position he held for the ensuing twenty-five years.

He exercised great charm. He ran 'a relaxed court', reported one of his biographers, Peter Howell. He allowed his colleagues to appear in the streets without the terrifying majesty – and summertime oppression – of top hat, frock coat and silver-topped cane. He also decreed that they could 'dine, smoke and have their hair cut in public establishments', activities that these god-like beings had previously been required to keep hidden from the everyday world. While he was Chancellor of the University of Adelaide, between 1948 and 1961, he intervened in appointments in the History Department, supporting the appointment of George Rudé, a member of the Communist Party of Great Britain, as Senior Lecturer, and the promotion of Ken Inglis to Reader, even though Inglis had actively and publicly criticised Napier over his part in the Stuart case. Dame Roma considered that Napier's bark was far worse than his bite: 'he was really a very gentle sort of man', she mused, 'in the Criminal Court he'd bark about things but his sentences were always very light'.

Nevertheless, Napier ran an extremely – indeed, improperly – tight ship. He formed a small 'coterie' to resuscitate the Law Society that ensured that the legal profession policed itself, rather than suffering scrutiny from outside. He took lunch with his puisne judges every weekday, when they discussed the cases currently before the courts. This meant it was impossible for any appeal to the Full Court against one of his judgments to succeed. Senior counsel concluded, wrote Howell, that 'it was necessary to go to the High Court of Australia or the Judicial Committee of the

Privy Council to obtain an independent review of his decisions'. Deeply committed, was this Scottish South Australian Chief Justice, to maintaining 'the tradition that is our common inheritance from the Bench and Bar of England'; he cited English decisions before looking to Australian precedents and never considered relevant American cases. Nevertheless, he held that judges could exercise a 'law-creating function' within the constraints of that inheritance – as long as it was a function that he approved. On one occasion when he pressed counsel for the authority for a particular point, unsuccessfully,

> the barrister asserted that he was unable to help the Chief Justice with any cases and it seemed, so he said, that there was no authority on the issue. The immediate reply of the Chief Justice, according to the oral tradition at the Bar, was simply: 'Don't worry, there soon will be.'

Such assurance in the rectitude and security of his own authority was buttressed by his terms as Lieutenant Governor of South Australia, and Acting Governor, between 1942 and 1967. No doubt this assurance contributed to his professional insularity and profound political insensitivity in, himself, sitting on the commission of inquiry into the Stuart case, when it was the decision of the Full Court over which he had presided that was the subject of that inquiry. As legal historians Alex Castles and Michael Harris were to observe, '[t]he notion that [Napier] or his colleagues might have the regrettable but human capacity to err seemed to many involved hardly to impinge on the chief justice's thinking.' 'I think he [thought he] had sort of become omnipotent', Dame Roma recalled. 'He didn't ever expect any of his judgments to be over-ruled. I remember the High Court over-ruled one. He couldn't forgive them.'[11]

He had three sons. The eldest was killed in action while flying with Coastal Command off Italy in 1943. He wanted to elevate the youngest above the stigma that he had inherited from his own father's rejection by the OAFs, so in 1960 he recommended him for silk, even though being a QC was beyond R.M. (Bob) Napier's capacities. Shortly afterwards, a lawyer friend told Jack Elliott that the whole profession was snubbing the unfortunate Bob Napier QC; he was not getting any briefs.[12] The profession also responded by attempting a palace coup.

The Law Society Council suggested a change in the way in which people could be made QC. In future, they proposed, all appointments to silk should be initiated by candidates applying to the Chief Justice and the Law Society, both at the same time, and that the Law Society should have the right to tell the Chief Justice what they thought of the applicants. Sir Mellis Napier agreed in principle; his only provision was that the Law Society was not to 'assume the role of a judge and veto any requests'. But he was bluffing; he was not going to allow any such whittling away of his autocracy. Subsequently he claimed to have agreed only to the suggestion that he invite people to apply for silk as and when he saw fit, and that applicants could inform the Law Society only if they thought they had been overlooked. Also, he added, he did not want disappointed persons applying to be made silk after they had complained to the Society; this would lead to 'undesirable results'. Finally, he thought that the 1960 agreement, which – in his words – 'the Society had clearly misunderstood', should be cancelled and the profession notified accordingly. The Council had appointed a sub-committee consisting of Roma Mitchell, G.C. Harry and E.W. Palmer to draw up the proposal in the form of a regulation and notify the rest of the profession, but when it became clear that Napier CJ was not having a bar of it, they rescinded the measure.[13] The coup had failed.

Before Bob Napier's elevation, there had been speculation in the press about new QCs. 'Rumour predicts that Miss Roma Mitchell may be among the "likelies"', reported the 'State Roundsman' for the Adelaide *News*. This piece went on to assure its readers that Crown Solicitor J.R. Kearnan was a certainty, and that other names heard among the rumours included Charles Bright, J.F. Astley and R.M. Napier.[14] Miss Mitchell cut it out of the paper and stuck it in her scrapbook, writing 'premature' below it on the page. But then Kearnan, Astley, Bright and Napier were all appointed to silk. Premature maybe, but not simply nonsense.

Two years later, she and Sesca Zelling attended a meeting of the Law Society Council at which the Society raised a question that the Chief Justice did not want to answer. So he distracted his colleagues by raising one that was entirely different. 'I can't remember what it was the Law Society had put to the Chief Justice', Dame Roma noted, but

> the wily old man gave a non-committal answer on that and [then] said, 'How would the Society view a woman being appointed as Queen's Counsel?' Obviously just to, you know, give them something else to think about. And I said, 'Well I think perhaps I better withdraw while you discuss this', and Sesca Zelling was on the Council and she said 'I'm not withdrawing, I'm staying'. So I withdrew and time went on and on. I was sitting in one of the other rooms reading but I got more and more furious. I thought 'What are they talking about, why didn't they immediately say, yes that's O.K.?' And then when someone eventually came to me, they said, 'Sorry, we forgot you were out there!' I was so cross.[15]

Napier put her name forward, together with those of Sangster, Zelling and Wells. She received the letter from the Chief Secretary's Office appointing her 'one of Her Majesty's Counsel learned in the law', presumably in the morning post. Hugh Gooch's Secretary left him a note that read:

> Mrs Gooch phoned.
>
> The Premier's Secretary phoned Miss Mitchell a little while ago to say everything was all right.
>
> Also, would you please go home early as you have people coming in for drinks.

Roma Mitchell QC, Vice President of the Law Society of South Australia addressing a sitting of the full court on the retirement of Judge Pellew, President of the Industrial Court, *Advertiser* 15 December 1964, published with permission of the *Advertiser*.

Mrs. Gooch has put a bottle of Champagne in the refrigerator and would like you to make Champagne Cocktails.

What – no pink gins!!![16]

A Woman on the Crest of a Wave

The second story begins with the National Council of Women [NCW] and the League of Women Voters [LWV]. Both were organisations established in the wake of the victorious campaigns for women's suffrage as a means of maintaining links and solidarity among women across Australia and beyond, and counteracting other claims on their loyalties and energies by the political parties forming in the early years of the twentieth century. The various state branches of the NCW were offshoots of the International Council of Women established in Washington DC in 1888, and the LWV was, at first, called the Women's Non-Party Political Association. The NCW was a conservative body: its understanding of 'non-party' most often meant 'anti-labour or anti-socialist', while the LWV was committed to reform, but gradually. In Adelaide, both organisations had taken a prominent part in activities to mark the centenary of the arrival of British settlers on the Kaurna plains in 1836, notably in compiling *A Book of South Australia: Women in the First Hundred Years*. This work was distinguished from centenary volumes produced in other Australian states by the number of Ladies with titles among the contributors. There had been, too, a tussle over the essay in it concerned with Aboriginal Australians. Constance Cooke had joined the committee organising contributions to the volume as a representative of the Aborigines' Protection League. She wanted the book to include some recognition of Aboriginal women. More ambitiously, she wanted the centenary celebrations to include the return to the Aborigines of

> a portion of the land that has been taken from them so that they may become self-supporting and enabled to work out their own destinies in their own communities.

She was rebuffed. No land was returned to South Australia's Aboriginal people at this time, and while the centenary volume did include attention to Aboriginal women, it appeared in an article by

Daisy Bates who referred to 'our natives' as 'a dying race'.[17] Reactionary over race relations, these women's organisations were, then, as well as generally conservative, despite their commitment to advancing the rights of women.

However, as the Second World War brought wider recognition of the need for equal pay for women, both the NCW and the LWV participated actively in the Women's Charter Conferences of 1943 and 1946. They also, like other far less conservative bodies, took heart and inspiration from international affirmation that 'the inherent dignity and ... the equal and inalienable rights of all members of the human family [are] the foundation of freedom, justice and peace in the world'. Such international optimism, seared and seasoned though it undoubtedly was, prompted the United Nations Conference on International Organization in San Francisco in 1945. Like the Australian Women's Charter Committee, the NCW and the LWV sent cables to the Secretary-General of the United Nations conference, the Charter Committee requesting that all post-war plans incorporate 'The Democratic Principle Of Equality Of Status, Opportunity, And Reward For Men And Women, And Elimination Of All Discriminations Based On Sex'. They and their international allies were successful. The *Preamble* to the *Universal Declaration of Human Rights* includes a reaffirmed faith in 'the equal rights of men and women', and in 1946 the Commission on the Status of Women was established 'to prepare recommendations and reports to the [Economic and Social] Council on promoting women's rights in political, economic, civil, social and educational fields'. The new United Nations' bureaucracy also included an Office of the Status of Women in the Division of Human Rights at the Secretariat in New York. From 1950 to 1958, that office was headed by a South Australian, the St Aloysius old scholar who had preceded Roma Mitchell as prominent in the Law, Mary Tenison Woods.[18]

In Australia, the Women for Canberra Movement's efforts to install women in the Federal Parliament met with little success. But slowly events overtook them. The election of 1943 saw Dorothy Tangney from Western Australia gaining a seat in the Senate for the Australian Labor Party, and Dame Edith Lyons from Tasmania occupying one in the House of Representatives for the United Australia Party. In the following year, Lilian Fowler, an enthusiastic disciple of J.T. Lang, and Australia's first woman mayor, of Newtown, won a seat in the New South Wales Parliament. Just over a decade later, Nancy Buttfield – born into the family of prominent motor car manufacturer, Sir Edward Holden, member of the South Australian Legislative Council from 1935 to 1947 – revivified conservative politics in the Liberal Party Adelaide Women's Branch and won a seat in the Australian Senate.[19]

Then, at the end of the 1950s, two women gained endorsement from the major parties to contest a seat – the same seat – for the South Australian Legislative Council. They were Jessie Cooper for the Liberal-Country League and Margaret Scott for the Australian Labor Party. A major debate ensued about whether the 1894 legislation – which not only gave women in South Australia the vote, but also the right to stand for election themselves – applied to elections to the Legislative Council (which still had a property franchise). This debate was conducted largely in court, so it provoked interest throughout the legal profession. Indeed, it was heard by the Full Court of three judges. Dr John Bray QC appeared for the two men who had challenged women's right to sit in the Legislative Council. Crown Solicitor Roderic Chamberlain appeared for the electoral Returning Officer who had accepted nomination papers from those women. Mrs Cooper was represented by Tacky Hannan QC and Jean Gilmore, Mrs Scott by C.K. Stuart and Don Dunstan, a young lawyer who was, by then, himself a member of the House of Assembly for the Australian Labor Party. Jessie Cooper and Margaret Scott sat together in the court while the debate dragged on for six days, with the election looming. Chamberlain was able to conclude, eventually, that Dr Bray was arguing that women had – though no-one had realised it – been given the right to vote by South Australia's 1855–1856 Constitution, but that the Parliament then took it away when they passed the 1894 suffrage legislation. 'That', pronounced Chamberlain, 'was unthinkable'. The court agreed – more or less. On 3 March 1959, only four days before the election, it brought down its decision. It would not grant the order that the two men had sought, refusing women the right to contest seats in the Legislative Council; it found that there was no express provision in any of the legislation under consideration that prevented women's candidature. But it refused to decide whether women were eligible to sit in the Council. Instead, it turned that question over to the Parliament to be resolved. Both women did contest the election; each was at the top of her party ticket. As the seat was strongly non-Labor, Jessie Cooper, wife of a local brewing clan, won.

A third woman stood in these elections, Mrs Joyce Steele. But she was contesting a seat in the House of Assembly, and no-one sought to prevent her candidacy, so she was spared the insult offered to the aspirants to the upper house. She also had endorsement from her party, the Liberal-Country League, and the seat that she sought was Burnside, an LCL stronghold, so she won comfortably.

Both Jessie Cooper and Joyce Steele took their seats in the South Australian Parliament. That Parliament then passed legislation removing any legal doubt about women's eligibility for election to the Legislative Council. 'Hullo, girlie', said Premier Playford when he ran into Joyce Steele in the lobby on her first day. By the early 1960s the number of women who had gained seats in the parliaments of Australia had risen to fifteen.[20]

Jessie Cooper, retiring MLC 5 July 1979, photograph by Lewis, published with permission of the *Advertiser*.

Mrs Joyce Steele, 23 April 1968, published with permission of the *Advertiser*.

Besides watching these events at home, Roma Mitchell kept an eye on those women overseas who were, like Mary Tenison Woods, her intellectual and professional predecessors. She also remained in touch with Aline Fenwick, with whom she had gone hunting for a place of Catholic worship in Tokyo in 1962. Aline was another St Aloysius old scholar, ten years younger than Roma, who had gone on from Law at Adelaide University to a stint at the London School of Economics and Political Science and had then, like Woods, joined the United Nations Secretariat. Roma and Aline had spent time together at the Ottawa conference, and it was through Aline that Roma learned about the Tokyo conference. Two other Australians were there as well, both friends of Roma's: Molly Kingston, a solicitor from Melbourne, previously from Perth where until 1938 she and Sheila McClemans had run the first all-woman legal practice in Australia, and Zeta Walsh, who had gone sightseeing with Roma once or twice in London; she was in Tokyo as an NCW observer.[21]

Decades later, Dame Roma was to recall this conference.

> The participants were all from Asian countries with the addition of Australia and New Zealand. The Asian delegates were concerned at the inadequacy of childminding facilities for women employed in industry, but Australia and New Zealand really could not contribute to that session because we did not have married women employed in industry, and therefore there was no call for childminding centres there or in the public service.[22]

Those Australians and New Zealanders still subscribed to the widespread myth, encouraged by historical assumption and government policy, that the baby-boom mothers were all bare foot, pregnant and chained to the new Simpson-Pope washing machine or the new Hill's Hoist rotary clothesline at home. That myth, and their belief in it, ignored the effects of the post-war economic yeast in the cultural and social dough, enhanced by the arrival of immigrant women, also wives and mothers, seeking livelihoods by working in industry. The proportion of Australian wives and mothers already employed in industry, and needing, or lacking, childcare – this was the period of 'latch-key children', blamed for a rise in juvenile delinquency, something lawyers might have noticed – had almost trebled between 1947 and 1961. Even such a large increase was still not so very large, to be sure: it was a rise from 6.5 per cent of married women in the population to 18.36 per cent. But such an increase was a harbinger of far greater change: that proportion was to treble again in the next five years, and again in the following five years.[23]

Yet however unaware she might have been of the – so far, latent – changes in the nature of the labour market in the 1950s, Roma Mitchell could hardly have avoided noticing by 1962 how much conditions of life in Adelaide were changing. It was not only the rapidly growing population, the shifting cultural mix with new immigrants from Europe, the gradual alteration in ways of eating, drinking and entertaining with new restaurants opening in the city: now it was possible to eat quite excellent curries at the Ceylon Hut in Bank Street in the city, and an Italian restaurant calling itself The Mediterranean opened on O'Connell Street in North Adelaide. It was not only the new ways of getting about – trams were being replaced by diesel buses, a new airport at West Beach replaced Parafield so that planes now flew in and out over the city, and roads were filling up with privately owned cars, in which whole families could go to a drive-in movie theatre, and young couples would steam up the windows with their passions. Nor was such change appearing only with working-class bodgies and widgies, with teased hair and motorbikes, or with rock'n'roll – 'Rock Around the Clock Tonight' bawled Bill Haley and his Comets from increasingly miniaturised and portable radios, or with the Penny Rockets performing in cinemas with everyone dancing in the aisles – though they were all part of that change. It was also the veritable explosion in access to information, in education and in communication.[24]

Post-war prosperity encouraged more and more families to keep their children at school for longer than an earlier generation did. The number of schools grew. More and more school leavers looked for further education at university. Successive governments in Canberra established and then extended the Australian Universities Commission and a system of financing tertiary education. Post-secondary education was to increase exponentially. In South Australia, Premier Playford happily embraced such a development: he announced plans for a new university campus at Bedford Park on the southern edge of Adelaide in 1960. Jean Whyte wrote to her good friend Roma from the Fisher Library at the University of Sydney: would Roma find out about the plans for the new university, she asked. Would there be any opportunity for her to apply for the position of Librarian? Expanding opportunities for education were more than matched by accelerating access to information about events in Adelaide and about the world beyond. Television arrived in Australia, in Melbourne and Sydney, in 1956. The Australian Broadcasting Service opened in Adelaide in 1959, watched by 6124 holders of viewers' licences, and all their friends and relations. By June 1960 there were three channels and the number of licenses issued had risen to 84,967.[25] World events could now arrive – directly, it seemed – in people's households.

Women were in the forefront of this wave of change. The contraceptive pill appeared on the general market in 1960, so women had access to a more certain means of controlling their fertility than had ever been available before.[26] The effects of this development were not recognised immediately, but they were immense and far-reaching. And they underpinned others that could be seen more readily. Women, including middle-class women, including wives and mothers, were essential to the new labour force, and their earnings were just as essential to expanding domestic markets for consumer durables. Both brought major alteration to the shape and nature of domestic life as well as to that of the labour market. Women were gaining hitherto unprecedented access to university education – with implications that were, in 1962, still to erupt. Women were appearing in the nation's legislatures, determining public policy. Women were flying off to major international conferences – the FIDA conference that Roma Mitchell attended in Manila in 1960, the United Nations conference at which she represented Australia in Tokyo in 1962, just for instance. There she was, right on the crest of that wave, Miss Roma Mitchell, the first woman in Australia and one of the first in the world to be made a QC. She was already exceptional by virtue of her talent. Now the great changes underway allowed that talent to gain recognition.

News of her appointment appeared in the local, interstate and overseas press. Telegrams and letters poured in offering congratulations. Indeed, so many were there that Miss Mitchell contacted the post office to suggest staff wait until they had a bundle of telegrams, then bring them to her office all together, to save the frequent trips that the telegram delivery boys were having to make. Over and over again these messages referred to her sex. A lawyer from Naracoorte, Foster Skewes, wrote:

> I suppose it is indeed an honour to have been the vehicle by which the (weaker?) sex has at last invaded preserves which mere man had always regarded as peculiarly his own – in this country at any rate.

'The powers that be in South Australia are rather reluctant to give women equality with men … though they don't mind accepting their services', opined Helen Mayo and Constance Finlayson. Yet another letter, from Sydney barrister Bryce Ross Jones observed that 'your appointment … in addition to being well merited, is a major break-through into the otherwise exclusive male preserves'. One correspondent, Doris West, saw Miss Mitchell's appointment, optimistically, as part of a general trend:

> I have felt recently that at long last there were sure signs that women in Australia were breaking through. This appointment confirms it! We now need at least one woman holding a University Chair, then that barrier will be down.

Another, Ralph Newman from the Local Court in Adelaide, told her that pride was justifiable since she had 'blazed the trail for those of your sex in this realm'. Those of her sex agreed. Aline Fenwick and Molly Kingston sent telegrams. So did others whom she did not know as well: Sheila McClemans wrote, 'you have brought distinction on us all. I am sure that all women who practise law will happily bask in your reflected glory', and Mary Tenison Woods sent her love and applauded: 'you are indeed making history'. The Mercy Old Scholars Association gave a dinner at the South to celebrate her; Merle Jenkins, Molly and Margaret Brazel and Helen Devaney welcomed Miss Mitchell QC, who was wearing pelican pink splashed with chrysanthemums. Her old teacher, Sister Mary Ignatius, wrote of the pride of the whole community, and her own in 'one of my first and most successful pupils'. 'It is amazing', she continued,

> that a Q.C. has been awarded to a woman. I never believed that male complacency could bring itself to give honour where honour is due. The first lady Q.C. has reason to be very satisfied with her achievements. The first woman Q.C. of Australia! What a remarkable distinction.[27]

Never again would Roma Mitchell be so entirely her own person as she had been before this elevation. Now she was marked out as an exception far more clearly and prominently than when she had graduated with distinction from university, a much greater rarity even than when she was a practising barrister. Now she had become both a symptom and a symbol of social change, a representative of – a point of reference for – a whole spectrum of hopes about changes in the position of women, about recognition for women's abilities, about alteration in the conditions governing women's lives. Now, and for the rest of her life, there would be people who sought to own her, to claim her for their own desires.

To conclude this second story, let us return to the National Council of Women. Within a year of her appointment, Miss Mitchell had taken up arms in the struggle to have women allowed to serve on juries. There were two obstacles to overcome. One was the moss-covered belief among chivalrous patriarchal men that information provided in some court cases was too 'sordid' – sexually explicit – for the delicate and sheltered sensibilities of women. Some women believed this too, as did Premier Playford, who had said to previous deputations, 'I wouldn't like my wife to serve on a jury.' The other was the equally whiskery excuse that there was 'no accommodation' in the court houses for women – no lavatories. In 1960 the League of Women Voters and the NCW renewed their campaign. Roma Mitchell had no doubt, as she was to tell the Women Justices Association of South Australia, that 'Women should do jury service'. Preparing for the deputation to Playford in 1962, she 'worked out the arguments that would appeal to him'. Playford had a reputation for leading members of a deputation to argue amongst themselves, so they resolved upon only one speaker.[28] On 20 August 1963, Jessie Cooper and Joyce Steele introduced the deputation, with Marjorie Oldham of the LWV at its head. Their one speaker, Miss Roma Mitchell QC, presented their case.

The NCW represented thousands of women, she said, and they were unanimously in favour of women serving on juries. It would be an economical move, she pointed out. Many of the women who served would not be employed, so the new measure would minimise the loss of manpower in productive industries. And those women who *were* employed would be on lower wages than men so that their jury service would actually reduce the costs of running the service. She added another point, too, one that would have choked her, given her refusal to concede any intrinsic difference between the sexes, if it had not been a device calculated to appeal to the Premier's assumption of absolute difference between the sexes: 'there were cases, such as sex crimes, where women would be able to assess the veracity of young, attractive women less emotionally than men'. In conclusion, she gave him a major concession: women with children of school age might seek exemption, she suggested, and a judge could decide that the nature of a case required a single-sex jury to prevent jury-room discussion being inhibited. Playford was persuaded. 'Well, yes', he said, 'I don't see why we shouldn't amend the law'.[29]

It was a victory for women's equality with men, even though Playford did not manage to take it much further. Efforts to legislate foundered over the source of the names of women who could be invited to take part in jury service: the rolls of electors to the Legislative Council, which still had a property franchise, as was the case for men, or the fully democratic rolls of electors to the House of Assembly. Juries Act Amendment bills failed until, under a different government in 1965, the legislation passed, and was as fully democratic as it could be with the exemptions designed to persuade Playford included in it.[30]

A Female Silk at Work

Meanwhile, there were other changes underway in Roma Mitchell's life. Almost as though she were preparing for her new status, on 19 December 1961 she became a member of the exclusive, and expensive, Queen Adelaide Club. The election process required that she be proposed and seconded by women who were already members, and then voted for. The Gooch connection with the OAFs swept her in, though, as political analysts Neal Blewett

Queen Adelaide Club, published with permission of the Adelaide City Council

and Dean Jaensch have noted, by this time the acronym OAFs was something of a misnomer. The Old Adelaide Families had been supplemented by 'a number of families of less antiquarian origin, admitted through wealth and advanced through intermarriage', and though the wealth among the ranks of the South Australian Establishment might have often originated with land, it was increasingly drawn from 'commercial, financial and even industrial ventures'. The female equivalent of the Adelaide Club, the Queen Adelaide Club occupied a graciously furnished building on the corner of Stephens Place and North Terrace in the city. It could function as a refuge for the women who belonged to it, a place away from family responsibilities and burdens. It provided fine meals, too, with wine if you brought it yourself, bottles clinking as you came through the green door, and you could leave your bottle of sherry there for whenever you called in.[31] Handy for a hard-working professional woman, still excluded from so many men-only places for eating and drinking, wanting somewhere to have a quiet coffee and sandwich, or an evening meal, before she went back to her office.

Miss Mitchell's office was changing, too. Her partnership with Joe Nelligan had become impossible. By the early 1960s he was doing almost no work, and bringing in almost no earnings. Miss Mitchell felt close to breakdown under the pressure to keep up the firm's income. Nelligan & Mitchell had two young lawyers serving their articles, David Haese and Doreen Curnow (now Bulbeck). Miss Mitchell wanted to advance their careers. It would help with the income, too, if they made them partners. But Joe Nelligan would not hear of it. Eventually, in the winter of 1962, reluctantly and with immense distress, she terminated their partnership. It must have felt like leaving her father. They had worked together for twenty-seven years. Two years later, Nelligan accepted an appointment to the Adelaide Magistrates' Court. Miss Mitchell did not tell anyone her reasons for separating from him until long after his death.

She set up a new office at 82 Waymouth Street: a tidy and comfortable place, chartreuse carpet covering the floor, a grey blind keeping out the sun, a Utrillo print in one of the few spaces on the walls not covered by books, and an antique mahogany desk, which had belonged to Arthur Blackburn VC, a reminder of her first success in court. At the age of almost fifty – if she had been a man this could have been considered very late for setting up alone, though the war doubtless delayed many men's careers as well – she was the heart of a new firm: Mitchell, Haese & Curnow.[32] This firm was younger, better attuned to the new world in which, in the 1960s, the law was being practised.

For the legal profession in Adelaide was changing as well. Four of the members of the Bench who had been judges during the Stuart case had gone: three retired at the age of seventy, a compulsory requirement for those who had opted into the generously funded state superannuation scheme, and one had died. Only Napier and Sir Herbert Mayo, both in their unsuperannuated eighties, remained from those troubled Stuart-case years. Jim Brazel and Roderic Chamberlain, both elevated to the Bench in 1959, were conservative, as might have been expected of appointments made by Playford's Governments. Playford did not share Napier's Protestant suspicion of Catholics; he had failed to persuade Napier to accept Tacky Hannan's appointment to the Supreme Court, but he succeeded in his second attempt with Brazel. Subsequent judicial elevations included Leo Travers (1962), leader of the criminal Bar, also a Catholic, who had criticised Playford and his Government over the Stuart case; Roma Mitchell's

Charles H. Bright

good friend, another Catholic, David Hogarth (1962); and her friend and contemporary, the urbane and witty – non-Catholic – Charles Bright (1963).[33]

She would entertain them all in her new modern flat at 287 Melbourne Street, a few doors along from her cousins: Merle Jenkins, now on the executive of the NCW, and Beryl Jenkins, nursing still at the Royal Adelaide Hospital. The Gooches came to her parties, too. Charming, people found Ruth, 'attractive, feminine and intelligent', said one; she 'always left me with a feeling of happiness when we met'.[34] Others thought her 'neurotic': 'nutty as a fruitcake';[35] Pamela Villeneuve Smith remembers her frequently complaining of being ill in the middle of a dinner party and leaving early.[36] Ruth's health certainly was unreliable; it had been uncertain for most of her life, a worry to her younger sister. Another friend thought that being 'thin-skinned and sensitive' was an effect of being 'afflicted with the ghastly cross of depression'.[37] Life devoted largely to keeping house for Hugh Gooch, however much love, security and status he offered her – and however much prevailing attitudes pronounced marriage to be the only, unselfish, condition of life for an adult woman – might not have presented as much interest and excitement as the lives of her unmarried cousins, or her sister.

Roma Mitchell remained very close to Ruth and Hugh, writing to them frequently when she travelled to attend international conventions that, now, were for practitioners who were, or were the equivalent of, silks. In 1963, she flew to Athens as a participant in the American Bar Association World Conference on Peace through Law. There were over 100 participants, but the Cold War could still chill, so while some 'Iron Curtain countries' were represented, there were no participants from China, Hungary or Russia. Here, she spent time with Bruce Piggott, a Tasmanian commercial lawyer deeply committed to the ideals with which the

United Nations was founded who would chair the Tasmanian Law Reform Commission in the 1970s and 1980s, and made friends with Paul and Margaret Toose, also Australians – he was a judge of the Supreme Court of New South Wales – with whom she endeavoured to break down the national barriers between delegates by having a party for the Asians. It didn't work. She found some of the delegates 'hard to take' as they were 'very tied to their policies', pronouncing the government line, rather than engaging in independent discussion. Overall, she found the discussions depressing: 'rule of law or no rule of law one becomes a little despairing of world peace', she told Ruth and Hugh.[38]

Even the 'inevitable' cocktail parties – followed by dinners at different expensive restaurants with views of the floodlit Acropolis – wore a bit thin, though she was impressed by a 'Sound and Light' performance at the Acropolis. She enjoyed the sightseeing, however, truanting from the conference to tour the Acropolis with Simon (Sammy) Isaacs, a QC from Sydney.[39]

In the following year, she went to the Tenth Conference of the International Bar Association in Mexico City, and also visited H.N. Sanyal, Solicitor-General of the Congress Party Government in India, in New Delhi; she must have been shocked when she pasted a clipping about his murder in her scrapbook, and wrote beneath it 'Two weeks after I had visited Mr Sanyal at his home'. She went off to Brisbane, too, to escape the Adelaide winter with George and Noni Farwell and Bruce Piggott. George was restless: while she was in Athens she checked the cost of essentials to see if he and Noni would be able to afford to live there, but concluded they would starve.[40]

While travelling was one kind of adventure, her new status and work was another. Roma Mitchell would now wear a silk gown in court. Before her elevation to 'silk', her gown had been made of 'stuff' – fine wool. On ceremonial occasions her uniform was extremely elaborate. It consisted of a coat made of black superfine cloth in the same style as a man's, except that it was not skirted but short, as in a ladies' ordinary suit, reported *New Idea*. With that she wore a plain white blouse with a lace frill and ruffles at the wrist, a plain black skirt also of superfine cloth, black silk stockings, black patent leather ladies' court shoes with cut-steel buckles, a black silk gown, full-bottomed wig and white gloves. Her wig bag was to be made of black silk. The press photographed her in that full-bottomed wig many times, both with her glasses and without, clearly fascinated by the juxtaposition of apparently contradictory images: the harsh horsehair wig with all its associations of the masculine majesty of the law, and Roma Mitchell's incontrovertibly feminine face. Her height made her a commanding figure. Feminine, though, noted *New Idea*, anxious that

Roma Mitchell, published with permission of the *Advertiser*

however exceptional and modern a woman she might be, she would still conform to traditional expectations of womanliness. Outside court, this magazine continued, she displayed a flair for clothes and had most of her outfits specially made.[41]

She was having the time of her life, being a QC. She remained in her firm, Mitchell, Haese & Curnow, expanded to include Ted Mullighan, who had joined them as a junior. Now, her practice was all court work, and she did that only after being briefed by a solicitor. They had to be well prepared, wrote Mullighan,

> and to have thoroughly researched the matter before conferring with her. She gave direction politely and relevantly but, undoubtedly, could become irritated if her directions were not followed.

She had kept many of her clients, including two large trade unions, when she split with Nelligan, and her practice as a silk grew quickly; 'practitioners who had dealt with her over the years had no hesitation in briefing her and she received briefs in a wide variety of jurisdictions'. The Supreme Court's scale of fees specifies higher fees for the work of senior counsel; her clients would be able to recover these, if they succeeded in obtaining an order for costs. She also insisted on compliance with the time limits for proceedings, a requirement necessitating great efficiency among her juniors and solicitors, but one that also served to contain any costs that her clients might incur. On one occasion she appealed on behalf of a plaintiff before Judge Hogarth for leave to deliver interrogatories to the defendant, in order to shorten the conduct of the case and thus reduce expenses. 'Her attitude was that of the true legal professional; the interests of the client came first', observed Mullighan.[42]

Two cases stood out in her memories of this time. One was a source of indignation and distress, even decades later. A small boy with a fractured arm was being treated in a country hospital where his crying was regarded as a nuisance rather than an expression of pain. Eventually, his wound became gangrenous, and his arm had to be amputated. Miss Mitchell acted for the boy, and managed to persuade two doctors to give evidence that the child's treatment had been negligent. But, she lamented, 'in those days it was practically impossible to persuade any member of the medical profession to give evidence concerning alleged negligence on the part of another member of the medical profession'. Ranged against the two who supported her case were about six others who contradicted their evidence. 'I don't think that the people who gave evidence for the defence should have', she said brusquely. 'I don't think they were honest.' The judgment went against her. 'And I've always felt it was a wrong judgment', she said. She took it on appeal, and established that the judge had made an error in one particular crucial fact, but even then, the High Court 'didn't feel that it was sufficient to interfere'. Yes, Dame Roma told her interviewer, 'that's one I feel very strongly about'.[43]

The other case was a triumph that she was still celebrating in the last years of her life. South Australian Clyde Cameron tells the

Clyde Cameron

tale like this. Cameron had begun his working life at the age of fourteen shearing in some of the Kidman sheds. In 1946, when he was only thirty-three, he was elected President of the South Australian Branch of the Australian Workers' Union, which had been for nearly a century the largest, wealthiest and most powerful union in Australia. By the mid-1960s, he was also a Labor Party politician in the Commonwealth Parliament, member of the House of Representatives for Hindmarsh in South Australia, a seat that he held from 1949 until 1980. In 1958, Cameron told the Parliament a long story about the corrupt practices of someone he referred to as 'the unnamed tsar of an unnamed union'. It was not difficult to identify Tom Dougherty, the General Secretary of the Australian Workers' Union. Dougherty sought revenge by trying to expel ten of Cameron's friends in the union. These were Cameron's brother, Donald, Jack Wright, Reg Groth, Jim Dunford, Alan Begg, Mick Young, Claude Brine, Glen Chandler, Reg Wray and Ern Gehan. In 1964, they defeated Dougherty's supporters, led by Eric O'Connor, the Branch Secretary, in a ballot for official positions in the South Australian branch of the union. O'Connor then applied to the Commonwealth Industrial Court, alleging that there had been irregularities in the ballot and asking for an order directing that a fresh one be held. Dougherty subsequently sent a summons to Don Cameron and his nine colleagues requiring them to appear before the union Executive Council to show why they should not be removed from office or expelled from the union for alleged breaches of union rules. Clyde Cameron asked for advice from Don Dunstan, fellow member of the Australian Labor Party, and by this time – 1965 – Attorney-General in the new South Australian Government of Premier Frank Walsh. Dunstan told them to go to Miss Roma Mitchell QC and ask her to advise them, and to represent them in any legal proceedings that might arise. This was asking a lot of men schooled in public interactions that were almost exclusively homo-social, as the story about the 'threepennies' made more than clear. Nevertheless, Miss Mitchell took them on.

She sought and obtained a ruling from the Industrial Court that declared parts of two of the union rules to be invalid. She drafted letters to Dougherty for each of the ten to send him, asking for particulars of the allegations against them that had prompted him to summons them; Dougherty's reply, observed Clyde Cameron, was rambling and merely repeated the original charges. Then, in preparation for their appearance before the Full Bench of the Commonwealth Industrial Court, she helped each of them prepare a statement of defence against those charges in which each presented a detailed narrative of the events in which they had been involved, and instructed them that they must read these statements to the court. Heard one after another, those statements constituted a clear account of the corrupt operating methods of the union officials, Dougherty and his mates. She said that she did not think that they had 'a hope of winning'. But they did. On 29 September 1965, Spicer CJ, Dumphy J and Smithers J ruled with a 2–1 majority against the actions of the AWU Executive Council, revoking all the dismissals and expulsions, vindicating the South Australian Ten, and awarding costs against the Executive Council. Subsequently, Don Cameron was elected to the Commonwealth Parliament, to the Senate; Mick Young was elected to the House of Representatives and became a minister in the Government of R.J. Hawke; Reg Groth, Jim Dunford and Jack Wright were elected to the South Australian Parliament, and Alan Begg was elected Federal President of the Australian Workers' Union.[44] Roma Mitchell and 'her boys' celebrated that victory, calling it 'Smithers Day', with dinner at 'a good restaurant' every year for the next thirty years.

Of course, as always, she ensured that life was not all work. Or not all work around the South Australian courts. In November 1962, she was elected to the Standing Committee of the Senate of the University of Adelaide, a new body required to explain proposed changes to the University's increasingly voluminous and complex rules and regulations to the meetings of the Senate. Fellow lawyers elected were Richard Blackburn and Sam Jacobs. Roma Mitchell received the fourth highest number of votes.[45] The University of Adelaide also invited Miss Mitchell QC to address a commemoration ceremony in April 1965; she took advantage of that platform to lament the 'wastage among women graduates' and argue that the University should provide refresher courses that would ease women's return to their careers after they had spent time out of the workforce having children.[46] She was not arguing for childcare, but she was, now, recognising that women wanted not merely to earn their livelihoods but also to forge careers, as well as to marry and raise children.

Another commitment made in the same year was probably the result of lobbying by the NCW. Roma Mitchell embraced it; it expressed her distinctly un-Irish Anglophilia. For Roma Mitchell was at her most multiple and contradictory when, an Australian, an observing Catholic, and a committedly modern woman, she was also ardently British and traditionalist, fervently loyal to the British Commonwealth of Nations. In this case, her enthusiasm was for the Winston Churchill Memorial Trust to perpetuate and honour the memory of the man who, as prime minister, had presided over the British conduct of World War Two.

Following initiatives in various parts of Britain and the Commonwealth, a committee of influential men organised a massive door knock appeal across Australia to raise funds. It took place on the weekend following Churchill's death in January 1965 and collected more than £2 million. It was 'the largest charitable fund-raising effort ever'. These funds were to provide

> Winston Churchill Memorial Travelling Fellowships which will enable men and women in all parts of the Commonwealth and the United States to further their education in another part of the Commonwealth or United States. The awards, which will be made without regard to race, creed, colour or social background, will not be confined to students or scholars in accredited institutions but will be open equally to those whose business or calling would be increased through personal overseas study and travel.

> Persons chosen for participation in any of these programmes will be selected for qualities of character, intellect and responsible leadership, in addition to their academic qualifications.

The fellowships were to be open to citizens of Australia 'showing promise and ability in their calling and occupation'; they were open, too, to 'persons from Papua/New Guinea and Territories under the control of the Commonwealth of Australia'. There were no fewer than 1200 applications in the first round; forty-nine fellowships were awarded.[47] To make these selections, committees were established in each state and territory, with a national committee in Canberra.

Miss Mitchell was appointed deputy chairman of the South Australian committee, and a member of the Trust's otherwise all-male national committee, appointments that 'delighted leaders of SA women's organisations', reported the *Advertiser*, going on to quote Miss Ruth Gibson, Vice-President of the International Council of Women, also a member of the South Australian committee, and Dr Dorothy Adams, President of the League of Women Voters. Miss Gibson said that the NCW wanted women to be represented on the committee as the fellowships were open to women as well as men. Their reason was an assertion of the need to accept and include gender difference. 'We want to see that the woman's viewpoint is not overlooked,' she said. 'A woman ... has a different approach to the matter.'[48]

Roma Mitchell would not have agreed with them. She never believed, she said towards the end of her life, 'that women have a monopoly of certain qualities and that men have the monopoly of other qualities'. Nevertheless, she 'was quite in favour of some affirmative action',[49] and she ensured that women applying to the Churchill Trust gained more of a hearing than they might well have if she had not been there, and that more women were appointed to the committees. 'She was a forerunner of the women's lib movement', commented Bill Park, one of her colleagues on the Trust's National Committee.

> She never, ever gave up supporting women ... She did it in a way that was quiet, sincere and that did not upset people. In the end she

> succeeded in winning over male chauvinist pigs like me to the side of having women, both in the selection process and in the fellows.[50]

Her responsibilities with the Law Society grew, too. She added a stint on the Complaints Committee to her work with the Etiquette Committee and the Legal Assistance Scheme. In 1963 the members elected her their vice-president, the first woman to hold that position. In it she also acted as the South Australian representative on the Executive Committee of the Law Council of Australia, again being the first woman to appear among those men, a cause of some 'shock, horror' she noted with amusement. They recovered and then made her their vice-president. So it was that when the Third Commonwealth and Empire Law Conference began in all its pomp and majesty in the Sydney Town Hall on 25 August 1965, and more than 100 judges, clad in red, processing through an enormous audience and onto the stage, there were among them two women: Judge Edra Sanders Ferguson of Willowdale, Ontario, and Vice-President of the Law Council of Australia, Miss Roma Mitchell QC of Adelaide. And Miss Mitchell – whose fan club surrounded her – was about to become the first woman to be elected President of the Law Society of South Australia.[51] Indeed, plans were underway for her induction on 27 September of that year. And she had the position of first woman president of the Law Council of Australia firmly in her sights.

But it was not to be. Why ever not? Not because an accident befell her. Or not in the conventional sense. Nothing like that.

Because – out of the blue – came a proposal to make her a judge.

A judge! How did this happen?

Let us tell you a third story.

The Nureyev of Australian Politics

This one begins with Don Dunstan. In 1965 Dunstan was thirty-nine years old, the only member of Cabinet under the age of fifty. He would become premier in 1967, and again in 1970, remaining so until 1979, the most flamboyant political leader in Australia in an era of outstandingly spectacular political personalities. He was 'one of the most charismatic, courageous and progressive Australian politicians of the 20th century', wrote one observer,

'The Nureyev of Australian Politics', said another, 'the sexiest political leader in Australia', wrote a third.[52]

Don Dunstan with his father, Fiji, published with permission of the Flinders University Library

He was born in 1926 in Suva, Fiji, to two South Australians: Ida May Dunstan, born Hill, and Frances Vivian Dunstan MBE, a Branch Manager of a firm of general merchants, Morris Hedstrom Ltd.[53]

At least, that was his story. Since he was to provoke interminable gossip, it's probably not surprising that lunch tables in Adelaide can still hear an alternative account.

This claims that his mother was actually Patricia Hackett, the barrister who opened her own theatre, the Torch, in Gawler Place in the City of Adelaide in the 1930s. She was the daughter of Sir John Winthrop Hackett and Deborah Drake-Brockman. She was born in 1908 and spent her first eight years in Western Australia where her father worked as an editor and a politician. When he died in 1916, he left almost half a million pounds to the University of Western Australia, and endowed a chair of Agriculture; the grateful University would name Winthrop Hall after him in 1932 and daughter Patricia delivered the dedication in Latin. After her father's death, her mother married Frank Beaumont Moulden, Mayor of Adelaide from 1919 to 1921, so the young Hacketts moved to Adelaide where their mother held court at 'Lordello House' in Brougham Place, North Adelaide (later St Anne's College). Patricia Hackett began studying Law at Adelaide University but was dismissed for sitting her sister's Latin exam for her. She subsequently took her Bar exam in London, was admitted as a barrister in 1930, then returned to Adelaide where she set up a legal practice and went on to acquire a quite wonderful reputation as an eccentric actor, theatre director, playwright, entrepreneur and poet.

As a young lawyer in 1952, Don Dunstan accepted her invitation to share her chambers in the city and remained with her for some years, also appearing in a number of the performances in her theatres. By the time she died in 1963, Pat Hackett was famous for many things. She had flung an inkwell at the parliamentary roundsman from the Advertiser *for criticising her performance in a 1934 theatre production. She had taken a 100-year lease on the Island of M'bangai in the Solomon Islands, and visited from time to time, until the advent of the Second World War. She had extracted a public apology from Max Harris for a rude review of her performance in another play, this time in 1944. She had established a household on Hackney Road, Hackney – directly across the road from Botanic Park – with her partner, Mildred Mocatta, a medical practitioner twenty-five years older than she was, someone she had known since she was a child. There, she brought up her sister's three children, and in its basement she established a salon theatre and produced a number of plays. She and Dr Mocatta acquired a superlative art collection. Pat Hackett also became famous for her addiction to heroin, doubtless a consequence of her crippling arthritis.*

She had conceived Don Dunstan – the lunch-table story relates – during a stormily passionate night in Fiji, described in some of her poems published as These Little Things *(1938), and subsequently arranged for him to be adopted by the family that he claimed as his own. The date of his birth means that this conception would have had to have taken place when she was only eighteen, and the location transfers her Pacific enthusiasms from the Solomons to Fiji.*

Dunstan knew that people speculated about his origins.

> *The first of many rumours promulgated assiduously by the Adelaide Establishment in an attempt to discredit me personally was that I was not Australian at all, that having been born in Fiji, I was really 'a Melanesian orphan half-caste bastard' who had been brought up and educated by an unnamed elderly philanthropist, and had grown to bite the hand that fed me, a traitor to my adopted class.*[54]

He dismissed the stories.

An uncle, Sir Jonathon Cain, had been Lord Mayor of Adelaide, and two aunts lived at Murray Bridge, so the first schools he attended were Murray Bridge Infant and Primary Schools, before he went back to Fiji and his parents and attended Suva Boys' Grammar. His parents sent him back to Adelaide to finish his schooling at Saints. There in 1943 he matriculated among the top thirty in the state, gained accolades in the school magazine for his performance in the school's production of John Drinkwater's play, *Abraham Lincoln*, and as a member, he said, of 'an informal group organised by the Simpson family', handed out how-to-vote cards for leading conservative Archie Grenfell Price.[55]

He arrived at Adelaide University to take courses in Arts and Law. Dunstan's politics were, as his support for Grenfell Price would suggest, initially deeply conservative. He founded a journal of his own, called *Grist*, in which he attacked the surrealist modernism of the Angry Penguins, and when he was articled, it was to arch conservative Sir Collier Cudmore, leader of the Liberal-Country League in the Legislative Council from 1944 until 1959.[56] But, as with so many students, his political views fluctuated wildly. He also joined the student branch of the Communist Party, though he remained for only three meetings. He began to settle down when he read H.V. Evatt's biography of the silver-tongued socialist, William Arthur Holman, Premier of New South Wales from 1913 until 1920, 'a study of political idealism and an analysis of the forces and struggles of social change'. This book influenced him very considerably. 'By the time he left university he regarded himself as a Fabian and social reformer "in the Chartist tradition that I feel was then still strong in SA".'[57]

He was admitted to the Bar in Adelaide in 1948, but then rushed back to Fiji to be with his father: his mother had just died of cancer after an illness lasting two years, and his father was alone and grieving. He set up practice in Suva. 'It was good fun', he wrote in his autobiography, *Felicia*: 'My practice was lively, fascinating, and gave me satisfaction – providing intellectual stimulation, a sense of contest, and at times giving service.' In 1949 he married Gretel Ellis, daughter of Robert and Marcelle Elsasser, refugees from Germany who had changed their name when they arrived in Australia ten years earlier, and they had the first of their three children, a daughter, Bronwen. But he decided that he wanted to be more useful than he was being in Fiji, so he and his wife came back to Adelaide, arriving at the beginning of 1951. He knew how staid and quiet was the society to which he was returning: one of his aunts, he recalled, had told him that he must not roller skate on the streets on a Sunday, and she was not even religious.[58]

Don Dunstan then established himself in Norwood. His great-grandmother had lived there, his grandmother lived close by, his father had played in the local cricket team, Gretel Dunstan had lived there, too, and her parents still did, so the family had strong connections with this district.[59] Moreover, it had been a swinging seat for the South Australian House of Assembly, changing from the Labor Party to the Liberal-Country League quite regularly, and Dunstan had determined to go into politics. He had to overcome prejudice against his slight build ('Till I was thirty-five I weighed 9½ stone', he related); his educated, slightly plummy, accent; and the power in Norwood – with its population of Irish Catholics and pre-Second World War Italians among the retired soldiers from the First World War, the old-age pensioners, and the blue collar workers – of the Industrial Groups.

In the eastern states, principally in Victoria, Industrial Groups were formed in trade unions during the 1940s and 1950s by the highly secret and secretive Catholic Social Studies Movement, established in 1942 by Archbishop Daniel Mannix of Melbourne and administered by B.A. (Bob) Santamaria. Industrial Groups were a central element in the Movement's efforts to combat Communism, also a force in some unions. The struggle between Catholic and Communist factions of the Australian Labor Party would split the Labor Party in 1955, leading to the formation of the right-wing Democratic Labor Party. South Australia also saw Industrial Groups set up in unions during the 1940s, but in South Australia, the person who took on the chairmanship of the ALP committee overseeing the Groups was the erstwhile shearer, Clyde Cameron, who was also president of the South Australian branch of the Labor Party. Cameron, brought up Presbyterian and influenced by his Quaker mother, was suspicious of organised religion. His politics made him even less sympathetic to the Groups, for, while he was not a Communist, he certainly was strongly committed to the socialist objective of the ALP. He worded the Groups' charter carefully so that it committed them less to fighting Communism within the trade unions than to teaching workers about the socialist plank on the ALP's platform. This meant that Industrial Groups gained little power in South Australian unions, except for two that had only tenuous connections with the ALP. When Cameron led an attack on the Groupers in 1951, accusing them of engaging in anti-Labor activities, their charter was withdrawn. Cameron, and Catholic Archbishop Matthew Beovich of Adelaide who refused to support any party about to break away from the ALP, ensured that South Australian Industrial Groups were not going to figure in the Split in the ALP, four years later.[60] They may have been a nuisance to Don Dunstan, but they were not about to give him serious trouble.

Dunstan was also involved in Labor's campaign against the efforts of the national Menzies Government to dissolve the Communist Party of Australia, contributing to the reputation that he said he had acquired among Adelaide's conservative legal establishment as not merely red but 'bright bloody vermillion'. In 1953 he was elected to the House of Assembly, a seat that he would hold for the next twenty-six years.

Twelve years later, in 1965, as Attorney-General, Dunstan could begin to fulfil a number of the goals that he aspired to. One was to bring about change in the criminal justice system. He had spoken fiercely in Parliament against both the police and the Government during the Stuart trial and its aftermath; had protested about police 'moving on' innocent citizens having conversation in the street, including, on one occasion, Olympic swimming champion Dawn Fraser; and had introduced into Parliament a bill abolishing capital punishment, though without any success.[61] He would begin with the Bench.

First he consulted the Chief Justice, Sir Mellis Napier, about the retirement of Sir Herbert Mayo, next in seniority to Napier himself. Both were eighty-three, and the Law Society had told Dunstan that Mayo was showing signs of his age in court. Napier agreed to speak to his brother, reported Dunstan.

> But then added, 'Of course he may say – "well it's all very well to say I'm too old and should not continue – but what about you." I regarded him steadily and said, 'Well sir, of course he may. I will have to leave you to answer that.'[62]

Mayo did retire, passing on his ceremonial robes to the new judge, Roma Mitchell; she responded by hoping that his mantle would descend on her in more ways than one.[63] But Napier hung on for another two years, meeting with the Attorney-General on occasion, perhaps even teasing him.

> 'You know Don,' he said to me at one interview, 'I'm, I'm very worried about my judges.' (He spoke in what the profession called 'the baritone whisper', and at times with a stammer which was not an impediment but a mannerism). 'In some forty-odd years on the bench I have never been in the – the minority in the Full Court. But lately – well you saw this last case. I wrote – wrote to Lord Reed about it (an English law lord and fellow octogenarian) and he quite – quite agreed with me. Of course some may say – well, well, it's you who are out of touch but ...' Pregnant silence from the Attorney-General.[64]

Once the Government discovered Napier believed he couldn't afford to retire, they arranged a pension for him. Then it was merely a matter of time.

In the meantime, the Supreme Court's workload was so heavy that the Government had resolved to increase its number of judges from six to seven. With Mayo's retirement, that meant that there were two places to fill. One went to George Walters, who had been Roma Mitchell's colleague briefly in the 1940s, and had since been a magistrate and then Master of the Supreme Court. Then Attorney-General Dunstan made a move that also expressed his commitment to widening opportunities for women. 'I had the Government nominate Roma Mitchell QC', he wrote. She was 'a first-rate lawyer', and had been 'outstanding at the bar'.[65]

There had been lots of speculation about who the new seventh judge would be, Dame Roma would recall.

> Always was in the profession. And it didn't occur to me it was at all likely, at all possible that I would be invited because oh, no woman had ever been on the bench and ... Don Dunstan ... asked me to have lunch with him in Parliament House. And I did. And much to my surprise he asked me if I'd accept an appointment.

'Yes', she repeated, she had been 'absolutely surprised'. And more than a little dismayed.

> I really didn't want it at that stage. I was enjoying life as a Queen's Counsel and I really didn't want to go onto the bench. And I was very

> unhappy for the six weeks preceding my going on the bench ... And I thought I wouldn't enjoy it. And I knew I did enjoy my life as it was ... There's no excitement in connection with a judge's life.

Nevertheless, she said yes, immediately. 'I thought I should accept the appointment. I thought I owed it to women.' She also knew that there was a tradition in the legal profession that 'if a barrister was offered such an appointment, he had a moral obligation to accept'.[66]

Would this have happened without Don Dunstan? Probably not. Roma Mitchell would certainly not have sought it. She was achieving exceptional distinction through positions on the state and national councils of the law societies, and that was where she was directing her ambitions. Her new appointment made those positions impossible, now. Besides, as she said herself, she was enjoying herself as a QC. She thought that being a judge would lift her out of the gossip network, and, she told an interviewer, it would impose great constraints on her social life.

> *I remember one friend of mine who was and still is a bachelor who, when he heard the news said, 'oh, this'll be dreadful. There'll be so many things you won't be able to do', and I said, 'oh I don't know. I've only thought of one. I don't think I'll be able to go to', and I named a restaurant, I can't even think of its name, perhaps just as well, and that's why I made you take me there last week. Because it was in the Hindley Street area and it, although they had good food, it was frequented by some of the lower life in Adelaide, not that there's a great deal of lower life in Adelaide. And I didn't go back there.*

It is unlikely that anyone else in the governments of Frank Walsh, or Dunstan himself, once he had become Premier in 1967, would have thought of such a move, even those who were to support the Dunstan Governments' measures to increase rights for women. For this was a move that was characteristic of Dunstan's unique flair for the dramatic, the unexpected, the charismatic, the qualities that made him so attractive to the new visual medium of television. It might also have given this clever young man something of an alibi for a still more dramatic and unexpected legal appointment that he was to make two years later.

It was Sir Mellis Napier who administered the oath of office to Miss Roma Flinders Mitchell QC at a meeting of the Executive Council on 23 September 1965. He was Lieutenant Governor; the Governor was away on the west coast of the state, so he was deputising. He had not known ahead of time who he was to swear in, and he was stunned. Journalists from press, radio and television were waiting outside the meeting. How was she to be addressed, they asked. Will you be called 'Mr Justice' like other judges. 'I hope not', shot back Miss Mitchell, quick as a flash, 'it would interfere with my social life'. Also, she noted, '"Miss Justice" sounds like an invitation to appeal'. But joking with the media was probably not a good idea for a judge: she asked them not to report what she had said, and, unlike journalists later in the century, they didn't.[67]

Miss Mitchell congratulated on her appointment. From left: Works Minister Mr Hutchens, Premier Mr Walsh, Miss Mitchell, Chief Justice Sir Mellis Napier, Chief Secretary Mr Shard, Attorney-General Mr Dunstan, 23 September 1965, published with permission of the *Advertiser*

The question of how she would be addressed caused a great deal of silliness. British precedent led the way. The British had appointed a woman to the bench just weeks before, and had determined that she was to be addressed as Her Lordship Mr Justice Elizabeth Lane. Following suit, Napier decreed that Roma Mitchell be addressed as Mr Justice Mitchell, though he could not decide whether she could be called His Honour or Her Honour. Many of her legal friends thought this ridiculous. Howard Zelling

> could not disagree more with the Chief's pronouncement. That anything as delightfully feminine as yourself should be called *Mr* Justice is fit only for Mr Bumble's famous saying that the law is an ass. It is like saying that Elizabeth II should be called His Majesty the King. I hope you will judicially overrule this in due course!!

The press interstate chimed in. 'Why must this legal lady be called Mr?' asked Martin Collins in the *Australian*. 'To do Miss Mitchell justice, justice has to be done.' The *Canberra Times* editorialised: 'It was sensible of [South Australians] to choose a woman, but it would hardly be wise for them to pretend now by their mode of address that their new judge is not really a woman at all.'[68]

Her Honour Justice Mitchell presented her commission and took her seat on the Bench of the Full Court in Court Room No. 1 on 27 September 1965. Addressing her, Attorney-General Dunstan observed that

> The idea that positions in our society, and in public life, should be exclusively, or predominantly, the province of males is an absurd one, but because it dies hard your assumption of the high office of Supreme Court Judge is significant indeed, not only in this state, but in the whole Commonwealth.

Her Honour saw her elevation in a similar light: it was a breakthrough for women in their long battle for equality. But she held firmly that such an appointment must be made because the individual was good at her work, not because she was female, and hoped to live long enough to see a similar appointment arousing little interest, at least on the basis of the sex of the person appointed. She concluded by referring to President John F. Kennedy's inaugural address, echoing him in asking for God's blessing and His help, 'but knowing that here on earth God's work must truly be our own'.[69] Several of the Sisters of Mercy were there, including three of her teachers from St Aloysius.

Her most noteworthy accolade came from Justice Herbert Mayo at the special sitting of the Full Court to mark his retirement just three months after she had joined the Bench. He held that 'the most impressive event that has happened during my association with the law, judicious and judicial, is the appointment of Roma Mitchell. That appointment has been approved by all.'[70] Indeed it had: letters and telegrams applauding her new position came flooding in, all 482 of them, she counted (and she would have replied to each one). Gough Whitlam, then deputy leader of the Australian Labor Party, telegraphed: 'Proud of Portia's Promotion'. Tom Kellock reaffirmed his participation in her fan club. John Stack of the Victorian Supreme Court joined that club. The future Chief Justice Len King felt 'a special personal pleasure in the elevation of my former principal'. Another, her old friend John Bray, predicted: 'You are clearly destined to historic fame'.[71] As he was.

For two years later, when Napier finally gave in and retired, the Walsh Government made an even more controversial appointment to the Bench of the Supreme Court. Against all expectations that Napier's successor as Chief Justice would be Roderic Chamberlain, the Walsh Government appointed Dr John Bray, erudite, cultured, bohemian, a poet. There was more controversy than most people knew over this appointment, controversy that was not to surface until a decade later, in a context saturated with anxieties over sexual politics. For the moment, though, there was great delight among Bray's friends, many of whom were authors, actors and artists, and many of the younger members of the legal profession. He marked the change that he would bring to the Court immediately, telling his Bench at their first meeting:

His Honour Chief Justice John Bray with Premier Don Dunstan, published with permission of the Flinders University Library

> I think that judges of this court have for too long subjected themselves to far too many self-denying ordinances. So I shall tell you what I shall do. I am dyslectic, do not drive a car and when I choose, from time to time, will go by public transport ... And when I wish, during lawful

> trading hours, to meet my friends in a licensed public house, I shall do so. In fact (looking at his watch) I'm going there now.[72]

Accordingly, for the next eleven years, much of her time on the Bench, Justice Mitchell was a member of what became known as the 'Bray Court', a time considered a golden period for justice in South Australia, indeed in Australia.

Roma Mitchell was now literally Roma the First. Her friend, Peter Kelly, sent her a clipping from *La Fiamma* for 28 September 1965. 'Viva Roma' it read:

> Adelaide – regno di linarello: una donna e stata nominata giudice dell Corte Suprema.
>
> La signorina Roma Mitchell – cosi si chiama il gentile magistrato – e la prima donna in Australia chiamata a ricoprire una carica cosi importante.
>
> Ancora una volta, Roma e la prima.[73]

Chapter Six
The Golden Years

A Woman on the Bench

The Honourable Justice Mitchell left Waymouth Street and moved into chambers in the Supreme Court. It was a stately building with an imposing Palladian façade on the corner of King William and Gouger streets in the south-west corner of Victoria Square, but by now it had an ugly new cream brick extension and that was where Justice Mitchell established herself. 'I chose chambers that

Supreme Court, published with permission of the Adelaide City Council

had a loo, a dressing room and an air conditioner', she remarked. 'I had to have a separate lavatory from the male judges.'[1] Here she got down to work. Working conditions were relatively primitive. There were only two secretaries to do any typing needed by seven judges, including their judgments, so it was difficult for any judge to have a letter typed, and junior judges went to the bottom of the queue. Neither of the secretaries took shorthand, so senior judges – who, of course, could not type – wrote their drafts by hand. The more junior judges had acquired at least a modicum of technological experience: they demanded tape recorders so that they could dictate their work. At last this was all deemed impossibly slow. By 1970, the judges were allocated a secretary each. Peggy Harvey, appointed to Justice Mitchell's staff, remained with her until she retired. Judges had other kinds of help, too: Tipstaves and Associates. Tipstaves were general assistants; Associates had a legal education and were to spend a term, like an apprenticeship, assisting in legal and court matters and anything else that might crop up. Justice Mitchell's first Tipstaff, Harry Palmer, was about to retire. Her second, Reg Soan, remained with her for the next seventeen years, his duties varying wildly, on occasion including shopping for her groceries, paying her bills and driving her to

Front row: Tipstaff Reg Soane, Associate Piers Plumridge, Dame Roma Mitchell, Secretary Peggy Harvey; standing from left: John O'Grady, Vivian Cocks, Elizabeth Wilkins, Simon Stretton, Lindy Powell QC, Helena Jasinski, Mary England, David White, Margaret Ross, from the Law Society of South Australia Bulletin, June 1996, p. 12, published with permission of the Law Society of South Australia.

meetings.[2] She had a total of thirteen Associates over the ensuing eighteen years, all from Adelaide University's Law School.

Judges usually choose their Associates according to some principle involving merit. No doubt Justice Mitchell did too. One who was to do especially well was Lindy Powell. She joined Roma Mitchell in January 1974. Twenty years later she herself took silk, and in 1998 became President of the Law Society of South Australia, the first woman to achieve that office, for although Miss Mitchell had been in line for it in 1965, she had to relinquish the prospect once she was a judge.[3] Often, too, Justice Mitchell seems to have chosen her Associates partly because she had some connection with their families. Michael Smith, who joined her in May 1972, was a son of Mervyn and Fairlie Smith, an Adelaide University association, for Mervyn, a surgeon, was to serve on the University of Adelaide Council for almost thirty years, his last three (1994–1996) as Deputy Chancellor. Mary Walters, later Mary England, joined her in 1975. She was the daughter of Roma Mitchell's fellow judge and old colleague, George Walters. David White became her Associate in 1976; he was the son of another fellow judge, Michael White. Margaret Ross, granddaughter of retired Justice Sir Bruce Ross, was her Associate in 1981, and John O'Grady, her godson and son of her former legal partner, in 1982. Sometimes, as well, Roma Mitchell seems to have chosen her Associates because having them attached to her staff might be able to assist them in making their way in the law, and the world.

Jillian O'Dea, the Associate who joined her only two weeks after she began work on the Bench, was a Catholic, and as Roma Mitchell knew from her own experience, being both Catholic and female were not the greatest advantages with which to begin a career in the law in Adelaide. Helena Jasinski, too, was a Catholic; she joined Roma Mitchell as her Associate in 1977 at a time when she was going out with Mike Rann, a politically gifted member of Don Dunstan's staff. They were both to move on: in the early 1980s Helena Jasinski took on the unsuccessful defence of Bevan Spencer von Einem in a case of horrific serial murders,[4] and at the beginning of the twenty-first century Mike Rann is himself Premier of South Australia. Simon Stretton suffered no disadvantage from his sex or his religion (or lack of it), but he was having difficulty finding work after he had been admitted to the Bar. His father, Hugh Stretton, had been a client of Miss Mitchell's when he sought to divorce his first wife and gain custody of his two sons. His connection to her continued through the University of Adelaide where he taught, and through the Winston Churchill Memorial Trust Fellowship Committee of which they were both members. He asked Justice Mitchell to help Simon to find an associateship. Simon had resolved to go into the law to help prevent the anguish that he saw his mother suffering when she and his father parted so acrimoniously, motivation that would have been close to Roma Mitchell's heart. He joined her in 1980. He was to do especially well. In June 2005, he was appointed Crown Solicitor of South Australia.[5]

Justice Mitchell had no Associate at all following Jill O'Dea until she took on young Piers Plumridge in February 1969. He was the elder of two sons of Harry Plumridge, an urbane and charming journalist, a friend. Harry and his second wife Bonnie were worried about curly headed, deep-voiced, amusing and engagingly courteous Piers. He had finished his schooling and enrolled in law, but was not pursuing his studies with particular application. He began working as Roma Mitchell's Associate in March 1969. No doubt that helped him concentrate, and, initially, on a more readily achievable goal: he gained his Final Certificate in Law seven months later. He was admitted as a practitioner of the South Australian Supreme Court in June 1970. He remained Justice Mitchell's Associate for a year or so until he took off for Europe. He returned to her, too, in 1972. He became a close friend. Later, he joined Margaret Nyland's firm; she was, herself, on her way to the Supreme Court Bench. Piers and Margaret married. They were at Roma Mitchell's for dinner quite often, and they both travelled with her as well. Later, after he and Margaret Nyland had parted company, Roma Mitchell took Piers with her to lunch at Pam Cleland's from time to time. Roma was 'particularly fond' of

Dame Roma with Piers Plumridge, copied from Dame Roma Mitchell's Scrapbooks in Master Peter Norman's chambers 2001

him, said Pam Cleland. 'I remember her saying to me, "He is very good value".' 'They got a lot from each other', said Sir Walter Crocker. She could mother him; he could be a son to her. She would appoint Piers Plumridge one of the two executors of her will, and she would leave him her books and furniture.[6]

The great gong still echoed – a habit of the heart, far more than any effort of will. She took care of her cousins as well as Ruth and Hugh. She took care of various friends and colleagues. Now she would take care of her Associates. She would teach them: as one explained, she 'was the sort of person who allowed you to participate. She would allow you to understand how her thought processes were working, which is a wonderful insight for a young practitioner wet behind the ears.' Another held that what he had learned from her was the importance of compassion and clarity in court. She quoted to him Howard Zelling saying that 'the most important aspect of the Court's work "was that the person who lost felt that they had been treated fairly"'. 'She could be very bossy' in the process of taking care of them. Some thought that she expected too much of them; more than one succumbed to tears; at least one told herself that she would resign. 'She was very sharp with a couple of her Associates', observed Pam Cleland. 'She wouldn't suffer fools gladly.' Yet, they said, 'it was always loving bossiness. Having Dame Roma's confidence and support in one's "chosen" career path was a great source of comfort and inspiration.' They stuck with her, too, joining together to celebrate her birthday for decades after their terms with her were over.

Miss Mitchell's Associates tell two stories about her. Both have become legend. Here is the first. Roma Mitchell always went out for lunch on Thursdays, a legacy from the Thursday Girls' meetings perhaps. But one Thursday she came back to her chambers unexpectedly early to find her Associate and a companion locked together in a tangle of half-discarded clothes on the table. 'Oh really!' she expostulated. 'That's where I eat my lunch!'[7]

And here is the second, a story that Lindy Powell tells.

> When we were in Sydney, we were going out, and while Dame Roma changed, she asked me if I would pop into the laundry and pick up her washing that she'd ... stuck in the dryer. When I picked it up,

> I discovered it was leopard-print underwear. So I dashed back to the room. 'Roma, you're wearing leopard-print underwear!' She said, 'Yes, I know. Isn't it gorgeous?'[8]

Being a judge meant preserving a distance from other people and their concerns in case it might be necessary to sit in judgment on them at some time. Roma Mitchell gave up horse riding with her old school friend, Lorna Williams, when she visited the Williamses in Melbourne; if she were to hurt herself it would interrupt any legal procedures that she was involved in. And her status got badly in their way when she and Lorna were driving between Melbourne and Newcastle to visit Lorna's daughter, Adrienne McMahon, Roma's goddaughter. Harold Williams' sister died suddenly, so they had to turn back. That left them needing to find somewhere to spend the night in New South Wales on an Australia Day weekend. It took them well out of their way. Roma vetoed Lorna's suggestion that they park in the main street of Goulburn and sleep in the car because she feared that they would be arrested for loitering. She also refused to stay in the only hotel with a vacancy because she thought that criminals stayed there. They did try to sleep in the car in a rest stop a few miles from the town, but were driven away by mosquitoes. Not until they had travelled on as far as Liverpool could they find somewhere that Her Honour considered satisfactory.

Roma Mitchell on horseback, note above 'Quelle derriere', copied from Dame Roma Mitchell's Scrapbooks in Master Peter Norman's chambers, 2001

Yet, for all this, she did not, after all, find life on the Bench as different as she had feared. You 'didn't hear the gossip so quickly' she noted. A Melbourne judge had written congratulating her on her appointment but cautioning, 'You'll find it a lonely life'. 'I thought lonely!' exclaimed Justice Mitchell. 'My chambers were like a railway station with the number of people shunting in and out.'[9]

One change made a big difference. She was on a salary – £6000 a year[10] – instead of having to earn her living from fees. By 1969 she decided to buy somewhere to live. She had always rented until now. She may have considered buying before this, but she knew that 'women seeking to obtain a mortgage from a bank or building society … need[ed] a male guarantor, irrespective of the fact that the woman's employment may provide a higher income and that she may have higher employment prospects'. This was absurd, a good reason for 'legislation to prohibit such practices'.[11] She was not going to allow the banks to patronise her with such a requirement. Indeed, she was going to astonish them: she paid for her new home in cash. It was a unit, number two, in a cream brick block of units at 256 East Terrace, the well-to-do side of the city of Adelaide, looking east across the road to the gum trees and olive groves around Victoria Park Racecourse, almost next door to St Corantyn, a large and stately dwelling that had once belonged to Sir John Lavington Bonython, though by this time it was a Mental Health Services Day Hospital.[12] From there she could walk to St Francis Xavier's Cathedral on Sundays, and closer to home, she could easily attend daily Mass at the Daughters of Charity's chapel on Hutt Street.

She would live in this unit for most of the rest of her life. The front room had an antique mahogany desk, carver chair, half a dozen other chairs, some covered in red linen and some in green, and a book case also in mahogany that she filled with precious ornaments. The sitting room held a Victorian *chaise longue* covered in linen tapestry, some small tables, a Georgian rosewood clock, a mirror over the mantelpiece, several oil paintings and a collection of books. The dining room was, of course, fitted out for dinner parties – she was able to seat at least ten – with various silver jugs, a crystal decanter, a pair of sterling silver Georgian berry spoons and in a cabinet between the dining room and the kitchen no fewer than sixty crystal glasses. The sterling silver cutlery was kept in the kitchen. Upstairs were two bedrooms – one containing a pair of single beds – and a bathroom.[13] Here, she was scarcely half an hour, by foot, away from Victoria Square and the courts.

Supreme Court judges in South Australia rotated through the different jurisdictions. One month, for example, Justice Mitchell would sit in the Criminal Court. The next, she would do civil work: damages claims, for instance, and claims for breach of contract, and the like. Another month she would sit as the single judge hearing appeals, chiefly from the Magistrate's Court, and spend time in her own chambers preparing for cases due to be heard, and doing Motions and Petitions, which were mainly processes of winding up companies. She would spend yet another month sitting on the three-member Full Court. And, for now anyway, she would also spend a month in the Matrimonial Causes jurisdiction, though that would disappear altogether with the passage of the Australian Family Law legislation, creating a whole new jurisdiction in the Federal court system. So there was variety as well as intellectual challenge even if she had lost the excitement of winning or losing that went with life at the Bar. Life on the Bench was 'nothing like the Bar', she noted, it 'is not exciting'. But it had its compensations, 'and I was never bored with it'.[14]

Criminal trials were a relatively new experience, and she wondered how her colleagues regarded her performance. The Crown Prosecutor E.B. (Eb) Scarfe QC was famous for his caustic comments on newcomers on the Bench. She caught Kevin Duggan, a prosecutor for the Crown, completely off balance when she called him aside and said, 'I suppose Eb has been saying frightful things about me.' Without thinking, Duggan replied: 'On the contrary, he thinks you have taken to the criminal court like a duck to water.' After a dreadful silence, Justice Mitchell 'threw her head back with that trademark chortle, "So that's how the Crown thinks of me".'[15]

She looked fierce enough, facing the court in her long black robe and horsehair wig with fashionably heavy black-rimmed glasses. But her fierceness was most often reserved for counsel not doing their job properly. A barrister returning ten minutes late after an adjournment met a stinging rebuke, though on another occasion when Associate Piers Plumridge, realising that he would be late, sent her a frantic message – he was stuck in a lift – she did just smile. She was impatient with counsel who had not prepared adequately; 'poor counsel', she commented, meant that 'you've got to do more of the work for yourself of making sure that the legal angle is right'. Anyone wasting her time would elicit an impatient drumming of fingers on the bench. The *National Times* was to report:

> Some years ago, an inexperienced young private investigator appeared in court in a divorce case before Justice Roma Flinders Mitchell. He told her that he'd hung about outside a bedroom, and had heard the unmistakable sounds of sexual intercourse.
>
> 'And what,' asked Justice Mitchell, 'are the unmistakable sounds of sexual intercourse?'
>
> She can be a bit testy in court.[16]

If the investigator's testimony was meant to embarrass the lady on the Bench, it didn't work.

She could be impatient with the whole system, especially when delays made the process more expensive for the clients involved. In April 1975 she took the unprecedented step of calling over the entire civil list of 459 actions waiting to be heard in the Supreme Court to determine which of them could be removed to the Local Court and heard more promptly. She was annoyed at the waste of time, and the unnecessary expense, when petitioners or their counsel failed to turn up; she was particularly concerned, she told a court room packed with more than fifty lawyers, about delays in cases awarding damages for personal injuries.[17] She also wrote her judgments as soon as possible after each case concluded. She believed that she owed a prompt decision to those who appeared before her. She considered that leaving too long an interval meant that 'you lose impressions'. When she sat on the Court of Appeal she saw, she said, 'judges who've clearly lost touch with the case when they've gone to write their judgment'. She was not troubled by the possibility of an appeal against her decision; she considered that judges who seemed to look over their shoulders to the Appeal Court showed a 'complete lack of courage, a lack of self-confidence'. One colleague was to say that he thought that she did not allow enough time for reflection. Dame Roma said, simply, 'I am punctual, I don't like putting things off.' Accordingly, 'I didn't amass large numbers of reserved judgments for myself.'[18]

Towards the offenders before her, though, she was not impatient: she was determinedly open-minded. She conceded that she might be prejudiced against some crimes. 'I can only remember having one case of blackmail but I think ... it's a horrible crime because ... it really has only, gain is its only motive.' She was certainly conscious of 'the terrible effect upon the victims and the friends and relatives' in criminal cases, but she still generally held that serious criminals were not 'monsters': 'when you see them, sometimes they're just pathetic'. Despite the strength of her opposition to capital punishment, the law compelled her, on occasion, to pronounce the death penalty for a murder conviction. But she was able, also, to tell the condemned man that it was the policy of the government not to carry out such penalties.[19] The times had changed since the horrors of the Stuart case.

The Age of Aquarius

For now came 'the dawning of the age of Aquarius', the cultural revolution of advanced industrial capitalism, an explosion of cultural and political protest against everything that smacked of established authority, restrictions on ideas and sexual repression. 'I got Life!' they sang. 'Let the sunshine in'.

These were titles of songs in a musical called *Hair*, first staged in April 1968 in New York City. It broke a host of taboos, men appearing with wild long hair, men and women naked, singing about hashish, about racial politics, and about gay sex – 'Sodomy' they crooned – songs recorded and sold across the world. Jim Sharman produced *Hair* in Adelaide only two years later; always supporting the leading edge of modern culture, Roma Mitchell took four friends with her to see it. Men had already begun to wear their hair longer than the military-looking short-back-and-sides of the 1950s, especially after the Beatles visited Australia in 1964, and the hem lines of women's skirts had risen so close to their panty lines that receptionists' desks had to have modesty panels installed. 'It seems', wrote Australian poet, Judith Wright,

> as though the whole of 'Western' society is in a ferment of change and challenge to accepted moral attitudes, religious and legal institutions, time-hallowed views of war and sex. Every taboo is being questioned, dragged to the dock and put through a process of naked examination and self-justification. Most of them look old and flabby, and to the young examiners they look pretty ugly up there in the light ... no use trying to scuttle off and put your clothes on again; they know what you

look like under them now, those judicial wigs; those corsets and business suits and military uniforms.[20]

There were other changes as well. During the same year, 1968, sixty young women took buses across the United States to Atlantic City to protest against the Miss World Pageant being staged there. People in Australia knew about this because many of them – a vast majority of those aged between ten and seventeen – watched television. And those young television watchers saw other images, too, during that year: images of the students taking over the streets of Paris in protest against both the stultifying conditions and nature of their education; of the assassination of black leader, Martin Luther King, in the racial conflicts of the United States; and of Russian tanks rolling into Prague to re-establish Stalinist control over the liberalising politics of Alexander Dubček's new regime in Czechoslovakia; and then, in 1969, of the moratorium marches against the United States' war in Vietnam, and Australia's participation in it. In March 1970 about fifty young women calling themselves members of Women's Liberation echoed the Atlantic City protest by picketing the 'Miss Fresher' contest held as part of the Orientation Week celebrations at Adelaide University.

It was the birth of the counter culture. It would develop into the new social movements – activist collectivities demanding rights and recognitions for particular identities: youth, women, blacks, gays and lesbians, and around particular political issues: the green and peace movements protesting the degradation of the environment, the proliferation of war, the expansion of nuclear weaponry.[21] The movements were energetic and irreverent, determined to unveil the hidden, to read the forbidden, to speak the unspoken – most urgently against war, against censorship, against racial and gender injustice, and in favour of unfettered sex. They were determined, too, to live – to enact – the social, political and intellectual changes that they sought. They brought radical change to Australian society for the rest of the twentieth century. In South Australia they were important forces in both the Dunstan Decade and the Bray Court.

The Dunstan Decade effectively began in 1965 with the election of the ALP Government of Frank Walsh, for Walsh was 'a Neanderthal figure in the television age' while Dunstan – especially after he began weight training at the American Health Studios and accepted advice about his previously neat 1950s haircut – was distinctly glamorous ('a pocket-size Adonis'), and excelled as a television performer. He became the symbol of the Government and of the ALP, projecting a 'progressive, professional and middle-class image', pioneering a major change in style for the traditionally horny-handed, blue-collar ALP, a change that would be adopted by other ALP leaders: Gough Whitlam in Federal politics and Neville Wran in New South Wales. Indeed, this style appeared among the South Australian conservatives as well, after Playford stepped down as leader of the LCL in 1966, to be replaced by the handsome and youthful Steele Hall.

Street procession led by Gough Whitlam, Don Dunstan and Bob Hawke c. 1972, published with permission of the *Advertiser*

Dunstan was the youngest and most energetic in the new, inexperienced, but very senior Walsh Cabinet, and he was determined to make the most of his portfolios as Attorney-General, Minister for Aboriginal Affairs and Minister for Social Welfare. It was not Dunstan who set out to liberalise gambling, liquor and entertainment laws – legislation that would make the greatest impact on the everyday lives of the majority of the population – but Walsh. And he cautiously subjected the proposed changes to popular enquiry: a referendum on gambling and a royal commission on licensing reform. But it was Dunstan who represented in the popular mind all the progressive changes that followed from the final demise of the Playford regime, including the end of the six o'clock swill in pubs, and the transformation of eating and drinking throughout the city with a gradual spread of cafés, bars and restaurants, eventually spilling onto the pavements.[22]

Dunstan succeeded Walsh as leader of the parliamentary party in 1967, but lost the election of 1968 to Steele Hall. Bi-partisan commitment to electoral reform to eliminate the 'playmander' followed, and after that, Dunstan swept back into power in May 1970. There followed four Dunstan governments lasting until 1979 – a period of liberal reform and increasing governmental activity, in a context of national – indeed international – social and cultural upheaval.

Writing at the invitation of the editor of the Melbourne *Herald* in 1974 to provide an *apologia pro vita sua*, to match one already published by Jim Cairns (the highly controversial socialist treasurer in Prime Minister Gough Whitlam's ALP Government), Dunstan reaffirmed his commitment to socialism and democracy. 'As a socialist', he declared,

> I am concerned to secure
>
> full and stable employment for those who can work;
> care for the aged, poor and sick;
> education for children;
> balanced development for the nation's resources;
> personal liberty and the opportunity for everyone to develop to the full his or her human potential;
>
> These are the traditional concerns of the Australian Labor Party, the prizes for which it struggled through decades of war, depression and adversity . . .
>
> Most importantly of all we have to be vigilant in the preservation of personal liberty. This is not a static concept but an evolutionary one.[23]

Much of the decade's legislative and administrative effort – and it was incontrovertibly a mighty effort – was devoted to these goals. They were not especially new for anyone on the left of the political spectrum, though to have them spelled out by someone in government with power to implement them was unprecedented.

Dunstan's Governments introduced reforms in relation to Aboriginal land rights, consumer protection, education, housing, licensing laws, welfare and anti-discrimination and equal opportunity. He had argued fiercely in Parliament against capital punishment during the Stuart case; now his Government would abolish it. In the fields of health, education, planning and community welfare, Dunstan 'moved South Australia from rock bottom to Australian pre-eminence'. In 1978 he introduced historic legislation to recognise the inalienable rights of the Pitjantjatjara people to their land in the north of the state. He gave strong support to the Festival of Arts, the Art Gallery and the State Theatre Company, and found funding to ensure the completion of the new and innovative Festival Centre building on the banks of the Torrens, just north of Parliament House in Elder Park, at a time when government support for creative work was an innovation. He went further, too, by establishing the South Australian Film Corporation, a leader in the 1970s renaissance of Australian film making. But it was his last goal – expanding the very concept of individual liberties – that most distinguished Dunstan's vision from that of the ALP's traditions and brought him closest to the movements flourishing in the community in which he lived with Gretel and their three children, now teenagers. As he was to write himself:

> South Australia, in the Commonwealth as a whole, had rightly come to be regarded as a social crucible, with a Government in favour of protecting the right to dissent and to depart from accepted social norms as long as one didn't hurt others, and encouraging commitment to social issues and participation in finding solutions by interested citizens.[24]

And it was for his Governments' commitment to, and indeed his own enactment of, an evolving concept of personal liberties that he attracted most notice and is best remembered.

Dunstan was flamboyant and theatrical, famous for appearing in Parliament one hot summer day wearing shorts – pink shorts – and surrounding himself with others who were also sexy and good looking. His Governments were likened, 'half seriously', to Florence under Lorenzo I, where close staff were personal friends. 'Dunstan likes to be chummy with his staff', wrote the *National*

Times: 'that way he can feel a trust'. He appointed as his executive assistant the handsome Peter Ward, a recruit from advertising, public relations, radio and then journalism with the national weekly, the *Bulletin*. A gay man, sharing his life and house on Kingston Terrace in North Adelaide with Dimitrios (Dimitri) Theodoratos, 'in those days, a defiant statement', Ward was to comment. A bachelor, noted the *National Times*, who 'has a touch of the Madison Avenue ad executive about him'. He 'fitted very well with the swish Dunstan image'. He was fun, too. Dunstan was to recall a moment when Ward set out to take the mickey out of Max Harris. Harris had just reviewed a book about recent elections in South Australia, observing 'If ever a leader needed critics rather than sybarites at the moment it is the Don in full flood', the last four words presumably supposed to invoke associations with Nobel Prize winner Mikhail Sholokov, a socialist-realist writer in the Soviet Union, author of *And Quiet Flows the Don*. Peter Ward found Harris at the pub, holding forth to a group of friends and – here Dunstan, who is recounting this tale, reveals himself as an intellectual snob – teachers' college students.

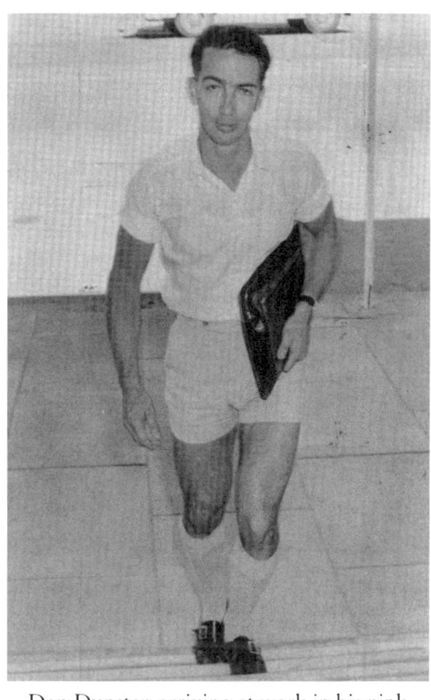
Don Dunstan arriving at work in his pink shorts, published with permission of the Flinders University Library

> 'Say Max – what's a sybarite?', he asked. 'Oh, it's a rather awful sort of person – lacking in criticism of others – connotations of sucking up to them' Max pronounced. 'Well' said Peter, 'What's a sycophant?' Shouts of laughter.[25]

Dunstan told Ward that he needed 'special kinds of human responses' from the friends around him in the office. Ward reminded him of this when, in 1972, after Don and Gretel had decided to split up, Dunstan brought into both the Premier's Department, and possibly into his flat for a time, a young man whom he had met some years earlier at a city gym. John Ceruto was recruited – ostensibly – to be trained into developing fine dining and tourist facilities. Ceruto was 'very, very strange', noted Ward. He was also given to dressing for maximum effect, being reported as saying, himself,

> I had on a white silk shirt, open almost to the waist, a fairly ordinary amount of jewellery, like chains and bracelets, some of that beautiful Aztec stuff, y'know, and a pair of very tight, bright red silk slacks with a gold zipper down the front and down both sides, and big gold rings on the zips.

This was to accompany Dunstan on a visit to Prime Minister Gough Whitlam, who was visibly shocked and (again in Ceruto's account) told Dunstan that it was bad for his image and that of the ALP for him to be getting about accompanied by someone looking like 'some sort of Hollywood stud'. Ward was blunter: first he told Dunstan, 'you must know and accept that John's manner is, to all kinds of people, unattractively sycophantic and camp'; second, and here he warned that the press was also watching closely, 'the truth is that, unlike previous candidates, people really do believe you are fucking John. They're not just stirring.' Earlier in that year the *Sydney Morning Herald* had fallen into a froth of excitement over Dunstan's own clothing. 'And the Premier wore white lace', read the headline to a report on the Festival of Arts, noting that 'citizens of Adelaide' were now claiming to be 'the Athenians of Australia'. 'South Australia, once regarded as a stuffy, backwoods sort of place where nothing very much happened, is now building itself a reputation of a different sort', the paper elaborated.

> What other State in Australia has ... a Premier who appears in the evening in a see-through white lace shirt, bulging over his pectorals, skin-tight black trousers, and ornate silver rings?[26]

Such sartorial radicalism went far further than anything that Whitlam or Wran would ever even contemplate, especially as such over-excited reportage – which made the Sydney press sound quite wonderfully stuffy and provincial – was clearly coded to inform its readers that Dunstan was gay.

Don Dunstan never came out as gay. This is hardly surprising: for most of his public career, homosexual acts between men were criminal offences. Moreover, his sexuality was no simple matter. Peter Ward said that for some time he hadn't known what Dunstan's sexuality was, though eventually, he concluded that Dunstan was bi-sexual. He was married twice, the second time at the end of 1976 to Adele Koh, an English graduate from Singapore, expelled by President Lee Kwan Yew when he closed the *Singapore Herald* where she had been features editor, recruited onto Dunstan's personal staff in 1973. She died of cancer tragically young, in October 1978. He was the father of three, and could

Don Dunstan with Adele Koh, published with permission of the Flinders University Library

well have considered their lives would be less complicated without scandal about their father's sex life. Besides, he is said to have considered that coming out as gay would jeopardise other, important, causes to which he was committed.[27] Nevertheless, Don Dunstan consistently supported gay rights and during the last decades of his life he set up house, and business – a restaurant called Don's Table – with chef Steven Cheng, dedicating his memoirs to 'Steven without whom I would not have survived'.

This was a clear enactment of an evolving concept of personal liberties, and an enactment possible only following changes wrought by his time in government. For the Dunstan Governments swept in a swathe of measures to improve the position and recognise the rights of homosexuals as well as Aboriginal Australians and women. As a dimension of that immense liberalisation, those governments also sought to effect far-reaching change to relations between the people, the police, the criminal justice system, and the legal profession. The Bray Court was one, important, aspect of those changes.

When John Bray wrote to Roma Mitchell on 23 September 1965 to congratulate her on being made a judge, she answered him the next day, in green ink on Judges' Chambers letterhead:

> Dear John,
> Thank you for your generous remarks and wise advice about loosening the trammels of judicial office. The advice I propose to adopt wherever practicable.
> I can only hope that your unique legal talents are being reserved for a higher field.
> Yours sincerely,
> Roma Mitchell.

She was being disingenuous; she knew what Dunstan had in view. Indeed, her knowledge meant that she was embarrassed at an art opening in White Studios in Gawler Place when a friend, gay ballet dancer and teacher George Viggers, taunted Bray, observing that Roma Mitchell had been made a judge, asking 'Why didn't you get the appointment, John Bray?' Bray replied, 'Because I know people like you'. It was, Peter Ward noted, 'a very famous put-down'.[28] History made it more, too: it turned out to be all too close to a simple statement of fact. Roma Mitchell rejoiced at Bray's appointment in 1967, even though, with the law as it still was, she was not able to join him at the pub where he celebrated.

John Jefferson Bray

That was the Sturt Arcade Hotel in Grenfell Street, Bray's favourite watering hole, roughly midway between Shakespeare Chambers at 123 Waymouth Street that housed the firm of Genders, Wilson & Bray and what was subsequently named Bray House at 56 Hutt Street where, a bachelor, he lived with his mother until her death in 1970.[29] At the Sturt Arcade Hotel a week earlier, he had held a private party, attended, recalled Peter Ward,

Bray House, published with permission of the Adelaide City Council

> by perhaps a hundred of his close acquaintances – writers and lawyers, actors and academics, artists and journalists, and plainspun drinking friends. It became a rowdy Falstaffian feast that left publican Peter Wallin's Tap Room in great disarray the following morning.[30]

His appointment shook Adelaide to the core. There was no question about how well he qualified for the position. As Dunstan observed, 'he was pre-eminent in every field. You could brief John Bray QC in a criminal case, a divorce, a company law tangle, a taxation matter, a constitutional contest, or a running down case and expect to get the best.'[31] But John Bray also presented to both the Establishment and the legal profession a quite wonderful assemblage of contradictions. He was born into the Establishment. His grandfather, Premier of South Australia for what was then a record term, 1881–1884, was knighted in 1890 and appointed Agent-General in London in 1892. His aunt married a Bonython, an OAF family. His mother was a Stow, descended from the pioneering Congregational minister after whom Stow Memorial Church (now Pilgrim Church) in Flinders Street in the City of Adelaide was named. His father, even though he was counted 'no worldly success', still made a comfortable enough living to send his sons to Saints, to maintain the Hutt Street household with servants during the Great Depression, and – when John Bray graduated for the third time in 1937, this time adding a PhD to his earlier ordinary and then honours Law degrees – to give him a five-month trip to England and Europe as a congratulatory gift. John Bray conformed to his background in voting conservative, at least in Federal elections. Yet he refused to join the Adelaide Club, or, following his elevation as Chief Justice, to act as Lieutenant Governor, deeming this inconsistent with the independence of the judiciary. And while he was quite prepared to adopt the necessary regalia when occasion demanded, not quibbling even over knee breeches and buckled shoes – his refusal to wear a hat mattered only because there were regulations and precedences about judges doffing their hats to each other – he was also to be seen in a shirt, slacks and sandals, with a towel over his shoulder, heading for the Glenelg tram to take him to the beach for a swim.[32] He would write in 1979: 'Fortunately we are all much more Bohemian now. I am about to go down to the shop in shorts, T-shirt and sandals. I could not have done that 40 years ago. I would have been the object of public disapprobation. Stones might have been thrown.'[33]

John Bray with towel, copied from *A Portrait of John Bray: Law, Letters, Life* (Wakefield Press), 1997, page facing the index

Napier had promised Roderic Chamberlain that he would succeed him as Chief Justice, so Chamberlain was outraged by Bray's appointment. Indeed, Chamberlain's good friend, and co-worshipper at Stow Memorial Church, Brigadier John McKinna, Commissioner of Police – a Playford appointment who had kept his title from his rank in the forces in the Second World War – endeavoured to prevent it, as we shall learn shortly. Chamberlain never spoke to the Premier again. His remaining days at work, wrote Dunstan, 'were punctuated by remarks from the bench critical of Government policy'. Once he had retired, he continued to write to the *Advertiser* condemning Dunstan and his Governments.[34]

Roma Mitchell rejected Bray's description of himself as 'physically clumsy and lacking in dexterity'. 'No one expected sporting activity on his part', she noted, 'but he did not appear clumsy'. He was, she continued, 'of good height, not overweight, not stooped although he always had a tendency to carry his head slightly inclined, with thick, dark hair, expressive brown eyes. Whenever,' she remembered, 'late at a party, he claimed descent from the Princess Pocahontas and suggested that we call him "Highness" his appearance gave support to the proposition'.[35] Barrister Jack Elliott recalled seeing him 'almost daily eating a snack lunch, absorbed in reading a book'.

> He was said to have a photographic memory and dabbled in poetry. He had never learned to drive a motor car, nor owned a wireless set and had no intention of acquiring a television.[36]

Bray did much more than 'dabble' in poetry. Poetry was second only to the law, if it was second to anything, in his life. He wrote poetry himself, principally in classical mode, and during the two decades between 1945 and 1965 led a life that he would have considered bohemian already. He was fast friends with gay classicist Charles Jury, also a poet, who, from 1946 to 1949, had occupied the Chair of English Literature that his mother had endowed at Adelaide University; with Brian Medlin, a younger poet who would become Professor of Philosophy at Flinders University in the mid-1960s; with Colin and Gwenneth Ballantyne, leaders of Adelaide's amateur theatre world during the 1940s and 1950s; and with the artist Wladyslaw Dutkiewicz. 'There was much dining and wining, poetry reading including regular sessions of Virgil in Latin, and long discussions about life and letters', at Jury's rooms on North Terrace, or at his house in Archer Street, North Adelaide; at Bray's in Hutt Street; and in the saloon bar of the South. The Ballantynes held open house every month at 77 Kingston Terrace, North Adelaide, next door to Peter Ward and Dimitri Theodoratos, facing the parklands, and Dutkiewicz, too, threw 'more rowdy and bibulous' parties. There were wild parties at Pam Cleland's, as well, in Norwood before she moved to Waterfall Gully.

One time Bray vetoed Pam Cleland's suggestion that she

include Roma Mitchell at a Norwood party, saying 'Oh, no. Don't ask her. She'll ruin my rebellation [sic] and pleasures.' But if he found Roma's presence inhibiting at Pam Cleland's, that was not part of the story about times when they both went to Nell's. Nell Dowd was reputedly a Communist. She was also a hospitable *bon viveur* who would counter the early closing laws by opening her house to the local intelligentsia, especially artists and members of the legal profession, willing to suffer her rigorous cross-examination about their views. Once admitted, people could buy a bowl of some sort of stew, and coffee cups of port, if they had not brought their own liquor with them. Max Harris might be there, and Dutkiewicz, and Dave Dallwitz the jazz musician, various journalists, and John Bray, and Roma Mitchell. Everyone sat about on couches and cushions, in one room listening to someone reading poetry, or a whole group conversing about morals, or politics, or arts, or the law, and in the other room playing or listening to live music. One evening the talkers took over the music room and sent it up: Roma Mitchell playing a washboard in imitation of a guitar, accompanied by John Bray on a double bass made from a tea chest, while someone else kept time by tapping on the floor with a broom handle with beer bottle tops nailed to it.[37]

At the end of the 1950s, Jury died, Medlin sailed for Oxford, and Bray took silk. By then he had stopped lecturing on Jurisprudence and on Legal History at Adelaide University, but he took on lecturing on Roman Law on Saturday mornings.[38] So bohemia and its poetry morphed into regular Saturday lunch at the Sturt Arcade Hotel, where Bray met with 'Ballantyne's "school" of photographers, journalists, academics, teachers and artists', including Max Harris. He also met with a select group of about a dozen known as 'The Poetry' who gathered at Hutt Street on the first Wednesday of the month to hear one of their number read works of a poet that he or she had chosen. Bray joined in the organisation of the first three Writers' Weeks, too, participating himself, reading his poetry to the growing gatherings in the shade of marquees on the lawns of the Women's Memorial Gardens just north of Government House on King William Road, next to the Torrens Parade Ground. And when new, modernist Festival Director Anthony Steel organised a major celebration for the opening of the new drama theatre in the Festival Centre in 1973, there was an effusion of enthusiasm: Peter Ward, 'having announced that he was also the Premieral Bard', wrote a blank verse introduction to Premier Dunstan, and Bray composed a poem for Dunstan to recite from the stage.[39]

By contrast with such conviviality, Bray's fellow judges – the men – found him shy. 'There was an air of courtesy between him and the puisnes', wrote Puisne Judge Charles Bright, 'but there was a little reticence on his part'. So far was he from Napier's practice of lunching with his judges every week day, and discussing their cases, that while Bray would discuss Banco cases – cases heard by three judges sitting as the Bench together – he would usually do this only once and only after judgment had been reserved, and 'he made no attempt to dissuade a fellow judge from a judgment with which he did not agree'. He did not lunch with the other judges, nor did he linger at the court for a drink at the end of the day.

> He worked, rapidly but incessantly, from the time that he arrived until 6.30 p.m. or thereabouts. When the day's work was done he reverted to being a private man. Then he had other and more congenial friends with whom to discuss other and more congenial topics in other and more congenial surroundings.[40]

Off to the Sturt Arcade Hotel, it was, and once six o'clock closed the pub, he would frequently go to dinner in Hindley Street with Peter Ward. They were both members of the Fellowship of Australian Writers, therefore with much to discuss. They attracted attention though, Ward was to recall, because 'I was a young and apparently handsome person and there was obviously a disparity between the senior QC and the young radio journalist'.[41]

Bray also presented an intellectual contradiction: it was Roman law that he taught to university students on Saturday mornings during the 1960s, but it was as 'the Herculean common-law jurist' that he made his greatest and most lasting contribution to the law in the Australian Commonwealth and in 'the greater common law world beyond'.[42] Roman law was primarily concerned with private law, codified by the Emperor Justinian as the *Corpus Juris Civilis* that formed the basis of all later systems of civil law. Bray considered it important for students to learn about Roman law because, he told the Classical Association, it is

> the foundation of the legal systems of all the countries of western Europe with the exception of England, and [of] their extensions outside Europe – Roman-French law in Quebec and Louisiana, Roman-Spanish law in South America, and Roman-Dutch law in South Africa and Ceylon. Even Scots law has a Roman foundation at least in the theoretical part of it.[43]

The legal system brought to Australia with the earliest waves of Anglo-Celtic settlers was entirely different. It was the English common law, 'a morass of past decisions' compiled, preserved and evolved over centuries, since the time when the Norman kings of England established courts to resolve the disputes that their subjects brought to them. In the common law the focus is on the single, individual case, so the common law's effectiveness depends principally on the capacity of its practitioners 'to assemble and deal with the many arguments that may be presented in relation to the individual case'. This, of course, requires an encyclopaedic knowledge of all relevant cases in the past, their arguments and the decisions reached in them. And a practitioner will benefit mightily from an understanding of the concepts and principles, and their origins and rationale in the past, which inform those arguments and decisions. Bray had, legal academic Andrew Ligertwood argues, a phenomenal capacity to assemble all the relevant arguments, and, High Court Judge Michael Kirby maintains, 'a great depth of insight'.[44]

A later Chief Justice, John Doyle, thought that Bray might well have been tempted to change the law with his judgments.

> For a man of his intellect and inclinations, it would have been easy ... to play the part of the spectacular reformer. Perhaps there were some who hoped he would. It is fair to say that he resisted that temptation, but this resistance was never at the expense of the proper development of the law and the proper performance of the judicial role that expresses itself in appropriate judicial creativity.[45]

But he did not. Charles Bright explained.

> He applied the law as it stood, giving expression to its requirements as accurately as he could. Where it brought about stupid consequences he would say so. He was not prejudiced in favour of the social status quo. When he considered that the status quo involved conflict between law and common sense, or law and currently accepted mores, or law and fair play he did not hesitate to say so. He was in no way resistant to the tide of social change that was surging through the community; but I have never known him to bend the law to bring about change.[46]

Roma Mitchell agreed: 'His role, as he saw it, was to indicate, where appropriate, the need for legislative reform and to leave it to Parliament to pass legislation, if it saw fit.'[47] Her own experience made the difference especially distinct. For Roma Mitchell, like Bray, was engaged in performing 'the judicial role' with the law as it stood. But, unlike John Bray, Roma Mitchell was also to explore ways in which the law might be changed to relieve inequality between women and men, and to indicate – indeed explicitly to recommend – to the government where legislation should be introduced to reform the whole criminal justice system. Here we consider her work as a judge administering the law as it was. We will move on to her work as a reformer of the law in the next chapter.

Justice Mitchell's Judgments

Roma Mitchell has never been known as a great or radical jurist. She was no theorist; her feet were far too firmly on the ground. She was a practical, pragmatic, hardworking and efficient judge. Our reason for considering her judgments, here, is to know more of her and the life that occupied her mind and imagination for the greater part of her days.

Like Bray, Justice Mitchell saw no reason to resist 'the tide of social change ... surging through the community': 'of course', she observed, 'the common law has to be interpreted in the light of changes in the times and in community values'.[48] It was not always obvious that she considered the law in this way. She did not, for instance, join with Bray in his onslaught on censorship in a succession of cases in the late 1960s concerning the possession or dissemination of obscene material among consenting adults, one such case concerning the staging in Adelaide of the raunchy revue, *Oh! Calcutta*, which Bray defended from the Bench with fervour. Nor did she join in the public battle between Bray and the conservative Justice Leo Travers over what kind of clothing or hair length could be worn in court, Bray insisting that it was no part of the justice system's brief to regulate such matters. The controversy raged in the press for almost a week. Of course, there was no particular reason for her views to be recorded since she did not sit on these cases. Like the rest of the Bench, she also remained silent when Steele Hall's brief Liberal Government refused, in 1967, to accept Bray's recommendation that they make Elliott Johnston a QC, the refusal made on the grounds of Johnston's membership of the Communist Party. There was a furore, Bray politely informing the Executive Council that while he could not prevent it adopting a course that he considered wrong, he was entitled to refrain from making any further recommendations for silk until his previous recommendation had been adopted. All the judges supported Bray – who had, innovatively and democratically, held a meeting to learn their views on who should be recommended – though without making any public statement.[49] Johnston was appointed to silk immediately the Dunstan Government regained power in 1970. But however quiet she was on these issues, Roma Mitchell did bring to her decisions about cases emerging from the social and political upheaval around Australia's participation in the war in Vietnam a careful sympathy.

One case in 1968 concerned a young man who had been distributing anti-war pamphlets outside the General Post Office opposing national service and urging young men not to register for the draft. When the police arrested him he went limp and had to be carried to the paddy wagon. A magistrate convicted him of a breach of a city bylaw and of disorderly and offensive conduct. His appeal to a single judge was dismissed. His subsequent appeal to the Full Court also failed, the majority – consisting of Justices Chamberlain and Walters – dismissing it. But Justice Mitchell dissented. She 'held that the bylaw prohibiting distribution of pamphlets exceeded the bylaw-making power of the council and that the appellant's conduct was neither disorderly nor offensive'.[50]

Another case arose from the mass moratorium demonstration in September 1970, an event in which Police Commissioner Brigadier McKinna ordered the 4000 or so demonstrators forming a solid block at the intersection of King William Street and North Terrace to disperse, then ordered the mounted police to ride at them. The *Advertiser*'s front page featured Bray's good mate, philosopher and poet Brian Medlin, in the forefront of the marchers shouting 'No Violence', and headlines announcing that the police had arrested 130 people. It was, Dunstan was to reflect, 'the ugliest [scene] Adelaide had seen since the beef riots of the depression years, with demonstrators being roughly treated and forced into police vans'.[51] He ordered a royal commission into the encounter, headed by Charles Bright. The case that came to Justice Mitchell concerned a young man who was charged with refusing to comply with the police direction to disperse, and with hindering the Police Inspector who gave that direction 'while dispersing a crowd pursuant to Section 59 of the Police Offences Act'. This young man – possibly an anarchist, or one of the Flinders University Maoists – had refused to plead, stating that he did not recognise the court. Even so, an appeal reached the Full Court, which easily dismissed the appeal against the conviction for failing to disperse. But in relation to hindering the police, Justice Mitchell turned to the question of timing. Clearly the defendant had hindered the police before they had given the order to disperse. 'But', as Len King points out,

> the charge had been particularised as hindering 'while dispersing a crowd'. Justice Mitchell was not satisfied that the evidence proved any act of hindering after the direction to disperse. There was power to amend the conviction to found it on the earlier hindering, but as the appellant had had no opportunity to answer that allegation she declined to amend.[52]

At least once, in 1969, she evinced an almost maternal concern, this time for an old woman facing abortion charges, and passed a sentence that showed imagination. The woman was aged seventy-eight, had been charged with abortion offences six times between 1932 and 1968, had been found guilty of five of those charges, and had served four terms in prison. Justice Mitchell, noting her age and poor health, stated that she considered that the woman was not, on this occasion, entirely responsible for what had taken place: 'you were sought out and persuaded to undertake the abortion', she observed. 'You have got to realise you are coming towards the end of your life and you do not want to be doing these things now.' She ordered that the woman be released on a bond of $500, with a surety of the same amount, to be of good behaviour for three years, that good behaviour to include moving from her home. Such a move would render her less vulnerable to persuasion by people seeking abortions, but she had lived there for forty-six years, so this was a considerable hardship.[53]

The Hon. Len King, Roma Mitchell's old friend and colleague, was Premier Dunstan's Attorney-General from 1970 to 1975, and then the Chief Justice who succeeded Bray in 1978, while Roma Mitchell was still on the Bench. He has surveyed her judicial decisions, pointing out a number that were important in the law, the fine-grained detail necessary to these decisions offering a vivid glimpse of the intellectual world that Justice Mitchell inhabited for most of her waking hours during these years. Her decision in *Kellogg v Austral Steel Co.* was 'a question of law of importance to workers seeking common law damages following receipt of workers compensation', he noted. The criminal case of *Drymalik v Feldman* was 'a germinal case' because 'it considered for the first time the meaning and effect of the word "forthwith" in the section of the *Police Offences Act* that prescribes the duty of a police officer exercising the statutory power to arrest on suspicion'. Interpretations of this word affected decisions about evidence that the police may have obtained from the person arrested. If they had detained the person arrested for longer than could be considered properly or lawfully encompassed by the word 'forthwith', then any evidence that they had obtained during that time was also improper or unlawful – inadmissible in court. This was a question that she revisited in her last judgment of significance during the Bray Court period, King writes, in *The Queen v Barker*. Here Justice Mitchell decided that a trial judge may, at his or her discretion, exclude evidence illegally or improperly obtained, and that this rule also applied to confessions obtained while the accused was unlawfully detained. Her view was vindicated later, King notes, by judgments of the High Court. She maintained this view in a later case, too, even though the other judges sitting with her disagreed, and even though, as Charles Bright had observed of some of John Bray's judgments, applying the law as it stood brought about stupid consequences. It does seem to me, she observed,

> that there is a case for giving to the police power to do legally what nowadays they can do only illegally, although possibly with the best motives, namely question a person whom they have arrested before charging him when they have had no opportunity of questioning him prior to his arrest.[54]

During her years in the King Court, she resolved a number of contentious but entirely practical issues. Here are just three examples. Is the householder liable for injury to a milkman who tripped on an uneven pathway while delivering milk? No, she decided, for an uneven pathway was not an unusual danger. Can a third-party insurer intervene in an action between a passenger injured in a car that has been involved in a collision and its driver, on the grounds that the driver was intoxicated and the passenger voluntarily accepted the risk of travelling with him? No, she determined,

> the issues in relation to the plaintiff's action could be completely adjudicated upon if the insurer exercised its right to take over the defence, and ... the plaintiff's action was not the proper vehicle for the resolution of issues between the insurer and the insured.

Can officers of the state government's Department of Lands be held liable for losses sustained by soldier settlers on Kangaroo Island who followed the advice given by those officers about the land being suitable for production of fat lambs and wool? Yes, she resolved: those officers owed a duty of care to the soldier settlers, and had failed to exercise that duty.

Len King asked himself whether or not the judgments of Justice Mitchell, the first woman judge on an Australian Superior Court, 'were influenced by her gender'. Overall, he decided that, as should be expected of any judge, there was not 'the slightest trace of bias in favour of women'. But he went on to establish that her experience and tastes as a woman influenced her interpretation and application of the law in relation to liquor licensing. The new *Licensing Act* of 1967 gave a central place in the licensing system to the hotel or full publican's licence. A retail outlet wanting to sell liquor could not obtain a bottleshop licence if there was a pub in the vicinity, nor could it obtain a licence in a new or expanding community if that licence would then make it more difficult for a pub to be established. Justice Mitchell, of course, regarded the pub as a bastion of male separatism. This did not mean that she never entered one, though the pub in which Bray's former legal partner, Alec Genders, recalled dancing with her was a new and innovatively civilised establishment – the Hotel Australia opened in 1960, on the crest of the hill at Brougham Place, with stunning views south-east across the city. 'Her preference', however, noted King, 'was to avoid hotel bottle departments and to purchase her supplies from liquor stores'. He went on, then, to demonstrate how in no fewer than five cases her judgments were influenced by that preference. Roma Mitchell elaborated this point herself when relating an exchange that she had had with John Bray. He was a great supporter of pubs, she said.

> For some years any store seeking a liquor licence in South Australia had to run the gauntlet of opposition from nearby hotels and some not so near. Appeals in such matters came to the Full Court – I thought them a shocking waste of the Court's time. Once, as we walked off the Bench at lunch time, I gave vent to my feelings, saying: 'What dreadful nonsense this is. The legislation is simply designed to protect the hotels and what have they done for us? We couldn't get decent meals until the restaurants established themselves. We couldn't get comfortable rooms and particularly bathrooms until there were motels.' John's immediate reply was 'They gave us counter lunches.'[55]

There were other moments, too, when the difference between a male and a female perspective were clear in Justice Mitchell's decisions, moments that King CJ did not tackle. Such difference could be encapsulated by contrasting one of John Bray's comments while he was still a barrister with one of Roma Mitchell's judgments. Bray was arguing an appeal case before the Full Court, including Herbert Mayo, which involved defending a man who had shot another in self defence against what he believed was to be a homosexual attack.

> Although prepared to accept that a woman could kill a man who was attempting to ravish her, Justice Mayo ... observed that, 'The risks

> with sodomy are quite different from the consequences of rape.' To this John Bray responded: 'But would not the wound to the man's honour be even greater? In the case of the woman it can be, one may say, regarded as a back-handed compliment.'[56]

By contrast with this breathtakingly misogynist utterance, Roma Mitchell never had any doubt that violent rape deserved the maximum penalty, and was quite prepared, with entirely reasonable provisos, to penalise the kind of behaviour that is often a preliminary to rape.

> I suppose that many young and many not so young men regard it as a pleasurable pastime to seek to attract a woman by parading before her in a motor car. If the attempt is successful and she is enticed into the motor car it cannot be said that the conduct has been offensive to her. And, if the attempt is abandoned when the woman displays annoyance, fear or lack of interest, it seems to me that the conduct cannot be characterised as being offensive to a reasonable person. But where a girl or a woman makes it clear by her words or actions that she has no wish to be pestered with the attentions of a man and he persists in following her in his motor car, then I believe that his conduct is calculated to arouse in her anger and resentment.[57]

The yawning gulf between Bray's comment and Mitchell's argument is also a gulf between the late 1950s and the early 1970s. For the beginning of the 1970s saw the eruption of the Women's Liberation Movement across Australia.

Feminism

In Adelaide, the demonstration against the Miss Fresher contest at the University of Adelaide in March 1970 was the beginning of a multiplicity of meetings, sometimes at the University, sometimes in a bookshop on Melbourne Street in Lower North Adelaide, sometimes in the Women's Liberation Centre set up in Bloor Court in the city, from which young women ran a referral service for women seeking abortions, organised conferences on women and sexist education, initiated plans for a specifically feminist refuge or shelter for women needing to escape from violent husbands, and for a women's health centre, and produced a newsletter.[58] There was a multiplicity of actions, too. In December 1970 a group of

Women's Liberationists attempted to liberate the front bar of a hotel, still considered a male preserve, where the beer was two cents cheaper than in the 'ladies' lounge'. In February 1972 groups prepared leaflets about women's right to reproductive control and to state-funded child care and distributed them everywhere. Early in 1973, another feminist force appeared, first in Melbourne but then throughout the country: Women's Electoral Lobby [WEL], less revolutionary than Women's Liberation, but nevertheless committed to radical change to the position of women and relations between women and men, initially through the electoral process. In March 1975 in Adelaide, Premier Dunstan – who had come top of a WEL questionnaire addressed to politicians about their views on an array of issues of concern to women[59] – made the Festival Centre available to women's groups to celebrate International Women's Day, and South Australian feminist singer-songwriter Robyn Archer sang to them. Towards the end of 1975, University of Adelaide graduate Anne Summers published *Damned Whores and God's Police: the Colonization of Women in Australia*, an analysis of the oppressions of women and their causes. In 1976 the Dunstan Government appointed Deborah McCulloch Advisor to the Premier on Women's Affairs. She did not plan on 'going around ... ramming her opinions down women's throats', reported the Adelaide *Advertiser*. But she had an impressive array of statistics demonstrating how disadvantaged women still were.[60]

Singer/song-writer Robyn Archer, published with permission of the *Advertiser*

The groups of women who made up the Women's Liberation Movement were predominantly – though far from exclusively – young. They were usually – in party political terms – off the left-hand side of the page. They sought to transform the world entirely, eliminating forever all differences of power between women and men. 'Smash the Family', declaimed one demonstration banner. 'The vaginal orgasm is a myth', declared a pamphlet brought from the United States, typed onto a stencil, roneoed onto sheets of paper smelling of methylated spirits and handed out to people watching an International Women's Day demonstration. 'Equal Pay', they shouted, marching down the street in their filmy Indian cotton shirts. Then, contradictorily, they made buttons that read 'To Demand Equality is to Lack Ambition!' and pinned them onto their jackets. Their anthem was Helen Reddy's 'I Am Woman'.[61] Poet, novelist and anti-war campaigner, Glen Tomisetti, wrote them another: 'Don't Be Too Polite, Girls', sung to the tune of 'Click Go the Shears'. In the beginning, at least, there appeared to be a vast distance between them, with their noisiness and impatience, and the older women's organisations like the National Council of Women and the League of Women Voters that had continued campaigning – politely and with a well-honed, but cautious, appreciation of the politically possible – for improvement in the position of women.

It was an entirely new context for the public person who was the first woman to take silk in Australia, the first woman to be made a judge. What was so important about being 'the first woman' – an isolated individual – to do anything? asked Women's Liberation. Wasn't it more important to build a mass movement of Women's Liberationists who would change the world? Besides, some held, it was a waste of time to expect the state or the law to be anything but a hindrance to the total social and political transformation that Women's Liberation sought.

Roma Mitchell was accustomed to being the woman on whom the camera lens focused, the woman invited to launch the South Australian division of the Miss Australia Quest, for instance, to open the triennial meeting of the Australian Council of the Girl Guides Association, to address an annual meeting of the South Australian Country Women's Association, the national triennial convention of the Young Women's Christian Association in Perth, the Soroptomists' Convention in Hobart, and to being the guest of honour at the Women Lawyers' Association of New South Wales' luncheon. She was no mere figurehead. She took advantage of these platforms to argue for the education of women and their continuing participation in the workforce (though she was troubled about the welfare of families if women worked full time), for equal pay, and for equality. But she did not behave like the adherents of Women's Liberation. The most extreme gesture that had ever occurred to her was at a State dinner where the organisers had, as usual, sat people in marital pairs 'husband-wife, husband-wife'. Justice Mitchell thought this tedious – 'I think it's less boring at these official functions if you can walk around and talk to people and that's easier to do if you're on your own' – so she would never agree to nominate someone to be invited as her partner. On this occasion she found herself sitting with Joyce Steele MHA who had brought with her, not a husband, but her daughter. 'I said "Let's get up and shout 'Votes for Women'"', remembered Miss Mitchell, but Joyce Steele didn't think it was a good idea. No, indeed, women had been voting for more than seventy years by this time: it would have been an embarrassingly dated gesture. Was the Women's Liberation Movement about to displace Roma Mitchell's centrality, rendering her a relic of an old and now superseded order? What did she think of Women's Liberation?

She tells us, in no uncertain terms.

Moved by the sudden noisy presence of women all over society's public spaces, the Adult Education Board of Tasmania invited Justice Roma Mitchell to present to them 1971's annual Sir John Morris Memorial Lecture. They considered a judge an appropriate choice for a memorial to Tasmania's Chief Justice and Administrator, 1940–1956, and Australia's first female judge being especially appropriate for the topic they had chosen – 'Women's Liberation and the Law'. This lecture was a quite wonderful piece of artful rhetoric, akin to her successful persuasion of Premier Playford to allow women to sit on juries.

She began by referring to the achievement of votes for women in her home state in 1894 and in Tasmania in 1903, achievements that some would have said gave women freedom, and to small groups of women since that time who continued to agitate for equal pay for equal work, a campaign though that was 'not sufficiently clamant nor sufficiently well supported to arouse full public interest'.[62] Now, however,

> there are a number of women, and the number appears to be growing, who claim that women's liberation is still but a dream. They say that

> they would prefer to abdicate from the role of voters, that nothing has been gained by suffrage for women who are still enslaved.

It is difficult, she said, to establish a clear picture of the complaints and aims of the protagonists of women's liberation. Nor does it seem that Women's Liberation is a single homogeneous group. Then she positioned herself. 'In some respects I find myself uncommitted', she announced, reassuringly for any conservatives in the audience. But immediately she added, 'On the other hand those who attempt to write satirically about the movement succeed only in clouding the issues', and moved on to quote from some of the earliest and most influential works of the Women's Liberation Movement in the United States: *Notes from the First Year* (1968), *Notes from the Second Year* (1970), Robin Morgan's anthology, *Sisterhood Is Powerful* (1970) and Betty Friedan's *The Feminine Mystique* (1966). It was a rhetorical move that she repeated. 'Some ... of the ideas in the literature to which I have referred, and in the other literature of the movement, will be abhorrent to people of my generation', she noted, offering more reassurance. But she followed that by stating unequivocally that 'some of us' nevertheless thought that the position of women in our society was open to substantial criticism. 'It is useless to adopt an "ostrich-like" attitude to the Women's Liberation Movement. It will not be quelled by ridicule.' This is 'not just a movement to "burn the bra" or to ban degrading beauty competitions', she observed. These women were serious.

She listed the eight demands in the Bill of Rights published by the United States' National Organization of Women [NOW]: equality of women with men under the law; equal employment opportunity with men; women's right to paid maternity leave and reinstatement in employment after child birth without loss of seniority benefits; tax deductions for home and childcare expenses for working parents; free childcare facilities; full education for women; job training, housing and family allowances for women on equal terms with men; and the 'right of women to access to contraceptive information and devices, and to abortion'. She announced her support for most of those demands, with some qualifications. Then she made those demands appear utterly reasonable by pointing out that for more extreme feminists, like Robin Morgan, the membership of NOW was too exclusively middle class and in danger of following those women in the past who campaigned for women's suffrage into a '"bourgeois feminist movement that never quite dared enough, never questioned enough, never really reached out beyond its own class and race".'

This led Justice Mitchell into a historical *excursus*, a clever move as it presented the opponents of women's suffrage under the reign of Queen Victoria as obstructionist and silly, the analogy with current opposition to Women's Liberation merely hinted, but unmistakeable. She related the story of the struggle that Joyce Steele and Jessie Cooper had had to engage in – not to be elected, but for their election to be recognised as legitimate. It is, she observed mildly, 'startling to realise that in 1959 it could seriously be contended that a person might, by reason of her sex, be disqualified from sitting as a member of Parliament'. She pursued her own earlier argument about the importance of women fulfilling the obligations of all citizens by undertaking jury duty. She elaborated a case for women's education, noting that Women's Liberation rejected arguments against women's higher education in favour of their confinement to 'the arts and skills of a homemaker', and observed, perceptively, 'Perhaps it is because they feel that women are deprived of the opportunity of complete development of their intellectual faculties, that many women's liberationists claim that women should be entitled to abortion on demand.' She detailed current statistics about women moving into the labour market, including women who were wives and mothers; it was, she said, a 'tendency ... not likely to be reversed'. This would give added force to women's demands for equal pay for equal work. She paused over Germaine Greer's exhortation to women seeking to ameliorate their condition: 'they must refuse to marry ... if independence is a necessary concomitant of freedom, women must not marry'. 'If I were asked to play the soothsayer', hazarded Justice Mitchell, again providing reassurance, 'I would say that if women have to choose between independence and marriage they are likely to choose the latter.' Nevertheless, 'Certain it is that divorce is becoming more commonplace, and more children are living with one parent alone.' She took account of Women's Liberation's emphasis on 'the need for sexual equality in the many aspects of sexual gratification', remarking dryly, 'Legislation cannot ensure the enjoyment of sexual relationships, though it may, by imposing penalties on those who perform certain acts, restrict enjoyment by some persons.' She went on to note that the law penalised the female prostitute but not her male client.

And at two moments she offered a prediction that ran directly counter to her conservative reassurances. One could – she suggested – be considered light hearted.

> It may be that I view this matter too seriously, but I have been asked ... to look forward. What I have read of the Women's Liberation Movement in the United States convinces me that if it is not taken seriously at this stage, there may be a grave erosion into the whole of the social life of the community in the not too far distant future. The manifesto of SCUM (The Society for Cutting Up Men) may not be intended to be taken too seriously. The opening paragraph contains this suggestion:
>
>> 'Life in this society being at best an utter bore and no aspect of society being at all relevant to women, there remains to civic-minded, responsible, thrill-seeking females only to overthrow the government, eliminate the money system, institute complete automation, and destroy the male sex.'
>
> However, women, disgruntled by discrimination in wages by reason of sex, might take heart from the claim that 'if a large majority of women were SCUM they could acquire complete control of this country within a few weeks simply by withdrawing from the labour force, thereby paralysing the entire nation.'

What is this, if not a thinly veiled threat?

The other was a plea: the heart of her case. 'In general', she said,

> My plea is that the law should, where necessary, be amended so as to ensure that women do not suffer any disabilities under the law merely by virtue of the fact that they are women. If this does not happen then it may be that the revolution sought by some members of the Women's Liberation Movement will become a reality.

Such a prediction might seem 'ludicrous'. But then

> how many of us ten years ago would have believed that in the year 1971 we would be living in a society in which otherwise law-abiding people would find themselves impelled by conscience to demonstrate against such issues as conscription, involvement in a particular war, or exchange of sporting teams with a country practising apartheid?

There may be many attracted to the 'doctrines' preached by Women's Liberation.

> Some men and women may feel, as I do, that what the Women's Liberation Movement is seeking should be examined carefully, and that where inequalities are shown to exist merely by reason of sex these should be eradicated, in the same way as should be plucked out those inequalities which exist merely by reason of race or religion, or for some other reason quite extraneous to the value of the particular person.

A clear, uncompromising statement, this was. In it, as Elizabeth Evatt was to observe, Roma Mitchell 'nailed her feminist colours to the mast'.[63] She might not be at the camera's central focus on the streets with Women's Liberation, but she was still well and truly in the picture. She became, in this new context, the acceptable 'face' of the new feminism, the woman whom the Australian Broadcasting Commission would invite to present the Boyer Lectures during 1975, International Women's Year.

Her stand took courage. Look at the views of her leader, the Chief Justice. The stereotypes of his education and youth 'lingered on', Ward was to observe. Bray was happy to take advantage of the ways in which the Dunstan Decade revolutionised eating and drinking in Adelaide, but he preferred the homo-social world of his early bohemian days. He

> greatly enjoyed the lingering pre-war hotel culture of smoke-filled bars redolent with stale beer. In the liberating early seventies he was even reluctant to concede that public bars should be open to both sexes.

His misogyny also lingered on in his treatment of the women involved in cases of sexual assault brought before him. As Andrew Ligertwood notes, Bray 'might be criticised' for taking too great a care of the interests of the men accused, too little of the women victims, thereby making the law a positively destructive resort for women who had been raped. Furthermore, 'Bray was instrumental in making mandatory a warning to juries of the danger of acting upon the uncorroborated testimony of victims of sexual assault', Ligertwood observes. Bray simply could not see the disadvantages that women still encountered at every turn. For him, Women's Liberation was anathema. He said so in a scolding poem addressed 'To the Feminists'.

> Felicitations on your victory, ladies.
> Or should I say fellow-citizens of the feminine gender?
> The fortress has fallen, the pride of the penis is chastened, the male capitulates.
> You can follow any career you choose, from ditch-digger to deacon.
> ...
> Why then all these beatings of drums, blaring of trumpets, blasts of defiance, banging of gauntlets, bugles of separatism?
> You are battering unbarred gates, disarm, demobilize, enter into the promised land.
> The year of Boadicea is over; these are the days of Demeter.
> In all public and social areas you are accepted as gender-free citizens.
> Behave as if you were.[64]

He refused to use the word 'Ms' when feminists sought its introduction to obviate distinctions between women who were or were not married, referring to it as 'that pathetic monosyllable'. Roma Mitchell said publicly and in print that she did not understand his difficulty over this, a comment that was both a condemnation of his view and, at the same time, a fond tease.[65] And it was fond: she regarded this brother judge as a good friend.

Shadows

That meant that, as with her other friends, she would look after him, when he needed it. And the moment when he needed it occurred in the late 1970s. Events had been building towards this moment for more than a decade, events that resonated far beyond South Australia. For this was when the liberalism, even libertarianism, of the cultural revolution of the late 1960s and early 1970s in the West ran smack into the authoritarianism, even residual totalitarianism, of the years of the Cold War, embodied in the forces of law and order, supported by conservatives among the citizenry who desired a return to the apparently unshakeable certainties of the 1950s. In Britain, the clash was encapsulated in the Profumo Affair in 1963, a political scandal around the Tory Secretary of State for War who had a brief affair with a showgirl called Christine Keeler, who was also involved in a relationship with an attaché at the Soviet Embassy and therefore a security risk. John Profumo lied to the House of Commons about his connection with Keeler, but was found out and had to resign.[66] In Australia, the national encounter of these forces occurred between the Attorney-General in the Whitlam Federal Government, Lionel Murphy, and the Australian Security and Intelligence Organisation [ASIO] on 15 March 1973. In South Australia, it came to a head on 17 January 1978 when the Dunstan Government sacked its Commissioner of Police, Harold Hubert Salisbury, again over questions around security.

What became known as 'The Salisbury Affair' occupies an important place in any narrative of Roma Mitchell's life because it all landed on her desk to fix, and because – and this is what is entirely new to an understanding of these events – the emotional intensity driving them arose (as in the case of Profumo) from their association with sex, and, in South Australia, sex that was considered illicit at the time. It also arose from the hitherto unrecognised need for the protection of John Jefferson Bray CJ.

For the Salisbury Affair began well before Harold Salisbury received his comeuppance. We present a mere sketch of these events, here; we do not, for instance, explore the part played in them by the deteriorating friendship between the Premier and Peter Ward, nor the detail of the exchanges between the Premier and the Police Commissioner. Rather, we present only what is needed to understand Justice Mitchell's part in the proceedings. These events can be pictured as the shadows clustered at the edges of the Golden Years of the Bray Court and the Dunstan Decade, causing Roma Mitchell great concern

Salisbury to replace McKinna as Commissioner of Police 1972

One of the several means by which Dunstan Governments sought to liberalise relations between the people, the police, the criminal justice system and the legal profession was by reforming the police.

Dunstan was already highly critical of the police, especially in relation to civil liberties, even before Labor won government in 1965. He was even more critical after the violent clash between the police, headed by Police Commissioner Brigadier McKinna, and anti-war demonstrators in September 1970. The ensuing Bright Commission recommended that the police must be made 'subject to appropriate ministerial direction on policy', and the Government duly enshrined that recommendation in legislation. The Government also determined to replace McKinna, who was due to retire, with a very different appointment, someone who was, Dunstan wrote later, 'able, intelligent, experienced, and with sufficient education to understand what we were about'.[67]

Police Commissioner, J.G. McKinna, published with permission of the *Advertiser*

No locals were up to the job, the Government learned. So they undertook a search in England. There, eventually, they settled on the fifth person, last on their list, who 'interviewed well ... though he was not as bright or flexible and was very much more pukka than others we'd seen'.[68] This was Harold Hubert Salisbury. By 1968, he had risen through the ranks of the English police to be Chief Constable of the amalgamated forces of York and the North-East Yorkshire Police, numbering 1300, approximately the same size as the police force in South Australia. In 1970 he received the Queen's Police Medal for

Police Commissioner Harold Salisbury, published with permission of the *Advertiser*

distinguished, efficient service. He was fifty-five, and, in the words of South Australian journalist, Stewart Cockburn, 'ruggedly handsome, 6'2" [1.83 m] and powerfully built ... still physically and mentally very fit'. At this time chief constables in Britain were increasingly retiring at the age of sixty, but Salisbury wanted to work for longer. Dunstan outlined to him the relationship that was to exist between the police commissioner and the government following the Bright Report. He raised with him the need for change in police treatment of Aboriginal people. He suggested a general education program for police officers. Salisbury responded positively to all of this so they appointed him.[69]

The culture of the police

Salisbury and his wife arrived in Adelaide on 1 July 1972 – to a major upheaval involving the police. It was also a major upheaval around the continuing criminality of homosexuality, triggering campaigns across Australia for legislative change. This was the tragic death of Dr George Duncan, forty-one-year-old Lecturer in the Law Faculty at Adelaide University. On 10 May 1972, George Duncan, Wesley James and another man were set upon, bashed and thrown into the River Torrens opposite the Torrens Parade Ground, at a spot known to homosexuals, and to the police, as 'No. 1' beat. George Duncan drowned. On 30 June three officers of the Vice Squad refused to answer questions at the coronial inquest into Duncan's death and were suspended from the police force. The Coroner delivered an open finding. The three Vice Squad officers resigned, a move that – as a subsequent inquiry pointed out – meant that they could not be compelled to give evidence that might incriminate them.

LOTTERY MAJOR PRIZES

THE NEWS

Adelaide: Wednesday, July 5, 1972

LAST

VIOLENCE IN DUNCAN DEATH

But finding open

Dr. George Ian Ogilvie Duncan drowned in the River Torrens on May 10 "due to violence on the part of persons of whose identity there is no evidence."

This was the open finding of the Coroner, Mr. T. E. Cleland, today at the conclusion of the inquest into the death of the 42-year-old Adelaide University law lecturer.

Costly

THEY'RE OFF TO ENGLAND!

• Police accept Vice Squad man's resignation, Page 5; Inquest continued, Page 5.

To the knowing the usual means St Agnes Brandy

Front page of the *News*, 5 July 1972, with photograph of Dr Duncan, published with permission of the *Advertiser*.

Salisbury took up his new post while the inquest was still underway.

He persuaded the Dunstan Government to ask Scotland Yard for help. Two senior English detectives came to Adelaide, carried out enquiries, and submitted a report – effectively a whitewash for the police – which said that Dr Duncan's death had been the result of a 'high-spirited frolic that went wrong', the so-called 'frolic' involving the three former members of the Vice Squad who had already resigned. The Scotland Yard detectives were not entirely squeaky clean, it would turn out. Later, they were convicted of offences themselves: one for fraud, the other for corruption.[70]

In 1972 what remained was – for Dunstan and his allies – an ominous and clearly marked opposition between the aspirations of the libertarian Dunstan Government, and the culture within the South Australian police force. The police held themselves to be autonomous, entitled to impose their own ideas about morality upon the public, regardless of government and statute law. As Peter Ward was to remark, 'the police were very censorious'. 'I don't think they were corrupt', he went on, 'but they did regard themselves as not only the police force, but [also] the morals police of South Australia.'[71] Salisbury fitted into that culture as neatly as if McKinna, not Dunstan, had appointed him, and began making other friends outside the force among members of the Jaguar Drivers Club of South Australia.[72] Perhaps a collision between the police and the government was inevitable. It took two chains of events to make it happen.

Government enquiries about Special Branch activities 1975–1977

The first chain of events bringing government and police into conflict began in August 1974 when Whitlam's Government in Canberra instigated a royal commission to inquire into ASIO, presided over by Justice Robert Hope.[73] On 27 May 1975 that Royal Commission asked Dunstan's Premier's Department to obtain certain information about security work undertaken for ASIO by the South Australian police. The Premier's Department referred the request to Salisbury who, in turn, referred it to Special Branch, the small intelligence unit within the South Australian Police Force, established in 1939. Two Special Branch officers drafted a reply and Salisbury used that as a basis for his answer to the Premier. On

18 August 1975, Justice Hope went to talk with Dunstan, telling him that he was not satisfied with the information that Salisbury had provided, and, Dunstan related, 'that he believed that the Police Special Branch was involved in security activities to an extent he thought it unlikely I would know about'. Dunstan had the Premier's Department send further questions to Salisbury about the work of Special Branch. Salisbury sought advice from a legal officer within the police force about whether or not the Premier could require such information from him. The advice that he received was that yes, indeed, the Premier certainly could do so, under the *Police Regulations Act* as amended (following the Bright Commission) in 1972. Salisbury ignored this advice and sent another memorandum to the Premier purporting to provide answers to the new questions that the Premier had asked.

There matters rested, even though the whole issue of police surveillance and the work of Special Branch surfaced again during 1976, when two branches of the ALP asked if Special Branch was keeping watch on some of their members. The Premier's Department replied using the most recent of Salisbury's memoranda, a reply that Salisbury had written himself, based on the very incomplete information provided to him by his Special Branch officers. But during the following year, the second chain of events brought questions about Special Branch and its activities onto the front pages of the local, even the national, press.

Peter Ward's questions about Special Branch activities 1977

This second chain of events began with Peter Ward's friendship with Dunstan during the late 1960s, when both were involved in, among other things, the Council of Civil Liberties, a body strongly opposed to any kind of socio-political surveillance. As a gay man, living openly with his lover, Ward had good personal reasons for such opposition; Dunstan was to write of him that he 'lived with a constant paranoia, and allowed it to colour his view of things'.[74] Beginning in 1974, Ward's interests were shifting away from the Premier's Department, and Dunstan found that he needed more from an executive assistant than Ward was providing. A succession of semi-detached arrangements ensued, but when Ward's partner, Dimitri Theodoratos, quit the government Wildflower Garden where he had been employed and returned to Greece, Ward's financial arrangements meant that he needed a full-time job again. So he resigned from the Premier's Department altogether, returning to journalism, taking charge of the Adelaide desk of the Murdoch press's national daily, the *Australian*.

On 1 September 1977 Ward sent a list of questions about police surveillance of private citizens to the Premier's Department. The Department referred it to Salisbury, who replied that the answers had been provided in the memorandum of 1975. The Premier's Department did nothing with this reply.[75] Peter Ward was not to be dismissed. On 3 September 1977 the *Australian* published an article headed: 'Exposed … the Secret Police Dossiers on Demonstrations'. It suggested that Dunstan had special and secret reasons for being unwilling to investigate questions about the activities of Special Branch. Ward also telephoned Robin Millhouse MP, the only member of the South Australian Parliament who belonged to the Australian Democrats, a party founded in May 1977 with the principal aim of 'keeping the bastards honest', the bastards in government that was. Millhouse put a list of similar questions on notice in the House of Assembly. The Government asked Salisbury for answers and he sent some; Chief Secretary D.W. Simmons replied to Millhouse with these answers on 1 November 1977.

Peter Ward was not giving up. On 3 November 1977 another article appeared in the *Australian* over his by-line headed 'Secret Police Files a Nettle for Dunstan to Grasp', alleging that the Premier was failing to ensure that 'such surveillance of political dissenters and political terrorists as is necessary is conducted under the right kind of supervision, with the correct degree of care'. Dunstan was overseas. His Cabinet colleagues decided to act. On 8 November 1977 they appointed Acting Justice J.M. White to conduct an inquiry into the records held by the Special Branch of the South Australian Police Force. White moved swiftly. He handed a copy of his report to the Premier on 21 December 1977. Dunstan scanned it and decided that it was 'pretty hair-raising'.[76] But it needed proper attention, and he was tired and jet-lagged, so he put it away until he returned from his Christmas break at the end of the first week in January 1978.

And then everything blew up.

Acting Justice White's Report on Salisbury's answers about Special Branch activities

As Dunstan was to observe, when reporting all of this to the Parliament, 'it is not possible to have an open inquiry into the content of security files'. What the Government could do was, as it had quite properly done, 'have a judicial officer investigate', and what White AJ discovered from his investigations showed that the answers that Salisbury had provided to the Government on each of the occasions when he had been asked about Special Branch had been wrong, 'very seriously wrong'. There was 'a mass of records ... relating to matters, organizations and persons having no connection whatever with genuine security risks'. 'Since 1953–4', reported Justice White,

> the time of the Petrov Commission, Special Branch has maintained extensive records, not only about extreme left and right wing activities, but also about organizations perceived to be 'left' of its own point of view; for example, ALP and trade union organizations and personalities, members of universities, Council of Civil Liberties members, Peace movement members and many other categories of people.

The Petrov Commission had followed the defection to Australia of Vladimir and Evdokia Petrov, who had been Cold War Warriors, spying for the USSR from its embassy in Canberra. But South Australia's Special Branch had not uncovered any activity of that kind. Rather, Justice White observed, 'Special Branch criteria for recording material after 1953–54 were not based on the possibility of violence or force to overthrow the Government. Nor were they based on any real suspicion of possible espionage'. Instead,

> they were based ... on the unreasoned assumption that any persons who thought or act[ed] less conservatively than suited the security force were likely to be potential dangers to the security of the nation in that they might possibly give direct or indirect comfort to the enemy, Communism. Suspicion of direct or indirect comfort was based on unrealistically nervous grounds.

'Some well known moderate figures (often senior Members of Parliament) have recorded about them scandalously inaccurate opinions about their political standing', he added. Were there records about Dunstan himself, perhaps? Special Branch records were not secured, Justice White pointed out; most of the information had been or could be passed on to ASIO.[77] Moreover, he added, 'Material which I know to be inaccurate, and sometimes scandalously inaccurate, appears in some dossiers and on some cards. Some of this information appears to have been used in "vetting" procedures.' Acting Justice White 'refrained from mentioning some specific glaring examples for fear of identifying individuals'.

And there we are, abruptly, at the core of the emotions radiating throughout these events: moralistic police opinions, sometimes 'scandalously inaccurate', treated as though they were factual information, 'used in "vetting" procedures' about people who could not be named because it would be too damaging to their reputations. For this was how Brigadier McKinna had endeavoured to prevent John Bray's elevation to the position of Chief Justice in 1967.

Ten years earlier, 1967

At the time when Dunstan had proposed that the next Chief Justice should be John Bray, and not Roderic Chamberlain, Police Commissioner Brigadier McKinna, friend of His Honour Justice Roderic Chamberlain, had gone to Premier Walsh with what Dunstan described as 'a very defamatory allegation' about Bray. Dunstan had been outraged at what he was to call 'his baseless scandal-mongering', 'walking up & down, shouting & threatening him with a court action for having libelled Bray to the Premier', demanding to know what basis it could have. McKinna told Walsh and Dunstan simply that 'it was a matter which was common talk amongst senior officers of his Force. He said particularly that some senior officers of the Force had said that they would not allow their sons to associate with the person concerned', that is with Dr Bray.[78]

McKinna had been despatched to see if he could provide evidence, rather than gossip. Dunstan told Cabinet that it was nonsense, malicious rumour, and that if Cabinet took any notice of it, he would resign. But there was immense alarm and distress. At the Sturt Arcade Hotel, Bray said to Peter Ward,

> 'Look, come outside, something really serious has happened. The government has received a report from McKinna which has been thrown out because there was no evidence, which was linking me with a homosexual. And that probably means you.

Well, there were quite a number of other homosexuals that it could have referred to, Ward thought. But Bray thought it was him. Peter Ward

> went straight over to Dunstan's house. His house was in an uproar. Gretel had taken to bed with the vapours ... The whole Dunstan house was in an uproar. The kids were crying. But it was quite serious because Dunstan had put his career on the line.[79]

There were more dramas over the weekend, but then – mercifully – an anticlimax. McKinna came back with three stories from police patrol reports, two referring – testified Dunstan – 'to the person concerned; the other referred to an occasion at which he was not present at all'. All three were, in Dunstan's words, 'completely innocuous'.[80] Such talk, especially once it had become the subject of a legal inquiry, was shrouded in anonymity to protect Bray's reputation. Nevertheless, the stories were recorded. Bray's indiscretions were, Ward relates, extremely minor, and indiscretions, not crimes. The reports were

> about John Bray being seen outside the Palais drinking in a car, in the parklands near the Palais, which young men did because you couldn't get any drinks in the Palais. And the other was that he was seen with a bearded gentleman on the verandah of his house late in the evening drinking. This was in Hutt Street. And then he helped this bearded gentleman behind some shrubbery in the front, and they emerged later brushing their clothes. In fact it was John Davey, the blind lawyer, and he was helping him urinate.[81]

There was a third incident, too, but, as Dunstan was to observe, in this incident – when the police arrived at a house in Hutt Street adjacent to Bray's to encounter some transvestites – John Bray was not even present.[82]

These reports were so innocuous that they failed altogether in the purpose for which McKinna had brought them up. Bray's appointment had been able go forward, and Dunstan had not needed to resign. Indeed, Dunstan was to complain to the press subsequently that 'he had been given information by the Police Commissioner, Mr. McKinna, from files containing the names of people who had not committed a crime'. Those files were from 'routine reports by officers', 'patrol report files' they were to be described as later, the same kinds of files that could have been kept by the members of the Vice Squad who drowned George Duncan at 'No. 1' beat on the Torrens in May 1972. These were not Special Branch files.[83] Peter Ward's letters and articles in the *Australian* were not supposed to implicate his good mate, John Bray.

Now in 1977 again: Sacking Salisbury

Nevertheless, when Acting Justice White reported to the Government in December 1977 that the files compiled and kept by Special Branch contained inaccurate information, material that White considered to be 'scandalously inaccurate', then all of the fears raised by McKinna's attempts to smear John Bray ten years earlier resurfaced. All about sex were the stories that he had told. And sex that would have been illegal at the time. Such stories must not gain circulation.

Dunstan was appalled. White's report spelled out Salisbury's refusal to comply with the Premier's requests for information: 'On three occasions the Premier sought information from the Commissioner about categories of files. On each occasion, reference to the sensitive files on political, trade union, university and other matters was avoided.'[84] Dunstan went to see Salisbury, gave him a copy of the White Report, told him it was clear that he was in the same position as a Minister of the Crown would be if he had misled the Parliament. He would have to resign. He told Salisbury to read the White Report and then come back and see him. When Salisbury did so, he tried to wriggle out of the whole affair, arguing that there were records on members of conservative political parties as well as on members of the Government, fulminating against Robin Millhouse and Peter Ward, endeavouring to win Dunstan over by abusing the press. But he did acknowledge that he may have 'pulled' his answers to the Premier's requests for information 'somewhat'.[85]

He adopted a different tack, as well, for a time, apparently assuming that anything deriving from England would be considered superior to anything local. He cited Justice Denning's report on the Profumo case, and, again referring to English precedents, noted that 'MI5 did not provide information to the Home Secretary or the Prime Minister and that the Treasury in England did not provide certain information to the Chancellor of the Exchequer'.[86] He seemed to have believed that, as Governor General Paul Hasluck was to point out, he was quarantined from answerability to the government, even though the 'highest military personnel in Australia are subject to civilian control'. And he seemed to have continued to believe this, even after the legal advice provided to him from within the ranks of the police themselves told him it was not so, even though, too, he continued – in effect – to lie to the government, rather than telling them frankly that he was not willing to give them the information that they had asked for.[87] Dunstan was not impressed. After all, both of Salisbury's English examples ignored the over-riding power that his Government's legislation had given to the government, requiring that the police force conform to government direction, following the Bright Report's recommendations. And he had, he said, consulted Salisbury about this new law, in interviewing him for the job of Police Commissioner. Dunstan took the White Report to Cabinet and Cabinet decided that it should be published, that Acting Justice White's recommendations about Special Branch should be implemented, and that Salisbury should be asked for his resignation.

But Salisbury did not want to resign. Even after he had been told that he would not suffer any monetary penalty – a decision that cost the South Australian Government of 1978 $160,000 – he did not want to go. So the Government dismissed him.

But it turned out that Salisbury had some powerful allies. They included the Dunstan-appointed former Governor of the State of South Australia, Sir Mark Oliphant, journalist Stewart Cockburn (former press officer to Prime Minister Menzies), the Murdoch press in general, the members of the Jaguar Drivers Club, and the members of the police force whose autonomy had been called into such severe question by Acting Justice White's report. Together they made Salisbury into a rallying point for all the conservative forces to have been alarmed by the transformations being wrought by the Governments of Premier Dunstan, by what Liberal Leader David Tonkin called 'a Dunstan Establishment'.[88] Salisbury held a press conference, and announced that he had believed that 'the duty of the police is solely to the law'. The Police Association passed a resolution that he should have an inquiry into his dismissal and whether it was not 'harsh, unjust and unreasonable'. There was a demonstration in Victoria Square of between 10,000 and 15,000 people demanding a 'Fair Go for Salisbury'. Stewart Cockburn told the *Sydney Morning Herald* that he had received many letters from migrants – implicitly fugitives from iron curtain countries – saying, in effect, 'We have been through all this before in Europe!'[89]

No-one doubted the gravity of the events under dispute. One Liberal parliamentarian pointed out that that the White Report drew analogies between the FBI under J. Edgar Hoover in the United States and the activities of ASIO and Special Branches in Australia. An anti-Communist witch hunt, in other words, victimising political innocents. Dunstan himself announced that at issue were 'principles that lie at the heart of our free and democratic way of life'. The Liberal Party thought that they could use their majority in the Legislative Council to demand appointment of a select committee of inquiry.

That could take months and months. Such a committee could call anyone before it. Already Liberals were asking what Dunstan and the Government had to hide. A select committee could foment allegations and rumour. At least so Dunstan thought. That must not be allowed to happen. He had, he recalled, taken to Cabinet the suggestion that there be a royal commission. They had rejected it, considering that 'to appoint one would be admitting that there was something to investigate'. They spent hours in the Parliament arguing against it. But something had to forestall the Liberals. Dunstan changed his mind: 'a Royal Commission would pre-empt them, as the matters before it would be sub judice'.[90]

Justice Roma Mitchell and the Salisbury Commission

And so it was that on 10 February 1978 the new Governor of South Australia, Keith Douglas Seaman, appointed Justice Roma Mitchell a Royal Commission to inquire into and report upon whether Harold Salisbury misled the Government about the nature and extent of the operations of Special Branch; whether the Government's decision to dismiss Salisbury was justifiable; and whether there was reason to modify the prerogative rights of the Crown to dismiss the Commissioner of Police. Ted Mullighan, her former junior, and incoming President of the Law Society, was appointed to assist her.[91] Cairns Villeneuve Smith wrote to her from Melbourne: 'Does this appointment mean that you are one of the judges not on Special Branch files? How dull! Don't get a complex about it!'[92]

She submitted her report to the Governor on 30 May 1978. 'Yes', she wrote, Salisbury did mislead the Government. 'Yes', the Government's decision to dismiss him was justifiable in the circumstances. And 'yes', the *Police Regulation Act* 1952–73 should be amended to provide for the Commissioner of Police to be removed from office by the government. She had considered legal precedent in an array of case law. She had consulted the Hope Royal Commission into ASIO as well as the White Report. She consulted a wide range of written authorities. She did not, though, include any reference to Lord Denning's report on the Profumo Affair.[93] Everyone concerned, including Salisbury, including Dunstan, including Ward (who had hailed the dismissal as a victory for the press), including a representative of the Liberal Party, was examined and cross-examined by counsel in public hearings. She had not – and, as she pointed out, properly not – interviewed Acting Justice White about his Report.

She had even done what Salisbury had consistently failed to do:[94] she had gone to Special Branch, in the bowels of Police Headquarters,[95] and looked at the immense array of cards and files kept there. Her purpose, she said – in response to arguments advanced by counsel for the Communist Party of Australia and the Socialist Party of Australia South Australian Branch – was not 'to decide what records should have been or should, for the future, be kept by Special Branch'. Nor was it for her to 'determine what motives inspired the keeping of any part of the records of Special Branch'. 'It is not for me to say whether Special Branch was right or wrong in keeping specific records or types of records', she maintained. Rather, her task was to determine the accuracy of those parts of the White Report that counsel asked her to check, as part of her overall task of determining if Salisbury's dismissal was justifiable on the grounds of his misleading the government. And she found that, with some minor quibbles, 'the statement of White A.J. ... appears to me to be substantially correct'.[96]

Amidst all of this, she had also learned that many beliefs about the Special Branch files were 'misconceptions'. In particular, the 'patrol report files, which were relevant to a particular appointment in 1967' were just that, and not files kept by Special Branch; any threat of scandal to John Bray lay in the files of ordinary police patrols, not in the records kept by Special Branch. But she was angry with Peter Ward for taking action that, however inadvertently, could have caused trouble for John Bray. She rejected his views as less than helpful.

> Mr Ward's statements, not only in his article but also repeatedly in evidence before me, were so inaccurate ... that they necessarily affect Mr Ward's credibility. Where he is in conflict with other witnesses I find it impossible to rely on his evidence.[97]

She had also established that the card and file kept on Premier Dunstan did not contain all of the information that they might once have held; she reported that the officer examined about this card had said that 'one reason for culling the Premier's card [was] the possibility that the Premier might insist on seeing his own file'. Roma Mitchell had a sardonic wit. 'This is certainly a good reason', she observed, 'for removing from that file matter which might reasonably be considered to be scandalously inaccurate'.[98] And she had ensured that John Bray was never mentioned by name, that the police patrol reports used by McKinna to query his elevation to the position of Chief Justice were referred to only as an 'incident relating to a particular appointment in the '60s'.[99] She interrupted McKinna, when he was being interviewed, for this purpose.

> Mr. Mullighan: There is just one matter – I do not want to go into detail about this but was there an occasion in 1967 when you gave some information to members of the Cabinet.
>
> Mr. McKinna: Yes.
>
> Mr. Mullighan: That information that you gave, was that information from Special Branch itself or from some other section.

> Mr. McKinna: No, it was not from Special Branch; it was from a patrol report – you are concerned, I think, concerning the appointment –
> The Commissioner [Justice Mitchell]: We do not want the details.[100]

Premier Dunstan gave evidence about that appointment, and he, of course, made no mention of the name of the person being appointed.[101]

Justice Roma Mitchell was to comment that Salisbury's belief that his responsibility was to the law, to the Crown, and not to any politically elected government, 'suggests an absence of understanding of the constitutional system of South Australia or, for that matter, of the United Kingdom'.[102] His dismissal, observed legal historians Castles and Harris, 'was an important, indeed an essential, reaffirmation of a basic precept of responsible government'. The Government passed the *Police Regulation Act Amendment Act* 1978, inserting a new section into the previous legislation to provide that the Governor may remove the Commissioner, or Deputy Commissioner, of Police from office for incompetence, neglect of duty, misbehaviour or misconduct, or mental or physical incapacity.[103]

When it was all over

It could be thought that Dunstan chose Roma Mitchell as the Salisbury Commissioner because he thought that she would feel compelled to protect his Government. After all, he had appointed her.[104] Such a speculation ignores Roma Mitchell's rectitude and commitment to justice. It also ignores her refusal of the traditional alignments of party politics: 'I've never had any political affiliations. I've never been interested in politics really', she declared.[105] If there were any extraneous impetus for her in taking on this commission, it was her desire to protect those who depended upon her, even when such dependence was never spelled out. A feminist she was, certainly. But she was also as strongly an individualist as was John Bray. And she let Bray know what her reasons had been for taking on the Salisbury Commission.

After it was all over, she wrote to him. 'I had no objection to your showing Peter [Ward] a copy of the report', she noted, though she added, 'Indeed I assumed that you would use your discretion as to whether to burden him with it or not.' She believed, she told him, that all her findings were 'inevitable upon the evidence', and she 'endeavoured to make them as mild as possible'. But then she let him know of the tension she had suffered in weighing her loyalty to him in a balance against her commitment to the law, of the strain of choosing between her achieved status as an insider and her belief in justice. 'My own wish' she continued,

> would have been not to have accepted the Royal Commission. I knew that I must receive opprobrium from one quarter or another and this has not been entirely absent. But I hoped that I could avoid any adverse publicity for you which would have been monstrously unfair. And I was not confident that anyone who was not fully apprised of the disgraceful performance of the then Police Commissioner and others in 1967 would have done this. As it was, with the assistance of counsel, and by dint of interrupting one or two willing witnesses I succeeded in this and in my view any subsequent vilification was a small price.

To this startlingly uncompromising admission, she then added what can only be construed as a reprimand for Peter Ward. 'I am quite unable to understand how any friend of yours could have put you in danger of false reports as to your behaviour whatever the reason for the newspaper articles.' 'Yours', she concluded, 'Roma'.[106] She forgave Ward, though, he told us. Two years later, she took him and John Bray to lunch in a restaurant in Hutt Street, and apologised to Peter Ward. 'She even cried'.[107]

There is, of course, a great silence at the heart of these events, a silence that changing times can now render voluble. In 1978, the same year as the new legislation was passed allowing the government to dismiss the commissioner of police, John Jefferson Bray CJ retired, four years ahead of time, his health beginning to fail and his desire to write becoming imperative.[108] At the beginning of the next year, on 15 February 1979, Don Dunstan resigned as Premier of South Australia on the grounds of ill health. The Golden Years of the Bray Court and the Dunstan Decade were over. Roma Mitchell could only have been grieved at the damage done to such giants of those times by the longstanding prohibition on homosexual relations, and at the limits to her ability to take care of them. All the stronger an imperative, this was then, to reform the law in this as in so many other ways.

Chapter Seven
Roma the Reformer

Punishment vs Reform: The Theory

Careful, her Honour the Judge might have been. Careful of her friends, her family, her Associates, taking care of them, protecting them; people in the legal profession in the eastern states referred to her as 'Auntie Judge'. Careful of her own reputation. But she was also and at the same time, courageous, even daring.

Roma Mitchell had made her way from the ranks of the Catholic Outsiders into the heartland of the Protestant Adelaide Establishment, and she had taken her Catholicism with her, defining for herself a place in which 'Catholic' did not mean 'anti-British' or 'disloyal', indeed could include the ecumenical. Always ambitious, she had also created a place for herself – a woman – in a world peopled almost exclusively by men, certainly dominated by men. In doing so, she had created a new way of being a professional person, for herself and for other women.

She was proud of pioneering a new kind of womanhood. In her scrapbook, she pasted a clipping from the National Times *describing her as 'the uncontested godmother and pathfinder for women in the [legal] profession'. Another clipping, also in her scrapbook, from the Adelaide* Advertiser, *was headed 'They Sought New Fields'. It noted her first as a silk. And then it surrounded her with other pioneering women: in*

Science, Dr Violet Plummer, a founding member of the Women's Non-Party Political Association and the first woman to practise medicine in Adelaide; South Australia's first policewoman, Kate Cocks; May Douglas, the only Australian to serve in the four women's services and the first woman in South Australia to become a lieutenant colonel; and under the heading 'Politics' it produced an extensive list beginning with Catherine Helen Spence, 'the Grand Old Woman' of Australasia, and concluding with Joyce Steele and Jessie Cooper.

Pioneering a new kind of womanhood was not for the timid, the fainthearted, the cautious. It required confidence, a sang-froid, *a willingness to stand – not alone, but in a place that she had fashioned for herself, among friends she had chosen for herself. 'Why should* I *be modest!' she was to exclaim.*

'I'm sure religion has helped', she was to observe. 'It is always there, somewhere in the background'. She never missed Sunday Mass, and attended Mass on weekdays as often as possible. As central to her being as breathing was her faith. She adjourned the court in Mount Gambier in June 1969 so she could attend a special Requiem Mass for Senator Robert Kennedy at St Paul's Church.

There was the memory of her mother, too.

There was also modesty and generosity alongside her ambition and pride. Not for her the claims associated with some, that their exceptional eminence was a just reward for their exceptional abilities. 'I certainly don't take the attitude, "I got there, you can get there too"', she commented. There was no question about Roma Mitchell's abilities. But she was far more inclined to emphasise hard work as the means to achievement and recognition, and to allude to the support of an imagined collectivity – 'Other trailblazers encouraged me', she said, going on to mention Thursday Girl, Dumps Somerville, by then in her nineties. Miss Mitchell and some other women lawyers arranged an annual dinner for women law students and articled clerks, a gathering that introduced them to women already practising the law; some gained offers of articles from those occasions. She gave good parties, herself, generous in her hospitality; she was famous for pouring gin-and-tonics that were half gin. She took care of her Associates, bossing them, teaching them to laugh at pretension, and to relish her own ready wit. People spoke of her trademark chortle. She made friends with other high-achieving women, recognising the element of loneliness in their distinction: Fay Gale, for many years the first and only woman at Adelaide University to have achieved the rank of Professor; ten years later, Mary O'Kane, the first woman to be Vice-Chancellor of Adelaide University.

A colleague during the 1980s, Human Rights Commissioner Elizabeth Hastings, was to write of Roma Mitchell as though appreciating a fine wine.

> *When I was still young enough to enjoy cask and flagon wine, I would often give consideration to what makes a person desirable. In those days I thought it would be quick wit, preferably a bit wicked; intelligence and incisive thinking; professional success and confidence; and independence of mind. All of these Roma has in abundance. As I have grown older and my taste in wine and people has matured, my list has developed somewhat and now includes kindness and generosity of heart; warmth towards and interest in other people; dignity of bearing and autonomy of action; firmness of resolve and strength of spirit. All these, too, are integral to Roma's being. The characteristics at the top of these tasting notes are kindness, and generosity of heart.*

Generosity: taking care. It was a habit of the heart that impelled her to take advantage of her own eminence to make her world a better place – more just, more helpful – and more fun. And her world stretched from the law in all its ramifications to her own carefully guarded private life.

The law concerning crime and punishment in common law jurisdictions oscillates between two poles: retribution and rehabilitation. Retribution – punishment – emphasises the offence rather than the offender, and seeks to take revenge upon the offender for his or her offence against society and its law. Retribution is associated with notions of deterrence; punishments are supposed to 'fit' the crime in ways that deter other people from committing them. Rehabilitation – reform – at the opposite pole, focuses primarily upon offenders and how they think about their actions and place in society; rehabilitation endeavours to find ways of reforming offenders so that they can resume a place in society and fill it usefully, refraining from committing any more crimes.

Attitudes to the law concerning crime and punishment likewise oscillate between these two poles. At times, the complete independence of the judiciary from other arms of government, combined with the – apparently contradictory – involvement of both government and judiciary in administering the law concerning crime and punishment produces conflict. A government committed to a strong law-and-order policy emphasising retribution for a wrong committed may find itself in conflict with a judiciary passing a minimal sentence on an offender whom the court perceives as likely to respond positively to merciful treatment. And vice versa. Conversely, there are times at which both governments (and the people who elect them) and the judiciary converge in a view of how the criminal law and the penal system should function. Such a convergence occurred in South Australia in the late 1960s and early 1970s.

Indeed, there were demands for change to the criminal law and penal systems at this time across the western world. The National Deviancy Conference in Britain, the Radical Criminologists in the United States, Michel Foucault's illuminating analysis of 'the birth of the prison' in France, all produced sweeping critiques of assumptions governing current policing and punishing practices.[1] Yet again, the highly local narrative of Roma Mitchell's life is also, and simultaneously, a story about shifts and changes across the globe. In Australia, reform was held to be imperative. The Commonwealth Government of Gough Whitlam swept into action. One of its first acts after convening Parliament in February 1973 was to introduce legislation abolishing capital punishment in the Territories and under Commonwealth law.[2] It went on to eliminate appeals from the High Court to the Privy Council in England, an assertion of national independence; to establish the Federal Court of Australia (to be next in seniority to the High Court, and to take over part of the High Court's jurisdiction and all of the jurisdiction of the Australian Industrial Court and of the Federal Court of Bankruptcy), a streamlining effort; and to set up the Commonwealth Law Reform Commission. It also moved into the field of human relations, passing the *Racial Discrimination Act* of 1975, and the *Family Law Act* that, in 1976, established a new federal Family Court. All the work that had formed the bulk of Roma Mitchell's practice as a solicitor and barrister concerned with matrimonial matters in the Supreme Court of South Australia was, from this time on, the work of a new federal jurisdiction, initially headed by Justice Elizabeth Evatt.[3]

Reform of the criminal law and penal system had been on the agenda in South Australia since the horrors of the Stuart case in the late 1950s. The appointment of Norval Morris as Bonython Professor of Law at almost the same time, and the expansion of the staff of the Law School, brought a breath of fresh air to legal education in Adelaide; one of Morris's students described his arrival as 'comparable to the advent of colour T.V.'.[4] Morris moved on in 1961, to Melbourne University, then, following appointments in London, Harvard and Tokyo, to become Julius Kreeger Professor of Law and Criminology at the University of Chicago. But in 1970, he and Gordon Hawkins, Professor of Criminology at Sydney University, published a book called *The Honest Politician's Guide to Crime Control*. This was an extreme version of the rehabilitation approach to their subject.

'The first principle of our cure for crime is this: we must strip off the moral excrescences on our criminal justice system so that it may concentrate on the essential.' The criminal law's prime function, they continued, is to protect persons and property. It should not be intruding upon the 'spheres of private morality and social welfare'; when it does so, 'it exceeds its proper limits at the cost of neglecting its primary tasks', and that makes it 'expensive, ineffective, and criminogenic'.[5] They went on to make an extremely persuasive case for decriminalising public drunkenness; the acquisition, purchase, possession and use of any drug (though they excluded dealing in drugs); gambling; disorderly conduct and vagrancy; abortion; sexual activities between consenting adults; juvenile delinquency (which rendered criminal a whole array of behaviours that were not crimes if performed by adults); and for establishing a 'Standing Law Revision Committee'. This would, they maintained, halve the swollen number of arrests currently being made.[6] They criticised alarmist and misleading announcements about the numbers and costs of criminality, mocking research into the causes of crime, as though criminality were akin to a disease infecting individuals, and quoting Lord Atkins (Lord of Appeal in Ordinary in Britain from 1928 until his death in 1944):

> The domain of criminal jurisprudence can only be ascertained by examining what acts at any particular period are declared by the State to be crimes, and the only common nature they will be found to possess is that they are prohibited by the State and that those who commit them are punished.[7]

They did not abandon social regulation altogether; they recommended the introduction of breathalysers and a minimum sentence of twelve months' disqualification from driving for anyone found driving with a blood alcohol content greater than 0.08 per cent. But in relation to punishments – prison is at present, they observed, 'the core of the penal system'[8] – they sought to eliminate prisons almost entirely, abolishing imprisonment instead of bail before trial; introducing community treatment programs instead of institutionalisation for those offenders convicted of minor offences, the majority of offenders; and building a new set of penal institutions to house only felons convicted of an offence carrying no less than one year's imprisonment as its penalty. Those prisons should have 'modern industrial programs', and imprisonment should be accompanied by expanded work release, graduated release and furloughs that would necessitate a major increase in the number of probation and parole officers, and the availability of probation and parole programs.[9]

Don Dunstan had wanted to set about reforming the law as soon as he gained power. He was still Attorney-General in Walsh's Cabinet when he asked the newly appointed Justice Mitchell to chair a committee on law reform. She was too new, she decided, sensibly, and suggested that he ask a more senior judge. Accordingly, it was David Hogarth who headed the committee established in 1967 to streamline South Australia's criminal law and court procedures, removing unnecessary old offences. But the government fell before he was able to make any recommendations.

The Liberal-Country League Government of Steele Hall undertook its own reforms: three innovations introduced chiefly to speed up the work of an over-burdened criminal court, among them the *Prisons Act Amendment Act* (no. 2) 1969 that established a Parole Board.[10] This Government also introduced the appointment of Acting Justices to ease the workload of members already on the Bench. Howard Zelling, for instance, was an Acting Justice from 27 March to 22 October 1969 before being appointed to the Bench on 23 October 1969; Andrew Wells acted for seven months before gaining permanent appointment on 21 May 1970; Keith Sangster acted for seven months during 1970–1971, and was then appointed to the Bench on 24 June 1971.[11] Zelling was appointed to chair the Law Reform Committee of South Australia as well. A body concerned principally with the civil law, it continued its work under the Governments of Don Dunstan when he returned to power in 1970.[12]

Dunstan had read Morris and Hawkins's book, published in Australia in 1971. What he wanted to achieve, once he was back at the helm, was nothing less than reform of the entire criminal law and punishment system to bring it into line with prevailing social conditions and knowledge.[13] Could his Attorney-General, Len King, tackle Roma Mitchell again? King needed little prompting. He had been a member of the Law Society's Committee on Law Reform throughout the 1960s. And he had known Roma Mitchell for decades. She would be a good choice. She had

> a practical humanity, a deep and abiding sympathy with the weaknesses of those who come before the court, and with the hardships and vicissitudes of the lives of many of them, a sympathy qualified nevertheless by realistic understanding of the requirements of justice.[14]

This time she assented: 'Oh all right then, I have been on the Bench long enough'.[15]

The Criminal Law and Penal Methods Reform Committee was gazetted on 14 December 1971 with Justice Mitchell in its chair.[16] There were two other members. Colin Howard was Hearn Professor of Law at the University of Melbourne. He had a Master of Laws from London University, a PhD from Adelaide University and a Doctorate in Laws from Melbourne University, and had spent time as Visiting Fellow at Harvard Law School and Visiting Professor at the Texas and Wayne Law Schools in the United States. He was also author of several books, including one titled simply *The Criminal Law* – 'the standard text on criminal law and constitutional law then being used in Australian universities'[17] – which was in its second edition in 1970, and its third by the time the committee submitted its fourth and final report in 1977.[18]

David Biles's inclusion gave earnest of the breadth of scope intended for this inquiry, for his qualifications were in psychology, rather than law. Senior Lecturer in Criminology at Melbourne University, he had a Master of Arts from La Trobe University and a Bachelor of Education from Melbourne University.[19] He had helped establish education systems in several Victorian prisons, and was interested in the operation of correctional systems, the effectiveness of prisons, and the parole of offenders. They were to be paid: Howard would earn $3000 a year and Biles $1800. Justice Mitchell chose not to accept remuneration for this work.[20]

Geoff Muecke, later a judge in the District Court of South Australia, was seconded from the Attorney-General's office to be their Secretary and Research Officer. He was to comment:

> Roma Mitchell and Colin Howard shared a mutual respect ... It was a privilege, and somewhat disconcerting sometimes, to watch debate between them during meetings of the committee. There was sometimes a clash of wills between the fine minds of these two members, but there was never a clash of respect.

He thought David Biles a 'practical and friendly man' who made 'an immense contribution'. Biles and Roma Mitchell formed 'a close and enduring friendship'.[21]

They worked extremely hard. All of them continued in their other, full-time jobs; Howard retired from the committee early, but only a couple of months before they had finished their final report. Over five-and-a-half years, they received and considered submissions from around 170 organisations and individuals, interviewed ninety people, received suggestions from around twenty judges, justices and magistrates, and visited twenty-three prisons and police cells in South Australia and twenty-six institutions and people in an eight-day whistle-stop journey to New Zealand. Justice Mitchell also visited three prisons when she was in England in August 1972. At all of the prisons and other institutions they visited they met prisoners – without prison officers or officials being present – and talked with them informally. They read an immense body of statute and case law, and literature on the law, police and correctional systems, providing themselves with interstate and international comparisons, and – unusually for lawyers – historical comparisons as well. They produced four reports – on *Sentencing and Corrections*, on *Criminal Investigation*, on *Court Procedure and Evidence*, and on *The Substantive Criminal Law* – and a total of 907 recommendations. Len King was to praise Roma Mitchell's 'prodigious and perspicacious labours' in this work.[22]

Their reports provide an illuminating insight into the social order of their times. They consider the place of legal sanctions in that order – their limitations as well as their capacities. They describe the delicate balance between popular opinion and emotion, government policy, the operation of the criminal law and penal system, and the welfare of people who fall foul of the criminal law. They also offer insight into the political and intellectual world, the world of the imagination of the three authors, and – since many of their examples allude to real cases – their experience, too. They are, in terms of the polar opposition between retributors and rehabilitators – punishers and reformers – firmly aligned with the reformers. Yet, at the same time, they affirm the centrality of the courts and the process of adversary trial against any more radical reforms that might be suggested. Pragmatic, perhaps. Realistic, certainly. Here we meet Roma Mitchell the reformer. She was not a radical – opined labour lawyer Gordon Barrett QC (later a judge) – any more than was John Bray. But, Barrett then added, she was the more reforming.[23]

The Mitchell Committee's world is already a thoroughly liberal consensus society, 'basically orderly and self-regulating' with 'well-established conventions for the transfer of political power', so 'Australians accept that as much scope for individual freedom of action should be allowed' as is compatible with maintaining widely accepted rules of communal conduct. The law, police, courts and prisons assist in maintaining those rules, and helping to preserve public order and decorum. Most offences against such rules are slight; people who seriously infringe against the criminal law constitute 'a small minority'. The police, the courts and the penal processes all – usually – enjoy support from the community, and they, in turn, support the community by imposing sanctions upon people convicted of offences. In a democracy, sanctions need to satisfy the voting citizens, as well as to protect them from danger.[24]

The committee makes an uncompromising statement of faith.

> The purpose of adversary trial is to test the evidence. It is a basic principle of justice in common law courts, and one which we have no intention of departing from, that a person accused of a criminal offence must be proved guilty before he can be lawfully convicted, as opposed to his being required to disprove the accusation before he can be lawfully acquitted. In our opinion no better way has yet been devised of testing the adequacy of the case advanced by the prosecution than subjecting it to adversary contest by the defendant before an impartial tribunal.[25]

Later, they elaborate.

> No member of the committee has had personal experience of working in a system often referred to as 'inquisitorial', in which there is a judicial investigation of the case for the prosecution and for the defence before the trial, and a report of the investigation is prepared for the trial judge who then conducts the questioning at the trial on the basis of the report.[26]

No-one has suggested to them that the inquisitorial system be introduced, so they abide by their initial view: the adversarial trial is the best possible system. This is their foundation stone. Upon this they build structures that, carefully – but not cautiously – challenge the status quo.

Their concerns are of the moment. South Australia in the 1970s is 'a modern developed community', they declare. In 'the courts of today', their reports announce, 'modern sentencing policy' focuses on the offender rather than the offence. They illustrate their point graphically in relation to criteria for imposing prison sentences.

> Age, present and probable future personal circumstances, and presence or absence of a previous criminal record are relevant. And perhaps most important of all, the circumstances under which the offence was committed ... the circumstances may be unique, as where a son seeks to defend one parent against the other and in the heat of the moment goes too far; or where distress at the sufferings of a close and loved relative brings resort to euthanasia; or where an unlawful homicide is

> committed because of an overstrained personal relationship between the offender and the deceased.

Further, they observe,

> Danger to the public can be a concept which goes beyond physical violence. It can reasonably be argued that large-scale fraud or theft, drunken and dangerous driving and the sale of dangerous drugs are activities sufficiently dangerous to the public to justify imprisoning an offender if there appears to be no other way of protecting the community from him.[27]

Indeed, this committee has decided that any effort to make the punishment fit the crime, rather than the criminal offender, 'implies a certain primitiveness of thought' in relation to sentencing people convicted of criminal offences. '[S]entencing is a matter which gives rise to strong emotions', they note: rage, grief, shame, desire for revenge – just for instance. 'Strong emotions produce a yearning for simple solutions.' But 'there are no simple solutions'. So, in a recommendation that, this time, runs directly counter to those of Morris and Hawkins, who had argued for sentences to be fixed by legislation, that is, by statute, they decide that sentencing is best made the exclusive prerogative of the courts, accustomed as they are to the complexities of the common law. Statute law should be confined to prescribing maximum sentences, or fixed sentences only for such summary offences as are connected with road traffic legislation. One of the 'main avenues of advance in correctional methods' in 'the present day', they announce, is 'the recognition of variations between offenders as well as between offences'.[28]

The people passing sentences are still to be the judges and magistrates, then. But the judges and magistrates are to be brought up to date. There has been criticism of judicial sentencing. Individual differences of judicial personality may result in very different sentences, even though both offender and offence are similar. Judges may impose sentences with far too little knowledge of the offender's personality or background, or with too little knowledge of the actual working of the correctional system to which an offender is consigned by his sentence. Judges and magistrates don't know enough criminology to make the best use of information provided to them, even when that information is in itself adequate. The Mitchell Committee review these criticisms and decide that they are grounds for improving the practice of judges rather than grounds for replacing the courts with any other sentencing authority (they are very rude about the new Parole Board). Accordingly, they draw attention to 'an effective machinery of appeal', and recommend that judges attend seminars on sentencing and make regular visits to correctional institutions.[29]

In such a modern, and modernising, society, views are changing, and that should require a review of the whole of the criminal law, not only to make it 'more accessible' but also to 'facilitate its natural development as a consensus of the community'. The changing times appear in advances in medical science, making it possible to 'keep people technically alive', something that then has bearing on questions about the cause of death. The changing times appear in their observation that

> the view that the consent to sexual intercourse given upon marriage cannot be revoked during the subsistence of the marriage is not in accord with modern thinking. In this community today it is anachronistic to suggest that a wife is bound to submit to intercourse with her husband whenever he wishes it irrespective of her own wishes.

In these times, there are 'newer forms of dishonesty which have been promoted by the advent of computers, credit cards and the increasing tendency towards the provision of goods and services on trust that the consumer will pay'; the defects in the present law in relation to theft, they comment, 'are that it is unduly complex, lacks coherence in its basic elements and has not kept up to date with techniques of dishonesty'. The police agree with them, they observe, quoting a paper on 'Tomorrow's Policeman' that Commissioner Salisbury presented to a conference in 1974: 'it must be anticipated that the rate of serious crime may increase'; 'the offences of housebreaking and office breaking become more rife with the expansion of the city'.[30]

So, now, as ever, there needs to be a delicate balance maintained between, on the one hand, a police force that enjoys general support in the community, such support making the task of the police easier, and, on the other hand, a police force whose efficiency in detection and prosecution of crime could encroach upon 'the degree of individual freedom of action which we wish to preserve'. 'If every person who drove his motor car away from licensed premises at closing time were followed by a uniformed policeman driving closely behind him', they suggest, by way of example, 'it may be that the incidence of traffic accidents would decline, but the community at large would not be likely to endure such a surveillance if it were made a permanent police duty'. Similarly, the committee refers explicitly to the Vietnam moratorium demonstration of 18 September 1970 and police activity that was perceived as having 'political overtones', the ensuing Bright Royal Commission, and the amending legislation following Charles Bright's recommendations. They then discuss 'those street offences which may have political implications and which in our view warrant amendment', and proceed – sounding just like Morris and Hawkins, and Don Dunstan in the 1960s – to recommend abolition of the offences of loitering and behaving in a disorderly manner, and moderation of rules governing distribution of literature in the streets and removal of unruly people in a meeting. Their survey of Police Offences likewise leads them to recommend eliminating a list of offences that are quite simply out of date. They also consider that good will towards the police would be enhanced if someone else were to take charge of giving driving tests and tests of road-worthiness of cars, acting as court orderlies, clerks of court, bailiffs, and issuing 'bull, dairy and bee licenses'. It would be less costly, too, they note, a touch recalling Justice Mitchell's argument for women on juries to Tom Playford, and her consistent efforts to keep clients' costs to a minimum. But they recommend, as well, toughening some provisions: 'assault punishable by law' should include verbal assault, and the police should be empowered to remove to a safe place anyone whose presence 'arouses hostility in a crowd'.[31]

In general, they reiterate, the police need to be far better educated; the current requirement for recruitment is only three years of secondary schooling. Exchanges with other police forces would bring in 'new ideas' and provide an 'antidote to inbreeding', they observe, a glancing reference to the inward-looking and smug self-referentiality that Roma Mitchell would encounter a few years later when she was sitting as a Royal Commission into the dismissal of Police Commissioner Salisbury. It has already been decided to expand the role of women within the police force, but this needs to allow for women to be employed 'in the ordinary work' of the force, as well as in specialist 'preventive and general social work'. Further, they observe that the police find 'considerable difficulty in its relations with the aboriginal population of South Australia'.

> The aborigine is likely to see the policeman as a representative of the white Australian and as not representing the aborigine. This situation might change if a sufficient number of aborigines became and remained members of the Police Force.[32]

It is a hope, but a forlorn one. There *are* Aboriginal members of the police force in the early twenty-first century, but not enough to achieve the effects that the Mitchell Committee hoped for.

The Mitchell Committee's overall alignment with the reformers causes them to give an associated emphasis to what they refer to as 'the mental element', the '*mens rea*', the state of mind of the accused. The 'main line of evolution', they note in relation to the law relating to murder, quoting Sir Owen Dixon (who sat on the High Court from 1929, and was Chief Justice from 1952 until his retirement in 1964),[33] is a shift from 'an almost exclusive concern with the external act which occasioned death to a primary concern with the mind of the man who did the act'; a concern with the offender, rather than the offence. They repeat the point in their recommendation that 'assaults be defined in terms of intention and recklessness'. Similarly, in relation to rape, they quote South Australian Justice Andrew Wells noting that

> It may, at first sight, appear strange that none of the traditional definitions – I should rather call them descriptions – of rape contained an overt reference to a guilty mind.[34]

But in relation to this offence, the need to establish the state of mind of the accused causes some difficulty.

They prepared their chapter on 'Rape and Other Sexual Offences' in their Fourth Report initially in response to a request from a new Attorney-General, Peter Duncan – Len King having moved on from Parliament to the Bench – on 2 December 1975.

Peter Duncan was a young firebrand – only thirty years old in 1975 – with a background in student politics, Young Labor and opposition to the war in Vietnam while he was taking his Law degree at Adelaide University during the 1960s. After a couple of false starts, he won Labor Party endorsement and then a seat in the South Australian Parliament for the northern satellite city of Elizabeth in the election on 10 March 1973.[35] He resigned his membership of the Law Society when he entered Parliament, considering there was a conflict of interest in belonging to both bodies at the same time. A radical reformist, he embraced elements of the politics of the social movements of the 1970s, campaigning for rights for homosexuals and for women, and against capital punishment and uranium mining. Once elected, he did more than campaign. Twice he introduced legislation to decriminalise homosexual behaviour between men, finally succeeding in having his bill passed in 1975. He was not responsible for the *Sex Discrimination Act* of 1975, which prohibited 'less favourable treatment of women (and men) which proceeds from sex-based stereotypes of people's social status and capabilities',[36] but he became the minister responsible for the Commission for Equal Opportunity that that legislation set up, for on 9 October 1975, he joined the Dunstan Cabinet as Attorney-General. His was the bill to abolish capital punishment, as recommended by the Mitchell Committee,[37] introduced in November 1976. And he was one of the prime movers in the formation of the Labor Against Uranium Group in August 1979, anticipating – though mistakenly, as it turned out – that Premier Dunstan might have reversed his own opposition to uranium mining during his visit to Europe, to check out reports on safe disposal of high-level atomic wastes in Sweden.[38] Duncan would go on to membership of the Federal Labor Party Governments of R.J. Hawke during the 1980s. His request to the Mitchell Committee followed a public outcry about the law relating to rape.

The occasion was an English case, *D.P.P. v. Morgan*, in 1975.[39] A member of the Royal Air Force, a man, invited three of his friends, also men and members of the RAF, to his house specifically to have sex with his wife. He had persuaded his mates that his wife was a willing participant in the occasion by telling them not to be surprised if she struggled a bit 'as she was "kinky" and this was "what turned her on"'. In the events that happened, observed the Mitchell Committee, 'it appeared that the wife was subjected to what must have been a horrible ordeal'.[40] The four men were convicted of rape, but then appealed their convictions. Five Law Lords were divided in their determination on the appeal. Three held that

> if a person accused of rape believed that the woman against whom he was alleged to have committed the crime had consented, whether or not that belief was based on reasonable grounds, he could not be found guilty of rape.[41]

In the press, that judgment was described as 'a green light for rapists'.[42]

It could have been expected that the – reformist – Mitchell Committee would agree with the outcry against those Lords' decision. But they don't. They point out, first, that in spite of the general ruling that the majority of the Law Lords had made, they had rejected the appeal on the ground that 'no reasonable jury would have believed that any of the appellants had an honest belief that the woman consented to the acts of intercourse'.[43] Second, the Mitchell Committee agrees with South Australian Justice Andrew Wells' definition of rape:

> A person commits rape when he has unlawful ... carnal knowledge of a female without her consent, knowing that she is not consenting, or recklessly indifferent as to whether she is consenting or not.

The rapist's *mens rea* is reckless indifference. Third, they note that 'where the alleged victim has voluntarily accompanied the accused and has consented to some form of familiarity, and there is no credible evidence of the use of force or threats, the Crown has a difficult task in establishing that the woman was not consenting to sexual intercourse'. This is the phenomenon that feminist journalist Anne Summers referred to as 'petty rape' or 'rape by fraud'.[44]

The Mitchell Committee considers that 'this should continue to be the situation'. Why? For two reasons. One is that, they say, 'Rape has always been regarded as a very serious crime. In South Australia the maximum penalty is life imprisonment.' This means, though they do not say so, that juries will be reluctant to convict without proof beyond reasonable doubt. Since juries should not be willing to convict without proof beyond reasonable doubt of *any* crime, no matter what the sentence attached, this could seem a specious argument – if it were not also pragmatic and thence realistic. The second reason is a legal distinction between whether it is the Crown or the victim that has to prove that the accused had 'guilty intent', his state of mind. 'This ingredient', they observe, 'constitutes the *mens rea* of the offence'. That is, not his determination to have sex with the woman, but his determination to do so against her consent, or whether she consented or not. They point out:

> If the onus of establishing that he believed that the woman was consenting was cast upon the accused, then the Crown would bear the burden of proving only that the accused had unlawful carnal knowledge of the woman, that is that he had sexual intercourse with her ... and that she did not consent to such intercourse. The Crown would be absolved from the obligation which it now has to establish a guilty intention on the part of the accused.

And that, they decide, is 'in principle' wrong. For the criminal law does not require an accused to defend himself against accusations of 'negligence or unreasonable belief' in relation to any other offence carrying so serious a sentence. Besides, it was asking too much of a jury to require them to decide whether or not the accused's belief in the woman's consent was reasonable or reckless.

They anticipate objections to their view. Sometimes, they observe, a rape trial is regarded as a 'contest' between 'the prosecutrix and the accused', and this means that the acquittal of the accused is seen as being 'in some way a censure of the prosecutrix'. This is wrong. It 'is no more the case than the acquittal of a person charged with murder on the ground that the act which caused the death was not the voluntary act of the accused is in any way an impugnment of the deceased'. Then, to emphasise their point, they suggest that 'the general public' doesn't understand that what is at issue in a trial on a charge of rape is a conflict between the Crown and the accused, not between the victim and the accused. It follows, they continue, that

> as far as the law is concerned, the verdict of not guilty results in no consequences to the prosecutrix, whereas the verdict of guilty is likely to result in a severe penalty being imposed upon the accused.

They accept that the 'prosecutrix' in a rape case may find her reputation 'defiled by an act of intercourse which took place against her will'. Unenviable, they decide.

> An attitude towards the victim of rape which regards her as soiled by the act of rape should change, but this is not a reason to require a less stringent standard of proof of this offence than of any other less serious offence carrying a penalty of lengthy imprisonment.[45]

But there is more to this chapter in the Mitchell Committee's *Fourth Report* than that last, distinctly helpless, observation. Later, they give considerable attention to the victim's 'ordeal', and her further ordeal when endeavouring to report it. They make recommendations about how the police and the medical profession might be trained to treat a complainant with respect and sympathy. And they draw attention to their earlier recommendation that the right of the accused to make an unsworn statement to the jury be abolished.[46] It must be, they observe,

> a most unedifying spectacle for a jury to see and listen to a young girl, the prosecutrix in a charge of rape, being stringently cross-examined and subsequently to hear the accused merely read a statement giving his version of what happened without being exposed to any questioning at all.[47]

Further, this committee takes time to consider a question for which they and the Dunstan Government – or rather, Duncan – becomes famous. This is the question of rape in marriage. The Mitchell Committee's very attention to such an idea is radical; their decision about it, though, is much less so: a husband may be charged with rape of his wife, they decide, but only if he and his wife are living apart.[48]

They are far less cautious in their discussion of sentencing. Sentences, of course, include a whole array of determinations, ranging from fines through probation, suspended sentences and parole to imprisonment. Here, in their first report, appears one of the imperatives for the Mitchell Committee being set up. For, even though they declare the chief goal of 'modern sentencing policy' to be not sending offenders to prison, but, on the contrary, 'wherever possible keeping them out of prison', they do not see an end to the need for incarceration: inevitably, some offenders are going to fetch up in the prison system. And that, in South Australia in 1972, is in an appalling condition.[49]

There are eight prisons: the Adelaide Gaol, a half-panopticon structure on the north-west edge of the city; Yatala Labour Prison on the northern outskirts of the Adelaide suburbs; prisons in Mount Gambier in the south-east of the state; in Gladstone in the north; in Port Lincoln and in Port Augusta, the industrial 'iron triangle' in the north-west; the Cadell Training Centre on the River Murray; and the Women's Rehabilitation Centre, also on the northern edges of the Adelaide suburbs. Conditions in these institutions vary wildly.

Adelaide Gaol, published with permission of the Adelaide City Council

> Some prisoners spend up to 17 hours a day in solitary confinement in their cells while others are housed in pleasant dormitories and are never isolated. Some buildings of recent construction are almost lavish in their facilities while others are so old and dilapidated that … their conversion into museums appears to be the only reasonable course of action. Some prisoners are kept hard at work while others are idle. Some prisoners are studied and classified while others are perfunctorily

> assigned to places and tasks. Some prisoners are encouraged to improve their education while for others there are no educational facilities available. Some prisoners occupy single cells with pleasant furniture, toilet, wash-basin and two-way radio, while others are crowded four to a cell with none of these facilities.

This immense variation causes 'an understandable sense of injustice' among prisoners in the worse institutions and that 'militates against the attainment of constructive correctional aims'.[50]

Just how bad were conditions in some prisons appears in the Committee's recommendation that 'minimum standards of accommodation' should be provided 'with the least possible delay'. What they had in mind, they state, are 'such simplicities as adequate ventilation, sewerage, light, room, a degree of privacy, and reasonable facilities for reading and study'. And when those 'simplicities' have been provided, then there are such matters as properly balanced diets, medical, dental, optical and psychiatric services, and a staff of prison officers large enough to allow its members to have proper entitlements to rostered duty and leave. At Adelaide Gaol, the committee notes, pre-trial defendants who have not been granted bail are locked in their cells for an 'indefensible' proportion of each day, because of the shortage of prison officers. Such observations make the Committee's earlier recommendations for the establishment of post-secondary-school education courses for prison officers sound utterly utopian, since it emerges that most of the prison officers currently employed in such grossly inadequate numbers have not even completed their secondary schooling.[51]

A twenty-first-century reader not acquainted with any elements of the history of prisons turns the pages of this report with growing horror. The chapter concerning what the Mitchell Committee wants to call the Department of Correctional Services – rather than the Prisons Department – concludes tellingly by noting that the legislation governing the prison system and its regulations is 'absurdly out of date', that this is 'undesirable ... in any part of the law', and that it is even more so 'when questions of liberty and human rights are affected'. They recommend that new legislation be framed and minimum standards for prison administration be set, paying close attention to the *Standard Minimum Rules for the Treatment of Prisoners and Related Recommendations*, issued by the Department of Economic and Social Affairs of the United Nations in New York as long ago as 1958.[52] Things are clearly in an indefensibly atrocious condition.

But there is yet worse to come.

The *First Report* concludes with the chapter, 'Special Problems'. These are endured by the Aboriginal peoples of South Australia.

> Aborigines in South Australia, as in all other mainland States and the Northern Territory, are poor in circumstance, opportunity and economy. The reasons are embedded in the history of this country and are not admirable. Conditions have not been improved significantly by measures taken in recent years by federal and State governments or by private organizations ... South Australia shares with the rest of the nation a history of neglect and ill-treatment of aborigines, and of discrimination against them.

However, South Australia's criminal law is 'not founded on criteria of racial discrimination'. On the contrary: 'it is unlawful to discriminate against aborigines or other racial minorities'. Yet Aboriginal people form an entirely disproportionate component of the prison population in this state in 1972 as they still do in the early years of the twenty-first century.

In a total population of approximately 1.2 million people, Aboriginal South Australians number about 9100, that is approximately three-quarters of one per cent. By the end of the 1960s, twenty-five per cent of men admitted to prison were Aboriginal, and that proportion 'continues to rise', observes the Mitchell Committee. Figures for women in prison in 1972 show Aboriginal women to be more than half that population; in Port Augusta they are almost the entire population of women in the prison.

The Committee members acknowledge that the causes of this deplorable state of affairs lie largely outside the scope of the criminal law and its enforcement, and so, too, outside their own terms of reference. But they nevertheless draw attention to it, forcefully and in some detail. They make recommendations for immediate action, and even utter a threat. Their recommendations are three: 'minor palliatives', they remark ruefully. First, they note that public drunkenness is 'overwhelmingly' the most common offence among Aborigines and recommend abolishing public drunkenness as an offence against the law. Such a measure would halve the number of Aboriginal people in prison. They go on to urge establishment of detoxification centres, 'State-owned overnight houses for insensible and exhausted drunks', and associated regulations for running them. Here, they echo Morris and Hawkins again, but with entirely different and far more imperative reason. Second, they recommend that 'far greater use be made than at present of supervised probation' instead of short-term imprisonment for Aboriginal people. Third, they recommend that separate statistics be kept of Aboriginal offenders, particularly those imprisoned. 'Whilst we agree with the sentiment which has been expressed to us', they aver, 'that there are no aborigines in prison, only people' – such a 1970s' belief that you can achieve equality by assertion – 'we regard it as a hindrance rather than a help in this particular application'. They observe, too, a fact that finally achieved national attention and concern a decade or so later, that Aboriginal people become depressed when they are locked up in single cells, that they are held in conditions of far greater security than is necessary, and that they would do better if provided with dormitories, lacking in Port Augusta. Further, the committee urges, whether they are concerned with Aborigines in prison or out of it,

> all agents of the law have a special duty to ensure that aborigines who are charged with or convicted of an offence understand what is happening and why. All too often they are inarticulate and ill-informed and unquestioningly accept whatever orders they receive. It is quite possible that many of them are technically unfit to plead because they do not understand the proceedings and have no idea what is the purpose of imprisoning them. These are not reasons for placing them outside the law. They are reasons for taking the view that all law enforcement officers should take a special responsibility for the welfare of these singularly disadvantaged citizens.

Here, at last, we learn what Roma Flinders Mitchell probably thought of the Stuart case at the end of the 1950s.

The Mitchell Committee's threat was to add incentive for urgent steps to be taken immediately. 'The human suffering, social damage, danger to public health and economic waste involved are becoming widely recognized', they observe. 'Moral community responsibility for aborigines as fellow citizens and human beings is generally accepted in principle, even if action does not as yet match aspiration.' But the urgency proceeds from more than morality; politics could be involved as well.

> It would be a simple exercise to present the foregoing data as purported proof that the practical impact of the criminal law is discriminatory. Such a demonstration in the hands of skilled advisers could be a powerful instrument of publicity, the use of which might not always be in the best interests of the aborigines themselves, the community generally or the correctional system.[53]

Do something! And do it now! Or someone will call the whole system into question.

These are the most imperative and straightforward of all of their recommendations. In many other instances, they are more pragmatic. They are – to a twenty-first-century eye – extremely liberal about a person who has committed an offence while 'completely deprived of effective power of control over his actions by provocation, duress or intoxication'; 'he should be acquitted altogether of the offence with which he is charged', they announce.[54]

Being so drunk that you can't control yourself means that you should be acquitted of murdering your wife while in that condition? Apparently so. There are moments when the Law takes a lay person's breath away!

They argue against random breath testing, for instance, saying that such a practice would be an infringement of human rights, and that 'compulsory submission to tests by persons who displayed no aberration from normal driving standards would be liable to rouse animosity in them, and to detract from good public relations of the Police Force with the community'. They recommend both further inquiry into the accuracy of breath analysis and inquiry into the possibility of blood testing instead. In relation to the offence of causing death by dangerous driving, they note that experience has taught them that juries are extremely reluctant to convict a driver of manslaughter and often resort to conviction of a lesser offence, such as driving without due care and attention. 'The case of the motorist has proved to be a very special one in our community', they note. 'If juries have been reluctant to convict homicidally dangerous drivers of manslaughter by criminal negligence, it seems to us unlikely that they will convict the defendant of any other form of manslaughter.' So their determination has to balance that evidence of community attitudes against the logic of the law.

In relation to abortion, they give a summary of the present state of the law, and refer to submissions that they have received, but

> [l]ess for analytical reasons than because ... discussion of abortion tends to raise wide and contentious policy issues, we have concluded that policy recommendations on this subject are beyond our terms of reference.

Yet, they do also 'record our view that the factual assertion that in practice abortion is now obtainable on demand appears to be substantially correct', and they make no recommendation that would alter that state of affairs. Justice Mitchell's Catholicism does not register, here. Similarly, they decide that euthanasia is also beyond their terms of reference, but they note, as well, that under the law as it currently stands it would be possible for a jury to convict someone of a 'mercy killing' and for the court to 'release the offender on parole immediately after the sentence'.[55]

The sentiments of Mitchell, Howard and Biles were, Geoff Muecke recalled, 'novel, even alarming, to many involved in the criminal justice system and to the public in the early 1970s in South Australia'.[56] Some approved of them. Ngaire Naffine, a lawyer attached to the Office of the Women's Adviser to the Premier during the 1980s, considered that several of the Mitchell Committee's decisions in relation to the law concerning rape – extending the definition of sexual intercourse, making rape non-sex specific, and removing the immunity of spouses from prosecution – were unprecedented reforms.[57] Others disagreed. Chief Justice Bray objected strongly to their recommendation to abolish the unsworn statement.[58] Charles Bright observed that while only some of the recommendations were controversial, conservative opposition to them made it difficult to implement even the proposals that were not.[59] And – infuriatingly – the Director of what had been renamed the Department of Correctional Services declared the South Australian prison system 'the best system in Australia', needing little change.[60]

But if the Mitchell Committee upset the conservatives, they did not altogether delight the radicals. Their argument that education should prevent victims of rape feeling defiled is impeccably logical, but utterly antipathetic to other arguments being developed at the time among the radical feminists establishing Rape Crisis Centres in cities across Australia. The Mitchell Committee did invite contributions to their deliberations from women's groups, but they did not receive any; many feminists in the early 1970s would have regarded cooperation with a government enquiry anathema. Similarly, the Committee's relatively sympathetic attitude to persistent sexual offenders, considering them as unfortunates rather than a social menace, would shock early twenty-first-century opinion that has learned to consider many such offences as sexual abuse of children.[61] Peter Duncan decided they had been unduly 'swayed by what they saw as the community attitude' in relation to their recommendation about rape in marriage. He introduced legislation applying all of the Committee's recommendations concerning rape also to rape within marriage. This legislation was passed, attracting intense interest and controversy across the country, indeed across the common law world.[62]

Punishment vs Reform: In Practice

These endeavours were, by any count, an immense work. Roma Mitchell was indisputably on the side of the reformers, but she was cautiously so, and those cautions meant that the Mitchell Committee's recommendations were never as radical as Dunstan had hoped. They would have needed to be less pragmatic, and less protective of the centrality of the judiciary, to have achieved his ambitions, even though many of those recommendations were too controversial to achieve acceptance among conservatives. They would also have needed Dunstan to be in better health than he was by the time the Mitchell Committee presented its final report. It would have helped, too, if Duncan had been closer to his leader than he was finding it possible to be.

Peter Duncan wrote to Dunstan in November 1977 of his 'concern and frustration' over the Mitchell Committee's recommendations. The Premier had referred to them, promising progressive implementation in his policy speeches in each of the elections of March 1973, July 1975 and September 1977, he reminded him. But the recommendations were being stalled by bureaucratic resistance. Efforts to draft a Treatment of Offenders Bill has been brought to a standstill, first by opposition from the Director of Correctional Services, and later, in 1978, by the Chief Secretary arranging a trip to 'undertake a study of the extent to which the Mitchell Committee's Recommendations could and should be revised in the light of developments and experience overseas': 'I personally find it a great embarrassment', Duncan continued,

> to have to defend the prison system in South Australia and the argument that we are in the process of reforming the whole system is wearing very thin after seven years in office and nearly five years since the receipt of the First Report dealing with this matter.

Further, there were likely to be the same kinds of obstructiveness when they tried to implement the recommendations of the *Second Report*, as they would involve the Police Department.[63] Clearly, Duncan had developed as jaundiced a view of the police as Dunstan had himself. But by the time Dunstan received this letter, he was already being plagued by the events that would culminate in the dismissal of Police Commissioner Salisbury.

Despite Duncan's frustration, some of the Mitchell Committee's recommendations did find their way into the statute books. There was the abolition of capital punishment.[64] There were the *Criminal Law (Sexual Offences) Amendment Act* of 1976, the *Evidence Act Amendment Act* and the *Justices Act Amendment Act*, both of 1976, and some recommendations were incorporated in the *Children's Protection and Young Offenders Act* of 1979. Mitchell Committee recommendations continued to be incorporated into legislation, even after the end of the Dunstan Decade,[65] and its reports have been cited by the Law Reform Commission of Western Australia in 1976,[66] the New South Wales Law Reform Commission in 1985, 1996, 1997 and 2003,[67] the Law Reform

Commission of Victoria in 1991,[68] and the Legislative Council Select Committee on Correctional Services and Sentencing in Tasmania in 1998.[69]

These reports and recommendations were influential, no doubt, but they certainly did not become the blueprint for reform of the criminal justice system across Australia as Dunstan and King hoped. Geoff Muecke was to comment that

> There is a real sense in which much of the work of the Mitchell Committee was done too well ... the minds of its chairperson and its members were well ahead of their time. Such was their progressive imagination and foresight that it was probably inevitable that the Mitchell Committee's recommendations would not and could not be implemented other than over a period of several decades.[70]

Peter Duncan, for one, would no doubt have contested such a view.

Events provided a challenging context for the recommendations. One series of events followed the retirement of conservative Sir Roderic Chamberlain from the chair of the new Parole Board. The Mitchell Committee had recommended abolishing the Parole Board altogether and giving its functions to the judiciary. Instead, what the Dunstan Government did was appoint as Chamberlain's replacement the Board's most prominent critic – Justice Mitchell. She must have taken a very deep breath, and then decided that – well, at least questions of granting parole were still to be within the purview of a judge. And being on the Board would give her an opportunity to assist introduction of reforms in the prisons. It was wrong to put a person in prison and then forget about him, she told the *Sunday Mail*. Rather, offenders needed to be retrained during their terms in prison; much more work needed to be done to implement this policy.[71]

Others on the Parole Board when she joined it were a psychiatrist, a trade union representative, a businessman and a psychologist. They met every three weeks. But the Mitchell Committee's recommendations increased the Parole Board's work: prisoners could now appear before the Board, and if their parole was refused, then they had to have the reasons explained to them. Soon Parole Board meetings lasted almost all day. The Committee's recommendations also prompted the Board to 'take a chance on people' if they believed that they could do so without putting the public at risk.[72]

The public, and the press, were quick to make a fuss, though, if ever there was reason to consider that a paroled offender did constitute a public risk. Rupert Max Stuart, for instance – probably the best-known prison inmate in South Australia, ever since the late 1950s – had broken his parole twice before. It could have been thought there was no guarantee that he would not do it again, but Justice Mitchell's Parole Board released him on parole again and defended their decision.[73] She had to defend a Parole Board decision again when, in mid-May 1979, 150 prison officers at Adelaide Gaol and Yatala Labour Prison walked off the job in protest at the parole of a prisoner, convicted of armed robbery, who had taken part in a sit-in at Yatala.[74] However, these occasions shrank in significance when compared with the shocking events that ensued after the release on parole of Christopher Robin Worrell.

A fresh-faced twenty-year-old – his first names evoking the England of Pooh Bear and Piglet and songs of innocence about stairs and prayers – he was first convicted of one count of armed robbery. He had stolen $1.50 from a female hitchhiker. It was his first offence, so his two-year sentence was suspended and he was placed on a good behaviour bond under the supervision of a parole officer. Within three months he was back before the Supreme Court, charged with attempted rape and indecent assault. Justice Sangster called him a 'miserable and contemptible creature', revoked the suspension of his previous sentence, and sentenced him to a further four years' imprisonment. In prison, he met and became close friends with James William Miller.

Worrell's first application for parole was rejected. But his second, after a psychiatric examination, succeeded. He was released on 12 October 1976. In mid-December he joined Miller, working as a labourer for Unley Council. Then, on 20 February 1977, he and his girlfriend were killed in a car accident. But that was only the dreadful beginning of this quite terrible story.

Between 25 April 1978 and 26 April 1979 the bodies of four young women were found near Truro, a small town in the mid-north of South Australia. In May 1979, police interviewed James Miller. He took them to the site at which a fifth body was buried.

By the end of that month, police had found two more bodies. Seven young women, all murdered – the police decided – between December 1976 and February 1977. They accused Miller and Worrell. The murders had begun just ten weeks after Christopher Robin Worrell was released on parole.[75]

Not surprisingly, there was a furore. Letters to the press fulminated. The Secretary of the Police Association announced that there was no confidence in the Parole Board.[76] And when the Liberal Party Government of David Tonkin extended Justice Mitchell's appointment to chair the Parole Board for a further five years, even her friends and former colleagues expostulated. Jessie Cooper MP told Sir Walter Crocker – whom Dunstan had appointed Lieutenant Governor in 1973, finally replacing Mellis Napier – that she was shocked, and Sesca Zelling, at dinner, really let rip. Crocker noted it all with relish.

> Mrs Zelling, a lawyer, said she no longer practices and her health failing (which her appearance bore out). I suspect that Z had little time for Roma Mitchell & no doubt that what Mrs Z said about RM reflected this. She described her as over-rated, trendy, and insatiably ambitious & pushing and also subjective ... Her doings on the Parole Board were lamentable ... The former led Mrs Z to criticize Tonkin for renewing her headship of the Parole Board.[77]

Crocker's own views were entirely patriarchal, often misogynist; over and over again his diary shows him believing that the only truly civilised conversation takes place in the company exclusively of men, or at least when any women present keep silent. It is in accord with such an approach to the world that he attributes Sesca Zelling's views to her husband. And that means that he missed altogether the envy and disappointment rising like a sour steam from the pages on which he inscribed his report.

Women who were more or less contemporaries of Roma Mitchell were accustomed to social and political pre-eminence arriving only as a dimension of their marriages to the men who rose to fame and reward brought by their work, the women were the help-meets, the powers-behind-the-throne. They did not achieve such prominence themselves. Or, if they did, then they must be 'insatiably ambitious' and 'pushing'. No man attracted such venom for achieving social and political prominence; when David Hogarth decided that the knighthood bestowed on Charles Bright in the New Year's Honours List for 1980 should have been his instead, he complained volubly to Sir Walter Crocker, but, Crocker noted, he was 'never petty or malicious'. Sesca Zelling's 'trendy', of course, meant no more than that Roma Mitchell was – as she would have described herself – modern. If Sesca Zelling was shocked at Justice Mitchell's appointment being extended by the Liberal (Tonkin) Government, then no doubt, Sesca Zelling was a conservative soul who believed, as did many men as well, that with Dunstan gone, everything would – or should – revert to its proper place in the world, including her former friend and fellow-Thursday Girl. Roma Mitchell may have made herself a place in the heartland of the Adelaide Establishment, but that did not guarantee unqualified Establishment approval, especially from the wife of a man who had written to Roma Mitchell praising her femininity.

Of course, Justice Mitchell was not universally approved. That would not have been possible for anyone but a total nonentity. And even though people maintained that they would never know how she voted – Crocker noted that she opposed Margaret Thatcher, but because she (Roma Mitchell) was opposed to capital punishment,[78] rather than on account of any general opposition to Thatcher as a Tory – there were a number of pointers. Her long association with Joe Nelligan, her alignment with Dunstan and King, her recommendations as chair of the Criminal Law and Penal Methods Reform Committee, and of the Parole Board, to say nothing of the eventual outcome of the Salisbury Commission – all ensured that she was perceived as one of the progressives – the reformers. She was, then, admired or derided according to the political persuasions of those expressing opinions. She made such opinions difficult to form, though, for she also, contradictorily, accepted alignment with reforming elements in the Liberal Party, both in South Australia and federally, and she was also firmly in favour of such traditions as the system of imperial honours, conferring upon colonial eminences recognition for achievement and service, and status. She received such honours herself, with pleasure and pride.

Chapter Eight
Citizen of the World

Voice for the Nation?

In 1975, the Honourable Justice Roma Mitchell CBE – Commander of the Civil Division of the Most Excellent Order of the British Empire, an imperial award made in 1971 for services to law[1] – was invited to present the Boyer Lectures. The Australian Broadcasting Commission had initiated these – modelled on the English Reith Lectures – in 1959, and renamed them in 1961 as a memorial to Sir Richard Boyer who, as chair of the ABC, had been one of the chief instigators of the project. Five lectures would be broadcast, one a week, for five weeks, to stimulate thought, discussion and debate. Each year, they chose a prominent Australian, a 'great mind' according to their website, to examine 'key issues and values'.

Her Honour Justice Roma Mitchell CBE, published with permission of the *Advertiser*

This was the moment when Roma Mitchell, already well known throughout the common law world, and very well known at home in South

Australia, could have become a national figure. Giving the Boyer Lectures would establish her in the minds of the entire nation as the woman who ranked in public esteem alongside such other Boyer Lecturers as Professor Julius Stone (1960), Sir MacFarlane Burnet (1966), Robin Boyd (1967), Sir Zelman Cowan (1969) and Dr H.C. Coombs (1970). A public intellectual, she would be, respected and admired across Australia. She was the first woman to have received such an invitation, and remained the only woman to have given the lectures until prize-winning novelist, Shirley Hazzard, joined the list in 1984.[2]

The ABC undoubtedly chose her as a gesture to International Women's Year. Justice Mitchell's one specific reference to International Women's Year in these lectures repeated a point she had made before on several occasions. There should be parity between men and women in responsibility to accept jury duty. 'Women do not need the somewhat patronising protection of the law which enables them, at their whim, to refuse jury service', she stated caustically. Then she amplified the point by wondering 'whether we would be able to retain the right to trial by jury if all men could opt out of jury service without giving a reason'.[3] But she did not use these lectures to repeat any of the points that she had made so splendidly in her lecture on Women's Liberation and the Law in Hobart in 1971, and she did not embark upon any new discussion of the position of women. It would be enough that she was, a woman, giving the lectures. 'The Web of the Criminal Law' she titled them, and based them firmly in the work that she was already engaged upon for the Mitchell Committee. A South Australian she was, and would tell the nation about law reform in South Australia. After all, the principles involved in that work were immediately relevant to all common law jurisdictions, beyond as well as across Australia.

In her first lecture, she attended to some of the issues prompting particular concern among social movement activists at that time. Sexual offences, for example. There are many people, she told Australia, 'who advocate that consensual acts between adults should not be subject to prosecution merely because they may breach moral precepts'. Most protest of this kind has focused on 'homosexual acts'. She was enjoying being shocking on the national broadcaster.

> Such acts between females have not been made the subject of prosecution under the criminal law. Perhaps the draftsmen of the various criminal codes and those who enacted them, who were almost certainly all men, did not recognise or refused to recognise that lesbianism existed. Perhaps homosexuality between males was regarded as more inhibiting to population growth than similar acts between females.

Anomalous, now, she commented, and went on to inform her listeners of South Australia's leadership in gay law reform: under legislation passed in 1972, homosexual acts between adult men in private were no longer criminal offences in South Australia. This had not satisfied those who held that 'homosexuality as such should not give rise to prosecution', though, she noted, so there was still room for further reform.[4]

She paused – and there was no joking here – over the age at which a girl could consent to heterosexual sex: seventeen in South Australia, or eighteen if the man was a guardian, teacher or schoolmaster. There had to be a limit to the extremities proposed by some rehabilitators: 'I doubt if the most ardent reformers would wish to make actual consent by a child of 10 years a defence to a charge of carnal knowledge or to a charge of a homosexual offence', she observed dryly. She touched on incest and bigamy, both offences that her committee had recommended removing from the statute book on the ground that they were adequately covered by other legislation and did not need special consideration, particularly since divorce had become so much more easily obtained. When she turned to abortion and rape, she simply repeated opinions that would also appear on the public record in the Mitchell Committee's reports. Later, in the 1980s, she would have to revisit the question of the rights of the unborn child, as distinct from the rights of the mother – central in debates over rights to abortion – in a new context of human rights.[5]

Composing these lectures was extra work, on top of her day job on the Supreme Court Bench and her role as chair of the Mitchell Committee. Her exclusively South Australian focus ensured that, at least at this moment, she effectively rejected the opportunity that the ABC's invitation offered for her to become a female voice for Australia. The principles involved in the reforms that she described and discussed had far wider application, no doubt, but since she did not spell that out, or add examples from other places, the lectures inevitably sound parochial. Her focus is hardly surprising; she was already so busy that only a combination of ambition and a sense of obligation could have compelled her to accept the invitation in the first place. Her days had already been a whirl of engagements almost from the moment at which she arrived on the Bench ten years earlier.

There had been the Fourteenth Australian Legal Convention in July 1967. This brought to Adelaide such luminaries as former United States Attorney General, Justice T.C. Clark, Dean Griswold, Dean of Harvard Law School, and Lord Denning, England's Master of the Rolls and President of the Court of Appeal. Justice Mitchell did not give a paper herself, though she did read Charles Bright's on breach of contract for him (he was overseas), and hosted a dinner party for fourteen at her Melbourne Street apartment, wearing a white crèpe hostess skirt offset by a black jersey top embroidered with white beads in a leaf design. The social pages loved her, reporting on her black suit with a turquoise velvet hat for the mayoral reception; her small camel domed hat with a camel and spiced apricot checked jacket suit for lunch at Ernest's Restaurant at the weir that dammed the River Torrens to the west of the city; her burnt orange Italian knit suit with black accessories for another lunch; and for the Law Council's reception at the Hotel Australia a black corded silk dress.[6] Her hosts for the last occasion were Justice Howard Zelling, President of the Law Council of Australia, and his wife, Sesca; this was the same Sesca Zelling who was so whole-heartedly to condemn Justice Mitchell at dinner with Walter Crocker, once her former friend had become a reforming judge. There were other legal conventions – in Brisbane in 1969, Melbourne in 1971 and Perth in 1973.

Then there had been all her non-legal involvements; as she had told Joe Nelligan all those years ago, it didn't do to become too exclusively focused because then one was narrow-minded. In 1969–1970, for instance – the same year as she moved from Melbourne Street to East Terrace – she had been inaugural vice-president of the newly formed Friends of the Art Gallery of South Australia. In 1969, she was appointed a member of the Committee of Enquiry into Education in South Australia established by Joyce

Steele, Minister of Education in the Hall Government, a body named after its chair, Emeritus Professor Peter Karmel, Vice-Chancellor of Flinders University.[7] The Committee submitted its report in February 1971, not to the Government that had set them up but instead to the magisterial Hugh Hudson, Minister of Education in Dunstan's second Government, who would go on to use it as a template for the Commonwealth Schools Commission.[8] Later in the decade, she would accept other appointments too: as a Trustee of the Brian Jordan Scholarship Fund, which awarded scholarships for the further education of diocesan priests; as the first chair of the newly formed State Heritage Committee; as a member of the Board of Governors for the 1982 and 1984 Adelaide Festivals of Arts; and from 1979 until 1990, as a member of the Council for the Order of Australia, the body that vetted nominations for the local Australian honours that eventually superseded the imperial awards.[9] Even with all of that going on, she was intensively involved, as well, in four other non-legal activities: the Ryder-Cheshire Foundation and the Churchill Trust, the Council of the University of Adelaide and her regular travels. Efficient, impatient, generous, and energetic, her work might be focused intensively upon South Australia, but her imaginative compass already extended far beyond a single Australian state and its judiciary.

Internationalist

The Ryder-Cheshire Foundation was – like the Churchill Trust with which she also continued to work, endowing her own fellowship for the Arts[10] – a post-Second World War philanthropic effort spreading across the world among the countries of the British Commonwealth of Nations. It was the work of Leonard Cheshire and Sue Ryder. Group Captain Cheshire, son of the Vinerian Professor of English Law at Oxford University from 1945 to 1949 who wrote various legal textbooks, was one of the dambuster flyers in the Royal Air Force. The most highly decorated member of the RAF at the end of the war, he had watched the atom bomb drop on Nagasaki. Changed by these scaring experiences, he became a Catholic and devoted the remainder of his life to establishing services to support people with disabilities. Lady Ryder,

CMG, OBE, had begun her work for charity in 1945, caring for sick and displaced people in Europe. They met in 1955, married in Mumbai (then Bombay) in 1959, and together set up Raphael, a series of homes for orphans and people suffering from leprosy, tuberculosis and cerebral palsy, in Dehra Dun in India. Such an undertaking needed help with fundraising. Roma Mitchell hosted the inaugural dinner of the Australian arm of the Ryder-Cheshire Foundation at the South Australian Hotel on 11 November 1970. The 220 guests included sundry legal friends, and she persuaded her friend and Melbourne Street neighbour, grazier Russell Longmire, to act as vice-president, and long-time friends Mary Bleechmore and Zeta Walsh to help with fundraising.

While Leonard Cheshire, tall and dignified, and Sue Ryder, small, dynamic and dogged, continued to travel the world raising money and opening homes in other countries too, the Australians took on responsibility for funding Raphael. Roma Mitchell visited in 1971, when she went to the Fourth Commonwealth and Empire Law Conference in New Delhi, and met the young leprosy victim whom she supported. She took to fundraising with gusto, pressuring her friends to help. She held the position of South Australian president from 1971 to 1980. And even though she had said firmly in 1975 that she could not take on the federal chairmanship, she succumbed in 1981 and became national president, a position she held for the next ten years. She also became friends with Leonard Cheshire and Sue Ryder, lunching with them when she was in London in 1977, arranging their accommodation when they visited Adelaide in 1978 and 1979. Such personal connection meant that she responded indignantly to suggestions in the early 1980s that the name be changed, or that it be merged with a larger overseas aid agency, since no-one knew what 'Ryder-Cheshire' represented any more, making it difficult to raise funds for it.[11]

On the Council of the University of Adelaide in the late 1960s, she had helped establish Kathleen Lumley College, named after the sister of her old friend Sir Kenneth Wills, Deputy Chancellor of the University from 1961 to 1966, Chancellor from 1966 to 1968; Mrs Lumley had donated £30,000 of the wealth that she had gained from her husband's family's insurance business to found the college, a residence for postgraduate students in Lower North

Adelaide. Miss Mitchell's major contribution to the Council, at this time, was to the Finance Committee, which she served 'with great perspicacity'.

Here, too, as with the criminal law, she participated in reform. The University of Adelaide had increased in size; Vice-Chancellor Geoffrey Badger observed that 'there are ten times as many university students in Australia today as there were just before the war'.[12] The 'student troubles' of 1968–1969, with their protests against authority and hierarchy, brought about a radical redistribution of power throughout the institution, with academic departments becoming self-determining units, and all decision-making bodies including students among their representatives. In 1971, the Dunstan Government passed new legislation, the *University of Adelaide Act*. Among the changes introduced was an expansion of the University's governing body, the University Council. The twenty-five members were increased to thirty-three. Twenty-two of them were to be elected by a convocation of all graduates, all postgraduate students and everyone employed in the University. Those twenty-two were to consist of eight members of the academic staff, one member of the non-academic staff, one postgraduate student and twelve people who were not employed in the University at all. Another four members, themselves undergraduate students, would be elected by the undergraduates.[13]

The conservatives on the council included Sir Walter Crocker. He hated the new arrangements. In the old days, he complained, 'members of the University Council sat around an oval table and were there as a committee'. Now, with thirty-plus members, they 'took to speech making'. Moreover, he held, 'students were at the University not to play campus politics but to acquire knowledge and training'. He could tell, though, that Roma Mitchell regarded him and his few supporters as an unfashionable minority; she treated them as a judge treats a hostile witness, he said.[14] Briskly, impatiently, no doubt.

Driven? Of course she was. But such a judgment suggests someone without friends or any kind of private life, and that would ignore the array of friends and relations with whom Roma Mitchell maintained frequent contact. Closest, always, were Ruth and Hugh. Hugh was in his seventies by this time, his health becoming less robust, and Ruth was beginning to show signs of the dementia that would so cruelly take her away long before she died. Close they were, but also a source of anxiety and anguish. Her Jenkins cousins were, themselves, working extremely hard. Merle Jenkins had spent two years at Manchester University in England during the 1950s on a research grant, and had returned to Adelaide as a specialist teacher of education, and Beryl Jenkins had taken charge of the Outpatients Department of the Royal Adelaide Hospital in 1962. Roma wrote regularly to her MacDonald cousins; she and Ruth went to visit Jean MacDonald once when Jean was living in Canberra, and then went on to Goulburn to visit Arch MacDonald, who was brim-full of family news.[15]

There were the Williamses and Villeneuve Smiths, and lawyer Molly Kingston, in Melbourne, and goddaughter Adrienne McMahon in Newcastle. Godmother Roma decided that Adrienne had produced enough children with her fourth, and told her so, regardless of her church's attitudes to contraception.[16] Jean Whyte had not gained an appointment in the library of what had been planned as the Bedford Park campus of the University of Adelaide but became an independent university soon after it was opened in 1966: the Flinders University of South Australia. Instead, she moved on from the Fisher Library at Sydney University, first, in 1972, to the National Library of Australia in Canberra, where she was appointed Director of Information, Reference and Research, one of but two – and 850 men – in the second division of the Commonwealth Public Service, and then, in 1975, to an appointment as Foundation Professor in the Graduate School of Librarianship at Monash University in Melbourne. Billie Whyte continued to teach English at Adelaide Girls High School.[17]

Roma continued firm friends with the Farwells, too. In April 1969, after she had presented a paper on the Family and the Law at the New Zealand Centennial Law Conference in Rotorua, she went on to stay with George and Noni in Fiji. They were living in a bungalow on the outskirts of a village of thatched huts clustered around a church at Korotogo. The Chief was impressed at the presence of a judge and invited Roma and George to visit. They were entertained in a room with two chairs on which they sat looking – she feared – like the pictures of Queen Elizabeth and

Prince Philip on the wall, while the Chief's brother mixed kava root and water into a milky and muddy brew. The Chief's wives sat at the far end of the room with their backs towards the visitors and were never introduced. The brother scooped liquid from the bowl and offered it to the Chief. He clapped his hands three times, said, 'Na bula vinaka', and drank the yagona in a single draught. First Roma and then George had to follow suit. 'It is said', George observed, 'that if you drink enough yagona, the head remains clear but you lose the use of your legs'. So after four bowlfuls, Roma decided not to drink any more. George continued to drink as long as the Chief.

> When we rose to shake hands, murmur pleasantries in English and Fijian, walk steadily into the afternoon glare of the sun, we decided that we were both sober as judges. Back home Noni was less convinced. We giggled too much, she said.[18]

The Farwells joined Roma and other Librans, drama critic Harry Kippax and Maurie Isaacs, brother of Justice Simon Isaacs of the Supreme Court of New South Wales, for dinner in Sydney each year to celebrate.

Librans at dinner, Noni Farwell on left, from right George Farwell, Roma Mitchell, and one we have not identified, photograph in Dame Roma Mitchell's Scrapbooks, copied in Master Peter Norman's chambers, 2001

> There was no legal talk on these festive occasions, but heated discussions about the merits or otherwise of the latest plays, operas, books and ballets on offer. The highlight of these evenings was the exchange of birthday gifts. Initially a limit of $2 was set, rising in the last year to $5. At one dinner, Roma handed out miniature, floral painted cow bells she had bought in Switzerland, but was trumped by Maurie with long cylinders of black peppercorns.[19]

Roma Mitchell caught up with other friends on her travels, combining legal conferences with tourism when she could. The Law Association for Asia and the Pacific (LawAsia), which her friend Paul Toose helped to form in 1966, held its first conference in Kuala Lumpur in 1968. Roma attended it on her way to the International Bar Association Conference in Dublin where, among many other activities, she went to a performance of Brendan Behan's *Borstal Boy*, banned in Australia because of its obscene language. It was 'excellent', she told Ruth and Hugh, writing while at the hairdresser's, not at all offensive because it was 'played so naturally & without emphasis on the language'. Afterwards, she and Pam Cleland and Pam's husband went touring through the Boyne Valley to Tara in a hired car with Theo Ruoff. In London Roma went on long walks with Ruoff and his wife, and lunched with the Lord High Chancellor, Lord Gardiner.[20]

She became a regular at the LawAsia conferences, travelling to Manila in 1971, following the Fourth Commonwealth and Empire Law Conference in New Delhi; to Djakarta in 1973, to Colombo in 1979, to Bangkok in 1981. In 1975 she gave an address at a lunch hosted by the Federation of Women Lawyers for the twenty-five delegates to the Commonwealth Magistrates Conference in Kuala Lumpur, then went on to the Fifth United Nations Congress on Crime Prevention and the Treatment of Offenders in Geneva – overseas homework for the Criminal Law and Penal Methods Reform Committee – a trip that she managed to stretch to Spain and England. In 1976 she spent time in Greece and Sweden as well as visiting London, and in 1977 she was away twice, the first time representing the Supreme Court of South Australia at an International Conference of Appellate Magistrates in Manila, visiting Hong Kong on the way, and the second time combining her annual holiday – which included London, where Lord and

Lady Denning returned the hospitality she had extended to them during their Adelaide visit – with a legal convention in Edinburgh. From there, she wrote to John Bray (who ventured away from Australia on only three occasions in his life), suggesting that the Scots held their convention on the first week of their vacation and the last week of the English term specifically to avoid being overrun by the English judiciary: there was not a member of the English Lords to be seen there.[21]

She travelled easily. 'How strong she is!' Walter Crocker exclaimed to his diary. He was now one of Roma Mitchell's neighbours in the East Terrace flats, and he had run into her when she was just back from five weeks in England, the long flight and 'all the to-do flowing from the Air Hostess' strike': she still looked 'fresh'. '"Yes", she said in reply to my observation, "I feel fine. I slept over 11 hours straight off last night." She can always sleep, she told me before.'

Roma Mitchell and Walter Crocker were, on the whole, good neighbours to each other. She often invited him, a divorced man living alone, to join lunches or dinners on occasions like Christmas Day, usually taken up with familial gatherings. He appreciated her hospitality at such times, and, on occasion, tried to help with Ruth and Hugh. He also helped at the times when someone broke into her flat while she was away. He told his diary that she was 'a fairly good – if fussy – neighbour. If I fell & broke a limb etc she would not spare herself'.[22] But he was often extremely critical of her. And while she probably liked having the Lieutenant Governor of South Australia next door, she must have been critical of him – at least once. He told the story himself.

> [T]here was a hedge facing East Terrace. Roma was against it, I was for it. I thought we needed some sort of coverage from eyes peering into where the toffs were living. One day I clipped the hedge and left the clippings on the footpath, which would have been taken away on the Monday (I clipped the hedge on the Friday or Saturday). I thought it was fine to leave them, being lazy. Roma disapproved. She didn't say anything. She went out – I can still see her put on a sun hat – and she herself picked up the clippings and put them in a wheelbarrow and took them away. A bigger and more tasteful reprimand I couldn't imagine.[23]

He hated her voice – so definite, with a faint trace of that childhood lisp in the roll of her tongue – though his diary entries suggest that it was often the feminist sentiments that she expressed that were the major irritant. He should probably have been living somewhere more secluded: he also disliked the sound of many voices if she was entertaining, even the sound of her wireless.[24]

She entertained, often, when she was at home. These were substantial parties. Twelve or more for dinner on 24 March 1974, including Russell Longmire, the Plumridges, Hugh Gooch, May Douglas, just for example. She cooked herself, when she entertained at home. Sometimes she made a huge pot of minestrone that she and her guests could eat before or after going to the opera. 'I do it very well', she would say. But Pamela Villeneuve Smith thought that occasionally her cooking left something to be desired, as on the occasion when she served a chicken with the blood still running. She always had a cleaner, which would have helped when she was entertaining; she would take a broom to her balcony herself, though, from time to time; she complained of the dust raised by the Formula One Grand Prix, the car race that the government introduced in the 1980s into an inner city circuit, including the Victoria Park Racecourse immediately in front of her unit. 'It is extraordinary that this senior judge & scholar & citizen of the world is so good a cook & so efficient & unruffled a housekeeper', commented Crocker,[25] who, although he was often so critical of her,[26] considered her hospitality 'generous & in good taste'.[27] For larger dinner parties – twenty or so, sometimes – she resorted to the Queen Adelaide Club.[28]

Romance?

Was it now, amid all this highly demanding work, travel and extensive sociability, that Roma Mitchell was also – befitting the generalised but intense sexiness of the period, the sexual revolution of the late 1960s and early 1970s – swept up into an affair of the heart? There had been speculation about her sex life for most of her adult years; we've observed already that there is a long tradition of popular denial when confronted with the spectacle of a woman who seems not to need the comforts of a heterosexual relationship or the support of a man. Alec Genders, for instance, insisted that she had an affair with Jim Brazel. Roderic

Chamberlain, talking with Walter Crocker, referred to her as 'the Virgin Judge' and then hastily added that she had been 'the mistress of a well-known lawyer for some years'. A doctor, wanting her to have had the particular happiness of a sexual relationship, told us his mother 'knew' she had had a relationship with Russell Longmire. Certainly, Longmire turns up often in the lists of people that she invites to dinner, once she has moved to East Terrace. But other people laughed dismissively at that suggestion, commenting that while Roma and Russell were good friends and often accompanied each other to parties and performances – he would escort her until he lost the use of his legs; after that she would push him in his wheelchair – there was nothing more between them. A senior member of the South Australian bureaucracy, and a senior judge of a federal court, both also wanting her to have had the pleasures of a sexual relationship, insisted that she had had a relationship with a woman: Billie Whyte. 'Nonsense!' said former Associate Lindy Powell QC, on ABC-TV, going on to utter a reproof:

> *I don't consider there is any truth in any of the rumours about Dame Roma's preference for other women in terms of her sexual proclivities. People make assumptions about that sort of thing because a woman is unmarried, because a woman doesn't have children. I think people were just loath to accept that she was a person dedicated to public service and accordingly that was her life.*

Otherwise, though, her Associates will not speak of such matters. Yet their silences, like Noni Farwell's, are nervous, as though there is, indeed, a secret in the air, a secret that might provoke criticism among those who wish to be moralistic or judgmental. On some days Justice Mitchell would come to work especially beautifully dressed, and would not allow anyone else to answer the phone. Was this a fabrication of ill-wishers, wanting to tarnish her reputation? Was it scuttlebutt among prisoners idling away their time with fantasies of bad behaviour among those who had put them behind bars? Was it a fantasy that well-wishers dreamed for her? Or was this a daring delight that brought rapture to Roma's early 1970s? We have been told enough to ask the questions, indeed enough to furnish answers to them, but we have not found anyone willing to go on the record as providing those answers. So we have made up a story. Of course, it could be said that we have made up everything in this book. Indeed, we have. But we have written or oral evidence supporting everything else we have written. The people who provided the oral evidence for this story are not willing to own up to it.

It was at the opening of an exhibition of paintings by Sidney Nolan at Kym Bonython's new gallery, in Jerningham Street, Lower North Adelaide. The pictures, themselves, were exciting, even though Nolan's dramatic figurations of the Ned Kelly story were fairly well known by this time. The rooms of the little house were crowded, and the wine was fine and plentiful. Roma and – let us call him – Patrick found themselves standing side by side, admiring Nolan's sexy *Leda and the Swan*. They had, they realised, known each other when they were children, living in North Adelaide – a long time ago. He was older than she was. A father-figure perhaps, just like her sister Ruth's husband. There was a spark, there, each coming from the world of the senior professional; Patrick was a surgeon. He was quick, and witty, too. And there was a flash of warmth from a sense of a shared past; like her, he had ancestors who had played a part in the law and the public affairs of the colony. They could go on talking, just a block away in Melbourne Street at Decca's, Derek Jolley's new and trendy restaurant, over dinner and an excellent bottle of shiraz from the Barossa Valley. Several groups of people did just that; no-one took particular notice of these two. Patrick drove her home afterwards. They promised each other that they would do it again, soon.

And so they did. She would go to work especially beautifully dressed, and he would telephone and appoint the place and time to collect her.

One time when Patrick drove Roma home to East Terrace, he came in for a nightcap. That was the moment when they stepped through the moral shimmer in the air dividing the forbidden from the free, and into each other's arms.

So liberated, she felt. In her late fifties, there was no question of pregnancy, and these moments of rapture were not about to detract, or even seriously distract, from her passion for her work. On the contrary, she could talk to him about it; he said that he was in love with her mind.

So powerful, she was. Look at how she was reshaping the criminal law to suit the culture of her times. Sexually permissive and sexually intense, her times invited her to reshape her personal life, even if only for a moment.

And these moments of ecstasy were all the more intense, because they had to be secret.

Patrick was already a husband, and a father of three. His wife was an invalid, he told Roma. He was not about to leave his domestic responsibilities.

> 'Nothing can ever come of it', he said.
> – Outside the window, the white rose waved its head.
> A late bird sang, insouciant, in the tree.
> The sunset stained the river red.
>
> 'There is no future, none at all', he said.
> – She stretched her arms up from the tumbled bed:
> 'What future has the river or the rose?' said she,
> 'The bird's song is, and nothing comes of red.'
>
> He held her as the river holds the red
> Stain of sunset; as, when the bird has fled,
> The tree holds the song. 'Listen,' said she,
> 'Bird, rose and sunlit water sing from this bed.'[29]

So they had to be discreet. Extremely discreet. For although the times invited sexual adventures of all kinds, there were still people who made a great moral huffing and puffing about them. Keith Seaman, the Superintendent of the Central Methodist Mission, was spotted going into the new Arkaba Motel for an assignation, and was brought before his church's authorities to explain himself. They counselled him, but allowed him to remain 'a minister in good standing'. However, when Don Dunstan appointed him Governor of South Australia soon afterwards in 1977, Robin Millhouse MP decided to make as much fuss as possible about Seaman's indiscretion. Dunstan dismissed Millhouse's clamour as 'muck-raking'. But neither Roma the judge, nor Patrick the husband and father, wanted attention of this kind to themselves.

Roma wanted to take care of him as well as to love him. He needed care, too: so much older than she was, and not nearly as strong. His life was to end in the late 1970s.

Conferences in another city were a wonderful opportunity for inversion of the everyday requirements of rectitude and duty, for carnival and play. They could spend a whole night together in the same room, in the same hotel, even if they booked in separately and into separate rooms. Civilised, luxurious – and private.

But they were sprung. Patrick's wife telephoned while Patrick was in the shower, and Roma – who had just placed an order with the hotel for dinner to be brought to their room – answered the phone. Patrick's wife hung up, without speaking. But she had recognised Roma's distinctive voice and diction. After that, nothing could be the same again. The wronged wife was distraught. She told the whole story to a good friend, and the friend told her god-daughter. Roma and Patrick had to part, to deny that it had ever been. He bought her a diamond ring, but it was a farewell. She wore it often –

> Though I could hardly bear
> The pain, I still was thinking
> Of the silence you have kept since parting-day.[30]

Grief and Rage

The years between the mid-1970s and the early 1980s brought Roma Mitchell great grief, for this was a time of major transitions, of several sad endings in her life.

By the mid-1970s, Ruth's health had deteriorated to such an extent that the Gooches sold their house in Prospect and bought the unit next to Roma in East Terrace. There Roma could look in on them every day and ensure that they were well cared for. Then, a shock: George Farwell died, unexpectedly, on 6 August 1976. Roma went to Noni as soon as she heard. The police will freeze your bank account, she told her; regular procedure in a case of unexpected and sudden death. Here is a cheque. Roma had written and signed a blank cheque and gave it to Noni to meet all and sundry expenses. It turned out not to be necessary; the Farwells had already made provision for disaster. Noni told the story, all the same, to show the open-hearted generosity of her friend.[31] 1978 brought the complications and difficulties of the Salisbury Commission with attendant criticisms that left Roma still smarting two years later.[32] There was, too, John Bray's early retirement in

October 1978, to be followed by Charles Bright less than two months later, and then David Hogarth in September 1979, depriving Roma of the three closest friends she had on the Bench, leaving her with only George Walters and Howard Zelling as her contemporaries, and reminding her that she, herself, would have to retire in 1983, the year of what she called her 'statutory senility',[33] when she would turn seventy.

In the new year of 1979, a year that might also have brought Roma knowledge of the death of her paramour, her beloved sister Ruth collapsed and had to go to a nursing home. Hugh Gooch was stricken as well, soon afterwards, and nearly died, but then recovered in hospital. Ruth's cat came to live with Roma. She would feed it ice cream, even though the vet told her that was bad for its dandruff.[34] Sometimes Noni Farwell came and lived in Ruth and Hugh's flat; now Noni could 'baby sit' the unit when Justice Mitchell went travelling, and organise Hugh's laundry deliveries, with supplies of gin and wine in the same suitcase.[35] A year later, Roma had both Gooches back at East Terrace for New Year's Day. This must have been a dreadful, and dreadfully prolonged, heart break. Ruth apparently 'took in nothing', reported Walter Crocker, come to help his neighbour. 'Didn't recognise me. Sat in a stiff corpse-like way; most difficult to get her from taxi into the wheelchair'. Crocker continued to visit Hugh Gooch, who went to live in Abingdon Hospital with his wife: 'What horrible places these geriatric hospitals are', he exclaimed. In January 1982 he found Hugh sitting 'with his head down unable to see, let alone read ... While with him I could hear his wife Ruth screaming like a child, & keeping it up.' Hugh died of pneumonia at the age of 92 on 29 April that year. Roma organised a requiem Eucharist for him in St John's Anglican Church in Halifax Street, just around the corner from East Terrace. 'Church nearly full', noted Crocker.[36] Six weeks later, Ruth died. Roma donated new doors to St John's, and gave a chalice and paten to the Daughters of Charity in Hutt Street – the church that she visited often during the week – in memory of Ruth. 'She had such care for you,' wrote Jill O'Dea, Roma's first Associate, 'as you did for her, & the void left must be immense'.[37]

An immense void, yes, but it was an emptiness that had been creeping coldly around her for some years now as the sister she had known all her life gradually disappeared into her dementia. Alone, she was, with the familial buffers between her and the world all gone.

She would have been glad of some buffers during these years. It was in October 1979, ten months after Ruth had been admitted to hospital, that Roma Mitchell – uncharacteristically – burst into tears at a special meeting of the University of Adelaide Council. Something physicist Harry Medlin had said struck her as a personal attack.[38] And she had more substantial reasons for feeling especially emotionally fragile. That same year saw the publication of a book, *The Salisbury Affair*, by prize-winning *Advertiser* columnist, Stewart Cockburn. This work rejected Royal Commissioner Mitchell's findings, declaring that a grave injustice had been perpetrated upon the Police Commissioner. Hugh Gooch told Walter Crocker that Roma was 'so furious' about this work that 'she explodes at the mention of it'. This was a long fuse. Two years later, at dinner in the Adelaide Club, at which Crocker decided she had drunk too much, she 'made an impassioned attack on S[tewart] Cockburn':

> She used to find him a good journalist, now she finds him not only not intelligent enough for what he takes on but unreliable & in effect misrepresenting, in fact untrustworthy. She was contemptuous.[39]

Questions about Salisbury and his dismissal continued to surface, especially after Dunstan's resignation and the subsequent change of government. Eventually, Premier Tonkin asked his Attorney-General, Trevor Griffin, to investigate the repeated gossip that Dunstan had had something to hide, and prepare a report. Griffin delivered it in September 1980. This was not his finest hour. Even after asserting that 'Mr Dunstan must have been influenced in his actions by his fears of public disclosure of [John] Ceruto's position of influence', which in itself is hardly a strong or conclusive claim, he could not recommend reopening the royal commission. The *Advertiser* editorialised that the whole exercise would have been 'Better Not Done'.[40]

Roma Mitchell could have been forgiven for believing that Stewart Cockburn was making her a particular target. For he also took up another issue in which her judgment was subjected to criticism. This was the Splatt case. Edward Charles Splatt was convicted of the brutal murder of an elderly woman in her home in 1978 and sentenced to life imprisonment. Roma Mitchell was the presiding judge, and, in the view of barrister Jack Elliott, acting for the defence, she adopted such a tone of severity in her questions to the witness that she was effectively assisting the prosecution. The whole process, Elliott raged, could be called a 'joint cross-examination'. Cockburn instigated a campaign in the *Advertiser* against Splatt's conviction and sentence, extending his efforts so far as to arrange for the foreman of the jury in the case to appear on ABC-TV. That, coupled with the appearance of new forensic material, prompted Attorney-General Chris Sumner in the new Labor Government of John Bannon to institute a royal commission, and when the commission delivered its decision on 4 March 1984, it quashed Splatt's conviction because of problems with the scientific evidence. This overturned Justice Mitchell's judgment. She may have derived a kind of back-handed satisfaction from such a result as the Mitchell Committee had recommended more specialist and scientific expertise in dealing with forensic evidence a decade earlier. Elliott was undoubtedly pleased with the outcome, though he was disappointed that it did not attribute any fault to her conduct of the case.[41] Cockburn could well have seen it as a victory for the press. But even before the royal commission's report appeared, Cockburn's intervention had provoked Roma Mitchell – again uncharacteristically – into an open expression of rage.

In his retirement, Charles Bright had written a book about his wife's great-grandfather, Charles Flaxman, who had emigrated to South Australia in 1838 as the agent of G.F. Angas.[42] Sadly, Justice Bright died before it was published, but Betty Bright and son David had it published and launched on 28 February 1984 at the University of Adelaide Club with a small dinner party to follow. Roma Mitchell was there, and so was Stewart Cockburn.[43] The next day Cockburn wrote to 'Dear Roma'.

> It was probably my fault that things took the turn they did during last night's dinner. I should have avoided, scrupulously, raising the jury issue with you and risking this leading on to the Splatt case. Nevertheless, it was perhaps good that you should have got off your chest the anger that you have had to bottle up for so long. I could

> hardly be unaware that *The Salisbury Affair* would have infuriated you and I have always accepted your right to hit back at me.
>
> Why I write now is that I cannot be sure what you were trying to do by accusing me openly and repeatedly of 'dishonesty', and I want you to make your purpose clearer to me. I do not object strenuously to being called 'irresponsible', 'misguided', 'inaccurate', 'wool[l]y-minded' … That sort of thing. But what happens to my self-respect if … Roma Mitchell accuses me in the presence of witnesses of being dishonest and professionally incompetent and goes on to inform me that she is, or has been, in the habit of saying so privately whenever it seemed appropriate – and I then do nothing about it?

She was extremely angry with Cockburn. She must also have felt safe in her company, for there is no suggestion that anyone was inclined to scold her for such a party-stopper. Her attack was clear and incisive: positively clinical. Even Walter Crocker, usually so ready to find fault, reported only that they walked home together after dinner and that she gossiped 'against S. Cockburn'.[44]

Cockburn's letter went on to reiterate his disagreement with Roma Mitchell's findings in the Salisbury Commission report: his terms for her were 'selective', 'undue stress on some aspects', 'underplaying other aspects'; his description of his own work was as 'a piece of advocacy and a protest at what I was and remain convinced was a gross injustice done to Salisbury'. 'I withdraw nothing', he declared stoutly, but then added, 'I do not propose to debate the contents of the book at this stage'. What did he expect to achieve with this letter, then? He told her that his reputation was as 'precious' to him as hers was to her, and listed three awards that he had received over the previous decade. He told her that he could forgive her anger at his book, but then, he wrote, 'I cannot accept your right to say to anyone in the future what you said to me last night.' Finally he got to the point.

> What I suggest is that we let the dead bury their dead, draw a curtain over the past and regard last night's dinner as having been (as it was) an entirely private affair. I would enjoy being able to resume friendly and relaxed personal relations with you without hard feelings … So far as I am concerned, we have had a bitter but honest disagreement. Can we not agree to leave it there and be done with it?

Even here, he blurred this question with two other issues: he suggested that if they could make up and be friends, then one day he would write a profile of her for his newspaper series, 'a profile that would please you', and he defended himself for mentioning her religion and that of Mr Justice White in his book.

Roma Mitchell replied, writing by hand in case he would prefer 'that it not be published to any other person'. Yes, it was unfortunate that he had raised the subject of his book with her; she herself would never have mentioned it to him or to anyone else, and no-one had mentioned it in her presence for some years. No, she would not have asked him to withdraw anything that he wrote in that book: 'I would have regarded it as incompatible with my dignity as a Supreme Court Judge and as a person to do so.' It had not caused any damage to her reputation, as could be seen in the honours and positions of importance to which she has been appointed by 'governments of both parties'. She did not accuse him of being professionally incompetent, she wrote. But there *was* the question of his honesty.

> It must be obvious to you, even if it has not been hitherto, that I vehemently dispute the accuracy of your assessment and many of the statements in your book ... I find it impossible to believe that any competent journalist could have honestly made some of the statements that I find offensive, if he was apprised, or had the opportunity of being apprised, of the evidence given to the Commission.

Lazy, rather than incompetent, then? Or dishonest?

> In your letter you say that I was selective in the finding which I made in the Royal Commission. That is an allegation of grave dishonesty on my part. I am interested that you have confirmed in your letter the impression which I, in common with others, gained from perusing your book.

She rejected his offer to write a profile about her. 'If ever I were seen to have collaborated with you in any article concerning me, people who may be interested in my life and career at some future time would be justified in believing that I accepted as accurate your assessment of my work as Royal Commissioner. I do not.' She quoted his reference to her religion, Justice White's religion, and his observation that White played tennis with other Catholic lawyers '"who have since been appointed to prominent public positions"', making it clear that this could readily be understood as a slur, and noted, 'I would not want you to think that I am other than proud of my religion'. Finally, outdoing him completely in what clearly had elements of a competition in magnanimity, she wrote:

> I am not a person who harbours ill feelings. In my view they do more harm to the person who retains them than to the person against whom they are directed. That is why, after an interval, I have found it possible to meet you on easy terms. I hope this will continue.

That might have been an end of it, but Cockburn couldn't leave it alone. He wrote three days later saying that he was glad to have had her letter and took it 'as an assurance that you do not intend to make further accusations of dishonesty against me'. One could wonder how carefully he had read the letter. Roma Mitchell responded with due annoyance and impatience: 'I gave no assurance that I would not, in the future, express my opinion as to the dishonesty apparent in your book', and concluded, 'I find this correspondence tedious and unproductive. If you decide to reply to this letter please do not infer that any failure on my part to answer your further letter implies that I agree with its contents or any part thereof.' Cockburn had to have the last word, expressing surprise and disappointment, but also threatening to sue her if he ever heard of her reflecting on his honesty again.[45] She did not reply. But about three years later, she did write to him again, after his first wife, Beatrice, had died. He thanked her for a letter that was 'kind, thoughtful, perceptive in its appreciation of Beatrice's outstanding qualities, and a great comfort to me'.

How bleak and lonely she must have felt, with Ruth effectively gone, her friends on the Bench gone on to other occupations, or, like Charlie Bright, gone to meet his maker, and her own career as a judge drawing to a close that would also mean no more Associates. It was at about this time that she acknowledged that she suffered from nightmares.[46] Her letters to Cockburn in 1984 are haughty and chilly, no doubt, but they also sound strained.

That darkness was shot through with flashes of light, though. There was her visit to China, in company with twenty-three others, mainly lawyers, in July 1978 – it was still a major achievement to visit China at all, so soon after the fall of the Gang of Four in the wake of the Cultural Revolution.[47] There was her invitation to join the World Conference of Women Leaders in Jerusalem in June 1979. Organised by the Council of Women's Organisations in Israel, the conference was to examine whether the struggle for increased women's participation had been vindicated, and how that participation would change society. There were 140 delegates, from Africa, North and South America, Asia and Europe; five from Australia. Margaret Guilfoyle, Minister for Social Security in the Liberal-Country Party Coalition Government of Malcolm Fraser gave a speech at the conference opening. Beryl Beaurepaire, Convenor of the National Women's Advisory Council, addressed one of the plenary sessions. Yolana Klempfner, Co-ordinator on Women's Affairs in the Victorian Government, answered questions about being an adviser to the premier. Roma Mitchell was the vice-chair of the Steering and Recommendations Committee that met throughout the gathering and presented its final recommendations. At the closing dinner, she was seated next to Israel's Foreign Minister, Moshe Dayan.[48]

There was light closer to home, too. For in August 1981 Jean and Billie Whyte, as 'close as siblings', had joined with her to buy a block of land on the seafront at Carrickalinga, a secluded cluster of houses about eighty kilometres south of Adelaide on the Fleurieu Peninsula, over the seductively curved Sellicks Hill and south towards Cape Jervis. There they would build a kit home, its external walls made of treated pine logs – fashionably rustic – with an extra room, for Jean Whyte was now keeping company with Hector Monro, Foundation Professor of Philosophy at Monash University, a widower, and, like Jean, a poet; he would accompany her sometimes when she came for weekends. They were good friends with others living at Carrickalinga; artist Barbara Robertson was to paint Billie Whyte sitting pensively naked.[49]

And there was her new appointment. Even before she had come to the end of her career on the Bench, in September 1981, Senator Peter Durack, Attorney-General in Fraser's Government, announced the establishment of an entirely new body, the Human Rights Commission, with Justice Roma Mitchell CBE in its chair.[50]

During her last years on the Bench, Roma Mitchell had moments of being the Acting Chief Justice, when Len King CJ was away, moments that – once again – made her the first woman in Australia to hold such a post. The second time occurred just before she retired herself, so she moved into Len King's chambers for the ten weeks of his absence. Now, in 1983, there was no problem about the lavatory: she simply asked for a latch to be put on the door so that everyone would know that it was being used.[51] She had come a long way from that tramp across Victoria Square to her chambers to be able to be able to go to the loo.

Another flash of light was her title. A letter dated 7 June 1982 told her that Queen Elizabeth II had approved her nomination for appointment as Dame Commander in the Civil Division of the Most Excellent Order of the British Empire: a DBE, the female equivalent of a knighthood. She was the second-to-last Australian to receive this honour; the number of women receiving such awards was always small, and Australia dispensed with imperial honours ten years later. This one made her Dame Roma Mitchell. She was quite happy to make fun of it, declaring it all 'a bit of a pantomime', evoking the comic pantomime dame. But she was proud of the number of letters that arrived to congratulate her: 600, she told Walter Crocker. And – contradictorily, for a Catholic, a feminist and a reformer – she prized very highly the honour and the stature that this traditional imperial, Anglican Insider, title conferred upon her. From now on, she would be known – and insist on being known – as Dame Roma.[52]

The letter telling her of the award was forerunner for the official announcement: that was made on 12 June 1982. Ruth died the next day. It must have been a relief. But that would not diminish her sadness. Roma had no family with her when she attended the investiture at Government House in Canberra. Sir Ninian Stephen imparted 'special warmth' to his greeting to her, but those who accompanied her were her long-time Secretary, Peggy Harvey (who might well have felt like a family member by this time), and a fellow member of the Churchill Trust, Justice Fox, and his wife. 'I should have conceded my grief', she told Noni Farwell. Instead, she used the publicity surrounding her honour to reinforce her case for advancement for women. Yes indeed, women were better off now, but that did not mean that they could relax. 'Results of past discrimination, where women did not easily get the opportunity to fit themselves for positions, are going to take a long time to reverse.'

She fled away, spending a week on Bribie Island with Joan Gooch, Hugh's niece, who had retired there, then flying on to England where, as well as her usual hectic round of visits and theatre performances in London, she spent time touring Winchester, north Cornwall and Bath, walking in the New Forest in the rain and on the Downs in blustery winds, and visiting Oxford with Zelman and Anna Cowan.[53] A restorative, it was, eventually, after the loss of her sister.

Connecting the Nation with the World

By then she knew that when she returned, she would pick up work that would be far more engaging – exciting even – than her last days on the Bench of the Supreme Court of South Australia, or the succession of occasions – eleven in all, running from 1969 until 1981 – on which her appointment to the Bench of the High Court was canvassed, unsuccessfully. The first woman to be appointed to the High Court was Mary Gaudron, and that was not until 1987.[54] No South Australian has ever been appointed. But for Roma Mitchell there was to be something quite different and entirely new, and so entirely appropriate for the reforming chair of the Mitchell Committee, the feminist activist on the Council of the University of Adelaide, the chair of the Parole Board who risked letting Aboriginal Rupert Max Stuart out of prison on parole again. The Australian Human Rights Commission would offer her a larger stage, more international concerns than she had habitually dealt with so far, perhaps even an opportunity to make change happen more rapidly than any following from the work of the Mitchell Committee. It is here, in this work, that we meet Roma the Reformer on a national, nay an international, stage.

The Human Rights Commission was proclaimed on 10 December 1981, the date that the United Nations had declared to be Human Rights Day.[55] Its pre-history included efforts towards human rights legislation made by both the Whitlam and Fraser governments during the years between 1973 and 1980, and the connections being established between those governments and the United Nations. The Universal Declaration of Human Rights that the General Assembly of the United Nations adopted unanimously in 1948 had acquired more-detailed definition and supplementation during the 1960s, 1970s and 1980s with such undertakings as the *Convention on the Elimination of All Forms of Racial Discrimination* (1965), the *International Covenant on Civil and Political Rights* (1966), the *International Covenant on Economic, Social and Cultural Rights* (1966), the United Nations' *Declaration on the Rights of Disabled Persons* (1975) and the *Convention to Eliminate All Forms of Discrimination Against Women* (1980). The United Nations also acquired many more member states during those decades, and such expansion inevitably brought into international consideration important issues of cultural diversity and difference.[56] Successive Australian governments during the 1970s and 1980s endeavoured to bring Australia into line with these conventions, covenants and declarations. Such efforts entailed conflict between the two ruling political parties, between the Federal government and the governments of the various Australian states, and between governments and members of sundry churches and other interest groups. Not surprisingly, they took a considerable time.

One legacy from those efforts was a number of compromises, making the Human Rights Commission [HRC] weaker than its promoters would have wished. Neither the Whitlam nor the Fraser governments had succeeded in their goal of establishing a comprehensive Bill of Rights, so the HRC had no statutory regulations to administer and enforce; it was not a prosecuting or judicial body. Its functions were to listen to complaints, enquire, conciliate, research and educate. It had no mandate at all over the states, even though many considered that the principal violations of human rights occurred within state jurisdictions.[57] Australia's shadow Attorney-General Senator Gareth Evans described it as a 'paper mouse' with no power to take even the 'grossest' breaches of human rights to court.[58] A second legacy was its 'sunset' clause, giving it only five years of life from the date of its proclamation. A third was Al Grassby.

Energetic, ebullient, outspoken and spectacular, he had been Whitlam's Minister for Immigration until the election of 1974 when, following a viciously ethnocentric campaign against him, he lost his seat. Whitlam then made him Commissioner of Community Relations, with a brief to administer the Australian *Racial Discrimination Act* passed in 1975, and he remained in that position during the rest of the 1970s, setting up and supporting sixteen Consultative Committees on Community Relations spread about the country, to hear complaints and conciliate them. Under the Act establishing the HRC, Grassby's fiefdom remained semi-autonomous, but now was to operate under the general direction of the HRC.[59] Evans considered the Fraser Government's failure to appoint Grassby to the HRC the 'most disgraceful feature of its creation'.[60]

These negatives found counterweights, though. One was that the compromises broadened the mandate of the Commission to include two further United Nations declarations: on the *Rights of the Child* (1959) and on the *Rights of Mentally Retarded Persons* (1971).[61] Another was the successful working relationship established between Al Grassby and the Commission. Grassby was expected to work with the Commission, but without being a commissioner. 'I'm told that you have to keep me in order', he said to one of the commissioners, and so they did, but chiefly by inviting him to attend their meetings regularly, by continuing to provide support to his Consultative Committees on Community Relations and their work. A member of the ALP, Grassby was sometimes outspokenly critical of the Fraser Government. Even so, he and the HRC sustained good relations until his term expired in October 1982 and he was replaced by Jeremy Long, a Sydney University graduate who had been, from 1969 to 1982, Deputy-Secretary of the Federal Department of Aboriginal Affairs.[62]

The third, and principal, positive aspect of the HRC when it was established was the talent of its commissioners. Only one was full time. Tall, lanky Peter Bailey OBE, a Rhodes Scholar at Oxford after training as a lawyer at Melbourne University, had been Special Adviser on Human Rights since 1978 and had headed the Human Rights Bureau established as a temporary measure in Attorney-General Durack's department in 1980. Now he was to be Deputy Chair of the Commission, which he would administer.[63] He and Durack consulted about others to include on the

The Human Rights Commission: seated from left: Elizabeth Hastings had qualifications in Psychology and Psychotherapy, Dame Roma Mitchell, Christopher Gilbert, Senior Lecturer in Constitutional and Administrative Law at the University of Queensland; standing from left: Peter Bailey OBE, had been a Rhodes Scholar at Oxford; Eva Geia was Director of the Aboriginal Housing Service in Townsville and a member of the Aboriginal Development Commission and the National Aboriginal Conference; Peter Boyce, Professor of Politics at the University of Western Australia and an executive member of the Australia-New Zealand Foundation; Norma Ford was a solicitor in Traralgon in rural Victoria, Deputy Chair of the National Status of Women and Decade [for Women] Committee of the United Nations Association and occasional member of the Equal Opportunity Board of Victoria; and Manuel Aroney OBE, Associate Professor of Inorganic Chemistry at the University of Sydney, photograph in Dame Roma Mitchell's Scrapbooks, copied in Master Peter Norman's chambers, 2001

Commission as early as March 1980. Durack, a member of the Western Australian Parliament, 1965–1968, Senator in the Federal Parliament from 1971 to 1993, Attorney-General from 1977 to 1983, contributed importantly to the *Freedom of Information Act* and the *Administrative Decisions (Judicial Review) Act*, as well as the legislation establishing the HRC.[64] He wanted all Australians to feel as though they 'owned' the Commission, so he wanted commissioners drawn from each of the states, and representing community concerns with a number of those disadvantages that had surfaced earlier in the socio-political movements that grew out of the counter culture of the 1960s: concerns with women's rights, with indigenous rights, with the rights of ethnic minorities, with the rights of the disabled. The HRC was to deal with questions resonating with international law, so the commissioners needed, if possible, to have had a tertiary education. The HRC was to receive complaints and make efforts to conciliate conflicts, so the commissioners needed experience of working effectively with people. They would want to embody principles of equality in their own composition, so the Commission was 'carefully constructed to demonstrate a balance of sexes, politics, interests, ages and backgrounds'. Since they were appointed part time, they would need to be exceptionally energetic to take on this work as well as their day jobs. One, Elizabeth Hastings, pointed out caustically that four of them 'comprised two people with disabilities, an Aboriginal woman and activist, and Roma who was nearing 70', three of those four being women. Their selection demonstrated, in her view, 'the delicate sensibilities (or lack thereof) of the Parliament of the day'. Opposition speakers deemed them as 'likely to prove incapable of manning [sic] a rowboat, let alone of rocking the ship of State'.[65]

Hastings was one of two members – the other was Christopher Gilbert – who had contracted polio when they were children and were now confined to wheelchairs. Gilbert was a Senior Lecturer in Constitutional and Administrative Law at the University of Queensland, had been actively concerned with human rights issues, and had worked for the Committee for the International Year of Disabled Persons. Hastings had qualifications in Psychology and Psychotherapy, and worked as a student counsellor at LaTrobe University, was a member of the Victorian Executive Committee of the Australian International Year of Disabled Persons, 1981, and a founding member of Disabled Peoples International. She would go on to become Australia's first Disability Commissioner in 1993.[66] A third commissioner, Manuel Aroney OBE, Associate Professor of Inorganic Chemistry at the University of Sydney, was a foundation member of the Ethnic Communities Council of New South Wales. Eva Geia was Director of the Aboriginal Housing Service in Townsville and a member of the Aboriginal Development Commission and the National Aboriginal Conference. Norma Ford, a solicitor in Traralgon in rural Victoria, Deputy Chair of the National Status of Women and Decade [for Women] Committee of the United Nations Association, and occasional member of the Equal Opportunity Board of Victoria, was the fifth. Sixth was

Peter Boyce, Professor of Politics at the University of Western Australia, and an executive member of the Australia–New Zealand Foundation.

If all states were to be represented, then the person chosen to fill the chair would have to come from South Australia or Tasmania. Peter Bailey had a few names but had done nothing about them when Durack told him with delight that he had persuaded Roma Mitchell to take the job. Bailey could 'hardly believe [his] ears': he thought that she 'was probably too big a fish … to hope for'. He first met her at Government House in Canberra.

> I was told to go in by a … side entrance, and you go up … a long flight of stairs … And I looked up the stairs and here's this tall woman at the top of the stairs, dressed in some boots and a dress, a fairly long … skirt, and she was standing there just looking. So I looked up and I said, 'Are you Justice Mitchell?' She said, 'I am'. And she said, 'You must be Peter Bailey' … So I walked up the stairs and we met … That … picture has stayed with me because she was a kind of regal-looking person and she would often use that capacity in her role as Chair of the Commission. Not in the Commission meetings at all, but when we had public meetings and sometimes they got a bit stroppy and she would draw herself up in that way, and she was an impressive looking person.

Elizabeth Hastings was also impressed, though she was less reverent: 'when it is necessary she achieves her effect rather in the way of another great Australian, the frill-necked lizard, drawing herself up into an astonishment of "Presence" which cannot be gainsaid'.[67]

It was still there, then, perhaps even more so: the capacity that Len King had noticed when she was but a solicitor and just bounced that aggressive and abusive husband right out of her office.

She met the other commissioners before they were formally inaugurated. 'I believe her first words were "Good morning, my name is Roma"', recalled Hastings. Those words were 'uttered in such a firm voice that none of us dared to use the Dame word for the whole of the next five years',[68] though, of course, the 'Dame word' was not part of her, when she first met them. Their first official meeting took place on the day that the HRC was proclaimed. The Government was to allocate space for them on the seventh floor of the AMP Building in Canberra. But the commissioners could not meet there – this was an irony that should have embarrassed the Government – because these offices did not have lavatories accessible to wheelchairs.[69] All the commissioners except Roma Mitchell and Peter Bailey stayed at the Canberra International Motor Inn, so meetings of the HRC were held at the Motor Inn. Peter Bailey lived in Canberra. Justice Mitchell stayed at the Commonwealth Club; her membership of the Queen Adelaide Club gave her reciprocal membership and accommodation in an elegant building on the edge of Lake Burley Griffin.

The commissioners met approximately nine times a year, only four or five of those occasions being in Canberra. Other meetings were mostly held in the capital cities of other states. Progressively, the HRC set up cooperative arrangements with the anti-discrimination and equal opportunity agencies in New South Wales, Victoria and South Australia, and, eventually, Western Australia, giving those agencies responsibility for administering the Commission's legislation.[70] In states with no anti-discrimination legislation, the HRC established regional offices, first in Brisbane, then – for a time – in Perth, and co-opted representatives in Darwin and Hobart. This gave the commissioners local representatives and access to meeting space in each of the cities that they visited. An office was established for Dame Roma on the tenth floor of 25 Grenfell Street, which had earlier housed the Local and District Criminal Court, now moved to Victoria Square in the refurbished Moore's building on the south-west corner of Victoria Square.[71]

Hastings recalled:

> Roma was meticulous about meetings and was always fully prepared regardless of how high was the mountain of papers she received, often very shortly beforehand. Indeed, the day after receiving them she would be ringing Peter to ask questions or make comment: sometimes Peter was leafing through the documents for the first time while trying to respond with the astuteness and knowledge Roma was already displaying.

She was 'so quick' remembered Peter Bailey, 'so quick, whether she had really absorbed the stuff or whether she had thought it through'; she, for her part, thought that he suffered from never having been in legal practice, possibly implying that she found him slow. So there was space for heated discussion. 'Roma exercised ... iron control over what could only be called at times a passionate and unruly lot', noted Hastings, 'she was very firm on occasion with the peccadilloes of the members, and would not allow us to be too idiosyncratic or ego ridden, sometimes to our chagrin!'[72]

She also entertained the commissioners when they visited Adelaide, hosting one of the parties that Walter Crocker objected to hearing through his wall.

The seventh floor of the AMP Building housed the secretariat – office accommodation for Peter Bailey and the HRC's staff: thirty-five people, five of whom were part time. Their brief was to review Commonwealth and Territory legislation for its consistency with the UN's instruments on human rights; to receive complaints, inquire into them and, where appropriate, to conciliate the opposing parties; to provide advice; to evaluate international instruments; to report; to promote human rights; to carry out research; and to cooperate with non-government organisations in related fields. The Community Relations Commission had already set up centres and processes for hearing and conciliating complaints under the racial discrimination legislation, and could, if conciliation failed, issue a certificate of conciliation that the complainant could take to court. The HRC established similar investigation and conciliation processes for other complaints under the international covenants.[73] This was to be their major work. Visits of the commissioners and research projects and reports were aimed at countering the conditions that led to the complaints in the first place.

Issues around discrimination against Aboriginal Australians were number one on their agenda. By March 1982, the HRC had decided that they would begin with a study of the problems of Aborigines in country areas. A small group of experts, half of whom were Aboriginal, set out on a field trip in the Murray Valley, in Gippsland and in southern New South Wales. 'If the study leads to a recognition of their rights and responsibilities and the rights and responsibilities of residents who are not Aboriginals', said Dame Roma, 'we will, I hope, have begun an education process which should spread throughout Australia'.[74] Some field officers inquired into prejudice against Turks, Italians and Greeks, but the group's chief focus was prejudice against Australia's first inhabitants.[75]

It was in pursuit of similar understanding that the HRC held one of its non-Canberra meetings in Cairns in North Queensland, so that the commissioners could see first hand the people and places from which a number of complaints had originated. On that trip, they also visited Mantaka, Kowrowa and Palm Island, places with long histories of dispossessed and displaced Aboriginal people. Much as it might have wanted to, the HRC could not intervene in the struggle for Aboriginal land rights in Queensland, because land rights came under state control.[76]

In its first six months the HRC received no fewer than 381 complaints of racial discrimination, two-thirds of which were prompted by distribution of racist propaganda. Dame Roma was appalled by the attitudes and behaviours that she encountered. She labelled Western Australia and the Northern Territory 'neglected centres of racial intolerance'. She explained to the Sydney University Law Graduates Association how the simply unthinking, apparently frivolous, can nevertheless be extremely offensive.

> 'As an example I refer to the description of a shade of color as "nigger brown", an expression which I have been guilty of using since childhood,' she said.
>
> 'But then I remind myself that I have never been referred to as a nigger. If I had been, and my skin had been brown or black, I should regard it as an offensive epithet.'

The HRC had called for submissions on the sometimes conflicting right to freedom of expression and the right not to be discriminated against on racial or religious grounds, as preparation to making recommendations for revision to the Racial Discrimination legislation. When they made their recommendations to the Federal government, the press had a field day: 'Telling Irish jokes could be illegal if Govt. adopts proposal', announced headlines in the *Advertiser*.[77] John Bray joined them, writing to his friend Roma:

> Your proposals outlaw derogatory stereotyping on racial grounds. But stereotyping is part of life. We have not only stupid Irishmen, mean Scotsmen, avaricious Jews, braggart Americans, excitable Italians, lascivious Frenchmen, but nagging wives, tyrannical mothers-in-law, effeminate homosexuals, sour old maids, grasping moneylenders, shyster lawyers, bullying policemen, and so on. Stereotyping is a crude attempt to make sense of life by categorizing human types and there is often some real fire underneath a cloud of noisome smoke. After all people are conditioned by their ethnic, cultural and occupational backgrounds and I think everyone ought to be prepared to put up with a certain amount of ill-natured jeering. I realize that if the recommendations become law the authorities are not likely to pursue bar-room jests. But they will have an inhibiting effect on the stage, particularly the vaudeville stage, the cartoonist, the press, the electronic media and the night-club. In one aspect this could be regarded as yet another manifestation of the humourless Puritanism that seems to be endemic in Anglo-Saxon communities, if that's not a racist sentiment.[78]

Which of course it was, as Dame Roma observed. Addressing a seminar organised by the Media Law Association, she quoted Bray and commented on his last sentence: 'Well, that criticism is put in more picturesque language than we normally hear. It doubtless will appeal to many, but I think mainly to those of Anglo-Saxon origin whom the critic blames for humourless Puritanism.' All good fun, indeed, but she went on to say:

> But they are not the complainants whom the HRC sees. We hear from the Aborigines, the Greeks, the Italians and the Asians. They do not enjoy the ill-natured jeering. They believe that it has deleterious effects upon them and upon their children. I do not think we can afford to do nothing.[79]

Racist slurs were but the first of the discriminations that the HRC addressed. The human rights of the disabled involved some careful, and innovatory, distinctions between, for instance, mental illness and intellectual disability. The HRC's review of the Mental Health Ordinance proposed for the Australian Capital Territory in 1981 resulted in a number of revisions, including safeguards in relation to such invasive treatments as Electroconvulsive Therapy (ECT). The HRC also investigated, and then recommended, that terminally ill patients have access to heroin, a drug that had been outlawed in 1953 but had become a widely used, illegal, recreational drug during the 1970s. They considered

> the legal and ethical aspects of the management of newborns with severe disabilities; the treatment of disabled persons in social security and taxation law; ethical and legal issues in guardianship options for intellectually disadvantaged people; affirmative action for people with disabilities; the rights of hearing-impaired people in the workplace; and, finally, alternative accommodation for intellectually disadvantaged persons – a study in Human Rights and discrimination.

'In many of these areas', observed Hastings, 'the Commission reports were the first published consideration in Australia of disability issues in relation to Human Rights rather than welfare rights'. They were forerunners for later legislation on Disability Services and Disability Discrimination.[80]

Then there was the whole matter of sex discrimination. This marked a moment when mainstream politics and activist feminism met. One of the characteristics of Australian feminism has been the interconnectedness of political movement with activism in government bureaucracy (the 'femocrat phenomenon') and in parliaments. Accordingly, the Australian sex discrimination legislation represented an achievement of the Women's Movement as well as of the Labor Party Government of R.J. Hawke – both personified by Susan Ryan.

The Honourable Susan Ryan AO

The Federal ALP, with Hawke at its helm, swept into power on 5 March 1983, the same night as the drought broke – symbolism that took strong hold of the imagination in the parched eastern states. Hawke's first Attorney-General, Gareth Evans, became responsible for the HRC that he had condemned while in opposition. He had been a senior lecturer in Constitutional Law at the University of Melbourne before his election to the Senate in 1977. He was also a strong civil libertarian, and thence, also, a strong supporter of human rights. Now, he proposed to give the HRC some teeth, he said, expatiating on revised legislation to allow human rights to be enforced, looking forward to the possibility of enacting a national Bill of Rights, and announcing the new functions that the HRC would exercise under sex discrimination legislation already before the Parliament.[81]

Hawke had included Susan Ryan in his first Cabinet, with charge of the Education and Youth Affairs portfolios, and responsibility for advising the Prime Minister on policies affecting women. Ryan was a member of Women's Electoral Lobby [WEL], the constitutional element of the Women's Movement, and the first Labor Senator for the Australian Capital Territory. In 1983, she introduced a Sex Discrimination Bill into the Senate. It had attached to it the text of the International Convention of the Elimination of All Forms of Discrimination Against Women [CEDAW] that had been adopted at a conference in Copenhagen in 1980 to mark the middle of the UN's Decade for Women. Australia ratified CEDAW on 28 July 1983, shortly after the Ryan Bill had its first reading. Its attachment ensured the bill a solid constitutional base; it exceeded CEDAW's objectives by reaching to discrimination against men.[82] These objectives, and Australia's extensions, were, of course, of integral concern to the HRC.

The debate that ensued was, at that time, the longest in the history of the Australian Senate and occupied popular attention for months. Some of that attention came from elements who were way to the right of mainstream politics. A group called Women Who Want to be Women deluged the Parliament with letters on pink paper. One of the letter writers, Mrs Betty Hocking, a member of the Family Team in the Australian Capital Territory House of Assembly, issued a statement asking, 'Is there no-one who can see that the women who hate men are castrating them with their sex discrimination Bills and making them eunuchs in their own kingdoms?' Then, even more memorably, she announced: 'Delilah cut off Samson's hair and made him her slave. The Sex Discrimination Bill cuts off far more than that.' Her concern with anatomy met its match when leading Democrat feminist member of Parliament, Janine Haines, startled members of what the press described as the 'relaxed red-leather Senate chamber, known for its air of a gentleman's club' by declaring:

> I cannot see how it [the bill] can possibly end all differences between men and women. Despite the Freudian remarks about assertive women, that they suffer only from penis envy, I have yet to meet a woman who suffers from that or who has any particular desire to acquire that section of male anatomy.[83]

The pink paper organisations mobilised such local heavyweights as Lachlan Chipman, Founding Professor of Philosophy at the University of Wollongong, and the Very Reverend David Roberts, Anglican Dean of Perth. Roberts declared that

> Susan Ryan's drab and humourless Utopia ... has lost sight of the complementary delights of being male and female ... It would be tragic for our humanity if we allowed ourselves to be remodelled by an Amazonian reformism which legislates against the weakness of men and apparently counts as ineffectual the real strength of women – the humanising and civilising power of their femininity.

'Whatever can the Dean have been reading as the Sex Discrimination Bill?' expostulated Dame Roma. 'Certainly not my copy.'[84] The pink paper people also brought to Australia two veterans of the struggle against the Equal Rights Amendment in the United States – Phyllis Schlafly and Michael Levin (Professor of Philosophy at the City College of New York). They toured Australia giving seminars and addresses against the Ryan Bill. Levin went so far as to proclaim that 'feminists are not women', and announced that '[s]exual harassment is a problem that simply does not exist'. Since these addresses were often at universities, he met strong opposition. At Queensland University students pelted him with eggs.

Members of the parliamentary Liberal Party generally supported the Ryan Bill. But they had problems with it, and introduced amendments. One such amendment wanted reference to CEDAW removed, since, they believed wrongly that it undermined the legislative autonomy of the Australian government by introducing external powers into Australian lawmaking. Susan Ryan elaborated their contention in her autobiographical memoir.

> The gist of the opposition was: the convention was an instrument of the United Nations; the United Nations was dominated by Communists, especially the Russians; Communists were dedicated to the destruction of the family through the provision of 24-hour-a-day child-care. Susan Ryan, the weapon of this mass destruction, must be stopped.[85]

Such a view would oppose all aspects of the work of the HRC.

The Women's Movement, or at least the constitutional and liberal elements of it, were enthusiastic. By September 1983, vociferous affirmation had arrived from WEL, from the Australian Federation of University Women, from the National Council of Women, from the United Nations Status of Women Committee, from the Union of Australian Women, from Women and Development Australia, and from the Young Women's Christian Association. Zonta, a worldwide service organisation of executives in business and the professions working to advance the status of women, joined them towards the end of that month, and a group of Western Australian women academics a week later.

The bill passed the Senate on 17 December 1983, with eleven members of the Liberal Party crossing the floor to vote with the Government. It then passed rapidly through the House of Representatives at the beginning of 1984, in time for a celebration in front of Parliament House with a giant cake on International Women's Day, 9 March 1984. Sex Discrimination Commissioner, Pamela O'Neill, joined the HRC on 28 July 1984. In the first ten days from the Act's proclamation, the HRC received 15,400 letters requesting information about the new law.[86]

As Chair of the HRC, Dame Roma was at the cutting edge of the changes that it was to introduce to Australia. Peter Bailey set these out. 'Change', he held, was the 'raison d'être' of the HRC.

> It looks for change in interpersonal relations – between the parties to a complaint about racial discrimination or about violations of human rights; it stands for change in departmental practice where these infringe human rights or are discriminatory; it stands for change in the law, where the law is inconsistent with human rights, and it stands for change in government policy, where this is required before there can be a change in the law.[87]

Dame Roma was at the cutting edge of change in a quite different sense, as well. For when she became a judge, Roma Mitchell had been enjoined to live quietly and discreetly, in a manner befitting her function. She had taken up positions in a number of other bodies, but few of them were subject to public scrutiny, or required much in the way of public promotion. With the HRC, though, she encountered diametrically opposed requirements.

The HRC was scarcely three months old when Justice Michael Kirby, at the time Chair of the Australian Law Reform Commission, urged the commissioners to adopt 'a frankly high public profile' so that it would engage the 'imagination' of ordinary Australians. If the HRC was to work 'quietly upon administrative tasks and the complaints that are neatly typed or written by articulate middle Australia', he said, they would 'leave untouched the many people who are precisely those for whom the international human rights debate is a desperately serious issue'. It was 'vital', he urged, that the HRC

> bring to the four corners of Australia the message that it will seek out relevant complaints where people feel they have suffered an injustice that amounts to a deprivation of basic rights, will investigate these complaints fearlessly and bring considered and reasoned decisions about the complaints to the notice of parliament.

The Commission's reports should be 'a continuing stream of education on human rights' that should be 'widely ventilated, thoroughly debated and, where appropriate, strongly justified in the Australian media'.[88] A fortnight later Roma Mitchell began a formidable list of public addresses, explaining and promoting understanding of human rights and the work of the HRC. That list is all the more remarkable when we notice that she gave two such addresses shortly before the death of her brother-in-law, just before she finally lost her much-loved sister, and that it begins when there were yet another eighteen months before she would retire from the Bench of the Supreme Court of South Australia. And that was merely a beginning.

'We have been characterized variously as a "toothless watchdog", "paper mouse" and "limp, toothless pussy-cat commission"', she told the Women Lawyers Association of New South

Wales, going on to explain the limitations to the HRC's powers, then setting out goals so ambitious as to suggest that this new body might well become 'the mouse that roared'. The *Canberra Times* had been scathing about the new Commission: it 'scarcely has a profile at all – certainly not on the street'. Other attitudes to human rights were similarly dismissive, said Dame Roma: 'They associate human rights with "do gooders" whom they regard as troublesome persons who will not let well alone.' She went on to urge that 'The full observance of human rights will occur only if a belief in, and a dedication to, the rights of others are inculcated in earliest childhood and cultivated throughout the whole of life.' She converted her speech at an award-granting ceremony at the South Australian College of Advanced Education into an exposition of the meaning of human rights, quoting from President Roosevelt's 'historic Four Freedoms Speech to Congress in 1941', naming as the four essential freedoms Freedom of Speech, Freedom of Religion, Freedom from Want and Freedom from Fear, and on other similar occasions in Sydney, Canberra, Melbourne and Perth she instructed graduating students on specific aspects of human rights. 'The United Nations Convention on the Elimination of All Forms of Discrimination Against Women is "a political diatribe ... full of unctuous political sentiments"' she announced, provocatively, at Monash University, but then assured her listeners that these were not her words, and provided instead words of her own to explain and illustrate the provisions of CEDAW.[89]

There was controversy, of course. 'Suggestions that "Cupid had been robbed of his arrow" by new laws against sexual harassment were arrant nonsense', she scoffed; harassment had to do with power and oppression, it 'had nothing to do with romance'.[90] When pink paper ally Lachlan Chipman accused the HRC of threatening freedom of speech, the HRC issued a press release quoting her.

> Proposed amendments to the *Racial Discrimination Act* were designed to protect people from being publicly vilified because of their racial origins, the Chairman for the Human Rights Commission, Dame Roma Mitchell said today ...

> 'There is no attempt by the Human Rights Commission to stifle freedom of speech, newspaper reporting or genuine academic discussion. This has been made absolutely clear in our Report,' she said ...
> 'Professor Chipman has his Big Brothers mixed up. There are some people and groups in our community who are nothing short of bullies attacking other groups on racial grounds because they are a minority and can't hit back.'
> 'In the future, these Big Brothers might have to take on someone more their own size, like the Human Rights Commission,' Dame Roma said.

The question of free speech had cropped up earlier, too, in March 1983, when the Australian League of Rights, a body that described itself as 'Australia's most influential conservative group', working to expose, among other things, 'the link between Monopoly Capitalism, Political Zionism and Communist Revolution', mounted an exhibition in Adelaide's Constitutional Museum, the old Parliament House on North Terrace. One portion of the display alleged that the Holocaust – the Nazi extermination of six million Jews during the Second World War – was 'a hoax'. The Secretary of the South Australian Campaign Against Racial Exploitation declared the exhibition 'racist insulting nonsense': it was, he said, 'anti-Semitic, anti-Asian and anti-black, and only underlines the need for government action to make incitement to racial hatred an offence under law'. The Museum's Director, Suzanne Brugger, said in response: 'Our role is not to censor displays according to our personal whims, but to encourage people to put their views forward and have them examined by the general public.' Nevertheless, when the Executive Council of Australian Jewry wrote directly to Dame Roma at the HRC, the HRC sought to intervene, only to find the law inadequate to their wishes.[91]

The following year brought a major row over immigration. Distinguished historian Geoffrey Blainey announced to the Warrnambool Rotary Club that the level of Asian immigration to Australia should be severely reduced. It was not exactly comparable to the moment in 1968 in Britain when Tory politician Enoch Powell declaimed against immigration and the Race Relations Bill before the Parliament, prophesying that the streets of England would run with 'rivers of blood', but it did polarise and re-politicise views around immigrants in ways that were anathema to the HRC.

Dame Roma told Sir Walter Crocker that she blamed Blainey for racialism in Australia, especially for hostility to the Vietnamese. Blainey responded to hostility to his views by publishing *All for Australia*, arguing that immigration policy was being designed in secret by faceless politicians and bureaucrats, without the knowledge of Parliament or people. He became a figurehead for those who found the policies of the Hawke Governments, and later those of Paul Keating, Hawke's Labor successor, to be too inclusive, too orientated to Asia.[92] This polarisation was to enter national politics within a couple of years, with important implications for the HRC.

In the meantime, Queensland brought Dame Roma and the HRC several especially fiery moments. When the HRC distributed human rights teaching kits, offering $1000 to each teacher willing to initiate a course on human rights, to help defray costs and compensate him or her for extra preparation, assessment and reporting work, the Minister of Education in the profoundly conservative National Party Government of Joh Bjelke-Petersen attacked them. 'Bribery!' he charged. 'Arrant nonsense!' retorted Dame Roma, again. When the Queensland police raided two clinics in Queensland believed to provide abortions, and seized 47,000 medical records, Dame Roma declared their action 'an arbitrary interference with the right to privacy', in breach of Article 17 of the *International Covenant on Civil and Political Rights*. When the Queensland Government introduced legislation requiring workers in its Electricity Commission to do whatever work the Commissioner directed at any time, the workers responded with not only a strike but also a blockade halting all flights and postal, rail and sea services into and out of Queensland. In response, the Government proposed draconian new industrial legislation that threatened electricity workers with 'forced and compulsory labor'. The HRC stormed in to the rescue, urging the Federal Government to consider legislation of its own to override Queensland's tough new industrial laws. 'Dame Roma Mitchell ... said in Brisbane yesterday the commission believed parts of the legislation expressly contravened the International Covenant on Civil and Political Rights'. Bjelke-Petersen responded by calling for Dame Roma Mitchell's resignation: 'the commission was nothing more than a feeble fabrication doing the bidding of the A.L.P. and the unions', he fumed. Dame Roma, of course, did not even contemplate resigning. On the contrary, only three months later she condemned Bjelke-Petersen outright, this time for his 'derogatory remarks about Aboriginal citizens':

> Dame Roma Mitchell ... said Sir Joh's remarks were particularly deplorable because they came from someone holding an office of such responsibility.
>
> 'Outbursts such as these are inexcusable', Dame Roma said.
>
> 'They cause serious distress to their victims and create tension and division within the community.'[93]

She was clearly outraged. Usually she expressed her views coolly and coherently, but on occasion even the magisterial 'presence' that Elizabeth Hastings so admired, her capacity to remain 'calm (even when very angry indeed!)', failed and she lost her temper. In an interview on the Australian Broadcasting Commission's program, *Nationwide*, she accused Australians in general of 'intolerance' and 'narrow-mindedness'. A press report about that interview observed that there was 'No mistaking the depth of her feeling ... Her words probably shook many TV watchers, coming straight without any softening frills': people would be 'jolted by the considered opinion [that] Australians are bigoted, prejudiced, intolerant and narrow-minded where racial, social and moral issues are concerned'. Peter Bailey thought that, having been a judge and therefore accustomed to deference, used to having her own way, she was readily annoyed by criticism of the Commission, and her anger made her uncomfortable in unruly press conferences and public consultations. He noted that 'towards the end of a long day and ... a torrid session with hecklers' she was inclined 'to snap a bit'. Walter Crocker described one of her appearances on television as 'humiliating ... her loss of temper, judgement, & dignity'.[94] As with his reiterated criticisms of her voice, this could well have been an expression of his own distaste for the substance of her remarks, as much as for her manner of making them.

Given the HRC's sunset clause, there was always a question in the background about what shape the future of human rights in

Australia would take. During Gareth Evans's term as Attorney-General, this focused on arguments around a Bill of Rights, such as Lionel Murphy had endeavoured to introduce during his own term as Attorney-General in the Whitlam years. A Bill of Rights would be based on the UN's *International Covenant of Civil and Political Rights*. It would ensure that, for instance, every person was 'entitled to equality before the law, irrespective of race, color, sex, language, religion, political or other opinion, national or social origin, property, birth or status'. It would guarantee people freedom of worship and privacy; it would guarantee everyone the right to marry, and also the right not to be coerced into marriage. It would be a charter against which practice could be assessed and found wanting, therefore a means of enforcing civil liberties. Opponents – and the opposition was vehement – included conservative politicians like John Howard, who was to become Prime Minister of Australia in 1996; nationalists, who feared anything introduced into Australia from the United Nations, deeming it 'un-Australian'; states-rights politicians, who feared that this potential legislation would override legislation in the states; Catholic bishops, who, like the Law Council of Australia, considered the Bill 'seriously defective'; Sir Harry Gibbs, Chief Justice of Australia, who said weightily:

> If society is tolerant and rational, it does not need a Bill of Rights. If it is not, no Bill of Rights will preserve it.

And, of course, opponents included Geoffrey Blainey. He announced that such a measure would lead to 'a system of neighbourhood spies and secret courts', and a 'brain laundry in which incorrect opinions would be steampressed', and people could wake up feeling fresh and refreshed.[95]

Before any of these laudable possibilities could be effected, Gareth Evans was moved to Foreign Affairs, following the election of 1984. His successor, Lionel Bowen, secured Cabinet approval for a draft Bill of Rights that was considerably weaker than Evans's had been, but still including a provision allowing a new Human Rights body to investigate and conciliate complaints against state laws. The states would never accept this. So ultimately the Government allowed the Bill to lapse. Senator Evans lamented its failure as a victory for the 'troglodytes, the Neanderthals, the drones and the thugs'. Dame Roma, like a good common law lawyer, had believed that

> the common law could do justice and that the proper approach was to rely on the legislators to intervene when it became apparent that the principles of the common law were inefficient in any particular sphere.

But her work with the HRC had made her wonder if she might have been wrong. Now, she said, 'I would like to see [a Bill of Rights] in existence, but I readily admit that it would not be a panacea'.[96]

Legislation was eventually passed in November 1986, a month before the HRC would have simply had to close down. It created a new body, the Human Rights and Equal Opportunity Commission [HREOC]. Its members would be three full-time commissioners headed by a part-time president, and its secretariat would move from Canberra to Sydney. Pamela O'Neill was relieved because the new Act ensured what she described as 'full protection of women's rights', an ambitious claim. At least she was a member of the new body. The only other element of continuity was the new part-time president, Marcus Einfeld, AO, QC, PhD; Dame Roma was sceptical about his doctoral qualification, and it has been called into question by others since then. Einfeld had joined the HRC early in 1986 when Peter Boyce resigned to attend to his new day job as Vice-Chancellor of Murdoch University. Boyce commented that the new legislation had abandoned the 'opportunity for State representatives to act as watchdogs of regional or minority interests or as generalists with an ear to the public mood'. He pointed out that there was now no promise of specific attention to issues around disability. Eva Geia, too, was disappointed: the fact that HREOC did not include anyone who was Aboriginal, she said, 'would further retard the fight against racial discrimination'. Roma Mitchell stressed that it was important for the new body to 'remain independent and free of political influence'. But any disappointment that she might have felt was countered by the announcement on the same day that the Solicitor-General of New South Wales, Mary Gaudron QC, was to join the High Court of Australia, the first woman in such a position, an appointment made possible, said the press, perhaps more than any other woman's, by Dame Roma's achievements.[97]

One side of the coin reads 'human rights', she liked to observe, but the other says 'human responsibilities', and each is integral to the other. Addressing Amnesty International in Hobart, she commented, with a wonderful mixture of optimism and resignation, and total deafness to any consideration of gender-inclusive language: 'Human rights will not be won by spectacular pyrotechnics but by gradually warming the heart of man towards fellow man.'[98]

Women organised dinners to celebrate Dame Roma and her human rights work, in Adelaide, of course, and in Sydney, as well. She has acquired a status equivalent to that of H.C. Coombs or J.G. Crawford, expostulated an appalled Walter Crocker: 'god-like'.[99] The celebrations offered her admiration for her courage in daring the displeasure of premiers and politicians, to say nothing of her old friends and colleagues, and in making a place for herself in a world where women had formerly had no place, and in doing so – changing the world. At the Adelaide dinner, she responded to a toast in her honour by encouraging everyone there, all women, to nominate women for honours such as she had received herself – sharing the information about how to do it, offering encouragement.[100]

Chapter Nine
Contradictions and Continuities

Global Star: Loyal Local

'Nor was her influence by any means confined to this state', said the Honourable Len King, Chief Justice of the Supreme Court of South Australia,

> or indeed to this country. The influence and example of this outstanding woman lawyer and judge spread not only throughout Australia but throughout those parts of the world which possess similar legal systems.[1]

Roma Mitchell's stage covered far more of the globe than the red coloured patches that used to map the colonies of the British Empire. Her 'fan club' extended across a common law world defined by the International Bar Association, the American Bar Association and LawAsia, as well as the Commonwealth and Empire Law Conferences.

It even encompassed the Republic of Kiribati – pronounced 'Kiribas', the local approximation of 'Gilberts', part of a former British colony[2] – an array of coral atolls in the Pacific about halfway between Australia and Hawaii. For three years, from 1987 to 1990, Dame Roma travelled there, with two brother judges, Sir Harry Gibbs and Sir Sydney Frost, to serve for a week or so as visiting 'resident' appeal court judges. There she would be driven to court past the village square where women sat fanning the fish they hoped to sell, and along a causeway from which, recalled Gibbs, 'one sees the deep blue of the ocean on one side and the green of the coralline waters of the lagoon on the other; the contrast is striking and beautiful'. They delivered joint judgments, and they delivered them before they went home again. This meant working fast. They would choose one of their number to write the first draft of each, then all three would consider it and agree on its final form. Sir Harry Gibbs found Dame Roma 'quick and capable', and noted that she did more than her fair share in preparing the drafts, going out of her way to take care of Sydney Frost who was, by this time, 'showing the effects of ageing' and finding it difficult to complete his drafts in time.

> Roma virtually shepherded him so that he was able, with her assistance, to do his share of the work and she did so unobtrusively and gently and in a way that could not have possibly caused him embarrassment or offence.

She was, he reported to his diary, 'a tower of strength'.[3]

Len King was speaking at a special sitting of the Supreme Court of South Australia to mark Justice Mitchell's retirement from the Bench on 28 September 1983. The list of her involvements 'outside of the ambit of her judicial work' defeated him – too formidable, it was, for him to itemise. Among other things, it would have included her active work for both the Churchill Trust and the Ryder-Cheshire Foundation, international philanthropies that connected her with their activities in India and South Africa.

It would have included, too, another array of international networks: the countries comprising the International Federation of Women Lawyers (FIDA); United Nations circles concerned with the rights and status of women; participants in the 1979 World Conference of Women Leaders. For always, now, as ever since she was made a silk, she presented – just as she presented to King, just as she presents to us today – not one subject but two. A career lawyer, she was, a Queen's Counsel, a judge, a Boyer Lecturer – a ship in full sail breasting the waves. And always there, rippling along at its side, was the ship's reflection, telling us that she was a woman, an exception: the first woman to take silk, the first woman to be made a judge in a superior court, the first woman to give a Boyer Lecture – a woman pioneering a new kind of womanhood, with the shapes of women's lives changing in her wake.

Look at them! The Honourable Elizabeth Evatt AC, LLM – younger than Roma Mitchell – but already enjoying a stellar career as Chief Judge of the Family Court of Australia from 1976 to 1988, President of the Law Reform Commission 1988 to 1993 and concurrently a member of the United Nations Committee on the Elimination of Discrimination Against Women 1984 to 1992. She readily and warmly acknowledged Dame Roma's friendship and support. The Honourable Justice Catherine Branson, Crown Solicitor of South Australia and Chief Executive Officer of the South Australian Attorney-General's Department from 1984 to 1989, appointed a judge in the Federal Court in 1994. The Honourable Justice Mary Gaudron. The Honourable Justice Jane Matthews, sworn in in the Supreme Court of New South Wales in 1987, wrote to Roma Mitchell: 'I feel I owe a great deal to the influence which you've exerted over the years. And all the more now that I've clambered – somewhat clumsily – into the shoes which you wore for so many years'. An example, was Roma Mitchell, of what a woman could attempt, and an inspiration to make such attempts.

The Honourable Elizabeth Evatt AC, LLM

It was her international vision and sympathy, together with the professionalism and detachment that she combined with her feminism, that made her so appropriate a choice by the Fraser Government to head the Human Rights Commission and its efforts to link Australia with United Nations' international human rights covenants. Such vision and sympathy made her, as Chair of the HRC, so appropriate a choice by the Hawke Government to chair a Royal Commission into what became known, popularly if inaccurately, as 'The Greek Conspiracy Case'.

This was an international scandal, extending from Sydney and Canberra to Athens, involving the Australian Commonwealth Police [COMPOL], the Australian Department of Social Security

[DSS], the Australian Attorney-General's Department and their Ministers, approximately a thousand Australian citizens – some of whom were medical practitioners, many of whom had been born in Greece – and an uncounted number of lawyers. It must have tasted extremely sour to Dame Roma, for many people suffered badly, and the only people to benefit were lawyers. Criminologist P.N. Grabosky provides an incisive analytical account.[4]

The mid–late 1970s were years of economic contraction. When the Australian Auditor-General estimated in 1975–1976 that unemployment benefits had been over-paid to the tune of $40 million, DSS determined to crack down on 'dole bludgers'. At about the same time, the relatively newly established COMPOL was anticipating a visit by Sir Robert Mark, former Commissioner of the London Metropolitan Police, to advise the Fraser Government on police organisation; the Australian police wanted to show that they were already competent, had 'runs on the board'. The two imperatives came together towards the end of 1976 when the Sydney office of DSS was told that an arrangement existed between medical practitioners and members of the Greek community to defraud the Australian welfare system. The medicos, this story alleged, would provide certificates testifying to inability to work, in return for extraordinary payments; the people obtaining those certificates would use them to gain invalid pensions. In December 1976, COMPOL were told that DSS had been authorised to provide information to COMPOL to help investigate this alleged fraud.

By September 1977, COMPOL had passed on to DSS allegations from an informant who estimated that the fraud involved eight medical practitioners, at least 500 people 'of Greek extraction', and a cost to the taxpayer of between $2.5 and $5 million a year. Following some further preliminaries, which included a cash payment to the informant for his cooperation, COMPOL acted. A team of over 100 police in Sydney made early morning raids on some 160 households and five doctors' surgeries. The police invited the tabloid *Sun* to attend. They arrested 181 people, almost all of Greek background, and charged them with conspiracy to defraud the Commonwealth of Australia. The media dubbed the operation 'Don's Party', after Detective Chief Inspector Don Thomas who had led it. On 3 April 1978, eighty-three of those charged appeared in Central Court in Sydney. On the steps outside, Detective Chief Inspector Thomas held a news conference. This was 'the greatest breakthrough in the history of the police force', he announced. He 'heralded the possibility of a further thousand arrests, and the extradition of a further 300 people from Greece'. Police were stationed at all major airports to prevent other fraudsters leaving the country. There were more arrests over the following weekend. A total of 699 people had their social security benefits withdrawn. The publicity ensured a moral panic about welfare cheats and about government prosecutors, and – among non-Greek Australians – about Greeks in the community. And the Greek community, one of the largest ethnic minority groups in Australia, was both distraught and outraged.

But this affair was not the grand triumph that Chief Inspector Thomas proclaimed. Instead, it gradually unravelled into a sordid and shameful instance of dishonest opportunism coupled with public ethnocentric prejudice. There were no more arrests. The 181 charged were mostly people of very modest means, and the costs to the government of providing them with legal representation ended up at around $10 million. The 699 people who lost their pensions did so abruptly, and without any warning or opportunity to defend themselves. Some suffered extreme hardship. Home owners, unable to meet their mortgage payments, were forced to sell their houses. Tenants were threatened with eviction. Some were so reduced that they had to scavenge in rubbish bins.

What surfaced during the long-drawn-out court hearings about police procedure was shocking. When Don Thomas was cross-examined, it emerged that the informant who had initially approached COMPOL, providing information in return for indemnity and a cash reward, was actually a police agent, acting on Thomas's instructions. Questions followed about entrapment, as they did, too, after the courts learned of recorded telephone conversations between police agents and people alleged to be conspirators, and of police bugging the surgeries of two doctors. Other questions revolved around personal documents, passports and bank statements.

Eventually – the informant flew back to Greece, first-class, at the Australian tax-payers' expense; the court told Thomas it would ask the Attorney-General to institute proceedings against him for both perjury and conspiracy to pervert the course of justice; a decision to proceed against four doctors was quashed; of the 181 people initially charged with conspiracy to defraud the Commonwealth of Australia, four were convicted on that charge and thirty-three were convicted of lesser charges of imposition. The four included three patients who each pleaded guilty and were placed on good behaviour bonds, and a doctor who was convicted on a conspiracy charge and sentenced to a term in prison. The thirty-three convictions were for minor irregularities, some almost trivial; eight of them were fined and the rest were placed on good behaviour bonds. Distress among the Australian Greek community clearly needed – and warranted – redress.

The change of government in March 1983 set that need firmly on the agenda. On 31 January 1984, Attorney-General Gareth Evans and Don Grimes, Minister for Social Security, announced the appointment of a judicial inquiry to determine appropriate compensation for anyone who had been wrongly prosecuted as a result of 'Don's Party'. The Chair of the Human Rights Commission, Dame Roma Mitchell, would head it, and for this purpose would have the powers of a royal commission. She had now retired from the Bench, though she was deeply engaged with the HRC. Over the next two years she spent more time away from Adelaide than at home, in Sydney, and in Athens, reviewing relevant files held by DSS and COMPOL, hearing submissions from individual complainants, and holding public hearings so that the legal representatives of the claimants could make oral submissions.

What she heard was heartbreaking. Many of the people arrested were charged for no better reason than that they were pensioners who had names that appeared to be Greek, and who had been treated by one or more of the doctors at the centre of the police investigation. Grabosky describes them:

> Most were born in Greece, with elementary formal education, and with limited ability to speak or understand English. A number had not adjusted well to life in Australia; they tended to come from village

> backgrounds and coped poorly with the stresses of urban living. Many had worked for a number of years in heavy labouring jobs, and had suffered disabling physical injury from industrial accidents. A number also suffered from psychiatric illness, thereby compounding these difficulties.

Dame Roma heard of men frightened by large policemen (who had not bothered with search warrants) arriving several together, making jokes that sounded like threats. When those men were brought into the lock-ups, police took identification photographs of them, and added to those photographs not only a number but also a sign with the word 'Greece' written on it. Friends and relatives of those arrested sought to raise bail for them, but it was a weekend, they were invalid pensioners so the $1000 required was well beyond their means, and in any case the police had confiscated their bank books. In the lock-up, they were put in cells that were already overcrowded with people who appeared to be vagrants or drunks. There were no private toilet facilities, and the cells were putrid. One person who had been receiving psychiatric treatment at the time when he was arrested subsequently committed suicide.

Dame Roma's awareness of the processes and effects of discrimination was especially acute at this time; she spent days each month with the other members of the HRC discussing ways of preventing it. Hearing the evidence presented to her as the Royal Commissioner into the so-called Social Security Conspiracy case must have been sickening.

Ultimately, on 30 April 1986, she presented a report to the Governor General that recommended payment of compensation totalling $6.1 million. As well, she recommended payment of an additional $1.24 million for 'legal costs that had thus far been borne privately by the medical practitioners who had been implicated in the alleged conspiracy'. The only real winners, observed Grabosky, were 'those members of the legal profession whose good fortune it was to have become involved in the various legal proceedings which were as lucrative as they were protracted'. Detective Chief Inspector Don Thomas had a good eye for the main chance. He was not prosecuted. Instead, he resigned his position and joined the New South Wales Bar. Over all, Grabosky notes, mildly enough:

'The total cost to the Australian tax-payer approached $100 million, a sum vastly in excess of that which was originally alleged to have been fraudulently acquired.' Dame Roma told Sir Walter Crocker that she was going to ask 'an ex-Taxing Master' to go through the claims for legal costs because her staff had found that 'one of the not few lawyers involved had padded his bill 300 per cent'.[5]

Yet none of this work overseas, or her extensive travelling within Australia for the HRC, ever made Dame Roma wish that she had or could live anywhere else but in South Australia. 'Have you ever felt like a big fish in a small pond?' asked an interviewer.

> Have you ever thought about going to one of the bigger states or even internationally, given that somebody of your ability, stature, confidence, could have done well outside the relatively small community of South Australia?

'No', she replied, without missing a beat. 'I never had any aim to do so'. She had enjoyed 'working in other places', but, no: 'I haven't ever felt – oh, it would be good to make my mark elsewhere'.[6]

She was far too busy even to contemplate such a thought. When she was not travelling the world or the nation, or working in Sydney, then she was flat out at home. She was entertaining – on one occasion all of the Human Rights Commissioners and Al Grassby, as well; on another, the stepdaughter of her old friend Jim Brazel. This was Amanda Vanstone, elected to the Senate in 1984.[7] She was going to concerts, the opera, and to the theatre with old friends like Russell Longmire, or former colleague Doreen Bulbeck and her husband Paul, or Piers Plumridge and Margaret Nyland, or more recent friends like Geography Professor Fay Gale; they would go out for supper afterwards to one of the restaurants mushrooming around the city. These days everyone liked the kind of food, like eggplant, that had seemed so exotic to Professor Campbell's students in the 1930s. During the early 1980s, theatre supremo Jim Sharman gave the State Theatre Company a new name – Lighthouse – and in two seasons gave premieres of large-scale new works by Patrick White, Bill Harding, Louis Nowra and Stephen Sewell, as well as reinterpretations of the classics, equally large-scale Shakespeare, Kleist, Beaumarchais, Lorca, and Rodgers and Hart. Directors of the Festivals brought to Adelaide such English talents as Christopher Hunt and Lord Harewood (who had married Patricia Tuckwell, sister of that maestro of the French horn, Barry Tuckwell; she had been an Australian model known by the name 'Bambi'). Don Dunstan recommended to the Trustees of the Festival Centre that they invite another brilliant Englishman, Anthony Steel, to Adelaide to run some festivals. At Steel's festivals, Dame Roma could have heard the Polish Chamber Orchestra, watched Jiri Kylian's Nederlands Dans Theatre, and in 1988 take rugs and sleeping-bags to the quarry where Peter Brook was staging *The Mahabharata*, a performance that took all night. She joined audiences who flocked to the Barossa Music Festival, born in 1990, nurtured by the talents of local violinist Brenton Langbein; he and his colleagues organised concerts of chamber music and gastronomic delights in the wineries and old churches of the Barossa Valley, north of Adelaide. Even walking from her flat on East Terrace to the shops on Hutt Street could become a major excursion, because so many people wanted to stop her and chat. She would meet Noni Farwell for lunch or coffee at a café there called Roma's: 'I'll meet you at *my* café', she would tell Noni. Walter Crocker was vividly rude about how she looked: 'Roma Mitchell with her quick short-step walk reminds me more and more of a rooster wearing spectacles'.[8] Short steps for high-heeled shoes, something beyond Crocker's ken.

She was spending time at Carrickalinga with Jean and Billie Whyte, peaceful weekends, walking across sand so silky it squeaked, swimming in a gentle swell, then trudging through the tufty sea grass to their cabin for a gin-and-tonic, a meal of local crayfish and salad with a frosted bottle of riesling, and a nap. Later she would be back in the water, pleased if she could swim twice in a day, and around sundown, she would visit another retired judge, Andrew Wells who, with his wife Eleanor, also had a place there, and they would drink sherry before dinner. Once when Roma wanted to go to the butcher's shop, Billie – who was growing vague – asked for directions. 'We go round the roundabout', said Roma, and so Billie drove round and round and round the roundabout, chuckling. Sometimes Dame Roma organised a seaside trip with her former Associates. Lindy Powell remembered how she would ring and say, 'Lindy, I think we're going to Carrickalinga this weekend', and there was never a chance for Lindy to say, 'But Dame Roma, I was going to a party.' And at Carrickalinga, even if they stayed up late, drinking and talking, 'we always had to be up and off to church in the morning', said Helena Jasinski, who, being Catholic, would go with her to Normanville, where the nearest service was.[9]

She was lunching at the Queen Adelaide Club where she might meet Heather Bonnin, Chair of the Board of the Art Gallery of South Australia; Heather remembered telling her about the time when she effectively proposed marriage to Jim, her doctor husband. 'She had that all too rare gift of being able to make the person she was talking to feel special about themselves', said Amanda Vanstone. 'She used it widely, although not indiscriminately'. 'Oh he was a bastard!' she exclaimed in a conversation about the father of Joe Steele, a young artist, partner of novelist and artist Barbara Hanrahan. She understood all too well, Vanstone noted, with some relish, 'how to convey through what was said, what was not said and through body language, just how little or how much she thought of someone'.[10]

Amid all this activity, Dame Roma was working. For there were new challenges and demands ahead of this tireless seventy year old.

The recession that was held to have triggered the Social Security scandal in the late 1970s, the recession that had prompted Premier Dunstan to try to find out if there was any way of making it safe for his Government to support development of uranium mining at Roxby Downs – that recession was an international phenomenon. The long economic boom that followed the Second World War throughout the advanced industrial nations had come to an end. By the mid-1980s, conservative regimes in Britain under Margaret Thatcher, and in the United States under Ronald Reagan, had discarded the Keynesian economics and the commitment to welfare that characterised the boom years in the West, and had adopted, instead, policies labelled variously 'economic rationalism' or 'economic liberalism'. It was a huge shift and one that drew political authority from the collapse of the USSR and the fall of the Berlin Wall in the late 1980s – both together signalling and symbolising the end of the decades of Cold War between the socialist East and the capitalist West. These policies reeled back state protectionism, turning the operation of the economy over, increasingly, to the market. Talk of needs and justice and rights vanished; now, talk was all about efficiency, deregulation and privatisation.[11]

The Labor Government of R.J. Hawke in Canberra was of an entirely different political hue from the Thatcherite Tories and the Reaganite Republicans. But it still had to deal constructively with an economy undergoing successive recessionary crises. In 1985 its Treasurer, Paul Keating, deregulated the Australian banking and financial system, opening them up to the global economy. In the late 1980s, the Hawke Government also began to dismantle what had begun life as the Commonwealth Arbitration Commission, the nation's central wage-fixing mechanism, proud boast of the protectionist Australian labour movement for almost a century. In its place they introduced the practice of 'enterprise bargaining' with negotiations to take place directly between managers and workers over wages and conditions in individual enterprises, in individual workplaces. And those enterprises and workplaces were, increasingly, governed not by national laws and institutions but, rather, by the market. After the Federal Liberal-National Party Coalition under John Howard won the election of 1996, these processes were extended further. Belief in a right to social welfare faltered, defeated by the appearance of programs such as work-for-the-dole. Commentators diagnosed a breakdown in social cohesion, especially in precisely the relations concerning racial and ethnic difference that Dame Roma was working to improve with the HRC during the early 1980s.[12]

In South Australia, the election called soon after Dunstan's resignation in 1979 brought the Liberal Government of David Tonkin to power. But only three years later, another election returned another Labor Government with John Bannon at its head. They held power from November 1982 until September 1992. So it was the Bannon Labor Government that bore the brunt of this huge shift in the Australian economy and economic culture, and in relations between the market, the state, and civil society, coupled with major economic recessions in 1983 and 1991–1992.

There were similarities to be found between Dunstan and Bannon, to be sure: educated at Saints and the Adelaide University Law School, amateur experience in the performing arts, just for a start. But the start was all the similarities there were. Fair-headed, blue-eyed, marathon runner John Bannon, son of the Art Master at Saints, had been an undergraduate in the days when the Law School was enjoying the effects of Norval Morris's arrival. He had joined with Frances Nelson – who was to become a QC, the second woman in South Australia after Roma Mitchell to take silk, and the longest-serving Chair of the Parole Board – in debating 'That the nudity of domestic animals is desirable', 'That virginity is a state of mind' and 'That there is no sin except stupidity'. He was to be heard mixing the 'Internationale' with Gilbert and Sullivan when drinking with his mates, and, being a German scholar, on occasion at parties, 'doing near-perfect imitations of Herr Hitler'. He had edited the student newspaper, *On Dit*, and had been a leader in the fierce and innovative student politics of a time that saw student unions give birth to the Australian Overseas Student Travel Scheme. His undergraduate years were a moment of the joyous counter-cultural rebellion and adventure of the 1960s, quite different from the post-Depression, wartime seriousness of Dunstan's time at university. In another signal of the differences between his times and Dunstan's, Bannon had married Robyn Layton – herself a Law graduate on her way to being a judge, first in the Industrial Court, subsequently, in 2005, on the Bench of the Supreme Court of South Australia.

Bannon had held a number of advisory positions, including one in the Federal Department of Labour and Immigration when its minister was South Australian Senator, Clyde Cameron, in the Whitlam Government. He was a white-collar professional, one of 'a new set of decision makers from outside of the trade unions'. So young was he, when he was elected Premier, that some spoke of him as 'the Boy Wonder'. But this was not a reference to glitter or glamour. Rather – and ironically, given his carefree student years – he was extremely sober and careful: the Carnival was well and truly Over. He was an 'ever cautious Treasurer' said one of his ministers, an economic 'dry', convinced of the necessity for 'economic rationalism', 'lecturing his Cabinet at the annual seminar on the allegedly parlous condition of the State's finances', questioning his senior bureaucrats about where the money was going.[13]

The sad state of the South Australian economy in the early 1980s would seem to have warranted caution. It was in an even worse condition than the national economy, and throughout the Bannon years unemployment was higher than for Australia as a whole. The whitegoods industries had gone, relocated off shore. The motor manufacturing industry was shrinking under the same pressures from the market. Mining at Roxby Downs did go ahead, but the Government endeavoured to maintain a distance from a source of jobs so immensely unpopular with environmentalist electors. Bannon and his Cabinet focused on a few large-scale developments that political commentator Andrew Parkin characterises as 'Playford-style' projects, intended to 'stimulate the economy and symbolise growth and renewal'. Parkin lists them:

John Bannon running a marathon race, published with permission of the *Advertiser*

> the large public–private joint venture to develop the Golden Grove housing estate, the huge development of the Adelaide Railway Station area to include a Hyatt hotel and a convention centre, a bid to win a submarine construction project and the advent of the Formula One Grand Prix to the inner Adelaide street circuit.

There were others, too, but – except, perhaps, for the huge Entertainment Centre built at the city end of the road to Port Adelaide – they had little success, at least at that time: tourist development in the ecologically delicate environment of the Flinders Ranges, north of Port Augusta; another attempt at a tourist magnet, a cable-car from the Adelaide plains up the scrub-covered slopes of the Adelaide Hills to the pinnacle of Mount Lofty, again a project threatening a fragile environment; developments along the Adelaide foreshore – those wonderful beaches of Dame Roma's childhood; and the Multi-Function Polis, an idea initiated in Japan but with quite beguiling vagueness about who would provide the funding for it, and how, allocated to South Australia by a national committee that determined that a swampy area called Gilman, north-west of Adelaide, its underground water table lethal with industrial waste, would be a good site for a high-technology retirement city for Japanese people. And then there was the combination government–corporate venture, the State Bank, ultimately such a disaster that it dumped a huge debt onto the South Australian economy and onto young Bannon's desk.[14]

Consequent economic imperatives meant that, even though government funding for community services – health, education and welfare – roughly doubled during the Bannon Decade, there were still severe cuts in funding allocations from the mid-1980s on. These clipped the wings of one energetic and adventurous reformer, John Cornwall, Minister of Health from 1982 until 1988. He instituted an array of inquiries,[15] and engaged the help of Dame Roma – emblem of the contradictory combination of reform, tradition, and parsimony with other people's money.

She chaired a body titled graphically but puzzlingly the Very Difficult Clients Liaison and Research Committee. Its concern was with the problems of the mentally ill and homeless, people who would once have been incarcerated in psychiatric hospitals but were now de-institutionalised, left to wander the streets. Among them, Dame Roma was shocked to learn, were 'a significant number of homeless children'. Next, she sat on a Management Assessment Panel for Behaviourally Disordered Persons, and headed an advisory committee appointed to deal with objections to the establishment of an alcohol detoxification centre in the respectable eastern Adelaide suburb of Joslin, recommending measures to ensure that patients would not have any contact with children from nearby schools or cub and scout troops, and meeting fear with information, prejudice with sweet reason. Many of the protesting residents' submissions, she explained in her report, exhibited a stereotypical image of drug withdrawal as 'screaming, terrified patients in extreme physical and mental distress who … would do anything to get their drug'. The reality would be quite different: 'patients ... would be, on average, very tired people who had suffered from long periods of sleep deprivation and who felt generally unwell'.[16]

She accepted the politically tricky job of chairing a steering committee appointed to produce a plan for the amalgamation of two hospitals that had stubbornly refused all attempts to integrate them into the management structure of the South Australian Health Commission – the century-old Adelaide Children's Hospital and the illustrious Queen Victoria Maternity Hospital, founded by Audrey, Lady Tennyson, wife of South Australia's Governor, in 1902, a 'model fifteen-bed maternity hospital'. It was not Cornwall who proposed her for this post, but Judith Roberts, chair of the Queen Victoria Hospital Board, a former member of the Liberal Party. Judith Roberts had been considered likely to make her mark in conservative politics, but had resigned in protest against her party's reluctance to endorse women to contest safe Liberal seats. She and Dame Roma were natural allies. Dame Roma was successful: the plan was complete by the end of 1988, the physical removal of the Queen Victoria Hospital's services to North Adelaide to be effected by 1993, funded by the sale of the vastly expanded Queen Victoria building that began the twenty-first century as a block of apartments.[17]

Dame Roma headed the new Child Protection Council, too, a body that the Child Sexual Abuse Task Force had recommended establishing in 1986, its charter to focus on psychological as well as physical abuse, its members to include Sue Vardon, Director-General of the Department of Community Welfare, and Josephine Tiddy, Commissioner for Equal Opportunity. Dame Roma's successor in this important position was the former principal of Pembroke School, the co-educational independent Protestant school in the eastern suburbs, formed when King's College for boys and Girton Girls' School were amalgamated in 1974.[18] This was Didi Medlin, wife of Harry, with whom Dame Roma worked extensively, and often arduously, on the Council of the University of Adelaide.

Chancellor of the University of Adelaide

That council, Dame Roma was to confide to Basil Hetzel, Chancellor of the University of South Australia, was 'the most demanding committee she had ever chaired'.[19] She had been elected Deputy Chancellor in 1972. Precedent could have led her to expect – or at least hope for – elevation to the top position, in time. Two chancellors, Sir George Coutts Ligertwood and Sir Kenneth Wills, had both moved seamlessly from the position of Deputy Chancellor to that of Chancellor in the late 1950s and 1960s, and no fewer than five of nine men appointed to the chancellorship, including Sir Mellis Napier and John Bray, had come from the ranks of serving or retired Supreme Court judges. But Roma Mitchell's path to this post was far from smooth.

The first obstacle had occurred even earlier. In 1968 Sir Kenneth Wills was retiring as Chancellor and John Bray was being elected to take his place. Kenneth Wills and Roma Mitchell were old friends. He encouraged her to stand for election as Deputy Chancellor. But the University of Adelaide still nurtured the presumptions and attitudes about the position of women that had characterised her years as an undergraduate, even though she had since lectured so successfully to generations of students in the Law School. There were very few women on the academic staff, and those few generally occupied the most junior, and often temporary, ranks. Where women were to be found in substantial numbers was among the administrative staff, as secretaries – handmaidens to the male academics. The even tenor of these gentlemen's ways was about to be disrupted by the anti-authoritarianism of the counter culture and the leftist opposition to the war in Vietnam. But the resulting democratisation of those bodies charged with making decisions did not alter the profound conservatism of the institution's culture; democratisation meant only that everyone, even those who disagreed, became complicit in the conservative policies resolved upon by the majority. Further, such democratisation was a process that involved only men; women were hardly – yet anyway – registering as intelligences on these gentlemen's radars. Accordingly, when Justice Mitchell was seriously proposed as a candidate for the position of Deputy Chancellor, the gentlemen set about to discredit her. Roma Mitchell's defeat in 1968 was engineered by a smear campaign against her alleging that she was a lesbian and a drunk.[20]

By 1972, though, with young female students organising demonstrations of the Women's Liberation Movement, and female postgraduate students combining to offer courses in Women's Studies, Her Honour Justice Roma Mitchell appeared in a very different light. Familiar, she was, and respectable: knew how to behave. Moreover, homophobia in a culture that prized John Bray as its Chancellor, and judgmentalism about alcohol consumption among academic gentlemen who consumed quite so much wine at lunch time, looked at least inconsistent now, if not inaccurate and unjust. Further, electing her Deputy Chancellor would provide them with an alibi against charges about the absence of women in their ranks.

She was not going to allow such acceptance to inhibit her, however. She took occasion in her addresses to the four commemoration ceremonies of 1972 to make clear assertion of the justice of some of the current demands of the Women's Movement. She deplored the fact that women applying for jobs in commerce and industry were often asked only if they could type, and hoped that soon 'the sex of an applicant would no longer be regarded as relevant to an appointment to any position'. Later she emphasised that she did not favour 'token' appointments, but held that a woman's sex should not operate to her disadvantage. 'Universities that said they always had one woman dean', she said, 'were like curators who said "this zoo always has one giant panda".'[21]

As the second obstacle to her advance from Deputy to Chancellor was her old friend John Bray, Justice Mitchell hesitated to dislodge him. For Bray had early in his career sought appointment as a Professor of Law, and when that proved unsuccessful he had prized those connections that he had been able to maintain – with the Law School as lecturer, with the University as a member of the Classical Association, as a member of the English Association – Adelaide Branch, and, ultimately, as its Chancellor.[22] He was elected unopposed in 1968 and re-elected, again unopposed, in 1973 and 1978.

He defined his role, and that of the Deputy Chancellor, as 'ceremonial heads' of the University, to be quite distinct from the

Vice-Chancellor, who was 'the executive head'. Accordingly, he noted, 'I held aloof from the day-to-day running of the university', even during what Dame Roma was to refer to, so gently, as 'some turmoil at the time of the Vietnam War', leaving it to the Vice-Chancellor 'to calm passions'. When students invaded Council meetings to claim a right to representation there, 'Council adjourned for some period', recalled Dame Roma, 'and John and I departed to the Richmond Hotel (but not the bar) and left it to the then Vice-Chancellor, Professor Geoffrey Badger, to entertain the protesting students to tea and biscuits and sort matters out'.[23] Subsequently, Bray considered that there was no foundation for disquiet over student members of Council whose presence followed from the turmoil; on the contrary, their contributions to debates had, he observed, 'been marked by moderation and good sense'.

Yet however hands-off a Chancellor he was, being Chancellor was a great deal of work. No doubt Dame Roma was writing of her own experience as well when she described John Bray's.

> University Council meetings are not occasions for relaxation. There is a prodigious quantity of papers to be perused before each meeting, and many become available only shortly before the meeting. The Chancellor, who is to preside, needs to have a good working, if not detailed, knowledge of what is involved in each item on the agenda. John Bray's speed of reading and of mastering facts stood him in good stead in this regard. In relation to many of the items for discussion there are a number of members eager to speak, sometimes with opposing views, sometimes to reiterate what has already been said. As Chancellor John Bray had an inexhaustible supply of patience at such meetings. There was at least one member of council who, at times, wished it were otherwise! The Chancellor did sometimes bemoan the inordinate amount of time spent on minutiae of administration as opposed to that devoted to matters of research and teaching, but he realised that the tide was against him and he accepted that position with good grace.

Academics can be extremely wordy, she intimated, to say nothing of being pompous and self-important; they often insist on contributing to debate, even when their point has been made already by someone else, sometimes already made several times by several other people.

One academic who became prominent on the University of Adelaide Council during these years was Harry Medlin, older brother of John Bray's good friend, Brian Medlin the poet. An electrician who joined the Royal Australian Engineers in February 1938, Harry Medlin spent three years and seven months of his time on active service as a prisoner of war in Timor and Java. The Commonwealth Reconstruction Training Scheme brought him to Adelaide University where he gained degrees including a PhD with a thesis on crystal structure, and an academic post to teach Physics. He knew at first hand of the struggle necessary for many seeking further education; he devoted a great deal of his energies and his years at the University – 'with obstinacy, tenacity, imagination and dedication, and assisted by an elephantine memory' – to efforts to assist others in that struggle. He was elected to the University Council in 1967, and was then re-elected continuously until 2003. His intense commitment to rights for the underdog, his involvement with an immense array of activities related to the University – ranging from the Federation of Australian University Staff Associations to the Tertiary Institutions Child Care Centre, from the Adelaide University Theatre Guild to the Adelaide University Union Bookshop – and his concern with administrative detail, could irritate some members of the Council. Mervyn Smith told Sir Walter Crocker that 'Medlin ... has done enormous damage since the student unrest in the 'sixties threw him up'. To be sure, Medlin allowed conviction to outweigh chivalry on at least one occasion when his remarks about members of selection committees being 'politically managed' reduced Deputy Chancellor Justice Mitchell to tears. Not you, he hastened to reply, and not Sam Jacobs (by then a judge on the Supreme Court Bench) either; they, after all, were two of the three people he considered to have been the 'young "Turks"' who had set up the Standing Committee of the University Senate in 1961. But then he made it all worse.

> I say however as deliberately as I can and with complete respect that it is not necessarily to be taken as meaning that they, or anyone else, cannot be politically managed. In my opinion no special political acumen attaches to lawyers. Even a judge cannot expect it to be

> accepted that he carries with him his absolute impartiality when he steps from the bench into other arenas.[24]

Nevertheless, in 1978, Council created a new position and elected Medlin to it. They made him Second Deputy Chancellor – to fill any possible gap created if both John Bray and Roma Mitchell had to be absent on Supreme Court business at the same time – making it more than clear that even in so conservative an institution, there were others who did not share the disparaging views of him that Walter Crocker recorded. In 1984, they elected him Senior Deputy Chancellor, a position he held until 1997.

One of the most intransigent matters facing the Council during these years was the relationship between Adelaide University's North Terrace campus, where the bulk of its teaching and research took place, and the Waite Institute of Agricultural Research near Urrbrae, in the south-eastern suburbs, not far from the foothills that young Roma Mitchell had climbed when she was a child living at Kingswood. Vice-Chancellor Geoffrey Badger had once referred to the Waite as 'the jewel in the crown and the mill-stone around the neck' of the University. Staff at the Waite felt isolated and undervalued, their institution not adequately funded for the important work they did. They were told that their independence was under attack. In 1978 Council appointed Justice Mitchell head of a committee of enquiry into the relationship between the two bodies. Others on her committee were Justice Jacobs, the noted conservationist Warren Bonython, and the Hon. Anne Levy MLC. The committee's review of issues over funding, administration and academic matters clearly exercised a calming influence. The Waite's Director, Professor J.P. Quirk, thanked them 'for the orderly, dignified and patient way in which they had conducted the enquiry and for the manner in which they had negotiated the labyrinthine ways of complex and intricate issues'; the Council accepted their report on 13 June 1980.

Yet trouble soon surfaced again. Quirk considered his emolument inadequate. Previous directors had lived in Urrbrae House, which not only saved on housing costs but also provided free repairs and the services of a gardener. If he had to live somewhere else, then he should receive a compensatory financial allowance. A second committee produced an alternative formula for funding the Waite. But Quirk preferred the formula that the Mitchell Committee had recommended. The squabbling was to drag on until August 1986 when Dame Roma definitively closed it down, announcing that 'the Council was perfectly satisfied that the Waite Institute had received its proper share of University resources'.[25]

Once he had settled into it, Medlin set about making use of his new position. He was tired of Bray's focus on Classics and the Law, he said, and his lack of interest in the rest of the University. In May 1983, he suggested to the Council that it was time to 'engage in the exercise of determining who shall be the Chancellor of the University from 1 November 1983'. Bray equivocated about whether or not he would stand again. Medlin tried to discourage him. He and Dame Roma and Alex Castles, who was also a member of Council, had been plotting. Medlin and Mitchell would nominate each other for election to the position of Chancellor: Medlin and Castles nominated Dame Roma, and Dame Roma and Castles nominated Harry Medlin. No-one nominated John Bray, and Harry Medlin's nomination carried a proviso: 'if, at the close of nominations, there is only one other nomination, namely that of Roma Flinders Mitchell, then his nomination is to lapse'.[26] So Bray did not stand, and Dame Roma was elected unopposed at the meeting of the University of Adelaide Council on 9 September 1983.

She was the first woman to be chancellor of an Australian university. When she donned the robes of office, splendidly embroidered in gold, she reflected on the predecessor who had donated them to the University.

> I certainly did not anticipate, when I graduated, that I would one day wear the robes which belonged to the then chancellor, Sir George Murray. Nor, I am confident in saying, did he. He was the Chief Justice of South Australia, an elderly, scholarly bachelor. Although he was a man of impeccable courtesy, I wonder whether his courtesy would have survived an intimation in December 1934 that one of his successors, five down the line, would be a young woman upon whom he had just conferred the LL.D. degree.

She was, of course, long accustomed to the robes of judicial office, but she knew well that by donning the 'black-with-gold robes designed specially for the office and the mortar-board with a gold tassel' of what Virginia Woolf had called 'the procession of learned gentlemen', she was, yet again, a woman moving onto a path that had previously been the exclusive preserve of men.[27]

Bray declared, 'Now the course is set for the University to sail serenely into the computer era with Dame Roma Mitchell at the helm. I am sure that she will be a more vigilant navigator than I.' Her view of what the position required was indeed of a more active engagement than Bray's had been, even though – as he knew very well – she knew nothing about computing. She likened being Chancellor to being the chairman of a board; she was more than a mere ceremonial figurehead, she was an advisor to the Vice-Chancellor and, like the Vice-Chancellor, available to the University as a whole.[28] And the University as a whole was about to encounter more of an upheaval than followed the rapid spread of microcomputers to which John Bray had alluded, and the related development of electronic communications systems. The University was about to sail into very turbulent waters.

The Vice-Chancellor when she took office was Don Stranks. A compelling and popular teacher, he had been appointed to Adelaide University's foundation Chair of Inorganic Chemistry in 1964. His academic standing gained him membership of numerous national committees, among them the Australian Research Grants Committee, predecessor of the Australian Research Council. He was an active member of Community Aid Abroad, and already knew Dame Roma from the time they both spent on the South Australian Committee of the Churchill Memorial Trust. In the mid-1970s, he left for the University of Melbourne, his *alma mater*, as Professor of Inorganic Chemistry and Chair of the School of Chemistry, but returned to Adelaide when he was appointed Vice-Chancellor in 1977. He liked Dame Roma, valued her 'friendly and incisive counsel' and looked forward with pleasure to 'a long and continuing personal association'. '[Y]our service now as Chancellor is adding new dimensions to the role of that Office', he told her.[29]

Besides the running sore of relations between North Terrace and the Waite, there was another issue that Vice-Chancellor Stranks and Chancellor Dame Roma needed to tidy up. This concerned the Research Centre for Women's Studies, established in

1983 with what were described as 'windfall monies' that had become available to the Faculty of Arts.[30] The Faculty had appointed a director to establish a research centre for women's studies, and allocated the windfall to pay her salary for the next three years. But it had not considered that such a centre might need funding for anything else – a typewriter, perhaps, paper, pens, access to photocopying, telephone and postage – and it had not even thought about what was to happen to the centre at the end of its initial three years when the windfall funds would run out. But when it became clear that this centre could bring in funds from outside the university system, and win credit for an institution having to meet some of the requirements of government-funded bodies, following from the sex discrimination legislation of 1984, some members of the University campaigned for its continuance.

Fay Gale, Professor of Geography and the only senior woman on the academic staff, personally visited the dean of every faculty to try to persuade them to vote funds for the director's post to be continued. It was a tribute to the esteem in which she was held that they heard her at all: funds were extremely tight. They would not promise her that they would vote *for* such a proposal, but some did promise that they would not vote *against* it. The Director of the Research Centre, Susan Magarey, wrote to her friends and contacts all over Australia, indeed, all over the world, telling them of the centre's plight, and they wrote to Vice-Chancellor Stranks urging him to ensure that the Centre's good and important work would continue; he was to say that if he had had $10 for every letter that he had received, then the Research Centre for Women's Studies would be securely funded for the next ten years. The students, marshalled by Dr Carol Johnson, Lecturer in Politics, planned a demonstration, and threatened to hold it on a highly sensitive public occasion.

Professor Emerita Fay Gale AO

At the graduation ceremony in May 1985, the University would celebrate the centenary of the graduation of its first female graduate, Edith Dornwell, BSc, and at the same time would confer upon its recently elected Chancellor, Dame Roma Mitchell, the degree of Doctor of the University. But people attending this widely publicised ceremonial occasion now appeared likely to encounter a student picket, with support from members of the staff of the Working Women's Centre, the Women's Studies Resources Centre, the Women's Studies Unit in the Philosophy Department at Flinders University, and people teaching Women's Studies courses at the South Australian College of Advanced Education – all gathered at the doors of the Bonython Hall, their placards and chanting calling into question everything that the celebration was trying to establish about the University's rather hastily formed commitment to the rights and well-being of women. Something had to be done, and quickly.

The records don't show Don Stranks consulting Dame Roma, but there can be no doubt that he did. She knew about the Research Centre for Women's Studies. Indeed, she had contributed to one of its first efforts to establish what Women's Studies was, for a university that seemed not to know anything about women and the 'New Modes of Thought' by then being so widely developed in tertiary and secondary education that the Academy of the Social Sciences in Australia had devoted a conference to them in 1983. The Research Centre's effort was a series of public lectures in 1984 by senior feminist intellectuals from interstate, and one distinguished local: Roma Mitchell's lecture was titled 'Consideration of gender in changes in the law'. Stranks also consulted Fay Gale. Then, with only a few weeks to go before the graduation ceremony, he summoned Susan Magarey and asked her if she would accept tenure in the post of Director of the Research Centre for Women's Studies. She said yes, of course. So in the event, the demonstration around the doors of the Bonython Hall on 1 May 1985 was far smaller than had been threatened, and instead of protesting, the banners congratulated the University of Adelaide on its commitment to Women's Studies. Dame Roma told the participants in the graduation ceremony that she was gratified by the University's decision to commit further funding to the Research

Centre for Women's Studies, suggesting that it echoed the enlightened thinking of the earlier administrators who had admitted such students as Edith Dornwell to degrees. But she did, also, lament that the University of Adelaide was 'so backward in appointing women to the professorial staff', a plaint that she could have continued throughout her time as Chancellor.[31]

Don Stranks was clearly an adept politician. With Dame Roma's backing, he was appointed to a second term as Vice-Chancellor. He was elected Chair of the Australian Vice-Chancellors' Committee, too. But on Saturday 9 August 1986, playing tennis with his son at the courts at Memorial Drive, he suffered a heart attack and dropped dead. Shocked and stricken members of the University filled St Peter's Anglican Cathedral to capacity for a thanksgiving service and listened to Dame Roma's moving eulogy. 'Dear Don', she concluded, 'Go in peace'. John Bray wrote to congratulate her on it – 'a model of what such a speech should be. It was comprehensive, generous & compassionate', he affirmed, and then exclaimed: 'Who would have thought twenty-five years ago that you would be addressing a highly distinguished audience from the pulpit of the Anglican cathedral?'[32]

The *interregnum* called for Dame Roma to play a far more active part in the University's administration than John Bray could ever have imagined. Most importantly, she had to determine who should fill Don Stranks's shoes while the University went through the processes of finding his successor. She settled upon Kevin Marjoribanks, Professor of Education, with degrees from Harvard and Toronto universities, four years' teaching at Oxford University where he laid the foundations of his international reputation for research into the interaction of families and schools in determining the educational outcomes for children from diverse social and cultural backgrounds. He was a rugby player who

Vice-Chancellor Kevin Marjoribanks

enjoyed red wine and told good jokes. Here is just one – a very Adelaide joke.

> I recall standing near three undergraduates, whom I knew, at the cricket final earlier in the year, at the university oval. One of the young men was a former student of St Peter's College, one was from Prince Alfred College, and the other was from Woodville High School.
> A woman came to watch the game. The young undergraduate from PAC asked the woman if she would like a chair; but didn't do anything about it.
> The student from Woodville High – he didn't say anything but went and fetched a chair.
> And the student from St Peter's College – he sat on the chair.

He was also a gentle and generously perceptive man. He had been at Adelaide University since 1974, serving as Dean of Education, Chair of the Academic Board, Chair of the Education Committee, the University's academic decision-making body, and in 1986, as one of two Pro-Vice-Chancellors. He was invited to take on the job of Acting Vice-Chancellor, and when the selection processes added an invitation – which, Fay Gale told Susan Magarey, Dame Roma regarded as her own achievement – to take on the top job in his own right, he became Vice-Chancellor in 1987. They liked each other, Roma and Kevin. He considered her a 'valued friend', appreciated her 'understanding', her being 'caring and honourable', her steadfast backing – especially when he had to argue against 'vigorous and even unpleasant opposition'.[33]

And that he was bound to encounter. It was on his watch that the University met some of the consequences of the great changes in the Australian economy, polity and civil society. These represented another apparent contradiction. Labor Treasurer Keating's decision to open the Australian finance system, indeed the entire Australian economy, to the international marketplace was a move that could more readily have been expected of a conservative government. Similarly, the changes that became known as the 'Dawkins Reforms' – often with scare quotes around the word 'reforms' – were a strategy that might have been expected of an economically rationalist government seeking to reduce the costs of tertiary education, except for two factors: at least initially, these 'reforms' caused a major expansion of the number of student places in post-secondary education institutions, and, again, at least initially, funding from the Australian government increased markedly.

The demand for more, and more advanced, education during the three decades or so following the end of the Second World War had brought into being two new kinds of educational institution: colleges of advanced education and institutes of technology. Initially, people could assume, as did John Bray for one, that the 'theoretical departments of learning' should belong to the universities that awarded degrees, while institutes and colleges 'should qualify people technically for various occupations' in which people could earn diplomas.[34] But growth and change had blurred the distinctions in this dual system. Colleges of advanced education had begun to offer a comprehensive range of degrees, including higher degrees, and had adopted some of the titles and procedures of universities. They also engaged in research. Universities, in turn, had responded to ideas of open university and continuous learning by developing more flexible entry requirements, greater opportunities for external and part-time study, and a wider range of courses.[35] The Whitlam Government had abolished fees in an effort to make tertiary education more democratic, and student numbers did increase – indeed, the number of women gaining access to tertiary education increased more than the number of men, as the Australian Democrats were to point out when the Hawke Government reintroduced fees – but despite their growth, a number of individual colleges still remained uneconomically small. By the mid-1980s, the Commonwealth Government, which provided the bulk of higher education funding, had responded to recession by making cuts in its allocations, introducing stringent means testing for student-income support, and acknowledging that research funding was inadequate. In December 1987, Senator John Dawkins, the bright-eyed, darkly handsome Minister for Employment, Education and Training, issued a green paper titled *Higher Education – A Policy Discussion Paper*.

It was a serious critique of the comfortable ways of academic gentlemen in universities. The number of graduates was unjustifiably low by international standards and would need to increase to keep pace with projected demographic changes and international competitiveness. That would require reforms to existing structures and administrative arrangements and practices. A further imperative for change came from the need to provide better participation in higher education for low-income earners, Aboriginals, women 'and other disadvantaged groups'. The green paper made it clear that the Federal Government would use its financial dominance over the States and Territories to force the changes that it considered necessary. They were to abolish the distinction between universities and colleges, amalgamating some, and developing a 'unified system of universities'.

There ensued extensive, intense and highly emotional debate among academics at all three kinds of institution, all with a strong sense of urgency as Dawkins was to issue a white paper, *Higher Education – A Policy Statement*, only six months later. This, in effect, changed the verbs in the green paper from proposals to imperatives. Mergers between institutions abolishing the binary system and installing a 'unified system' were to be the primary means of introducing structural and efficiency gains for the sector. They were to be effected by 1990. There would be an emphasis on autonomy and accountability, and funds would be earmarked for equity and specified performance contracts. Institutions were, themselves, to seek out merger partners. At the end of this process, any institutions that fell outside the unified national system would be denied access to Commonwealth Government funding.

Vice-Chancellor Marjoribanks had been endeavouring to revivify the professoriate and its leadership within the University of Adelaide – leadership that, since the early 1970s, it had ceded to colleagues elected to head departments and higher committees – by instituting a series of inaugural lectures to be given by newly appointed professors. These enabled Marjoribanks, he would recall, 'to test out on a wide university audience a range of issues such as reactions to the early mergers'. He read the temper of his institution acutely and accurately. He summoned everyone employed in the University of Adelaide to a packed meeting in the Elder Hall and presented to them a lecture in which he meditated upon the nature of a university, and the relationship that he believed should exist between universities and governments.

'Universities must be able to examine the problems of our time, free from the necessity of appearing to be relevant or popular, or even, finally, correct', he announced. Research, for instance, should not be defined and limited by preconceived ends. If it is 'solely directed towards specific, practical, marketable and speedily achieved results, then it can be argued the research ... could distort the teaching and research activities of departments'. Universities should always, of course, listen to governments and industry, he acknowledged. They should assist them in achieving their social and economic goals – where appropriate.

> But they must not become a tool of governments or industry, otherwise we betray the very essence of what it is to be a university. It is always important to emphasize that universities are for the long run. They are custodians of the rational process itself. They stand for the worthwhileness of the intellectual pursuit of truth. It is important, therefore, that universities must always be prepared to challenge the government's creeping control of the intellectual agenda through its patronage of particular lines of enquiry and its unnecessary involvement in what should best be left to universities.

Universities 'are for the long run'. They were not to be 'the playthings of ephemeral ministers'. At the end of his term, he made the same point again. 'During my seven years as Vice-Chancellor there have been four Commonwealth Ministers responsible for higher education and four State Ministers': 'I rest my case.' He concluded by announcing that he and the Chancellor, Dame Roma, were writing to the other 'established universities' inviting them to 'join us in a common protest about the government's threat to the autonomy of the nation's universities'. Then, to a wildly enthusiastic standing ovation, he tucked his lecture under his arm and marched down the central aisle of Elder Hall like a knight heading for a white charger snorting on the lawn outside the front door, just waiting to carry him off to do battle against Canberra.[36]

It was an amazing moment, possibly unique in the history of universities in Australia. Of course, Marjoribanks did not lead the vice-chancellors of the Australian universities against Dawkins and the Government; it was Melbourne University's Vice-Chancellor Penington who took on that battle, with quiet but important support from Peter Karmel, former Vice-Chancellor of both Flinders University and the Australian National University. And they lost. Amalgamations were to go ahead.

The Dawkins Reforms brought a new philistinism to university education, converting education into training and research into precisely the kind of knowledge production that Marjoribanks condemned. His opposition to these changes did not represent any antagonism on Marjoribanks's part to government social justice imperatives; he was especially pleased, at the end of his seven years, that the University of Adelaide had adopted a policy of accepting a minimum of fifteen per cent of its initial student intake on special entry bases, and with the development of an Aboriginal Access Scheme. Similarly, in 1985, his Chancellor, Dame Roma, already well known as a campaigner for justice and human rights, had taken special pleasure, she said, in being able to confer the degree of LLB upon Mrs Irene Margaret Watson, the first Aboriginal woman graduate from Adelaide University.[37] But their participation in the negotiations over amalgamation was extremely reluctant.

During 1989, all four higher education institutions in South Australia established a merger implementation committee with Dame Roma as its Convenor. Flinders University had always been seen 'in academic terms as the "daughter" university of Adelaide';[38] that, and the rivalry between them, made any amalgamation of those two institutions an unhappy prospect. Instead, Flinders University and the South Australian Institute of Technology explored the possibility of merging with each other, while Adelaide University considered amalgamating with Roseworthy Agricultural College and with the South Australian College of Advanced Education. There were endless discussions, especially around questions of real estate, seniority and control, at every level of the institutions, and very great anxiety about resources. Kevin Marjoribanks and Dame Roma also discussed potential outcomes, at length. Ultimately, Marjoribanks decided that it would be a good idea for both to amalgamate Adelaide University with Roseworthy. At the same time, he determined that an amalgamation between Adelaide University and the South Australian College of Advanced Education – 'an institution as large as or even larger than itself', with, moreover, 'very different academic strategic objectives' – would benefit neither. Further, he noted, proposals to reduce higher education in South Australia to a 'two-university organisational structure' would make vulnerable 'the pre-eminent academic standing of the University of Adelaide'. He knew that there would be immense opposition to his view. But not from his Chancellor. She knew, he said, the importance of seizing the day and showing determination. Together, they withdrew the University of Adelaide from the Merger Implementation Committee's deliberations.[39]

In the end, it was the South Australian College of Advanced Education that was divided up. The amalgamations that did take place in 1990 were between its Kintore Avenue campus, next door to Adelaide University's North Terrace campus, Adelaide University and Roseworthy College; between the college's Sturt campus, adjoining Flinders University, and Flinders; and between the rest of the College of Advanced Education and the Institute of Technology. For the next fifteen years, South Australia would be a three-university state, the proportion of the funding coming from the Commonwealth government to each of those institutions shrinking dramatically, just as it did to universities across Australia. All were compelled to turn for survival to the market and student fees, increasingly paid by students from overseas. By the mid-2000s, tertiary education had become an important export commodity for Australia.

Dame Roma and Kevin Marjoribanks had one other serious trouble to deal with during their years together at Adelaide University's helm. The Department of Anthropology had been mourning the loss of its Foundation Professor ever since he had gone off to London University. Its members had developed into an inward-looking, quarrelsome and highly defensive community, unable to agree on almost anything, ranging from candidates to replace their professor to principles for marking students' work. A review was in order. The University appointed a Review Committee with the highly respected and popular Fay Gale – now a Pro-Vice-Chancellor – at its head. But so deep had the rifts become, and so scandalous the mutual accusations, that Professor Gale felt compelled to a drastic solution: the department would be disbanded and each academic distributed to another department nearest to his or her area of specialism, though the match was sometimes a bit rough and ready. Dame Roma, fearing for the reputation of the whole University, recommended that the records of the review be pulped. Courses in anthropology continued to be offered, but with difficulty. And Kevin Marjoribanks, with immense patience and care, went to see individual members of that department, regularly and frequently, counselling them, until – after a few had gone off to jobs in other places – the department could be brought together again.[40] By then, Dame Roma had been obliged to relinquish her position as Chancellor for that of Visitor to the University of Adelaide, for she had moved on to even higher office.

The Daily Round at Seventy-Plus

Let us pause, for a moment, to imagine a few days in the life of this unstoppable seventy-five year old. She was, of course, not the only former judge to fill her retirement so supremely. Charles Bright, for instance, had been elected Chancellor of Flinders University in 1971 and held that position until 1983, after his retirement from the Bench in 1978. He went on to serve part-time on the Health Commission; as special adviser to the government on health matters; as President of Minda, a home for the intellectually disabled; Vice-President of the Red Cross Society in South Australia; and Convenor of the Committee on the Rights of Persons with Handicaps.[41] David Hogarth, made a Companion of the Order of Australia in 1982, spent the first ten years after his retirement in 1979 on the time-consuming and exacting preparation of an index to the South Australian *State Reports* – the published records of precedent-setting trials. He continued his membership of the Council of Aquinas College, and, after being Inaugural Chairman of the Council of the Sturt College of Advanced Education, was made an honorary life fellow of the South Australian Colleges of Advanced Education in 1982. He also gave his time as Vice-President of the Australian–Asian Association (SA), Vice-President of the Malay Language and Cultural Association (SA), a member of a committee of the Australia–Japan Association and Convenor of the Committee for the Introduction of Japanese Language into

School Curricula in South Australia. But his great love was community sports and he served as President and later Patron of the South Australian Hockey Association, Chair of the Committee for the Duke of Edinburgh's Awards (SA), Director of the Royal Caledonian Society and Vice-President of the Adelaide Highland Games.[42] John Bray had told his good friend Roma Mitchell of the attractions of '[r]everie and introspection' in retirement, observing

> I now feel astonished at my former energy & feel less & less inclined to bestir myself, not on account of any lessening of any intellectual interest so much as avoidance of all the mechanics of its practical application.

Nevertheless, his retirement saw the publication of three collections of his own poetry, a selection of his poetry and prose, a collection of his occasional addresses, his continuing participation in The Poetry, in gatherings and readings of the Friendly Street Poets and in Writers' Week, and the completion of a work of massive scholarship, a biography of the bizarre Roman emperor, *Gallienus: A Study in Reformist and Sexual Politics*.[43]

Yet even compared with those of such thoroughly occupied, learned and philanthropic citizens, Dame Roma's days were quite extraordinarily busy. She always rose early, scanned the newspapers, wrote letters, made telephone calls. On the first of the days we are imagining, she was in Canberra. She had been at a meeting on the previous day of the Churchill Memorial Trust, of which she was now National President, and was due to fly home as soon as the fog lifted enough for the plane to take off. The fog made her late arriving back in Adelaide. And that mattered particularly because in 1987 she had signed on as a volunteer for Meals on Wheels, a charitable service providing hot meals at midday to frail aged people still living at home. She didn't drive, of course. But Billie Whyte had retired from teaching in 1985, so these childhood friends could do the work together. They continued it for three years. On the morning of the fog in Canberra, Billie had to meet her at the airport: 'we just made it', said Dame Roma to a journalist from the English magazine *New Woman*. 'You have a certain number of people to get around to in a certain time and you can't keep hungry people waiting'.[44] After that the two of them went back to East Terrace and had lunch at Roma's. Then Billie went home because Dame Roma was going to Marigold Rathbone, the hairdresser, for a cut, wash and blow dry – no perms, now – ready for the party that she was giving that evening at the Queen Adelaide Club. In the interval between Marigold's attentions and her walk into the Club in Stephens Place, she wrote – by hand, with her fountain pen; no computer keyboards here – the address she was to give at the opening of the Refugee Week Program, supporting 'Our Australia', a project 'designed to reinforce the positive attitudes which Australians have towards migration and its contribution to Australia'.[45]

Her dinner party was for people to meet Peter Bassett and his wife. She had met Peter in 1981, when he was Australian High Commissioner in Rangoon, and she was, with Piers Plumridge and Margaret Nyland, about to visit Myanmar (Burma) on their way home from a LawAsia conference in Bangkok. As they left Thailand, they encountered a strong suggestion that any difficulties with immigration and customs in Burma might be overcome by 'the simple expedient of proffering bottles of whisky and boxes of cigarettes to the black-marketeers who moved unhindered and unheeded in the midst of officialdom'. Oh no. 'Justice Mitchell declared (in a tone reserved for such occasions) that she had never in the past resorted to such measures and was not going to start now'. They despatched a message to the Australian Embassy in Burma. Peter Bassett came to meet them: 'on the tarmac of Rangoon Airport, our friendship began'. It was a friendship cemented when she was to visit Kiribati as an Appeal Court Judge in 1987. By then, Peter Bassett was High Commissioner, living at the capital, Tarawa. He wrote to Dame Roma, telling her of the generally minimal requirements for formal clothes – short dresses in the evenings – and the need for sunburn cream and medicine to combat diarrhoea; she brought the antibiotic powder that saved Sir Harry Gibbs's wife from a tropical infection when she cut her leg, too. Bassett also invited the Australian Appeal Court judges to stay at his own residence, far more comfortable than the one hotel where the lavatories and showers, their New Zealand brother judges told them, operated only when the tide was in.[46] The Bassetts were in Adelaide to visit family, and Dame Roma was returning their hospitality, in spades! Twenty or thirty people, reported Walter Crocker, from seven o'clock to ten thirty '& liquor was in generous supply'. He considered the guests well chosen, except for Irishman Frank O'Neill, Registrar of the University, someone Crocker disliked ('loudmouthed pushing'): he watched with appalled fascination when, at the end of the evening, moustachioed O'Neill kissed Dame Roma goodnight 'effusively'.[47]

Crocker thought Dame Roma had had 'rather more than enough to drink' by the end of her party. But she was up early the next day, as every day. This day she was at her desk, writing to Aline Fenwick, to Fay Gale who had gone off to Perth to be Vice-Chancellor of the University of Western Australia, and to Molly Kingston about her next visit to Melbourne, telephoning Jean Gilmore to arrange to meet for lunch, making arrangements for fundraising for the Ryder-Cheshire Foundation, sending a donation to the Mary Potter Foundation for a hospice at Calvary Hospital, sending a donation to the Save the Flinders Ranges Campaign – which did not help the attempt to develop tourist facilities there – and sending to WEL a paper-bound copy of her second Boyer Lecture for them to auction to raise funds. The ABC had decided in the previous year, the bicentenary of British settlement in Australia, to invite outstanding speakers from the previous twenty years to contribute a half-hour lecture each, looking forward from the bicentennial year. Dame Roma's lecture reiterated her earlier opposition to indeterminate sentencing and her strong support for community service orders as alternatives to prison sentences, believing in the importance of reforming anyone convicted of a crime, rather than simply locking them up.[48] Towards the end of the day, she walked along Halifax Street to the Daughters of Charity's chapel on Hutt Street for Mass, pleased to see the chalice she had given them in memory of Ruth. Then home again to ring Lorna Williams and Cairns Villeneuve Smith, to catch up, and to talk about the visit to Melbourne where she would stay with Jean Whyte.

In August 1989 she was up early to attend court as an Auxiliary Supreme Court Justice, retired judges being invited by the Chief Justice to take on court work for a month at a time, a measure introduced 'to clear up some backlog' in the over-burdened court system.[49] After lunch, she spent the afternoon working on the text of what would be the inaugural Mitchell Oration. This had been Josephine Tiddy's idea. Beautiful, delicate-featured Josephine Tiddy had moved on from being a counsellor at the Adelaide Children's Hospital to being the second South Australian Commissioner for Equal Opportunity. She proposed to establish an annual oration to demonstrate the 'philosophical, historical and analytical basis for the enormous changes in equal opportunity and human rights that had occurred over the preceding twenty years' and to 'honour Dame Roma's many achievements in public life'. She and her colleagues would choose as orators, she wrote, 'members of the community whose erudition, commitment and high public standing would be certain to attract credibility and respect'. They had immediately agreed that there could be 'no more suitable person after whom to name it' than Dame Roma, 'nor could there be a better choice as inaugural Orator'.[50] Dame Roma was touched. She did hope, she would say at the beginning of the inaugural Mitchell Oration in November that year, that 'an oration upon topics relating to equal opportunity and human rights would before long, become otiose'. It was a later version of the argument that she had been advancing ever since she said that she hoped that when the next woman was made a silk, this would not be cause for attention. But she went on to argue for measures to eliminate discrimination – primarily racial discrimination, though she also referred to discrimination against migrants, women and people with disabilities – beginning, as had the Human Rights Commission, and as did the South Australian Equal Opportunity Commission, with efforts at conciliation. 'Many people who offend in this area do so through thoughtlessness rather than malice', she declared. And those who are malicious 'may glory in a prosecution in which they have an opportunity to flaunt their racial prejudices'. But this was no mere revisiting of the arguments she had advanced as Chair of the HRC. For, and characteristically, she moved from the moderate case to one that was startlingly radical: the Commonwealth government had failed to develop a Bill of Rights, she observed, so 'those who wish to promote the recognition of human rights would do well to consider the advisability of enshrining such rights in our State legislation'.[51] A challenge for the Bannon Government, one coming out of the blue.

Another morning, her work was a response to a request from the South Australian Aboriginal community. They had asked her, a year ago, to enquire into the Aboriginal Legal Rights Movement in South Australia, and the ways in which it was run. It was supposed to provide representatives for Aboriginal people in court proceedings. But its funding was inadequate in the first place, since so many more Aboriginals than other kinds of Australian were brought into the courts, and the Legal Rights Movement was now having to compete with other demands on the limited grants made available for Aboriginal services, like provision of housing. All of these services were, at the time, being overshadowed by the Royal Commission into Aboriginal Deaths in Custody. Dame Roma was entirely in sympathy with the goals of the commission, but she also held fiercely that the only way to reduce the disproportionate number of Aboriginal people appearing in the courts was to ensure that they had adequate legal representation, that the number of those legal representatives who were themselves Aboriginal was increased, and that there be more Aboriginal paralegal practitioners. She made this case in her inaugural Mitchell Oration, too.[52]

After lunch, Billie came and collected her in her car and they set off down South Road. They were going to Carrickalinga, but on the way, they would stop at Reynella, a village off the main road about half an hour's drive from the city. Here was – indeed, still is – Woolcock's, a shop offering extremely elegant women's clothes imported from Europe, its clients coming from all over Australia, as they had done for one, two and three generations. Mr Woolcock prized Dame Roma's custom. He went to the trouble of bringing her clothes to try on at Carrickalinga; 'winter clothing to buy in temperatures of 30 C!' she exclaimed, one January Monday.[53] This time, Dame Roma would buy a new silk suit, and – this time, too – consider their out-of-season clothes for travelling.[54] For, of course, she would soon be off and away overseas again.

Last year, 1988, she had gone to England and Europe, catching up with Theo Ruoff, having lunch with old friend Gwenneth Stokes and her husband, eating at the Inner Temple and the House of Lords, visiting Hugh's remaining relations in Yorkshire or Torquay. Such a relief it was, when she arrived at Margie Clover's in Torquay. It was hot and she was in her London clothes, but Margie lent her a pair of shorts, distinctly skimpy, she said, and a T-shirt. Then they could settle down on the terrace with a gin-and-tonic.[55] As usual, she went to an array of galleries: the exhibition of late Picassos at the Tate, of early Cezannes at the Royal Academy and French paintings from the USSR at the National; the Winter Palace in what was still called Leningrad had a quite wonderful collection of French Impressionists. Off to the theatre, of course: Tom Stoppard's *Hopgood* was the most *avant garde* play she saw; others were Shaffer's *Lettice and Lovage* starring the wonderful Maggie Smith, Ostrovsky's *Too Clever By Half* and the Royal Shakespeare Company's production of *Julius Caesar*. She caught up with George Viggers, too, ballet dancer and teacher, former partner of wealthy Adelaide businessman John Alison, the subject of John Bray's famous put-down when she had been made a judge and Bray had not – yet. Viggers's health was less certain, these days; he had suffered what she described as a 'slight cerebral incident' just before she arrived. But that did not deter him. He summoned her to lunch on the day that she landed, and several other times as well.[56]

In the next year, 1990, she would fly to Europe again, this time to attend the Festival of Early Music at Innsbruck, concerts in the evenings and tours exploring the countryside around them during the day. Then, in August, she moved on to Italy, to Verona, where there is a Roman amphitheatre, open to the stars, to which you gain entrance through a tunnel lit by flaming torches. Dame Roma was to watch a 'splendid ballet', *Zorba the Greek*, there. But she could have been forgiven for being distracted because her trip had been interrupted earlier that day by a message: a 'Mr. Cannon' had telephoned and left a number for her to ring. She did ring it, but there was no answer; time differences between Australia and Italy set Verona several hours behind Adelaide. The contact was not absolutely unexpected, she would remark; just before she left Australia, she had dined at Government House in Yarralumla, residence of the Governor General in Canberra, and one of the other guests, an advisor to Premier Bannon, had asked about her travel plans, saying that he might want to get in touch with her. He didn't say why, though. Still, she was sure the message was from

John Bannon. There was another message when she got back to her hotel. So she tried ringing again. It was his home number. She found herself speaking to his second wife, Angela.

> It was midnight Verona time, but fairly early in the morning South Australian time, and the Premier had just left for his office. I asked Mrs Bannon if it was too much trouble to her to telephone the Premier's Office and tell him that I would now be for some hours at the telephone number at which he had attempted to speak to me. She readily agreed. I then sat up in bed and read until about 1 a.m. Verona time, when the Premier telephoned me and asked if I would be agreeable to my name being put forward to Her Majesty The Queen as the next Governor of South Australia. I assented.[57]

At least that was her story. Another seeps out through the letters of congratulation, or rather, one of those letters. Mary Gaudron had been in Adelaide in August 1990 to deliver the second Mitchell Oration – 'In the Eye of the Law: the Jurisprudence of Equality' – an occasion that Dame Roma would have been extremely reluctant to miss. Indeed, when they asked her to, she wrote an introduction to Justice Gaudron that Crown-Solicitor Catherine Branson read for her. In it, Dame Roma offered an excuse for being away.

> 'A strange set of priorities,' you may say, 'And why can not a woman who has retired alter her plans in order to enable her to attend a function which she has told the Commissioner for Equal Opportunity that she is desolated to miss?'
>
> In reply to such an observation I can but say 'Wait until you have retired and have assumed the various commitments which seem inevitably to follow retirement. Then see if you can find it practicable to alter holiday arrangements, particularly those which involve others.'[58]

Who could argue with that? Only someone noticing that there did not seem to be any 'others' particularly involved in this holiday of Dame Roma's. Mary Gaudron clearly did not find the excuse entirely persuasive. On 19 October, after Dame Roma's new appointment had been announced, she wrote to her.

> Your Honour, Your Excellency,
> You Foxy Old Thing,
> Well, of course, all is now revealed. How wonderful. And how lucky to get that holiday in as a private citizen. And all the while, while you were doing Europe, poor Len King had to fend off rumours – even advanced to his face at the Mitchell Oration – that he was to be Governor. Of course you will be magnificent. You always have been a hard act to follow and I imagine that your vice-regal successor will come to wish that she/he did not have to live up to your demanding standards.
> All the very best.[59]

If Mary Gaudron is right in intimating that Dame Roma had taken herself away deliberately, at precisely the moment when Bannon and his colleagues were considering who to make the next Governor – just as she had, all those years ago, removed herself from the room at the Law Society in which her colleagues were to discuss whether or not a woman could be made a Queen's Counsel – then Dame Roma had more than an inkling of what was in the wind. And that would suggest that this appointment was something that she wanted very much indeed.

And why ever not? This was 'the greatest honour which I, as a South Australian, could have received', she was to say. A culminating achievement for the Catholic Outsider defining herself in a world still dominated by the muscularly masculine values derived from the Protestant Insiders, a major victory for the woman making a new way of being a woman in a world dominated by men. And, always of course, a quite wonderful encapsulation of the contradiction between her commitment to liberal and democratic reform, on one hand, and on the other, her conservative traditionalism, her attachment to Britain and the hierarchies of Britain's lost empire. In her seventy-eighth year, Maude Mitchell's bluebird of happiness had arrived at the highest pinnacle in her world. Roma Mitchell's heart must have swelled at the thought of her mother's pride.

Just over two months after Bannon's phone call, at 8 pm on 18 October 1990, Queen Elizabeth II signed the necessary documents. On 6 February 1991, Her Excellency The Honourable Dame Roma Mitchell, AC, DBE would be sworn in as the thirty-first – and sixth Australian-born – Governor of South Australia.

Chapter Ten
A Very Good Retirement Occupation

Governor of South Australia

There was, of course, immense fanfare. Back from Europe at the end of September 1990, she had had time to prepare for the packed and excited press conference almost three weeks later. When he spoke to her in Verona, Bannon had asked her if she would have the energy for this job, so she had a medical check-up to make sure. She could answer the journalists with confidence. No, she said, she didn't think she was too old. 'I think if one is healthy and has the qualifications it is one's duty to accept ... I can say I'm healthy because I have had a full medical just in case there was something hidden. There is not.' A few noted the contradiction between her being appointed to the state's most important post at an age when she was disqualified, by age, from being a judge, a premier, or a prime minister.[1] But most of an already

Dame Roma Mitchell at media conference, published with permission of the *Advertiser*

ageing population accepted the *Advertiser*'s pronouncement: 'She is our most distinguished older citizen. Our emerging ageing society can be proud that age has proved no bar to her appointment.'

Yes, she did have regrets. She would, she said,

> take a while to get accustomed to the fact that I will have to live in more isolation and I won't be able to move quite as freely as I have in the past which I always like doing. I like moving among everybody.[2]

She would have to give up her positions with the Churchill Trust and the Ryder-Cheshire Foundation, and with the University of Adelaide. She would have to stop delivering Meals on Wheels; Billie would do it without her, now. But Roma Mitchell had been here before – disengaging and withdrawing from her extensive, and intricate social interconnections – when she was first made a judge. This time, though, she would have to withdraw from explicit public campaigning, promoting human rights at every possible opportunity. Would she be 'more contentious' than her predecessor, one journalist asked. 'I hope I won't be', she replied. 'I will certainly make an effort not to be', as a governor 'has to act with some restraint': the Queen 'gives a marvellous example of that'.[3] 'If I start offering personal opinions, praise or criticism, then I think I should expect to be met on equal terms and I don't think it would work out.' No doubt she had in mind one of her predecessors: nuclear scientist Sir Mark Oliphant, appointed Governor by the Dunstan Government in 1971. He had a host of personal views – ranging from the folly of the Government's attempt to develop a satellite city at Monarto, near Murray Bridge, to its mistake in sacking Harold Salisbury, an event in which he intervened even though he was no longer Governor – and he had not hesitated to voice them loudly and publicly, a practice that, Dame Roma knew, had proved awkward for the government. At least one journalist didn't believe her disclaimer: 'After all, being Governor provides a lifelong public crusader a soapbox which cannot be ignored.'[4] And he, as it turned out, was right.

The announcement that Dame Roma was to be the next governor drew widespread and enthusiastic acclaim; '[l]istening to many comments it must be the most popular appointment ever', her friend, Kate Hannaford, told her.[5] The role of governor had not had a good run, ever since Don Dunstan had endeavoured to break the mould by choosing someone other than a member of the armed forces. After Oliphant, he chose Douglas Nicholls, KCVO, OBE, a clergyman and a footballer, and the country's first Aboriginal person to hold such a post. But Sir Douglas was in such poor health that he remained at Government House for only six months. Dunstan then chose another gentleman of the cloth, Methodist minister Keith Seaman, KCVO, OBE. But the scandal about Seaman's personal life made opponents of the Government believe Dunstan was trying to reduce the importance of the post. Dunstan's successor, Labor Premier Des Corcoran, reverted to convention, appointing a former army officer – and no relation of the retired premier – Lieutenant-General Donald Dunstan, AC, KBE, CB. After almost nine years, it was now time for him to retire. Bannon and his Cabinet, especially Attorney-General Chris Sumner, who lobbied for her, knew Dame Roma would be a controversial appointment. After all, she was already ten years older than the retiring Governor, she was unmarried and she was a woman. But they also knew she was widely known and much admired, so much so that there were fond jokes about her, told so often that they had become legend.

There was the story from her early years on the Supreme Court. A 'somewhat brash journalist' asked her, 'You are not married?' 'I am not', she replied tersely. 'And you do not drive a car?' 'I do not.' Undeterred, the journalist pressed on. 'The Chief Justice, Dr Bray, is also unmarried. Is there any chance that the two of you might get together?' 'No', responded Roma Mitchell, 'that would be no good at all. He doesn't drive a car either.'[6] Later, when she was first appointed to the Human Rights Commission, the Chief Justice of New South Wales, Sir Laurence Street, noted that her age was a great mystery – even her entry in *Who's Who* did not reveal the date of her birth, he remarked. Then he told the story that has been repeated so often since. The Federal Attorney-General's Department sent a telegram to the South Australian Attorney-General requesting this information. 'How old Roma Mitchell?' it asked. Back came the telegraphed reply that, in some versions, is attributed to Dame Roma herself: 'Old Roma Mitchell very well. How you?'[7]

There was, as well as her age, her religion. She was only the second Catholic in South Australia's history to become Governor. The local Catholic hierarchy was, of course, delighted. Monsignor Robert Aitken, Administrator of St Francis Xavier's Cathedral, where Roma Mitchell had worshipped since she began attending school next door, saw 'real value in having two pews reserved for the Governor and her Aide-de-Camp' as it would highlight for the congregation both the dignity of her new office, and the important place in her life of 'the worship of God'. But her faith attracted little media attention in what was so predominantly secular an era. Comment came from those who had known earlier and different times. John Bray hoped that her 'sex and religion' would 'strike yet another blow to the crumbling taboos of the establishment', and Brian Stanley from the Industrial Court of South Australia joked that 'there must be a few old Masons turning in their graves to know that a Catholic will be occupying the position of governor.'[8]

What did emerge prominently in the media, though, was the fact that she was single. 'Who would undertake the many duties ordinarily imposed upon the Governor's wife? Who indeed!' She would have to do some of the things normally undertaken by the governor's wife, as well as the duties of the governor: 'I suppose everything new one does is a challenge in some respects and I think it is a challenge to follow the present incumbent and Lady Dunstan as I've got to follow two of them.' It would be more work, she acknowledged breezily: 'It makes it difficult to be in two places at once'. She would turn it into a joke.

> One radio interviewer asked me whether I thought I could cope in my unmarried state. He was not tactless enough to add 'and as a woman'. I pointed out that Tasmania had had as Governor comparatively recently a bachelor, the distinguished former diplomat Sir James Plimsoll, who had been completely successful in his role as Governor. Then I added, 'But of course, he did die in office'. I thought that Sir James' situation had been, in one respect, more difficult than mine. He was, as I was, President of the Girl Guides Association and Chief Scout. While there are female and male scouts, there are no male guides![9]

And of course, some of the concern about her lack of a wife was precisely what it disclaimed: concern about her being female.

She noticed 'a certain feeling of dismay' at her appointment, 'particularly among elderly women of some social standing'. Did she know that the ranks of the dismayed included her old friends Sesca Zelling, Eleanor Wells and Toby Hogarth? Her willingness to accept this most important and prominent position challenged every assumption in their lives about the necessary subordination of women, every decision about women being second to men in which they might have acquiesced. So tall, she stood, so fearless and independent: the first woman in Australia to be made Governor of an Australian state, her very presence announcing how much was changing for women throughout their society. Any 'new appointment for a woman is a good thing', she said, 'it is one more recognition of the fact that nothing should be barred to a woman'. 'By the time I became Governor', she was to tell a valedictory assembly at a girls' school,

> *people had ceased to offer me unwanted advice but I was slightly amused at the effrontery of some women who told me, after I had completed my term, that they had not approved of my appointment. They expected me to be complimented by the statement that they had changed their minds. In fact I was shocked, not only by their presumption but also their fossilised views.*

The media made much of her being 'the first woman'—yet again. But the times had changed since the press had clamoured about how she was to be addressed now that she was a judge. She was not a 'token woman', they noted—terminology deriving directly from the Women's Movement—the News *editorialising that 'gender is virtually a secondary consideration': she was, it announced, 'The right person for the job.'*

For she was no longer quite so exceptional—so alone—as she had been, being the first woman. Those dismayed women had daughters whose lives were often quite different from those of their mothers. They might be the women who gathered at dinner at Chloe's Restaurant to congratulate Dame Roma on concluding her work with the Human Rights Commission: Catherine Branson, South Australian Crown Solicitor; Lindy Powell, who would become a QC; Fay Gale, Professor of Geography at Adelaide University. They might be women from the women's services organisations that gathered at the front of the Bonython Hall to celebrate the University of Adelaide's decision to continue its Research Centre for Women's Studies: the Working Women's Centre, the Women's Information Switchboard, the Women's Health Centre. They might be those women who worked with Dame Roma on the Child Protection Council: Sue Vardon, Director-General of the Department of Community Welfare, and Josephine Tiddy, and her successor as Equal Opportunity Commissioner, Linda Matthews. They might be the women appointed as Women's Advisers to the Premier: first Deborah McCulloch, then Rosemary (Wodie) Wighton, and later Carol Treloar. They might be the Women's Advisers appointed in the Education Department and the Health Commission as well, in this decade of the 'femocrat' (initially, feminists taken into government posts to advise on policies concerning women). Increasingly, other women were also moving into positions previously held exclusively by men. In the South Australian Parliament between the election of Anne Levy in 1975 and that of Liberal Bernice Pfizner in 1990, another ten women gained seats, three Liberals, one member of the Australian Democrats, and six members of the Labor Party. In 1985, the Bannon Government appointed Legislative Councillor, Barbara Wiese, to the portfolio for Tourism and Local Government, the first woman in its Cabinet. In 1986 the members of the Legislative Council elected Anne Levy their President, the first woman to hold the post of presiding officer in an Australian legislature. Adelaide University went so far as to make a second female professorial appointment: Marcia Neave, Professor of Law. Flinders University appointed educationist Sister Deirdre Jordan, another St Aloysius old scholar, as its Chancellor.

These women – South Australians who made a signature impact upon their times – were but the tip of a growing iceberg. For more and more women, including women who were also wives and mothers, worked not only at housework, childcare and husband maintenance in their own households, but also in the labour market for wages or salaries. Their households, increasingly, depended upon their incomes as well as those of their husbands. They still worked disproportionately in the secondary labour market – characterised by part-time work, insecurity and lower earnings. Many worked in appallingly exploited conditions. In 1983, Judith Roberts chaired a Speak-Out for Immigrant and Refugee Women of South Australia at which more than 200 women told of their sweated out-work, toiling over sewing machines at home, or in their own kitchens, producing garments, cakes and confections for pitiful returns. In 1989, the Bannon Government legislated to bring these workers within the ambit of the Industrial Commission so that their hours, rates of pay and conditions of work would be regulated and adequately compensated. But increasingly, the market's demand for particular skills, without any concern with the gender of the worker exercising those skills, meant that there were some women gaining better-paid jobs than their husbands, achieving positions of influence, even power. Like a flotilla, they sailed in the wake of Dame Roma Mitchell, Governor of South Australia. No wonder those women of social standing were dismayed; it must have seemed as though the world that they had known and helped preserve was disappearing altogether.

In December, the new Governor told Walter Crocker that the letters of congratulation reaching her now totalled 880. There would be more, too, for on 26 January 1991, she was awarded Australia's highest honour, being made a Companion of the Order of Australia (AC) in the Australia Day honours list, which also included her friend and ally, Michael Kirby.[10] Aline Fenwick wrote, expecting that she would be especially pleased with this honour as it was for 'services to law', and 'at the end of the day I imagine you will rank your achievements as a lawyer above everything else'. She went on to tell Roma of a dinner party in Sydney – 'a great gathering' – given by senior legal women for two of their number who were retiring. 'We spoke of you', she told Roma. Mary Gaudron was there, and

> Mary was adamant that you didn't quite approve of her + wish she had better manners. You will be glad to hear that this view was considered by all to be quite erroneous! I quietly think Mary could do with a bit more polish but she is a warm-hearted + generous woman + that is what counts.[11]

It hardly matters whether Dame Roma would have agreed with Aline Fenwick – or not. What is important in this observation is the glimpse that it offers of how those senior Sydney women lawyers regarded her – a touch aloof, perhaps, and, mingling with her easy friendliness, a desire to preserve old-fashioned formalities:

Adelaide good manners. As Tony Baker, former Press Secretary to Don Dunstan, observed:

> She is a perfect appointment …
>
> She is looked on kindly by both the Adelaide Establishment, or what remains of it, and by reformers.[12]

Now Dame Roma, always generous, so 'overwhelmed with joy at the appointment & with plans for entertaining and hav[ing] house guests', had just three months to prepare for her new occupation and her new residence. In October the Dunstans invited her to Government House to see where she would be living and working; Walter Crocker had the impression that the visit was 'not matey'. Not matey, no. Crocker told his diary that Sir Donald Dunstan was 'a bully, unbalanced about personal loyalty to him, unfair, unjust, violent temper'. During his term, twenty-five or twenty-six members of staff at Government House had been sacked. Crocker thought Dunstan lucky to have escaped censure. The Dunstans may have been among those dismayed over Dame Roma Mitchell; they were to refuse the many invitations she extended to them to visit Government House during her time there, and since vice-regal invitations normally enjoyed the status of a command, such refusals were exceptionally rude. Dame Roma certainly considered them a snub. She still had questions after that visit, so she asked Crocker, since he had, as Lieutenant Governor between 1973 and 1982, been Acting Governor from time to time, and had lived at Government House.[13]

In November she resigned as Chancellor of the University of Adelaide. Senior Deputy Chancellor Medlin gave her a long service medallion for her twenty-five years of work and the members of Council conveyed their appreciation and admiration by acclamation and a standing ovation.[14] It was not the end of her connection, though; as Governor, she would become the Visitor to all three South Australian universities, officially charged to 'investigate complaints that relate to the internal or domestic management' and any allegations that the statutes, rules and regulations have not been applied or have been applied wrongly.[15] Fortunately, nothing would require her to exercise this function.

She was eager to get on with the job. But she was frustrated because the Dunstans, who were supposed to have departed by the end of December, were still in occupation on 9 January 1991. She spent the last two weeks of January packing and arranging things in her apartment on East Terrace, selecting pieces of her own furniture for Grace Brothers Removals to take to Government House for her private rooms there. She had been at it 'night & day' observed Crocker. 'In spite of her 78 years she remains as strong as a horse; but she looked a little weary today.' He invited her in for a cup of tea as 'a final friendly gesture before she leaves for Govt House' because, while he disagreed with most of her public work, and considered her boring and egotistical, he did, he wrote, 'want to express my appreciation – which is also the feeling of the other three flat owners in this complex – for her as a neighbour'. Then he had a sudden burst of generosity himself: 'Roma so happy about the Govship that one can be happy with her.'[16]

At last Wednesday 6 February 1991 arrived, clear and sunny: pleasant at 10.45 in the morning when the official Rolls Royce arrived to collect her from East Terrace, though it would be hot later. Police motor cyclists escorted her to Victoria Square. There the police greys took over, pennants fluttering in the breeze, clip-clopping ahead of the big car north down the centre of the city to the entrance of Government House – across King William Road from Parliament House, across North Terrace from the Adelaide Club, diagonally across the intersection from where the South Australian Hotel used to stand, and just south-east across the road from the Festival Centre. This was the heart of Adelaide. Many people travelling by train into the city to work would walk past her front gate.

At 10.50 am they drove her up the curving gravel driveway to meet exactly 1002 guests seated on the eastern lawns with century-old Moreton Bay Fig trees beyond, flower-beds full of colour beside them, facing a dais. The guests were arrayed in order of importance from front to back. On the left, precedence went from the partners of Cabinet ministers through four rows of judges, six rows of state parliamentarians, two rows of federal parliamentarians, and four rows of others who had been sent gold invitations. Behind them was an aisle, then a further thirteen rows for the guests who had green entrée cards. On the right, in the first five rows sat people with honours – knights from the imperial system or

ACs from the Australian system – together with people for whom Dame Roma had requested invitations. They included Sister Judith Redden, Principal of St Aloysius College, and some of the nuns who had offered their community Mass that morning for 'Roma's intentions', and 'invoked God's blessing upon her'.[17] Dame Roma wanted them there to affirm her life-long loyalty to them. But she had not been in the chair of the HRC for nothing; she would also have been all too aware of the visual theatricality of a group of nuns (even without habits), Aboriginal people and refugees seated beside the sea of Anglo-Celtic faces beneath their hats: '[r]ed, green, black, purple, white, orange and of course natural straw hats'. She wore a hat herself, 'black with a stylish band', and a two-piece skirt with a matching loose jacket in black and white, with white gloves and a black handbag.[18]

In the Morning Room, she joined the Vice-Regal party: Crocker's successor as Lieutenant Governor, Sir Condor Laucke, and his wife, and two people who would necessarily be very close to her, at least at the outset – her Personal Assistant, David Neal, and her Secretary, Don Mackay. They took up their positions on the dais next to Premier John Bannon, Chief Justice Len King, the members of Bannon's Cabinet and other members of Parliament. The Guard Commander ordered the Royal Salute: ranks of soldiers presented arms. The 4th Military District Band played the National Anthem – 'Advance Australia Fair'. The Clerk of the Executive Council (Bruce Guerin) read the Governor's Commission: to exercise 'the powers and responsibilities of the Queen in our State system of government', and to personify 'the ongoing rule of law and unity of the State, irrespective of changes of governments'.[19] Then, before Chief Justice King, sweltering in his ceremonial robes and wig, Dame Roma took the three oaths of office – of Allegiance, the Official Oath and the Judicial Oath – and signed on as Governor. Now everyone could sit down. But only briefly. For the timetabling for the speeches of welcome by the Premier, by the Leader of the Opposition, Dale Baker, and by the Lord Mayor of Adelaide, Steve Condous, allowed them only three minutes each. Sensible in the February heat when it would be almost noon. Dame Roma was allowed twice as long: all of six minutes.

She was proud to be South Australian, she told them. She thanked the previous speakers. She was delighted that she would still live in the City of Adelaide in this beautiful house, and she hoped to emulate those who had gone before her 'by entertaining as many South Australians as possible within these garden walls'. Of course, 'South Australia consists of much more than Adelaide'. She had visited various rural cities and towns, she noted, reminding them of points in her career,

Dame Roma Mitchell with Chief Justice Len King at her swearing-in as Governor, published with permission of the *Advertiser*

> as a Supreme Court Judge on circuit, as a Member of the Karmel Committee on Education, as Chairman of the Criminal Law and Penal Methods Reform Committee of South Australia, as Chairman of the Human Rights Commission of Australia and as a Member of a committee looking at Aboriginal Legal Aid.

And she had holidayed in more remote parts of the state, too, away from cities and towns. She looked forward to renewing her acquaintance with people in places she had already visited, and meeting others there and in places that she did not yet know.

This was all very much as could be expected. But then Dame Roma offered a flash of the steel behind such graciousness. They were in the middle of a period of acute economic crisis. There are many suffering economic hardships similar to those of the Great Depression, she observed.

> I pray that, during my term of office, Australia will be able to work its way out of the present problems and enter a period of prosperity in which the will to work will be a guarantee of success.

From the economy, she turned to the Hawke Government's engagement in the war in the Persian Gulf.

> I should be remiss if I did not mention the sorrow which we share by reason of the involvement of Australia, along with other members of the United Nations, in the Gulf War. Probably most of us present have lost some whom we have loved in earlier wars and, in any event, we must all grieve that once again much of the world is immersed in war. Those of us who believe in prayer must surely pray for a speedy and true peace.

Then she returned to 'happier topics'. But the journalist who had deemed her a 'crusader' had been perceptive. Being Governor was not going to stop her. Indeed, the *Advertiser* had editorialised encouragement for crusading that very morning. She would of course take seriously 'her formal duties as the Queen's surrogate in our governance and society', the newspaper announced, but went on to comment that 'as a feminist and an unmarried woman, she might cause the upending of some of the stuffy protocol clichés associated with the job' which would be 'a refreshing change'.

> Her lively mind, banned by the isolation attending upon such a lonely office from many of its usual pursuits, cannot be allowed to vegetate in Government House. We must hope she uses her position to keep offering her thoughts, and some social leadership to a confused and often rudderless community.
>
> Politicians might also be put on notice that Dame Roma, supporting a famous passion for human justice with an equally famous juristic brilliance, is unlikely to be a mere rubber stamp when it comes to the constitutional performance of the Queen's ministers.
>
> We are entitled to expect that life with Dame Roma, a fine model for South Australians, will be both constructive and progressive.

After that, what Dame Roma actually said was quite mild. She expressed her pleasure that some of the Aboriginal community with whom she had worked were present, and another Australian citizen, holder of an Order of Australia award, who had come to South Australia in 1939 as a Jewish refugee from Nazi Germany. 'I thank you all for attending this ceremony', she concluded. 'With God's grace I shall serve you to the best of my ability'.[20]

They loved it. 'Very well spoken', murmured Len King. 'Yes, it was', said Attorney-General Chris Sumner. Everyone heard them because the public address system was still on. Finally, after the soldiers had presented arms again and the band had played once more, nineteen guns on the Torrens Parade Ground nearby fired a salute, and blue-singleted workers on the other side of North Terrace, high on the $570 million Myer–Remm development overlooking Government House, cheered and whistled.[21] Daniel Thomas, Director of the Art Gallery of South Australia, burst into an effusion of enthusiasm.

> Dear Dame Roma, we are immensely proud of you. Not only because your experience of law and academic scholarship is a more attractive symbolic qualification than other Governors' more usual military experience. (Not everyone sympathises with the necessary evil of killing.) Nor because you are yet another South Australian first, the nation's first Vice-Regal appointment of a woman.
>
> It's also, very simply, because you look the part. You hold your head well. You chose terrific clothes for your inauguration: the black straw hat, the bold-patterned dress, the beautiful shoes. It's a look we saw when the President of the Republic of Italy and his consort were here from Rome a couple of years ago. I call the look Grand Roman Flash.[22]

There was a dinner party at Government House that first night to entertain Premier Bannon, some other public figures and a few personal friends. This showed her how easy it was going to be, with the help of a superlative cook, Diane Walheim, and a staff to wait upon her guests.[23] Afterwards, she retreated upstairs to the three rooms that she was making her own. Workmen had been in to repaint and recarpet them, and she had furnished them with the pieces that she had brought from East Terrace, and some of her paintings, books and personal treasures. A bedroom, a study and a sitting-room, all for herself – but a lot less space than she had occupied in her apartment on East Terrace. For the rest of this stately old house consisted of the formal state rooms; quarters for her two principal members of staff; quarters for visiting VIPs and their staff, and for several footmen; and rooms for staff working late at night. The formal rooms were the ballroom, used for receptions, concerts and investitures; the dining room that could seat twenty-eight; three interlinked drawing rooms; a library; the Governor's study; a morning room; and a Royal Suite on the east side of the building, used by any members of the royal family who might visit. There was a billiard room, too, an office for the private secretary, a porter's hall and a strongroom, and the cottages – Palm, Peppertree and Pine Cottages – which housed her chauffeur, her butler and her secretary, with their families. There was a swimming pool, which Dame Roma was to use often, and the garden enjoyed the attentions of four full-time gardeners. It is 'a small village', Peter Bassett was to observe, with 'quite a friendly feel to it. It's a home as well as an office.' 'It's not too big or too grand like some of the others (Government Houses)', she told the *Sunday Mail*. It's 'a beautifully proportioned, elegant house which is not intimidating'.[24]

She had to begin by learning the ropes. But she soon had changes in view. Some were urgent: the fabric of Government House was suffering badly from salt damp as well as age, so repairs were called for. '"Dame Roma thought it important to see the work tackled properly, otherwise we might have been looking at some very expensive ruins in a few years," says a staff member'. Throughout the following five years, engineers, builders, plumbers and painters would be 'an almost permanent fixture': a 'scaffolding here, a drip sheet there. The Governor, and the 20 house staff, have had to operate in and around the repairs.'[25]

Some changes were to meet the needs of a household that did not have 'a wife'. Despite her jokes with the journalists, she was not going to try to be both Governor and Governor's wife herself. She created the position of Comptroller, someone who would oversee the running of the household, including arrangements for accommodating and entertaining guests, and would live in, at least during the week. This was not because she was concerned about security, though there was at least one occasion when security issues arose; she requested the Police Commissioner to visit to 'discuss week-end security following problems of Under Butlers with intruders to house'. Rather, it was because 'she hated dining alone when there were no official functions in her programme'. If there was no-one else, she would ask one of the voluntary aides to keep her company. But it was preferable to have someone she knew better, and being able to share her dining table with Barbara Habel – who brought her two Cairn terriers and her two Siamese cats with her to the post of Comptroller – also meant that Dame Roma could 'keep in touch with matters affecting the running of the household'. They became good friends. One time, Dame Roma took Barbara with her to see a photographic exhibition, and then spent a '[p]leasant evening at home' with her; another, they went shopping together – Dame Roma wanted to replace some buttons that had worn out, but she also bought some evening shoes: '$290' she noted; on yet another occasion, they walked Barbara's dogs for a couple of hours; there was the evening when they watched a video together, *An Enchanted April*; then the evening when they walked through Rundle Mall and Rundle Street East together – looking in the shop windows, no doubt. Barbara Habel would accompany Dame Roma on the last of her overseas adventures, too: in 1999, they travelled to Africa.[26]

Some other changes followed at least partly from her commitment to equality of employment opportunity. 'Now that we have a woman Governor, can we expect to see a woman aide-de-camp in this traditionally entrenched male role?' asked Christabel Hirst of the *Sunday Mail*. 'I would hope so if and when it comes to replacement, I would hope that we would have at least one woman', replied Dame Roma.[27] Had she forgotten her own remark to Adelaide University about zoos and 'one giant panda'? She was to achieve many more than one woman. But not as aide-de-camp. Traditionally, this post had been filled by an officer from the armed services, usually the army. Dame Roma wanted, instead, a civilian with a background in the law; someone who might be a research assistant for her, should she need one, as well as carrying out the usual duties relating to her engagements and protocol. She appointed Simon Hardy, young, highly competent, and heart-meltingly handsome. She changed the occupant of the Official Secretary's post, too. Towards the end of her first year, knowing that the Bassetts had retired from the foreign service and wanted to return to Adelaide where they had family, she suggested to Peter that he consider taking this on. Initially, it seemed that there would not be room for him with his wife, Carol, and their son at

Government House so she suggested that they move into her flat on East Terrace, 'paying only basic running costs' while she was at Government House. In the event, Peppertree Cottage was restored to its proper function, and the Bassetts moved in there. This meant that the three most senior posts at Government House were filled by lawyers, a cause of jokes over the next four years, and, presumably, a source of quick understanding – of camaraderie among them.[28]

Peter Bassett

She combined her equal opportunity measures with a gesture towards de-militarisation. Peter Bassett explains.

> The practice had been to appoint several honorary Aides-de-Camp from the Defence Force Reserves to accompany the Governor to functions after normal working hours and at weekends. These officers provided unpaid service on top of their own professional commitments, and therefore were highly valued. Dame Roma enjoyed greatly her relationship with these young men and women but was keen to see that their generosity was not exploited. She also felt there should be gender balance. Therefore, she expanded the corps of Honorary Aides to include two officers, male and female, from each of the Defence Force Reserves, and two from the South Australian Police Force. The use of Police Honorary Aides was a novelty at the time but the Police Commissioner, David Hunt, was strongly in favour.

This staffing initiative broke new ground, observes Bassett, and Government Houses in other Australian states soon emulated it.[29] Indeed, Government Houses in other Australian states rapidly did away with military aides altogether, a far more extreme move than Dame Roma's.

The last major change in senior personnel took place in April 1992, when Basil Hetzel replaced Sir Condor Laucke as Lieutenant Governor. The Lieutenant Governor's job was to take on the vice-regal duties when a governor's appointment was in process, or when the governor was away or incapacitated. Basil Hetzel, who also became Chancellor of the new University of South Australia in 1992, was a distinguished doctor and medical academic with an international reputation for his research into the effects of iodine deficiency. Another professional who did not come from the armed forces in the senior Government House ranks, then, but this one – at least – was not a lawyer.

With her infrastructure in place, Dame Roma could establish a routine. She began by getting up at 7 am, having a light breakfast in her upstairs rooms, then coming downstairs. In the beginning, she wasn't sure how much walking she would be able to do. Would she walk up King William Street to Victoria Square for Executive Council meetings, asked the *Advertiser*'s Political Editor, Rex Jory. 'I am going to try to walk to church first', she replied. 'I could walk up to the Cathedral in Wakefield Street. I'll see how I go with that.'[30] That went just fine. When Peter Bassett moved into Government House a year later, he spent his first three months, before his wife could join him, occupying the Gloucester Room, directly opposite Dame Roma's rooms. He woke regularly each morning to the sound of Dame Roma slamming her bedroom door as she left to walk to Mass in St Francis Xavier's Cathedral before breakfast.[31] It amused her friends, the slammed doors, and slammed telephone receivers, too; a habit born of impatience.

From nine on the dot, she was at work. 'A thick folder, the "bible" of the Governor and her staff, holds details of hour-by-hour duties, squeezing in hairdressing appointments in what are often seven-day working weeks.'[32] When Parliament was in session, two or three hours were set aside every Wednesday afternoon or evening for her to prepare for her meeting with the Executive Council first thing the next morning. Other mornings were usually devoted to visits from local or foreign dignitaries, industrialists or business people, and afternoons to launching exhibitions or making official visits.

On Thursday 21 February 1991, for instance, she had a meeting of Executive Council in the morning and in the evening Leonard Cheshire and Sue Ryder arrived to stay, labelled 'HG' – House Guests – in the bible. Lord Cheshire was already ill; a year or so later, Dame Roma told him that she had sought the intervention of Mary MacKillop, founder of the Sisters of St Joseph, for him. He was, Peter Bassett considers, the 'one person in the world for whom she reserved a unique admiration'.[33] Had he recovered, then Dame Roma's petition would have helped, as well, with the case being advanced at the time for MacKillop to be made a saint. Another HG arrived in the middle of the next day: the Honourable Leycester Meares, a retired judge from the New South Wales Supreme Court, and an old friend. At the LawAsia conference in Manila in 1971, Roma Mitchell had added to the evening's mirth when she presided over a contest near the swimming pool at the conference hotel between Leycester Meares and Ronald Wilson: they were competing to see who could perform 'with style' the greater number of push-ups. On the day Leonard Cheshire and Sue Ryder departed from Government House, Marigold Rathbone came to do Dame Roma's hair at midday; from half past two to half past four, she attended the opening of a Meals on Wheels kitchen, at which she made a speech; and that evening there was an annual dinner for Legacy.[34] On the next day, Sunday 24 February, she took Leycester Meares to Carrickalinga – 'BH' for Beach House in the bible – for the day and a night, in the Rolls no doubt (the chauffeur presumably staying in a bed-and-breakfast place in nearby Yankalilla), returning the next morning.

She prepared her speeches herself. She would either dictate into a tape recorder, as she had as a barrister and solicitor since soon after the Second World War, or she would prepare a draft in longhand. It would be typed as a draft, she would correct it by hand, and that was then typed as the final version. She liked to prepare speeches well ahead of time, so organisations requesting her to make speeches for them had to provide all relevant information at least two months in advance of their occasion. They had to provide minutely detailed accounts of where and when the Governor would arrive, too, and where and when she would move, and speak, and where and when she would leave; Simon Hardy would check with event organisers and walk over the steps with them.

She was even busier than she had been before moving into Government House. She did have help with all the busyness, now. But there is a relentlessness about the succession of events and their highly public nature that could have been very draining. In any single month, she attended up to fifty functions within and away from Government House, and she received overseas and interstate representatives as well. However, she was, she had told

Crocker, a good sleeper; he had already marvelled at her strength. And her staff soon learned that if her right eye began to twitch, they should leave her alone to rest.[35]

She had to make time for friends, and for personal maintenance. Friends sometimes came to lunch on Sundays when she was in town – Noni Farwell now and again, and Billie Whyte often. Some occasionally came for a quiet evening during the week; Russell Longmire and Prue Bonnin came to dinner on Thursday 13 January 1994; Toby Hogarth, despite her opinion of Dame Roma, was not too proud to come to dinner on 14 January 1994; Mary Bleechmore came to supper in June that year, when her husband John was in hospital for a hip replacement; Piers Plumridge and Margaret Nyland spent an evening with her to tell about their travels when they had been away overseas. Friends as well as official visitors came to stay – Cairns and Pamela Villeneuve Smith from Melbourne one time, Merilee MacDonald from Perth another, their presence being woven into, or away from, the days' commitments.

On Tuesday 5 March she made a 'private visit' to Jack Davey, the blind lawyer whose need for a pee had caused such a scandal with the police keeping an eye on John Bray, all those years ago. On Wednesday 6 March, Mrs Fantini, a dressmaker, came to call; Dame Roma had thought that she would be able to go shopping in the stores along Rundle Mall, if she took someone with her, and she did that too, from time to time.

> Rather than do a Bob Hawke and buy contact lenses and stop drinking, the Dame recently was spotted shopping at the hipper-than-hip Miss Gladys Sym Choon fashion boutique in trendy Rundle St.
>
> She bought a dinosaur necklace (for the non-trendies among you, it's chunky, beady stuff – similar to what the Flintstones wear), and a wide-brimmed 'really groovy' Audrey Hepburn-style hat.
>
> That's how one of the boutique assistants described it, anyway.[36]

On other occasions Mr Woolcock and his assistant brought clothes from Reynella to Government House for her to try on. On Friday 15 March 1991, Marigold Rathbone came to do her hair at five o'clock, ready for her to go to the Hyatt International Hotel, west along North Terrace just past the Railway Station and the Casino, for a dinner of the Barons of the Barossa – a fraternity begun in 1974 to foster and publicise grape growing and wine making in the Barossa Valley. Two appointments with the dentist appear in the bible in March, and early in April all appointments were cancelled for two days because she was not well. But the morning after the second of those days, she was at the Warrawong Wildlife Sanctuary in the Adelaide Hills at half past five in the morning to see where those shyest of Australian native animals, platypuses, were being encouraged to breed. She was, clearly, having a wonderful time.

Serious business had begun almost immediately. On Saturday night, 9 February, John Bannon asked her to be available to commission the Auditor-General to carry out an inquiry into what was called cryptically 'aspects of the State Bank'.[37] The job that had those workers cheering her from the Myer–REMM construction site across North Terrace should have been finished long ago. The project had been designed around 'an American concept of shopping and amusement', but it was situated in a couple of city blocks where the consulting rooms of medical specialists sat side by side with the headquarters of the Liberal Party, next door to the Adelaide Club, heartland of what was left of the Adelaide Establishment, and that meant that there was resistance to change so strong that it had caused delays before construction could even begin. More importantly, this was a project in which the joint government–corporate State Bank of South Australia was so heavily involved that there had been anxiety about potential financial losses to South Australia since 1988. On 17 January 1991, the Board of the State Bank was informed that the Bank now stood to lose $249 million on this project, and that was before they calculated the fees necessary for the capitalisation of the debt. Dame Roma had been planning to go to Carrickalinga for the weekend – Jean Whyte would have been in town for her Swearing-In Ceremony, and they'd have wanted to catch up away from the crowds – so the timing of the Executive Council meeting was altered so that she could still set off for the seaside, but a bit later than expected.[38]

There was another meeting of Executive Council, the body of government ministers that gives effect to the laws passed by the legislature, less than a week later, the regular meeting that took place every Thursday. One of her most important functions as Governor was to preside over Executive Council and she prepared with scrupulous care. Graham Gunn, a member of the Liberal Government of John Olsen, later during Dame Roma's term, once delivered some bills to her and then had to defend himself as being 'only the messenger, not the architect of these opinions' when she asked a series of difficult questions about them. Trevor Griffin, Attorney-General in that same Government, reported that it was 'not uncommon for her to phone ministers to discuss a point arising from some submissions or to phone the Attorney-General to discuss a legal point or two'. Mike Rann, then Leader of the Opposition, told a farewell dinner in her honour that 'Dame Roma always asked the best questions on Thursday mornings, particularly of the Attorney-General, and sometimes with a twinkle in her eye'. On one occasion, she pointed out an error on page 46, paragraph 4, clause 8 in a bill about the keeping of bees, 'and indeed there was'.[39]

Her official functions had been laid down by the Australia Acts promulgated in each Australian state in 1986. These determined that the head of each state was the Queen of Australia (and not the British government, nor the Australian Governor General), represented in each state by its Governor. A governor is appointed by the Queen, on the recommendation of the premier of that state. The role required her to summon and to dissolve the Parliament, to call elections, to appoint the premier and the ministry, to assent to legislation, and to make regulations and appointments – on the specific advice of the ministers and in accordance with constitutional conventions. All of this was routine. Only in such exceptional circumstances as a constitutional crisis would there be any call for the governor to do anything that was not an entirely regular part of her weekly round. 'Nobody has given me any indication of a constitutional crisis', she told the Adelaide *Advertiser* in 1990, 'but common sense, of course, says that a constitutional crisis can occur at any time'.[40]

There were precedents for such exceptional circumstances, of course. They ranged from Governor Sir Philip Game's intervention against the actions of Premier Jack Lang in New South Wales during the Great Depression, to Governor-General Sir John Kerr's dismissal of the Federal Whitlam Government in 1975. And the state of the Bannon Government, at the time when Dame Roma moved into Government House, did not prompt unqualified confidence. There was a 'hung' Parliament: in the forty-seven seat House of Assembly, the Government survived on the casting vote of the Speaker and the support of the Chairman of Committees, both positions held by Independent Labor members. In the Legislative Council, the balance of power lay with two members of the Australian Democrats. It was, commented the *Australian Magazine*, 'a fragile situation, fraught with possible constitutional complications. In any crisis, the Governor's role will be crucial in the exercising of the Monarch's reserve powers.'[41]

The situation was about to become even more fragile. On 10 February 1991 Bannon announced that the taxpayers were going to have to bail out the State Bank to the tune of $970 million (a sum that rose to $3.1 billion). The Auditor-General would investigate the reasons for the Bank's losses. Only two days later, at a media conference, Bannon also announced a Royal Commission, to be headed by recently retired judge, Sam Jacobs. Eventually, Jacobs's first report blamed the Premier who was also the Treasurer and therefore should, Jacobs maintained, have kept a closer eye on the Bank's activities, so that he could have prevented the staggering blowout of its debts to the government. But this did not develop into a constitutional crisis. As Dame Roma had chuckled: 'This is South Australia. We do not have constitutional crises'. Instead, on 4 September 1992, John Bannon determined that the buck would have to stop on his desk, and resigned his commission. Lynn Arnold was sworn in to replace him as ALP Premier on 1 October. There was not ever, Dame Roma observed, a situation 'which would call for any intervention'.

Did it not call for 'some wise counsel?' asked her interviewer. 'If anybody had known in time I suppose it might have', Dame Roma replied, 'but nobody did realise, I don't think anybody realised the problems we were in financially'. No wonder the State Bank's collapse was so spectacular, then.

In general, she considered the governor's task to be 'to watch, to warn', or, 'as it's sometimes said, not to warn, about legislation that the Government may be going to introduce'. But it was for the Parliament to decide whether such legislation should pass or not.[42] And she thought that the governor did not have any role in questioning legislation that was presented for assent to the Executive Council, except to approve it.

> Providing it is not outrageous, of course. You can imagine if we had a Hitler regime. I suppose you would have a role then. I suspect a Governor has more of a role in regulations and probably should advise if a regulation appears not to be authorised by the statute.[43]

Nevertheless, 'at least one premier of that era recalls some spirited private discussions'.[44]

On the evening of her second Executive Council meeting, the Government gave an enormous formal state dinner in the Banquet Room at the Adelaide Festival Centre in the new Governor's honour. They would eat roulade of whiting with scallop mousse and lemon butter sauce; loin of lamb filled with spinach and served with rosemary *jus*, with fresh seasonal vegetables; brandy snap baskets with fresh fruits and mango *coulis*. They would drink Seppelt's Great Western Champagne, Hardy's Siegersdorf Rhine Riesling, Wolf Blass Yellow Label Cabernet Shiraz, Peter Lehman Sauterne and Mt Rufus Port – wines made in South Australia and on their way to world fame. The entire Parliament was there; all the judges of the Supreme Court and their wives; the President of the Industrial Court and the Senior Judge of the District Court, and their wives (they *were* all wives); the chiefs of the armed forces and their guests; seven senior bureaucrats and their partners; four media leaders, three with wives, and one, Peter Ward – by now Chief of Staff on the *Australian* – alone; church le
arts organisations; ethnic organisations; Aboriginal organisations, including lawyer Polly Sumner and her partner, Polly Dixon; education leaders – Chancellor Deirdre Jordan with Sister Judith Redden; and there was the Secretary of the United Trades and Labour Council and his wife.

There were also twelve men under the heading of 'Business Leaders', all with wives who shared their last names, their ambits extending from Santos (a mining company) to the Adelaide Steamship Company, from South Australian Brewing Holdings to

Britax Rainsfords (manufacturer of automotive parts), from Kinhill Engineers to Adelaide Brighton Cement.[45] These names offer a snapshot of where financial power lay in South Australia under a Labor government. The forceful and alarming Tim Marcus Clark, Managing Director of the State Bank, was there. Otherwise, except for two representatives of the Chamber of Commerce and Industry, there were no obvious descendants of the families who would have been OAFs, unless they appeared under some other hat as well; it was some time since large acres up-country had been a source of economic power or influence. And the industrial base of South Australia's economy represented at this gathering was extremely narrow. There was little a governor could do about this, except – and here it was clear that Dame Roma was, just as at the University of Adelaide, no mere ceremonial figurehead – use her position to promote South Australia. She had begun thinking about how to do this already. She had a 'secret ambition', she told Rex Jory. 'The Queen Mother is patron of the Adelaide Festival and Dame Roma would like her to visit South Australia to attend a future Festival.' It was not her position to make such a suggestion to the government, she acknowledged; all she could do, officially, was approve its recommendations.[46] But, by telling a journalist, she had made her suggestion anyway.

She set out to promote cohesion and optimism throughout South Australia by travelling all over the state, to country towns, isolated communities and into the outback. 'I think it's a very good retirement occupation', she was to say:

> I visit all parts of the State. So that I'm seeing different people all the time. And getting a lot of interest out of it. I think that's the main thing that I really like about it.

Her visits delighted many: 'Usually they only see officials when there is something wrong, or when there is a political reason', reported a member of her staff. 'But when the Governor turns up, just to see them, those people feel remembered.' She enjoyed these visits herself: 'one of the best things' about being the Governor, she said, was that it provided 'an opportunity to go right through the state'. 'You can do that as a private citizen but when you do it as governor, people show you things and you get a lot more interesting information than you would otherwise.' 'It's an opportunity for people to air their problems and have some chance of being heard', she noted. 'Also, they like to show their achievements.'[47] The first school function she attended was the opening of new rooms at Kalori School, run by the Sisters of St Joseph at Wallaroo on the Yorke Peninsular;[48] the Sisters of St Joseph had been founded by Mary MacKillop, the potential saint whose intercession she sought for Leonard Cheshire. During her first year on the job, she made no fewer than five expeditions to country areas well away from Adelaide.

The first, filling four days in July, probably in the Rolls, was to the location of her earliest memories, to the fruit-growing regions of the Riverland on the Murray. A couple of weeks later, she went to Kangaroo Island for a day, visiting Kingscote Museum, attending a flag-raising ceremony at Reeves Point, having lunch at the Ozone Hotel – where her parents had honeymooned – and visiting the Kangaroo Island General Hospital and the Cook Health Centre. In August, she flew off to the Northern Territory where she stayed at Government House – an elegant timber building on a headland with one of Darwin's most beautiful views – toured the new Supreme Court Building, and made a speech at a lunch-time gathering for the Women's Advisory Council and the Office of Women's Affairs. She also toured about – flying to Daly River, where she attended Mass at a local Catholic church and opened the Daly River Nauiyu Arts Festival; to Katherine, where she toured Katherine Gorge; to Bathurst Island, where she visited the Tiwi Ngaripuluwamigi Keeping Place, Tiwi Designs and Pottery Production, the Patajili Heritage Museum, and St Therese's School; and to Melville Island, where she visited the Jilamara Art & Craft Museum, the Milikapita Women's Centre and School, and spent three-quarters of an hour watching traditional Tiwi dancing. In August, she visited the towns in the south-west of South Australia, travelling from Cowell to Port Lincoln, and then westwards to Ceduna before turning back to Wuddina. And in September, she went on from a trip to the Monarto Zoo, near Murray Bridge, to the south-east of the state: to Naracoorte, the Coonawarra wine district around Penola, and Mt Gambier – where once she had sat as a circuit judge.[49]

In November 1993, she travelled to the Anangu Pitjantjatjara Aboriginal Lands in the north of South Australia to open the Murputja Delivery Centre. She was, she said, delighted to know that the children were being taught in schools in their homelands for three days each week, and then in the Murputja Centre for two days a week where they were taught in the Anangu language and their lessons emphasised traditional Aboriginal learning.[50] Another time, she attended an Executive Council meeting that was held over several days in what were then called familiarly 'the AP lands', 'APY lands' more recently. The army went ahead of the members of the Government to set up tents; they all camped out. Widely admired Aboriginal activist, Professor Lowitja O'Donoghue, suggested that she and Dame Roma fly in from Alice Springs, attend the meeting, and then fly back to spend the night in a comfortable hotel. O'Donoghue herself was certainly not interested in camping out with no bathroom; she had been there, done that in her days as a bush nurse. But Dame Roma was having none of that. She told Professor O'Donoghue that she had already packed her swag and fully intended to sleep under the stars. She ignored the freezing temperatures as she sat beside a campfire at a tiny place called 'Talking Creek', listening to the dreaming stories of the Elders. They made her Patron of the Women's Council.[51]

She had already, Peter Bassett observed, 'an encyclopaedic knowledge of old Adelaide and, in a trice, could say who was related to whom – a useful skill at Government House', and important in choosing some of the guests for the large formal dinners that she held every month. But only some of those guests, for she ensured that the guest list 'spread ... well beyond a narrow band of what might have been called usual invitees'.[52] Democratising Government House functions, she was. She also had a quite extraordinarily good memory, and used it to advantage. Dean Brown, Premier of the Liberal Government following the South Australian elections in December 1993, in the wake of the State Bank debacle, told of visiting a township in the country south-east of Adelaide, not far from the Coorong and the mouth of the River Murray.

> Langhorne Creek had not had a visit from a Governor since 1938 so this day was a very special day for the people of Langhorne Creek.

> Virtually the entire township turned out to meet her. She went to the school; she sat down with the vignerons and had lunch; then she met with the entire community for afternoon tea after an extensive visit of the district ... She went from person to person talking with each about their family's history with Langhorne Creek, their involvement in the wine industry and a range of other activities.

A feature of this visit in Dame Roma's diary was the Bleasdale winery, and lunch being held in a Wine Vat.[53]

Under a Liberal Government, she met industrialists who had not been at the state dinner when she was first appointed. Gerard Industries Limited at Bowden, for instance, she found a 'most impressive organisation, forward thinking & obviously good employer'. She visited Dynek Limited, makers of surgical needles, and George Chapman's meat factory at Nairne. Walker Australia manufactured exhausts: she was 'impressed with attitudes of all'. When she went to the Levi Strauss factory, manufacturers of jeans, at Elizabeth, she noted approvingly that their 500 employees included 'a number of women in management positions'.[54] The South Australian economy needed far more, though.

Dame Roma extended such work well beyond the state, too, indeed beyond Australia. Her visit to New Zealand in 1993 was for the celebrations of their centenary of legislation giving women the vote, and an international conference of women judges, rather than to promote economic collaboration. She stayed with the Governor General, Dame Catherine Tizzard, who entertained her 'right royally', and dined with Mary Robinson, President of Ireland at that time, and her husband, Nicholas.[55] Mary Robinson shared Roma Mitchell's commitment to human rights; she would be made United Nations High Commissioner for Human Rights when her time as president ended. In 2002, shortly after she had retired from that post, she came to Adelaide to deliver the Mitchell Oration.

A couple of years later Dame Roma made an official visit to the People's Republic of China, attending the LawAsia conference being held that year in Beijing as well, and this time there were economic benefits to follow. In Shandong, they stayed in its capital, Jinan, in a 'forbidden city' of sprawling pavilions, ornamental lakes and high walls ... with ... cavernous bedrooms, brobdingnagian staircases and 1960s plumbing'. Dame Roma found that her age – 'an object of wonderment and respect in Chinese society' – meant that wherever she went, two handmaidens accompanied her, clutching her elbows, and evincing great distress when she managed to get down some stairs without their assistance. On this visit, because she was able to 'achieve a level of access at the highest political level', she was able to make positive and practical opportunities 'to promote South Australia's commercial and educational interests', her role as governor being that of a door opener.[56]

Even more productive was her visit to Indonesia the following year. This was an initiative of Dr B.J. Habibie, Minister for Research and Technology in the Government of Indonesia, who visited Adelaide primarily because he was interested in South Australia's defence-based industries. He was, observed Bassett, 'a mercurial figure, an aeronautical engineer educated in Germany, a protégé of President Suharto and, unlike most Indonesians, an indefatigable talker'. Partly because of her age and wit, suggests Bassett, and partly, perhaps, because of her work with the Human Rights Commission – human rights being, at that time, a subject of great moment in Indonesia – he was most taken with Dame Roma. He called her 'Lady Governor', and he invited her to visit Indonesia. He even offered to send his private jet to collect her.

And he did send the jet. He had Dame Roma and her party taken in this luxurious plane first to Irian Jaya to inspect the huge Freeport copper mine, principal source of wealth for those with wealth in Indonesia, then to Bali, then to Jakarta, where President Suharto received her and she met members of the Indonesian Human Rights Commission, and finally to Yogyakarta, Bandung and Bogor. 'Hot on her heels was a delegation of 40 SA business-people, all anxious to stitch up deals in Indonesia' in trade and the arts. 'More and more', noted Bassett, 'we are being seen in government as a resource to be used. The role is changing, beyond social and ceremonial aspects. It is a useful tool for the development of this State.'[57]

Of course there were also the traditional connections among the post-imperial members of the British Commonwealth of Nations to be maintained. Dame Roma was, she said herself, 'a staunch loyalist and always will be. And while we have the present Queen', she added, 'I can't understand how anyone could think otherwise'.[58]

She was host to Queen Elizabeth II and Prince Philip in February 1992, to the Duke of Gloucester in March 1993, to Prince Edward in March and then again in November in 1994, and in April 1995, Princess Michael of Kent stayed for an unprecedented nine days.[59] Once she had settled in, reorganised her senior staff, and appointed Simon Hardy and Peter Bassett, she could revert to what had been an established custom – a holiday of five or six weeks during the northern hemisphere summer. As soon as he knew her plans, Peter Bassett would write to Queen Elizabeth's Private Secretary, letting him know that the Governor would be in London should Her Majesty wish to see her. 'The Queen always wished to see Dame Roma', he noted. In 1992 she invited Dame Roma to lunch at Windsor Castle. Simon Hardy was in London at the same time. Dame Roma had promised to take him to lunch at the Ritz, to 'mark his splendour in morning suit', and, having found herself sitting next to the former Governor General, Sir Ninian Stephen, and his wife Val at the Trooping of the Colour, invited them along as well. But she put even that occasion in the shade by taking Simon Hardy to Windsor with her to lunch with Queen Elizabeth II, bursting with pride at having such a fine young South Australian escort. At lunch, she sat between Prince Philip and Prince Charles. Afterwards, she and Princess Michael of Kent drove in an open landau to the races at Ascot, where they sat in the Queen's Box – 'all very comfortable and pleasant'. She was at the Queen Mother's table for afternoon tea.[60] Such visits became an

Dame Roma Mitchell and Queen Elizabeth II, published with permission of the *Advertiser*

annual event. In July 1994, the Queen was, Dame Roma reported in her diary, 'her usual interested and cheerful self – looked wonderful and remarkably well informed'.[61]

Yet, for all that she nurtured these traditional imperial connections with such care and delight, Dame Roma was also – as had become habitual for her – 'forging what many believe is a new path', in this case, 'making governors more relevant to the community'.[62]

This was, however unstated, an intervention in the politics of the time. For Dame Roma's term as Governor of South Australia was also the time of a resurgence of republicanism throughout Australia. Paul Keating, who had (after a tussle) succeeded Bob Hawke as Labor Prime Minister in 1992, went into the elections of 1996 committed to the creation of an Australian republic, at least to the extent of severing the traditional ties with Britain. The Liberals, officially monarchist, won that election, but the resulting Government of John Howard promised to hold a referendum on the subject. This was not to take place until after Dame Roma had left Government House, but, as Peter Bassett observes, 'the republic debate ... was building a head of steam in the mid 1990s'; he and Dame Roma often discussed the constitutional issues surrounding it, he recalls. And while they could not participate in the debate, they could, and did, make Government House 'much more accessible to the public' and they used media and public events 'to explain the responsibilities of the Governor'.[63]

Dame Roma's visits to the people on the APY Lands, and her extended consultations with them, were also – however implicitly – political interventions. For these were the years that saw a major change of heart among non-Aboriginal Australians about relations between Aboriginal Australia and the island-continent they had cared for over the previous 40,000 years, and between Aboriginal and non-Aboriginal Australians. When the Report of the Royal Commission into Aboriginal Deaths in Custody was presented in 1992, Recommendation 339 stated that

> if ever the division, discord and injustice that scarred this country, and had scarred it for two hundred years, was to be resolved, there had to be a political commitment in the hearts of all politicians throughout the country to a process of reconciliation.[64]

In September that year, the Australian Parliament passed legislation establishing the Council for Aboriginal Reconciliation. Less than a year later, in the case of *Eddie Mabo and Others v State of Queensland*, the High Court brought down its ruling that the lands of the Australian continent were not – as all previous assumptions and rulings had accepted – *terra nullius* or 'practically unoccupied' in 1788, when Anglo-Celtic settlers first began taking possession of them. Claims that Aboriginal people made to rights to their land thenceforth took an entirely different course from earlier efforts. 'Thanks to Mabo', said Sir Ronald Wilson, 'Aboriginal Australians can now come to the negotiating table with their heads held high – because their rights as the original owners have been acknowledged'.[65] Another initiative was the National Inquiry into the Separation of Aboriginal and Torres Strait Islander Children from their Families. The Keating Labor Government requested the body that had succeeded the HRC – the Human Rights and Equal Opportunity Commission – to undertake this investigation in 1995. The head of HREOC then was Sir Ronald Wilson, the judge who had been doing stylish push-ups by the pool for Roma Mitchell to assess at the LawAsia conference in Manila almost a quarter of a century earlier. He was the second Mitchell Orator. He had also been Moderator of the Presbyterian Church of Western Australia

Lowitja O'Donoghue with Dame Roma Mitchell behind her, photograph from Dame Roma Mitchell's Scrapbooks, copied in Master Peter Norman's chambers, 2001

and was the first lay person to be President of the National Assembly of the Uniting Church in Australia, from 1988 to 1991. He and Mick Dodson, Social Justice Commissioner in the Aboriginal and Torres Strait Islander Commission, and himself Aboriginal, would present their heart-rending report, *Bringing Them Home*, in 1997. While she was still in Government House, Dame Roma could not make an explicit contribution to any of these processes. But simply by being there at the visits to the APY lands, she could, and did, make clear the commitment to justice for Aboriginal people that she had formulated at least twenty years earlier, as well as her continuing friendship with the Aboriginal people who had sought her aid before she became Governor. In August 1994 she ignored the virus that was troubling her to fly to Tjikurla for an Aboriginal Women's Meeting at which about 300 women, one set after another, presented their Dreaming dances: 'very interesting and serious'.[66] She and Professor Lowitja O'Donoghue hugged each other when they met.[67]

Similarly, while she could not comment too outspokenly on developments in and around the Women's Movement, she could still lend her support to its goals and activities. By 1993, Anne Levy was not only Minister for the Arts in the Bannon Government but also Minister for Women, the first such appointment in Australia. The Bannon Government determined to celebrate the centenary of the achievement of women's suffrage in 1894 in South Australia, and appointed a Steering Committee, with Jean Blackburn at its head, to develop celebratory events and projects. Jean Blackburn was an economist and educationist with strong left-wing views; in her youth she had been a member of the Communist Party of Australia. But her committee also included people with political views diametrically opposed to hers, and many at different points on the spectrum in between, so the events and projects that eventuated varied considerably. The committee had been meeting for more than a year when the elections of December 1993 brought the Liberal Government of Dean Brown to power. The new government dismissed Jean Blackburn. Susan Magarey resigned from the Steering Committee in a temper, writing to Dame Roma to explain that she saw this action as unfair. Dame Roma had been at Carrickalinga on the weekend when the new government announced its decision. 'I would have advised against doing that', she told Susan Magarey, 'but I was away'.[68]

The Women's Suffrage Centenary celebrations began on Friday 11 February 1994; Dame Roma attended the special ecumenical service at St Peter's Cathedral that evening. 'The Almighty referred to as "She"!' she exclaimed to her special Women's Suffrage Centenary Diary. Three days later, Government House hosted a garden meeting of the Multicultural Forum to honour women from Non-English Speaking Backgrounds who did notable work in South Australia. Bernice Pfitzner MP thanked Dame Roma for her opening speech, pointing out that she was wearing the women's suffrage colours: a dress of purple with a large gold-coloured amber necklace. On Saturday 12 March, Dame Roma went to the Morphettville Race Day, an event organised because two members of the Steering Committee were avid race-goers, rather than because there was any clear connection between horse racing and votes for women in South Australia. On Friday 15 April she opened the premises of the Working Women's Centre, now renamed after Augusta Zadow, the first woman in South Australia to be an inspector of factories, ancestor of her friend Jeanette Sandford Morgan and Jeanette's brother, Brenton Langbein, one of the founders of the Barossa Music Festival. On 20 April, she launched a tapestry designed by Kay Lawrence to be woven by as many hands as could be found over the coming months and then placed in Parliament House. Two days later she opened an exhibition at Old Parliament House about Women in Politics. On 7 May she went to Myer Department Store to open an Exhibition of a Century of Housework, and, since she was there, bought some shoes. In October, she hosted a reception for delegates to an international conference – '[s]ome very interesting & important women' – and the next day went to the first plenary session to hear Glenda Jackson, the superlative English actor turned Labour Party politician. She didn't like her: 'Glenda Jackson spoke appealingly but too party political. Attack on Margaret Thatcher in doubtful taste when latter not present', she told her diary. There was a Women's Suffrage Night at the Greyhound Racing Club; another visit to Parliament House to see the tapestries – now depicting three suffrage campaigners, Mary Lee, Elizabeth Webb

Nicholls and Catherine Spence, and now hung in the House of Assembly; a garden party at Government House; a launch at Flinders University of an anthology titled *Hope and Fear*; and finally on the morning of Sunday 18 December, in gruelling heat – it was 35° she noted; the heat was hindering people trying to install a bust of suffrage leader, Mary Lee, just outside the gate to Government House – a ceremony on the steps of Parliament House to close the centenary.[69]

'I don't think they (governors) should speak out on public issues because of the fact that they are appointed rather than elected', she told the *Advertiser*'s Tony Baker.[70] But in relation to women's rights, Dame Roma was often as frank and direct as ever. Even though Australian women were supposed to have achieved equal pay for equal work, she pointed out in a women's suffrage centenary speech,

> there is still leeway to be made up in the evaluation of work ordinarily performed by women and in affording to women equal opportunities for promotion with due regard to the fact that women as mothers will ordinarily undertake the major role as child carers and many necessarily have to put on hold their professional advancement while their children are young.[71]

And when launching a book that Susan Magarey had co-edited with the newly appointed Deputy Vice-Chancellor of Flinders University, Professor Anne Edwards, she uttered an exclamation of delight at something that had changed, absolutely, since her time in a university. The contributors, she noted, all experts in their fields, were almost all employed in universities. And that, she exclaimed, was cause to marvel – for they were all women.

> To a person of my generation the fact that Australia can boast so many outstanding women academics is in itself *mirabile dictu* ...There are Professors, Associate Professors, Senior Lecturers, a Deputy Secretary in the Department of the Prime Minister and Cabinet and a number of postgraduates.
>
> For most of my professional life women did not hold similar positions in Australia. It is a source of gratification to me that there are now sufficient highly placed women academics to be able to offer, as the

editors say, 'critical analysis rather than personal views or a particular policy agenda'.[72]

It was as though arguing for justice for women, celebrating moments when women had made some gains, was as unpolitical as arguing for peace, for it did not align her with left or right, with Labor or Liberal. But even arguing for peace could be highly political, as Dame Roma knew.

Mercifully, this job was not all hard work. On one occasion, Lord and Lady (George and Patricia) Harewood[73] were staying at Government House, and preparing to go out. 'Where are you going? Shall I come too?' So they all piled into the Rolls Royce and drove the two hundred metres or so along North Terrace to the Art Gallery. Curator Angus Trumble had not been expecting a vice-regal visit; he was dressed in his denims. Dame Roma told him to stop apologising: 'Don't be silly'. And invited herself to lunch as well, which was 'long, gossipy and highly enjoyable'.[74] She was a familiar figure at the Art Gallery. Its Director, Ron Radford, 'knew that soon after an exhibition had been installed, there would be a phone call from Dame Roma enquiring about the possibility of a preview'.[75] On another occasion, she was scheduled to attend the official lunch for the Adelaide Grand Prix, an extremely noisy event that used to annoy her by covering her front veranda at East Terrace with dust. She did not have to stay for more than about half an hour into the race. But she enjoyed it, so she stayed far longer, until the race was driven and won.[76] After a lifetime of relying on her own feet or someone else for transport, she took great pleasure in having a car and a driver at her personal disposal. Sir William Deane, another Catholic who had also been a judge, appointed Governor General of Australia in 1996, told of 'driving around the vineyards with her in the Rolls Royce from which she derived such infectious delight'.[77]

Each Easter Monday she was off to Oakbank Racecourse for the Great Eastern Steeplechase. She had gone to the races with Jean Whyte when they were young women, but she had clearly not absorbed any of the culture of such events. At Oakbank, she would give tips: 'I've heard that in race number four ... something or other is the best horse, it's an outstanding mare', and sometimes she would ask someone to place a bet for her. But not one horse she tipped came anything but last or second to last. After some years, Mike Rann pointed this out. Oh yes, she admitted. 'They're not my tips. They come from my footman.'[78]

John Bray had marvelled at her decision that she would like 'even the moral obligation to attend race meetings, test matches, football finals, boy scout jamborees and military reviews', or if not actually 'like' them, then at least not find them 'unbearably irksome'.[79] She was highly gregarious; as she had said, 'I like moving among everybody'. And she had the gift, as Amanda Vanstone pointed out, of 'being able to make the person she was talking to feel special themselves'.[80] That clearly included the boy scouts, the girl guides, and the people representing almost any charity one can think of, as she became *ex officio* patron of so many. But there was one kind of event that she could not manage well. Everyone knew that she 'hated football and had no idea what was going on at all', Mike Rann was to remember.

> There was one year when I think I was Leader of the Opposition and she and I were sitting next to each other at a South Australian National Football League Grand Final, and both of us fell asleep for the entire third quarter. In a packed stadium of nearly 50,000 people there were ... two people asleep and they were sitting next to each other. And so many people remarked on it.[81]

Concerts were a different matter. She had seats reserved in the front row of the dress circle at the Adelaide Symphony concerts at the Adelaide Town Hall, and would often invite friends to join her party. And other kinds of performance, too. During the 1992 Adelaide Festival, she managed to attend twenty-two performances in three weeks, ranging from the outrageously bawdy *Cementville*, a glamorous and gruesome play about the world of female wrestling, to the American baritone James Maddalena singing in the new opera, *Nixon in China*.[82] They played the national anthem when she and the vice-regal party were going to be there. Peter Ward was to report that when this happened, 'republicans rose from their seats, claiming that they did so "not for the song but for Roma"'.[83]

She entertained endlessly: sometimes small gatherings, as when she had Noni Farwell to lunch, or Mary and John

Bleechmore to dinner without anyone else,[84] sometimes – at least once a month – the full twenty-six that the dining room could accommodate. And even though she was known as a champion of reform, she was, noted Peter Bassett, 'unyielding' on 'matters of protocol'. 'Lindy, you *will* curtsey', she told her former very fondly regarded Associate through clenched teeth, as Lindy Powell reached her on the reception line. Even Billie Whyte had to curtsey, Bassett recalled.[85] It meant that everyone knew exactly where they were, even if this marked Government House in South Australia as especially staid and formal when compared with others.

> She had been brought up to observe correct form and courtesies, and her years at the bar and on the bench had reinforced this. She did not approve of the relaxation of protocol at some other Australian vice regal establishments and, to this extent, was quite happy to be thought old fashioned. She had accorded past governors full courtesies and she expected no less in her own case.

It mattered especially because 'She was sensitive to any hint of difference in treatment between her and her male predecessors.'[86] Government House staff, similarly, addressed her as 'Dame Roma' or 'Your Excellency': 'They won't be on first name terms with me and I don't think they would want to [be], quite frankly. People have got to be at ease with what they are doing and they would not be at ease.'[87] Later female governors may have been far less inclined to preserve such formalities, but Dame Roma was the first, making the rules for herself.

She was far from being rigid, though. When Clyde Cameron received an invitation to a Government House reception, he rang her Secretary and said he couldn't come because he didn't have a dinner suit. Her Secretary checked with Dame Roma who said, 'Of course he can come without a dinner suit. Tell him he can come in his pyjamas if he likes.' So he came in his ordinary suit, and took great delight in telling some of the other guests, including Dame Nancy Buttfield, doyenne of the Liberal Party in South Australia, that he was staying after the reception for dinner as well. 'I knew she was a bloody Labor appointment', he reported Dame Nancy saying – but he just might have made that up.[88] Other occasions could be funny, too. At dinners with members of Bannon's

Cabinet, Bob Gregory, Minister for Labour, would turn up in a kilt with a dagger in his sock. Unlike everyone else, he called her Roma, and instead of addressing him as 'Minister' as she did the others, she called him Bob. Like Cameron, he was the former head of a union, and she kept the rapport that she had established with those members of the Australian Workers' Union for whom she had acted in her last case as a QC. She was less formal with Mike Rann, too; he was so young, and only a junior minister: she called him 'dear'. He was a former journalist, and a former press secretary; she could assume that he would know all the gossip, and she would ask him to tell her, and giggle when he did. In return, she would tell him stories that she learned from her contact with the English royal family – stories about the stories behind the news, at the time of the messy break-up of Prince Charles and his first wife, Lady Diana Spencer.[89]

There were quieter pleasures. She liked nothing better, recalls Peter Bassett, 'than to go into the cutting gardens with trug and secateurs to cut flowers for her sitting room'. She sent flowers, as well, to friends and acquaintances, to members of staff if they were ill.[90] And there were moments of escape to the beach house. On Friday 23 December 1994, she set out for Carrickalinga 'replete with turkey, ham, salmon, Christmas pudding, Christmas cake etc. Full house – Jean Whyte, Hector Monro, Billie Whyte & self'. She was pleased that Mass on Christmas Day was early – ten o'clock. That, she noted, 'allowed me time to cook turkey after return'. But then, on New Year's Eve, it was time for others as well as the members of her elective family. The house must have been bursting: they entertained two former judges and their wives – Andrew and Eleanor Wells and Sam and Mary Jacobs; Dame Roma's Lieutenant Governor and his wife – Basil and Ann Hetzel; her former colleague and the colleague's husband – Doreen and Paul Bulbeck; and Eric Von Schranck and his wife: a table of fourteen.[91] And here they were doing the cooking and serving and pulling the corks out of the bottles themselves, without the Government House staff.

Dame Roma's other major refuge from her so-occupied public life, during her time as Governor, was overseas on her annual holidays. Of course, going to London was now to visit the Queen. But it was also to catch up with George Viggars, who would arrange all kinds of cultural adventures in Europe, making the bookings and escorting her. 'George is certainly a good guide', she wrote to Noni Farwell. 'He knows the important points of interest in each city and how to find them without wasting time'. They traversed the leading theatres and galleries of Germany, in 1992.[92] The next year, Viggars arranged for them a similarly rich cultural feast, principally in Italy. 1994 brought an eight-day cruise on the Douro River and visits to Salamanca and Santiago, her first visit to Spain and Portugal, and in 1995 she spent several days in the Hotel du Louvre in the Place André Malraux, visiting galleries, seeing *Giselle* at the new Opera de la Bastille, and the Frankfurt Ballet at the Châtelet; she had seen the Frankfurt Ballet before – in Adelaide, at the last Festival. Such a long time ago, it was, that she could think of Adelaide as a cultural backwater.

She spent time in England, too: visiting descendants of the Kidmans, old friends from Law School, going to the theatre – though she was disappointed at how little new and interesting fare was on offer. She did catch the latest Tom Stoppard play, *Arcadia*, on her 1994 visit: 'very clever and very well acted' she decided, though she found the nudity and 'strong language' in the first act of *Dead Funny*, 'an incredibly explicit comedy' starring Zoe Wanamaker, 'inexpressibly vulgar'. Thankful, she was then, that the second half brought it all together into 'a good play'. Apart from her visits to the Queen, the high spots in these returns to England were her encounters with the Churchill Fellowship scholars for whom she had, herself, provided the funds. One was Tobias Cole, 'a charming and cerebral young man of 22 who has a beautiful alto voice' who had been studying at the English Royal College of Music. She took him to a lunch provided by the Agent-General for South Australia, at which they were entertained by the very witty Neil Blewett, who was to be made Australian High Commissioner in London the next year; former Labor Party *apparatchik*, David Coombs, now a representative for Southcorp, the principal marketer for Australian wines; and Nicola Kutapan, treasurer of the 300 Group, a body dedicated to having 300 women elected to the British Parliament.[93] Her hosts wanted her to approve their enterprises and goals.

The most important event for Roma Mitchell, in all of these overseas activities, was her visit to her father's grave in France in July 1995. It would be an official event, organised through official channels. Being a public figure would help her with the complex emotion that it was bound to provoke. This would hardly be grief, since she had scarcely known him. But there was a monumental sadness at her mother's grief, resonating with – giving bass notes to – her own continued mourning at her mother's death. She had always found the Anzac Day commemorations harrowing, because they filled her heart with her mother's grief, again and again.[94] Ruth and Hugh had made their acknowledgements at Harold Mitchell's grave long since. Now it was Roma's turn.

The Australian Embassy provided a car. Chargé d'Affaires, Mark Pierce, and representatives of the Prefet de la Somme attended her. Various military officials, a representative of the Commonwealth War Graves Commission, and sundry local mayors accompanied them. At Millencourt, she walked between the members of a guard of honour to lay her wreath on her father's grave. They played 'The Last Post' and 'Reveille'. Then they took her on a veritable tour of the region – to the Australian memorial at Villers Brettoneux, where her cousin, older brother of Noel Paternoster, was buried; to the Historial de la Grand Guerre at Peronne; and to a luncheon that Mark Pierce hosted. It was not at all what the Diplomatic Service in Australia thought proper; the Australian Embassy in Paris had been 'at sixes and sevens', and 'the poor young military attaché' who was supposed to accompany her was, instead, recalled 'as a mark of anger', even though he was only halfway through his term. Fortunately, Dame Roma did not collapse in hysterical laughter – or tears – at all the muddle and excess. The emotion was too strong for that. She could not have borne it years ago, she told Jean Whyte and Noni Farwell, but it was so distant, now, that she 'could take it': it was 'very poignant'.[95] Two years later the President of the Republic of France appointed her Commander dans l'Ordre de la Légion d'Honneur.

Eventually, the time came: Dame Roma's term in Government House drew to a close. By then, so widely loved and admired was she that a former Lord Mayor had tried to have part of Hindley Street renamed after her; the *Telephone Directory* had filled its

Statue of Dame Roma Mitchell on North Terrace, published with permission of the *Advertiser*

front cover with a picture of her standing in the driveway holding the hand of a person in a wheelchair; and at her final Executive Council meeting, Premier Brown handed her a tribute book signed by thousands of ordinary South Australians.[96]

There were already other material acknowledgements of her achievements scattered around Adelaide: the Roma Mitchell Building at St Aloysius College, the Market Street Chambers renamed the Mitchell Chambers, the Dame Roma Mitchell Garden at the back of the Old Adelaide Gaol, providing for the needs of people in the Adelaide Day Centre for Homeless Persons, founded by Sister Janet Mead.[97] There were to be many more. The City Council – with Jane Lomax-Smith as Lord Mayor – was to commission not merely a bust but a whole statue of her to be cast in bronze and installed on the northern side of North Terrace, just outside the walls of Government House. Subsequently, no fewer than three large buildings would be named after her: the Roma Mitchell Building that houses the Office for Women and the Women's Information Switchboard, opposite the Railway Station on North Terrace; the Roma Mitchell Arts Building on Light Square; and the tall ochre and opal Roma Mitchell Commonwealth Law Courts Building just east of Victoria Square.

Her Government House staff loved her, a major tribute. She had remembered their birthdays with small gifts and bought them Christmas presents. An aide on leave visited to show her new baby. Look at the expression on the face of the officer walking behind her as she reviews the ranks of soldiers. They wept when she

Dame Roma Mitchell inspects soldiers outside Parliament House prior to opening Parliament, 3 August 1993, photograph by Adams, published with permission of the *Advertiser*

walked out of that front door and away.[98] Her term had redefined the nature of this office. Sir William Deane, himself a much-loved Governor General, was to reflect: 'For my part, I venture to suggest that there has been no better loved vice-regal representative in the whole history of this land'.[99]

Chapter Eleven

A Private Citizen Again

Growing Older

Now that she was no longer the Governor, she could, she thought, recover the pleasures of acting spontaneously. 'I suppose one thing one feels in the office of Governor is that you can't do anything on the spur of the moment – now I can.' Surely she must also have had some moments of being glad of taking things a little more slowly? She was now eighty-three. There had been *mementi mori*. Dumps Somerville had had a stroke from which she never recovered – on the very day that Dame Roma was sworn in as Governor. Leonard Cheshire had died soon after she had visited him in 1992. John Bray had died while she was in London in 1995. And Joan Gooch, who had suffered a long illness, had a stroke and died in the same year. Even Dame Roma, herself, had suffered moments of less than perfect health over the past few years: a virus when she returned from England in 1994, lingering on so that she had to go so far as to cancel some of her engagements; the tendon that she pulled in her foot, necessitating the attentions of a physiotherapist; tests of the blood flow in her right temple because of anxieties about her sight.[1]

Perhaps she and Jean and Billie could spend more time at Carrickalinga. They bought things for their seaside establishment:

Roma had purchased a microwave oven; Jean had caught the plane from Melbourne carrying a birdbath.[2] One hot February day, Roma had bought a birthday present for Billie: a Burmese kitten '8 weeks old & beautiful', she reported. Billie brought the kitten with them to Carrickalinga: 'settled in well', Roma had commented. Even when it was cold and unpleasant on the beach, they could escape to the beach house, and Roma would do some gardening.[3] But after she had left Government House, the Rolls was no longer at her command to take her to the beach. She did ask Noni to drive her there – once. But never again. Parts of the journey are along narrow roads with steep hills, curves and blind corners; Noni had drunk about half a bottle of brandy. Roma would rely on Billie. But Billie was becoming less reliable. Once when they were there, she drove over Roma's foot. Fortunately the driveway was sandy, so the foot was not injured; Roma was cross, rather than hurt. Another time, Billie couldn't get the car to start. What to do? Roma had to get back. At her wit's end, she rang Pam Villeneuve Smith in Melbourne. Pam suggested that the battery might be flat. Oh no. Roma pooh-poohed that idea. It was, though, and, Pam Villeneuve Smith said crossly, Roma didn't even apologise.[4]

Having a car and driver at her personal disposal was a luxury that Dame Roma was finding it difficult to do without. Sometimes she walked, as she had in the past, far more than she had been able to as Governor. But there were moments when she engaged the services of a car-hire firm to bring her home from a dinner or a party. Chivalrous, they were. More than once she woke the next morning to realise that her gentle driver had not only carried her in from his car, but also carried her upstairs and put her to bed.

Sadly, Roma realised, Billie's memory was failing, failing quite badly. Early in 1997, Jean Whyte noted the names of both of Roma's executors – Piers Plumridge and Nancy Detmold – in her diary, with a phone number for Piers; perhaps he would help remind Billie of appointments, if Roma was not there to do so. In March, it seems that Billie came to Carrickalinga to join Jean, but travelling by bus rather than driving her car; she probably failed her last driving test. In May, Jean recorded Billie's appointment at the dentist – to telephone and remind her to go, perhaps. 'I told her to ring me before she set out to collect me', Dame Roma recalled,

The Hon. Dame Roma Mitchell, AC, DBE

256 East Terrace
Adelaide
South Australia 5000
Tel (08) 8232-4273

30th January
1997

Dear Pam,

Thank you for a splendid luncheon party. Your choice of guests was excellent and the fare, as provided by Gulf Sea Foods, admirable. Of course the wines had to be superb.

You were very kind to Bettie and I am sure that she enjoyed the

P.O. Box 7030 Hutt Street
South Australia 5000

Roma Mitchell to Pam Cleland, 30 January 1997, kindly given to us by Pam Cleland occasion. Unfortunately she is so slow now in putting her thoughts together that when she wants to join in the conversation it has flowed past her.

Your house and forest are beautiful. What an achievement it has been!

love from

Roma.

'so that I could be downstairs and ready for her. But she didn't, and when I asked, she didn't remember what I'd said. That was when I realised.'[5] After this, Roma would take on small tasks on Billie's behalf, writing a sympathy letter to their Carrickalinga neighbours from both herself and Billie, for instance. In a bread-and-butter letter to Pam Cleland, also thanking Pam for her kindness to Billie, she wrote: 'Unfortunately she is so slow now in putting her thoughts together that when she wants to join in the conversation it has flowed past her.'[6]

But, she said, 'You don't think about ageing. I think you are yourself all the time, and ageing is not a thing that intrudes very much', except, she added, 'when you find that you can no longer run'. 'I've been old for such a very long time now that it's hard to know how to define it; but, no. I don't think I ever feel old.'[7] She certainly had no conception of retiring. She had scarcely settled back into her refurbished flat – she installed a Bang and Olufsen music system, 'a terrible extravagance and a lovely indulgence', she said[8] – before she was back at work.

Still at Work.

At a dinner in 1993, she had been seated next to David Wotton, Member of the House of Assembly for Heysen since 1975, now the new Minister for the Ageing in the Brown Government. She spent the evening telling him what she would expect of such a position. He decided to ask her to act on her own advice, and invited her to be the Presiding Officer of the Ministerial Advisory Board on Ageing, established under legislation passed in 1995 to set up the Office for the Ageing. 'Since I have told you what to do', she responded, 'I have very little option but to accept this position'.[9] The board held its first meeting in August 1996. It was to 'advise the Minister and the State Government on issues affecting older people', and to 'advise, assist and monitor the implementation of the 10 Year Plan on Ageing' that Dame Roma had helped to prepare.[10] The other members – Val Ball, to focus on rural areas; Mark Reid, on mental health; Marj Tripp, on Aboriginal issues; Basil Taliangis, on people of non-English-speaking background; and Barbara Garrett, who had close connections with the wine industry – linked this board with the executive of the non-government Council on the Ageing. They set to work far more energetically than anyone had expected.

They consulted people from Naracoorte to the Riverland, from Kangaroo Island to Port Augusta, from Yankalilla to Wudinna. They also consulted a spectrum of organisations involved with ageing, so that they could agree to a platform of shared concerns. Senior government ministers and heads of public service departments found themselves being quizzed about how they were going to implement the plan. Dame Roma telephoned Minister Wotton frequently to tell him about the discussions on her board and, more importantly, to find out what action he intended to take.[11]

Dame Roma was to tell people how impressed she was by the success of Aboriginal women on the APY lands in persuading their families to reduce the amount of flour and sugar in what they ate, to reduce the occurrence of diabetes. In October 1998, she and Barbara Garrett went to the opal mining town of Coober Pedy in the north-west of South Australia to listen to the participants in a first Aboriginal Elders' Conference talking about issues that their communities faced. 'Our first aim', she told the Australian Reconciliation Convention in 1997 – going right back to basics – 'must be to assist them to attain old age';[12] life expectancy for Aboriginal people was, and still is, far shorter than for non-Aboriginals. She opened a Healthy Ageing Day at the Murray Bridge Nungas Club early in 1999. And towards the end of that year, in November, a 'vigorous, challenging and committed' Dame Roma presided over a Seminar on Rural Ageing held at Bungaree Station, just out of Clare.

And this was just one of the strings to her bow. Central to her interests, as always, was the law. She continued her subscription to the *Australian Law Journal* that brought her the High Court judgments, and she continued to speak at legal gatherings covering an immense range throughout these years. One lecture was the ninth in a series dedicated to the memory of Sir Richard Blackburn; he had still been in the Law School when she had inherited his war-hero father's desk. Blackburn's son Tom wrote to Dame Roma: 'There have been many distinguished speakers over the years, but none, if I may say so, who possessed that quality and who has known the family for so long. Dad would be (to use one of his own expressions) as pleased as punch.'[13] She opened a forum that Commissioner for Equal Opportunity, Linda Matthews, organised in conjunction with the South Australian Employers' Chamber of Commerce and Industry and the Australian Sex Discrimination Commissioner, Susan Haliday, titled 'Recruitment and Selection: Who's missing out and what's it cost?' Social justice, these days, needed to be couched in terms of economic costs and benefits.

At the opening of Law Week in May 1999, she delivered a stinging rebuke to the media over the comments that it disseminated about sentencing. Echoing arguments that she and her reform committee had formulated a quarter of century earlier, though more mildly then, she said that there was 'more ill-informed public comment about individual sentences than about any other aspect of judicial decisions'. It was irresponsible of the media to publish comments made by the injured party or their friends or relatives. They were made in the heat of the moment, and were likely to be underscored by the desire for revenge. A sentence, she emphasised, certainly is 'intended to be a deterrent not only to the offender but also to others who might be tempted to commit a similar crime'. At the same time, 'it must be remembered that if a term of imprisonment is imposed the offender will, in due course, be free to resume his or her place in society'. Accordingly, if a shorter sentence is more likely to rehabilitate an offender, then a shorter sentence will serve the whole society better than a long one.[14]

And of course, the law included the Constitution. Dame Roma was there at the Constitutional Convention eventually held in Canberra, in Old Parliament House, in February 1998. There were 152 participants, one-third of whom had been nominated by Prime Minister Howard, Dame Roma among them. Mike Rann remembered her as clearly aligned with the monarchists.[15] The monarchists were led by Brigadier Alf Garland and Bruce Ruxton from the reactionary Returned Services League, both of whom engaged in rude and offensive bullying, so she could not have been delighted by her allies. Perhaps that was why she insisted that she was not aligned with any group.[16] Her principal contribution emerged over the sovereignty of the states; she considered it important to retain a means of advancing the interests of each state within the system, something that she had already made clear in her final Proclamation Day Address as Governor.[17] And that determination meant that she thought any attempt to introduce the term 'president' to be entirely inappropriate.

'I do want to say something on that', she told the convention participants. 'I am taking the opportunity of doing so, especially, I remind people, it is the first time I have raised my voice in this gathering, and that is unusual for me.' She 'fervently desired' to retain the heads of individual states. It was not at all clear why that made the title 'president' so 'ridiculous'; 'constitutionally adventurous and dangerous' was how she characterised it, recalled Mike Rann. Perhaps she took it personally: if 'governor' had been just fine for her, and she had done such a good job, then everyone should want to retain the system, and the nomenclature, that had brought her to Government House. At the end of that session, the voting went strongly against her: thirty-seven in favour of retaining the title 'governor-general' and eighty-three in favour of 'president'.[18] Rann had voted for 'president'. Dame Roma sought him out afterwards in a fury and gave him 'a real sort of telling-off'. Ultimately, however, questions about Australia becoming a republic were put to the nation in a referendum that was defeated. South Australia's vote was distinguished by giving weaker support for the republic than any other state; there were those who speculated that this was because so many rejected the possibility of voting against Dame Roma. Meeting Dame Roma later, Rann found she held no animus against him for their disagreement: 'she was absolutely fine about it'.[19]

Equally central to her days – as always – was her faith. 'It is part of my life', she said, 'it always has been, and in that I'm fortunate'. It was 'a help', she attested – such a summary way of affirming the deep communion she enjoyed. It was a source of her unflagging commitment to justice for everyone, welfare for those who, like vagrants in Whitmore Square in Adelaide, were unable to find work, and 'the poor, especially' she said, 'those in [the] Third World and societies emerging from Communist Oppression'. 'The world must find concrete alternatives to war and build a culture of peace', she declared.[20] In 1991, fellow Catholic, Supreme Court Justice Michael White, asked her to speak to a gathering of the Australian Association of the Sovereign Military Order of Malta. This is a worldwide organisation of Catholic lay people, founded nine centuries ago, though in Australia as recently as 1974. It runs a system of charitable hospitals and care centres.[21] Dame Roma talked to them about three candidates for sainthood, two of whom were locals, and women: Mary Potter, founder of the Little Company of Mary after whom the Mary Potter Hospice at Calvary Hospital was named, and Mary MacKillop. This Order had Knights and Dames, 150 of them in Australia: prominent members of the community with a record of welfare service. Robert Britten-Jones, a medical man and a Knight of the Order, proposed that they give Dame Roma an award. In 1997, as a reward for upholding its 'historic traditions of chivalry and charity', Dame Roma Mitchell became the first woman in Australia to be invested with the distinguished Cross of Merit with Crown of the Sovereign Military Order of Malta. So many awards she was receiving – honorary degrees from Flinders University, the University of South Australia and Queensland University; a medal from the Institute of Engineers – all a source of pride and pleasure, but this one came from her heartland. She was 'thrilled',

Sir Walter Crocker congratulating Dame Roma Mitchell on her investment with the distinguished Cross of Merit with Crown of the Sovereign Military Order of Malta, 27 October 1997, published with permission of the *Advertiser*

she told Britten-Jones. Walter Crocker, one of only three other Australians to have received this honour, so far forgot his poor opinion of his erstwhile neighbour as to kiss her hand, a theatrical gesture captured by the press photographers.[22]

The End

In the New Year's Honours List in 2000, there appeared an announcement that Queen Elizabeth II had, on her personal initiative, appointed Dame Roma Mitchell Commander of the Royal Victorian Order in recognition of her outstanding service to the Crown during her time as Governor. This is the highest award the British monarch can bestow upon an Australian since the Hawke Government decided in 1986 that Australian governments would no longer recommend imperial honours. The South Australian Premier, now Liberal John Olsen, sent his congratulations. The *Advertiser* sent a reporter to find her on the beach at Carrickalinga, looking relaxed and healthy. 'I am fortunate in good health', she told him, adding, 'I think it (my health) is due more to good luck than anything'. But she was sitting down; quite possibly her back was hurting already. For the cancer that had claimed her mother and her two aunts had finally caught up with her. She must have known. This was agonising pain.

The doctors said 'tests'. She made appointments for them. She made her bookings for the next Festival of Arts, too, the second to be directed by Adelaide feminist singer and writer, Robyn Archer, to begin in March. There was still time to go to a concert; the Sandford Morgans offered her a lift home. She was carrying a stick, they noticed, and asked if she had hurt her back. 'I think it might be a bit more serious than that', she said, waving them goodbye.[23] There was still time to go to Harry Medlin's party: an occasion to be remembered 'with affection and gratitude', she wrote to Harry afterwards.[24] There was still time to go to dinner with the Harewoods to celebrate George's birthday; she had her stick then, too, and was walking slightly awkwardly. 'Oh, it's nothing dear. I have to go into hospital tomorrow for some tests', she said, dismissing their enquiries.[25]

She went into St Andrews Hospital, just round the corner from her unit, and had six days of tests. Then, when she heard the results, she told the press. 'It's terminal cancer, Dame Roma reveals', screamed the *Advertiser*'s headline on 22 February 2000. 'It's bone cancer', she had told the reporters. 'The only question now is whether it is worthwhile doing any (treatment) measures at all.' She was waiting to find out. 'In the meantime, I'm here being kept as pain-free as possible.'[26]

They decided that treatment was impossible. So then it was just a matter of time. Father Maurice Shinnick was her parish priest; he came every day to pray with her and give her holy communion.[27] Piers Plumridge cancelled his plans to travel overseas with his new partner, Thirza Thomas. Jean Whyte was already in Adelaide, staying at Roma's at East Terrace, so she could see her fairly easily – except for the numbers of others wanting to see her too. Piers expressed dismay at some of the people clustering, 'ingratiating themselves with the great and famous', he said, displacing his own overwhelming grief. She prepared for visitors: she was 'immaculately groomed and in a pretty, feminine bed jacket', remembered Patricia Harewood. Dame Roma's successors at Government House, Sir Eric and Lady Neal, brought roses from the Government House gardens. Everyone else sent flowers as well, so many that they overflowed her room into the passages and the rooms of other patients. Someone suggested telling people not to send any more. Oh no. 'Florists have to live, too', she decreed.[28] Noni Farwell arrived to find Roma being extremely practical: 'First things first'. She had the tickets that she had bought for the Festival and handed them over in a bundle. The Festival opened with a celebration in Elder Park on the banks of the Torrens. Robyn Archer told the crowd of 30,000 that the former Governor was ill in hospital. She called upon them for three cheers for Dame Roma – and the roar was deafening.[29] A friend rang Amanda Vanstone in Canberra; she flew back to Adelaide and arrived at the hospital the next morning.

> [W]hen I put a simple and direct question as to what were the circumstances of her illness, I got the unwanted but direct and matter-of-fact reply. My simple response was the exclamation that I was very unhappy with that state of affairs. Again it was met with a simple matter-of-fact reply accompanied strangely by a chuckle and 'well, I didn't expect you to be happy'.

It was not simply just a matter of time, though. When Patricia Harewood telephoned 'to commiserate', Roma said, 'Well it's terminal dear, and I have a great deal of work to do before I die.' Work? Surely there was not anything left to do with her estate? On 30 October 1986, she had written to Piers Plumridge that she had 'finally got around to executing an enduring Power of Attorney in your favour'; she sent him as well a direction that she had given 'pursuant to the Natural Death Act' – 'I hope that you enjoy these cheerful directions', she concluded. And she had made or revised her Will on 5 February 1998. She would leave valuable keepsakes to Noni Farwell, to Jean Whyte, to goddaughter Adrienne McMahon, to old friend Mary Bleechmore, to Margaret Nyland, to Doreen Bulbeck and to several of her former Associates, and she would leave substantial sums of money to members of her family, and friends and other former Associates. It must have made her very sad that by this time there was no point in leaving anything to Billie Whyte; Billie does not appear in this document. The largest sums would go to Monash University for research into librarianship, to Amnesty International, to the Ryder-Cheshire Foundation, to the Winston Churchill Memorial Trust, to the University of Adelaide, to St Aloysius College, and to the Roman Catholic Archbishop of Adelaide to divide among the Adelaide Day Centre for Homeless Persons, the Daughters of Charity St Louise's Centre and Catherine House, also a refuge for homeless women.[30] Nothing further needed to be done there.

But there were hundreds of letters: people were writing to tell her how important she was to them, to the time in which she had lived, to the state over which she had presided, to the world that she had helped to fashion. And perhaps there were other things that needed to be dealt with, as well. She told the Harewoods that she 'had been going to her house nearby with two of her associates to put her affairs in order'. Peter Ward happened to be at the East Terrace flat, visiting Jean Whyte. She had asked him to come and help her with the air conditioning and the CD player. Now, she was getting ready to go with him to the Art Gallery, and had suggested that, while she did so, Peter might like to go upstairs to see Roma's new Margaret Olley painting.

> Coming back down the stairs I heard voices and someone apparently breaking in via the back door. I was at the point of deciding whether to accost or run for the phone, when it turned out to be Roma in a nightie and dressing gown being led by a nun of middle years. Roma was then almost blind and said, 'Is that you, Jean?' I said, 'No, it's Peter Ward, Roma; I've been helping Jean with the air conditioning and the music system'. She said: 'Very good, very good', primly, and went through to the study where she and the nun set about arranging … papers and composing thank you notes for all the people who had sent her flowers. I got one a few days later.[31]

The second time the Harewoods went to see her, she said, 'I've done it and everything is neat and tidy.'

Amanda Vanstone came back, this time with oysters and lemon for lunch.

> Strangely, with something approaching the air of a picnic four of us sat around her hospital room having oysters. Her feet had been cold so I had brought her some bed socks and hadn't washed them before taking them to the hospital. I casually remarked that I was sure they would be okay despite the lack of washing. She immediately remonstrated with me for, in her view, clearly forgetting *Grant v Australian Knitting Mills*. How could I forget the famous product liability case in which the plaintiff suffered eczema through wearing unwashed clothing next to the skin?
>
> Suitably chastised, I sought to retrieve the socks with a promise to return the next day with newly washed socks. That was rejected as unrealistic because I might be called to Canberra. In desperation I even offered to wash them in her hand-basin. This was rejected and with considerable vigour she out-foxed me by thrusting the socks behind her and leaning back. I was defeated; I did not have it in me to wrestle bed socks from behind the back of an 8[6] year old titan.[32]

She was sinking, though; just as well the work – and whatever else was concerning her – was all tidied up. By the beginning of March, Father Shinnick was spending longer with her 'because she was physically "very low"': 'She was certainly finding comfort from some of the psalms that I was praying', he said.[33] Sir William and Lady Deane cut short their other plans and flew to Adelaide. They would invest Dame Roma with her Royal Victorian Order;

clearly it could not wait for the Queen's arrival in Canberra in a few months' time. Together with Archbishop Leonard Faulkner, and the Neals, they presented her with the award. 'That was a beautiful moment', said Faulkner.[34] Afterwards William and Helen Deane received communion with Roma, and were sitting with her on their own in silence.

> Roma had been fully conscious for the investiture but now her eyes were closed. As the time came for us to leave to return to Canberra, she opened her eyes and the courage, the thoughtfulness, the courtesy and the wonderful formality of the quintessential Roma shone through. 'Thank you Bill. And you too Helen', she said. 'It's been a very great pleasure.'

True to her practice throughout her life, she did not waste time. She died just before noon on Sunday 5 March 2000, listening to Father Shinnock reading the words of the Twenty-Third Psalm: '... and I will dwell in the house of the Lord for ever'.

There was a State Funeral, of course. On Friday 10 March 2000, in St Francis Xavier's Cathedral, with Archbishop Faulkner celebrating. Others also took part: the Anglican Archbishop, Ian George; Lieutenant Colonel Poke of the Salvation Army, Chairman of the Heads of Christian Churches in South Australia; the Reverend Michael Semmler, President of the Lutheran Church in South Australia and the Northern Territory; Dr. Lowitja O'Donoghue AC, CBE; the former Moderator of the Uniting Church in South Australia, the Reverend Margaret Polkinghorne; and Mrs Kathy McEvoy, Member of the Diocesan Pastoral Team.[35] The centre of Adelaide came to a standstill; streets nearby were closed off. The Cathedral holds 1400. It was full. A marquee was set up on its western side, with another 300 seats and large video screens relaying the service inside. Hundreds more stood in the blazing sun in tribute. People came from everywhere. There were diplomats from all over Europe, the Mediterranean and South-East Asia. There were Governors, Premiers, Chief Justices, members of governments and parliaments from all over Australia, representatives of all legal jurisdictions also from all over Australia, the Sisters of Mercy, representatives from Anglicare, representatives from the universities, from the arts and from the media.

There were hundreds of us ordinary folk whose lives had been lifted, strengthened, enlarged, delighted by having been touched by Dame Roma's. And there were members of her family, and her close friends: they had brought her the greatest joy, the people she had had fun with, she said: 'it's the company of friends really. The company of people you love'.[36]

The Honourable Len King gave the first reading.

> If you do away with the yoke,
> The clenched fist, the wicked word,
> If you give your bread to the hungry,
> And relief to the oppressed,
> Your light will rise in the darkness,
> And your shadows become like noon.

The Aboriginal community of Tandanya made a tribute for her.

> She walked paths others feared to tread.
> She was a legend in her own lifetime.
> And legends live forever.

Sir William Deane gave the eulogy. This is, he said, 'also an occasion for celebration. Celebration of the life of one of the greatest of all Australians. A life of wonderful achievements, including an incomparable number of nationally significant firsts. A life which blazed a trail for all Australian women ...'

Chapter Twelve
Epilogue

Roma Mitchell's life is a story about contradictions. A life-long and devout Catholic, she achieved prominence in a society justly known as a 'paradise of dissent'. Her religion aligned her with Irish working-class Outsiders, yet she gained a position at the heart of the Protestant Establishment, and prized the honours awarded her as a loyal member of the British Commonwealth of Nations. She was deeply committed to the common law, but she sought to change it. A reformer, she was also a traditionalist. An internationalist, she was also a ferociously loyal local. A woman, she gained authority in a world almost exclusively of men.

Two other possible contradictions might complicate the narrative further. Roma Mitchell held firmly that there were no intrinsic differences between the sexes.

> I've never believed that women have a monopoly of certain qualities and that men have the monopoly of other qualities. I think women can be considerate and compassionate but so can men. And women can be tough and hard hearted and so can men. So I've never really subscribed to this view that you have to have more women doing certain things because the qualities belong to women.[1]

Yet, we might see a different view in her correspondence with John Bray. He wrote to commiserate with her on the death of her sister, and congratulate her on her DBE, saying, 'I know you told me not to write a letter of congratulation. Nevertheless I think I'd prefer to do so, if only for the sake of the biographers.' His reference to 'biographers' in the plural implicitly included her in the world of the great and good which he, himself, inhabited. Roma replied, 'Dear John, Thank you for your two letters which I shall preserve for your biographer. But no biographer would find anything of interest in mine. I do not even emulate Lady Tennyson in her detailed descriptions of clothes and food.'[2] Of course, she may have been teasing. Flirting, even. This was after all the woman who 'managed' Joe Nelligan. Nevertheless, she is describing her place in a different world from his, invoking the feminine world of the wife of a previous governor of South Australia. It is a distinction that gives emphasis to the masculinity of Bray's world, and evades recognition that her achievements situate her firmly in precisely the same world, a public masculine world – even if it is changed because of her presence in it. It could imply recognition and acceptance of difference between the sexes, one that brings her view closer to those expressed more recently. Justice Mary Gaudron, for instance, told the inaugural meeting of Australian Women Lawyers in 1997:

> The truth is that, in some respects, we are the same [as men] but in others we are different. And when we admit that difference, when we assert our right to be different, we are going to be significantly better lawyers. Moreover, the legal profession is going to be a better profession and the interests of justice are going to be better served.[3]

Marilyn Warren emphasised difference, when she was appointed Chief Justice of the Supreme Court of Victoria in November 2003. She maintained that women offer the law unique skills: 'they identify issues quickly, persuade rather than dictate; they have "finely honed organisational skills", and bring the "typically feminine characteristics" of "energy, patience, humour and insight" to the law'.[4]

The second additional contradiction concerns us closely for it relates to her biography. Some of her friends and Associates told us

Dame Roma had said that she did not want anyone to write a biography of her. Yet, again in her correspondence with Bray, and in her subsequent actions, we encounter a different view. He wrote to congratulate her on being appointed to the Supreme Court of South Australia: 'You are clearly destined for fame', he predicted, '& my guess is that you will not have to wait as long as Sir Samuel Way for your biography.' (A biography of Way, Chief Justice of South Australia for nearly forty years from 1876, was not published until 1960.) In response to another letter in 1983, Roma Mitchell wrote to Bray telling him that both Jean Whyte and the State Library were petitioning her to deposit her personal papers in the South Australian archives: 'I shall cherish your more than generous letter to me and believe that the archives should have it in due course as anything in your hand, even if difficult to decipher, will be of inestimable historic value.'[5] She left that letter, and the hundreds of others that she received, together with various other personal papers, to be deposited in the Mortlock Library of South Australiana. And she annotated those letters so that any future biographer could readily know who each letter had come from, and what was the office that he or she held at the time, or was to achieve. This was a considerate and generous undertaking, and a considerable chore. In response, we have felt welcomed into those papers that she preserved. It has been a privilege for us to spend time in her company. Her sense of humour is wry and dry, her heart generous and her mind sharp and practical: it has been a great pleasure reading her papers.

Such an array of contradictions means that any narrative of her life must offer a kaleidoscope of differing selves in the one person. They are not all present, all at once in the same moment, of course. We have sought to show them emerging, retreating or developing, acquiring firmer definition or fading away, as some doors opened for her and others closed. We have endeavoured to show how she chose some doors, and not others, how she insisted on some doors opening although that was difficult, even degrading, and how some doors that she had not even noticed abruptly whooshed open before her.

At the same time, we have endeavoured to show the changing world and times that she inhabited: the ways in which they shaped her, and the ways in which she contributed to their changing shapes. For the central and most important dimension of her life was the way in which she enacted a new mode of living for women, a new, modern form of womanhood, and the ways in which she sought to expand the horizons of possibility for other women. We have endeavoured to show something of those women who, inspired by her example, joined the expanding flotilla sailing in her wake to positions of independence, even prominence and power, to make their own signature impact on their worlds.

One of them, Mary Gaudron, combined her tribute to Dame Roma with a declaration that she would follow her example. When she was sworn in as a Justice of the High Court on 6 February 1987, she said,

> Of the many women lawyers who were instrumental in advancing the status of women within the legal profession, Dame Roma Mitchell's contribution merits particular acknowledgment ... My constitutional duty is to all Australians but I hope that consistent with and by reason of the discharge of that responsibility, I shall be able to contribute as effectively to the status of women lawyers as has Dame Roma.[6]

Increasing the number and status of women in the legal profession will, necessarily, change – improve – the practice of the law and its commitment to justice. How? By making the profession itself more just: there are no good reasons for women to be denied access to any kind of opportunity or occupation. Indeed, excluding them both diminishes the expertise available to the justice system, and calls its legitimacy into question. Retiring High Court Justice Michael McHugh declared in 2005 that

> Unless we redress the present gender imbalance in judicial appointments, there is an ever increasing risk in the society of today that the public support on which the legitimacy of the judiciary rests will erode.

If people continue to see a legal system dominated by men and overwhelmingly occupied by men, McHugh warned, then they will be forced to conclude that the legal profession still suffers from systemic and structural discrimination against women. And that undermines the public confidence on which the whole legal system rests.[7] Similar warnings could be offered about the

Cover of the Law Society of South Australia *Bulletin*, December 1999. Group photograph organised by Lindy Powell QC during the final weeks of her presidency of the Law Society. Seated from left: Judge Helen Parsons (Industrial Court and Commission), former Judge Iris Stevens (District Court), former Justice Doreen Bulbeck (Family Court), former Justice Dame Roma Mitchell AC DBE QC (Supreme Court), Lindy Powell QC, Justice Margaret Nyland (Supreme Court), the Hon. Anne Harrison (Federal Industrial Commission, Sydney); standing from left: Ms Roseanne McInnes SM, Ms Charlotte Kelly (Judicial Registrar, Family Court), Ms Catherine Cashen (Senior Registrar, Family Court), Ms Susan O'Connor SM (Magistrates Court), Judge Ann Vanstone (District Court), Senior Judge Andrea Simpson (Youth Court), Ms Sue Raymond (President Office, Residential Tenancies Tribunal). Five individual portraits below, from left: Justice Christine Dawe (Family Court of Australia), Judge Christine Trenorden (Environment, Resources and Development Court), Former Judge Robyn Layton QC (Industrial court and AAT), Justice Catherine Branson (Federal Court of Australia) and Justice Kemeri Murray (Family Court of Australia). Absent were Justice Ann Robinson of the Family Court and recently-appointed Ms Elizabeth Bolton of the Magistrates Court. Published with permission of the Law Society of South Australia.

participation of women in other kinds of institution to which Roma Mitchell also contributed: universities, just for instance.

Women do make a difference to the nature of public life when they occupy prominent positions in the public gaze. For that gaze is formed by traditions and assumptions about differences in the proper occupations and locations of women and men; it has to assimilate something new and unfamiliar when it encounters women in prominent public circumstances. We are becoming far more accustomed to seeing women as state governors, as judges, as professors, as senior doctors, as parliamentarians, as vice-chancellors, as industrial leaders. But these women still stand out as exceptions. We still notice them. We applaud them. But, as Roma Mitchell said often, 'Women can't relax yet.'

Notes

Chapter One: Growing up Caring, Competitive and Catholic

1 Film Australia. *Australian Biography II*, 4 June 1993, shown on SBS Television, pp. 5–6. This is a transcript of a videotaped interview with Dame Roma Mitchell; we have silently removed the transcriptions of her voiced hesitations, and amended the transcribers' punctuation where that seemed appropriate; Susan Magarey, Interview with Mrs Lorna Williams (born Lorna Lumbers) and her daughter, Dame Roma Mitchell's god-daughter, Mrs Adrienne McMahon, 17 August 2001.

2 Card dated 2 October 1917, in Dame Roma Mitchell's Scrapbooks, State Library of South Australia [SLSA] PRG 778/22; K.A. Lenihan, 'The Saga of Roma', notebook containing stories about Roma Mitchell aged around four years, SLSA PRG 778/21.

3 H.F. Mitchell, Form D.16, 30 May 1918, World War I Service Records, National Archives of Australia [NAA].

4 Lenihan, 'The Saga of Roma'; Susan Mitchell, 'Dame Roma Mitchell', in Susan Mitchell, *The Matriarchs. Twelve Australian Women Talk about Their Lives* (Penguin), Ringwood, 1987, p. 30.

5 A.D. Hope, 'Australia', in *Collected Poems 1930–1965* (Angus & Robertson), Sydney, 1966, p. 13; Michael Ignatieff, *Isaiah Berlin: A Life* (Vintage), London, 2000, p. 301.

6 Kerrie Round, Telephone conversation with Ross Wickham, grandson of Maude Mitchell's brother, Harry, 28 October 2002; Glenda Condon, Interview with Dame Roma Mitchell, 27 March 1992, Mercy Archives, Adelaide, Box 165; on Mount Gambier, see Margaret Allen, 'She Seems to have Composed Her Own Life: Thinking about Catherine Martin', *Australian Feminist Studies*, vol. 19, no. 43, March 2004, pp. 33–35; Walter Crocker, Entry for 3 September 1981, MS Diaries, Barr Smith Library [BSL], Special Collections; John Playford, 'Smith, Francis Villeneuve (1883–1956)', *Australian Dictionary of Biography* (Melbourne University Press), Carlton, vol. 11, 1988, pp. 642–643. Villeneuve Smith was allowed to sit his exams only after Paris Nesbit, K.C. – a colleague of Samuel James Mitchell, father of Harold – had intervened on his behalf.

7 See entries on Samuel James Mitchell in J.J. Pascoe, *History of Adelaide and its Vicinity* (Hussey & Gillingham), Adelaide, 1901, pp. 481–482; H.T. Burgess (ed.), *The Cyclopedia of South Australia* (Cyclopedia Co.), Adelaide, 1907, pp. 221–222; Robert Thornton, 'Mitchell, Samuel James (1852–1926)', *Australian Dictionary of Biography* (Melbourne University Press),

Carlton, vol. 10, 1986, pp. 533–534; *Advertiser*, 4 October 1926; Dame Roma Mitchell to Zita Nalty, 7 June 1993, SLSA PRG 778/5/8. On the Liberal Democratic Union, see Dean Jaensch, 'Party, Party System and Federation: 1890–1912', in Dean Jaensch (ed.), *The Flinders History of South Australia: Political History* (Wakefield Press), Netley, 1986, pp. 203–207.

8 Dr A.J. Shinkfield, Headmaster, St Peter's College, to Roma Mitchell, 12 May 1983, SLSA PRG 778/4/1; *Kangaroo Island Courier*: 16 May 1908, 26 February 1910.

9 *Kangaroo Island Courier*: 15 August 1908, 14 December 1907, 21 December 1907, 14 August 1909, 5 December 1908, 19 December 1908, 5 June 1909.

10 Figures calculated from the 1901 Census provided in Wray Vamplew (ed.), *Australians: Historical Statistics* (Fairfax, Syme & Weldon Associates), Sydney, 1987, pp. 421, 422, 424.

11 David Hilliard, 'The Catholic Church and the Community in Adelaide', in Fay Gale (ed.), *Making Space: Women and Education at St Aloysius College Adelaide 1880–2000* (St Aloysius College in association with Wakefield Press), Kent Town, 2000, pp. 3, 7, 5, 6; Margaret Press, 'Catholic Church', in Wilfrid Prest, Kerrie Round and Carol Fort (eds), *The Wakefield Companion to South Australian History* (Wakefield Press), Kent Town, 2001, p. 97; Margaret Press, Interview with Dame Roma Mitchell, 19 March 1990, Mercy Archives; Kerrie Round, Telephone conversation with Jean Macdonald, granddaughter of Samuel and Eliza Mitchell, 10 December 2002; *Australian Biography II*, p. 11.

12 http://www.ewtn.com/library/CURIA/NETEMERE.HTM Accessed 25 February 2004; Harold and Maude were married on 8 August 1908 and Maude Mignon Flinders Mitchell was born on 16 March 1909: Marriage Certificate, Harold Flinders Mitchell and Maude Imelda Victoria Wickham; Birth Certificate, Maude Mignon Flinders Mitchell.

13 *Kangaroo Island Courier*, 1 May 1909.

14 *Kangaroo Island Courier*, 5 March 1910; *The Islander*, 13 February 1980.

15 *Eyre's Peninsula Tribune*, 7 April 1911.

16 *Eyre's Peninsula Tribune*: 9 February 1912, 29 March 1912, 21 June 1912; undated card advertising H. Flinders Mitchell, 'Solicitor and Notary, Mannum/Attends Palmer 2nd Wednesday and 4th Monday/Rhine Villa, 1st and 3rd Thursday, Swan Reach, 3rd Wednesday, Mount Pleasant, 2nd Tuesday', in Dame Roma Mitchell's Scrapbooks.

17 Birth certificate, Roma Alma Flinders Mitchell.

18 *Australian Biography II*, p. 96.

19 Bill Gammage, *The Broken Years: Australian Soldiers in the Great War* (ANU Press), Canberra, 1974, pp. 6, 18–19; Hilliard, 'The Catholic Church and the Community in Adelaide', p. 9.

20 H.F. Mitchell: Enlistment Form, Medical Form, World War I Service Records, NAA; C.E.W. Bean, *The Official History of Australia in the War of 1914–1918*. Vol. V: The A.I.F. in France: December 1917–May 1918 (Angus & Robertson), Sydney, 1937, p. 404; Dame Roma Mitchell, Speech at the Returned Services League 75th Anniversary Luncheon, 8 December 1991, SLSA PRG 778/17.

21 H.F. Mitchell: World War I Service Records, NAA; Department of Defence, *Standing Orders, Australian Imperial Force, and War Financial Regulations* (Government Printer) Melbourne, 1918.

22 Student record cards, University of Adelaide; Lenihan, 'The Saga of Roma'. All of the stories about the Mitchells' time at Hill Street are taken from this source unless otherwise noted.

23 Kate Walsh, Migration Museum, to Dame Roma Mitchell, 14 March 1989, SLSA PRG 778/5/5. Dame Roma donated these items to the Museum of Migration & Settlement, Adelaide, in 1989.

24 *Australian Biography II*, p. 8.

25 Returned Sailors' & Soldiers' Imperial League of Australia, Victorian branch, *War Pensions Handbook* (The League), Melbourne, 1936; Susan Mitchell, 'Dame Roma Mitchell', p. 30; *Advertiser*, 19 October 1990.

26 Dame Roma Mitchell, Speech at the opening of new gallery and restored youth centre, Mitcham Village Art and Crafts Association, 17 April 1994, SLSA PRG 778/17.

27 Playford, 'Smith, Francis Villeneuve', Playford has mistaken the sex of their first child; H.M. Whitington, 'Frank Villeneuve Smith Q.C. 1884–1956', Law Society of South Australia, *Bulletin*, September 1986, pp. 239–244; J.A. Cassidy and J.F. Corkery, *Alderman's Barristers & Solicitors. History of the Firm 1928–1988* (The Firm), Adelaide, 1988, pp. 23–24.

28 *Australian Biography II*, p. 9; Magarey, Interview with Lorna Williams and Adrienne McMahon; Kerrie Round, Interview with Pamela Villeneuve Smith (widow of Cairns), 13 August 2002; Dame Roma Mitchell, Speech at the opening of the Beachside Community Centre, Seaford Community Fund, 30 October 1993, SLSA PRG 778/17.

29 Press, Interview with Dame Roma Mitchell; David Hilliard, *Catholics in Kingswood: The Catholic Church in the Mitcham District 1869–1994* (Kingswood Catholic Parish Pastoral Council), Kingswood, 1994, pp. 15–16, 19–20; we are grateful to David Hilliard for providing us with a copy of this work, and for correcting our mistaken description of the Mitchell's parish church; Condon, Interview with Dame Roma Mitchell.

30 Mercy Archives; *Southern Cross*, 2 September 1927.

31 Dame Roma Mitchell, Speech at the opening of an exhibition at the Unley Museum, 22 September 1993, SLSA PRG 778/17; Stephanie Burley, 'The Classroom: Challenges and Changing Curriculum', in Gale (ed.), *Making Space*, p. 38; Anne McLay, *Women on the Move: Mercy's Triple Spiral: A History of the Adelaide Sisters of Mercy Ireland to Argentina 1856–1880 to South Australia 1880–* (Sisters of Mercy, Adelaide), Adelaide, 1996, p. 93; School Register, Mercy Archives; Stephanie Burley, 'None More Anonymous', M.Ed. thesis, University of Adelaide, 1992, p. 163; advertisement, *Southern Cross*, 30 September 1921; School Report, 1922, Mercy Archives; Sister Mary Carmel to Dame Roma Mitchell, 19 October 1990, SLSA PRG 778/3/8/1.

32 'The Most Necessary Prayers', *The Ideal Daily Missal with Vespers for Sundays and for Feasts* (Eason & Son Ltd), Dublin, 1952; Burley, 'The Classroom: Challenges and Changing Curriculum', pp. 47–48; Sister Carmel Bourke, Written Memoirs, 1991, quoted in Burley, 'None More Anonymous', pp. 106, 103.

33 Condon, Interview with Dame Roma Mitchell; Sister Carmel Bourke, Written Memoirs, quoted in Burley, 'None More Anonymous', p. 102; Burley, 'None More Anonymous', p. 103; M. Brigid Jones, *Reminiscences of the J.C.W.L.: Catholic Action for Girls (1929–1948)*, (J.C.W.L.), Adelaide, c. 1982, p. 1.

34 Fay Gale, 'Introduction', in Gale (ed.), *Making Space*, p. xii.

35 Dame Roma Mitchell, Speech at a book launch, Art Gallery of South Australia, 28 February 1991, SLSA PRG 778/17. The Waterhouse ' Circe' was one of the most popular pictures held in the Art Gallery of South Australia at the beginning of the twenty-first century.

36 Margaret O'Toole and Paul Sharkey, 'The Spirit that Nurtures the Mercy Vision', in Gale (ed.), *Making Space*, pp. 25, 26; Burley, 'The Classroom', in Gale (ed.), *Making Space*, p. 46.

37 Condon, Interview with Dame Roma Mitchell; McLay, *Women on the Move*, p. 84; Lenihan, 'The Saga of Roma'; Burley, 'The Classroom', in Gale (ed.), *Making Space*, pp. 47–49; Susan Mitchell, 'Dame Roma Mitchell', p. 30; photograph in Dame Roma Mitchell's Scrapbooks; *Sunday Mail*, 18 December 1986; Magarey, Interview with Lorna Williams and Adrienne McMahon.

38 Dame Roma Mitchell, Speech at the opening of the Beachside Community Centre, Seaford Community Fund; Nadine Williams, 'In memoriam', *Advertiser*, 24 March 2001; Magarey, Interview with Lorna Williams and Adrienne McMahon.

39 Susan Mitchell, 'Dame Roma Mitchell', p. 30; Dame Roma Mitchell, Presentation to Senior Secondary Assessment Board of South Australia, 19 February 1992, SLSA PRG 778/17; Burley, 'The Classroom', in Gale (ed.), *Making Space*, pp. 48–49; G.W. Cox, *The Athenian Empire* (Longmans, Green and Co.), London, 1923; A.M. Curteis (ed.), *Rise of the Macedonian Empire* (Longmans, Green and Co.), London, 1927; W.W. Capes, *Roman History – The Early Empire* (Longmans, Green and Co.), London, 1927; Sydney Herbert, *Modern Europe 1789–1914* (Macmillan and Co.), London, 1926; Ernest Scott, *A Short History of Australia* (Oxford University Press), Oxford, 1925; these books are in the Mercy Archives; the prize, *The Poetical Works of Thomas Moore* (Frederick Warne and Co.), London, nd, is held in Mercy Archives; *Advertiser*, 13 December 1934; Dame Roma Mitchell, Speech at the Speech Day of the Collegiate School of St Peter, 13 December 1991, SLSA PRG 778/17.

40 Mother Dolores, quoted in the *Advertiser*, 25 May 1996; Condon, Interview with Dame Roma Mitchell; Magarey, Interview with Lorna Williams and Adrienne McMahon; Susan Mitchell, 'Dame Roma Mitchell', p. 30; *Australian Biography II*, p. 3; Molly M. Gunson, 'What is Girl Guiding', *Golden Jubilee Wattle*, 1930, Mercy Archives; Mrs George Gunson, 'Girl Guiding', paper given to the Second Interstate Catholic Women's Conference, Adelaide, October 1929; A.C.M., 'The origin of the Angas Street Junior C.W.L.', *Catholic Women's League Magazine*, vol. 2, no. 7, 1938, pp. 10–11.

41 Press, Interview with Dame Roma Mitchell; Beryl Pickhaver to Roma Mitchell, 22 September 1962, SLSA PRG 778/3/1/1; Magarey, Interview with Lorna Williams and Adrienne McMahon; newspaper clipping, no source, nd, Dame Roma Mitchell's Scrapbooks.

42 Condon, Interview with Dame Roma Mitchell; Kay Brownbill to Roma Mitchell, 22 June 1980, SLSA PRG 778/5/1; Noni Farwell, 'Roma Mitchell and the Arts', in Susan Magarey (ed.), *Dame Roma, Glimpses of a Glorious Life* (Axiom Publishing in association with the John Bray Chapter of the Adelaide University Alumni Association), Adelaide, 2002, p. 240; Kay Brownbill to Roma Mitchell, 2 July 1980, SLSA PRG 778/5/1; Dame Roma Mitchell, Launch of *A Rich Tapestry of Lives*, MLC/Annesley College Old Scholars' Association, 30 August 1995, SLSA PRG 778/17; Mercy Archives, Box 162; Film Australia, *Australian Biography II*, p. 9; Dame Roma Mitchell to Sister Deirdre Jordan, 22 November 1991, Mercy Archives, Adelaide; *Sunday Herald*, 21 October 1990.

43 *Nationwide*, 'Dame Roma Mitchell', ABC Television, 5 March 1984; *Australian Biography II*, p. 15; Magarey, Interview with Lorna Williams and Adrienne McMahon.

44 Peter Norman, Interview with Dame Roma Mitchell, 22 March 1999.

45 Alison Mackinnon, 'The Streets and into the World Beyond', in Gale (ed.), *Making Space*, pp. 181–183, 188; Dame Roma Mitchell, AC, DBE, CVO, QC, 'Foreword', in Gale (ed.), *Making Space*, p. vii; Dame Roma Mitchell, Speech at St Peter's Girls' School Speech Night, 11 December 1992, SLSA PRG 778/17.

46 Kay Brownbill to Roma Mitchell, 2 July 1980, SLSA SRG 165/1/85.

47 Condon, Interview with Dame Roma Mitchell.

Chapter Two: Courses in Law, and Life

1 J.C. Caldwell, 'Population', in Wray Vamplew (ed.), *Australian Historical Statistics* (Fairfax, Syme & Weldon Associates), Sydney, 1987, p. 41.

2 A.G. Austin (ed.), *The Webbs' Australian Diary 1898* (Pitman), Melbourne, 1965, p. 93.

3 Walter Crocker, *Travelling Back* (Macmillan), South Melbourne, 1981, p. 17.

4 *Ever Yours, C.H. Spence: Catherine Helen Spence's* An Autobiography *(1825–1910), Diary (1894) and Some Correspondence (1894–1910)*, (eds) Susan Magarey, with Barbara Wall with Mary Lyons and Maryan Beams (Wakefield Press), Kent Town, 2005.

5 Simon Cameron, *Silent Witnesses. Adelaide's Statues and Monuments* (Wakefield Press), Kent Town, 1997, pp. 16, 19.

6 Hugh Stretton, *Ideas for Australian Cities* (Georgian House), Melbourne, 1970, p. 143; Arnold D. Hunt, 'Methodist Church', in Wilfrid Prest, Kerrie Round and Carol Fort (eds), *The Wakefield Companion to South Australian History* (Wakefield Press), Kent Town, 2001, p. 348; Dirk Van Dissel, 'The Adelaide Gentry, 1850–1920', in Eric Richards (ed.), *The Flinders History of South Australia: Social History* (Wakefield Press), Netley, 1986, pp. 335, 337, 364; Mark Peel and Janet McCalman, 'Who Went Where in *Who's Who 1988*', *Melbourne University History Research Series* No. 1 (1992), p. 43; Crocker, *Travelling Back*, p. 17; Thistle Anderson, *Arcadian Adelaide* (1905), With 'Thistle Anderson in Edwardian Adelaide', Derek Whitelock (Wakefield Press), Netley, 1985, p. 32; 'Emanuel Solomon', in Prest *et al.* (eds), *Wakefield Companion*, p. 500. Our thanks to David Hilliard for reminding us of the Solomons; Dean Jaensch, 'Party, Party System and Federation: 1890–1912', in Dean Jaensch (ed.), *The Flinders History of South Australia: Political History* (Wakefield Press), Netley, 1986, p. 180; Peter Ward, 'John Bray in Adelaide', in Wilfrid Prest (ed.), *A Portrait of John Bray: Law, Letters, Life* (Wakefield Press), Kent Town, 1997, pp. 3–4.

7 John Bray, '1930s', in Hometown Adelaide, a series of spoken recollections delivered at Adelaide Writers' Week, Adelaide, 1986, State Records of South Australia [SRSA] GRS

1132/3/P, Tape B27. See also *Licensing Act* 1932–1936. An earlier or less secular household had cold meals on Sundays so that the servants did not have to cook and could attend church said Susan Magarey's great-aunts Dorothy and Marjory Gilbert, telling her about growing up at Pewsey Vale in the Adelaide hills in the 1880s. By the 1930s, though, few households had domestic servants; see Joan Hancock and Eric Richards, 'Wealth, Work and Well Being: Some Historical Indicators', in Richards (ed.), *Flinders History: Social History*, Table 21.6; Don Dunstan, *Felicia: The Political Memoirs of Don Dunstan* (Macmillan), South Melbourne, 1981, p. 23; Stella Bowen, *Drawn From Life: Reminiscences by Stella Bowen* (Collins Publishers), London, 1940, p. 11; Alex Castles, Andrew Ligertwood and Peter Kelly (eds), *Law on North Terrace 1883–1983* (Faculty of Law, University of Adelaide), Adelaide, 1984(?), p. 30; photograph in Dame Roma Mitchell's Scrapbooks, SLSA PRG 778/22, for Roxy Simms, later Byrne, see *On Dit*, 15 June 1934 and Roxy Byrne to Dame Roma Mitchell, January, 1991, SLSA PRG 778/3/9/2; *Australian Biography II*, p. 25.

8 See Stuart Macintyre, 'Cricket', in Graeme Davison, John Hirst and Stuart Macintyre (eds), *The Oxford Companion to Australian History* (Oxford University Press), Melbourne, 1998, p. 162; John Mannion, 'Horseracing', in Prest *et al.* (eds), *Wakefield Companion*, p. 265; Bernard Whimpress, 'Australian Rules Football', in Prest *et al.* (eds), *Wakefield Companion*, pp. 58–60; P.W. Verco, *Thomas and Elisabeth Magarey* (LPH Adelaide), Adelaide, n.d., pp. 198–199; Andrea Rhode, 'Struggling to survive, or postponing pleasure: women and class in the Great Depression', BA Hons thesis, University of Adelaide, 1995, p. 42; Dylan Walker, *Adelaide Silent Nights. A Pictorial History of Adelaide's Picture Theatres during the Silent Era 1896–1929* (National Film and Sound Archive), Canberra, c. 1996, p. 31; http://www.adelaidecitycouncil.com/council/publications/Brochures/walktrailtheatre.pdf Accessed 18 April 2005; *Advertiser*, 23 March 1931; see John Hetherington, *Melba: A Biography* (Penguin), Ringwood, 1967.

9 http://www.adelaidecitycouncil.com/council/publications/Brochures/walktrailtheatre.pdf Accessed 18 April 2005; Nancye Bridges, *Wonderful Wireless. Reminiscences of the Stars of Australia's Live Radio* (Methuen), Sydney, 1983; *Year Book of the Commonwealth of Australia*, No. 23 (Australian Government Publishing Service), Canberra, 1931; 'Radio to Aid Musical Education', *News*, 19 August 1929; http://www.sydneyoperahouse.com/sections/whats_on/education/images/FamilyPromsJazz Accessed 18 April 2005; *Adelaide University Magazine*, VI, 24, 1930, pp. 38–39; Jo Peoples, 'Miss Patricia Hackett', *Journal of the Historical Society of South Australia*, no. 25, 1997, p. 134. See also Thelma Afford, *Dreamers and Visionaries: Adelaide's Little Theatres from the 1920s to the Early 1940s*, edited with additional research by Kerrie Round (Currency Press), Sydney, 2004, chapter 3.

10 Margaret Press, Interview with Dame Roma Mitchell, 19 March 1990, Mercy Archives; *Australian Biography II*, pp. 25–26; Jim Moss, *Sound of Trumpets: History of the Labour Movement in South Australia* (Wakefield Press), Netley, 1985, pp. 293, 295, 298; Rob Linn, 'Royal Adelaide Show', in Prest *et al.* (eds), *Wakefield Companion*, p. 466; Ray Broomhill, *Unemployed Workers. A Social History of the Great Depression in Adelaide* (University of Queensland Press), St. Lucia, 1978, p. 167; Susannah Farfor, George Dunford and Jill Kirby, *Adelaide & South Australia* (Lonely Planet), Footscray, 2005, p. 21; Stephanie Burley, 'The Classroom: Challenges and Changing Curriculum', in Fay Gale (ed.), *Making Space: Women and Education at St Aloysius College Adelaide 1880–2000* (St Aloysius College in association with Wakefield Press), Kent Town, 2000, p. 39; V.A. Edgeloe, *University Children of the 1880s* (Law), Adelaide, 1978, n.p.

11 Alan O'Shea, 'English Subjects of Modernity', in Mica Nava and Alan O'Shea (eds), *Modern Times. Reflections on a Century of English Modernity* (Routledge), London, 1996, p. 30, quoted in Jill Julius Matthews, *Dance Hall and Picture Palace: Sydney's Romance with Modernity* (Currency Press), Sydney, 2005, p. 200; quoted in the *Mail*, 22 July 1933; Russel Ward, *A Radical Life* (Macmillan), Melbourne, 1988, p. [illegible]; our thanks to Dr O.R. Varoneckas for her diagnosis of Ruth Mitchell's condition; *Australian Biography II*, p. 20; Ruth Flinders Mitchell, record card, Student Records Office, University of Adelaide.

12 *Advertiser*: 24 October 1932, 5 September 1933; Roma Flinders Mitchell, record card, Student Records Office, University of Adelaide; Peter Norman, Interview with Dame Roma

Mitchell, 22 March 1999; Susan Mitchell, 'Dame Roma Mitchell', in Susan Mitchell, *The Matriarchs. Twelve Australian Women Talk about Their Lives* (Penguin), Ringwood, 1987, p. 31.

13 *Penny Post*, 17 February 1931, in Dame Roma Mitchell's Scrapbooks; photograph of Ruth Mitchell in Dame Roma Mitchell's Scrapbooks; Dame Roma Mitchell, Speech at the Memorial Service for the Late John Bray, AC, QC, Tuesday 25 July 1995, printed in Susan Magarey (ed.), *Dame Roma, Glimpses of a Glorious Life* (Axiom Publishing in association with the John Bray Chapter of the Adelaide University Alumni Association), Adelaide, 2002, p. 91.

14 Kerrie Round, Interview with Pamela Villeneuve Smith, 13 August 2002; Press, Interview with Dame Roma Mitchell; *Australian Biography II*, p. 19; *Adelaide Telephone Directory*, 1933.

15 W.G.K. Duncan and Roger Ashley Leonard, *The University of Adelaide 1874–1974* (Rigby) Netley, 1973, pp. 13–14, 72–73; e.g. *On Dit*, 15 April 1932; Essay accompanying the exhibition 'Women at the University of Adelaide 1874–1985. Centenary of the First Woman Graduate', BSL, Special Collections; *News*, 2 December 1927; Castles *et al.* (eds), *Law on North Terrace*, pp. 36, 75; Dame Roma Mitchell, 'Reminiscences of a 1930 law student and practitioner'. Speech given to law students in 1993, p. 2.

16 Marilyn Lake, *Getting Equal: The History of Australian Feminism* (Allen & Unwin), Sydney, 1999, p. 173.

17 Jean Forward, '1932 – A Short History of the Tatler's Club – 1954', typescript. We are most grateful to Barbara Wall, still a member of the Tatler's Club in 2005, for lending us her copy of this history; Box 132, Aquinas Society and Box 80 Catholic Action, Catholic Archives, Adelaide; see also Michael Head, *Fire on the Hill: Aquinas College 1950–2000* (Aquinas College Foundation), North Adelaide, 2002, p. 177; Press, Interview with Dame Roma Mitchell; Margaret Press, *Colour and Shadow. South Australian Catholics* (Archdiocese of Adelaide), Adelaide, 1991, p. 152.

18 *On Dit*, 1 July 1932; Letter to the Editor, *On Dit*, 16 September 1932; Kerrie Round, Interview with Beryl Linn, 15 October 2002; *Register*, 17 November 1911; Kerrie Round, Interview with Cedric Isaacson, 28 October 2002; Castles *et al.* (eds), *Law on North Terrace*, p. 36; *Advertiser*, 23 April 1934 (the newspaper dealt with this refusal by taking two photographs and combining them into a single image.

19 *On Dit*, 13 May 1932; Liz Johnswood, *New Woman*, February 1991.

20 Mitchell, 'Reminiscences', p. 3; Duncan and Leonard, *The University of Adelaide*, pp. 62, 26; Doreen Bridges, *More Than A Musician: A Life of E. Harold Davies* (Australian Scholarly Press), Melbourne, 2006, p. 68; John Miles, *Lost Angry Penguins D.B. Kerr & P.G. Pfeiffer: A Path to the Wind* (Crawford House Publishing), Adelaide, 2000, pp. 12–13, 15; Bowen, *Drawn From Life*, p. 22; Elizabeth Butel, *Margaret Preston: The Art of Constant Rearrangement* (Penguin Books in association with the Art Gallery of New South Wales), Ringwood, 1985, p. 2; Michael Heyward, *The Ern Malley Affair* (University of Queensland Press), St Lucia, 1993.

21 Ward, *A Radical Life*, p. 82; Castles *et al.* (eds), *Law on North Terrace*, p. 47; *S.A. Dance News*, September 1935, quoted in 'Music! Dancing! An exhibition on Adelaide's Dancehalls and Nightclubs during the 1920s, '30s and '40s', presented by the Performing Arts Collection of South Australia, 26 February–21 March 1982, BSL, Special Collections; *A Handbook to the University of Adelaide*: 1931, 1935; *On Dit*: 30 June 1933, 15 June 1934.

22 Susan Mitchell, 'Dame Roma Mitchell', p. 31; Mary Wesley, *Jumping the Queue* (Macmillan), London, 1983 (Black Swan edition, London, tenth reprint 1993) p. 142; http://www.womenaustralia.info/index.html, Accessed 18 April 2005; Round, Interview with Beryl Linn; Mary O'Kane, *Adelaidean*, 13 March 2000.

23 *On Dit*, 22 April 1932.

24 Roma Flinders Mitchell, record card; Mitchell, 'Reminiscences', p. 4; Castles *et al.* (eds), *Law on North Terrace*, pp. 30–31; Howard Zelling, 'Campbell, Arthur Lang (1889–1949), *Australian Dictionary of Biography*, vol. 13 (Melbourne University Press), Carlton, 1993, pp. 353–354; Norman, Interview with Dame Roma Mitchell.

25 Margaret J. Jennings, 'Benham, Edward Warner (1872–1948)', *Australian Dictionary of Biography*, vol. 13 (Melbourne University Press), Carlton, 1993, pp. 162–163; Castles *et al.* (eds), *Law on North Terrace*, pp. 30, 31–3, 35; Mitchell, 'Reminiscences', pp. 6–7.

26 Round, Interview with Beryl Linn; *Australian Biography II*, pp. 9, 21; Joan Adams to Roma Mitchell, nd, SLSA PRG 778/3/4/4; Maj Povey to Dame Roma Mitchell, nd, SLSA PRG 778/3/2/1; Mitchell, 'Reminiscences', pp. 7, 11; Jason Hopton, *A History of Wool Auctions in South Australia and Seventy-Six Years in the Brookman Building Wool Exchange*, (Adelaide Woolbrokers' Association), Adelaide, 1977; Dame Roma Mitchell, Speech to the Girl Guides Association, nd, c. 1984, SLSA PRG 778/17/33.

27 *On Dit*, 3 May 1935, 1 July 1932, 13 September 1934, 4 August 1933, 27 July 1934, 12 October 1934; University Women's Union, Minute Book 1929–1934, 13 June 1933, 4 July 1933, 11 June 1934, University of Adelaide Archives; *Advertiser*, 13 December 1934.

28 Press, Interview with Dame Roma Mitchell.

29 Norman, Interview with Dame Roma Mitchell; *Australian Biography II*, p. 26; Round, Interview with Beryl Linn; Johanna Palmer to Roma Mitchell, 26 September [1962], SLSA PRG 778/3/1/1.

30 *Advertiser*, 6 April 1936; Norman, Interview with Dame Roma Mitchell; Mitchell, 'Reminiscences'.

31 Norman, Interview with Dame Roma Mitchell, p. 15; E.P. Mullighan, 'Before the bench', in Magarey (ed.), *Dame Roma*, pp. 42–43; Affadavit of Gladys Ethel Owen in the matter of Roma Flinders Mitchell, SLSA PRG 778/10/1. Bill Rollison, who died in 1936, left the firm in debt. Gerry Rollison, his nephew, did not wind up the firm. Instead he 'amended' the books, was caught, tried and gaoled. Roma Mitchell later gave evidence for him in an unsuccessful attempt to return his name to the rolls, Norman, Interview with Dame Roma Mitchell.

32 Mitchell, 'Reminiscences', p. 13; Castles *et al.* (eds), *Law on North Terrace*, pp. 46–47.

33 Katharine Massam, 'Catholic Church', in Davison, Hirst and Macintyre (eds), *Oxford Companion*, pp. 113–114; Hilliard, 'The Catholic Church and the Community in Adelaide', pp. 12–13; Moss, *Sound of Trumpets*, pp. 297, 299, 305; *Town Topics*, 6 November 1931; Thelma Afford, Adelaide 1930 Little Theatres and Their Visionaries, unpublished MS, nd., Performing Arts Collection, Festival Centre, Adelaide.

34 Jaensch, 'The Playford Era', in Jaensch (ed.), *Flinders History: Political History*, pp. 243–244; see also 'Archibald Grenfell (Archie) Price (1892–1977)', in Prest *et al.* (eds), *Wakefield Companion*, p. 427.

35 *Advertiser*: 11 December 1934, 13 December 1934, 17 December 1934; Castles *et al.* (eds), *Law on North Terrace*, photograph on p. 32.

36 Beryl Jenkins married Noel Paternoster in October 1931, *Town Topics*, 6 November 1931; newspaper clipping, no source, nd, Dame Roma Mitchell's Scrapbooks; Ellis Cafés, Menu, SLSA BRG277; newspaper clipping, no source, nd, Dame Roma Mitchell's Scrapbooks, SLSA PRG 778/22; Kerrie Round, Telephone conversation with Rosemary Wilkinson, 2 June 2003.

Chapter Three: World War Two

1 Dame Roma Mitchell, Speech at Commemorative Launch of Australia Remembers, 10 August 1995, SLSA PRG 775/17.

2 Dame Roma Mitchell, 'Reminiscences of a 1930 law student and practitioner'. Speech given to law students in 1993; Dame Roma Mitchell, 'Reflections on a career in law', in J.F. Corkery (ed.), *A Career in Law* (Federation Press), Sydney, 1992, p. 203; see also Hon. E.P. Mullighan, 'Before the Bench' in Susan Magarey (ed.), *Dame Roma, Glimpses of a Glorious Life* (Axiom Publishing in association with the John Bray Chapter of the Adelaide University Alumni Association), Adelaide, 2002, p. 42.

3 *Sunday Mail*, 19 May 1923.

4 Film Australia. *Australian Biography II*, 4 June 1993, shown on SBS Television, pp. 23, 97; Susan Mitchell, 'Dame Roma Mitchell', in Susan Mitchell, *The Matriarchs. Twelve Australian Women Talk about Their Lives* (Penguin), Ringwood, 1987, p. 33; J.A. Cassidy and J.F. Corkery, *Alderman's Barristers & Solicitors. History of the Firm 1928–1988* (The Firm),

Adelaide, 1988, pp. 9, 25–28; Board listing Presidents of Mercy Old Scholars, Mercy Archives, Adelaide; Peter Norman, Interview with Dame Roma Mitchell, 22 March 1999.

5 Jon Faine, 'Dame Roma Mitchell' in *Taken on Oath: a Generation of Lawyers* (Federation Press), Sydney, 1992, p. 6.

6 Mitchell, 'Reminiscences'; Stewart Cockburn assisted by John Playford, *Playford: Benevolent Despot* (Wakefield Press), Kent Town, 1994 (first published 1991), pp. 208, 305; B.A. Magarey, 'President's Report', Law Society of South Australia *Bulletin*, September 1971, p. 1; Graham Loughlin, 'South Australia's Queen's Counsel', BA Hons. thesis, University of Adelaide, p. 69.

7 Jim Moss, *Sound of Trumpets: History of the Labour Movement in South Australia* (Wakefield Press), Netley, 1985, pp. 306, 313, 314; Peter Spearritt, 'Lang, John Thomas "Jack"', in Graeme Davison, John Hirst and Stuart Macintyre (eds), *The Oxford Companion to Australian History* (Oxford University Press), Melbourne, 1998, pp. 377–378.

8 Kerrie Round, Interview with Len King, 29 April 2003; Len King quoted in E.P. Mullighan, 'Before the Bench' in Magarey (ed.), *Dame Roma*, pp. 43–44; Jack Elliott, *Memoirs of a Barrister* (Wakefield Press), Kent Town, pp. 5–6, 27; Norman, Interview with Dame Roma Mitchell.

9 *Advertiser*, 12 May 1936.

10 Faine, 'Dame Roma Mitchell', p. 4; Susanna de Vries, *Great Australian Women: from Federation to Freedom* (HarperCollins), Sydney, 2000, p. 323; *Australian Biography II*, p. 32.

11 Norman, Interview with Dame Roma Mitchell; *Australian Biography II*, p. 32.

12 See below, Chapter 4, pp. 105–106.

13 Mitchell, 'Reminiscences'; Norman, Interview with Dame Roma Mitchell; Dame Roma Mitchell, 'The Effect of the External Affairs Power upon the Balance of Power between Commonwealth and States', The Tenth Richard Blackburn Lecture, *Canberra Law Review*, vol. 2, no. 2, 1995, p. 104.

14 Norman, Interview with Dame Roma Mitchell; John Bray, 'The Bench and the Legal Profession', Law Society of South Australia *Bulletin*, March 1977, p. 4; *Australian Biography II*, pp. 26–28; Faine, 'Dame Roma Mitchell', p. 10; Lindy Powell, 'Dame Roma Mitchell, A Life in the Law', Law Society of South Australia *Bulletin*, February 1991, p. 7; Faine, 'John Bray', in *Taken on Oath: a Generation of Lawyers* (Federation Press), Sydney, 1992, p. 112; *Guardianship of Infants Act* 1940; Helen Jones, *In Her Own Name. Women in South Australian History* (Wakefield Press), Netley, 1994, p. 181; http://www.womenaustralia.info/biogs/AWE0665b.htm, accessed 27 October 2005.

15 Roma Mitchell, 'Self-education for Social Service', *Catholic Women's League Magazine*, vol. 2, no. 2, 1937, pp. 8–10.

16 Bruce Duncan, *Crusade or Conspiracy: Catholics and the Anti-Communist Struggle in Australia* (UNSW Press), Sydney, 2001, p. 25 (we are grateful to Stuart Macintyre and David Hilliard for telling us to read this book.); Stuart Macintyre, *The Reds* (Allen & Unwin), Sydney, 1998, p. 303. Aubrey Stevens was Stuart Macintyre's grandfather.

17 *Advertiser*, 17 August 1936, 18 August 1936; Amirah Inglis, *Australians in the Spanish Civil War* (Allen & Unwin), Sydney, 1987, especially ch.3; *Smith's Weekly*, 3 October 1936.

18 *Southern Cross*, April 2000.

19 E.J.L. Morgan to The Hon. Justice Mitchell, 12 June 1971, SLSA PRG 778/3/3.

20 *Australian Biography II*, p. 31.

21 Peter Norman and Susan Magarey, Interview with Clyde Cameron, 2002; *Nationwide*, 'Dame Roma Mitchell', ABC Television, 5 March 1984; Mitchell, 'Reminiscences'.

22 Susan Mitchell, 'Dame Roma Mitchell', pp. 31, 38. Joan Rosanove was made silk after eleven years of applying for such elevation; the delay may have had something to do with her politics, as well as her sex; see Heidi Zogbaum, 'Kisch Must Land', *Memento: News from the National Archives*, No. 29, May 2005, p. 12, where she is described as 'a barrister with Communist Party connections'. Once appointed, though, she used to modify the extreme masculinity of the clothes required for appearing in court by including a white frill at the top of the obligatory stiff white collars; see Isabel Carter, *Woman in a Wig. Joan Rosanove QC* (Lansdowne Press), Melbourne, 1970, p. 55. *Australian Biography II*, p. 61; Roma Flinders Mitchell, Passport, 24 February 1951, SLSA PRG 778/18/1; Laurel McGuire to Dame Roma

Mitchell, 22 October 1990, SLSA PRG 778/3/8/4; Clyde Cameron to Dame Roma Mitchell, 13 July 1982, SLSA PRG 778/3/4/3.

23 Dame Roma Mitchell, Speech given at the Tenth Anniversary Luncheon, Australian Woman of the Year, 1984, reprinted in *Women of the Year: A Collection of Speeches by Australia's Most Successful Women* (National Council of the Woman of the Year Luncheon), Buderim, Queensland, 1987, p. 192.

24 Sir Norman Young to Dame Roma Mitchell, 6 November 1990, SLSA PRG 778/3/8/2; Norman, Interview with Dame Roma Mitchell.

25 *Australian Biography II*, pp. 36–37.

26 Margaret Thornton, 'Women Practitioners', in Tony Blackshield, Michael Cooper and George Williams (eds), *The Oxford Companion to the High Court of Australia* (Oxford University Press), Melbourne, 2001, p. 722.

27 Faine, 'Dame Roma Mitchell', p. 6; Kevin Ward, 'First Steps in the Law', Law Society of South Australia *Bulletin*, February 1988, p. 8; Powell, 'Dame Roma Mitchell', pp. 5–6; Dame Roma Mitchell, Speech on the Golden Jubilee of Opening of State Bank of South Australia Head Office, 14 December 1993, p. 1, SLSA PRG 778/17; Susan Mitchell, 'Dame Roma Mitchell', p. 38; Beryl Linn, 'A Lady of the Law', Law Society of South Australia *Bulletin*, March 1998, p. 32; *Sunday Mail*, 2 June 1934; *Australian Biography II*, p. 29; Dame Roma Mitchell, quoted in Peter Ward, 'Brightly fades the Dame', *Weekend Australian*, 25–26 May 1996; Dame Roma Mitchell, Speech at the Opening of the Supreme Court and Federal Court Judges' Conference, 24 January 1995, p. 3, SLSA PRG 778/17.

28 Roma Mitchell to Ruth Gooch, 22 October 1939, 29 January 1949, SLSA PRG 778/11.

29 See, for example, E.P Thompson, Douglas Hay and Peter Linebaugh (eds), *Albion's Fatal Tree* (Allen Lane), London, 1975; Kathleen Bermingham to the Hon. Justice Roma Mitchell, 25 September 1965, SLSA PRG 778/3/2/5; Charles Bright, 'Dr John Bray in Context', *Adelaide Law Review*, vol. 7, 1980–81, p. 10.

30 Norman, Interview with Dame Roma Mitchell; *Australian Biography II*, p. 97.

31 Sesca Zelling, 'Friday and the Thursday Girls', Law Society of South Australia *Bulletin*, June 1996, p. 13; Macintyre, *The Reds*, p. 355; Alex Castles, Andrew Ligertwood and Peter Kelly (eds), *Law on North Terrace 1883–1983* (Faculty of Law, University of Adelaide), Adelaide, 1984(?), p. 40; Rosemary Wighton, '1940s', Tape B27, Writers' Week 1986, Hometown Adelaide, SRSA GRS 1132/3/P; Michael Heyward, *The Ern Malley Affair* (University of Queensland Press), St Lucia, 1993, p. 20.

32 Just for instance: on 12 January 1939 the temperature in Adelaide reached 117.7 degrees F (47.6 degrees C), the highest temperature recorded in an Australian capital city.

33 Roma Mitchell to Ruth Gooch, 19 January 1949, SLSA PRG 778/11; Susan Mitchell, 'Dame Roma Mitchell', p. 30.

34 *Australian Biography II*, p. 22; Roma Mitchell to Ruth Gooch, 12 December 1948, 2 January 1949; Maude Mitchell to Ruth Mitchell, 23 January 1935, SLSA PRG 778/11.

35 Jill Julius Matthews, *Dance Hall & Picture Palace* (Currency Press), Sydney, 2005, p. 311; Music! Dancing!: An exhibition on Adelaide's Dancehalls and Nightclubs during the 1920s, '30s and '40s, presented by the Performing Arts Collection of South Australia, 26 February–21 March 1982, BSL, Special Collections; Letters written by Professor E. Harold Davies to W.H. Gooch, SLSA D 6044(L); Thelma Afford, *Dreamers and Visionaries: Adelaide's Little Theatres from the 1920s to the Early 1940s*, edited with additional research by Kerrie Round (Currency Press), Sydney, 2004, pp. 80–81.

36 For information about Hugh Gooch's war career, we thank James Armstrong, Archivist, Honourable Artillery Company, London, letter of 29 July 2003, and Keith Miller, National Army Museum, Chelsea, London, letter of 5 August 2003; Kerrie Round, Telephone conversation with Katherine Dicker, current owner, Thargomindah Station, 22 September 2003; Kerrie Round, Interview with Sir Walter Crocker, 30 October 2002; Jill Bowen, *Kidman: the Forgotten King* (Angus & Robertson), Sydney, 1987, p. 323; H.N. Huffadine, *These Hundred Years. The Story of G & R Wills & Co. Limited during its First Century 1849–1949* (G & R Wills), Adelaide, 1949, pp. 10, 15.

37 *Australian Biography II*, p. 10.

38 *Grosvenor Hotel Limited, June 1918–December 1995*. Booklet produced by the Grosvenor Hotel, Adelaide, 1995; *Australian Biography II*, pp. 79–80; Last Will and Testament of Eliza Ann Mitchell, 5 March 1930.

39 *Australian Biography II*, pp. 10, 21–22.

40 Margaret Press, Interview with Dame Roma Mitchell, 19 March 1990, Mercy Archives; *Advertiser*, 11 October 1939; *Australian Women's Weekly*, 28 October 1939; Rosemary Miles, 'Women in Wartime', in *Greater than Their Knowing: a Glimpse of South Australian Women 1936–1986* (Wakefield Press), Netley, 1986, p. 78; Roma Mitchell to Ruth Gooch, 22 October 1939, SLSA PRG 778/11.

41 Joan Beaumont, 'Introduction', in Joan Beaumont (ed.), *Australia's War, 1939–45* (Allen & Unwin), Sydney, p. xx.

42 Joan Beaumont, 'Australia's War: Europe and the Middle East' in Beaumont (ed.), *Australia's War*, pp. 9–25; Judith Raftery, 'Catholics and Social Issues in South Australia in the 1930's', Seminar paper presented to the History Discipline, Flinders University of South Australia, 13 September 1985, p. 8; Rosemary Wighton, '1940s', Hometown Adelaide Session, Writers' Week, Adelaide, 1986; Joan Beaumont, 'Australia's War: Asia and the Pacific' in Beaumont (ed.), *Australia's War*, pp. 26, 29–30, 33–34; Elliott, *Memoirs of a Barrister*, p. 73; Kate Darian-Smith, 'War and Australian Society' in Beaumont (ed.), *Australia's War*, p. 54; Hilda Irving, *In Florrie's Footsteps: Adventures of a Trainee Nurse at Adelaide Hospital 1938–41* (H. Irving), Adelaide, 1985, p. 37; Papers of the Women's Air Training Corps, SLSA PRG 925; Dame Roma Mitchell, Speech at the Service of Remembrance, National Council of Women War Memorial Fund, 19 November 1995; Carol S. Fort, '"Equality of Sacrifice"? War Work in Salisbury, South Australia' in Bernard O'Neil, Judith Raftery and Kerrie Round (eds), *Playford's South Australia: Essays on the History of South Australia, 1933–1968* (Association of Professional Historians Inc.), Adelaide, 1996, pp. 215, 219, 221–223.

43 Obituary of George Walters, Law Society of South Australia *Bulletin*, October 1999, p. 22; Castles *et al.* (eds), *Law on North Terrace*, pp. 39, 41, 42, 45–46; Dame Roma Mitchell, Speech at the Service of Remembrance National Council of Women War Memorial Fund.

44 Howard Zelling to Rob Linn for the Law Society of South Australia, 'Legal Assistance Scheme 1933–1972 – an oral history', mimeo prepared for the Law Society of South Australia, 1997, p. 51.

45 Kerrie Round, Interview with Beryl Linn, 15 October 2002.

46 F.L Field, 'The Law Society in War Time', Law Society of South Australia *Bulletin*, July 1980, p. 1.

47 M.G. Montgomery, 'Obituary: The Honourable David Stirling Hogarth', Law Society of South Australia *Bulletin*, April 1989; *Advertiser* 14 March 1989; Toby Hogarth, 'A Terrific Friend', Law Society of South Australia *Bulletin*, April 2000, p. 12. Toby was a nickname; she had been christened Dorothy.

48 Dame Roma Mitchell, Speech at the Service of Remembrance National Council of Women War Memorial Fund.

49 Irving, *In Florrie's Footsteps*, pp. 37, 39; Wighton, '1940s', see Wighton, Rosemary on www.Austlit.edu.au.

50 Dame Roma Mitchell, Speech at the launch of 'Australia Remembers', 10 August 1995, SLSA PRG 778/17.

51 E.g. W.G. Sebald, *On the Natural History of Destruction with Essays on Alfred Andersch, Jean Améry and Peter Weiss*, translated from the German by Anthea Bell (Hamish Hamilton), London, 2003, especially pp. 3–32.

52 Beaumont, 'Introduction', pp. xx–xxi.

53 Marilyn Lake, *Getting Equal: the History of Australian Feminism* (Allen & Unwin), Sydney, 1999, p. 194.

54 Dame Roma Mitchell, Speech at the 27th Australian Legal Convention, 8 September 1991, SLSA PRG 778/17.

55 E.P. Mullighan, 'Before the Bench', in Magarey (ed.), *Dame Roma*, p. 47. Mullighan says that the dinner was probably addressed by a Judge of the High Court, possibly Sir Owen Dixon.

Chapter Four: Out of the Frozen Fifties

1 Film Australia. *Australian Biography II*, 4 June 1993, shown on SBS Television, p. 44.
2 Kerrie Round, Interview with Premier Mike Rann, 7 May 2003.
3 Susan Magarey, Interview with Lorna Williams (born Lorna Lumbers) and her daughter, Adrienne McMahon, 17 August 2001.
4 Dame Roma Mitchell's Scrapbooks, SLSA PRG 778/22.
5 Roma Mitchell to Mrs W.H. Gooch, 7 December 1948–25 March 1949, SLSA PRG 778/11.
6 Roma Mitchell to W.H. Gooch Esq., 12 December 1948 and Roma Mitchell to Mrs W.H. Gooch, 13 February 1949.
7 Roma Mitchell to Mrs W.H. Gooch, 29 December 1948–25 March 1949.
8 Kerrie Round, Interview with Pamela Villeneuve Smith, 13 August 2002.
9 Roma Mitchell to Mrs W.H. Gooch: 12 December 1948–18 March 1949; Roma Mitchell to W.H. Gooch Esq., 29 December 1948; Roma Mitchell to Mrs W.H. Gooch: 7 January–26 February 1949.
10 Susan Magarey and Kerrie Round, Interview with Pam Cleland, 22 May 2003; Kerrie Round, Telephone conversation with Sharon Polkinghorne of the *Advertiser*, September 2006; *Advertiser*, 20 August 1973; Good Neighbour Council, *Newsletter*, May 1964, copy sent to us by Sharon Polkinghorne to whom we are most grateful; Roma Mitchell to Mrs W.H. Gooch: 7 December, 16 December 1948; *Sands & McDougall Directory*, 1949.
11 Susan Magarey, Personal memory.
12 Roma Mitchell to Mrs W.H. Gooch and to W.H. Gooch Esq., 16 December 1948–13 February 1949; Magarey and Round, Interview with Pam Cleland; Alex Castles, Andrew Ligertwood and Peter Kelly (eds), *Law on North Terrace 1883–1983* (Faculty of Law, University of Adelaide), Adelaide, 1983, p. 47.
13 Roma Mitchell to W.H. Gooch Esq., 29 December 1948; *Advertiser*, 26 April 2003; Roma Mitchell to Mrs. W.H. Gooch, 20 December 1948–21 March 1949.
14 Roma Mitchell to Mrs W.H. Gooch, 7 December 1948–13 March 1949; Michael Shmith and David Colville (eds), *Musica Viva Australia – the First Fifty Years* (Playbill), Pymble, NSW, 1996, pp. 6–7; Leslie Halliwell, *Halliwell's Film Guide* (Grafton Books), London, sixth edition 1987, p. 774.
15 Kerrie Round, Interview with the Hon. Len King, 29 April 2003; Roma Mitchell to Mrs W.H. Gooch, 7 December 1948–18 March 1949; 'Obituary: George Walters AO', Law Society of South Australia *Bulletin*, October 1999, p. 22; it was Jack Elliott who described him as handsome, Jack Elliott, *Memoirs of a Barrister* (Wakefield Press) Kent Town, 2000, p. 209.
16 Peter O'Callaghan, 'Obituary, Cairns Villeneuve-Smith QC', *Victorian Bar News*, No. 116, Autumn 2001; Round, Interview with Pamela Villeneuve Smith; Castles *et al.* (eds), *Law on North Terrace*, p. 51.
17 Castles *et al.* (eds), *Law on North Terrace*, p. 53; Round, Interview with Len King.
18 Elliott, *Memoirs of a Barrister*, p. 215.
19 Entry for 20 January [1980], Diaries of Sir Walter Crocker, BSL, Special Collections.
20 Toby Hogarth, 'A terrific friend', Law Society of South Australia *Bulletin*, April 2000, p. 12.
21 Peter Norman, Interview with Dame Roma Mitchell, 22 March 1999; E.P. Mullighan, 'Before the Bench' in Susan Magarey (ed.), *Dame Roma, Glimpses of a Glorious Life* (Axiom Publishing in association with the John Bray Chapter of the Adelaide University Alumni Association), Adelaide, 2002; Lindy Powell, 'Dame Roma Mitchell. A Life in the Law', Law Society of South Australia *Bulletin*, February 1991, p. 5.
22 Letter in SLSA PRG 778/3/8/6. We have sought to preserve the privacy of letter writers by not giving their names in our text. Dame Roma said that she did not remember individual cases, *Australian Biography II*, p. 27.
23 Round, Interview with Len King; Norman, Interview with Dame Roma Mitchell; Alex C. Castles and Michael C. Harris, *Lawmakers and Wayward Whigs* (Wakefield Press), Adelaide, 1987, p. 343; Powell, 'Dame Roma Mitchell', p. 6; these letters are all in SLSA PRG 778/: 3/1/3, 3/8/7 and 3/1/2, see above note 22.
24 Powell, 'Dame Roma Mitchell', p. 7; The Hon. Justice Roma Mitchell, 'Divorce Law in Australia', *Lawasia*, vol. 1, no. 2, 1970, p. 84.

25 Round, Interview with Len King; Mullighan, 'Before the Bench', p. 49.
26 Mullighan, 'Before the Bench', p. 49.
27 Round, Interview with Len King; Dame Roma, quoted in Powell, 'Dame Roma Mitchell', p. 7.
28 Graham Loughlin, 'South Australian Queen's Counsel', BA(Hons) thesis, University of Adelaide, 1974, pp. 7, 44; Gerard B. Carter, *Law in Australia. The Question and Answer Book* (Blackstone Press), Sydney, 1992, p. 68; Jan Bowen, *The Macquarie Easy Guide to Australian Law* (Macquarie Library), Chatswood, 1987; Elliott, *Memoirs of a Barrister*, p. 33; J.R.S. Forbes, *The Divided Legal Profession in Australia: History, Rationalisation and Rationale* (Law Book Co.), Sydney, 1979, pp. 182–185.
29 'Obituary: George Walters AO', Law Society of South Australia *Bulletin*, October 1999, p. 22; Magarey and Round, Interview with Pam Cleland; Round, Interview with Len King.
30 Dame Roma Mitchell, Speech at the opening of the Pam Cleland Exhibition, Greenhill Galleries, 17 September 1995, SLSA PRG 778/17; Magarey and Round, Interview with Pam Cleland; Sheryl-Lee Kerr, *Advertiser*, 25 May 1996.
31 John Playford, 'Hannan, Albert James (1887–1965), *Australian Dictionary of Biography* (Melbourne University Press), Carlton, Vol. 14, 1996, pp. 376–377; Norman, Interview with Dame Roma Mitchell; Law Society of South Australia, Minutes of Council and Executive, Annual General Meeting, 29 September 1952; Minutes for 26 July 1948 of the Law Society Council and Executive, Ts., Law Society of South Australia.
32 Law Society of South Australia, Council Minutes, 3 November 1952; Elliott, *Memoirs of a Barrister*, p. 17; Dean Jaensch, 'Stability and Change, 1910–1938', in Dean Jaensch (ed.), *The Flinders History of South Australia: Political History* (Wakefield Press), Netley, p. 238; Rob Linn, 'Legal assistance scheme 1933–1972 – an oral history', mimeo prepared for the Law Society of South Australia, 1997, p. 7
33 Linn, 'Legal assistance scheme 1933–1972'.
34 Linn, 'Legal assistance scheme 1933–1972'.
35 John Murphy, 'Work in a Time of Plenty: Narratives of Men's Work in Post-War Australia', *Labour History*, no. 88, May 2005; Ann Game and Rosemary Pringle, 'Sexuality and the Suburban Dream', *Australian and New Zealand Journal of Sociology*, no. 15, 1979; Susan Magarey, 'Does the Family Have a Future?' in S.T Waddell (ed.), *Addresses Presented at Prospect 2000: A Conference on the Future* (ANZAAS (Western Australia Division), Perth, 1979, pp. 27–28; George Farwell, *Rejoice in Freedom* (Nelson), Melbourne, 1976, p. 273.
36 Michael Heyward, *The Ern Malley Affair* (University of Queensland Press), St Lucia, 1993, ch. 9.
37 *Australian*, 10 January 1967, newspaper clipping, no source, nd, Dame Roma Mitchell's Scrapbooks.
38 Carol S. Fort, '"Equality of Sacrifice"? War Work in Salisbury, South Australia' in Bernard O'Neil, Judith Raftery and Kerrie Round (eds), *Playford's South Australia: Essays on the History of South Australia, 1933–1968* (Association of Professional Historians Inc.), Adelaide, 1996, p. 215; Jaensch, 'Stability and Change', pp. 244, 250, 251–253; Eric Richards, 'The Peopling of South Australia, 1836–1986' in Eric Richards (ed.), *The Flinders History of South Australia: Social History* (Wakefield Press), Netley, 1986, p. 135; Barbara Hanrahan, '1950s' in Hometown Adelaide, a series of spoken recollections delivered at Adelaide Writers' Week, Adelaide, 1986, SRSA GRS 1132/3/P, Unit 13, Tape 11.
39 *Australian Biography II*, p. 19.
40 Roma Mitchell to Mrs W.H. Gooch, 5 February 1949; 'Jenkins, Merle Nona', *Who's Who in Australia, 1971* (The Herald and Weekly Times Ltd.), Melbourne, 1971, p. 521; Melbourne *Age*, 18 April 2003; Roma Mitchell to The Secretary, Committee on Fellowship Awards, American Association of University Women, 31 October 1952 and R.F, Mitchell 'To Whom It May Concern', 11 May 1956, Jean Whyte Papers, National Library of Australia [NLA], uncatalogued November 2004.
41 Manuscript, dated 11 February 1962, marked with stains of tea or coffee cups. Whyte Papers, uncatalogued.
42 *Australian*, 24 July 2001.

43 Information from Bill Pearce, Archivist, Adelaide High School, 14 July 2005; Susan Magarey, Conversation with Deborah McCulloch, 24 July 2007.

44 Magarey and Round, Interview with Pam Cleland; Kerrie Round, Interview with Mary Bleechmore, 16 December 2003; Peter Norman, Interview with Alec Genders, 23 September 1998; Susan Mitchell, 'Dame Roma Mitchell', in Susan Mitchell, *The Matriarchs. Twelve Australian Women Talk about Their Lives* (Penguin), Ringwood, 1987, p. 34.

45 George Farwell (ed. B. McArdle), *Around Australia on Highway One* (Thomas Nelson), Melbourne, 1966, pp. 116, 118; R.C. Adkins, *I Flew for MMA. An Airline Pilot's Life* (Self-published), Perth, 1996, pp. x, 42–43; Roma Mitchell to Mrs W.H. Gooch, 2 July 1952; George Farwell, *Rejoice in Freedom*, p. 281.

46 Dame Roma Mitchell, 'A Pleasant Sunday Afternoon', Maughan Methodist Church, no date, SLSA PRG 778/17/0; Speech given at St Ann's College, October 1986, SLSA PRG 778/17/71; *Advertiser*, 2 September 1955; Kerrie Round, Interview with Beryl Linn, 15 October 2002; Shorthand notebook containing list in Roma Mitchell's handwriting of all the people who sent congratulations on her appointment to the Bench, totalling 482 at the front of the notebook and 182 at the back. In between is a page listing things to wear, SLSA PRG 778/3/2/1.

47 'SA Woman was in Plane in Hurricane', newspaper clipping, no source, nd, Dame Roma Mitchell's Scrapbooks; *Advertiser*, 2 September 1955; Mullighan, 'Before the Bench', p. 55.

48 Humphrey Searle, *Quadrille with a Raven*. http://www.musicweb.uk.net/searle/lesley.htm Accessed on 17 February 2004; Roma Mitchell to Mrs W.H. Gooch: 11 June, 30 June, 31 August 1955.

49 'SA Woman was in Plane in Hurricane', *Advertiser*, 2 September 1955.

50 Law Society of South Australia, Council Minutes, 8 February 1960; Magarey and Round, Interview with Pam Cleland; Peter Ward, 'Brightly fades the Dame', *Weekend Australian*, 25–26 May 1996; Roma Mitchell to Mr and Mrs W.H. Gooch: 29 August–9 September 1960; *Australian Law Journal*: vol. 36, 1 June 1962, p. 47, and vol. 37, 25 July 1963, p. 99.

51 Roma Mitchell to Mr and Mrs W.H. Gooch, 17 September 1960; *Advertiser*, 18 October 1960; newspaper clipping, no source, nd, probably from a San Francisco newspaper, Dame Roma Mitchell's Scrapbooks.

52 Peter Howell, personal communication to Kerrie Round, 29 August 2003; Kerrie Round, Telephone conversation with Pamela Villeneuve Smith, 2 September 2003.

53 Special sitting on retirement of The Hon. Justice Roma Mitchell, SLSA PRG 778/30/2; Alex Castles *et al.* (eds), *Law on North Terrace*, pp. 61–62; The Hon. Justice Duggan, Law Society of South Australia *Bulletin*, April 2000, p. 10.

54 Farwell, *Rejoice in Freedom*, pp. 327–328; 335–336; Peter Ward, 'John Jefferson Bray' in Wilfrid Prest, Kerrie Round and Carol Fort (eds), *The Wakefield Companion to South Australian History* (Wakefield Press), Kent Town, 2001, p. 84.

Chapter Five: Roma The First

1 Quoted in Isabel Carter, *Woman in a Wig. Joan Rosanove*, QC (Lansdown Press), Melbourne, 1970, p. 154.

2 Film Australia. *Australian Biography II*, 4 June 1993, shown on SBS Television, p. 43. Dame Roma repeated this observation, see, e.g., Peter Ward, 'Brightly fades the Dame', *Weekend Australian*, 25–26 May 1996.

3 *Advertiser*, 21 September 1962, Editorial.

4 The International Federation of Women Lawyers (FIDA) was founded in 1944 by women lawyers from five countries in the Americas to improve conditions for women in developing countries and to raise awareness of human rights. http://www.iisd.org/50comm/commdb/desc/d29.htm Accessed 10 August 2007.

5 Susan Magarey and Kerrie Round, Interview with Pam Cleland, 22 May 2003; newspaper clipping, no source, nd, Dame Roma Mitchell's Scrapbooks, SLSA PRG 778/22; *Advertiser*, 31 August 1965.

6 Kerrie Round, Interview with Aline Fenwick, 29 November 2002.

7 Roma Mitchell to Ruth and Hugo Gooch, 14 July 1963, SLSA PRG 778/11.

8 Katharine Massam, 'Catholic Church', in Graeme Davison, John Hirst and Stuart Macintyre (eds), *The Oxford Companion to Australian History* (Oxford University Press), Melbourne, 1998, p. 113.

9 Peter Ward, 'John Bray in Adelaide', in Wilfrid Prest (ed.), *A Portrait of John Bray: Law, Letters, Life* (Wakefield Press), Kent Town, 1997, p. 13; Michael Abbott, 'Bray as Barrister', in Prest (ed.), *A Portrait of John Bray*, pp. 65–66.

10 Margaret Minney, 'Obituary: Alexander Keith Sangster QC', Law Society of South Australia *Bulletin*, February 1999, p. 27; Neville Rochow, 'Grand love of the Law', *Advertiser*, 17 November 2001; 'Mr Justice Wells', *Australian Law Journal*, vol. 58, September 1984, p. 534.

11 Rob van den Hoorn and John Playford, 'The Adelaide Hospital Row', in Dean Jaensch, *The Flinders History of South Australia: Political History* (Wakefield Press), Netley, 1986, appendix, pp. 215–225; P.A. Howell, 'Napier, Sir Thomas John Mellis (1882–1976)', *Australian Dictionary of Biography*, vol. 15 (Melbourne University Press), Carlton, 2000, pp. 461–463. All of the information presented here about Napier comes from this source unless otherwise indicated; Peter Norman, Interview with Dame Roma Mitchell, 22 March 1999; Graham Loughlin, South Australian Queen's Counsel 1865–1972, BA (Hons.) thesis, University of Adelaide, 1974, p. 87; Susan Magarey, Conversation with His Honour David Bright, 9 December 2005; e.g. K.S. Inglis, *The Stuart Case* (Black Inc.), Melbourne, 2002, first published Melbourne University Press, 1961, p. 312; 'Sir Mellis Napier', *Australian Law Journal*, vol. 40, 1967; Charles Bright, 'Dr John Bray in Context', *Adelaide Law Review*, vol. 7, 1980–81, p. 9; 'Sir Mellis Napier: Chief Justice 1942–1967', *Adelaide Law Review*, vol. 3, 1967, pp. 5, 4; Alex C. Castles and Michael C. Harris, *Lawmakers and Wayward Whigs: Government and Law in South Australia* (Wakefield Press), Kent Town, 1987, p. 371.

12 Norman, Interview with Dame Roma Mitchell; Jack Elliott, *Memoirs of a Barrister* (Wakefield Press), Kent Town, 2000, p. 211.

13 Law Society Council, Minutes, 26 April 1960, 9 May 1960; memorandum of 28 February 1963 accompanying Law Society Council, Minutes 25 March 1963; Law Society Circular no. 11/60, 29 November 1960; Law Society Council, Minutes 29 October 1960 [sic–1962], all quoted and cited in Loughlin, South Australian Queen's Counsel, pp. 23–25. By the time, in 2004, that we sought to read these minutes and those for the subsequent two years leading to Dame Roma's appointment as a QC, the Law Society had lost them. We are grateful to His Honour Judge Tom Gray for assisting our request to be allowed to carry out research among the Law Society's records, and sad that his efforts, like our own, produced so little useful information.

14 *News*, 2 May 1960.

15 Lindy Powell, 'Dame Roma Mitchell. A Life in the Law', Law Society of South Australia *Bulletin*, February 1991, p. 6.

16 Certificate issued by Lieutenant-General Sir Edric Montagu Bastyan on behalf of Queen Elizabeth II, SLSA PRG 778/2 O/S; Dame Roma Mitchell's Scrapbooks.

17 E.g. Leila J. Rupp, *Worlds of Women: The Making of an International Women's Movement* (Princeton University Press), Princeton, 1997, p. 15; Judith Smart, 'National Council of Women', in Barbara Caine, Moira Gatens, Emma Grahame, Jan Larbalestier, Sophie Watson and Elizabeth Webby (eds), *Australian Feminism: A Companion* (Oxford University Press), Melbourne, 1998, p. 463; Helen Jones, 'League of Women Voters', in Wilfrid Prest, Kerrie Round and Carol Fort (eds), *The Wakefield Companion to South Australian History* (Wakefield Press), Kent Town, 2001, p. 312; Louise Brown *et al.* (eds), *A Book of South Australian Women in the First Hundred Years* (Rigby), Adelaide, 1936; Susan Sheridan, 'Women Writers', in Laurie Hergenhan (ed.), *The Penguin New Literary History of Australia* (Penguin Books), Ringwood, 1988, p. 322; Marilyn Lake, *Getting Equal: the History of Australian Feminism* (Allen & Unwin), Sydney, 1999, p. 133.

18 *Universal Declaration of Human Rights*, http://www.unhchr.ch/udhr/lang/eng.htm Accessed 20 September 2005; Lake, *Getting Equal*, pp. 191–192; http://www.unhchr.ch/huricane.nsf/O/4454BACF6C1256B72002COF32?opendocument Accessed 18 November 2005; Norman MacKenzie, *Women in Australia* (F.W. Cheshire),

Melbourne, 1962, p. 205, note; Linda J. Kirk, 'Portia's Place: Australia's First Women Lawyers', *Australian Journal of Legal History*, vol. I, no. 1, 1995, p. 89.

19 Marian Sawer and Marian Simms, *A Woman's Place: Women and Politics in Australia* (Allen & Unwin), 1993, pp. 111–125; Jones, *In Her Own Name*, p. 323; Carol Bacchi, ' The "Woman Question"', in Eric Richards (ed.), *The Flinders History of South Australia: Social History* (Wakefield Press), Netley, 1986, p. 442.

20 All of this account is taken from Jones, *In Her Own Name*, pp. 326–349; Enid Campbell, 'The Legal Status of Women in Australia', Appendix in MacKenzie, *Women in Australia*, p. 366; Stewart Cockburn assisted by John Playford, *Playford: Benevolent Despot* ((Wakefield Press), Kent Town, 1994 (first published 1991), p. 252; Sawer and Simms, *A Women's Place*, p. 129.

21 Round, Interview with Aline Fenwick; Kirk, 'Portia's Place', p. 90; Roma Mitchell to Mr and Mrs W.H. Gooch, 29 August 1960, SLSA PRG 778/8/11.

22 Dame Roma Mitchell, 'Looking Back ... Looking Forward', The Inaugural Mitchell Oration, Adelaide, 11 October 1989, http://www.eoc.sa.gov.au/access/mitchell_oration89.html Accessed 18 November 2002.

23 Australian Bureau of Statistics, Census Data for 1947 and 1961.

24 Peter Donovan, 'Transport', in Prest *et al.* (eds), *Wakefield Companion*, pp. 555–556; John C. Radcliffe, 'Tramways', in Prest *et al.* (eds.), *Wakefield Companion*, pp. 553–554; e.g. Lesley Johnson, *The Modern Girl: Girlhood and Growing Up* (Allen & Unwin), Sydney, 1993, pp. 98–102; Stella Lees and June Senyard, *The 1950s ... How Australia Became a Modern Society, and Everyone Got a House and Car* (Hyland House), Melbourne, 1987, p. 127; Alison Painter, 'Entertainment. The Changing Scene', in Bernard O'Neil, Judith Raftery and Kerrie Round (eds), *Playford's South Australia* (Association of Professional Historians), Adelaide, 1996, p. 312.

25 David Hilliard, *Flinders University: The First 25 Years 1966–1991* (Flinders University of South Australia), Adelaide, 1991, pp. 8–13; Roma Mitchell to Jean Whyte, 4 April 1962; Alex Ramsay to Jean Whyte, postmarked 26 March 1962; both in Jean Whyte Papers, Box 4, National Library of Australia, uncatalogued; Eleanor M. Ramsay, Television in Australia: Public Service or Private Profit?, BA Hons thesis, University of Adelaide, 1970; Painter, 'Entertainment', p. 310.

26 Stefania Siedlecki and Diana Wyndham, *Populate and Perish. Australian Women's Fight for Birth Control* (Allen & Unwin), Sydney, 1990, p. 43.

27 For example, *Sydney Morning Herald*, 21 September 1962; *West Australian*, 21 September 1962; La Abogada 'Newsletter', Vol. 9, no. 1, October 1962; E.P Mullighan, 'Before the Bench', in Susan Magarey (ed.), *Dame Roma, Glimpses of a Glorious Life* (Axiom Publishing in association with the John Bray Chapter of the Adelaide University Alumni Association), Adelaide, 2002, p. 52; these letters can all be found in SLSA PRG 778/3/1/1 and PRG 778/3/1/2; *Advertiser*, 23 November 1962; Sister M. Ignatius RSM to Miss Roma Mitchell, 22 September 1962, SLSA PRG 778/3/1.

28 Minutes of meeting of National Council of Women, 10 August 1939, SLSA PRG 297/1; Playford, quoted in *Australian Biography II*, p. 40; Jones, *In Her Own Name*, p. 340; *Advertiser*, 21 May 1963; Cockburn with Playford, *Playford*, p. 256.

29 *Australian Biography II*, pp. 40, 62; *News*, 3 October 1963; Jones, *In Her Own Name*, pp. 339–340.

30 Jones, *In Her Own Name*, p. 339.

31 Susan Magarey, Telephone conversation with Mrs Lynn Nykiel, Secretary of the Queen Adelaide Club, 5 December 2005; Neal Blewett and Dean Jaensch, *Playford to Dunstan: The Politics of Transition* (F.W. Cheshire), Melbourne, 1971, pp. 8–9; Susan Magarey, Conversation with Mrs Audrey Abbie, November 2004.

32 Norman, Interview with Dame Roma Mitchell, Mullighan, 'Before the Bench', pp. 50 51; Kerrie Round, Interview with the Hon. Len King, 29 April 2003; *Advertiser*, 24 September 1965; *White Pages Telephone Book*, Adelaide, 1963.

33 *Australian Law Journal*: vol. 35, 1962, p. 385, vol. 36, 1962, p. 47; Law Society of South Australia *Bulletin*, May 1979, pp. 1, 7; see also Cockburn with Playford, *Playford*, pp. 221–223; *Australian Law Journal*, vol. 36, 1962, p. 110; M.G. Montgomery, 'The

Honourable David Stirling Hogarth', Law Society of South Australia, *Bulletin*, April 1989, pp. 89–90; *Australian Law Journal*, vol. 37, 1964, p. 325.

34 Isabel to Roma Mitchell, 16 June 1982, SLSA PRG 778/3/4/1.

35 These people asked not to be named.

36 Kerrie Round, Interview with Pamela Villeneuve Smith, 13 August 2002.

37 Tulla to Roma Mitchell, 23 June 1982, SLSA PRG 778/3/3

38 Roma Mitchell to Mr and Mrs Hugh Gooch, 5 July 1963; The Hon. Justice Michael Kirby AC CMG, funeral oration for John Bruce Piggott CBE LLB, June 2000, St David's Cathedral, Hobart www.hcourt.gov.au/speeches/kirbyj/kirbyj_piggott.htm Accessed 25 January 2006; http://www.aph.gov.au/hansard/senate/commttees/s1616.pdf Accessed 25 January 2006.

39 Roma Mitchell to Mr and Mrs Hugh Gooch, 2 July 1963

40 *Australian*, 12 September 1964; Roma Mitchell to Mr and Mrs Hugh Gooch, 10 July 1963.

41 *New Idea*, 7 November 1962.

42 Mullighan, 'Before the Bench', pp. 51–56. Unless otherwise noted, all of the information in this paragraph is drawn from this source; [1964] SASR 82.

43 *Australian Biography II*, pp. 33–34.

44 Jill Bowen, *Kidman: the Forgotten King* (Angus & Robertson), Sydney, 1987, p. 428; SM, 'Australian Workers Union', in Graeme Davison, John Hirst and Stuart Macintyre (eds), *The Oxford Companion to Australian History* (Oxford University Press), Melbourne, 1998, pp. 52–53; *Australian Biography II*, p. 35; Adelaide *Advertiser*, 30 November 1965; Clyde R. Cameron, 'A Matchless Silk', in Magarey (ed.), *Dame Roma*, pp. 60–62; Bill Guy, *A Life on the Left. A biography of Clyde Cameron* (Wakefield Press), Kent Town, 1999. Guy claims that Cameron prepared their affidavits (p. 198), but Cameron does not confirm the claim. See also above, Chapter 2, pp. 18–19, below, p. 22.

45 Adelaide University Archives, Series 351 Standing Committee of the Senate.

46 *Advertiser*, 15 April 1965.

47 Margaret Walters Auchmuty, *A Perpetual Trust: The Story of the Winston Churchill Memorial Trust Travelling Fellowships*, no publication details, p. 13; Susan Magarey, Conversation with Paul Tys, Chief Executive Officer, Winston Churchill Memorial Trust, Churchill House, Canberra, 6 February 2004; The Winston Churchill Memorial Trust, *Second Annual Report* (Patria Printers), Canberra, 1966, p. 2; The Winston Churchill Memorial Trust, *First Annual Report – 1966* (Patria Publishers), Canberra, 1966, pp. 25–29.

48 *Advertiser*: 14, 15 July 1965, clipping in Dame Roma Mitchell's Scrapbooks.

49 *Australian Biography II*, pp. 62, 57.

50 Kerrie Round, Telephone conversation with Mr Bill Park, 29 January 2004.

51 Norman, Interview with Dame Roma Mitchell; *Law Institute Journal*, Vol. 39, No. 12, 1965, p. 449; *Advertiser*, 31 August 1965; see above, this chapter, p. 1

52 http://www.milesago.com/People/dunstan-don.htm Accessed 3 December 2004; http://www.brisbanewritersfestival.com.au Accessed 4 January 2006; Elizabeth Johnswood in *Woman's Day*, 1 December 1975, quoted in Stewart Cockburn, 'The Dunstan Factor', Ts. in Box 39, Dunstan Papers, Flinders University. A version of this appears as chapter 21 in Cockburn assisted by Playford, *Playford: Benevolent Despot*.

53 Ts, CV for Don Dunstan for *Who's Who* 1992, Box 39, Dunstan Papers, Flinders University Library; http://www.milesago.com/People/dunstan-don.htm Accessed 3 December 2004; Cockburn, 'The Dunstan Factor', an accompanying letter lists Don Dunstan's corrections to this typescript.

54 'Patricia Hackett', in Prest *et al.* (eds), *Wakefield Companion*, p. 237; Jo Peoples, 'Miss Patricia Hackett', *Journal of the Historical Society of South Australia*, no. 25, 1997. We are most grateful to Anna Ragosa of the History Trust of South Australia for finding this article for us and sending us a copy. See also Stephen Atkinson, 'Grande Dame of SA Theatre', *Adelaide Review*, 8–21 June 2007, p. 7, we are grateful to David Hilliard for telling us this piece; Don Dunstan, *Felicia: The Political Memoirs of Don Dunstan* (Macmillan), South Melbourne, 1981, p. 6.

55 Cockburn, 'The Dunstan Factor' (he served three terms as Mayor, from 1933 to 1937); Ts., co for Don Dunstan; Ts. Biography of Don Dunstan Q.C., M.P., 15 January 1979, Box 39, Dunstan Papers; Don Dunstan to Stewart Cockburn, nd, Box 39, Dunstan Papers.

56 'Collier Robert Cudmore', in Prest *et al.* (eds), *Wakefield Companion*, p. 136.

57 Stewart Cockburn, 'The Dunstan Factor', pp. 3–4.

58 Dunstan, *Felicia*, pp. vii, 24; Peter Monteath, *Dear Dr Janzow: Australia's Lutheran Churches and Refugees from Hitler's Germany* (Australian Humanities Press), Unley, 2005, pp. 108–109.

59 Dunstan, *Felicia*, p. 26. The rest of this paragraph is drawn from *Felicia* chapter 2, unless another source is given

60 'Movement', in Davison, Hirst and Macintyre (eds), *The Oxford Companion to Australian History*, p. 441; Malcolm Saunders, 'The Labor Party and the Industrial Groups in South Australia 1946–55: precluding the split', *Journal of the Historical Society of South Australia*, No. 33, 2005. Our thanks to David Hilliard for referring us to this article.

61 Cockburn, 'The Dunstan Factor', pp. 1, 7–8.

62 Dunstan, *Felicia*, p. 114.

63 Powell, 'Dame Roma Mitchell. A Life in the Law', p. 8

64 Dunstan, *Felicia*, p. 114.

65 Dunstan, *Felicia*, p. 115.

66 *Australian Biography II*, pp. 41–42; Dame Roma Mitchell, 'Reflections on a Career in Law', in J.F. Corkery (ed.), *A Career in Law* (Federation Press), Sydney, 1989, p. 207.

67 Powell, 'Dame Roma Mitchell. A Life in the Law', p. 7; Dame Roma Mitchell, Speech made while Governor of South Australia, quoted in Magarey (ed.), *Dame Roma*, p. 64.

68 *Advertiser*, 24 September 1965; Howard Zelling to Roma Mitchell, 23 September 1965, SLSA PRG 778/3/2/4; *Australian*, 24 September 1965; *Canberra Times*, 24 September 1965.

69 'Her Honour Justice Mitchell Presents Her Commission, Monday 27 September 1965, in Magarey (ed.), *Dame Roma*, p. 99; *Advertiser*, 24 September 1965; *Sydney Morning Herald*, 24 September 1965; Special sitting on presentation of Commission by Roma Flinders Mitchell, SLSA PRG 778/30/1.

70 *South Australian State Reports* (1965), p. x.

71 Gough Whitlam to Roma Mitchell, n.d., SLSA PRG 778/3/2/5; Tom Kellock to Roma Mitchell, 27 September 1965, SLSA PRG 778/3/2/2; John Stack to Roma Mitchell, 27 September 1965, SLSA PRG 778/3/2/4; Len King to Roma Mitchell, 23 September 1965, SLSA PRG 778/3/2/3; John Bray to Roma Mitchell, 23 September 1965, SLSA PRG 778/3/2/4.

72 Quoted in Dunstan, *Felicia*, p. 116.

73 Clipping in Dame Roma Mitchell's Scrapbooks; translated, with help from Sue Kentish for which we are grateful, this reads, in part: 'A woman has been nominated a judge of the Supreme Court. The lady Roma Mitchell – this is the distinguished lawyer's name – is the first woman in Australia to be asked to assume so important a burden. Once again, Roma is the first'.

Chapter Six: The Golden Years

1 Susan Marsden, Paul Stark and Patricia Sumerling (eds), *Heritage of the City of Adelaide* (Corporation of the City of Adelaide), Richmond, 1990, pp. 177–178; Susan Mitchell, 'Dame Roma Mitchell', in Susan Mitchell, *The Matriarchs. Twelve Australian Women Talk about Their Lives* (Penguin), Ringwood, 1987, p. 38.

2 Attorney-General for the State of South Australia, The Hon. K. Trevor Griffin MLC, Speech at a Special Sitting of the Supreme Court of South Australia to mark the Passing of Dame Roma Mitchell AC DBE CVO, 13 March 2000, transcript printed in Susan Magarey (ed.), *Dame Roma, Glimpses of a Glorious Life* (Axiom Publishing in association with the John Bray Chapter of the Adelaide University Alumni Association), Adelaide, 2002, p. 300.

3 List of the Associates of Mitchell J kindly sent to us by Herman Fundham, Training and Historical Collections Librarian, Supreme Court Library, South Australia. We are grateful to him for his help; E.P. Mullighan, 'Before the Bench', in Susan Magarey (ed.), *Dame Roma*, p. 41; Film Australia. *Australian Biography II*, 4 June 1993, shown on SBS Television, p. 44.

4 Kerrie Round, Interview with Premier Mike Rann, 7 May 2003; and see Bob O'Brien, *Young Blood: the Story of the Family Murders* (Harper Collins), Sydney, 2002.

5 Entry for 16 March 1980, Diaries of Sir Walter Crocker, Special Collectitons, Barr Smith Library, University of Adelaide; *Advertiser*, 25 June 2005.

6 Newspaper clipping, no source, nd, Dame Roma Mitchell's Scrapbooks, SLSA PRG 778/22; entry for 27 April 1971, Diaries of Sir Walter Crocker; Dame Roma with Piers Plumridge, Dame Roma Mitchell's Scrapbooks; Dame Roma with Margaret Nyland in Sri Lanka in Magarey (ed.), *Dame Roma*, p. 199; Susan Magarey and Kerrie Round, Interview with Pam Cleland, 22 May 2003; Kerrie Round, Interview with Sir Walter Crocker, 30 October 2002; Christine Cane to Dame Roma Mitchell, 12 February 1987, SLSA PRG 778/5/3; Dame Roma Mitchell's Will.

7 Senator Amanda Vanstone, Speech in launching *Dame Roma: Glimpses of a Glorious Life*, Bonython Hall, University of Adelaide, 7 March 2002.

8 Lindy Powell QC, on *George Negus Tonight*, ABC television, 2 August 2004.

9 Susan Magarey, Interview with Lorna Williams and Adrienne McMahon, 17 August 2001; Susan Mitchell, 'Dame Roma Mitchell', p. 39.

10 *Advertiser*, 24 September 1965. This is approximately $118,000 in 2006, http://www.bunburychryslerjeep.com.au/tools/Cost/Australia.htm, Accessed 8 September 2006.

11 Dame Roma Mitchell, Speech at Monash University, December 1983, SLSA PRG 778/17.

12 Marsden *et al.*, *Heritage of the City of Adelaide*, p. 211,

13 Entry for 24 March 1974, Diaries of Sir Walter Crocker; McKennas Antiques, typed valuation of the property of 'Dame Roma Justice Mitchell', 14 February 1983, SLSA PRG 778/46.

14 See below, chapter 7, p. 3; *Australian Biography II*, p. 51; Susan Mitchell, 'Dame Roma Mitchell', p. 39.

15 The Hon. Justice Duggan, 'Overwhelming Sense of Justice', Law Society of South Australia *Bulletin*, April 2000, p. 10.

16 His Honour Chief Justice John Doyle, 'Her Colleagues Fondly Remember', Law Society of South Australia *Bulletin*, June 1996, p. 14; Liz Johnswood, 'Dame Roma Mitchell Lays Down the Law', *Woman's Day*, December 1983; *Australian Biography II*, p. 45; Helena Jasinski, 'Magnanimity, Support, Friendship', Law Society of South Australia *Bulletin*, April, 2000, p. 11; Diana Georgeff, 'Roma Mitchell, Pathfinder for Women in Law, Takes on a New Task', *National Times*, 20–25 February 1978, p. 14, Dame Roma Mitchell's Scrapbooks.

17 *Advertiser*: 28 February, 1, 2 April 1975; Law Society of South Australia *Bulletin*, March 1975, p. 2.

18 Lindy Powell, 'Dame Roma Mitchell. A Life in the Law', Law Society of South Australia *Bulletin* February 1991, p. 5; This informant asked not to be identified; *Australian Biography II*, p. 45.

19 *Australian Biography II*, p. 47; Johnswood, 'Dame Roma Mitchell', p. 19; Jon Faine, 'Dame Roma Mitchell', in *Taken on Oath. A Generation of Lawyers* (Federation Press), Sydney, 1992, p. 12.

20 The original Broadway cast recording, *Hair: The American Tribal Love Rock Musical*, RCA Victor; Noni Farwell, 'Dame Roma Mitchell and the Arts', in Susan Magarey (ed.), *Dame Roma*. p. 244; Judith Wright, 'The Age of Aquarius – and Queensland', in Geoffrey Dutton and Max Harris (eds), *Australia's Censorship Crisis* (Sun Books), Melbourne, 1970, p. 105.

21 *Advertiser*, 30 March 1970; Barry York, 'Power to the Young', in Verity Burgmann and Jenny Lee (eds), *Staining the Wattle: A People's History of Australia since 1788* (McPhee Gribble/Penguin Books), Fitzroy/Ringwood, 1988, p. 234; *News*, 12 March 1970; Verity Burgmann, *Power and Protest: Movements for Change in Australian Society* (Allen & Unwin), St Leonards, 1993.

22 Neal Blewett and Dean Jaensch, *Playford to Dunstan: The Politics of Transition* (Cheshire), (Melbourne), 1971, p. 36; Des Ryan and Mike McEwen, *'It's Grossly Improper'* (WENAN Pty Ltd), n.p., 1979, p. 87; Les Wright quoted in Jack Elliott, *Memoirs of a Barrister* (Wakefield Press), Kent Town, 2000, p. 160; Andrew Parkin, 'The Dunstan Governments: A Political

Synopsis', in Andrew Parkin and Allan Patience (eds), *The Dunstan Decade: Social Democracy at the State Level* (Longman Cheshire), Melbourne, 1981, pp. 3, 4.

23 Ts. of article written in response to an invitation by J.A. Fitzgerald, Editor, *Melbourne Herald*, 25 June 1974, Dunstan Papers Box 23, Flinders University Library.

24 http://www.milesago.com.People/dunstan-don.htm Accessed 3 December 2004; Mike Rann, 'Don Dunstan, Maestro of the Possible', in *Don Dunstan, 1926–1999, Labor Herald*, http://www.eherald.alp.org.au/download/now/dd.pdf Accessed 10 April 2006; Don Dunstan, *Felicia: The Political Memoirs of Don Dunstan* (Macmillan), South Melbourne, 1981, pp. 177–178, 261.

25 Dunstan, *Felicia*, pp. 179, 242; *National Times*, 23–28 January 1978; Kerrie Round, Interview with Peter Ward, 19 April 2004.

26 Dunstan, *Felicia*, pp. 205–206; Ryan and McEwen, *'It's Grossly Improper'*, p. 119; Peter Ward to Don Dunstan, 19 June 1972, Ts among the materials collected by Allan Patience towards his biography of Don Dunstan, Dunstan Papers; *Sydney Morning Herald*, 16 March 1972, clipping in VF4 Drawer 2, Dunstan Papers.

27 See, for instance, 'The Real Don Dunstan', in *Outrage*, April 1999, copy in Patience material, Dunstan Papers; Round, Interview with Peter Ward; http://schools.emergingleaders.com.au/ddunstan Accessed 18 August 2006; Dunstan, *Felicia*, pp. 218, 309.

28 Round, Interview with Peter Ward.

29 Michael Abbott, 'Bray as Barrister', in Wilfrid Prest (ed.), *A Portrait of John Bray: Law, Letters, Life* (Wakefield Press), Kent Town, 1997, p. 50; Peter Ward, 'John Bray in Adelaide', in Prest (ed.), *A Portrait of John Bray*, p. 4.

30 Ward, 'John Bray in Adelaide', p. 15.

31 Dunstan, *Felicia*, p. 116.

32 Round, Interview with Peter Ward; 'Thomas Quinton Stow', in Wilfrid Prest, Kerrie Round and Carol Fort (eds), *The Wakefield Companion to South Australian History* (Wakefield Press), Kent Town, 2001, p. 518; Ward, 'John Bray in Adelaide', p. 10; Charles Bright, 'Dr John Bray in Context', *Adelaide Law Review*, 7, 1980–81, p. 14; see also Portrait of John Jefferson Bray CJ, in the main staircase of the Supreme Court, Adelaide.

33 Quoted in Ward, 'John Bray in Adelaide', p. 5

34 Round, Interview with Peter Ward; Dunstan, *Felicia*, pp. 185, 116.

35 Dame Roma Mitchell, Speech at the Memorial Service for the Late John Bray, AC, QC, 25 July 1995, in Magarey (ed.), *Dame Roma*, p. 91.

36 Elliott, *Memoirs of a Barrister*, p. 203.

37 All of this account of Bray's life is taken from Ward, 'John Bray in Adelaide' unless otherwise indicated Magarey and Round, Interview with Pam Cleland; Rex Jory, *Advertiser*, 6 March 2000; Kerrie Round, Telephone conversation with Alek Mathieson, 27 November 2003.

38 Alex Castles, 'Times Are "A Changin"', in Alex Castles, Andrew Ligertwood and Peter Kelly, *Law on North Terrace* (Faculty of Law, University of Adelaide), Adelaide, 1983, p. 62.

39 Dunstan, *Felicia*, pp. 245–246; on Steel, see *Advertiser Review*, 14 January 2006.

40 Bright, 'Dr John Bray in Context', p. 14.

41 Round, Interview with Peter Ward.

42 Michael Kirby, 'Bray's Impact on Australian Jurisprudence', in Prest (ed.), *A Portrait of John Bray*, p. 95.

43 Quoted in Andrew Ligertwood, 'Bray the Jurist', in Prest (ed.), *A Portrait of John Bray*, p. 73.

44 Ligertwood, 'Bray the Jurist', pp. 71, 73, 75; Kirby, 'Bray's Impact on Australian Jurisprudence', pp. 94, 100.

45 Quoted in Mitchell, Speech at the Memorial Service for the Late John Bray', p. 95.

46 Bright, 'Dr John Bray in Context', p. 15.

47 Mitchell, Speech at the Memorial Service for the Late John Bray, p. 95.

48 Mitchell, Speech at the Memorial Service for the Late John Bray, pp. 95–96.

49 Ligertwood, 'Bray the Jurist', pp. 83–88; *Advertiser*: 3, 4, 5, 6, 7 July, 27 November 1967; Bright, 'Dr John Bray in Context', p. 15; Susan Magarey, Telephone conversation with Elliott Johnston 9 June 2008.

50 Len King, 'The Judicial Career of Dame Roma Mitchell', in Magarey (ed.), *Dame Roma*, pp. 72–73.

51 *Advertiser*, 19 September 1970; Dunstan, *Felicia*, p. 185.

52 King, 'The Judicial Career of Dame Roma Mitchell', p. 73; all of this account of Roma Mitchell's judicial decisions is drawn from King's article unless otherwise specified.

53 See Barbara Baird, "'Somebody was going to disapprove anyway": rethinking histories of abortion in South Australia, 1937–1990', PhD thesis, Flinders University, 1998, pp. 28–31. I am grateful to Dr Baird for giving me this information.

54 (1966) SASR 34; (1966) SASR 227; (1978) 19 SASR 448; (1979) 22 SASR 321.

55 Peter Norman, Interview with Alec Genders, 23 September 1998; Mitchell, Speech at the Memorial Service for the Late John Bray.

56 *R v Howe*. Transcript of argument before Court of Criminal Appeal, 14 April 1958, p. 6, quoted in Abbott, 'Bray as Barrister', p. 54.

57 *Sunday Mail*, 21 December 1986; quoted in King, 'The Judicial Career of Dame Roma Mitchell', p. 69.

58 All of the information in this paragraph comes from Susan Magarey's research material for A History of Women's Liberation in Australia, a project in process. See also Susan Magarey, 'Reading Straight and Reading Queer: Liberty Bodiss in Queen Adelaide's Town', in Joy Damousi and Katherine Ellinghaus (eds), *Citizenship, Women and Social Justice: International Historical Perspectives* (History Department, University of Melbourne), Melbourne, 1999, pp. 175–182; Sandra Lilburn, Susan Magarey and Susan Sheridan, 'Celebrity Feminism as Synthesis: Germaine Greer, *The Female Eunuch* and the Australian Print Media', *Continuum: Journal of Media & Cultural Studies*, vol. 14, no. 3, November 2000, pp. 335–348; Susan Magarey, 'Feminism as Cultural Renaissance', *Hecate: An Interdisciplinary Journal of Women's Liberation*, vol. 30, no. 1, 2004, pp. 231–246; Susan Magarey, 'The *Sex Discrimination Act* 1984', *Australian Feminist Law Journal*, vol. 20, June 2004, pp. 127–134; Susan Magarey, '"Holding the Horrors of the World at Bay": The Feminist Food Guide', *History Australia*, vol. 1, no. 2, July 2004, pp. 245–255; Susan Magarey, 'Memory and Desire: Feminists Re-membering Feminism', *Lilith: a Feminist History Journal*, no. 14, 2005, pp. 1–11.

59 Newsclipping, 4 March 1973, Women's Liberation Movement Archive, South Australia, WL,a 1/19/4

60 *Advertiser*, 24 April 1976.

61 See Michelle Arrow, ' "It Has become My Personal Anthem": "I Am Woman", Popular Culture and 1970s Feminism', *Australian Feminist Studies*, Vol. 22, no. 53, July 2007.

62 All of this account is taken from the Hon. Justice Roma Mitchell, *Women's Liberation and the Law*, the Sir John Morris Memorial Lecture (Government Printer), Tasmania, 1971.

63 The Hon. Elizabeth Evatt, 'A Woman's Perspective', in Magarey (ed.), *Dame Roma*, p. 282.

64 Ward, 'John Bray in Adelaide', p. 14; see also above, chapter 2, p. 11; Ligertwood, 'Bray the Jurist', p. 79; *John Bray Collected Poems 1962–1991* (University of Queensland Press), St Lucia, 2000, p. 237.

65 John Bray, 'Quindecadal Reflections: Address to the University Senate, 1983', in John Bray, *The Emperor's Doorkeeper: Occasional Addresses*, edited by Barbara Wall and Douglas Muecke (The University of Adelaide Foundation), Adelaide, 1988, p. 187; Roma Mitchell, Foreword to Bray, *The Emperor's Doorkeeper*, p. 2. Our thanks to Barbara Wall for lending us her copy of this book.

66 http://news.bbc.co.uk/onthisday/hi/dates/stories/june/5/newsid_2660000/2660375.stm, Accessed 5 August 2007.

67 Dunstan, *Felicia*: pp. 186, 201.

68 Dunstan, *Felicia*, p. 201.

69 Stewart Cockburn, *The Salisbury Affair* (Sun Books), Melbourne, 1979, p. 74; Dunstan, *Felicia*, p. 133.

70 R.J. McGowan, Detective Chief Superintendent, Criminal Investigation Department, New Scotland Yard, Metropolitan Police, *Report to Commissioner of Police, Adelaide, on enquiries into the death of Dr George Ian Ogilvie Duncan, 2 October 1972*, released 29 May 2002; the

Hon. M.J. Atkinson (Attorney-General), Ministerial Statement to the House of Assembly, South Australian Parliament, 15 July 2002.

71 Round, Interview with Peter Ward.

72 John Summers, 'The Salisbury Affair', in Dean Jaensch (ed.), *The Flinders History of South Australia: Political History* (Wakefield Press), Netley, 1986, p. 343.

73 The following account is taken from South Australia *Parliamentary Debates*, 7 February 1978, pp. 1360–1421; Dunstan, *Felicia*, chapter 13, which quotes verbatim from the Parliamentary Debates and the *Transcript of Proceedings*, Royal Commission on Dismissal from the Office of Commissioner of Police, SRSA GRG 108; and Cockburn, *The Salisbury Affair*, chapter 9, unless otherwise specified.

74 Dunstan, *Felicia*, p. 168.

75 Dunstan, *Felicia*, p. 285.

76 Dunstan, *Felicia*, p. 285.

77 S.A. *P.D.*, 7 February 1978, pp. 1364, 1369–1371.

78 Evidence of D.A. Dunstan to the *Royal Commission 1978: Report on the Dismissal of Harold Hubert Salisbury*, *Transcript of Proceedings*, p. 694; Dunstan, *Felicia*, p. 185; Entry for 17 December 1979, Diaries of Sir Walter Crocker.

79 Round, Interview with Peter Ward.

80 Evidence of D.A. Dunstan, *Transcript of Proceedings*, p. 694.

81 Round, Interview with Peter Ward.

82 Dunstan, *Felicia*, p. 133; entries for 2 April 1978, 27 April, 23 May, 28 May 1979, 20 April, 3 August, 24 September 1980, 14 May 1981, 13 June 1988, Diaries of Sir Walter Crocker.

83 *News*, 9 October 1968; *Transcript of Proceedings*, pp. 384–385, 1290; also Dunstan, *Felicia*, p. 307; Hon. Mr Acting Justice White, *Special Branch security records: initial report to the Hon. Donald Allan Dunstan, Premier of the State of South Australia [the White Report], 7.3.1*; Dunstan, S.A. *P.D.*, 7 February 1978, p. 1368.

84 *White Report*, 7.3.1.

85 Dunstan, *Felicia*, p. 294.

86 Dunstan reporting Salisbury, S.A. *P.D.*, 7 February 1978, p. 1366; Dunstan, *Felicia*, p. 295.

87 Alex C. Castles and Michael C. Harris, *Lawmakers and Wayward Whigs* (Wakefield Press), Adelaide, 1987, p. 290; Gordon Hawkins, 'The Salisbury Affair – a blinkered view', *Australian*, 28–29 April 1979.

88 D. Tonkin, S.A. *P.D.*, 7 February 1978, p. 1372.

89 P.N. Grabosky, 'Political surveillance and the South Australian Police', in *Wayward Governance: illegality and its control in the public sector* (Australian Institute of Criminology), Canberra, 1989, pp. 113–128. http://www.aic.gov.au/publications/lcj/wayward/ Accessed 10 April 2006; *Advertiser*, 26 January 1978; *Sydney Morning Herald*, 25 January 1978.

90 S.A. *P.D.*, 7 February 1878, pp. 1360–1421; Dunstan, *Felicia*, p. 299.

91 Cockburn, *The Salisbury Affair*, p. 206.

92 Cairns Villeneuve Smith to Roma Mitchell, 15 February 1978, SLSA PRG 778/5/1.

93 Richard G. Fox, 'The Salisbury Affair: Special Branches, Security and Subversion', *Monash University Law Review*, vol. 5, June 1979, p. 264.

94 Fox, 'The Salisbury Affair', 255; Cockburn, *The Salisbury Affair*, pp. 211–212

95 Grabosky, 'Political surveillance'.

96 *Royal Commission 1978: Report on the Dismissal of Harold Hubert Salisbury*, pp. 125, 130.

97 *Transcript of Proceedings of the Royal Commission*, Minutes of Evidence, pp. 1290, 1297; see also Dunstan, *Felicia*, p. 307; *Royal Commission 1978: Report on the Dismissal of Harold Hubert Salisbury*, p. 106.

98 *Royal Commission 1978: Report on the Dismissal of Harold Hubert Salisbury*, p. 134.

99 *Transcript of Proceedings*, p. 693.

100 *Transcript of Proceedings*, pp. 384–385.

101 *Transcript of Proceedings*, pp. 693–695.

102 Quoted in Summers, 'The Salisbury Affair', p. 345.

103 Castles and Harris, *Lawmakers and Wayward Whigs*, p. 294; Louis Waller, 'The Police, The Premier and Parliament: Government Control of the Police', *Monash University Law Review*, vol. 6, June 1980, p. 267.

104 Entry for Saturday 17 June [1978], Diaries of Sir Walter Crocker.
105 *Australian Biography II*, p. 101.
106 Roma Mitchell to John Bray, 9 June 1978, original shown to Kerrie Round by Peter Ward, who was John Bray's Executor.
107 Kerrie Round, Conversation with Peter Ward, 19 April 2004.
108 Ward, 'John Bray in Adelaide', pp. 17–18; Mitchell, Speech at the Memorial Service for the Late John Bray, p. 96.

Chapter Seven: Roma the Reformer

1 See for example Howard S. Becker, *Outsiders* (Collier–Macmillan), New York, 1963; A.K. Cohen, *Deviancy and Control* (Prentice Hall), New Jersey, 1966; Stanley Cohen (ed.), *Images of Deviance* (Penguin Books), Harmondsworth, 1971; Ian Taylor, Paul Walton and Jock Young, *The New Criminology: For a Theory of Deviance* (Routledge & Kegan Paul), London, 1973; Michel Foucault, *Discipline and Punish: The Birth of the Prison*, first published as *Surveiller et punir: Naissance de la prison*, 1975, translated by Alan Sheridan (Allan Lane), London, 1977.
2 Roma Mitchell, Colin Howard and David Biles, Criminal Law and Penal Methods Reform Committee of South Australia, *First Report: Sentencing and Corrections* (Government Printer), Adelaide, 1973, p. 160.
3 Alex C. Castles and Michael C. Harris, *Lawmakers and Wayward Whigs: Workings of the Law in South Australia in the Twentieth Century* (Wakefield Press), Netley, 1987, pp. 358–361, 376.
4 Alex Castles, Andrew Ligertwood and Peter Kelly, *Law on North Terrace 1883–1983* (Faculty of Law, University of Adelaide), Adelaide, 1983, pp. 58–61, 64.
5 Norval Morris and Gordon Hawkins, *The Honest Politician's Guide to Crime Control*, first pub, University of Chicago Press, 1970, (Sun Books), Melbourne, 1971, p. 1.
6 Morris and Hawkins, *The Honest Politician's Guide to Crime Control*, pp. 3–4, 27.
7 Morris and Hawkins, *The Honest Politician's Guide to Crime Control*, p. 45.
8 Morris and Hawkins, *The Honest Politician's Guide to Crime Control*, p. 111.
9 Morris and Hawkins, *The Honest Politician's Guide to Crime Control*, pp. 112–113.
10 CLPMRC, *First Report*, pp. 42–45.
11 (1969) SASR; (1970) SASR; (1971) SASR.
12 Charles Bright, 'Law Reform', in Andrew Parkin and Allan Patience (eds), *The Dunstan Decade: Social Democracy at the State Level* (Longman Cheshire), Melbourne, 1981, p. 150; Geoff Muecke, 'On the Criminal Law and Penal Methods Reform Committee' in Susan Magarey (ed.), *Dame Roma, Glimpses of a Glorious Life* (Axiom Publishing in association with the John Bray Chapter of the Adelaide University Alumni Association), Adelaide, 2002, p. 106.
13 Kerrie Round, Conversation with Peter Ward, 19 April 2004.
14 King CJ, 'Transcript of Proceedings at Special Sitting On the Retirement of Her Honour Justice Mitchell, 28 September 1983', in Magarey (ed.), *Dame Roma*, p. 181.
15 Lindy Powell, 'Dame Roma Mitchell. A Life in the Law', Law Society of South Australia *Bulletin*, February 1991, p. 4
16 Bright, 'Law Reform', p. 149.
17 Muecke, 'On the Criminal Law and Penal Methods Reform Committee', pp. 106–107.
18 See, e.g., CLPMRC: *Second Report: Criminal Investigation* (Government Printer), Adelaide, 1974, p. xxvii; *Fourth Report: The Substantive Criminal Law* (Government Printer), Adelaide, 1977, p. xlvi.
19 Muecke, 'On the Criminal Law and Penal Methods Reform Committee', p. 107.
20 *Advertiser*, 18 December 1971.
21 Muecke, 'On the Criminal Law and Penal Methods Reform Committee', p. 107.
22 King, 'Transcript of Proceedings at Special Sitting On the Retirement of Her Honour Justice Mitchell, 28 September 1983', p. 182.
23 Kerrie Round, Telephone conversation with Gordon Barrett QC, 25 June 2003.
24 CLPMRC: *First Report*, p. 63; *Second Report*: pp. 203, 3; *First Report*, pp. 66–68; *Second Report*, p. 3; *First Report*, pp. 60, 68, 79.
25 CLPMRC, *Second Report*, pp. 3–4.

26 CLPMRC, *Third Report: Court Procedure and Evidence* (Government Publisher), Adelaide, 197?, p. 2.
27 CLPMRC, *First Report*, pp. 6, 208, 164, 67, 85, 124, 66–67.
28 CLPMRC, *First Report*, pp. 8, 10, 20.
29 CLPMRC, *First Report*, pp. 19, 20, 20–22.
30 CLPMRC: *Fourth Report*, pp. 10, 53, 110, 157, 153; *Second Report*, pp. 24, 177.
31 CLPMRC: *Second Report*, pp. 3, 7, 10–11; *Fourth Report*, pp. 80–81; *Second Report*, pp. 17–20, 13–14.
32 CLPMRC, *Second Report*, pp. 39, 40.
33 Melbourne University Publishing, http://www.mup.unimelb.edu.au/catalogue/0-522-85045-6.hml Accessed 15 August 2006.
34 CLPMRC, *Fourth Report*, pp. 154, 10, 7, 64, 101.
35 Robert Holmes, 'A Political Biography of Peter Duncan', research project essay in Politics II: Party, Party Systems and Society in Australia, Flinders University, July 1977, in Alan Patience's notes towards a biography of Don Dunstan, Flinders University Library. Our gratitude to Gillian Dooley for permission to copy this essay.
36 Helen Mills, 'Equal Opportunities', in Andrew Parkin and Allan Patience (eds), *The Dunstan Decade: Social Democracy at the State Level* (Longman Cheshire), Melbourne, 1981, p. 118
37 Muecke, 'On the Criminal Law and Penal Methods Reform Committee', p. 111
38 Don Dunstan, *Felicia: The Political Memoirs of Don Dunstan* (Macmillan), South Melbourne, 1981, pp. 312–313; Geoff Stokes and Richard Cox, 'The Governing Party: The ALP and the Politics of Consensus', in Parkin and Patience (eds), *The Dunstan Decade*, p. 275.
39 [1975] 2 All E.R. 347.
40 Quoted in CLPMRC, *Fourth Report*, p. 99
41 CLPMRC, *Fourth Report*, p. 99.
42 CLPMRC, *Fourth Report*, p. 100.
43 CLPMRC, *Fourth Report*, p. 100.
44 Anne Summers, *Damned Whores and God's Police: The Colonization of Women in Australia* (Penguin), Ringwood, 1975, pp. 201–218
45 CLPMRC, *Fourth Report*, pp. 102–104.
46 CLPMRC: *Third Report*, pp. 123–130; *Fourth Report*, p. 149.
47 CLPMRC: *Third Report*, pp. 123–130; *Fourth Report*, pp. 148–149.
48 CLPMRC, *Fourth Report*, pp. 109–111.
49 CLPMRC, *First Report*, pp. 164, 64.
50 CLPMRC, *First Report*, pp. 190–191, 191.
51 CLPMRC, *First Report*, pp. 191, 198, 176.
52 CLPMRC, *First Report*, pp. 200–201.
53 CLPMRC, *First Report*, pp. 202, 202–204, 207, 209, 209–211, 205, 205, 206, 207, 204.
54 CLPMRC: *Fourth Report*, pp. 64–65.
55 CLPMRC: *Second Report*, pp. 158–159; *Fourth Report*, pp. 70–71, 86, 93, 57–58.
56 Muecke, 'On the Criminal Law and Penal Methods Reform Committee', p. 110
57 Ngaire Naffine, *An Inquiry into the Substantive Law of Rape* (Women's Adviser's Office, Department of Premier and Cabinet), Adelaide, 1984, p. 1
58 Quoted in The Honourable Dame Roma Mitchell, Final Address to the Criminal Law Conference, 18 June 1988, SLSA PRG 778/17/82.
59 Bright, 'Law Reform', p. 149.
60 Attorney-General Peter Duncan to Premier Don Dunstan, 15 November 1977, Dunstan Papers VF6 DR1, Flinders University Archives.
61 See CLPMRC, *First Report*, pp. 92–93.
62 Duncan Chappell and Peter Sallmann, 'Rape in Marriage Legislation in South Australia: Anatomy of a Reform', *Australian Journal of Forensic Sciences*, vol. 14, no. 3, 1982, pp. 56, 51.
63 Duncan to Dunstan, 15 November 1977.
64 *Statutes Amendment (Capital Punishment Abolition) Act* (1976), (SA).
65 In the *Criminal Law Consolidation Act Amendment Act* (1980), the *Correctional Services Act* (1982), the *Juries Act Amendment Act* (1984), the *Public Intoxication Act* (1984), the *Bail Act*

(1985), the *Police Offences Act Amendment Act* (1985), the *Criminal Law Consolidation Act Amendment Act* (1986), and the *Criminal Law Consolidation Act* (1992), see Attorney-General's Department, *The Recommendations Made by the Criminal Law and Penal Methods Reform Committee of South Australia: an Account and an Audit* (Attorney-General's Department), Adelaide, 1990.

66 http://www.lrc.justice.wa.gov.au/References.P43.PDF Accessed 15 February 2005.

67 http://www.lawlink.nsw.gov.au/lawlink/lrc/ll_lrc.nsf/pages/LRC_reports Accessed 15 February 2005.

68 http://www.lawreform.vic.gov.au/CA256902000FE154/Lookup/Homicide_Final_Report/$file/Chapter_2.pdf Accessed 25 January 2005.

69 http://.justice.tas.gov.au/cc.corrections1.htm Accessed 17 February 2005.

70 Muecke, 'On the Criminal Law and Penal Methods Reform Committee', p. 123.

71 *Sunday Mail*, 12 February 1978.

72 *News*, 23 July 1976.

73 *News*, 23 July 1976.

74 *Advertiser*, 20 May 1979.

75 *Advertiser*: 31 May 1979, 1 April 1979, 3 June 1979.

76 Charles Cornwall, *The Punishment Fit the Crime* (Peacock Publications), Adelaide, 2002, pp. 91–100; Letters to the Editor. Adelaide Advertiser, 31 May 1979; '"Too early" releases', Sunday Mail, 3 June 1979.

77 Entries for 12 April [1980], 6 April 1982, Diaries of Sir Walter Crocker, Special Collections, Barr Smith Library, University of Adelaide.

78 Entry for 29 July [1979], Diaries of Sir Walter Crocker.

Chapter Eight: Citizen of the World

1 M.L. Tyrrell, Official Secretary to the Governor-General to The Honourable Justice Roma Flinders Mitchell, LLB, QC, 4 June 1971, SLSA PRG 778/10/5; *Advertiser*, 12 June 1971

2 http://www.abc.net.au/rn/boyers/ Accessed 16 August 2006.

3 Justice Roma Mitchell, *The Web of Criminal Law. The Boyer Lectures 1975*, reproduced in Susan Magarey (ed.), *Dame Roma: Glimpses of a Glorious Life* (Axiom Publishing in association with the John Bray Chapter of the Alumni Association of the University of Adelaide), Adelaide, p. 156.

4 Mitchell, *The Web of Criminal Law*, p. 131.

5 Peter Bailey said that the legislation establishing the Human Rights Commission would not have passed without the support of Prime Minister Malcolm Fraser, because of the opposition of the Right to Life, Kerrie Round, Interview with Peter Bailey, 28 November 2002.

6 *Advertiser*, July 1967, Newspaper clipping, Dame Roma Mitchell's Scrapbooks, SLSA PRG 778/22.

7 *Education in South Australia – Report of the Committee of Enquiry into Education in South Australia 1969–70* (Government Printer), Adelaide, 1971.

8 *Advertiser*, 30 January 1969; Kerrie Round, Telephone conversation with Emeritus Professor Peter Karmel, 10 December 2003; Vice-Chancellor Professor Don Stranks, Speech at the presentation of the degree of Doctor of the University to Dame Roma Mitchell, 29 April 1985, SLSA PRG 778/4/2.

9 See Jordan–Kennedy Scholarship 1977–1989, SLSA PRG 778/6/31; Stranks, Speech at the presentation of the degree of Doctor of the University to Dame Roma Mitchell.

10 Mark McGuiness, 'Obituary: Hon Dame Roma Mitchell AC, DBE, CVO, QC', *Australian Law Journal*, vol. 74, May 2000, p. 333.

11 Josephine Collins, The Ryder-Cheshire Story in Australia: a Memoir, unpublished (March 1989).

12 W.G. K. Duncan and Roger Ashley Leonard, *The University of Adelaide 1874–1974* (Rigby), Adelaide, 1973, pp. 148, 155; Jill Thorpe, 'Kathleen Lumley College in the Spotlight', *'Clever Country' Journal*, June 2003, p. 4; Stranks, Speech at the presentation of the degree of Doctor of the University to Dame Roma Mitchell.

13 See, e.g., entry for 17 May [1972], Diaries of Sir Walter Crocker, Special Collections, Barr Smith Library, University of Adelaide; Duncan and Leonard, *The University of Adelaide*, p. 173.

14 Kerrie Round, Interview with Sir Walter Crocker, 30 October 2002.

15 Helena Jasinski, Interview with Noel Paternoster, cited in Susan Magarey and Helena Jasinski, 'Formations', in Magarey (ed.), *Dame Roma*, p. 30; Merle Jenkins, Entry in *Who's Who* (The Herald & Weekly Times Ltd), Melbourne, 1971, p. 521; Kerrie Round, Telephone conversation with Jean MacDonald, 10 December 2002.

16 Susan Magarey, Interview with Lorna Williams and Adrienne McMahon, 17 August 2001.

17 David Hilliard, *Flinders University: The First 25 Years 1966–1991* (Flinders University of South Australia) Adelaide, 1991, pp. 9, 24–27; Valmai Hankel, 'Pages of life an inspirational read: Jean Primrose Whyte AM', *Advertiser*, 26 April 2003.

18 George Farwell, *Rejoice in Freedom* (Nelson) Melbourne, 1976, pp. 368–370.

19 Noni Farwell, 'Dame Roma Mitchell and the Arts', in Magarey (ed.), *Dame Roma*, p. 243.

20 *Advertiser*: 3 and 30 July 1968, clipping in Dame Roma's Scrapbooks; Roma Mitchell to Mr and Mrs Hugh Gooch, 9 and 10 July 1968, SLSA PRG 778/11; List of places to visit in Letters Received – General 1952–1966, SLSA PRG 778/5/1; Handwritten note above 'Notices I on Orders of the Day, 17 July [1968]', Dame Roma Mitchell's Scrapbooks.

21 http://www.lawasia.asn.au/index.php?contentPKey=80, Accessed 15 August 2006; Malaysia, *New Sunday Times*, 17 August 1975; Passports and Travel Itineraries, SLSA PRG 778/18; Roma Mitchell to Noni Farwell, postcard, 28 August 1976 [though date not clear], SLSA PRG 778/38; Passport, 26 May 1972 to 16 May 1977, SLSA PRG 778/18; Engraved brass plaque in leather case, to the Hon. Roma Mitchell 'who participated in the International Conference of Appellate Magistrates, held in the City of Manila, Philippines, on January 10 to 15, 1977, as representative of the Supreme Court of South Australia', SLSA PRG 778/1/1; Roma Mitchell to John Bray, 4 August 1977, SLSA PRG 1098/1/11.

22 Sir Walter Crocker appears in the Adelaide telephone directory in Glen Osmond in 1977, but in East Terrace, Adelaide, in 1978; entries for 30 April [1981], 9 October 1978, 25 December 1978, 1 January 1981, 25 December 1981, 3 March [1982], 15 August [1982], 30 December [1982], 19 May 1990, Diaries of Sir Walter Crocker.

23 Round, Interview with Sir Walter Crocker.

24 E.g. entries for 8 January 1980, 8 September 1981, 6 December 1981, 28 May 1983, 15 March 1985, 19 March 1988, 3 July 1988, 19 May 1990, 17 October 1981, 2 December 1982, 29 April 1981, Diaries of Sir Walter Crocker.

25 Entries for Sunday 24 March [1974], 7 January 1987, 16 November [1982], 1 March [1981], Diaries of Sir Walter Crocker; Kerrie Round, Telephone interview with Pamela Villeneuve Smith, 13 August 2002; Susan Magarey, Conversation with Fay Gale, 6 September 2006.

26 Just for example, he wrote of her with extreme hostility in his entries for 23 September 1979, 12 October 1979 and 8 January 1980, Diaries of Sir Walter Crocker.

27 Entry for Monday 9 July [1984], Diaries of Sir Walter Crocker. See also entry for Saturday 5 May [1979]: 'Done with generosity & elegance as her parties always are'.

28 E.g. entries for Friday 19 May [1978], Thursday 20 August [1987], Saturday 22 April [1989] Diaries of Sir Walter Crocker.

29 Dorothy Auchterlonie [Dorothy Green], 'Present Tense', in Jennifer Strauss (ed.), *The Oxford Book of Love Poems* (Oxford University Press), Melbourne, 1993, p. 100.

30 Flexmore Hudson, 'Waiting for a Letter', in Strauss (ed), *The Oxford Book of Australian Love Poems*, p. 90.

31 Susan Magarey and Helena Jasinski, Conversation with Noni Farwell, 2002

32 Entry for 12 February 1980, Diaries of Sir Walter Crocker.

33 Quoted in Peter Bassett, 'Governor of South Australia', in Magarey (ed.), *Dame Roma*, p. 251.

34 Amanda Vanstone, 'A Good Friend', in Magarey (ed.), *Dame Roma*, p. 338.

35 Roma Mitchell to Noni Farwell, 6 August 1983, SLSA PRG 778/38; Magarey and Jasinski, Conversation with Noni Farwell.

36 Entries for New Year's Day, 1980, 7 January 1982, 12 January 1982, Entries for 30 April [1982], 3 May [1982], Diaries of Sir Walter Crocker.

37 Jill O'Dea to Roma Mitchell, 16 June 1982, SLSA PRG 778/3/4/3.
38 Entry for 12 October [1979], Diaries of Sir Walter Crocker.
39 Entries for 23 May [1979], 14 May [1981], Diaries of Sir Walter Crocker.
40 *Advertiser*: 6 February, 24 September 1980; John Summers, 'The Salisbury Affair', in Dean Jaensch (ed.), *The Flinders History of South Australia: Political History* (Wakefield Press), Netley, 1986, pp. 346–349.
41 Jack Elliott, *Memoirs of a Barrister* (Wakefield Press) Adelaide, 2000, p. 324, chapter 22 'Saga of the Splatt Case'; entry for 7 August 1981, Diaries of Sir Walter Crocker; Criminal Law and Penal Methods Reform Committee, *Second Report*, pp. 145–153; 'Face-to-Face-Chris Sumner', Law Society of South Australia *Bulletin*, November 1994, p. 10.
42 Charles Bright, *The Confidential Clerk: a Study of Charles Flaxman in South Australia and His Relationship with George Fife Angas* (Elizabeth H. Bright), Adelaide, 1983; David Hilliard, 'Bright, Sir Charles Hart', Ts. Entry for the *Australian Dictionary of Biography*; we are most grateful to David Hilliard for sending us this entry before it had been published.
43 Entry for 28 February [1984], Diaries of Sir Walter Crocker.
44 Entry for 28 February [1984], Diaries of Sir Walter Crocker.
45 Stewart Cockburn to Roma Mitchell: 29 February 1984, 10 March 1984, 13 March 1984; Roma Mitchell to Stewart Cockburn, 2 March 1984, 12 March 1984, the letters from Roma Mitchell to Stewart Cockburn are copies that she made herself, by hand, SLSA PRG 778/4/5.
46 Entry for 29 May [1990], Diaries of Sir Walter Crocker.
47 *Advertiser*: 7 August 1978, 4 September 1978; see also John Reid and Anne Gollan (eds), *Visiting China* (Waverley Offset Publishing Group), Canberra, 1969.
48 *Australian Jewish News*, 29 June 1979; Melbourne *Age*, 15 June 1979.
49 Hankel, 'Pages of life an inspirational read: Jean Primrose Whyte AM'; Ross Day and John Legge, 'David Hector Monro, 1911–2001', Melbourne *Age*, 10 June 2001; also entry for Christmas Day Friday [1981], Diaries of Sir Walter Crocker; Picture at Kensington Gallery, Norwood, South Australia.
50 *Advertiser*, 26 September 1981.
51 Susan Mitchell, 'Dame Roma Mitchell', in Susan Mitchell, *The Matriarchs. Twelve Australian Women Talk about Their Lives* (Penguin), Ringwood, 1987, p. 38.
52 David I. Smith, Official Secretary to the Governor-General, to Judge Roma Mitchell, 7 June 1982, SLSA PRG 778/3/4/3; *News*, 20 September 1983; entry for 13 July 1982, Diaries of Sir Walter Crocker; Dame Roma Mitchell to The Manager, GRE Insurance Ltd., 11 November 1986, SLSA PRG 778/4/4.
53 *Canberra Times*, 28 August 1982; Roma Mitchell to Noni Farwell, 1 October 1982, SLSA PRG 778/38; *Advertiser*, 12 June 1982.
54 Tony Blackshield and George Williams, *Australian Constitutional Law and theory, commentary and materials, third edition* (Federation Press), Sydney 2002, pp. 550–551; http://www.hcourt.gov.au
55 *Canberra Times*, 11 December 1981
56 Hilary Charlesworth, 'Human Rights and Reconciliation in International Perspective', in Susan Magarey (ed.), *Human Rights and Reconciliation* (University of Queensland Press), 1999, pp. 10–17.
57 Brian Galligan, *No Bill of Rights for Australia*, Papers on Parliament, no. 4, 1989, n.p.; Press Conference with the Attorney-General, Senator Peter Durack QC, National Archives of Australia [NAA]:CRS: M1853/90; Human Rights Commission Meeting no. 2, Paper no. 2, NAA:NSW: C3177/1; P.H. Bailey, Notes for Address to Melbourne Interest Group, 9 September 1982, NAA:CRS: M1859/100.
58 Justice Roma Mitchell, Address to Women Lawyers' Association of New South Wales, 27 March 1982, SLSA PRG 778/17/1.
59 Senator the Hon. Gareth Evans, Attorney-General, 'Discrimination and Human Rights', Paper presented to the 22nd Australian Legal Convention, Brisbane, 7 July 1983, NAA: CRS M1853/90.
60 *Canberra Times*, 11 December 1981; Galligan, *No Bill of Rights for Australia*, n.p.

61 P.H. Bailey, 'One World for Human Rights?', Address to United Nations Association of Australia, 7 December 1981, NAA:CRS: M1859/93; P.H. Bailey, 'HRCs and Their Roles', Sri Lanka address, 1987, NAA:CRS: M1859/171.

62 Meeting No. 2, Paper No. 2, NAA:NSW:C3177/1; Meeting No. 3, Paper No. 5, NAA:NSW:C3177/1; Round, Interview with Peter Bailey; E.g. '"Minnards' Morning" Friday, 5 February 1982', Meeting No. 3, NAA: NSW: C3177/1; http://www.aitsis.gov.au/__data/assets/pdf_file/2545/MS2534.PDF#search=%22%Jeremy%Long%22%20%22Human%20Rights%20Commission%22%22, Accessed 22 August 2006.

63 P.H. Bailey, *Human Rights: Australia in an international context* (Butterworths) Sydney, 1990, Preface.

64 http://www.familyrelationships.gov.au/agd/WWW/MinisterRuddockHome.nsf/Page/Media_Releases_2005_Third_Quarter_20_September_2005_-_Prominent_Australians_to_be_honoured_-_1712005, Accessed 16 August 2006.

65 Elizabeth Hastings, 'A Tribute to Dame Roma Mitchell', in Magarey (ed.), *Dame Roma*, p. 13; Mitchell, Address to Women Lawyers' Association of New South Wales, 27 March 1972.

66 '50 Great Australians', information provided by paffairs@humanrights.gov.au 13 April 2004.

67 Round, Interview with Peter Bailey; Elizabeth Hastings, 'A Tribute to Dame Roma Mitchell', p. 13.

68 Hastings, 'A Tribute to Dame Roma Mitchell', p. 13.

69 Roma Mitchell, Address to the Royal Australian Institute of Architects, 20 August 1982, SLSA PRG 778/17/4

70 'New Human Rights Director Appointed', Press Release No. 45/84, 25 September 1984, NAA: CRS, M1853/90; 'Combined Assault Against Discrimination', Press Release No. 4/85, 3 March 1985, NAA: CRS: M185391; *Advertiser*, 4 March 1985; Rod Goodall and Chris Fuller, 'Five Years in the Field', *Newsletter of the Human Rights Commission*, No. 19, December 1986, p. 10.

71 *Advertiser*, 16 January 1980.

72 Hastings, 'A Tribute to Dame Roma Mitchell', p. 13; Round, Interview with Peter Bailey; entry for 2 December [1982], Diaries of Sir Walter Crocker.

73 Human Rights Commission, NAA NSW C3177/1; Note on the Functions of the HRC, Meeting No. 1, Paper No. 7, Canberra 12 October 1981, NAA: NSW: C3177/1, Box 222; Hastings, 'A Tribute to Dame Roma Mitchell', p. 14.

74 *Canberra Times*, 21 March 1982.

75 Meeting No. 6, Field trip, May–June 1982, NAA:C3177/1, Box 223.

76 *Courier Mail*, 20 July 1982.

77 *Advertiser*: 4 December 1982, 28 September 1983; *Australian*, 27 October 1983; Dame Roma Mitchell, Speech to Sydney University Law Graduate Association 1982, SLSA PRG 778/17/4.

78 John Bray to Roma Mitchell, 13 June 1984, SLSA PRG 778/5/1.

79 Address to Media Law Association, 11 August 1984, SLSA PRG 778/17/31a; Letter to Editor, *Australian*, 10 November 1984.

80 http://www.abc.net.au/health/regions/features/heroin/history.htm Accessed 22 August 2006; Hastings, 'A Tribute to Dame Roma Mitchell', p. 15.

81 Address by the Attorney-General, Senator the Hon Gareth Evans, to the Conference on the Teaching of Human Rights, Adelaide 26 August 1983, NAA: CRS 1853/14.

82 Susan Ryan, *Catching the Waves: Life in and out of Politics* (Harper Collins), Sydney, 1999, p. 241.

83 Brisbane *Courier Mail*, 27 September 1983; *Sydney Morning Herald*, 22 October 1983.

84 Roma Mitchell, Address at Monash University, 10 December 1983, SLSA PRG 778/17/27.

85 Ryan, *Catching the Waves*, p. 242.

86 Susan Magarey, 'The Sex Discrimination Act 1984', *The Australian Feminist Law Journal*, Vol. 20, June 2004, pp. 127, 129, 130–132; Dame Roma Mitchell, Speech to the Federation of Women Lawyers, 26 August 1984, quoted in Einfeld, 'Human Rights', in Magarey (ed.) *Dame Roma*, pp. 203–204.

87 P.H. Bailey OBE, Deputy Chairman, Human Rights Commission, Notes for Address to Melbourne Interest Group, 9 September 1982, NAA: CRS M1859 100, pp. 12–13.
88 Australian National Commission for UNESCO: The Hon. Mr Justice M.D. Kirby, Chairman of the Australian Law Reform Commission, Book Launching: *Teaching Human Rights: a Framework for Law Reform*, 3 March 1982, Meeting No. 4, Box 222, NAA: C3177/1
89 Justice Roma Mitchell, 'The Human Rights Commission', Women Lawyers Association of New South Wales, 27 March 1982, SLSA PRG 778/17/1; *Advertiser*, 24 August 1982; Dame Roma Mitchell, Address to South Australian College of Advanced Education, NAA: C3177/1; Sydney University Law Graduates Association, 16 July 1982, SLSA PRG 778/17/4; University of New South Wales, May 1984, SLSA PRG 778/17/28; Canberra College of Advanced Education, 13 May 1983, SLSA PRG 778/17/26; Monash University, 10 December 1983, SLSA PRG 778/17/27; Murdoch University, March 1984, SLSA PRG 778/17/27.
90 *Advertiser*, 21 August 1984.
91 J. Glaros, Ethnic Affairs Officer, to the Assistant Secretary, Ethnic Affairs and Citizenship Branch, Canberra, 28 March 1983, copy to HRC; *Advertiser*, 29 March 1983; Isi J. Leibler CBE to Dame Roma Mitchell, 6 April 1983; Peter Bailey to Isi J, Leibler CBE, 12 April 1983, all in NAA, Display at the Adelaide Constitutional Museum, C3177/1, Box 225.
92 http://theoccidentalquarterly.com/vol1no1/ep-rivers.htm, Accessed 18 September 2006. What Powell actually said was: 'As I look ahead, I am filled with foreboding. Like the Roman, I seem to see "the River Tiber foaming with much blood"'; entry for 15 March [1985], Diaries of Sir Walter Crocker; See Graeme Davison, 'Blainey, Geoffrey Norman', in Graeme Davison, John Hirst and Stuart Macintyre (eds), *The Oxford Companion to Australian History* (Oxford University Press), Melbourne, 1998, p. 75.
93 Press release, HRC, 7 March 1985, NAA: M1853 91; *Advertiser*: 1 June 1985, 20 April 1985, 1 February 1986; Brisbane *Daily Sun*, 16 November 1985.
94 *Sunday Mail*, 11 March 1983; Round, Interview with Peter Bailey; entry for 6 July 1985, Diaries of Sir Walter Crocker.
95 *Examiner*, 31 July 1986; Brisbane *Courier Mail*, 15 August 1985; Melbourne *Sun*, 14 August 1986; Melbourne *Age*, 29 July 1986; Brisbane *Courier Mail*, 15 August 1985; Melbourne *Sun*, 14 August 1986.
96 *Sydney Morning Herald*: 18 August, 30 August 1986; Galligan, *No Bill of Rights for Australia*; Dame Roma Mitchell, Address to Council for Civil Liberties, 22 March 1985, SLSA PRG 778/17/45.
97 Press Release, 28 November 1986, NAA: CRS, M1853/91; Einfeld, 'Human Rights', in Magarey (ed.), *Dame Roma*, p. 197; *Australian*, 8 September 2006; *West Australian*, 23 October 1984; Melbourne *Age*, 15 November 1984; *Canberra Times*, 10 December 1986, clipping in Dame Roma Mitchell's Scrapbooks; *Australian*, 10 December 1986.
98 Justice Roma Mitchell, 'The Human Rights Commission', address to the Women Lawyers' Association of New South Wales, 27 March 1982, p. 11; Dame Roma Mitchell, Speech to Amnesty International, Hobart, November 1983, http://www.abc.net.au/btn/australians/rmitchell.htm, quoted in Einfeld, 'Human Rights', p. 198.
99 Entry for 8 May [1985], Diaries of Sir Walter Crocker.
100 Susan Magarey, Personal recollection of having organised that dinner.

Chapter Nine: Contradictions and Continuities

1 King C.J. at a Special Sitting of the Supreme Court of South Australia On the Retirement of Her Honour Justice Mitchell, 28 September 1983, Transcript of Proceedings, printed in Susan Magarey (ed.), *Dame Roma: Glimpses of a Glorious Life* (Axiom Publishing in association with the John Bray Chapter of the Alumni Association of the University of Adelaide), Netley, 2002, p. 180.
2 Peter Bassett, 'Governor of South Australia', in Magarey (ed.), *Dame Roma*, p. 254.
3 H.T. Gibbs, 'A Judge in Kiribati', in Magarey (ed.), *Dame Roma*, pp. 218–222.
4 P.N. Grabosky, 'The Great Social Security Conspiracy Case', in *Wayward Governance: Illegality and its Control in the Public Sector* (Australian Institute of Criminology), Canberra,

1989, http//www.aic.gov.au/publications/lcj/wayward/ch6t.html Accessed 18 October 2006. All of the account given here is drawn from this article.

5 Entry for 1 December [1985], Diaries of Sir Walter Crocker, Special Collections, Barr Smith Library, University of Adelaide.

6 Film Australia, *Australian Biography II*, 4 June 1993, shown on SBS Television, pp. 73–74.

7 Entry for 2 December [1982], Diaries of Sir Walter Crocker; Amanda Vanstone, 'A Good Friend', in Magarey (ed.), *Dame Roma*, p. 338.

8 Murray Bramwell, 'The Arts', in Andrew Parkin and Allan Patience (eds), *The Bannon Decade: The Politics of Restraint in South Australia* (Allen & Unwin), Sydney, 1992, pp. 299–300; Nick Enright, Rex Cramphorn Lecture, 2002, www.currencyhouse.org.au/documents/ch d rex2002.pdf Accessed 28 November 2006; www.hosking.wattle.id.au/~laurel/parahtml/conservation plan.html Accessed 29 November 2006; Dame Roma Mitchell, Dedication Speech, Opening Concert, International Barossa Music Festival, Saturday, 30 September 1995; Elizabeth Silsbury, 'Music', in Wilfrid Prest, Kerrie Round and Carol Fort (eds), *The Wakefield Companion to South Australian History* (Wakefield Press), Kent Town, 2001, p. 372; http://www.adelaidereview.com.au/archives/2004_10_15/theatre_story4.shtml Accessed 18 October 2006; Susan Magarey and Helena Jasinski, Conversation with Noni Farwell, 2002; see also *Advertiser*, 25 May 1996; entry for 18 November [1990], Diaries of Sir Walter Crocker.

9 For example, entry for 5 February 1994, Dame Roma Mitchell's Women's Suffrage Centenary Diary, SLSA PRG 778/32; Kerrie Round, Interview with Pamela Villeneuve Smith, 13 August 2002; Lindy Powell QC, on *George Negus Tonight*, ABC television, 2 August 2004; Susan Magarey, Conversation with Helena Jasinski, 2002; Entries for 16 January and 3 April 1994, Dame Roma Mitchell's Women's Suffrage Centenary Diary.

10 Vanstone, 'A Good Friend', p. 329; Susan Magarey, Conversations with Heather Bonnin and Susan Sideris, several occasions.

11 Anne Edwards and Susan Magarey, 'Introduction', in Anne Edwards and Susan Magarey (eds), *Women in a Restructuring Australia: Work & Welfare* (Allen & Unwin), Sydney, 1995, p. 4.

12 Paul Smyth and Bettina Cass, 'Introduction', in Paul Smyth and Bettina Cass (eds), *Contesting the Australian Way: States, Markets, and Civil Society* (Cambridge University Press), 1998, pp. 2, 5; Susan Magarey, 'Introduction', in Susan Magarey (ed.), *Human Rights and Reconciliation in Australia* (University of Queensland Press), St. Lucia, 1999, pp. 1–8; Robert Manne, 'Introduction', in Robert Manne (ed.), *Whitewash: On Keith Windschuttle's Fabrication of Aboriginal History* (Black Inc. Agenda), Melbourne, 2003, pp. 1–13.

13 Alex Castles, Andrew Ligertwood and Peter Kelly (eds), *Law on North Terrace* (Faculty of Law, University of Adelaide), Adelaide, 1983, p. 67; John Cornwall, *Just For The Record: The Political Recollections of John Cornwall* (Wakefield Press), Kent Town, 1989, p. 41 (our thanks to Wakefield Press for finding for us a copy of this book, now out of print, in their warehouse); http://www.parliament.sa.gov.au/pp/html/bannon.shtm. Accessed 10 October 2006; Vern Marshall, 'The Labor Party', in Andrew Parkin and Allan Patience (eds), *The Bannon Decade* (Allen & Unwin), Sydney, 1992, p. 37; Len Amadio (Director of the South Australian Department of the Arts, 1981–1991), Interview with Murray Bramwell, 7 November 1991, quoted in Murray Bramwell, 'The Arts', p. 297.

14 Andrew Parkin, 'Looking Back On The Bannon Decade', in Parkin and Patience (eds), *The Bannon Decade*, pp. 10, 11, 15, 22; G. McL. Scott, 'Economic policy', in Parkin and Patience (eds), *The Bannon Decade*, p. 75; Greg McCarthy, *Things Fall Apart: A History of the State Bank of South Australia* (Australian Scholarly Publishing), Melbourne, 2002.

15 Judith Healy and Francis Regan, 'Social Welfare', in Parkin and Patience (eds), *The Bannon Decade*, p. 223; Cornwall, *Just For The Record*, p. 97.

16 *Advertiser*: 4 July 1984, 2 February 1985, 17 July 1985, 1 July 1981, 3 February 1985, 1 July 1987; Management Assessment Panel for Behaviourally Disordered Persons 1987–1988, SLSA PRG 778/6/17; Roma Mitchell, 'Being Neighbours', *Adelaide Voices*, June 1987, p. 11.

17 Peter Howell, quoted in *Advertiser*, 24 January 1996; Helen Jones, *In Her Own Name: Women in South Australia* (Wakefield Press), Netley, first edition 1986, pp. 162–163; Susan

Magarey, Conversation with Mrs Judith Roberts AM, Deputy Chancellor, Flinders University, 4 November 2006. See also Cornwall, *Just for the Record*, pp. 59–60.

18 Dame Roma Mitchell, Speech at the Child Abuse Seminar, 1 December 1987, SLSA PRG 778/17/79; *Advertiser*, 23 May 1987; Department for Community Welfare, *Annual Report, 1985–86* (Government Printer), Adelaide, 1986; http://www.pembroke.sa.edu.au/framset.html?I_aims_body.html?intro Accessed 18 October 2006.

19 Basil S. Hetzel, *Chance and Commitment* (Wakefield Press), Kent Town, 2005, p. 238. Our thanks to Dr Barbara Wall for drawing this comment to our attention.

20 Committee to review the organization of Council business, Adelaide University Archives [AUA], No. 2663 Pt I; E.H. Medlin to Dr J.J. Bray, 5 April 1976; Kerrie Round, Conversation with E.H. Medlin, 21 April 2004.

21 *Advertiser*: 5 May 1972, 18 March 1978.

22 Roma Mitchell, 'Dr John Bray and the University of Adelaide', in Wilfrid Prest (ed.), *A Portrait of John Bray: Law, Letters, Life* (Wakefield Press), Kent Town, 1997, pp. 21–23, 33–36. All of the account of John Bray's term as Chancellor of the University of Adelaide comes from this article, unless otherwise specified.

23 Dame Roma Mitchell, Speech at the Memorial Service for the Late John Bray, AC, QC, Tuesday 25 July 1995, in Magarey (ed.), *Dame Roma*, p. 92.

24 The University of Adelaide, 'The Citation for the Award of the Degree of Doctor of the University to Edwin Harry Medlin, B.Sc.(Hons.), Ph.D., Bonython Hall, 1 May, 1987'; entries for 8 December 1972, 19 May 1980, Diaries of Sir Walter Crocker; Harry Medlin, Emeritus Senior Deputy Chancellor, Visiting Associate Professor in Physics and Mathematical Physics, and University Alumni Envoy to East and South East Asia, 'Address to Women's Club, 19 May 1999'; Committee to review the organization of Council business, AUA No. 2663 Pt.I.

25 Quoted in Professor Frank Jarrett to Miss Roma Mitchell, 18 May 1979, AUA Series 906; Dr J.H. Silsbury, Senior Lecturer in Agronomy, submission to the Mitchell Committee, n.d., AUA Series 906; Jones, *In Her Own Name*, p. 356; J.P. Quirk to the Hon. Mr. Justice Jacobs, Chairman, University of Adelaide Finance Committee: 21 December 1979, 29 October 1980; Minutes of the Meeting of the University Council, 8 August 1986, AUA Series 906.

26 Minutes of the Meeting of the University Council: 13 May 1983, 10 June 1983, AUA.

27 Address to Law graduates, University of New South Wales, May 1984, SLSA PRG 778/17/28; undated, unsourced newspaper clipping, Dame Roma Mitchell's Scrapbooks, SLSA PRG 778/22.

28 *Australian*, 6 July 1988.

29 *Advertiser*, 11 August 1986; D.R. Stranks to Dame Roma Mitchell, 1985, SLSA PRG 778/3/7.

30 All of this account is based on Susan Magarey's recollection of personal experience; she was Director of the Research Centre for Women's Studies for its entire life, 1983–2000; see also Susan Magarey, 'I Never Wanted to be an Administrator of Anything', *Women's Studies International Forum*, vol. 9, no. 2, 1986, pp. 195–202; Susan Magarey, 'Setting up the First Research Centre for Women's Studies in Australia, 1983–1986', *Australian Feminist Studies*, vol. 13, no. 27, April 1998, pp. 81–90.

31 Academy of the Social Sciences in Australia, symposium on 'Women and the Social Sciences: New Modes of Thought', Canberra, 1983; papers presented to this gathering were published in Jacqueline Goodnow and Caole Pateman (eds), *Women, Social Science and Public Policy* (George Allen & Unwin), Sydney, 1985; Roma Mitchell, 'Consideration of Gender in Changes in the Law', *Australian Feminist Studies*, No. 1, Summer 1985. The other lecturers were Marilyn Strathern, Kay Daniels, Meredith Edwards and Bettina Cass; all of their lectures published in the first issue of *Australian Feminist Studies*, see *Advertiser*, 1 May 1985; *Australian*, 1 May 1985.

32 Susan Magarey, Personal recollection, but see also Dame Roma Mitchell, Eulogy printed in The University of Adelaide, *On the death of Professor Donald Richard Stranks 18 July 1929–9 August 1986: A record of the Thanksgiving Service on Tuesday 12 August 1986 at St Peter's Cathedral; of the Tribute paid in the House of Assembly of South Australia on Tuesday 19 August 1986; and of the Commemoration of his Life and Work, in Bonython Hall at The*

University of Adelaide on Thursday 16 October 1986; John Bray to Roma Mitchell, 14 August 1986, SLSA PRG 778/5/1.

33 'Passionate educator and family man', *Advertiser*, 13 May 2006; Kevin Marjoribanks, Valedictory Lecture: "An Inaugural Lecture Revisited', University of Adelaide, 26 November 1993, typescript in Kevin Marjoribanks to Her Excellency the Hon Dame Roma Mitchell, 1 December 1993, SLSA PRG 778/5/1; Susan Magarey, Personal recollection.

34 *Advertiser*, 19 October 1983.

35 Department of Education, Employment and Training (Government Printer), Canberra, 1993, pp. 11, 13, quoted in Stephen Kendal, 'Implementing Educational Reforms in Australia: Relations between Policy Makers and Managers', presentation to the International Research Symposium on Public Sector Management, Edinburgh, April 2002, http://www.pcug.org.au/~kendal/edinburgh.html Accessed May 2002. All of the account given here comes from this paper, unless otherwise specified.

36 Marjoribanks, Valedictory Lecture, pp. 7–8; Susan Magarey, Personal recollection.

37 Marjoribanks, Valedictory Lecture, pp. 5–6; Dame Roma Mitchell, Speech as Chancellor to Graduation Ceremony, Adelaide University, 1985, SLSA PRG 778/17/113.

38 *Australian*, 6 July 1988.

39 Kevin Marjoribanks, '"I Shall Be A Member Of The University All My Life"', in Magarey (ed.), *Dame Roma*, pp. 232, 233.

40 Susan Magarey: Personal experience (the Research Centre for Women's Studies had two members of the Anthropology Department assigned to it in 1988); Conversation with Professor John Grey, Head of the Anthropology Department, 1999.

41 *Advertiser*, 18 May 1983.

42 Law Society of South Australia *Bulletin*, April 1989, p. 90; Fr Theo G. Overberg, SJ, Rector of Aquinas College, Tribute to Judge David Hogarth, 21 February 1989.

43 John Bray to Roma Mitchell, 28 March 1980, Dame Roma Mitchell's Scrapbooks; Peter Ward, 'John Bray in Adelaide' and [Wilfrid Prest], 'Publications of J.J. Bray, in Prest (ed.), *A Portrait of John Bray*.

44 *New Woman*, February 1991.

45 John Menadue to Dame Roma Mitchell, 6 April 1989, SLSA PRG 778/6/16.

46 Bassett, 'Governor of South Australia', pp. 253–254; Peter Bassett to Dame Roma Mitchell, 8 September 1987, SLSA PRG 778/6/1.

47 Entry for 22 April [1989], Diaries of Sir Walter Crocker.

48 Mervyn K. Smith to Dame Roma Mitchell, 9 March 1987, SLSA PRG 778/5/3; Stewart Cockburn, form letter with handwritten note, November 1988, SLSA PRG 778/5/5; WEL to Dame Roma Mitchell, January 1988, SLSA PRG 778/5/4; Malcolm Long, Director Radio, to Dame Roma Mitchell, 19 February 1988, SLSA PRG 778/38.

49 *Australian Biography II*, p. 69; *Government Gazette*, 27 July 1989.

50 Josephine Tiddy to Dame Roma Mitchell, 10 February 1989, Equal Opportunity – the Mitchell Oration, SLSA PRG 778/6/10.

51 Dame Roma Mitchell, 'Looking Back ... Looking Forward', Inaugural Mitchell Oration, 11 October 1989.

52 Mitchell, 'Looking Back ... Looking Forward'; also Dame Roma Mitchell, 'Renewal of the nation – citizenship in Australia', Plenary Session 3, Australian Reconciliation Convention 1997.

53 Entry for 31 January 1994, Dame Roma Mitchell's Women's Suffrage Centenary Diary.

54 Heather Britton, 'Changing with the Times', *SA Life*, July 2006, p. 57.

55 Margie Clover to Kerrie Round, n.d.

56 Roma Mitchell to Noni Farwell, 21 July 1988, SLSA PRG 778/38.

57 Dame Roma Mitchell, Speech to the Justices Association Dinner, Government House, 13 October 1992, printed in Magarey (ed.), *Dame Roma*, p. 269.

58 Dame Roma Mitchell, 'Introduction to the Hon. Justice Mary Gaudron, High Court of Australia', to be read at the Second Mitchell Oration, 24 August 1990, SLSA PRG 778/5/5.

59 Mary Gaudron to Dame Rome Mitchell, 19 October 1990, SLSA PRG 778/5/5.

Chapter Ten: A Very Good Retirement Occupation

1 Entry for 30 September [1990], Diaries of Sir Walter Crocker, Special Collections, Barr Smith Library; Kerrie Round, Interview with Premier Mike Rann, 7 May 2003; Adelaide *News*, 19 October 1990.
2 *Advertiser*, 20 October 1990.
3 *News*, 19 October 1990; *Advertiser*, 20 October 1990; *Sunday Mail*, 21 October 1990.
4 Don Dunstan, *Felicia: The Political Memoirs of Don Dunstan* (Macmillan), South Melbourne, 1981, pp. 247, 297; *Advertiser*, 19 October 1990.
5 Kate Hannaford to Dame Roma Mitchell, 3 November 1990, SLSA PRG 778/3/8/1.
6 William Deane, AC, QC, KBE, 'Memories', in Susan Magarey (ed.), *Dame Roma: Glimpses of a Glorious Life* (Axiom Publishing in association with the John Bray Chapter of the Alumni Association of the University of Adelaide), Adelaide, 2002, p. 17.
7 *Australian*, 17 July 1982.
8 Monsignor Robert Aitken to Dame Roma Mitchell, 29 April 1991, SLSA PRG 778/5/7; John Bray to Dame Roma Mitchell, 19 October 1990; Brian Stanley to Dame Roma Mitchell, 19 October 1990, SLSA PRG 778/3/8/6.
9 Dame Roma Mitchell, Speech given to the Lyceum Club of Adelaide, 11 June 1997, SLSA SRG 438/18; *Weekend Australian*, 20–21 October 1990; *Sunday Herald*, 21 October 1990.
10 *Advertiser*, 26 January 1991; *Weekend Australian*, 20–21 January 1991.
11 Aline Fenwick to Dame Roma Mitchell, Australia Day 1991, SLSA PRG 778/3/9/2.
12 *News*, 19 October 1990.
13 Entries for 15 October [1990], 17 April [1985], Diaries of Sir Walter Crocker (Crocker calls the cottage 'Peppermint'); Peter Bassett to Kerrie Round, email, 16 December 2004; Peter Bassett, 'Governor of South Australia', in Magarey (ed.), *Dame Roma*, pp. 264, 255.
14 Minutes of Council, 9 November 1990, AUA.
15 Kevin Marjoribanks, ' "I Shall Be A Member of the University All My Life" ', in Magarey (ed.), *Dame Roma*, p. 234.
16 Entries for 9 January [1991], 3 February [1991], Diaries of Sir Walter Crocker.
17 Sister Carmel Bourke R.S.M., 'The Hon. Dame Roma's "Swearing In" as Governor of South Australia', Ts., Mercy Archives.
18 *City Messenger*, 13 February 1991.
19 *The Governor of South Australia and Government House*, printed brochure, nd.
20 Dame Roma Mitchell, Speech at Swearing In Ceremony, Wednesday 6 February 1991; *Advertiser*, 6 February 1991.
21 *Australian*, 7 February 1991.
22 Daniel Thomas, 'Adelaide Observed: North Terrace Part 2: *The Heart*', *Adelaide Review*, March 1991.
23 *Advertiser*, 12 February 1991.
24 *Advertiser*, 7 November 1992; *Sunday Mail*, 17 February 1991; Dennis Coleman, 'Behind the Big Wall', *Adelaide Review*, 3–16 August 2007, p. 8.
25 *Advertiser*, 24 January 1996.
26 Entries for 3 February, 12 January, 26 April, 30 May, 1 June, 14 June, 10 November 1994, Dame Roma Mitchell's Women's Suffrage Centenary Diary, SLSA PRG 778/32; Bassett, 'Governor of South Australia', p. 264; Barbara Habel, MS Diary of holiday trip to South Africa, SLSA PRG 778/36.
27 *Sunday Mail*, 17 February 1991.
28 Bassett, 'Governor of South Australia', pp. 264, 255.
29 Bassett, 'Governor of South Australia', pp. 264–265.
30 *Advertiser*, 12 February 1991.
31 Bassett, 'Governor of South Australia', p. 256.
32 *Advertiser*, 24 January 1996.
33 Group Captain Lord Cheshire VC OM DSO DFC to the Hon. Dame Roma Mitchell, DBE, 23 March 1992, SLSA PRG 778/7; Bassett, 'Governor of South Australia', p. 257.
34 Attorney-General for the State of South Australia, The Hon. K. Trevor Griffin MLC, Speech at a Special Sitting of the Supreme Court of South Australia to Mark the Death of Dame Roma Mitchell AC DBE CVO, 13 March 2000, Transcript of Proceedings in Magarey

(ed.), *Dame Roma*, p. 302; Program of Government House Daily Programme, 4 January 1991–28 December 1991.

35 *Advertiser*, 24 January 1996; Kerrie Round, Interview with Peter Bassett, 8 December 2004.

36 Sundry entries in Dame Roma Mitchell's Women's Suffrage Centenary Diary; *Advertiser*, 12 February 1991; *News*, 15 January 1991, clipping in Dame Roma Mitchell's Scrapbooks, SLSA PRG 778/22.

37 *Advertiser*, 12 February 1991.

38 Greg McCarthy, *Things Fall Apart: A History of the State Bank of South Australia* (Australian Scholarly Publishing), Melbourne, 2002, pp. 202, 203; *Advertiser*, 12 February 1991.

39 Program of Government House Daily Programme, 4 January 1991–28 December 1991, Ts., SLSA PRG 778/33; Graham Gunn, Speech in House of Assembly, 28 March 2000, www.parliament.sa.gov.au Accessed 7 May 2003; Griffin, Speech at the Special Sitting of the Supreme Court to Mark the Death of Dame Roma Mitchell, p. 303; Mike Rann, Speech at the Farewell Dinner in Honour of Her Excellency, The Honourable Dame Roma Mitchell, 12 July 1996, copy kindly sent to us by Mike Rann; South Australia, House of Assembly, 28 March 2000, www.parliament.sa.gov.au Accessed 7 May 2003.

40 *Advertiser*, 12 February 1990.

41 *Australian Weekend Magazine*, 2–3 February 1991.

42 McCarthy, *Things Fall Apart*, p. 213; Dame Roma Mitchell, Speech to the Queensland University of Technology, Bar Practice Committee, 'The Reserve Powers of the Crown', 26 February 1997, SLSA PRG 778/17/144; Film Australia, *Australian Biography II*, 4 June 1993, shown on SBS Television, pp. 72–73.

43 *Advertiser*, 20 October 1990.

44 An unidentified English newspaper, May 2000, school file, Mercy Archives.

45 State Dinner in Honour of Her Excellency The Honourable Dame Roma Mitchell, AC, DBE, Governor of South Australia, Banquet Room, Adelaide Festival Centre, Thursday, 14 February 1991, photocopy of protocol arrangements.

46 *Advertiser*, 12 February 1991.

47 *Australian Biography II*, pp. 68, 70; *Advertiser*: 24 January 1996, 1 January 2000, 30 March 1994.

48 *Witness* (Pt Pirie Diocesan Monthly), March 1991; *Catholic Leader*, 5 May 1991.

49 Copy of Government House Timetable for 1991, SLSA PRG 778/33.

50 Dame Roma Mitchell, Speech at the opening of the Murputja Delivery Centre, 19 November 1993, SLSA PRG 778/17; Dorothy Kotz, Speech, South Australian House of Assembly, 28 March 2000, www.parliament.sa.gov.au Accessed 7 May 2003.

51 Melinda Brown, 'Achieving a reconciled Australia', *Law Institute Journal*, May 2001, p. 17; Bassett, 'Governor of South Australia', p. 259.

52 Bassett, 'Governor of South Australia', p. 258; *Advertiser*, 24 January 1996.

53 Dean Brown, Speech in South Australian House of Assembly, 28 March 2000, www.parliament.sa.gov.au Accessed 7 May 2003; Entry for 31 May 1994, Dame Roma Mitchell's Women's Suffrage Centenary Diary.

54 Entries for 3 August, 1 September, 19 October, 21 September and 16 November 1994, Dame Roma Mitchell's Women's Suffrage Centenary Diary.

55 Roma Mitchell to Noni Farwell, 9 July and 21 September 1993, SLSA PRG 778/38.

56 Bassett, 'Governor of South Australia', pp. 259–260; Bassett quoted in *Advertiser*, 24 January 1996.

57 Bassett, 'Governor of South Australia', pp. 260–261; *The Governor of South Australia and Government House*, nd, pamphlet issued by Government House; Bassett quoted in *Advertiser*, 24 January 1996.

58 *News*, 19 October 1990.

59 Kerrie Round, Telephone conversation with David Haines, 22 April 2003.

60 Roma Mitchell to Noni Farwell, 2 July 1992, SLSA PRG 778/38; Roma Mitchell to Sister Mary Carmel, 20 May 1992, Box 165, Mercy Archives; Roma Mitchell to Lady Catherine Wills, 21 June 1992, kindly lent to us by Judge Anthony Bishop; Peter Bassett, 'Governor of South Australia', p. 257.

61 Entry for 13 July 1994, Dame Roma's Women's Suffrage Centenary Diary.

62 *Advertiser*, 24 January 1996.
63 Wayne Hudson, 'Republicanism', in Graeme Davison, John Hirst and Stuart Macintyre (eds), *The Oxford Companion to Australian History* (Oxford University Press), Melbourne, 1998, p. 555; Bassett, 'Governor of South Australia', p. 266.
64 Sir Ronald Wilson AO, 'Epilogue', in Susan Magarey (ed.), *Human Rights and Reconciliation in Australia* (University of Queensland Press), St Lucia, 1999, p. 96.
65 See, e.g. M.A. Stephenson and Suri Ratnapa (eds), *Mabo: A Judicial Revolution: The Aboriginal Land Rights Decision and Its Impact on Australian Law* (University of Queensland Press), St. Lucia, 1993; Wilson, 'Epilogue', pp. 96–97.
66 Entry for 9 August 1994, Dame Roma Mitchell's Women's Suffrage Centenary Diary.
67 Bassett, 'Governor of South Australia', p. 259.
68 Susan Magarey, Personal recollection.
69 Entries for 11 February, 14 February, 15 April, 20 April, 22 April, 7 May, 7 October, 8 October, 13 October, 24 October, 24 November, 30 November, 8 December, 18 December 1994, Dame Roma Mitchell's Women's Suffrage Centenary Diary; Susan Magarey, Personal recollection.
70 *Advertiser*, 30 March 1994.
71 Dame Roma Mitchell, Speech at Launch of Women's Suffrage Centenary Tapestry, 20 April 1994, SLSA PRG 778/17.
72 Dame Roma Mitchell, Launch of book by Anne Edwards and Susan Magarey, The University of Adelaide [sic], Monday 20 November 1995; the book was a collection titled *Women in a Restructuring Australia* (Allen & Unwin), Sydney, 1995, and the launch took place at Flinders University.
73 Dame Roma refers to them as George and Patricia in her diary for 1994, SLSA PRG 778/32
74 Countess of Harewood to Kerrie Round, 3 December 2003.
75 Bassett, 'Governor of South Australia', p. 263.
76 Dean Brown, Speech to South Australian House of Assembly, 28 March 2000, www.parliament.sa.gov.au Accessed 7 May 2003.
77 William Deane, 'Memories', in Magarey (ed.), *Dame Roma*, p. 18.
78 Round, Interview with Mike Rann.
79 John Bray to Roma Mitchell, 19 October 1990, SLSA PRG 778/3/8/6.
80 Amanda Vanstone, 'A Good Friend', in Magarey (ed.), *Dame Roma*, p. 329.
81 Round, Interview with Mike Rann.
82 *Sunday Mail*, 29 March 1992.
83 *Australian*, 6 March 2000.
84 Entry for 21 May 1991, 'bible'.
85 Round, Interview with Peter Bassett.
86 Bassett, 'Governor of South Australia', p. 265.
87 *Advertiser*, 12 February 1991.
88 Susan Magarey and Peter Norman, Interview with Clyde Cameron, 2001.
89 Round, Interview with Mike Rann.
90 Bassett, 'Governor of South Australia', p. 258.
91 Entries for 23 December, 31 December 1994, Dame Roma Mitchell's Women's Suffrage Centenary Diary.
92 Roma Mitchell to Noni Farwell, 2 July 1992, SLSA PRG 778/38.
93 Roma Mitchell to Noni Farwell, various dates, SLSA PRG 778/38.
94 Roma Mitchell to Mike Rann, 25 April 1999, copy kindly sent to us by Mike Rann.
95 Roma Mitchell to Noni Farwell, 3 July 1995, SLSA PRG 778/38; Roma Mitchell to Jean Whyte, 6 July 1995, SLSA PRG 1335/51.
96 Roma Mitchell to Noni Farwell, 23 September 1991, SLSA PRG 778/38; *Advertiser*, 19 July 1996.
97 Law Society of South Australia *Bulletin*, October 1991, p. 16; Sister Deirdre O'Connor to Kerrie Round, June 2002.
98 Sir William Deane, Governor-General of the Commonwealth of Australia, Address on the Occasion of the Unveiling of the Dame Roma Mitchell Statue, Adelaide, 2 July 1999, in Magarey (ed.), *Dame Roma*, p. 23; entries for 19 April, 6 October, 23 November 1994, Dame

Roma Mitchell's Women's Suffrage Centenary Diary; photograph from Dame Roma's Scrapbooks, in Magarey (ed.), *Dame Roma*, p. 18; *Advertiser*, 20 July 1996.

99 Sir William Deane, Eulogy for Dame Roma Flinders Mitchell, 10 March 2000, www.gg.gov.au/speeches/textonly/speeches/2000/000310.html Accessed 29 November 2006.

Chapter Eleven: A Private Citizen Again

1 *Advertiser*, 19 July 1996; Roma Mitchell, 'A Balancing Act', in Tina Koch, Merilyn Annells and Marina Brown (eds), *Still Me: Twelve Women Talk about Ageing* (Wakefield Press), Kent Town 1999, p. 26; Sue Ryder to Roma Mitchell, 9 March 1992, SLSA PRG 778/5/7; Roma Mitchell to Noni Farwell, 3 July 1995, SLSA PRG 778/38; Kerrie Round, Interview with Pamela Villeneuve Smith, 13 August 2002; entries for 26 July, 5, 6, 7, 13, 14, 20, 28 August, 5, 9 September, 28 November, 2 and 9 December 1994, Dame Roma Mitchell's Women's Suffrage Centenary Diary, SLSA PRG 778/32.

2 Entry for 16 September 1994, Jean Whyte's Diaries, NLA, uncatalogued; entries for 8 September and 28 September 1994, Dame Roma Mitchell's Women's Suffrage Centenary Diary.

3 Entries for 6, 20 and 27 November 1994, Dame Roma Mitchell's Women's Suffrage Diary.

4 Round, Interview with Pamela Villeneuve Smith, 13 August 2002.

5 Dame Roma Mitchell, Conversation with Anne Levy and Susan Magarey during a dinner for the 1998 Fulbright Symposium, held at the University of Adelaide, which Susan Magarey organised.

6 Roma Mitchell to Pam Cleland, 30 January 1997. We are grateful to Pam Cleland for giving us this letter and three others that Dame Roma sent her.

7 Mitchell, 'A Balancing Act', p. 21

8 Peter Ward, email to Kerrie Round, 19 November 2004.

9 David Wotton, Speech, South Australian House of Assembly, 28 March 2000, www.parliament.sa.gov.au Accessed 7 May 2003.

10 Minutes of Annual General Meeting of the Council on the Ageing, 26 November 1996, SLSA PRG 778/17/141.

11 David Wotton, Speech, South Australian House of Assembly, 28 March 2000.

12 Dame Roma Mitchell, 'Renewal of the Nation – Citizenship in Australia', Australian Reconciliation Convention 1997, www.austlii.edu.au/cgi-bin/dis…d/MITCHELL Accessed 14 July 2003.

13 Tom Blackburn to Dame Roma Mitchell, 26 May 1995, SLSA PRG 778/5/9.

14 Dame Roma Mitchell, Speech at the Opening of Law Week, 18 May 1999, SLSA PRG 778/17/151.

15 Kerrie Round, Interview with Premier Mike Rann, 7 May 2003.

16 See for example, Transcript of Proceedings, Constitutional Convention, 6 February 1998, pp. 36–37, 64, www.aph.gov.au/hansard/conv/con0602.pdf, Accessed 13 April 2004; Unknown interviewer, Interview with Dame Roma Mitchell, recorded February 1999, www.uow.edu.au/law/civis/updates/roma_mitchell Accessed 26 October 2001.

17 Dame Roma Mitchell, Proclamation Day Address, 28 December 2005, SLSA PRG 778/17.

18 Transcript of Proceedings, Constitution Convention, 6 February 1998, pp. 22, 76.

19 Round, Interview with Mike Rann.

20 Dame Roma Mitchell, '1991 Turning Point', Speech given to the National Forum celebrating the centenary of the Papal encyclicals 'Rerum Novarum' (The Condition of Labour) 1891, 'Quadragesimo Anno' (The Reconstruction of the Social Order) 1931, and 'Centesimus Annus' (One Hundred Years) 1991, Adelaide 3 September 1991.

21 www.smom.org.au/history Accessed 6 December 2004.

22 Dame Roma Mitchell, Speech at Australian Association of the Sovereign Military Order of Malta, Saturday 6 July 1991, SLSA PRG 778/17; Kerrie Round, Telephone conversation with Dr Robert Britten-Jones, 2004, *Advertiser*, 27 October 1997.

23 Susan Magarey, Conversation with Jeanette Sandford-Morgan, November 2004.

24 Dame Roma Mitchell to Harry Medlin, 29 January 2000, copy kindly provided by Emeritus Professor Medlin.

25 Countess of Harewood to Kerrie Round, 3 December 2003.

26 *Advertiser*, 22 February 2000.
27 *Advertiser*, 2 March 2000
28 Peter Bassett, 'Governor of South Australia', in Susan Magarey (ed.), *Dame Roma: Glimpses of a Glorious Life* (Axiom Publishing in association with the John Bray Chapter of the Alumni Association of the University of Adelaide), Adelaide, 2002, p. 258.
29 Noni Farwell, 'Dame Roma Mitchell and the Arts', in Magarey (ed.), *Dame Roma*, p. 248.
30 Search Copy of the Last Will and Testament of Roma Flinders Mitchell.
31 Kerrie Round, Interview with Peter Ward, 19 April 2004.
32 Amanda Vanstone, 'A Good Friend', in Magarey (ed.), *Dame Roma*, p. 337.
33 *Advertiser*, 2 March 2000.
34 *Advertiser*, 2 March 2000.
35 *State Funeral: Funeral Mass for The Honourable Dame Roma Mitchell AC DBE CVO, 1913–2000, St Francis Xavier Cathedral, Adelaide, Friday 10 March 2000*.
36 Film Australia, *Australian Biography II*, 4 June 1993, shown on SBS Television, p. 86.

Chapter Twelve: Epilogue

1 Film Australia, *Australian Biography II*, 4 June 1993 (shown on SBS Television), p. 62.
2 John Bray to Roma Mitchell, 13 June 1982, SLSA: PRG 778/3/4/3; Roma Mitchell to John Bray, 15 June 1982, SLSA: PRG 1098/1/18. The reference to Lady Tennyson is to Alexandra Hasluck (ed.), *Audrey Tennyson's Vice-Regal Days: the Australian Letters of Audrey Lady Tennyson to her Mother Zacyntha Boyle, 1899–1903* (National Library of Australia), Canberra, 1978.
3 *Australian*, 10 February 2003.
4 Marilyn Warren, 'The feminine effect on the law', an edited extract from her speech at the Victorian Women Lawyer Achievement Awards presentation dinner, Parliament House, Melbourne, May 2003, Melbourne *Age*, 27 November 2003.
5 John Bray to Roma Mitchell, 23 September 1965, SLSA PRG 778/3/2/4; A.J. Hannan, *Life of Chief Justice Way: a Biography of Sir Samuel Way* (Angus & Robertson), Sydney, 1960; Roma Mitchell to John Bray, 14 October 1983, SLSA PRG 1098/1/19.
6 www.lawyersweekly.com.au/articles accessed 21 January 2005.
7 Adelaide *Advertiser*, 14 January 2005.

Bibliography

Archives

Catholic Archives, Adelaide

Aquinas Society, Box 132

Catholic Action, Box 80

Catholic Women's League Archives, Adelaide

Catholic Women's League Magazine

Second Interstate Catholic Women's Conference, Adelaide, October 1929.

Flinders University Library

Dunstan Papers

Law Society of South Australia

Minutes of Meetings, 1948–2000

Mercy Archives, housed in St Aloysius College, Wakefield Street, Adelaide

Dame Roma Mitchell's school records

School Register

Box 162

St Aloysius College Annual

National Archives of Australia

H.F. Mitchell, World War I Service Records

Human Rights Commission, New South Wales: C3177; CRS: M1853, M1859

National Library of Australia

Jean Whyte Papers, Uncatalogued

Performing Arts Collection, Festival Centre, Adelaide

Thelma Afford, Adelaide 1930 Little Theatres and Their Visionaries, unpublished ms, nd

State Library of South Australia

Papers of John Bray, PRG 1098

Papers of Dame Roma Mitchell, PRG 778

Papers of the Women's Air Training Corps, PRG 925

Ellis Cafes, BRG277

Professor E. Harold Davies, letters to W.H. Gooch, D 6044(L)

Liberal and Country Party, SRG 165

Lyceum Club, SRG 438

National Council of Women, SRG 297

State Records of South Australia
Adelaide Writers' Week, GRS 1132/3/P
Royal Commission on dismissal from the Office of Commissioner of Police, GRG 108
University of Adelaide
University Archives:
Committee to review the organization of Council business, Series 710
Standing Committee of the Senate, Series 351
University Women's Union, Series 687
Waite Agriculture Research Institute Mitchell Committee and Implementation Committee Papers, Series 906
Barr Smith Library Special Collections
Diaries of Sir Walter Crocker
Music! Dancing!: An exhibition on Adelaide's Dancehalls and Nightclubs during the 1920s, '30s and '40s, Fringe Club, 1982
'Women at the University of Adelaide 1874–1985. Centenary of the First Woman Graduate'
Transcripts of interviews carried out for this biography.
Winston Churchill Memorial Trust, Canberra, Australian Capital Territory
Women's Liberation Movement Archive, South Australia
WLA 1/19/4

Newspapers and magazines

Adelaide *Advertiser*, 1931–2006
Adelaide *City Messenger*, 1991
Adelaide *Sunday Mail*, 1923–1992
Adelaide *News*, 1927–1991
Adelaide *Register*, 1911
Adelaide Review, 1991, 2007.
Adelaide *Southern Cross*, 1921–1969
Adelaide Voices, 1987
Adelaidean, 13 March 2000
Adelaide University Magazine, 1933–1934
Australian, 1967–2001
Australian Jewish News, 1979
Australian Law Journal, 1962
Australian Women's Weekly, 28 October 1939
Brisbane *Courier Mail*, 11 December 1984
Canberra Times, 1965–1986
Catholic Leader, 5 May 1991
Catholic Women's League Magazine, 1937–1938
Eyre's Peninsula Tribune, 1910–1911
Kangaroo Island Courier, 1908–1910
Malaysia *New Sunday Times*, 1975
Melbourne *Age*, 1979–2003
Memento. News from the National Archives, 2005
National Times, 1978
New Idea, 1962
New Woman, 1991
On Dit, 1932–1934
Renmark Pioneer, 1916
St Aloysius College Annual, 1943, 1946
Smith's Weekly, 1936
Sunday Herald, 1990
Sydney Morning Herald, 1962
Town Topics, 1931
West Australian, 1962
Witness (Port Pirie Diocesan Monthly), March 1991

Unpublished manuscripts

Collins, Josephine. 'The Ryder-Cheshire Story in Australia: a Memoir', unpublished, March 1989.

Forward, Jean. '1932 – A Short History of the Tatler's Club – 1954', typescript in the possession of Barbara Wall.

Grosvenor Hotel Limited, June 1918–December 1995. Booklet produced by the Grosvenor Hotel, 1995.

Jones, M. Brigid. *Reminiscences of the J.C.W.L.: Catholic Action for girls (1929–1948)*, (unpublished), Adelaide, c. 1982.

Linn, Rob. 'Legal assistance scheme 1933–1972 – an oral history', mimeo prepared for the Law Society of South Australia, 1997.

McGowan, R.J. *Report to Commissioner of Police, Adelaide, on enquiries into the death of Dr George Ian Ogilvie Duncan, 2 October 1972*, released 29 May 2002.

Raftery, Judith. 'Catholics and Social Issues in South Australia in the 1930's', Seminar paper presented to the History Discipline, Flinders University of South Australia, 13 September 1985.

Royal Commission 1978: Report on the Dismissal of Harold Hubert Salisbury, Transcript of Proceedings

Hon. Mr Acting Justice White, *Special Branch security records: initial report to the Hon. Donald Allan, Dunstan, Premier of the State of South Australia (the White Report)*.

Theses

Baird, Barbara. '"Somebody was going to disapprove anyway": rethinking histories of abortion in South Australia, 1937–1990', PhD thesis, Women's Studies, Flinders University, 1998

Burley, Stephanie. 'None More Anonymous', MEd thesis, University of Adelaide, 1992.

Loughlin, Graham. 'South Australian Queen's Counsel 1865–1972', BA(Hons) thesis, University of Adelaide, 1974.

Ramsay, Eleanor M. 'Television in Australia: Public Service or Private Profit?', BA(Hons) thesis, University of Adelaide, 1970.

Rohde, Andrea, 'Struggling to survive, or postponing pleasure: women and class in the Great Depression', BA(Hons) thesis, University of Adelaide, 1995.

Schumann, Ruth. '"Charity, work, loyalty": a history of the Catholic Women's League in South Australia: 1914–1979', BA(Hons) thesis, Flinders University, 1979.

Websites

http://www.ewtn.com/library/CURIA/NETEMERE.HTM Accessed 25 February 2004

http://www.adelaidecitycouncil.com/council/publications/Brochures/walktrailtheatre.pdf Accessed 18 April 2005.

www.vatican.va/holy_father/pius_xi/encyclicals/documents/hf_p-xi_enc_31121930_casti-connubii_en.html, para.91 Accessed 18 July 2003.

Humphrey Searle, *Quadrille with a Raven*. http://www.musicweb.uk.net/searle/lesley.htm Accessed 17 February 2004.

International Federation of Women Lawyers (FIDA). http://www.iisd.org/50comm/commdb/desc/d29.htm Accessed 10 August 2007.

Kendal, Stephen. 'Implementing educational reforms in Australia: relations between policy makers and managers', presentation to the International Research Symposium on Public Sector Management, Edinburgh, April 2002 http://www.pcug.org.au/~kendal/edinburgh.html Accessed May 2002.

Universal Declaration of Human Rights, http://www.unhchr.ch/udhr/lang/eng.htm Accessed 20 September 2005.

http://www.unhchr.ch/huricane.nsf/O/4454BACF6C1256B72002COF32?opendocument Accessed 18 November 2005.

http://202.14.81.34/hansard/senate/commttee/s1616.pdf Accessed 25 January 2006.

http://www.bunburychryslerjeep.com.au/tools/Cost/Australia.htm Accessed 25 January 2006.

http://www.slsa.sa.gov.au/women_and_politics/polit6.htm Accessed 25 August 2006.

http://www.lrc.justice.wa.gov.au/References.P43.PDF Accessed 15 February 2005.

http://www.lawlink.nsw.gov.au/lawlink/lrc/ll_lrc.nsf/pages/LRC_reports Accessed 15 February 2005.

http://www.lawreform.vic.gov.au/CA256902000FE154/Lookup/Homicide_Final_Report/$file/Chapter_2.pdf Accessed 25 January 2005.

http://.justice.tas.gov.au/cc.corrections1.htm Accessed 17 February 2005.

http://www.abc.net.au/rn/boyers/ Accessed 16 August 2006.

http://www.lawasia.asn.au/index.php?contentPKey=80 Accessed 15 August 2006.

paffairs@humanrights.gov.au Accessed 13 April 2004.

http://www.mup.unimelb.edu.au/catalogue/0-522-85045-6.html Accessed 15 August 2006.

http://www.adelaidereview.com.au/archives/2004_10_15/theatre_story4.shtml Accessed 18 October 2006

http://www.pembroke.sa.edu.au/framset.html?I_aims_body.html?intro Accessed 18 October 2006.

Television and Radio

Nationwide, 'Dame Roma Mitchell', ABC Television, 5 March 1984.

Lindy Powell QC, on *George Negus Tonight*, ABC television, 2 August 2004.

Audiotapes

Bray, John, '1930s', in Hometown Adelaide, a series of spoken recollections delivered at Adelaide Writers' Week, Adelaide, 1986.

Hanrahan, Barbara. '1950s', in Hometown Adelaide, a series of spoken recollections delivered at Adelaide Writers' Week, Adelaide, 1986

Wighton, Rosemary. '1940s', in Hometown Adelaide, a series of spoken recollections delivered at Adelaide Writers' Week, Adelaide, 1986.

Parliament

South Australia, *Parliamentary Debates*, 1978–2000

South Australia State Reports (Government Printer) Adelaide, various years.

Interviews

(a) With Roma Flinders Mitchell

By *Australian Biography II*, 4 June 1993 (shown on SBS Television).

By Glenda Condon, 27 March 1992. Held in Mercy Archives.

By Peter Norman, 22 March 1999. Transcript in Special Collections, Barr Smith Library.

By Lindy Powell QC, 1991, Law Society of South Australia *Bulletin*, June 1996.

By Margaret Press, 19 March 1990. Held in Mercy Archives, Adelaide.

(b) About Roma Flinders Mitchell

Kerrie Round Interviews

With Peter Bassett, 8 December 2004.

With Mary Bleechmore, 16 December 2003. Transcript in Special Collections, BSL.

With Sir Walter Crocker, 30 October 2002. Transcript in Special Collections, BSL.

With Aline Fenwick, 29 November 2002.

With Cedric Isaachsen, 28 October 2002. Transcript in Special Collections, BSL.

With the Hon. Len King, 29 April 2003. Transcript in Special Collections, BSL.

With Beryl Linn, 15 October 2002.

With Harry Medlin, 21 April 2004. Tape in Special Collections, BSL.

With Premier Mike Rann, 7 May 2003. Transcript in Special Collections, BSL.

With Pam Villeneuve Smith, 13 August 2002.

With Peter Ward, 19 April 2004. Transcript in Special Collections, BSL.

Susan Magarey Interviews

(with Peter Norman):With Clyde Cameron, 2002

With Lorna Williams (nee Lumbers) and Adrienne McMahon, 17 August 2001. Transcript in Special Collections, BSL.

(with Kerrie Round): With Pamela Cleland, 22 May 2003. Transcript in Special Collections, BSL.

Telephone conversations

Kerrie Round

With His Honour Gordon Barrett, 25 June 2003.
With Robert Britten-Jones, 2004.
With Katherine Dicker, 22 September 2003.
With Denise Dundon, 7 October 2004.
With David Haines, 22 April 2003.
With Emeritus Professor Peter Karmel, 10 December 2003.
With Jean MacDonald, 10 December 2002.
With Alek Mathieson, 27 November 2003.
With Bill Park, 29 January 2004.
With Mrs Pam Villeneuve Smith, 2 September 2003.
With Peter Ward, 19 April 2004.
With Ross Wickham, 28 October 2002.

Susan Magarey

With Lynn Nykiel, Secretary, Queen Adelaide Club, 5 December 2005.
With Elliott Johnston, 9 June 2008.

Conversations

Susan Magarey

With Dame Roma and Anne Levy at dinner for the 1998 Fulbright Symposium, held at the University of Adelaide, April 1998.
With Audrey Abbie, November 2004.
With Heather Bonnin AO, various occasions.
With His Honour David Bright, 9 December 2005.
With Judith Roberts AO, 4 November 2006.
With Susan Sideris, various occasions.
With Paul Tys, 6 February 2004.
With Helena Jasinski and Noni Farwell, 2002.
With Deborah McCulloch, 24 July 2007.

Other interviews

Yvonne Abbott, interview with Dorothy Somerville, Lyceum Club, 1986.
Peter Norman, Interview with Alec Genders, 23 September 1998.

Dame Roma on Dame Roma

'Reflections on a Career in Law', in J.F. Corkery (ed.), *A Career in Law* (Federation Press) Sydney, 1989.
'Reminiscences of a 1930 law student and practitioner'. Speech given to law students, 1993.
'A Balancing Act', in Tina Koch, Merilyn Annells and Marina Brown (eds), *Still Me: Twelve Women Talk about Ageing* (Wakefield Press) Adelaide, 1999.

Dame Roma Mitchell: Speeches

A Pleasant Sunday Afternoon', Maugham Methodist Church, c. 1955
At the Perth Rotary Club's Australia Day luncheon, 26 January 1966.
Opening of the 37th Annual Meeting of the South Australian Country Women's Association, 28 August 1966.
'Women and Human Rights', Address given at the Annual General Meeting of the Western Australian Council for Equal Pay and Opportunity, 23 August 1968.
Address to the 11th Annual Convention of the Industrial Relations Society of New South Wales, 4 May 1969.
'The Human Rights Commission', Women Lawyers Association of New South Wales, 27 March 1982.
To Sydney University Law Graduates Association, 16 July 1982.
Address to the Royal Australian Institute of Architects, 20 August 1982.

At Canberra College of Advanced Education, 13 May 1983.
To Amnesty International, Hobart, November 1983.
At Monash University, 10 December 1983.
To the Girl Guides Association, c. 1984.
At Murdoch University, March 1984.
At University of New South Wales, May 1984.
To the Media Law Association, 11 August 1984.
To the Federation of Women Lawyers, 26 August 1984.
As Chancellor to Graduation Ceremony, University of Adelaide, 1985.
At St Ann's College, October 1986.
'Our destiny', Speech given at the Tenth Anniversary Luncheon, Australian Women of the Year. *Women of the Year. A Collection of Speeches by Australia's Most Successful Women* (National Council of the Women of the Year Luncheon, Buderim, Queensland, 1987).
At the Child Abuse Seminar, 1 December 1987.
At Swearing In Ceremony, 6 February 1991.
At book launch, Art Gallery of South Australia, 28 February 1991.
At the National Forum celebrating the centenary of the Papal encyclicals 'Rerum Novarum' (The Condition of Labour) 1891, 'Quadragesimo Anno' (The Reconstruction of the Social Order) 1931, and 'Centesimus Annus' (One Hundred Years) 1991, Adelaide, 3 September 1991.
At the 27th Australian Legal Convention, 8 September 1991.
At the Speech Day of the Collegiate School of St Peter, 13 December 1991.
To Senior Secondary Assessment Board of South Australia, 19 February 1992.
At the Justices Association Dinner, Government House, 12 October 1992.
At St Peter's Girls' School Speech Night, 11 December 1992.
At the opening of an exhibition at the Unley Museum, 22 September 1993.
At the opening of the Beachside Community Centre, Seaford Community Fund, 30 October 1993.
At the opening of the Murputja Delivery Centre, 19 November 1993.
On the Golden Jubilee of Opening of State Bank of South Australia Head Office, 14 December 1993.
At the opening of new gallery and restored youth centre, Mitcham Village Art and Crafts Association, 17 April 1994.
At the launch of Women's Suffrage Centenary Tapestry, 20 April 1994.
At the opening of the Supreme Court and Federal Court Judges' Conference, 24 January 1995.
At the Memorial Service for the Late John Bray, AC, QC, Tuesday, 25 July 1995.
At the Commemorative Launch of Australia Remembers, 10 August 1995.
At the launch of *A Rich Tapestry of Lives*, MLC/Annesley College Old Scholars' Association, 30 August 1995.
At the opening of the Pam Cleland Exhibition, Greenhill Galleries, 17 September 1995.
Dedication Speech, Opening Concert, International Barossa Music Festival, Saturday, 30 September 1995.
At the Service of Remembrance, National Council of Women War Memorial Fund, 19 November 1995.
At the launch of book by Anne Edwards and Susan Magarey, 20 November 1995.
To the Queensland University of Technology, Bar Practice Committee, 26 February 1997.
At the Lyceum Club of Adelaide, 11 June 1997.
To Lauriston Valedictory Assembly, November 1998.
At the opening of Law Week, 18 May 1999.
At 'Renewal of the nation – citizenship in Australia', Plenary Session 3, Australian Reconciliation Convention 1997 http://bar.austlii.edu.au/au/other/IndigLRes/car/1997/4/mitchell.html Accessed 20 July 2004.

Dame Roma Mitchell: written papers

'Self-education for Social Service', *Catholic Women's League Magazine*, vol. 2, no. 2, 1937.
'Divorce Law in Australia', *Lawasia*, vol. 1, no. 2, July 1970.

Women's Liberation and the Law, the Sir John Morris Memorial Lecture (Government Printer) Tasmania, 1971.
'Consideration of Gender in Changes in the Law', *Australian Feminist Studies*, No. 1, Summer 1985.
'Being Neighbours', *Adelaide Voices*, June 1987.
The Web of Criminal Law (Australian Broadcasting Commission, Sydney, 1975.
'Looking Back ... Looking Forward', The Inaugural Mitchell Oration, Adelaide, 11 October 1989.
'The Effect of the External Affairs Power upon the Balance of Power between Commonwealth and States', *Canberra Law Review*, vol. 2, no. 2, 1995.
'Dr John Bray and the University of Adelaide', in Wilfrid Prest (ed.), *A Portrait of John Bray: Law, Letters, Life* (Wakefield Press in association with the John Bray Law Chapter of the Alumni Association of the University of Adelaide; the University of Adelaide Foundation; and the Libraries Board of South Australia) Adelaide, 1997.

Dame Roma Mitchell: Papers and Reports written with others

Committee of Enquiry into Education in South Australia. *Education in South Australia. Report of the Committee of Enquiry into Education in South Australia, 1969–1970* (Government Printer) Adelaide, 1971 (Chairman: Peter Karmel).
Criminal Law and Penal Methods Reform Committee of South Australia. *First Report: Sentencing and Corrections* (Government Printer) Adelaide, 1973 (with Colin Howard and David Biles).
Criminal Law and Penal Methods Reform Committee of South Australia. *Second Report: Criminal Investigation* (Government Printer) Adelaide, 1974 (with Colin Howard and David Biles).
Criminal Law and Penal Methods Reform Committee of South Australia. *Third Report: Court Procedures and Evidence* (Government Printer) Adelaide, 1975 (with Colin Howard and David Biles).
Criminal Law and Penal Methods Reform Committee of South Australia. *Fourth Report: the Substantive Criminal Law* (Government Printer) Adelaide, 1974 (with Colin Howard and David Biles).
Criminal Law and Penal Methods Reform Committee of South Australia. *Special Report: Rape and Other Criminal Offences* (Government Printer) Adelaide, 1977(with Colin Howard and David Biles).

Books, book chapters and journal articles

Abbott, Michael. 'Bray as Barrister', in Wilfrid Prest (ed.), *A Portrait of John Bray: Law, Letters, Life* (Wakefield Press in association with the John Bray Law Chapter of the Alumni Association of the University of Adelaide; the University of Adelaide Foundation; and the Libraries Board of South Australia) Adelaide, 1997.
A.C.M. 'The Origin of the Angas Street Junior C.W.L.', *Catholic Women's League Magazine*, vol. 2, no. 7, 1938.
Adelaide University Union. *A Handbook to the University of Adelaide* (The University) Adelaide, 1931.
Adelaide University Union. *A Handbook to the University of Adelaide* (The University) Adelaide, 1935.
Adkins, R.C. *I Flew for MMA. An Airline Pilot's Life* (Self-published) Perth, 1996.
Afford, Thelma. *Dreamers and Visionaries: Adelaide's Little Theatres from the 1920s to the Early 1940s*, edited with additional research by Kerrie Round (Currency Press) Sydney, 2004.
Allen, Margaret. 'She Seems to Have Composed Her Own Life: Thinking about Catherine Martin', *Australian Feminist Studies*, Vol. 19, no. 43, March 2004.
Arrow, Michelle. ' "It Has Become My Personal Anthem": "I Am Woman", Popular Culture and 1970s Feminism', *Australian Feminist Studies*, Vol. 22, no. 53, July 2007.
'Atkins, James Richard', *Oxford Dictionary of National Biography*. http://www.oxforddnb.com/view/article/30492 Accessed 15 August 2006.

Attorney-General's Department. *The Recommendations Made by the Criminal Law and Penal Methods Reform Committee of South Australia: an Account and an Audit* (Attorney-General's Department) Adelaide, c. 1990.

Auchterlonie, Dorothy [Dorothy Green]. 'Present Tense', in Jennifer Strauss (ed.), *The Oxford Book of Love Poems* (Oxford University Press) Melbourne, 1993.

Auchmuty, Margaret Walters. *A Perpetual Trust: the Story of the Winston Churchill Memorial Trust Travelling Fellowships*, no publication details.

Austin, A.G. (ed.). *The Webbs' Australian Diary 1898* (Pitman) Melbourne, 1965.

Bacchi, Carol. 'The "Woman Question"', in Eric Richards (ed.), *The Flinders History of South Australia: Social History* (Wakefield Press) Netley, 1986.

Bailey, P.H. *Human Rights: Australia in an International Context* (Butterworths) Sydney, 1990.

Bassett, Peter. 'Governor of South Australia', in Susan Magarey (ed.), *Dame Roma. Glimpses of a Glorious Life* (Axiom Publishing in association with the John Bray Chapter of the Adelaide University Alumni Association) Adelaide, 2002.

Bean, C.E.W. *The Official History of Australia in the War of 1914–1918. Vol. V: The A.I.F. in France: December 1917–May 1918* (Angus & Robertson) Sydney, 1937.

Beaumont, Joan. 'Introduction', in Joan Beaumont (ed.), *Australia's War, 1939–1945* (Allen & Unwin) Sydney, 1996.

——. 'Australia's War: Asia and the Pacific', in Joan Beaumont (ed.), *Australia's War, 1939–1945* (Allen & Unwin) Sydney, 1996.

——. 'Australia's War: Europe and the Middle East', in Joan Beaumont (ed.), *Australia's War, 1939–1945* (Allen & Unwin) Sydney, 1996.

Becker, Howard S. *Outsiders* (Collier Macmillan) New York, 1963.

Blackshield, Tony and George Williams. *Australian Constitutional Law and Theory. Commentary and Materials* (3rd ed.) (Federation Press) Sydney, 2002.

Blewett, Neal and Dean Jaensch. *Playford to Dunstan: the Politics of Transition* (Cheshire) Melbourne, 1971.

Bowen, Jill. *Kidman: the Forgotten King* (Angus & Robertson) Sydney, 1987.

Bowen, Stella. *Drawn From Life: Reminiscences by Stella Bowen* (Collins Publishers) London, 1940.

Bramwell, Murray. 'The Arts', in Andrew Parkin and Allan Patience (eds), *The Bannon Decade: the Politics of Restraint in South Australia* (Allen & Unwin) Sydney, 1992.

Bray, John. 'The Bench and the Legal Profession', Law Society of South Australia *Bulletin*, March 1977.

——. *John Bray Collected Poems 1962–1991* (University of Queensland Press) St Lucia, 2000.

——. *The Emperor's Doorkeeper: Occasional Addresses 1955–1987*, edited by Barbara Wall and Douglas Muecke (The University of Adelaide Foundation) Adelaide, 1988.

Bridges, Doreen. *More Than a Musician: A life of E. Harold Davies* (Australian Scholarly Press) Melbourne, 2006.

Bridges, Nancye. *Wonderful Wireless. Reminiscences of the Stars of Australia's Live Radio* (Methuen Australia) Sydney, 1983.

Bright, Charles. 'Dr John Bray in Context', *Adelaide Law Review*, vol. 7, 1980–81.

——. 'Law Reform', in Andrew Parkin and Allan Patience (eds), *The Dunstan Decade: Social Democracy at the State Level* (Longman Cheshire) Melbourne, 1981.

——. *The Confidential Clerk: A study of Charles Flaxman in South Australia and his Relationship with George Fife Angas* (Elizabeth H. Bright), Adelaide, 1983.

Broomhill, Ray. *Unemployed Workers. A Social History of the Great Depression in Adelaide* (University of Queensland Press) St Lucia, 1978.

Brown, Louise (ed.). *A Book of South Australia: Women in the First Hundred Years* (Rigby) Adelaide, 1936.

Brown, Melinda. 'Achieving a Reconciled Australia', *Law Institute Journal*, May 2001.

Burgess, H.T. (ed.). *The Cyclopedia of South Australia* (Cyclopedia Co.) Adelaide, 1907.

Burgmann, Verity. *Power and Protest: Movements for Change in Australian Society* (Allen & Unwin) St Leonards, 1993.

Burley, Stephanie. 'The Classroom: Challenges and Changing Curriculum', in Fay Gale (ed.), *Making Space: Women and Education at St Aloysius College Adelaide 1880–2000* (St Aloysius College in association with Wakefield Press) Kent Town, 2000.

Butel, Elizabeth. *Margaret Preston: the Art of Constant Rearrangement* (Penguin Books in association with the Art Gallery of New South Wales) Ringwood, 1985.

Caldwell, J.C. 'Population', in Wray Vamplew (ed.), *Australian Historical Statistics* (Fairfax, Syme & Weldon Associates) Broadway, 1987.

Cameron, Clyde R. 'A Matchless Silk', in Susan Magarey (ed.), *Dame Roma. Glimpses of a Glorious Life* (Axiom Publishing in association with the John Bray Chapter of the Adelaide University Alumni Association) Adelaide, 2002.

Cameron, Simon. *Silent Witnesses. Adelaide's Statues and Monuments* (Wakefield Press) Kent Town, 1997.

Campbell, Enid. 'The Legal Status of Women in Australia', Appendix in Norman MacKenzie. *Women in Australia* (Cheshire) Melbourne, 1962.

Campion, Edmund. *Australian Catholics* (Penguin Books) Ringwood, 1988.

Carter, Isabel. *Woman in a Wig. Joan Rosanove, QC* (Lansdowne) Melbourne, 1970.

Cassidy, J.A. and J.F. Corkery. *Aldermans, Barristers & Solicitors: History of the Firm 1928–1988* (The Firm) Adelaide, 1988.

Castles, Alex, Andrew Ligertwood and Peter Kelly (eds). *Law on North Terrace 1883–1983* (Faculty of Law, University of Adelaide) Adelaide, 1984(?).

—— and Michael C. Harris. *Lawmakers and Wayward Whigs: Government and Law in South Australia* (Wakefield Press) Adelaide, 1987.

Chanin, Eileen and Steven Miller (with Judith Pugh). *Degenerates and Perverts: the 1939 Herald Exhibition of French and British Contemporary Art* (Miegunyah Press) Carlton, 2005.

Chappell, Duncan and Peter Sallmann. 'Rape in Marriage Legislation in South Australia: Anatomy of a Reform', *Australian Journal of Forensic Sciences*, vol. 14, no. 3, 1982.

Charlesworth, Hilary. 'Human Rights and Reconciliation in International Perspective', in Susan Magarey (ed.), *Human Rights and Reconciliation* (University of Queensland Press) St Lucia, 1999.

Cockburn, Stewart. *The Salisbury Affair* (Sun Books) Melbourne, 1979.

——, assisted by John Playford. *Playford. Benevolent Despot* (Axiom) Adelaide, 1991.

Cohen, A.K. *Deviancy and Control* (Prentice Hall) New Jersey, 1966.

Cohen, Stanley (ed.). *Images of Deviance* (Penguin Books) Harmondsworth, 1971.

Corkery, J.F. (ed.). *A Career in Law* (Federation Press) Sydney, 1989.

Cornwall, Charles. *The Punishment Fit the Crime: Memoirs of a Probation and Parole Officer* (Peacock Publications) Adelaide, 2002.

Cornwall, John. *Just For The Record: the Political Recollections of John Cornwall* (Wakefield Press) Kent Town, 1989.

Crocker, Walter. *Travelling Back: the Memoirs of Sir Walter Crocker* (Macmillan) South Melbourne, 1981.

Darian-Smith, Kate. 'War and Australian Society', in Joan Beaumont (ed.), *Australia's War, 1939–1945* (Allen & Unwin) Sydney.

Davies, Lloyd. *Sheila: a Biography of Sheila McClemans* (Desert Pea Press) Leichhardt, 2000.

Deane, William. 'Memories', in Susan Magarey (ed.), *Dame Roma, Glimpses of a Glorious Life* (Axiom Publishing in association with the John Bray Chapter of the Adelaide University Alumni Association) Adelaide, 2002.

Department of Defence. *Standing Orders, Australian Imperial Force, and War Financial Regulations* (Government Printer) Melbourne, 1918.

Donovan, Peter. 'Transport', in Wilfrid Prest, Kerrie Round and Carol Fort (eds), *The Wakefield Companion to South Australian History* (Wakefield Press) Kent Town, 2001.

Dowse, Sara. 'The Women's Movement's Fandango with the State', in Cora Baldock and Bettina Cass (eds), *Women, Social Welfare and the State in Australia* (George Allen & Unwin) Sydney, 1983.

His Honour Chief Justice John Doyle. 'Her Colleagues Fondly Remember', Law Society of South Australia *Bulletin*, June 1996.

The Hon. Justice Duggan. 'Overwhelming Sense of Justice', Law Society of South Australia *Bulletin*, April 2000.

Duncan, Bruce. *Crusade or Conspiracy? Catholics and the Anti-Communist Struggle in Australia* (UNSW Press) Sydney, 2001

Duncan, W.G.K. and Roger Ashley Leonard. *The University of Adelaide, 1874–1974* (Rigby) Adelaide, 1973.

Dunstan, D.A. *Felicia: the Political Memoirs of Don Dunstan* (Macmillan) South Melbourne, 1981.

Edgeloe, V.A. *University Children of the 1880s: Law* (no publisher) Adelaide, 1978.

Edwards, Anne and Susan Magarey. 'Introduction', in Anne Edwards and Susan Magarey (eds), *Women in a Restructuring Australia: Work & Welfare* (Allen & Unwin) Sydney, 1995.

Elliott, Jack. *Memoirs of a Barrister* (Wakefield Press) Adelaide, 2000.

Einfield, Marcus. 'Human Rights', in Susan Magarey (ed.), *Dame Roma, Glimpses of a Glorious Life* (Axiom Publishing in association with the John Bray Chapter of the Adelaide University Alumni Association) Adelaide, 2002.

Evatt, The Hon. Elizabeth. 'A Woman's Perspective', in Susan Magarey (ed.), *Dame Roma, Glimpses of a Glorious Life* (Axiom Publishing in association with the John Bray Chapter of the Adelaide University Alumni Association) Adelaide, 2002.

F. C. 'Collier Robert Cudmore', in Wilfrid Prest, Kerrie Round and Carol Fort (eds), *The Wakefield Companion to South Australian History* (Wakefield Press) Kent Town, 2001.

——. 'Mary Stewart (May) Douglas', in Wilfrid Prest, Kerrie Round and Carol Fort (eds), *The Wakefield Companion to South Australian History* (Wakefield Press) Kent Town, 2001.

——. 'Archibald Grenfell (Archie) Price', in Wilfrid Prest, Kerrie Round and Carol Fort (eds), *The Wakefield Companion to South Australian History* (Wakefield Press) Kent Town, 2001.

——. 'Thomas Quinton Stow', in Wilfrid Prest, Kerrie Round and Carol Fort (eds), *The Wakefield Companion to South Australian History* (Wakefield Press) Kent Town, 2001.

'Face-to-Face–Chris Sumner', Law Society of South Australia *Bulletin*, November 1994.

Faine, Jon. 'Dame Roma Mitchell', in *Taken on Oath: a Generation of Lawyers* (Federation Press) Sydney, 1992.

——. 'John Bray', in *Taken on Oath: a Generation of Lawyers* (Federation Press) Sydney, 1992.

Farwell, George (ed. B. McArdle). *Around Australia on Highway One* (Thomas Nelson) Melbourne, 1966.

——. *Rejoice in Freedom* (Nelson) Melbourne, 1976.

Farwell, Noni. 'Dame Roma Mitchell and the Arts', in Susan Magarey (ed.), *Dame Roma, Glimpses of a Glorious Life* (Axiom Publishing in association with the John Bray Chapter of the Adelaide University Alumni Association) Adelaide, 2002.

Field, F.L. 'The Law Society in Wartime', Law Society of South Australia *Bulletin*, July 1980.

Forbes, J.R.S. *The Divided Legal Profession in Australia: History, Rationalisation and Rationale* (Law Book Co.) Sydney, 1979.

Fort, Carol S. '"Equality of Sacrifice"? War Work in Salisbury, South Australia', in Bernard O'Neil, Judith Raftery and Kerrie Round (eds), *Playford's South Australia: Essays on the History of South Australia, 1933–1968* (Association of Professional Historians Inc.) Adelaide, 1996.

Foucault, Michel (translated by Alan Sheridan). *Discipline and Punish: the Birth of the Prison* (Alan Lane) London, 1977.

Fox, Richard G. 'The Salisbury Affair: Special Branches, Security and Subversion', *Monash University Law Review*, vol. 5, June 1979.

Franklin Harbour District Council 1888–1988. One Hundred Years of Local Government (The Council) Cowell, SA, 1987.

Gale, Fay (ed.). *Making Space: Women and Education at St Aloysius College, Adelaide, 1880–2000* (St Aloysius College in association with Wakefield Press) Adelaide, 2000.

Galligan, Brian. *No Bill of Rights for Australia*, Papers on Parliament, no. 4, 1989.

Game, Ann and Rosemary Pringle. 'Sexuality and the Suburban Dream', *Australian and New Zealand Journal of Sociology*, no. 15, 1979.

Gammage, Bill. *The Broken Years: Australian Soldiers in the Great War* (ANU Press) Canberra, 1974.

Gavell, K. *A Report on Professional Incomes in Victoria (June 1956)* (University of Melbourne Appointments Board) Carlton, 1957.

Gibbs, H.T. 'A Judge in Kiribati', in Susan Magarey (ed.), *Dame Roma. Glimpses of a Glorious Life* (Axiom Publishing in association with the John Bray Chapter of the Adelaide University Alumni Association) Adelaide, 2002.

Goodall, Rod and Chris Fuller. 'Five Years in the Field', *Newsletter of the Human Rights Commission*, No. 19, December 1986.
Goodnow, Jacqueline and Carole Pateman (eds). *Women, Social Science and Public Policy* (George Allen & Unwin) Sydney, 1985.
Grabosky, P.N. 'Political Surveillance and the South Australian Police', in *Wayward Governance: Illegality and its Control in the Public Sector* (Australian Institute of Criminology) Canberra, 1989. http//www.aic.gov.au/publications/lcj/wayward/ch6t.html Accessed 18 October 2006.
——. 'The Great Social Security Conspiracy Case', in *Wayward Governance: Illegality and its Control in the Public Sector* (Australian Institute of Criminology) Canberra, 1989. http//www.aic.gov.au/publications/lcj/wayward/ch6t.html Accessed 18 October 2006.
Griffin, Trevor. Speech to Mark the Passing of Dame Roma Mitchell, in Susan Magarey (ed.), *Dame Roma, Glimpses of a Glorious Life* (Axiom Publishing in association with the John Bray Chapter of the Adelaide University Alumni Association) Adelaide, 2002.
Gunson, Molly M. 'What is Girl Guiding', *Golden Jubilee Wattle* (St Aloysius College) Adelaide, 1930.
Guy, Bill. *A Life on the Left. A Biography of Clyde Cameron* (Wakefield Press) Adelaide, 1999.
Halliwell, Leslie. *Halliwell's Film Guide* (Grafton Books) London, sixth edition 1987.
Hancock, Joan and Eric Richards. 'Wealth, Work and Well Being: Some Historical Indicators', in Eric Richards (ed.), *The Flinders History of South Australia: Social History* (Wakefield Press) Netley, 1986.
Harris, Max. 'The Premier and his Mirror: the Armour Proper of Donald Dunstan', *Quadrant*, vol. xix, no. 5, August 1975.
Hastings, Elizabeth. 'A Tribute to Dame Roma Mitchell', National Foundation for Australian Women/Young Women's Christian Association, Adelaide, 15 November 1996, *Australian Feminist Studies*, vol. 12, no. 25, April 1997.
Head, Michael. *Fire on the Hill: Aquinas College 1950–2000* (Aquinas College Foundation) North Adelaide, 2002.
Healey, Judith and Francis Regan. 'Social Welfare', in Andrew Parkin and Allan Patience (eds), *The Bannon Decade: the Politics of Restraint in South Australia* (Allen & Unwin) Sydney, 1992.
Hetherington, John. *Melba: A Biography* (Penguin) Ringwood, 1967.
Hetzel, Basil S. *Chance and Commitment* (Wakefield Press) Kent Town, 2005.
Heyward, Michael. *The Ern Malley Affair* (University of Queensland Press) St Lucia, 1993.
Hilliard, David. *Flinders University: the First 25 years 1966–1991* (Flinders University of South Australia) Adelaide, 1991
——. 'The Catholic Church and the Community in Adelaide', in Fay Gale (ed.), *Making Space: Women and Education at St Aloysius College Adelaide 1880–2000* (St Aloysius College in association with Wakefield Press) Kent Town, 2000.
——. 'Freemasonry', in Wilfrid Prest, Kerrie Round and Carol Fort (eds), *The Wakefield Companion to South Australian History* (Wakefield Press) Kent Town, 2001.
Hogarth, Toby. 'A Terrific Friend', Law Society of South Australia *Bulletin*, April 2000.
Hoorn, Rob van den and John Playford. 'The Adelaide Hospital Row', in Dean Jaensch, *The Flinders History of South Australia: Political History* (Wakefield Press) Netley, 1986.
Hope, A.D. 'Australia', in *Collected Poems 1930–1965* (Angus & Robertson) Sydney, 1966.
Hopkins, Gerard Manley. 'No worst, there is none', *Poems and Prose of Gerard Manley Hopkins*, selected with an introduction and notes by W.H. Gardner (Penguin Books) Harmondsworth, 1953.
Hopton, Jason. *A History of Wool Auctions in South Australia and Seventy-Six Years in the Brookman Building Wool Exchange* (Adelaide Woolbrokers' Association) Adelaide, 1977.
Howell, P.A. 'Napier, Sir Thomas John Mellis (1882–1976)', *Australian Dictionary of Biography*, vol. 15 (Melbourne University Press) Carlton, 2000.
Hudson, Flexmore. 'Waiting for a letter', in Jennifer Strauss (ed.), *The Oxford Book of Love Poems* (Oxford University Press) Melbourne, 1993.
Hudson, Wayne. 'Republicanism', in Graeme Davison, John Hirst and Stuart Macintyre (eds), *The Oxford Companion to Australian History* (Oxford University Press) Melbourne, 1998.
Huffadine, H.N. *These Hundred Years. The Story of G & R Wills & Co. Limited during its First Century 1849–1949* (G & R Wills) Adelaide, 1949.

Hunt, Arnold D. 'Methodist Church', in Wilfrid Prest, Kerrie Round and Carol Fort (eds), *The Wakefield Companion to South Australian History* (Wakefield Press) Kent Town, 2001.
Ignatieff, Michael. *Isaiah Berlin: A Life* (Vintage) London, 2000.
Inglis, Amirah. *Australians in the Spanish Civil War* (Allen & Unwin) Sydney, 1987.
Inglis, K.S. *The Stuart Case* (Black Inc.) Melbourne, 2002 (1961).
Irving, Hilda. *In Florrie's Footsteps: Adventures of a Trainee Nurse at Adelaide Hospital 1938–41* (H. Irving) Adelaide, 1985.
Jaensch, Dean. 'Party, Party System and Federation: 1890–1912', in Dean Jaensch (ed.), *The Flinders History of South Australia: Political History* (Wakefield Press) Netley, 1986.
——. 'The Playford Era', in Dean Jaensch (ed.), *The Flinders History of South Australia: Political History* (Wakefield Press) Netley, 1986.
——. 'Stability and Change, 1910–1938', in Dean Jaensch (ed.), *The Flinders History of South Australia: Political History* (Wakefield Press) Netley, 1986.
Jasinski, Helena. 'Magnanimity, Support, Friendship', Law Society of South Australia *Bulletin*, April, 2000.
Jennings, Margaret J. 'Benham, Edward Warner (1872–1948)', *Australian Dictionary of Biography* (Melbourne University Press) Carlton, Vol. 13, 1993.
Johnson, Lesley. *The Modern Girl: Girlhood and Growing Up* (Allen & Unwin) Sydney, 1993.
Jones, Helen. *In Her Own Name: Women in South Australian History* (Wakefield Press) Adelaide, 1994.
——. 'League of Women Voters', in Wilfrid Prest, Kerrie Round and Carol Fort (eds) *The Wakefield Companion to South Australian History* (Wakefield Press) Kent Town, 2001.
Jordan, Deborah. 'Women's Policy', in Andrew Parkin and Allan Patience (eds), *The Bannon Decade: the Politics of Restraint in South Australia* (Allen & Unwin) Sydney, 1992.
King, Len. 'The Judicial Career of Dame Roma Mitchell', in Susan Magarey (ed.), *Dame Roma, Glimpses of a Glorious Life* (Axiom Publishing in association with the John Bray Chapter of the Adelaide University Alumni Association) Adelaide, 2002.
King CJ. 'Transcript of Proceedings at Special Sitting on the Retirement of Her Honour Justice Mitchell, 28 September 1983', in Susan Magarey (ed.), *Dame Roma. Glimpses of a Glorious Life* (Axiom Publishing in association with the John Bray Chapter of the Adelaide University Alumni Association) Adelaide, 2002.
Kirby, Michael. 'Bray's Impact on Australian Jurisprudence', in Wilfrid Prest (ed.), *A Portrait of John Bray: Law, Letters, Life* (Wakefield Press in association with the John Bray Law Chapter of the Alumni Association of the University of Adelaide; the University of Adelaide Foundation; and the Libraries Board of South Australia) Adelaide, 1997.
Kirby, The Hon. Justice Michael. Funeral Oration for John Bruce Piggott CBE LLB, June 2000, St David's Cathedral, Hobart. www.hcourt.gov.au/speeches/kirbyj/kirbyj_piggott.htm Accessed 25 January 2006.
Kirk, Linda. 'Portia's Place: Australia's First Women Lawyers', *Australian Journal of Legal History*, vol. 1, 1995.
Kirkby, Diane. *Barmaids: a History of Women's Work in Pubs* (Cambridge University Press) Melbourne, 1997.
Lake, Marilyn. *Getting Equal: the History of Australian Feminism* (Allen & Unwin) Sydney, 1999.
Lees, Stella and June Senyard. *The 1950s … How Australia Became a Modern Society, and Everyone Got a House and Car* (Hyland House) Melbourne, 1987.
Ligertwood, Andrew. 'Bray the Jurist', in Wilfrid Prest (ed.), *A Portrait of John Bray: Law, Letters, Life* (Wakefield Press in association with the John Bray Law Chapter of the Alumni Association of the University of Adelaide; the University of Adelaide Foundation; and the Libraries Board of South Australia) Adelaide, 1997.
Lilburn, Sandra, Susan Magarey and Susan Sheridan. 'Celebrity Feminism as Synthesis: Germaine Greer, *The Female Eunuch* and the Australian Print Media', *Continuum: Journal of Media & Cultural Studies*, vol. 14, no. 3, November 2000.
Linn, Beryl. 'A Lady of the Law', Law Society of South Australia *Bulletin*, March 1998.
Linn, Rob. 'Royal Adelaide Show', in Wilfrid Prest, Kerrie Round and Carol Fort (eds), *The Wakefield Companion to South Australian History* (Wakefield Press) Kent Town, 2001.

M. S. 'Australian Workers Union', in Graeme Davison, John Hirst and Stuart Macintyre (eds), *The Oxford Companion to Australian History* (Oxford University Press) Melbourne, 1998.

MacKenzie, Norman. *Women in Australia* (Cheshire) Melbourne, 1962.

Macintyre, Stuart. *The Reds: The Communist Party of Australia from Origins to Illegality* (Allen & Unwin) Sydney, 1998.

——. 'Cricket', in Graeme Davison, John Hirst and Stuart Macintyre (eds), *The Oxford Companion to Australian History* (Oxford University Press) Melbourne, 1998.

Mackinnon, Alison. 'The Streets and into the World Beyond', in Fay Gale (ed.), *Making Space: Women and Education at St Aloysius College Adelaide 1880–2000* (St Aloysius College in association with Wakefield Press) Kent Town, 2000.

Magarey, B.A. 'President's Report', Law Society of South Australia *Bulletin*, September 1971.

Magarey, Susan. *Unbridling the Tongues of Women: a Biography of Catherine Helen Spence* (Hale & Iremonger) Sydney, 1985.

——. 'Setting up the First Research Centre for Women's Studies in Australia, 1983–1986', *Australian Feminist Studies*, vol. 13, no. 27, April 1998.

——. 'Introduction', in Susan Magarey (ed.), *Human Rights and Reconciliation in Australia* (University of Queensland Press) St. Lucia, 1999.

——. 'I Never Wanted to Be an Administrator of Anything', *Women's Studies International Forum*, vol. 9, no. 2, 1986.

——. 'The Sex Discrimination Act 1984', *Australian Feminist Law Journal*, vol. 20, June 2004.

——. Ed. *Dame Roma: Glimpses of a Glorious Life* (Axiom) Stepney, 2002. It should be noted that while Susan Magarey edited the essays commissioned for this collection, the publishers subsequently decided to include a great deal of other material as well, some of which was poorly proofed and marred by spelling mistakes and wayward punctuation.

Manne, Robert. 'Introduction', in Robert Manne (ed.), *Whitewash: on Keith Windschuttle's Fabrication of Aboriginal History* (Black Inc. Agenda) Melbourne, 2003.

Mannion, John. 'Horseracing', in Wilfrid Prest, Kerrie Round and Carol Fort (eds), *The Wakefield Companion to South Australian History* (Wakefield Press) Kent Town, 2001.

Marjoribanks, Kevin. '"I Shall Be a Member of the University All My Life"', in Susan Magarey (ed.), *Dame Roma. Glimpses of a Glorious Life* (Axiom Publishing in association with the John Bray Chapter of the Adelaide University Alumni Association) Adelaide, 2002.

Marsden, Susan, Paul Stark and Patricia Sumerling (eds). *Heritage of the City of Adelaide* (Corporation of the City of Adelaide) Richmond, 1990.

Marshall, Vern. 'The Labor Party', in Andrew Parkin and Allan Patience (eds), *The Bannon Decade: the Politics of Restraint in South Australia* (Allen & Unwin) Sydney, 1992.

Massam, Katharine. 'Catholic Church', in Graeme Davison, John Hirst and Stuart Macintyre (eds), *The Oxford Companion to Australian History* (Oxford University Press) Melbourne.

Matthews, Jill Julius. *Dance Hall and Picture Palace: Sydney's Romance with Modernity* (Currency Press) Sydney, 2005.

McCarthy, Greg. *Things Fall Apart: a History of the State Bank of South Australia* (Australian Scholarly Publishing) Melbourne, 2002.

McGuiness, Mark. 'Obituary: Hon Dame Roma Mitchell AC, DBE, CVO, QC', *Australian Law Journal*, vol. 74, May 2000.

McLay, Anne. *Women on the Move: Mercy's Triple Spiral: a History of the Adelaide Sisters of Mercy Ireland to Argentine 1856–1880 to South Australia 1880–* (Sisters of Mercy, Adelaide) Adelaide, 1996.

McGowan, Detective Chief Superintendent R.J. *Report to Commissioner of Police, Adelaide, on enquiries into the death of Dr George Ian Ogilvie Duncan, 2 October 1972*, released 29 May 2002.

Miles, John. *Lost Angry Penguins* (Crawford House Publishing) Adelaide, 2000.

Miles, Rosemary. 'Women in Wartime', in *Greater than their Knowing: a Glimpse of South Australian Women 1936–1986* (Wakefield Press) Netley, 1986.

Miller, James William (Dick Wordley, ed.). *Don't Call Me Killer!* (QB Book) Maryborough, 1985.

Mills, Helen. 'Equal Opportunities', in Andrew Parkin and Allan Patience (eds), *The Dunstan Decade: Social Democracy at the State Level* (Longman Cheshire) Melbourne, 1981.

Minney, Margaret. 'Obituary: Alexander Keith Sangster QC', Law Society of South Australia *Bulletin*, February 1999.

Mitchell, Deborah. 'Wages and Employment', in Barbara Caine, Moira Gatens, Emma Grahame, Jan Larbalestier, Sophie Watson and Elizabeth Webby (eds). *Australian Feminism: a Companion* (Oxford University Press) Melbourne, 1998.

Mitchell, Susan. *The Matriarchs. Twelve Australian Women Talk about Their Lives* (Penguin) Ringwood, Vic., 1987.

——. *All Things Bright & Beautiful: Murder in the City of Light* (Pan Macmillan) Sydney, 2004.

Montgomery, M.G. 'Obituary: The Honourable David Stirling Hogarth', Law Society of South Australia *Bulletin*, April 1989.

Monteath, Peter. *Dear Dr Janzow: Australia's Lutheran Churches and Refugees from Hitler's Germany* (Australian Humanities Press) Unley, 2005.

Morris, Norval and Gordon Hawkins. *The Honest Politician's Guide to Crime Control* (Sun Books) Melbourne, 1971.

Moss, Jim. *Sound of Trumpets: History of the Labour Movement in South Australia* (Wakefield Press) Netley, 1985.

'Movement', in Graeme Davison, John Hirst and Stuart Macintyre (eds), *The Oxford Companion to Australian History* (Oxford University Press) Melbourne, 1998.

'Mr Justice Wells', *Australian Law Journal*, vol. 58, September 1984.

Muecke, Geoff. 'On the Criminal Law and Penal Methods Reform Committee', in Susan Magarey (ed.), *Dame Roma. Glimpses of a Glorious Life* (Axiom Publishing in association with the John Bray Chapter of the Adelaide University Alumni Association) Adelaide, 2002.

Mullighan, E.P. 'Before the Bench', in Susan Magarey (ed.), *Dame Roma. Glimpses of a Glorious Life* (Axiom Publishing in association with the John Bray Chapter of the Adelaide University Alumni Association) Adelaide, 2002.

Murphy, John. 'Work in a Time of Plenty: Narratives of Men's Work in Post-war Australia', *Labour History*, no. 88, May 2005.

Naffine, Ngaire. *An Inquiry into the Substantive Law of Rape* (Women's Adviser's Office, Department of Premier and Cabinet) Adelaide, 1984.

O'Brien, Bob. *Young Blood: the Story of the Family Murders* (Harper Collins) Sydney, 2002.

O'Callaghan. Peter. 'Obituary: Cairns Villeneuve-Smith QC', *Victorian Bar News*, 116, Autumn 2001.

O'Toole, Margaret and Paul Sharkey. 'The Spirit that Nurtures the Mercy Vision', in Fay Gale (ed.), *Making Space: Women and Education at St Aloysius College Adelaide 1880–2000* (St Aloysius College in association with Wakefield Press) Kent Town, 2000.

Painter, Alison. 'Entertainment. The Changing Scene', in Bernard O'Neil, Judith Raftery and Kerrie Round (eds), *Playford's South Australia* (Association of Professional Historians) Adelaide, 1996.

Parkin, Andrew. 'The Dunstan Governments: a Political Synopsis', in Andrew Parkin and Allan Patience (eds), *The Dunstan Decade: Social Democracy at the State Level* (Longman Cheshire) Melbourne, 1981.

——. 'Looking Back on the Bannon Decade', in Andrew Parkin and Allan Patience (eds), *The Bannon Decade: the Politics of Restraint in South Australia* (Allen & Unwin) Sydney, 1992.

Pascoe, J.J. *History of Adelaide and Vicinity* (Hussey & Gillingham) Adelaide, 1901.

Peel, Mark and Janet McCalman. 'Who Went Where in *Who's Who* 1988', *Melbourne University History Research Series* No. 1, 1992.

Peoples, Jo. 'Miss Patricia Hackett', *Journal of the Historical Society of South Australia*, 25, 1997.

Playford, John. 'Hannan, Albert James (1887–1965)', *Australian Dictionary of Biography* (Melbourne University Press) Carlton, Vol. 14, 1996.

——. 'Smith, Francis Villeneuve (1883–1956)', *Australian Dictionary of Biography* (Melbourne University Press) Carlton, vol. 11, 1988.

Powell, Lindy. 'Dame Roma Mitchell. A Life in the Law', Law Society of South Australia *Bulletin*, February 1991.

——. 'A Loving and Very Much Loved Person', Law Society of South Australia *Bulletin*, April 2000.

Press, Margaret. *Colour and Shadow. South Australian Catholics 1906–1962* (Archdiocese of Adelaide) Adelaide, 1991.

——. 'Catholic Church', in Wilfrid Prest, Kerrie Round and Carol Fort (eds), *The Wakefield Companion to South Australian History* (Wakefield Press) Kent Town, 2001.

Radcliffe, John C. 'Tramways', in Wilfrid Prest, Kerrie Round and Carol Fort (eds.), *The Wakefield Companion to South Australian History* (Wakefield Press) Kent Town, 2001.

Rann, Mike. 'Don Dunstan, Maestro of the Possible', in *Don Dunstan, 1926–1999, Labor Herald*, http://www.eherald.alp.org.au/download/now/dd.pdf Accessed 10 April 2006.

Reid, John and Anne Gollan (eds). *Visiting China* (Waverley Offset Publishing Group) Canberra, 1969.

Richards, Eric. 'The Peopling of South Australia, 1836–1986', in Eric Richards (ed.), *The Flinders History of South Australia: Social History* (Wakefield Press) Netley.

Round, Kerrie. *As Many Lives As A Cat? The University of Adelaide Theatre Guild 1938–1998* (The University of Adelaide) Adelaide, 1999.

Royal Commission. *Report on the Dismissal of Harold Hubert Salisbury* (Government Printer) Adelaide, 1978.

Rupp, Leila J. *Worlds of Women: the Making of an International Women's Movement* (Princeton University Press) Princeton, 1997.

Ryan, Des and Mike McEwen. *'It's Grossly Improper'* (WENAN Pty Ltd) n.p., 1979.

Ryan, Susan. *Catching the Waves: Life in and out of Politics* (HarperCollins) Sydney, 1999.

Sands and McDougalls Directories (Sands and McDougalls) Adelaide, various years.

Saunders, Malcolm. 'The Labor Party and the Industrial Groups in South Australia 1946–55: Precluding the Split', *Journal of the Historical Society of South Australia*, No. 33, 2005.

Saunders, Malcolm and Neil Lloyd. 'Remembering the Past and Hoping for the Future: Why there Was No Labor Split in South Australia in 1954–56', in Brian Costar, Peter Love and Paul Strongio (eds), *The Great Labor Schism: a Retrospective* (Scribe) Melbourne, 2005.

Sawer, Marian. *Sisters in Suits: Women and Public Policy in Australia* (Allen & Unwin) Sydney, 1990.

Sawer, Marian and Simms, Marian. *A Woman's Place: Women and Politics in Australia* (Allen & Unwin), Sydney, 1993.

Scott, G.McL. 'Economic Policy', in Andrew Parkin and Allan Patience (eds), *The Bannon Decade: the Politics of Restraint in South Australia* (Allen & Unwin) Sydney, 1992.

Sebald, W.G. *On the Natural History of Destruction with Essays on Alfred Andersch, Jean Améry and Peter Weiss*, translated from the German by Anthea Bell (Hamish Hamilton) London, 2003.

Sheridan, Susan. 'Women Writers', in Laurie Hergenhan (ed.), *The Penguin New Literary History of Australia* (Penguin Books) Ringwood, 1988.

Shmith, Michael and David Colville (eds). *Musica Viva Australia – the First Fifty Years* (Playbill) Pymble, NSW, 1996.

Siedlecki, Stefania and Diana Wyndham. *Populate and Perish. Australian Women's Fight for Birth Control* (Allen & Unwin) Sydney, 1990.

Silsbury, Elizabeth. 'Music', in Wilfrid Prest, Kerrie Round and Carol Fort (eds), *The Wakefield Companion to South Australian History* (Wakefield Press) Kent Town, 2001.

'Sir Mellis Napier', *Australian Law Journal*, vol. 40, 31 March 1967.

'Sir Mellis Napier: Chief Justice 1942–1967', *Adelaide Law Review*, vol. 3, no. 1, June 1967.

Smart, Judith. 'National Council of Women', in Barbara Caine, Moira Gatens, Emma Grahame, Jan Larbalestier, Sophie Watson and Elizabeth Webby (eds), *Australian Feminism: A Companion* (Oxford University Press) Melbourne, 1998.

Smyth, Paul and Bettina Cass. 'Introduction', in Paul Smyth and Bettina Cass (eds), *Contesting the Australian Way: States, Markets, and Civil Society* (Cambridge University Press) 1998.

Spearritt, Peter. 'Lang, John Thomas "Jack"', in Graeme Davison, John Hirst and Stuart Macintyre (eds), *The Oxford Companion to Australian History* (Oxford University Press) Melbourne, 1998.

Stephenson, M.A. and Suri Ratnapa (eds). *Mabo: a Judicial Revolution: the Aboriginal Land Rights Decision and its Impact on Australian Law* (University of Queensland Press) St Lucia, 1993.

Steward, H.D. *Recollections of a Regimental Medical Officer* (Melbourne University Press) Carlton, 1983.

Stokes, Geoff and Richard Cox. 'The Governing Party: the ALP and the Politics of Consensus', in Andrew Parkin and Allan Patience (eds), *The Dunstan Decade: Social Democracy at the State Level* (Longman Cheshire) Melbourne, 1981.
Summers, Anne. *Damned Whores and God's Police: the Colonization of Women in Australia* (Penguin) Ringwood, 1975.
Summers, John. 'The Salisbury Affair', in Dean Jaensch (ed.), *The Flinders History of South Australia: Political History* (Wakefield Press) Netley, 1986.
Tassie, Jane. *Out of Sight – Out of Mind: Outwork in South Australia* (Working Women's Centre) Adelaide, 1989.
Taylor, Ian, Paul Walton and Jock Young. *The New Criminology: for a Theory of Deviance* (Routledge & Kegan Paul) Longon, 1973.
The Ideal Daily Missal with Vespers for Sundays and for Feasts (Eason & Son Ltd) Dublin, 1952.
Thompson, E.P, Douglas Hay and Peter Linebaugh (eds). *Albion's Fatal Tree* (Allen Lane) London, 1975.
Thornton, Margaret. *Dissonance and Distrust: Women in the Legal Profession* (Oxford University Press) Melbourne, 1996.
——. 'Women Practitioners', in Tony Blackshield, Michael Coper and George Williams (eds), *The Oxford Companion to the High Court of Australia* (Oxford University Press) Melbourne, 2001.
Thorlby, Anthony. *The Penguin Companion to Literature*, vol. 2 (Penguin Books) Harmondsworth, 1969.
Thornton, Robert. 'Mitchell, Samuel James (1852–1926)', *Australian Dictionary of Biography* (Melbourne University Press) Carlton, vol. 10, 1986.
Thorpe, Jill. 'Kathleen Lumley College in the Spotlight', *'Clever Country' Journal*, June 2003.
Vamplew, Wray (ed.). *Australians: Historical Statistics* (Fairfax, Syme & Weldon Associates) Broadway, NSW, 1987.
Van Dissel, Dirk. 'The Adelaide Gentry, 1850–1920', in Eric Richards (ed.), *The Flinders History of South Australia: Social History* (Wakefield Press) Netley, 1986.
Vanstone, Amanda. 'A Good Friend', in Susan Magarey (ed.), *Dame Roma. Glimpses of a Glorious Life* (Axiom Publishing in association with the John Bray Chapter of the Adelaide University Alumni Association) Adelaide, 2002.
Verco, P.W. *Thomas and Elisabeth Magarey* (LPH Adelaide) Adelaide, n.d.
de Vries, Susanna. *Great Australian Women: from Federation to Freedom* (HarperCollins) Sydney, 2001.
Walker, Dylan. *Adelaide Silent Nights. A Pictorial History of Adelaide's Picture Theatres during the Silent Era 1896–1929* (National Film and Sound Archive) Canberra, c. 1996.
Waller, Louis. 'The Police, the Premier and Parliament: Government Control of the Police', *Monash University Law Review*, vol. 6, June 1980.
Ward, Kevin. 'First Steps in the Law', Law Society of South Australia *Bulletin*, February 1988.
Ward, Peter. 'John Bray in Adelaide', in Wilfrid Prest (ed.), *A Portrait of John Bray: Law, Letters, Life* (Wakefield Press in association with the John Bray Law Chapter of the Alumni Association of the University of Adelaide; the University of Adelaide Foundation; and the Libraries Board of South Australia) Adelaide, 1997.
Ward, Russel. *A Radical Life* (Macmillan) South Melbourne, 1988.
Watson, Sophie. 'Introduction', in Sophie Watson (ed.), *Playing the State* (Allen & Unwin) Sydney, 1990.
Wesley, Mary. *Jumping the Queue* (Macmillan) London, 1983.
Whimpress, Bernard. 'Australian Rules Football', in Wilfrid Prest, Kerrie Round and Carol Fort (eds), *The Wakefield Companion to South Australian History* (Wakefield Press) Kent Town, 2001.
Hon. Mr Acting Justice White. *Special Branch Security Records: Initial Report to the Hon. Donald Allan Dunstan, Premier of the State of South Australia (the White Report)* (Government Printer) Adelaide, 1978.
Whitelock, Derek. *Thistle Anderson, Arcadian Adelaide* (1905), *With 'Thistle Anderson in Edwardian Adelaide'* (Wakefield Press) Netley, 1985.

Whitington, H.M. 'Frank Villeneuve Smith Q.C. 1884–1956', Law Society of South Australia *Bulletin*, September 1986.

Whyte, Jean P. 'John Bray and the Libraries Board of South Australia', in *A Portrait of John Bray: Law, Letters, Life* (Wakefield Press in association with the John Bray Law Chapter of the Alumni Association of the University of Adelaide; the University of Adelaide Foundation; and the Libraries Board of South Australia) Adelaide, 1997.

Who's Who in Australia (Herald and Weekly Times) Melbourne, various years.

Williams, Peter N. *England. A Narrative History*. www.Britannia.com/history Accessed 23 March 2004.

Winston Churchill Memorial Trust. *First Annual Report* (Patria Printers) Canberra, 1966.

——. *Second Annual Report* (Patria Printers) Canberra, 1967.

Wilson, Ronald. 'Epilogue', in Susan Magarey (ed.), *Human Rights and Reconciliation* (University of Queensland Press) St Lucia, 1999.

Wright, Judith. 'The Age of Aquarius – and Queensland', in Geoffrey Dutton & Max Harris (eds), *Australia's Censorship Crisis* (Sun Books) Melbourne, 1970.

Year Book of the Commonwealth of Australia, No. 23 (Canberra) 1931.

York, Barry. 'Power to the Young', in Verity Burgmann & Jenny Lee (eds), *Staining the Wattle: a People's History of Australia since 1788* (McPhee Gribble/Penguin Books) Fitzroy/Ringwood, 1988.

Zelling, Howard. 'Campbell, Arthur Lang (1889–1949)', *Australian Dictionary of Biography* (Melbourne University Press) Carlton, Vol. 13, 1993.

Zelling, Jesca. 'Friday and the Thursday Girls', Law Society of South Australia *Bulletin*, June 1996.

——. 'Take a Bow. Dame Roma Mitchell', Law Society of South Australia *Bulletin*, June 1996.

Zogbaum, Heidi. 'Kisch must land', *Memento: News from the National Archives*, No. 29, May 2005.

Index

Wakefield Press is an independent publishing and
distribution company based in Adelaide, South Australia.
We love good stories and publish beautiful books.
To see our full range of titles, please visit our website at
www.wakefieldpress.com.au.